Microsoft®

MOS 2010 Study Guide for Microsoft® Word Expert, Excel® Expert, Access®, and SharePoint® Exams

John Pierce and Geoff Evelyn

PUBLISHED BY
Microsoft Press
A Division of Microsoft Corporation
One Microsoft Way
Redmond, Washington 98052-6399

Library of Congress Control Number: 2011934166
ISBN: 978-0-7356-5788-5

Printed and bound in the United States of America.

First Printing

Microsoft Press books are available through booksellers and distributors worldwide. If you need support related to this book, email Microsoft Press Book Support at mspinput@microsoft.com. Please tell us what you think of this book at http://www.microsoft.com/learning/booksurvey.

Microsoft and the trademarks listed at http://www.microsoft.com/about/legal/en/us/IntellectualProperty/Trademarks/EN-US.aspx are trademarks of the Microsoft group of companies. All other marks are property of their respective owners.

The example companies, organizations, products, domain names, email addresses, logos, people, places, and events depicted herein are fictitious. No association with any real company, organization, product, domain name, email address, logo, person, place, or event is intended or should be inferred.

This book expresses the author's views and opinions. The information contained in this book is provided without any express, statutory, or implied warranties. Neither the authors, Microsoft Corporation, nor its resellers, or distributors will be held liable for any damages caused or alleged to be caused either directly or indirectly by this book.

Acquisitions and Developmental Editor: Rosemary Caperton
Project Editor: John Pierce
Editorial Production: Waypoint Press
Technical Reviewer: Todd Meister; Technical Review services provided by Content Master, a member of CM Group, Ltd.
Copyeditor: Roger LeBlanc
Indexer: Christina Yeager
Cover: Jelvetica

Contents

What do you think of this book? We want to hear from you!
Microsoft is interested in hearing your feedback so we can continually improve our books and learning resources for you. To participate in a brief online survey, please visit:

microsoft.com/learning/booksurvey

Exam 77-887 Microsoft Excel 2010 Expert

1 Sharing and Maintaining Workbooks   161

2 Applying Formulas and Functions   185

Exam 77-885 Microsoft Access 2010 Specialist

1   Using the Access Workspace   309

2   Building Tables   347

3   Building Forms   395

Exam 77-886 Microsoft SharePoint 2010 Specialist

1   Creating and Formatting Content   497

**5   Integrating SharePoint 2010 Services and
Microsoft Office 2010 Applications   633**

What do you think of this book? We want to hear from you!

Microsoft is interested in hearing your feedback so we can continually improve our books and learning resources for you. To participate in a brief online survey, please visit:

microsoft.com/learning/booksurvey

Taking a Microsoft Office Specialist Exam

Desktop computing proficiency is increasingly important in today's business world. As a result, when screening, hiring, and training employees, employers can feel reassured by relying on the objectivity and consistency of technology certification to ensure the competence of their workforce. As an employee or job seeker, you can use technology certification to prove that you already have the skills you need to succeed, saving current and future employers the trouble and expense of training you.

Microsoft Office Specialist Certification

Microsoft Office Specialist certification for Microsoft Office 2010 is designed to assist employees in validating their skills with programs in the Office 2010 software suite. The following certification paths are available:

- A Microsoft Office Specialist (MOS) is an individual who has demonstrated proficiency by passing a certification exam in one or more of the Office 2010 programs, including Microsoft Word, Excel, PowerPoint, Outlook, and Access, or in Microsoft SharePoint.
- A Microsoft Office Specialist Expert (MOS Expert) is an individual who has taken his or her knowledge of Office 2010 to the next level and has demonstrated by passing a certification exam that he or she has mastered the more advanced features of Word 2010 or Excel 2010.

Selecting a Certification Path

When deciding which certifications you would like to pursue, you should assess the following:

- The program and program version(s) with which you are familiar
- The length of time you have used the program and how frequently you use it
- Whether you have had formal or informal training in the use of that program
- Whether you use most or all of the available program features
- Whether you are considered a go-to resource by business associates, friends, and family members who have difficulty with the program

Candidates for MOS-level certification are expected to successfully complete a wide range of standard business tasks, such as formatting a document or worksheet and its content; creating and formatting visual content; or working with SharePoint lists, libraries, Web Parts, and dashboards. Successful candidates generally have six or more months of experience with the specific Office program, including either formal, instructor-led training or self-study using MOS-approved books, guides, or interactive computer-based materials.

Candidates for MOS Expert-level certification are expected to successfully complete more complex tasks that involve using the advanced functionality of the program. Successful candidates generally have at least six months, and may have several years, of experience with the programs, including formal, instructor-led training or self-study using MOS-approved materials.

Test-Taking Tips

Every MOS certification exam is developed from a set of exam skill standards (referred to as the objective domain) that are derived from studies of how the Office 2010 programs or SharePoint are used in the workplace. Because these skill standards dictate the scope of each exam, they provide critical information about how to prepare for certification. This book follows the structure of the published exam objectives; see "Using This Book to Study for a Certification Exam" at the beginning of this book for more information.

The MOS certification exams for the Office 2010 programs and SharePoint are performance based and require you to complete business-related tasks in the program for which you are seeking certification. You might be told to adjust program settings or be presented with a file and told to do something specific with it. Your score on the exam reflects how well you perform the requested tasks within the allotted time.

Here is some helpful information about taking the exam:

- Keep track of the time. You have 50 minutes to complete the exam. Your exam time does not officially begin until after you finish reading the instructions provided at the beginning of the exam. During the exam, the amount of time remaining is shown at the bottom of the exam interface. You can't pause the exam after you start it.

- Pace yourself. At the beginning of the exam, you will be told how many questions are included in the exam. Some questions will require that you complete more than one task. During the exam, the number of completed and remaining questions is shown at the bottom of the exam interface.

- Read the exam instructions carefully before beginning. Follow all the instructions provided in each question completely and accurately.

- Enter requested information as it appears in the instructions, but without duplicating the formatting unless you are specifically instructed to do so. For example, the text and values you are asked to enter might appear in the instructions in bold and under-lined text, but you should enter the information without applying these formats.

- Close all dialog boxes before proceeding to the next exam question unless you are specifically instructed not to do so.

- Don't close task panes before proceeding to the next exam question unless you are specifically instructed to do so.

- If you are asked to print a document, worksheet, chart, report, or slide, perform the task, but be aware that nothing will actually be printed.

- Don't worry about extra keystrokes or mouse clicks. Your work is scored based on its result, not on the method you use to achieve that result (unless a specific method is indicated in the instructions).

- If a computer problem occurs during the exam (for example, if the exam does not respond or the mouse no longer functions) or if a power outage occurs, contact a testing center administrator immediately. The administrator will restart the computer and return the exam to the point where the interruption occurred, with your score intact.

Certification Benefits

At the conclusion of the exam, you will receive a score report, indicating whether you passed the exam. You can print with the assistance of the testing center administrator. If your score meets or exceeds the passing standard (the minimum required score), you will be contacted by email by the Microsoft Certification Program team. The email message you receive will include your Microsoft Certification ID and links to online resources, including the Microsoft Certified Professional site. On this site, you can download or order a printed certificate, create a virtual business card, order an ID card, view and share your certification transcript, access the Logo Builder, and access other useful and interesting resources, including special offers from Microsoft and affiliated companies.

Using the Logo Builder, you can create a personalized certification logo that includes the MOS logo and the specific programs in which you have achieved certification. If you achieve MOS certification in multiple programs, you can include up to six of them in one logo.

You can include your personalized logo on business cards and other personal promotional materials. This logo attests to the fact that you are proficient in the applications or cross-application skills necessary to achieve the certification.

For More Information

To learn more about the Microsoft Office Specialist exams and related courseware, visit:

www.microsoft.com/learning/en/us/certification/mos.aspx

Using This Book to Study for a Certification Exam

The Microsoft Office Specialist (MOS) exams for individual Microsoft Office 2010 programs are practical rather than theoretical. You must demonstrate that you can complete certain tasks rather than simply answering questions about program features. The successful MOS certification candidate will have at least six months of experience using all aspects of the application on a regular basis; for example, using Microsoft Outlook at work to send messages, track contact information, schedule appointments and meetings, track and assign tasks, and take notes.

This book has been designed to guide you in studying the types of tasks you are likely to be required to demonstrate in the MOS Expert exams for Microsoft Word 2010 and Microsoft Excel 2010 and the MOS Specialist exams for Microsoft Access 2010 and Microsoft SharePoint.

Each part of the book covers one exam. The coverage for each exam is divided into chapters representing broad skill sets, and each chapter is divided into sections addressing groups of related skills. Each section includes review information, generic procedures, and practice tasks you can complete on your own while studying. When necessary, we provide practice files you can use to work through the practice tasks. You can practice the procedures in this book by using the practice files supplied or by using your own files. (If you use your own files, keep in mind that functionality in some Office 2010 programs is limited in files created in or saved for earlier versions of the program. When working in such a file, *Compatibility Mode* appears in the program window title bar.)

As a certification candidate, you probably have a lot of experience with the program you want to become certified in. Many of the procedures we discuss in this book will be familiar to you; others might not be. Read through each study section and ensure that you are familiar with not only the procedures included in the section, but also the concepts and tools discussed in the review information. In some cases, graphics depict the tools you will use to perform procedures related to the skill set. Study the graphics and ensure that you are familiar with all the options available for each tool.

Features and Conventions of This Book

If you have worked with previous versions of Word, Excel, Access, or SharePoint, or if you need help remembering how to perform a particular task, the following features of this book will help you locate specific information:

- **Detailed table of contents** Scan a listing of the topics covered in each chapter and locate specific topics.

- **Chapter thumb tabs** Easily locate the beginning of the chapter you want.

- **Detailed index** Look up specific tasks and general concepts in the index, which has been carefully crafted with the reader in mind.

You can save time when you use this book by understanding how special instructions, keys to press, buttons to click, and other conventions are indicated in this book.

Convention	Meaning
1 2	Numbered steps guide you through step-by-step procedures.
→	An arrow indicates a procedure that has only one step.
See Also	These paragraphs direct you to more information about a given topic in this book or elsewhere.
Tip	These paragraphs provide a helpful hint or shortcut that makes working through a task easier, or information about other available options.
Interface elements	In procedures, the names of program elements (such as buttons and commands) are shown in bold characters.
Key combinations	A plus sign (+) between two key names means that you must hold down the first key while you press the second key. For example, "press Ctrl+Home" means "hold down the Ctrl key and press the Home key."
User input	In procedures, anything you should enter appears in bold characters.

Using the Book's Companion Content

Before you can complete the exercises in this book, you need to copy the book's practice files to your computer. These practice files, and other information, can be downloaded from here:

http://go.microsoft.com/FWLink/?Linkid=223407

Display the detail page in your web browser and follow the instructions for downloading the files.

> **Important** The Microsoft Word 2010, Excel 2010, Access 2010, and SharePoint 2010 programs are not available from this website. You should purchase and install those programs before using this book.

Practice files are organized by chapter (and by section number when necessary) in folders for Microsoft Word 2010, Microsoft Excel 2010, and Microsoft Access 2010. The names of the files you need to work with are provided in the practice tasks.

No practice files are provided for the section about Microsoft SharePoint 2010, although practice tasks you can perform on your own site are described in each chapter. To work through the SharePoint section, you need full access to a SharePoint 2010 team site, and because SharePoint 2010 is a server-based platform rather than a desktop application, you need access to a server or an online environment where SharePoint 2010 is installed or hosted. You can find information about SharePoint hosting services and the SharePoint trial edition at the start of that section of the book. The companion content also includes an appendix that provides an overview of SharePoint and its basic functionality.

Your Companion eBook

The eBook edition of this book allows you to:

- Search the full text
- Print
- Copy and paste

To download your eBook, please see the instruction page at the back of this book.

Modifying the Display of the Ribbon

The goal of the Microsoft Office working environment is to make working with Office documents as intuitive as possible. You work with an Office file and its contents by giving commands to the program in which the document is open. All Office 2010 programs organize commands on a horizontal bar called the ribbon, which appears across the top of an application's program window.

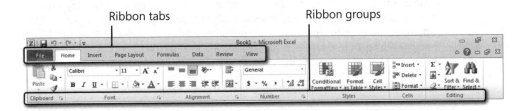

Commands are organized on task-specific tabs of the ribbon, and in feature-specific groups on each tab. Commands generally take the form of buttons and lists. Some appear in galleries. Some groups have related dialog boxes or task panes that contain additional commands.

> **Tip** Some older commands no longer appear on the ribbon but are still available in the program. You can make these commands available by adding them to the Quick Access Toolbar.

The appearance of commands on the ribbon changes as the width of the ribbon changes. A command might be displayed on the ribbon in the form of a large button, a small button, a small labeled button, or a list entry. As the width of the ribbon decreases, the size, shape, and presence of buttons on the ribbon adapt to the available space. For example, if you decrease the width of the ribbon, small button labels disappear and entire groups of buttons are hidden under one button that represents the group. Click the group button to display a list of the commands available in that group. When the window becomes too narrow to display all the groups, a scroll arrow appears at its right end. Click the scroll arrow to display hidden groups.

You can customize the ribbon or the Quick Access Toolbar to suit your working style and to make commands you use frequently easily available. To add a command to the Quick Access Toolbar, right-click the command on the ribbon and then choose Add to Quick Access Toolbar.

> **Tip** The screen images shown in the procedures in this book were captured at a screen resolution of 1024 × 768, at 100 percent magnification, and with the default text size (96 dpi). If any of your settings are different, the ribbon on your screen might not look the same as the one shown in the book. If differences between your display settings and ours cause a button on your screen to look different from the one mentioned in this book, you can adapt the procedures to locate the command. First, click the specified tab. Then locate the specified group. If a group has been collapsed into a group list or group button, click the list or button to display the group's commands. Finally, look for a button that features the same icon in a larger or smaller size than that shown in the book. If necessary, point to buttons in the group to display their names in ScreenTips.

To add your own tabs and groups to the ribbon, right-click the ribbon and choose Customize the Ribbon. In the program's Options dialog box (the one shown here is for Word), click New Tab to add a tab to the ribbon. The new tab will include a new group as well. Use the New Group button to add another group to the custom tab or to any of the built-in tabs shown in the Main Tabs list. You can add commands only to custom groups, not to any of the built-in groups.

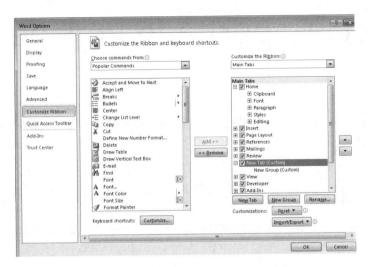

The Choose Commands From list provides options for displaying popular commands, commands not included on the ribbon, as well as all commands or commands on specific tabs. Select the command you want to add to a custom group, and then click Add. Click Remove if you want to remove a command from a custom group.

The Rename button opens a dialog box in which you can type a name for a custom tab or a custom group. For a custom group, you can also select a symbol to associate with the group.

If you want to return the ribbon and the Quick Access Toolbar to the default state, you can click Reset, Reset All Customizations.

How to Get Support and Provide Feedback

The following sections provide information on errata, book support, feedback, and contact information.

Errata & Book Support

We've made every effort to ensure the accuracy of this book and its companion content. Any errors that have been reported since this book was published are listed on our Microsoft Press site at oreilly.com:

http://go.microsoft.com/FWLink/?Linkid=221951

If you find an error that is not already listed, you can report it to us through the same page.

If you need additional support, please send an email message to Microsoft Press Book Support at *mspinput@microsoft.com*.

Please note that product support for Microsoft software is not offered through the addresses above.

We Want to Hear from You

At Microsoft Press, your satisfaction is our top priority, and your feedback our most valuable asset. Please tell us what you think of this book at:

www.microsoft.com/learning/booksurvey/

The survey is short, and we read *every one* of your comments and ideas. Thanks in advance for your input!

Stay in Touch

Let's keep the conversation going! We're on Twitter: *http://twitter.com/MicrosoftPress*.

Microsoft Word 2010 Expert

In the next five chapters, you'll build on the general skills required to create, edit, and format documents in Microsoft Word 2010. You'll learn more about the specific skills you need to be certified as a Microsoft Word 2010 expert. The areas covered are the following:

- Sharing and maintaining documents
- Formatting content
- Tracking and referencing documents
- Performing mail merge operations
- Managing macros and forms

What You Need to Know

In creating the exercises for this part of the book, we assumed that you are proficient using many of the features in Microsoft Word 2010. This level of proficiency includes familiarity with how to create and save documents, apply themes and other formatting, insert illustrations and other objects, and work with revision marks.

1 Sharing and Maintaining Documents

The skills tested in this section of the Microsoft Office Expert exam for Microsoft Word 2010 relate to sharing and maintaining documents. Specifically, the following objectives are associated with this set of skills:

1.1 Configure Word options
1.2 Apply protection to a document
1.3 Apply a template to a document

1.1. Configure Word Options

In the next two sections, you'll learn how to set program options that Word provides. These options control features such as spelling and grammar checking, the default file format, autocorrection, and many others. The first section examines general options, options related to document display, advanced options, and other categories. The second section covers spelling and grammar-checking options in detail.

Setting Default Program Options

The more experience you gain in Microsoft Word, the more apt you are to want to change program option settings so that Word appears and behaves as you want it to. You can make these changes in the Word Options dialog box. We don't cover every option in detail in this section, but we do highlight important options and explain the types of options you'll find on each page of the dialog box.

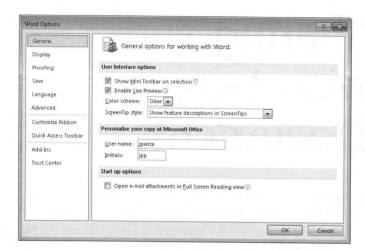

Click the information icon you see next to some options (such as the Enable Live Preview option shown here) to get more information about the option.

General

Two options on the General page, Show Mini Toolbar On Selection and Enable Live Preview, affect what you see on the screen as you work on a document. You also use the General page to define a user name and the initials that appear in comments and revisions, for example, and to specify how ScreenTips are displayed (or whether to display them at all).

> **Tip** The mini toolbar appears in outline when you select text in a document. When you point to the toolbar, it presents commands for formatting and other properties that you can apply to the text. If you prefer to use only the formatting tools on the ribbon or in dialog boxes, clear the check box for this option. Live Preview is the feature that shows you how formatting alternatives appear—for example, Word provides a choice of table styles; point to a style, and the Live Preview feature shows how the formatting for columns, rows, and headings will appear. Clear this check box to turn off this type of display.

Display

Use this page to control page display options, the display of formatting marks, and printing options. Show All Formatting Marks is the default setting. You can clear this check box to show no formatting marks, or clear it and then select the marks you want to see—for example, only paragraph marks, spaces, and tabs.

Proofing

This page provides an area that lets you specify how spelling is corrected in all the Office programs you use. Another section on the Proofing page gives you the options you can specify for Word.

> **See Also** For detailed information about setting spelling and grammar options in Word, see the next section.

Save

Options on the Save page control the default file format in which documents are saved and the default location; timing for the Save AutoRecover option, a feature that can help you prevent losing changes you make to a document; the AutoRecover file location; and settings related to offline editing of documents stored on a Microsoft SharePoint site. Click Browse on this page to change any of the file paths listed.

Language

If you work in multilingual groups, you might set or change some of the options on this page. For example, you can add dictionaries for other languages, which Word refers to when it checks the spelling of a document.

Advanced

This page is probably where you will spend the bulk of your time customizing program options to your liking. This page includes options related to editing document content; displaying documents on the screen; printing, saving, and sharing documents; and various other areas.

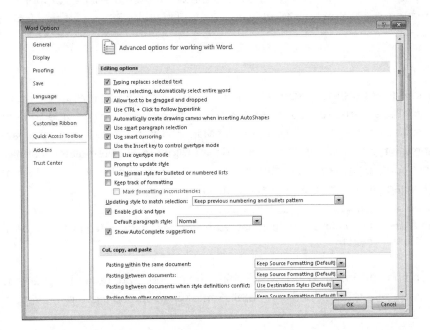

- In the list of editing options, you might want to enable the option Use The Insert Key To Control Overtype Mode if you are familiar with that technique. Select Keep Track Of Formatting if you want Word to track changes you make to the formatting of a document when you apply such attributes as bold and italics or change properties of the font being used.

- The Cut, Copy, And Paste section provides several lists that let you control how Word formats the content you copy in one document and paste in another. You can choose between keeping the formatting of the source document, merging the formatting, or pasting just the text (which picks up the formatting used in the destination document). This section also lets you turn off the display of the Paste Options button if you prefer to work without it.

- Among the options in the Display section are settings for the number of recent documents Word shows on the File tab, the default unit of measurement, and the width of the area that shows style names in Draft and Outline views.

- In the General area near the bottom of the page, click File Locations to make changes to the default locations where files and templates are stored, for example. Click Web Options to specify how web pages you create in Word are viewed in a web browser.

Customize Ribbon and Quick Access Toolbar

These pages let you make modifications to the Word user interface. For more information, see the section "Modifying the Display of the Ribbon" at the beginning of this book.

Add-Ins

Clicking Add-Ins displays a page that lists the add-in programs that are active in Word. You might see entries related to OneNote, for example. Add-ins provide additional features to an application. If you open the Manage list at the bottom of the page, you can see the types of add-ins available. Add-ins might include templates that have one or more complex macros, for example. You use the Manage list at the bottom of the Add-Ins page to select an add-in and install it.

> **See Also** For more information about templates, see "Apply a Template to a Document" later in this chapter.

You can find add-ins for Word by searching the Internet, but remember that not all add-ins are safe to download and install. Some might spread a computer virus, for example.

> **See Also** For more information about settings you can use to control add-ins, see the next section, "Trust Center."

Trust Center

The Trust Center page provides links to privacy statements and security information on Microsoft's website. Click Trust Center Settings on this page and you open the Trust Center dialog box, in which you can set options for how Word responds when you open a document containing macros, add-ins, or ActiveX controls. For most users, the default settings for macros and ActiveX controls are suitable. (Word prompts or notifies you before enabling the controls or macros.) For add-ins, you can require that add-ins are signed by a trusted publisher or choose the option Disable All Application Add-Ins. As the Add-Ins page indicates, choosing the Disable All Application Add-Ins option can keep you from taking advantage of the features an add-in is designed to provide.

The Trust Center also provides pages that let you designate trusted locations, trusted documents, and trusted publishers. The following list describes each of these designations:

- A trusted location is a folder on your computer (or possibly on your network, although creating a trusted location on a network is not recommended) from which a document can be opened without Word applying Trust Center settings. Documents in these locations do not open in Protected Mode. When Word opens a document in Protected Mode, you see a security warning that requires you to click Enable Content before you can fully edit the document or run macros, for example. Word lists several trusted locations, including the folder where templates are stored by default. You can also add, modify, and remove trusted locations by using command buttons on the Trusted Locations pages.

- A trusted document is a document for which you have enabled content. After you click Enable Content in the security warning and save the document, you won't see the warning the next time you open the document.

- A publisher is an individual or a company that sends you a document that contains content such as a macro or an ActiveX control. As a step you take in enabling the content in these documents, you can designate the person or organization as a trusted publisher so that Word trusts the documents sent by this source in the future.

➤ To set program options

1. Click **File, Options**.

2. In the **Word Options** dialog box, select the page you need to work with.

3. Select or clear the check boxes for the options you are setting, and specify any other information required for those options.

4. Click **OK** in the **Word Options** dialog box.

➤ To install an add-in

1. Display the **Add-Ins** page in the **Word Options** dialog box.

2. From the **Manage** list at the bottom of the page, select the type of add-in you need to install, and then click **Go**.

3. In the dialog box that appears, click **Add**.

4. In the **Add-In** dialog box, open the folder where the add-in you want to install is stored and then double-click its name.

5. In the list, select the check box for the add-in, and then click **OK**.

➤ To unload an add-in

1. Open the **Add-Ins** dialog box, and clear the check box for the add-in. This step removes the add-in from memory, but the add-in is still included in the list of available add-ins.

2. To remove the add-in from the list, click the add-in name and then click **Remove**.

Changing Options for Checking Spelling and Grammar

You set and change options for spelling and grammar on the Proofing page of the Word Options dialog box. One section of the dialog box is devoted to options that affect all Office applications. A second section lists options that pertain only to Word.

The options in the area for Microsoft Office programs are straightforward. If you have access to a special dictionary of technical or professional terms, for example, click Custom Dictionaries and then add the custom dictionary to the list that Office uses when you run the spelling checker in an Office application.

Use the Proofing page to specifiy options Word uses to check spelling and grammar and to make autocorrections. Click Settings to specify which grammar rules Word checks.

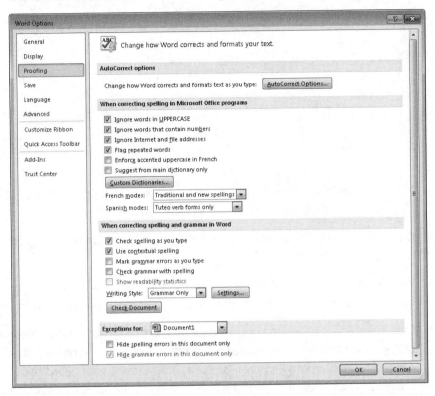

The following list summarizes the options in the area specifically for Word:

- **Check spelling as you type** With this option selected, Word places a jagged red line under a word you misspell as you type. You can continue typing, of course, or fix the mistake as soon as you notice it.

- **Use contextual spelling** This helpful option directs Word to highlight words that it detects are wrong based on context. For example, if you type **Wear are we going for dinner?**, Word flags the word "wear." Right-click on the word, and you'll see a menu that lets you correct the mistake by choosing the word *Where*.

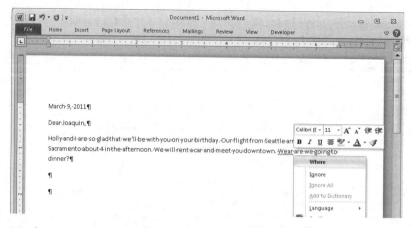

- **Mark grammar errors as you type** Select this option, and Word adds standard rules of grammar to the items it checks for as you type.

- **Check grammar with spelling** With this option, Word also checks grammar rules when you run the spelling checker.

- **Writing style** If you want Word to make suggestions that might improve your writing style along with your grammar, select Grammar And Style from this list.

- **Settings** Click the Settings button to open the Grammar Settings dialog box. This dialog box lets you specify, among other things, whether Word should check for a serial comma (Comma Required Before Last List Item), a standard convention but one that is not often used in magazine or newspaper publishing. You can tell Word whether it should check for fragments and run-on sentences, misused words, and the like.

- **Show readability statistics** If you select Check Grammar With Spelling, you can choose the option to Show Readability Statistics. If you choose this option, Word displays a readability score based on the average number of words per sentence and the average number of syllables per word.

The Grammar Settings dialog box provides a list of items that Word can check for when you check spelling and grammar.

At the top of the Proofing page is the AutoCorrect Options button, which leads you to the AutoCorrect dialog box and the tabs it contains with options for specifying the corrections Word makes and the type of formatting it applies as you type. In your regular work in Word, you have almost surely seen one or more of the default options in action—for example, when you start a numbered list, Word indents the number to set off the list, and when you press Enter, the next item is numbered automatically. When you start a sentence with a lowercase letter, Word changes it to an uppercase character for you. Some automatic corrections and formatting are very helpful, but others can be distracting or, in fact, be contrary to the effect you want to achieve.

Each tab on the AutoCorrect dialog box provides options for what Word can do for you as you type.

The AutoFormat tab lets you control built-in heading styles, the type of quotation marks you use, whether to replace two consecutive hyphens (--) with an em-dash (—), and whether to replace URLs and file paths you type with active hyperlinks.

➤ **To set spelling, grammar, and autocorrection options**

1. Click **File, Options**.

2. In the **Word Options** dialog box, click the **Proofing** page.

3. In the **When correcting spelling and grammar in Word** section, select or clear the check boxes for options you want to change or use.

4. To change options for the grammar rules Word checks, click **Settings** and then make the changes in the **Grammar Settings** dialog box.

5. To have **Word** check spelling and grammar so that words you ignored previously are checked again, click **Recheck Document**.

6. Click **AutoCorrect Options**.

7. In the **AutoCorrect** dialog box, use the tabs to change or set the options for autocorrection and autoformatting and then click OK.

8. Click **OK** in the **Word Options** dialog box.

Practice Tasks

The practice files for these tasks are located in the practice files folder for Microsoft Word. You can save the results of these exercises in the same folder. Change the file name so that you don't overwrite the sample files. When you are done, try performing the following tasks:

- Open a blank document in Word, and then click File, Options. Experiment with some of the options on the various pages in the Word options dialog box. For example, on the General page, change the setting for how ScreenTips appear, click OK, and then return to your document to see the effect this change has.

- Open the file Scene11.docx, which contains the dialog from a scene from the play *Romeo and Juliet* by William Shakespeare. Use the spelling and grammar options that Word provides to see how they affect the issues Word spots in this document.

1.2. Apply Protection to a Document

To apply permissions and protection to a workbook, you use commands on the Review tab or click Protect Document under Permissions on the Info tab in Backstage view. In the following sections, you'll learn how to restrict the editing of a document and how to manage user access to a document.

Controlling the Editing of a Document

Only in rare cases can you share a document and let any other user work with it at will by changing the formatting, adding or deleting content, inserting graphics, and the like. The majority of the time, you want to at least protect the content of important documents, and often you want to share a document only with certain users and to restrict what those users can do. Documents that contain important data or that you plan to use as the focus of a report or presentation should be protected before you share them.

To control how a document can be edited, you make settings in the Restrict Formatting And Editing pane.

The pane is organized in three sections:

- **Formatting Restrictions** Select the check box in this area to limit formatting to a specific set of styles and to prevent users of a document from modifying styles and from applying local formatting. Click Settings to open the Formatting Restrictions dialog box, and then use this dialog box to select the set of styles that should be available. Use the options at the bottom of the dialog box to block users from switching themes or substituting other quick styles.

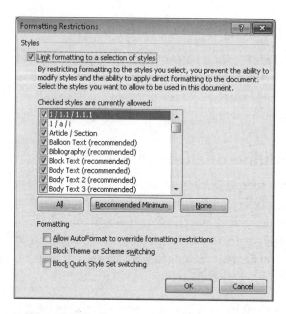

Clear the check box for any style you don't want to apply to a document. Use the Formatting options at the bottom of the dialog box to specify any exceptions for autoformatting, themes, and Quick Styles.

- **Editing Restrictions** Use the Editing Restrictions area to control the types of changes users can make to the document. The choices you have are No Changes (Read Only), Tracked Changes, Comments, and Filling In Forms. This area also allows you to define exceptions that apply to specific sections of the document. You can enable these exceptions for everyone working on a document or to specific people. To select individual users, click the More Users link. Type the names in the Add Users dialog box in the format *DOMAIN\username* or as an e-mail address.

  After you add a user, select the check box beside the user's name, and then click the down arrow at the right side of the text box. A menu appears that provides options for locating sections the user can edit and an option to remove editing permissions for the user.

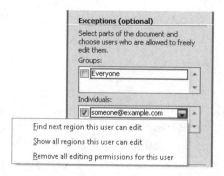

- **Start Enforcement** After you define the editing and formatting restrictions you want to apply to the document, click Yes, Start Enforcing Protection. In the Start

Enforcing Protection dialog box, enter a password that's required to remove protection from the document or choose User Authentication.

> **Tip** The Block Authors command in the Protect group can be applied to a document that is stored in a Microsoft SharePoint Foundation 2010 workspace. To use the command, open the document, select the part of the document you want to block, and then click Block Authors. To remove a block, click in the blocked section, click Block Authors, and then save the file.

> ➤ **To restrict editing and formatting**

1. On the **Review** tab, click **Restrict Editing**.
2. In the **Restrict Formatting and Editing** pane, select the options you want to apply:
   - To specify a specific set of styles users can apply, click **Limit formatting to a selection of styles** and then click **Settings**.
   - To control the type of editing allowed in the document, click **Allow only this type of editing in the document** and then choose from the options in the list. Define exceptions by selecting a section of the document and then choosing which users can edit a particular section.
3. Click **Yes, Start Enforcing Protection**.
4. In the **Start Enforcing Protection** dialog box, enter a password that's required to remove protection or click **User Authentication**.

> **Tip** Use a strong password that contains eight or more characters and uses a mix of uppercase and lowercase characters, numbers, and symbols.

Managing Access to a Document

Information rights management, a free service available from Microsoft, lets you restrict which users have access to a document (and other types of documents you create in Microsoft Office) and what those users can do to the content the document contains.

The first step in restricting user access is to set up information rights management on your computer. Microsoft Office takes care of this task the first time you click Protect Document, Restrict Permission By People on the Info tab. To use the free information rights management service from Microsoft, you must have a Windows Live ID.

> **Tip** You can sign up for a Windows Live ID by going to *live.com*. You can also register for a Live ID when you set up information rights management.

Setting Up Information Rights Management

If you want to use the information rights management service from Microsoft, you follow a few simple (and informative) steps. On the Info tab, when you click Protect Document, Restrict Permission By People, Restricted Access, you see a wizard page that introduces you to information rights management. To proceed, select the option Yes, I Want To Sign Up For This Free Service From Microsoft and then click Next. On the next page, you indicate whether you have a Windows Live ID or you can choose the option to register for one if you do not. Click Next and sign in with your Live ID. On the next page, specify whether you are using a private or public computer, review the licensing agreement and privacy statement, and click I Accept. After Office finishes setting up the information rights management service, click Finish.

You use the Permission dialog box to set up users with Read or Change permission. The dialog box describes the level of access each type of permission provides. Type e-mail addresses to identify users, or choose names from your address book. Click More Options, and Word displays a version of the Permission dialog box in which you can fine-tune options for specific users—for example, you can grant users the additional permission to print content from the document and allow users with Read access to copy information in the document to use in other documents—and designate an individual (using an e-mail address again) that users can contact to request additional permissions.

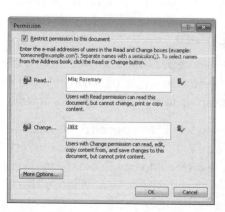
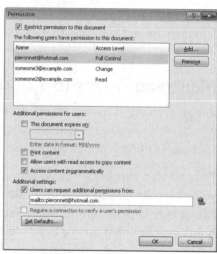

Use the dialog box at the left to specify which users can read or change a document. Click More Options, and then choose the options for any additional permissions you want to grant.

➤ **To restrict access to a document**

1. On the **Info** tab, click **Protect Document**, and then click **Restrict Permission by People**.

2. Click **Restricted Access**.

   At this point, if you have not set up information rights management, you'll walk through the wizard.

3. In the **Permission** dialog box, click **Restrict permission to this document** to enable the **Read** and **Change** areas.

   Read the descriptions below the text boxes for these areas to understand what permissions you restrict for the people you add to these lists.

4. Click **Read**, and then select the names of people you want to grant Read permissions to.

5. Click **Change**, and then select the names of people who need permission to read and edit the document.

6. Click **More Options**, and set the additional options you want to use.

Adding a Password to a Document

You can assign a password that users need to enter to open a document or to modify it. On the Info tab, you can also apply a password that encrypts the contents of a document, which means that the contents are protected unless a user enters the correct password.

➤ **To encrypt a file with a password, follow these steps**

1. Click **File, Info**.

2. On the **Info** tab, click **Protect Document**, and then click **Encrypt with Password**.

3. In the **Encrypt Document** dialog box, type the password you want to use and then click **OK**.

4. Reenter the password.

   Be sure to record the password in a safe place so that you can provide it to other users or refer to it yourself in the event you forget the password.

5. Click **OK**, and then save the document.

Practice Tasks

The practice files for these tasks are located in the practice files folder for Microsoft Word. You can save the results of these exercises in the same folder. Change the file name so that you don't overwrite the sample files. When you are done, try performing the following tasks:

- Open the file StoneworkProposal.docx, and then use commands on the Review tab to protect the document.

- Use the Restrict Formatting And Editing pane to define a section of this document that only you can edit.

1.3. Apply a Template to a Document

It should not surprise you that we used a template to create and format the documents we wrote for the chapters in this book. In fact, every document you create in Word is based on a template, whether it's the default Normal template (Normal.dotx), a sample template that comes with Word, a template from Office.com, or a template that you or another user design. When you base a document on a template, the template is attached to the document, and this association provides all the elements defined in the template to the document you are creating.

> **See Also** Word 2010 templates that include macros use the file-name extension .dotm. For more information about creating macros in Word, see Chapter 5, "Managing Macros and Forms," later in this section of the book.

You can define and organize a number of document elements in a template to facilitate consistency and the application of styles, maintain a set of specifications for page layout, emphasize graphics and other visual elements, and consolidate tools (including custom versions of the Quick Access Toolbar and the ribbon) and macros that you use frequently in building a document.

In the following sections, you'll learn more about using templates, how to modify a template, how to design your own template, and how to maintain templates by using the Organizer.

Using a Document Template

Like other Office applications, Word comes with several sample templates, and many additional templates are available online at Office.com. You can find these templates by clicking File, New. In Backstage view, you'll see links to some of the templates on Office.com and also a link to the sample templates. Use the search box to find additional templates on Office.com.

Type a phrase in the Search Office.com For Templates box to locate templates for the kind of document you are creating.

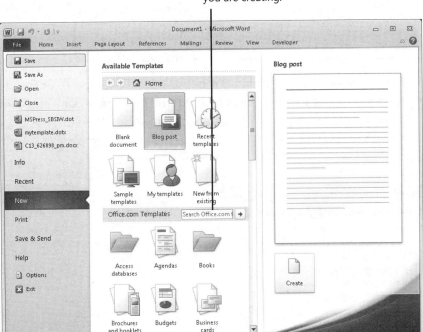

To start using one of the sample or online templates, double-click it. Word opens a new document, and you'll see the formatting, headings, fields, and other elements that are included in the template. Many templates also provide placeholder text that you replace with your own content.

When you click My Templates in Backstage view, Word displays a dialog box that shows the template files stored in the default location for templates (which is Users/*Username*/AppData/Roaming/Microsoft/Templates).

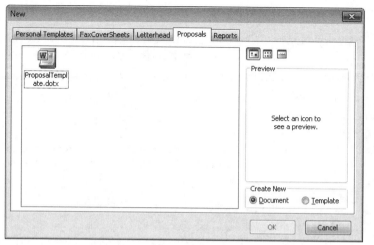

When you store templates in the default Templates folder, Word creates a tab in the New dialog box for each type of template.

In addition to using the New dialog box or the links to a sample or online template, you can attach a template to a document by using the Document Templates command on the Developer tab. When you click Document Templates, Word displays the Templates And Add-Ins dialog box. Click Attach, and then select the template you want to apply to the document.

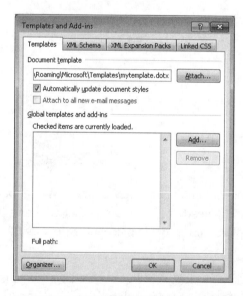

Tip If the Developer tab is not displayed on the ribbon, click File, Options, Customize Ribbon. In the Main Tabs list, click Developer. You can also attach a document to a template on the Add-Ins tab of the Word Options dialog box. In the Manage list at the bottom of the Add-Ins page, select Templates, and then click Go to open the Templates And Add-Ins dialog box.

➤ **To base a document on a sample template or a template on Office.com**

1. Click **File, New**.

2. Find the template you want to use from among the sample templates, or search for a template on Office.com.

3. Double-click the template file to create a document based on that template.

➤ **To base a document on a template on your computer**

1. Click **File, New**.

2. In Backstage view, click **My Templates**.

3. In the **New** dialog box, find the template you want to use and then click **OK**.

➤ **To attach a document to a template**

1. On the **Developer** tab, click **Document Template**.

2. In the **Templates and Add-Ins** dialog box, click **Attach**.

3. In the **Attach Templates** dialog box, select the template you want to use and then click **Open**.

4. In the **Templates and Add-Ins** dialog box, select **Automatically update document styles**.

5. Click **OK**.

Working with a Global Template

In general, the sample templates that come with Word (and the templates you can find on Office.com) are what Word refers to as *document templates*. The elements and settings in a document template are available only to documents that are based on that template. A template such as Normal.dotx is a *global template*, as is the Building Blocks template that comes with Word. A global template controls features such as macros, building blocks, and keyboard shortcuts. The settings in a global template can be applied to any document.

As you can see when you create a blank document, the Normal template contains no placeholder text, but this template does provide several default styles (which you can modify) and also uses the Office theme. When you create a macro, for example, or a new style, these modifications are saved with the Normal template by default.

You can make other templates available as a global template, which makes their features available to any Word document you are working with. To load a global template, you use the Templates And Add-Ins dialog box—the same dialog box you use to attach a document template to your current document. You might use an additional global template to provide a suite of macros you want to have available all the time, for example.

> **To load a global template**

1. On the **Developer** tab, click **Document Template**.

2. In the **Templates and Add-Ins** dialog box, under **Global templates and add-ins**, click **Add**.

3. In the **Add Template** dialog box, select the template you want to use and then click **Open**.

4. In the **Templates and Add-Ins** dialog box, click **OK**.

Modifying a Template

You can modify a template file to add elements to it, to remove any elements that aren't working to your satisfaction, or to change the formatting and properties of styles to better emphasize the information the template is designed to present.

You can open the template file from the Templates folder (or from whatever folder you've used to store the template) and make changes to it as you would another document. After you make these changes, you should attach the updated template to a new document and review the results. If you are testing the changes on an existing document, be sure to select the option Automatically Update Document styles in the Templates And Add-Ins dialog box. (To open this dialog box, click the Developer tab and then click Document Template.)

Another way to modify a template is to make changes to it while you are working on a document. For example, you might find that you need to distinguish more clearly the Heading 2 style from the Heading 3 style. When you adjust the style in the Modify Style dialog box, select New Documents Based On This Template. Word displays a message box when you save the document that asks whether you want to save the changes you made in the template. Click Yes when you see this message to save the changes you made to a document to the template the document is based on.

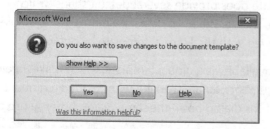

➤ **To change the template file**

1. Click **File**, **Open**, and then open the template file you want to change.
2. Make the changes you want to the template file.
3. Click **File**, **Save** (or click the **Save** button on the Quick Access Toolbar).

➤ **To change a template while working on a document**

1. In the **Styles** gallery on the **Home** tab, right-click the style you want to change and then click **Modify**.
2. In the **Modify Styles** dialog box, update the style with the changes you want.
3. At the bottom of the dialog box, select **New documents based on this template**.
4. Click **OK** in the **Modify Styles** dialog box, and then click **File**, **Save** to save the document.
5. If a message box appears, click **Yes** to confirm that you want to save changes to the document template.

Designing Your Own Template

If you want to design your own template, you have a few choices as your starting point. You can use a document you've created as the basis of the template, you can use another template file as your foundation, or you can create a template yourself from the ground up.

> **Tip** When you create a template, save the file in the Templates folder so that the templates are visible when you click My Templates in Backstage view or use the Templates And Add-Ins dialog box to attach a template to a document. By default, the template folder is located at Users/*UserName*/AppData/Roaming/Microsoft/Templates.

Here are some of the elements you should consider modifying or including in a template:

- **Styles** What styles do you need? Can you work with only the built-in styles, or do you need to define each style from scratch? Depending on the purpose of the template, you need to consider styles for headings, normal paragraphs, lists, tables, illustrations and images, and other elements.

> **See Also** For more information about creating styles, see Chapter 2, "Formatting Content," later in this section of the book.

- **Header and footer** Add page numbering, the date, a document title (for example, "Request for Proposal"), and other information (for example, the labels "Draft" or "Confidential") that you want each document based on this template to contain in these areas. To define a header and a footer, click Header or Footer on the Insert tab and then select the format you want to use.

> **See Also** For more information about defining headers and footers, see Chapter 2 later in this section of the book.

- **Images** Add a company logo or other graphic that should be part of each document. Click Picture on the Insert tab to add a picture to a document.

- **Page layout** Use the commands and tools on the Page Layout tab to set margins, the page orientation, page size, the number of columns, and other layout-related settings.

- **Document references** Add a placeholder table of contents, if applicable. If the template is for documents that include a number of illustrations, indicate whether captions are required and define a default style for captions.

- **Placeholder text** Add placeholder text for elements such as an address block, product references, agenda items, meeting notes, and other content that should be included in documents based on the template.

- **Tables** What type of table formats do you need? Can you use one of the built-in table styles provided by Word, or do you want to define your own?

- **Macros** Create macros that might be applicable for the template.

> **See Also** For more information about macros, see Chapter 5 later in this section of the book.

- **Building blocks** Building blocks are content elements or other document parts that are stored in galleries. You can save building blocks and distribute them with templates. When you send or make the template available to others, the building blocks you saved with the template are available in the galleries.

> **See Also** For more information on creating building blocks, see "Construct Reusable Content" in Chapter 2 later in this section of the book.

- **Content controls** You can add certain types of content controls to a template to help you and other users manage information. For example, you can add a drop-down list control to a template, define the items in that list, and then select the items you need as you build a document. By setting properties for a content control, you can restrict the content the control allows (only certain items in a list) or provide more flexibility. You can find more information about specific content controls in the next section.

Adding Content Controls

This section provides additional information about the types of content controls you can add to a template (or to a document). You add a content control by using the Controls group on the Developer tab, which lets you define elements such as a list, a date picker, or a rich-text control for a template.

> **Tip** To add content controls to a template, you need to show the Developer tab. Click the File tab, click Options, and then click Customize Ribbon. Under Customize The Ribbon, click Main Tabs, select the Developer check box, and then click OK.

Here's a quick rundown on some of the control controls you might use. Word displays a ScreenTip that you can read to identify each control:

- **Rich text** Used to hold text. You can format text as bold or italic, include multiple paragraphs, and add other formatting.

- **Plain text** Used to hold text. Use the plain text control if you want to limit what users can do with respect to formatting the text.

- **Combo box** Users can select from a list of defined choices or type their own information. If you select the Contents Cannot Be Edited check box in the properties for this control, users won't be able to add their own items to the list.

- **Drop-down list** In this control, users can select only from the list of defined options.

- **Building block** Use a building block control when you want people to choose a specific block of text. In a proposal, for example, you might include a building block control that indicates the length of time for which the proposal is valid or other types of boilerplate text. For more information about building blocks, see Chapter 5 later in this section of the book.

- **Picture** Use this control to embed an image file.

- **Date picker** This control inserts a calendar control that lets you select a date.

- **Check box** Use the check box control to provide a set of options in the template.

> **Tip** To group content controls, select the controls and then click Group in the Controls group. For example, if you want to keep three check boxes together as a unit so that they cannot be edited or deleted individually, select those controls and then click Group.

Working with Content Control Properties

Protecting the content controls you add to a template can prevent users from deleting or editing a content control or a group of controls. For example, you can set an option that lets a user edit the content in a control but not delete the control from the template or from a document that uses that template. Word also gives you an option with which users can delete the control but not edit its content. You might use the second option (delete but not edit) in documents that require specific wording but not in every instance.

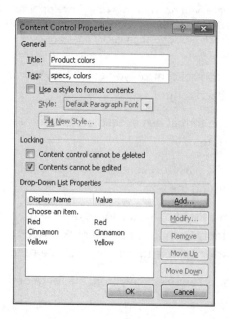

This dialog box shows how a list of items is defined.

Changing the Text in a Content Control

Content controls often include a simple text statement that tells users what the control is for. Changing this text so that it provides precise instructions helps users work with a template efficiently.

Changing the text is a simple operation. Open the template that contains the content control, and then click Design Mode in the Controls group on the Developer tab. Select the control whose text you want to change, select the text it contains, and then type the new text. This simple example shows how you can change the text in a content control to provide helpful information to users of your template.

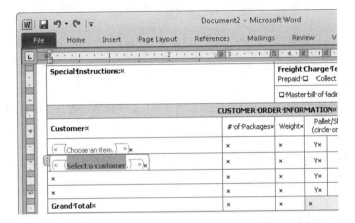

Protecting a Template You Design

Earlier in this chapter, in the section "Controlling the Editing of a Document," you learned how to apply a password to a document. You can also use the Restrict Editing command (on the Review tab or under Protect Document on the Info tab in Backstage view) to assign a password to a template. If you don't use a password, the work you've performed designing the template is subject to anyone's changes.

In the Restrict Formatting And Editing pane, click Yes, Start Enforcing Restrictions. (You don't need to set any restrictions unless you need them.) In the dialog box that appears, define the password you want to use to protect the template.

➤ **To create a template based on an existing document**

1. Click **File, New**.

2. In Backstage view, click **New from existing**.

3. In the **New from Existing Document** dialog box, select the document and then click **Create New**.

➤ **To create a template based on another template**

1. Click **File, New**.

2. In Backstage view, click **My Templates**.

3. In the **New** dialog box, select the template you want to use.

4. Under **Create New**, select **Template** and then click **OK.**

> ➤ **To create a template from scratch**

1. Click **File, New.**

2. In Backstage view, click **Blank document.**

3. Create the styles, placeholder text, and other elements you want to include in the template.

4. Click **File, Save.**

5. In the **Save As** dialog box, in the Save as type list, select **Word Template (.dotx)**, and then click **Save.**

> **Note** If you are saving a template that includes macros, choose Word Macro-Enabled Template (.dotm).

> ➤ **To add a text content control**

1. Click where you want to insert the control.

2. In the **Controls** group on the **Developer** tab, click **Rich Text Content Control** or **Plain Text Content Control.**

> ➤ **Insert a picture control**

1. Click where you want to insert the control.

2. In the **Controls** group on the **Developer** tab, click **Picture Control.**

> ➤ **Insert a combo box or a drop-down list**

1. Click where you want to insert the control.

2. In the **Controls** group on the **Developer** tab, click **Combo Box Content Control** or **Drop-Down List Content Control.**

3. Select the content control, and then click **Properties** in the **Controls** group.

4. In the **Drop-Down List Properties** area, click **Add**, and then use the **Add Choice** dialog box to define the first item for the list. Repeat this step to define each item required in the list.

5. Select options for other properties, and then click **OK.**

➤ **Insert a date picker**

1. Click where you want to insert the date picker control.

2. In the **Controls** group on the **Developer** tab, click **Date Picker Content Control**.

➤ **Insert a check box**

1. Click where you want to insert the check box control.

2. In the **Controls** group on the **Developer** tab, click **Check Box Content Control**.

➤ **Insert a building block**

1. Click where you want to insert the control.

2. In the **Controls** group on the **Developer** tab, click **Building Block Gallery Content Control**.

3. Click the content control to select it, and then click **Properties** in the **Controls** group.

4. Click the gallery and the category for the building blocks that you want to make available in the building block control, and then click **OK**.

➤ **To set or change the properties for content controls**

1. Select the content control, and then click **Properties** in the **Controls** group.

2. In the **Content Control Properties** dialog box, choose whether the content control can be deleted or edited when someone uses your template.

➤ **To customize the text in a content control**

1. In the **Controls** group, click **Design Mode**.

2. Select the content control you want to edit.

3. Edit the placeholder text, and apply any formatting.

4. In the **Controls** group, click **Design Mode** again.

Managing Templates by Using the Organizer

The Organizer is a dialog box that lets you modify and manage one template by using styles and macros already defined in another template or in another document.

In the example shown here, the template file Mytemplate.dotx appears in the Styles Available In list on the left. Below the list at the right, click Close File and then click Open File to open the Word template or document that contains the styles or macros you want to copy or use in Mytemplate.dotx. Select the styles in the list on the right, and then click Copy to include them in the open document. You can also delete styles or rename styles—for example, you might use names such as RFP_Heading 1 for your Request For Proposal template and Fax_Heading 1 for the style for your fax cover sheet.

➤ **To use the Organizer**

1. On the **Developer** tab, click **Document Template** in the **Templates** group.

2. In the **Templates and Add-Ins** dialog box, click **Organizer**.

3. In the **Organizer** dialog box, click the **Styles** or the **Macro Projects Items** tab.

4. Use the **Close File** and **Open File** buttons to open the template files or document files that contain the styles and macros you want to use.

5. Select the items you want to copy, delete, or rename, and then use the buttons in the middle of the dialog box to carry out these operations.

6. Click **Close**.

Practice Tasks

The practice files for these tasks are located in the practice files folder for Microsoft Word. You can save the results of these exercises in the same folder. Change the file name so that you don't overwrite the sample files. When you are done, try performing the following tasks:

- Click File, New, and then create a blank document. Design a template using the following elements:
  - Create a style named Regular Text.
  - Create three headings styles named Heading Level 1, Heading Level 2, and Heading Level 3, respectively.
  - Insert a header in the template that includes today's date and the page numbers.
  - Add a drop-down list content control with several items in the list.
  - Set the page layout options for the margins. Use a custom paper size of 7.38" x 9".
  - Restrict the editing and formatting of the document so that only the styles you define can be used.
  - Add a password to the template to protect it.
- Open the default Template folder at Users/*UserName*/AppData/Roaming/Microsoft/Templates. (You can enter this path in the search box on the Start menu to open the folder.) Create several subfolders, such as Budgets, Proposals, and Reports. Copy a Word template file into each of these subfolders. (These are just placeholders.) Click File, New, and then click My Templates. Note that the New dialog box displays tabs that match the subfolder names you used.

Objective Review

Before finishing this chapter, be sure you have mastered the following skills:

1.1   Configure Word options

1.2   Apply protection to a document

1.3   Apply a template to a document

2 Formatting Content

The skills tested in this section of the Microsoft Office Expert exam for Microsoft Word 2010 relate to formatting content in your documents. Specifically, the following objectives are associated with this set of skills:

2.1 Apply advanced font and paragraph attributes

2.2 Create tables and charts

2.3 Construct reusable content in a document

2.4 Link text boxes and sections

2.1 Apply Advanced Font and Paragraph Attributes

The next few sections describe ways that you can format text in Word 2010. Some of the basics are covered as a review, but the focus is on more advanced formatting, including changes you can make to character spacing, how to use ligatures, and how to apply effects such as shading and fills. You'll also learn about setting up styles.

Formatting Characters

Three of the keyboard shortcuts that many users of Word (and other Windows-based applications) learn from the start relate to character formatting: Ctrl+B for bold, Ctrl+I for italics, and Ctrl+U for underlining. For simple documents, these three formatting attributes might give you most of what you need, but they barely scratch the surface of the kinds of character formatting you can use in documents with special presentational needs.

To apply bold, italics, underlining, and many other formatting attributes to characters, you work with commands on the Home tab or in the Font dialog box, which you open by clicking the dialog box launcher in the Font group or by pressing Ctrl+Shift+F.

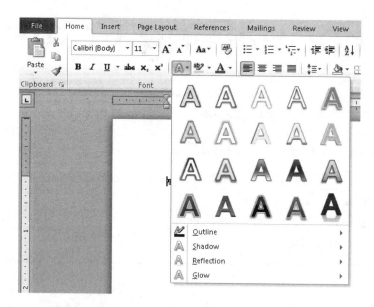

Use the Text Effects gallery to apply special character formatting from the Home tab.

Using the Font Tab

The Font tab of the Font dialog box lets you pick a font to use; a font style, size, and color; and a variety of text effects, including superscript, subscript, and small caps. Keep in mind, however, that applying local formatting to individual characters, words, or longer strings of text makes sense when you need to emphasize the text, but using character styles or paragraph styles is often more efficient and usually results in a document with a far more consistent appearance.

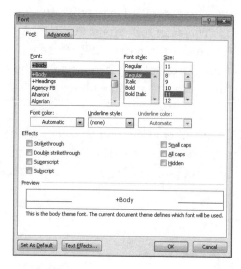

> **See Also** For more information about paragraph and character styles, see "Creating and Modifying Styles" and "Defining and Applying Character Styles" later in this chapter.

Applying Text Effects

Click Text Effects at the bottom of the Font dialog box to open the Format Text Effects dialog box. This dialog box provides detailed options for applying fills, outlines, shadows, reflection, and glow effects.

- Fills and gradients affect the color and fill patterns of characters.

- Outlines add a border to characters by using a specific line color, weight, and style.

- Shadow effects add a three-dimensional appearance to text so that it looks as though it is floating.

- Reflection effects show a mirror image of the text.

- Glow effects add radiance to characters.

To get a sense of the level of formatting detail you can apply, select the Gradient Fill option on the Text Fill page. The dialog box then displays controls for choosing a color, the type of fill, and the direction the fill pattern flows, as well as slider controls that let you adjust gradient stops, brightness, and transparency.

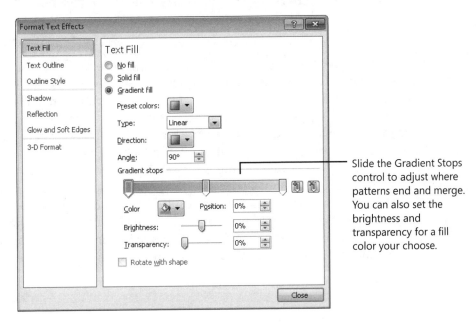

Slide the Gradient Stops control to adjust where patterns end and merge. You can also set the brightness and transparency for a fill color your choose.

Several of the other pages in the Format Text Effects dialog box include a Preset list. Use the galleries that appear when you display a Preset list to select an option for shadow effects, for example, that combines the detailed attributes you can refine on that page. You can, of course, use the detail controls to define and apply effects of your own making.

Applying Text Effects from the Home Tab

Another path to special text effects is through the Text Effects gallery on the Home tab. The gallery exhibits an array of built-in choices that combine fill colors and gradients, outlines, and shadows. Below the gallery are commands that lead you to additional options for outline, shadow, reflection, and glow styles. The galleries for these effects include links (Glow Options, for example) to their respective pages on the Format Text Effects dialog box.

To apply a fill color or gradient effect from the Home tab, click the arrow next to the Font Color button in the Font group.

Inserting a WordArt Object

Using a WordArt object is another approach to achieving special effects in formatting. To add WordArt to a document, select the text in your document, click WordArt in the Text group on the Insert tab, and then choose an option from the gallery.

The text effects you see in a WordArt object resemble the effects you can apply from the Home tab or from the Format Text Effects dialog box—and you can apply text effects such as a shadow or a glow effect to a WordArt object to enhance it even more. The decision to insert WordArt or format normal text with special effects should be informed by a couple of factors. If you apply text effects instead of using WordArt, you can search for the text, and Word includes the text when it checks the spelling in a document. You don't get these advantages with WordArt. Also, formatted text takes on the positioning and text wrapping of the text around it. You often have to move and tweak the position of a WordArt object. On the other hand, when you have a WordArt object looking like you want it to, you can copy it and use it in other documents or in other applications, and these applications might not provide the level of control over text effects that you have in Word.

Making Use of the Advanced Tab

The Advanced tab of the Font dialog box provides tools for adjusting character spacing, kerning, and other typographic features. These options come into play especially when you work with display type such as headings or need some special ornamentation.

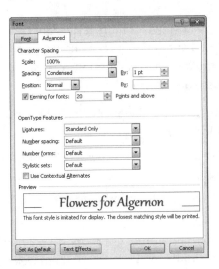

In the Character Spacing area, use the Scale list to specify a percentage by which characters are stretched to cover a larger area or squeezed together to conserve space. (The Preview area of the Advanced tab shows the effect of the selection you make, as it does for other options on this tab). To increase or decrease the spacing between characters, choose a setting from the Spacing list (Normal, Expanded, or Condensed) and then specify an amount in the By box. In a similar vein, to raise or lower characters above a baseline, choose Raised or Lowered from the Position box (Normal is the default option) and then specify an amount in this option's By box.

Kerning is another option for finely controlling the spacing of characters. Kerning won't be as noticeable in font sizes used in the body of a document, but in prominent headings that use a large-size font (and especially between certain sets of characters), kerning aids legibility. Select the Kerning For Fonts check box and then specify the point size at and above which you want Word to kern.

The settings in the OpenType Features area of the Advanced tab apply only to certain OpenType fonts. (OpenType fonts descend from TrueType fonts and are used on many different computer systems.) Some of these fonts are included in Windows and Office, such as Calibri, Cambria, Constantia, Corbel, and Gabriola. The following list describes the settings in the OpenType Features area:

- **Ligatures** A ligature is a character in which two or more letters are combined. Ligatures are used for aesthetic effect. Font designers can choose whether to include ligatures in one or more of the following categories. You can also choose options to use ligatures from all these categories or from none.

  ○ **Standard Only** Standard ligatures vary by language. In English, common ligatures join f, l, or i with a following f.

  ○ **Standard And Contextual** This setting includes character combinations designed specifically for the font.

  ○ **Historical And Discretionary** These ligatures included combinations (such as ct and st) that were once standard.

- **Number Spacing** Candara, Constantia, and Corbel use proportional number spacing by default. The varying widths of the numbers make them well suited for use within text. Calibri, Cambria, and Consolas use tabular spacing by default. Tabular numbers use the same width, making them well suited for aligning columns of numbers in tables of numerical data.

- **Number Forms** Numerical characters that use the "old style" vary in height and are often used when the numbers appear in text because they align easily with a mix of uppercase and lowercase characters. Lining-style numbers align on the baseline and are of equal height. They are used more for numerical data. The fonts Candara, Constantia, and Corbel use old-style numbers by default. Calibri, Cambria, and Consolas use the lining style as their default number form.

- **Stylistic Sets** Some fonts (Gabriola, for one) come with highly stylized combinations of characters for use in decorative text. Use the Stylistic Sets list to select one of the available sets. You'll often want to try more than one to get the effect you want, and you can apply different sets to different characters.

To check whether a font uses old-style or lining numbers by default, open Fonts in Control Panel and then double-click the font. The style for numbers shown in the font's sample text is usually that font's default style. Usually, fonts that use old-style numbers also use proportional spacing. Similarly, fonts that use lining-style numbers most often use tabular spacing as their default setting.

If you want to see whether any ligatures are included in a font, open Character Map in Windows. (In Windows 7, you can type **character map** in the Start menu's search box.) Select the font you want to examine, scroll to the bottom of the list of characters, and then check for fl and other ligatures.

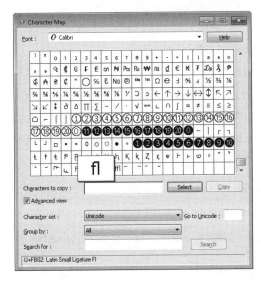

At the bottom of Character Map, you can see the ligatures that a font contains.

Adding a Drop Cap

For a dignified and classic look in a document, you can add a drop cap, an effect in which the first letter or first word of a paragraph is set in a larger size. To add a drop cap, the text must be formatted in a larger font and aligned with the top of the text in the rest of the paragraph.

Select the text you want to format, and then click Drop Cap in the Text group on the Insert tab. The options that appear let you wrap the drop cap within the paragraph or position it in the margin. Click None to remove a drop cap that's already present. Click Drop Cap Options to open a dialog box with the same positional choices and controls that let you choose a different font and fine-tune the position of the dropped characters.

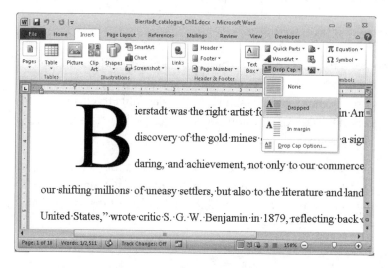

> ### To apply basic formatting to characters

1. Select the text you want to format.

2. Use the controls in the **Font** group on the **Home** tab to apply formatting such as bold, italics, font color, and others.

3. Click the **Font** dialog box launcher to open the **Font** dialog box. Use the **Font** tab to apply the formatting you need.

> ### To apply text effects from the Home tab

1. Select the text you want to format.

2. In the **Font** group, click the **Text Effects** button, and then choose the style you want to apply.

3. To work with other options for particular effects, click **Outline**, **Shadow**, **Reflection**, or **Glow**.

4. Select the effect you want to apply from the samples shown, or click the options link (not available for outlines) to open the **Format Text Effects** dialog box.

➤ **To use the Format Text Effects dialog box**

1. On the **Home** tab, click the **Font** dialog box launcher in the lower-right corner of the **Font** group.

2. In the **Font** dialog box, click **Text Effects**.

3. In the **Format Text Effects** dialog box, select the page for the effect you want to work with.

4. Apply the effects you want, and then click OK.

➤ **To apply advanced text effects**

1. On the **Home** tab, click the **Font** dialog box launcher in the lower-right corner of the **Font** group.

2. In the **Font** dialog box, click the **Advanced** tab.

3. On the **Advanced** tab, set options for character spacing and for OpenType features such as ligatures, number style, and number spacing.

4. Refer to the **Preview** area to see the results of your choices, and then click **OK**.

➤ **To add a drop cap to text**

1. Select the text you want to format.

2. On the Insert tab, click **Drop Cap** in the **Text** group.

3. From the menu, select the drop-cap style you want to use, or click **Drop Cap Options**.

4. In the **Drop Cap Options** dialog box, choose a position for the drop cap and specify settings for the font, lines to drop, and distance from the text.

Creating and Modifying Styles

Every paragraph in a Word document is assigned a particular style—and you can create an entire document that uses only the default Normal style and then dress up the text by adding bold or italic, increasing or decreasing font size, applying different fonts, and adding text effects. Even in a document that contains only one or two levels of headings and regular paragraphs of text, you need to do a lot of work to make elements of the same type consistent. Styles provide much more control and consistency, and after you apply styles, you can change style properties once and apply them throughout a document.

> **Tip** To see which style is applied to each paragraph in a document, you can switch to Draft or Outline view. You might need to increase the width of the style area pane in the Word Options dialog box. For more information about setting Word program options, see Chapter 1, "Sharing and Maintaining Documents," in this section of the book

The Styles gallery on the Home page displays several of Word's default styles, including the paragraph styles Normal, Heading 1, and Title (among others) and character styles such as Emphasis, Strong, and Subtle Reference.

> **See Also** For more information about character styles, see the next section.

To modify a built-in style that appears in the Style gallery, right-click the style name and choose Modify. This opens the Modify Style dialog box. In the dialog box, the style's properties are described below the preview box.

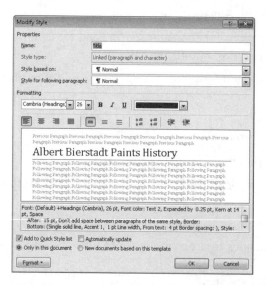

In the Modify Style dialog box, make changes to the style's properties by choosing a different typeface, for example, or setting a heading to a different font color, adjusting line spacing, setting indentation, and so on. To specify more detailed settings for a style, click Format at the bottom of the dialog box, and then choose Font, Paragraph, Numbering, or another option to open a dialog box with options you can set for that element of the style.

Be sure to review the settings in the check boxes and option buttons at the bottom of the Modify Style dialog box. Keep the Add To Quick Style List option selected if you have renamed a style and want to add it to the gallery on the Home tab. Select Automatically Update to apply the changes you made to all the paragraphs (and characters) that this style is applied to in the document. If you want to make this change more universal, select New Documents Based On This Template so that the changes you make to a style carry over to all documents you create from the current template. Keep the option Only In This Document selected if that's the scope you're working with.

> **See Also** For more information about working with templates in Word, see "Apply a Template to a Document" in Chapter 1 in this section of the book.

To create a style, click the Styles dialog box launcher on the Home tab, and then click New Style at the bottom of the Styles pane. Word opens the Create New Style From Formatting dialog box, which provides the same set of options as the Modify Style dialog box. Type a name for your style, and then select the type of style, a style to base this style on, and the style for paragraphs that follow paragraphs that use this style. Word assigns that style when you insert a paragraph break.

To create a style from text that you have formatted to fit the specifications you want for a style, select the text, click the More button in the Styles gallery, and then choose Save Selection As New Quick Style.

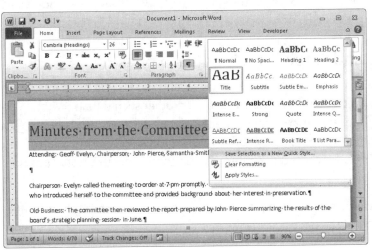

After you have text formatted the way you want to use it as a style, select it and save it as a Quick Style.

➤ **To modify a style**

1. In the **Styles** gallery, right-click a style and then choose **Modify**.

2. In the **Modify Styles** dialog box, revise the style's properties by changing the font, specific font attributes, indentation, line space, and other settings.

3. For more detailed settings, click **Format**, and then choose the command for the element you want to format—**Paragraph**, **Font**, **Border**, and other elements.

4. To update all the paragraphs the style is applied to, click **Automatically Update**.

5. To save the changes to this style to the current template, select **New documents based on this template**.

➤ **To create a style**

1. Click the **Styles** dialog box launcher in lower-right corner of the **Styles** group.

2. At the bottom of the **Styles** pane, click **New Style**.

3. In the **Create New Style From Formatting** dialog box, follow steps 2 through 5 in the preceding procedure to define the style's attributes.

➤ **To create a Quick Style**

1. Format the text with the attributes you want it to include as a style.

2. Select the text, and in the **Styles** gallery click the **More** button (which is the arrow at the lower-right corner of the gallery). Then click **Save Selection as a New Quick Style**.

Defining and Applying Character Styles

In many cases, you can capture all the formatting details you need in a paragraph style—indentation, font size, line spacing, and other such details. Within a paragraph, you can apply local formatting to characters by using the controls in the Font group on the Home tab or by choosing options in the Font dialog box, but you can also create styles specifically for groups of characters and then apply those styles as you format the document.

To define a character style, click the Styles dialog box launcher to display the Styles pane. At the bottom of the pane, click New Style.

In the Create New Style From Formatting dialog box, name the style (for example, Glossary Term) and then select Character from the Style Type list. When you make this selection, the options in the dialog box change so that they apply only to character styles.

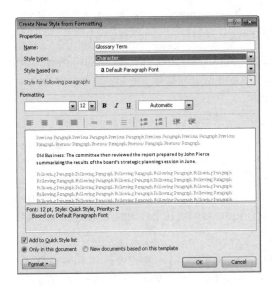

In the Style Based On list, you'll see Default Paragraph Font listed. Open the Style Based On list, and choose from among the built-in character styles if you want to use one of them as a starting point. You can then use the buttons and lists in the Formatting area of the dialog box to specify the properties you want to include in this style's definition.

➤ To define a character style

1. On the **Home** tab, click the dialog box launcher in the **Styles** group.

2. At the bottom of the **Styles** pane, click **New Style**.

3. In the **Create New Style From Formatting** dialog box, select **Character** in the **Style type** list.

4. Use the controls in the **Formatting** area to define the attributes for the style.

Practice Tasks

The practice files for these tasks are located in the practice files folder for Microsoft Word. You can save the results of these exercises in the same folder. Change the file name so that you don't overwrite the sample files. When you are done, try performing the following tasks:

- Open the file GreekText.docx. All of the text in this document is formatted with the Normal style. Follow the prompts in the file to create styles for specific document elements.

- Open the file GreekText.docx, and then open the Format Text Effects dialog box. Apply fills and gradients, outlines, shadows, and other effects to the text in the document. Specifically, increase the font size for the document's title to 26 points, and then add a blue outline and an outer shadow to the text. Then use the Text Fill page in the Format Text Effects dialog box to define a gradient fill for the text. Set the brightness to 10 percent, and set the transparency to 15 percent.

- One use of the options on the Advanced tab of the Font dialog box is to create a document for an occasion—for example, an announcement, invitation, or certificate. Open the file SaveTheDate.docx, and then open the Advanced tab of the Font dialog box. Select the text in this document, switch to the Gabriola font, and apply one or more of the stylistic sets. Increase the font size of one or more text blocks, and apply some of the settings for character spacing.

2.2 Create Tables and Charts

Some content in a Word document is best presented and formatted in a table or a chart. Defining and formatting tables and charts is especially important in a document whose content is supported by business statistics, financial results and trends, or other numerical data. In the following sections, you'll review the ways in which you can insert and format a table in Word and then move on to learn how to work with table data you create in Microsoft Excel, how to use formulas to calculate values in a Word table, and how to insert and format charts in a Word document.

Inserting and Formatting a Table

If you are unfamiliar with table design and layout in Word (or if you want a quick review), in this section we'll describe some of the fundamentals of how to insert and format a table.

You most often start by clicking Table on the Insert tab. Word then gives you the following options:

- Defining the rows and columns for a table by dragging through a grid.

- Opening the Insert Table dialog box, where you define the table's size (the number of columns and rows) and the table's AutoFit behaviors, which tell Word how you want it to adjust the columns and dimensions of the table. You can also specify a fixed column width. If this is a table layout you expect to use often, select the option Remember Dimensions For New Tables.

- Drawing the table. Choose this option, and your mouse pointer appears as a pencil. You can then draw table cells (and cells within cells if you need them).

- Converting text to a table. This approach is an easy way to convert a list arranged in two or three columns into a table—provided that the items in the list are separated by the same character, such as a comma, semicolon, dash, or tab space.

- Creating a table in Excel. For more information about this option, see the following section.

- Inserting a quick table. Use this option to display a gallery of table layouts you can choose from.

Among the ways you can add a table to a document is to define the table's dimensions and AutoFit behaviors in the Insert Table dialog box.

When you select a table in a document, the Table Tools tabs (Design and Layout) appear on the ribbon. Use the Design tab to apply and change table styles. The Table Style Options group includes a set of check boxes that you select or clear to specify that certain columns or rows receive distinctive formatting. For example, select Totals Row in this group if you are working with a table that shows a total in a row at the bottom of the table.

The Table Styles group provides a gallery of built-in table styles. If Live Preview is active, move through the gallery to see how each style affects the formatting in your table. Click Modify Table Style or New Table Style to add your own tastes or organizational standards to how tables appear.

The Draw Borders group extends the tools you can use to draw a table. You can change the pen color, line style, and weight; draw additions to the table; or erase portions of the table you need to correct or can do without.

You use the Table Tools Layout tab most often to add or delete columns and rows in a table, but it also lets you merge or split cells and to adjust cell size (the width of columns and the height of rows). The Layout tab also offers a few options that affect formatting, including the option to show or hide table gridlines and options for aligning the text in table cells.

➤ **To insert and format a table**

1. On the **Insert** tab, click **Table**.

2. From the **Insert Table** menu, use the grid to select the number of columns and rows in the table, or choose one of the alternative methods for inserting the table.

3. Select the table, and then use the **Table Tools Design** tab to apply a table style or to apply other formatting to the table.

4. On the **Table Tools Layout** tab, adjust the column and row widths, insert or delete columns or rows, and make other adjustments to the layout of the table.

Inserting Table Data by Using Microsoft Excel

When you need to present a table whose data is derived from or requires an array of mathematical or logical operations, you can use an Excel spreadsheet as the basis of that table.

Start this process by displaying the Insert tab in Word. In the Tables group, click Table, and then click Excel Spreadsheet. Word inserts a blank worksheet in your document and displays the Excel ribbon (absent the File tab).

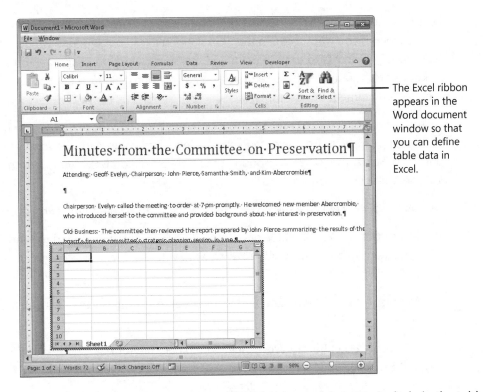

The Excel ribbon appears in the Word document window so that you can define table data in Excel.

In the blank worksheet that appears, type the data you want to include in the table—you have at your disposal all the features and functions that Excel provides.

To close the Excel ribbon and return to Word, click outside the boundaries of the worksheet. When you need to work again with the worksheet's data in Excel, right-click the worksheet and then click Edit, Open, or Convert on the Worksheet Object menu.

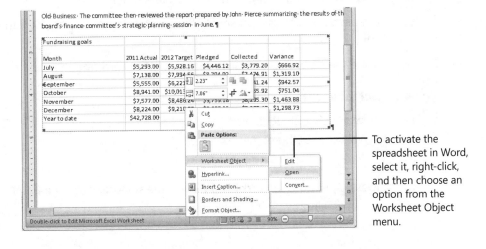

To activate the spreadsheet in Word, select it, right-click, and then choose an option from the Worksheet Object menu.

The Edit option opens the worksheet grid and displays the Excel ribbon within Word. Choose Open if you want to open the worksheet in Excel in a separate window. Choosing Open gives you access to the File menu in Excel, from which you can open other workbooks for reference, save the table as its own workbook, or send it to someone as an e-mail attachment, for example.

If you need to change the Excel data to a different format, choose Convert. In the dialog box that appears, you are presented with the following choices for the formats you can convert to. Select the Active As option in the Convert dialog box if you want to open the worksheet object in a different format.

- **Microsoft Excel Worksheet** The .xlsx format used by default in Excel 2010.

- **Microsoft Excel 97–2003 Worksheet** Use this option if you need to send the document to someone who needs to work with the Excel data in an earlier version of Excel.

- **Microsoft Excel Macro-Enabled Worksheet** A file format that lets you include macros.

- **Microsoft Excel Binary Worksheet** The binary file format (BIFF12) for Excel 2010 and Excel 2007.

- **OpenDocument Spreadsheet** A format that lets you work with the Excel data in another spreadsheet program, such as Google Docs and OpenOffice.org Calc.

➤ **To use an Excel spreadsheet as a table**

1. On the **Insert** tab, click **Table**, and then choose **Excel Spreadsheet**.

   The Excel ribbon is displayed within the Word document.

2. Type the table data in the spreadsheet, define formulas, and apply formatting and other features in Excel.

3. Click outside the object's boundaries to display the Word ribbon again.

➤ **To edit Excel table data in Word**

1. Select the worksheet object in Word, right-click, and then choose **Edit** or **Open** from the **Worksheet Object** menu.

   ○ Choose Edit to display the Excel ribbon in Word.

   ○ Choose Open to open Excel and display the spreadsheet in an Excel worksheet window.

2. To return to Word, click outside the spreadsheet object (if you chose Edit) or save the worksheet in Excel and exit Excel (if you chose Open).

> **To convert a worksheet object to a different format**

1. Select the worksheet object in Word, right-click, and then choose **Convert** from the **Worksheet Object** menu.

2. In the **Convert** dialog box, keep the **Convert** option selected or click **Activate As**.

3. Select the format you want to use, and then click OK.

Using Formulas and Calculations in a Table

You will probably use Microsoft Excel more often than Word to work with numerical data, but Word does provide the means for inserting formulas in tables to make calculations.

To insert a formula in a table cell in Word, use the Formula command in the Data group on the Table Tools Layout tab. The Formula command opens the Formula dialog box.

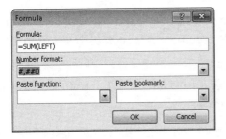

The SUM function appears in the Formula box if you select a cell at the end of a row of numbers or at the bottom of a column. Replace the SUM function with the function you want to use.

The Number Format list provides formats with and without comma separators (for thousands) and decimal places.

You can use the Paste Function list to create a formula that uses a mathematical function such as AVERAGE, COUNT, ROUND, or one of the available logical functions, such as FALSE, IF, NOT, OR, and TRUE. Each of the functions available is described in the following list:

- **ABS()** Calculates the absolute value of the value inside the parentheses.

- **AND()** Evaluates whether the arguments inside the parentheses are all true.

- **AVERAGE()** Calculates the average of the items identified inside the parentheses.

- **COUNT()** Counts the items identified inside the parentheses.

- **DEFINED()** Evaluates whether the argument inside the parentheses is defined. This function returns 1 if the argument has been defined and evaluates without error. It returns 0 if the argument has not been defined or returns an error.

- **FALSE** Takes no arguments. Always returns 0.

- **IF()** The IF function requires three arguments. It evaluates the first argument and returns the second argument if the first argument is true. It returns the third argument if the first argument is false.

- **INT()** Rounds the value inside the parentheses down to the nearest integer.

- **MAX()** Returns the maximum value of the items identified inside the parentheses.

- **MIN()** Returns the minimum value of the items identified inside the parentheses.

- **MOD()** Takes two arguments, which must be numbers or evaluate to numbers. It returns the remainder after the second argument is divided by the first. If the remainder is 0, MOD (short for Modulus) returns 0.0.

- **NOT()** Takes one argument. It evaluates whether the argument is true. It returns 0 if the argument is true or 1 if the argument is false. Mostly, it's used inside an IF formula.

- **OR()** Takes two arguments. If either is true, it returns 1. If both are false, it returns 0. Mostly, it's used inside an IF formula.

- **PRODUCT()** Multiplies the items identified inside the parentheses.

- **ROUND()** Takes two arguments. The first argument must be a number or evaluate to a number, and the second argument must be an integer or evaluate to an integer. It rounds the first argument to the number of digits specified by the second argument. If the second argument is greater than 0, the first argument is rounded down to the specified number of digits. If the second argument is 0, the first argument is rounded down to the nearest integer. If the second argument is negative, the first argument is rounded down to the left of the decimal.

- **SIGN()** Takes one argument that must be a number or evaluate to a number. It evaluates whether the item identified inside the parentheses is greater than, equal to, or less than 0. It returns 1 if it is greater than zero, 0 if zero, or –1 if it is less than zero.

- **SUM()** Calculates the sum of items identified inside the parentheses.

- **TRUE()** Takes one argument. It evaluates whether the argument is true. It returns 1 if the argument is true and 0 if the argument is false. Mostly, it's used inside an IF formula.

You can specify the table cells that you want a formula to operate on by using what Word refers to as *positional arguments*—LEFT, RIGHT, ABOVE, and BELOW. For example, to average the values to the left of a Totals cell, use the formula =*AVERAGE (LEFT)*. Combine positional arguments to specify a different range. For example, =*AVERAGE (LEFT, ABOVE)* averages the values in the cells to the left and above the table cell that contains the formula.

You can also refer to cells by using the name of a bookmark or by using cell references. For cell references, use the convention you might be familiar with from Microsoft Excel. The cell in the first row of the first column is cell A1, the cell in the fourth row of the third column is cell C4, and so on. To specify a range, use the colon operator as you do in Excel—for example, B2:D7. You can also use a convention using R and C values (RnCn). The following table summarizes this convention:

To Refer To	Use
An entire column	Cn
An entire row	Rn
A specific cell	RnCn
The row that contains the formula	R
The column that contains the formula	C
All the cells between two specified cells	RnCn:RnCn
A cell in a bookmarked table	Bookmarkname RnCn
A range of cells in a bookmarked table	Bookmarkname RnCn:RnCn

Note If you want to protect a formula, select the formula and then press Ctrl+F11 to lock the formula. To unlock the formula, press Ctrl+Shift+F11.

By default, you see the result of a formula when you insert it and when you open the document. But the formulas in a Word table are a type of field code, which means you can update a formula when you need to by using commands to update fields. Select a single formula (or more than one formula), right-click, and then click Update Field. To update all the formulas in a table, select the table and then press F9.

You can also right-click a formula in a table and choose Edit Field to open the Field dialog box. Click Formula in this dialog box to edit the formula.

Right-click a cell containing a formula and choose Toggle Field Codes to see the formula embedded within field-code markers—for example, {=SUM(LEFT)}. You can select text in the formula and edit it in the cell. If you take this step, right-click and choose Toggle Field Codes again to switch to showing field values. You then need to update the field to see the formula's result.

> **See Also** You can also find more information about fields in "Saving and Inserting Quick Parts" later in this chapter. Field codes are also used for index entries, for example, and for cross-references. For information about creating an index and cross-references, see Chapter 3, "Tracking and Referencing Documents," in this section of the book.

➤ To insert a formula in a table

1. Select the cell in the table.
2. On the **Table Tools Layout** tab, click **Formula** in the **Data** group.
3. In the **Formula** dialog box, type the formula in the **Formula** box.
4. To insert a function, click **Paste Function**, and choose the function you want to use from the list.
5. To refer to a bookmark in a formula, click **Paste Bookmark**, and choose the bookmark from the list that appears.

Charting Data in Microsoft Word

Government reports, dissertations, and many types of business documents need illustrations as well as text. The Insert tab includes a number of options in its Illustrations group for inserting an image, clip art, shapes (for illustrations such as block diagrams), SmartArt, screenshots, and charts. In this section, you'll learn more about creating and editing charts in Word.

Many users of Microsoft Office build charts in Excel. In Word 2010, you can use the same set of tools to create charts while you work in a document. Start the process by clicking Chart on the Insert tab. In the Insert Chart dialog box, select the type of chart and style of chart to use and then click OK. Excel opens and displays dummy data in a worksheet. The general layout of the sample data reflects the type of chart you selected. Replace the sample data with your own, and then close Excel to create the chart in Word.

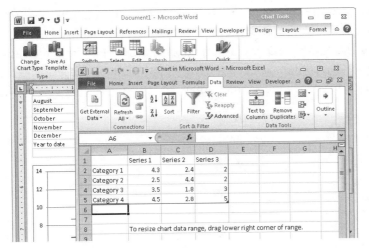

Word displays the Chart Tools tabs on the ribbon so that you can format and modify the chart in Word.

With a basic chart inserted in your document, you can select the chart and use the Chart Tools tabs (Design, Layout, and Format) to modify the chart's data, layout, and formatting. You can also change to a different chart type.

To change the type of chart you're using, click Change Chart Type. You see a different version of the Insert Chart dialog box (now titled Change Chart Type). Select the chart type and style, and then click OK.

Use the Select Data command on the Chart Tools Design tab to open Excel and display the Select Data Source dialog box. You can use this dialog box to change the cell range that contains the chart's data. The dialog box also provides controls you can use to make modifications to the chart, such as switching rows and columns or adding, editing, or removing a data series. Click Edit Data to open Excel so that you can make changes to the data itself. Close Excel when you finish making changes to the chart's data source or data.

The Chart Tools Design tab also provides a choice of chart layouts and chart styles that you can apply. Different chart layouts change the position of the legend, for example, and some display labels for the chart's data points. Click a layout option (scroll or click the More button to reveal others) to apply it to your chart and see which chart elements each layout includes.

The controls on the Layout tab let you further refine the elements in your chart. For example, use the buttons in the Labels group to adjust the position of the chart title and to specify whether and where to include a label for the horizontal or vertical axis. The Legend button reveals a number of choices for where to place a legend. At the bottom of each menu is a command (More Legend Options, for example) that opens a formatting dialog box for that type of label. The options in these dialog boxes give you another level of detailed control over the position and formatting for the labels, including formatting such as fill colors and patterns, shadows, and other effects. The Format Axis Title dialog box is an example of the dialog boxes you can open from the Labels group on the Chart Tools Layout tab. Select a formatting attribute on the left, and then use the controls displayed to specify the formats you want to use.

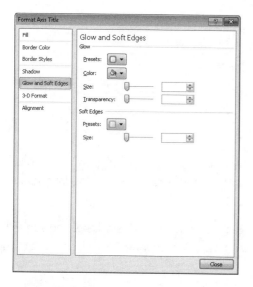

The Axes button opens a menu of built-in choices for showing data at a particular scale. For example, you can choose Show Axis In Thousands or Show Axis In Millions to condense the display of data (10 instead of 10,000,000). Here, too, you'll find a More option that opens a dialog box in which you can specify a number of axis options and apply formatting effects.

Use the buttons in the Background group to turn on or off the plot area, apply three-dimensional effects, and make changes to the appearance of the chart wall and chart floor. The chart walls and chart floor are background areas that anchor the placement of data in a three-dimensional chart.

On the Layout tab, use the Chart Elements list in the Current Selection group to select a chart element you want to format. Click Format Selection to open the element's format-ting dialog box. If you want to revert changes you make so that the element follows the chart style, click Rematch To Set Style.

When you have a chart set up just as you want it, you can save the chart as a template. Using a chart template can save hours of time if you are working on a document that contains a number of charts that you want to present consistently. Select the chart, and then click Save As Template in the Type group on the Chart Tools Design tab. Type a name for the template (using the .crtx file name extension, which is selected by default in the Save As Type list in the Save Chart Template dialog box), and then click Save. To create a chart based on this template, open the Templates folder at the top of the Insert Chart dialog box and then select the template you want to use. To delete, copy, move, rename, or distribute a chart template file, click Manage Templates in the Insert Chart dialog box, right-click the file, and then choose an option from the menu that appears.

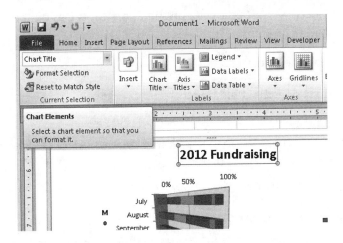

> ## To insert a chart

1. On the **Insert** tab, click **Chart**.

2. In the **Insert Chart** dialog box, select the chart type and style and then click OK.

   Microsoft Excel opens and displays sample data. A proxy for the chart appears in Word.

3. In Excel, enter the data for the chart.

   As noted in Excel, drag the lower-right corner of the sample range to resize the chart by adding or removing columns and rows.

4. Close Excel to return to Word, where the chart is selected and the **Chart Tools** tabs are displayed on the ribbon.

> ## To change the data source for a chart

1. Select the chart, and then click **Select Data** on the **Chart Tools Design** tab.

   Excel opens and displays the **Select Data Source** dialog box.

2. In the **Select Data Source** dialog box, change the range shown in the **Chart data range** box or select a new range by dragging in the Excel worksheet window.

3. In the **Legend Entries (Series)** area, use the controls to add, remove, change the range for, or reposition a data series.

4. In the **Horizontal (Category) Axis Labels** area, select a category and then click **Edit** to change the range for that category.

➤ To edit the data in a chart

1. Select the chart, and then click **Edit Data** on the **Chart Tools Design** tab.

Excel opens and displays the chart's data in a worksheet.

2. Revise the data, and then close Excel.

➤ To change the format of a chart element

1. Select the chart, and then click the **Chart Tools Layout** tab.

2. In the **Current Selection** group, open the **Chart Elements** list, select the item you want to work with, and then click **Format Selection**.

3. In the chart element's formatting dialog box, update the format for that element.

➤ To reposition the layout of chart elements

1. On the **Chart Tools Layout** tab, use the controls in the **Labels** group to change the position of elements, including the legend, chart title, axis titles, and data labels.

2. In the **Labels** group menus, click the **More** command for an element to open the element's formatting dialog box.

3. To show the data table with the chart, click **Data Table** in the labels group and then select **Show Data Table** or **Show Data Table with Legend Keys**.

4. Use the **Axes** command in the **Axes** group to turn on or off the display of an axis label, to format the axis, and to adjust its alignment.

5. Use the **Gridlines** command in the **Axes** group to turn on or off the display of major and minor gridlines. Click the **More Gridlines Options** commands to apply an array of formatting to the gridlines.

➤ To save a chart template

1. Select the chart in your document.

2. On the **Chart Tools Design** tab, click **Save As Template**.

3. In the **Save Chart Template** dialog box, type a name for the chart and then click **Save**.

Practice Tasks

The practice files for these tasks are located in the practice files folder for Microsoft Word. You can save the results of these exercises in the same folder. Change the file name so that you don't overwrite the sample files. When you are done, try performing the following tasks:

- Open the file TableFormulas.docx. In the cells at the bottom of the table in that document, insert formulas to calculate the values indicated. For example, use the MIN function to calculate the minimum amount of money raised over the months shown. You can use positional arguments or cell references in your formulas.

- Open a blank document in Word. Using the information in the file Fundraising.xlsx, create a table in Word that is based on an Excel spreadsheet. You can copy and paste information from Fundraising.xlsx into your document as necessary.

- Open the file Minutes.docx. Using the Worksheet Object menu, edit or open the Excel-based table in that document. Continuing with Minutes.docx, use the columnar chart in that document to experiment with chart formatting and layouts. Change the chart type to a line chart. Display the data table with the chart. Reposition the legend so that it appears on the left side of the chart. Use the generic line chart on page 2 of the document to practice editing chart data and modifying the chart's data source. For example, change the chart's data range so that it refers to cells A1:F6. Add additional data points in the new cells.

2.3 Construct Reusable Content in a Document

Very often, documents of the same type should use the same language in the same situation—for example, disclaimers and boilerplate language in a contract. Even in documents of different types, certain elements need to remain consistent in the information they present. An address block is one example. Being able to insert a ready-made piece of content when you are building a document saves time and works as an effective control to ensure that the document's elements are up to date and valid. In Word 2010, you can select a block of text, save it in a gallery, and insert it in a document time and time again with ease.

In this section, you learn about several kinds of content that you can reuse—building blocks, Quick Parts, and headers and footers.

Customizing Building Blocks

The galleries you work with in Word 2010 are filled with what are known as *building blocks*. Building blocks are available for document elements ranging from headers and footers to cover pages and tables. To add a building block to a document, you use commands on the Insert tab. (You've seen examples of how to use some of these commands in previous sections of this chapter. You also use other tabs to add certain types of building blocks.)

You can see the assortment of building blocks that come with Word by viewing the Building Blocks Organizer, a dialog box you open by clicking Quick Parts on the Insert tab and then clicking Building Blocks Organizer. Sort the list of building blocks by clicking a column heading. (The list is initially sorted by gallery.) Select a building block in the list to see a preview and a description. If you want to insert a building block in your document—for example, the Stacks footer—select that building block and click Insert.

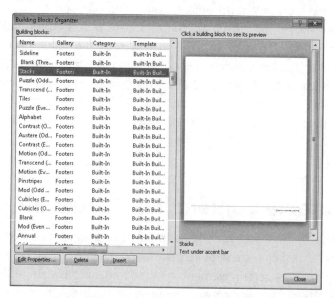

To make changes to a built-in building block—adding a cover page, for example—add it to your document, revise it, and then click Save Selection To Gallery (in this example, the Cover Page gallery). Word displays the Create New Building Block dialog box. (You can also click Quick Parts, Save Selection To Gallery on the Insert tab or press F3 to open the dialog box.)

Type a name for the building block, and then fill in the following fields:

- **Gallery** The Gallery list provides a long set of options for adding the entry to a built-in gallery (Headers, for example) if you don't want to stick with the default. Use these galleries to maintain building blocks in an orderly fashion.

- **Category** You can create categories within each gallery. Items in a gallery are grouped by their category.

- **Description** Use this field to enter a description that appears in a ScreenTip when you point the mouse to the item in a gallery and when you select the item in the Building Blocks Organizer.

- **Save In** Select the template in which you want to save the building block. Choose Normal.dotm to save it in Word's general template so that you can insert it in any document. Select the name of the template attached to the current document to store the building block there. This choice makes the building block available to new documents based on this template. Select Building Blocks.dotx to save it in the Building Blocks template. This choice also makes the building blocks available for all the documents you create.

- **Options** pecify how you want to insert the building block. The choices are Insert Content Only, Insert Content In Its Own Paragraph, and Insert Content In Its Own Page. The first of these choices places the building block at the cursor without adding a paragraph or page break.

> **Note** The Edit Properties button in the Building Blocks Organizer opens the Modify Building Block dialog box, which provides the same fields as the Create New Building Block dialog box. Although you won't often need to change the properties of built-in building blocks, you might do so for any building blocks you create. Still, if you work with any of the built-in building blocks regularly, you can use this dialog box to change its gallery affiliation (to a custom gallery, perhaps) or to recategorize it.

➤ **To create a custom building block**

1. Display the document element you want to create as a building block. This might be a cover page, an equation, a header or footer, a table, a text box, or a simple block of text.

2. Make any changes to this element, select it, and then click **Save Selection to Gallery** in the group for that element on the **Insert** tab. (The name of the element appears before **Gallery**.)

3. In the **Create New Building Block** dialog box, name the building block.

4. Make selections for the building block's gallery and category.

5. Type a description for the building block, and designate in which template the building block should be stored.

6. Choose an option for how to insert the building block, and then click **OK**.

Saving and Inserting Quick Parts

Quick Parts come in several varieties—AutoText entries (a type of building block), document properties, and fields. You gain access to Quick Parts by clicking that command in the Text group on the Insert tab.

> **See Also**   The Quick Parts command also appears when you work with headers and footers. For more information, see "Working with Headers and Footers," later in this chapter.

To define an AutoText entry, first select the text you want to save. Open the Quick Parts menu, click AutoText, and then click Save Selection To AutoText Gallery. You'll see the Create New Building Block dialog box, with the gallery you selected shown by default and with the Save In list showing Normal.dotm.

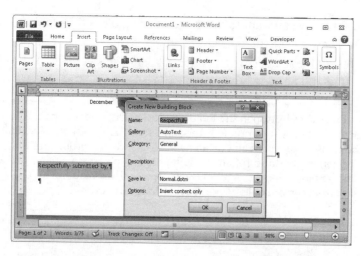

To insert an AutoText entry, click Quick Parts, AutoText on the Insert tab, and then select the entry you want to insert. A faster way to insert an AutoText entry is to type its name (or just the first few characters) and then press F3.

Select Document Properties from the Quick Parts menu to choose from a list that includes Abstract, Company, Keywords, Manager, Title, and others. Values for some properties (Author, for example) are filled in automatically by Word. You can specify values for other properties on the Info tab in Backstage view, in the document's Properties dialog box, or in the Document Panel that you can open from the Info tab. If a value hasn't been set for the property you choose, you can enter the value when you insert the property as a Quick Part. You can select the content control that defines a property and use the Save Selection To Quick Part Gallery to reuse it in the future.

Fields, the third type of Quick Part, are placeholders for specific types of content and data. The information a field contains can be updated automatically. The types of fields you can use is very broad, and Word uses fields for many different features that you might use regularly, including tables of contents, index entries, and the date and time. Use the Field dialog box to insert a field and specify formatting or other related information. You can view all fields or select a category from the list box at the top.

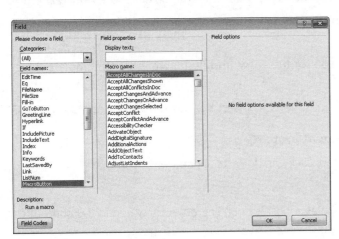

Fields can be used for a wide variety of operations, including adding a button to a document that runs a macro.

For example, to insert a field that shows who last saved a document, select LastSavedBy in the list of fields, specify the format you want to use (uppercase, lowercase, and so on), and then click OK. This bit of information might be helpfully placed on the first page of a document that a group is collaborating on or in the header or footer for that document.

To see the inner workings of a field, right-click the field and then click Toggle Field Codes. You'll see that the field's name appears along with a formatting reference and other information, depending on the field you are using. Fields are enclosed by curly braces—{author}, for example. You can enter field codes on your own by pressing Ctrl+F9, but using the Field dialog box is much easier. There, you see the required information as well as a description of the field.

➤ To insert an AutoText entry

→ On the **Insert** tab, click **Quick Parts, AutoText**, and then select the entry.

or,

Type the name of the entry (at least the first few characters), and then press F3.

➤ To save an AutoText entry

1. Select the text you want to define as AutoText.

2. On the **Insert** tab, click **Quick Parts, AutoText**, and then click **Save Selection to AutoText Gallery**.

3. In the **Create New Building Block** dialog box, name the AutoText entry.

4. Make selections for the gallery and category if you don't want to use the default options.

5. Type a description for the entry, and designate in which template the entry should be stored.

6. Choose an option for how to insert the AutoText entry, and then click **OK**.

➤ To insert a document property

1. On the **Insert** tab, click **Quick Parts, Document Property**.

2. Select the property you want to insert.

3. If the property's value hasn't been set, enter the value in the content control that Word displays for the property.

➤ To insert a field

1. On the **Insert** tab, click **Quick Parts, Field**.

2. In the **Field** dialog box, select the field you want to insert.

   Select a category to filter the list of fields that is shown.

3. Depending on the type of field you select, click **Options** or **Field Codes** to review and enter additional information.

Working with Headers and Footers

The information you define for a header or a footer is repeated on each page (or alternating pages) of a document or a document section. Page numbers are the simplest example of the type of information that a header or a footer presents (and whether you place page numbers in a header or a footer depends on factors such as page margins and page size, organizational preferences, or style conventions—the Modern Language Association, or MLA, for example, specifies that page numbers appear in the upper-right corner of each page).

Headers and footers can contain other information as well, including a document's title, a chapter's title, an author's name, the time and date, or labels such as Draft or Confidential.

Word 2010 provides a gallery of headers and footers that you can add to your documents as is (filling in particular information) or customize. You can also define your own headers and footers for a single document or as part of a template or in the headers or footers gallery if you use them regularly.

Headers and footers have their own group on the Insert tab. This group also includes the Page Number command, which lets you insert a page number in one of several locations and in a choice of formats.

More options for formatting page numbers are provided in the dialog box that appears when you click Format Page Numbers. Use this dialog box to change from the default format, which uses Arabic numerals (1, 2, 3...), to one that uses uppercase or lowercase roman numerals, letters (A, B, C...), or negative numbers (–1, –2, –3...).

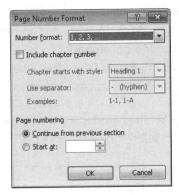

Another option in the Page Number Format dialog box give you control over whether a chapter number appears with a page number (a convention such as 3-1 or 3:1, meaning "page 1 of Chapter 3"). To use a chapter and page numbering scheme, select the Include Chapter Number check box and then select the style that marks the start of each chapter. (Only the built-in heading styles appear in this list.) In the Use Separator list, select the character that should separate the chapter number from the page number.

If sections are defined in your document, you can indicate whether you want pagination to continue from the previous section or that the next section of a document should start at a particular page number. Use this option if you set up a document in which elements such as the table of contents, foreword, preface, and other front matter use roman numerals and in which page numbers in the body of the document appear in Arabic numerals.

Headers and footers that include information in addition to page numbers (or that don't use page numbers at all) appear in galleries that Word displays when you click Header or Footer on the Insert tab.

Choose one of the built in headers or footers, click the option to find other styles on Office.com, or click Edit Header (or Edit Footer) to create one of your own. If you select one of the preset headers or footers, Word opens the header or footer area and displays placeholder text that you replace.

You work with custom headers and footers (as well as those that come with Word) by using the Header & Footer Tools Design tab, which makes an array of possibilities available. This tab includes the Header, Footer, and Page Number commands again, as well as various controls that let you define the header or footer you need:

- **Insert** Use the Insert group's commands to add the date and time (you can choose from a variety of formats), a Quick Part, a picture such as a company or department logo, or a piece of clip art.

  For Quick Parts, you might insert a custom AutoText entry you saved, such as "Confidential, For Internal Review Only," a document property (for example, the document's author or keywords that describe the document), or a field. The Quick Parts menu also gives you access to the Building Blocks Organizer, where you can select AutoText entries again or a building block from another category.

  > **See Also** For more information about saving AutoText entries and working with Quick Parts and building blocks, see the section "Saving and Inserting Quick Parts" earlier in this chapter.

- **Navigation** Use the controls in this group to switch between the header and the footer or to move between the header or footer on the next or previous page. Click Link To Previous to tie the current page's header or footer to the previous one.

- **Options** In some types of documents (generally long documents such as books), tradition calls for excluding a header or footer on the first page of a document section (or having only the page number) and to vary the information that appears on odd and even pages. For example, you might display the document title on even-numbered pages and section titles on odd-numbered pages. Options for both circumstances are included here. Also, clear the check box for the Show Document Text option if you want Word to hide the document's content so that you see only the information in the header or footer for the time being.

- **Position** Use the Header From Top and Footer From Bottom controls to set the position of a header or a footer. The Insert Alignment Tab command helps you gracefully arrange the elements of a header or a footer.

➤ To insert a preset header or footer

1. On the **Insert** tab, click **Header** (or click **Footer**).

2. Select the built-in header or footer format that you want to use. (Click the link provided if you want to find other samples on Office.com.)

3. In the Header or Footer area, replace the sample text and placeholders with information relevant for your document.

4. On the **Insert** tab, click **Close Header and Footer**.

➤ To define a custom header or footer or edit a header or footer

1. On the **Insert** tab, click **Header** (or click **Footer**), and then click **Edit Header** (or **Edit Footer**).

2. Use the **Header & Footer Tools Design** tab to insert or change elements for the header or footer:

   - Insert or edit the date and time, an AutoText entry, document properties, images, or clip art.

   - Set the options you need for whether the first page uses a different header or footer and whether a different header or footer appears on odd and even pages.

   - As necessary, set the position of the header in relation to the top of the document and the position of the footer in relation to the document's bottom margin.

3. On the **Insert** tab, click **Close Header and Footer**.

Practice Tasks

The practice files for these tasks are located in the practice files folder for Microsoft Word. You can save the results of these exercises in the same folder. Change the file name so that you don't overwrite the sample files. When you are done, try performing the following tasks:

- Open the file ContentReuse.docx. On page 1 of the document, insert the document property Company below the Author property. Using the Field dialog box, insert the LastSavedBy field below the content control for Company.

- Insert a document footer into ContentReuse.docx. Add a page number and the date, and then insert the text "For Internal Review Only." Select this text, and then save it as an AutoText entry. Save the header as a new building block in the Header gallery.

- Select the option to use a different header on odd and even pages. Set up a header for the next page that includes the page number, date, and the LastSavedBy field inserted as a Quick Part.

- Save the elements in this document as a new building block in the Cover Page gallery.

2.4 Link Text Boxes and Sections

If you use Word to create and edit a document such as a newsletter or a publication that uses columns for its layout, you can use text boxes to work with text that flows from page 1 to page 2 (or to a page later in the document or to another text box on the same page). In this section, you'll learn how to link and unlink text boxes, which helps you control the flow of text. You'll also learn how to create links between sections of a document, a technique you can use to navigate a long document.

Linking and Unlinking Text Boxes

To add a text box to your document, click Text Box on the Insert tab and then choose one of the text box styles that Word provides (others are available if you click More Text Boxes From Office.com) or Draw Text Box. If you draw a text box, use the mouse to define the box's boundaries and then use the handles that appear when the text box is selected to change its dimensions.

To facilitate the flow and editing of text in a text box, you can link two text boxes. When text boxes are linked, any text that does not fit within the boundaries of the first text box flows automatically into the linked text box. If you need to make changes to text—shorten or lengthen it, for example—the changes you make in one text box are carried through to the linked text box.

The process of linking text boxes involves a few easy steps: select the first text box, click Create Link on the Drawing Tools Format tab, scroll to the next text box, and then click in it. The mouse pointer changes during this process to resemble first an upright cup (when you click the first text box) and then a cup spilling letters, which is your clue that when you click again in the text box you've scrolled to, extra text will flow right along.

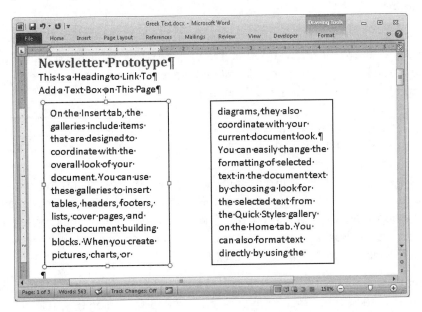

> **Note** You can link only to an empty text box. Word displays an error message if you try to create a link to a text box that already contains text.

When you need to break the link between two text boxes, select one of the text boxes and then click Break Link on the Drawing Tools Format tab.

➤ To link a text box

1. Select the text box you want to link to another text box.
2. On the **Drawing Tools Format** tab, click **Create Link** in the **Text** group.
3. Move to the text box you want to link to, and then click in that text box.

➤ To break a link between two text boxes

1. Select the text box you linked to another text box. (The text box you selected in step 1 in the preceding procedure.)
2. On the **Drawing Tools Format** tab, click **Break Link** in the **Text Group**.

Linking Document Sections

Moving from section to section in a long document can require lots of scrolling, and as you scroll you need to browse the document to find the text or section you are looking for.

You can take a couple of approaches to making navigation easier. One is to click Navigation Pane in the Show group on the View tab. This displays a document's heading (which in some cases correspond to section breaks). Click a heading in the Navigation pane to jump to that heading in a document.

> **Note** The Navigation pane also provides a search box that you can use to quickly search for a word or phrase in your document.

Another way to link sections in a document is to use bookmarks and hyperlinks. To set up these links, you use commands in the Links group on the Insert command. First define a bookmark by selecting the text (most likely a section heading or subheading) and then clicking Bookmark in the Links group. Type a name for the bookmark, which cannot include any spaces, and then click Add.

You can move to a bookmark by clicking Find, Go To on the Home tab, selecting Bookmark in the Go To What list in the Find And Replace dialog box, selecting the bookmark, and clicking Go To.

If you want to go one step further, you can create a hyperlink to a bookmark, possibly from a document's table of contents. After you create bookmark, click Hyperlink in the Links group. You then use the Place In This Document option in the Insert Hyperlink dialog box to specify the bookmark you want to link to.

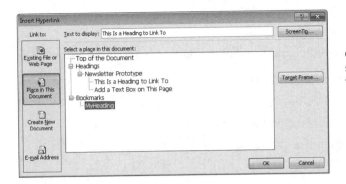

Create links between the sections in your documents to navigate more quickly.

➤ **To link document sections**

1. Select the text you want to link to, and then click **Bookmark** on the **Insert** tab.

2. In the **Bookmark** dialog box, name the bookmark, and then click **Add**.

3. Select the place in the document where you want to insert a hyperlink to the bookmark.

4. On the **Insert** tab, click **Hyperlink**.

5. In the **Insert Hyperlink** dialog box, select **Place in this Document**.

6. Select the bookmark to link to, and then click **OK**.

Practice Tasks

The practice files for these tasks are located in the practice files folder for Microsoft Word. You can save the results of these exercises in the same folder. Change the file name so that you don't overwrite the sample files. When you are done, try performing the following tasks:

- Open the file LinkingPractice.docx. Insert a text box on the second page of the document, and then link the text box on the first page to the text box you insert. Resize the first text box as necessary to see the text it contains flow into the second text box.

- Using the file LinkingPractice.docx, link the two section headings to the instances of those headings at the start of the document to create a dynamic table of contents.

Objective Review

Before finishing this chapter, be sure that you have mastered the following skills:

2.1 Apply advanced font and paragraph attributes

2.2 Create tables and charts

2.3 Construct reusable content in a document

2.4 Link text boxes and sections

3 Tracking and Referencing Documents

The skills tested in this section of the Microsoft Office Expert exam for Microsoft Word 2010 relate to tracking revisions in documents, merging documents, and creating references such as bibliographies, source citations, and indexes. Specifically, the following objectives are associated with this set of skills:

- **3.1** Review, compare, and combine documents
- **3.2** Create a reference page
- **3.3** Create a table of authorities in a document
- **3.4** Mark and compile an index for a document

In this chapter, you'll learn the mechanics for creating different types of reference material for a document, including bibliographies, cross-references, indexes, and tables of authorities (which are used in legal documents). Most of the tools you use for these tasks appear on the ribbon's References tab.

In the first section of this chapter, you'll learn details about tracking revisions in a document, including how to merge different versions of a document and review revisions in the combined document.

3.1 Review, Compare, and Combine Documents

In this section, you learn how to work with four groups of commands on the Review tab: Comments, Tracking, Changes, and Compare. You often use these commands when you work on a shared document with colleagues or coworkers, but you can use them effectively on your own when you need to annotate a document or compare and combine different versions of a document.

Adding Comments to a Document

A simple way to annotate a document is to insert comments. You might use a comment to indicate that a section needs revising, that information is missing, or that certain facts need to be checked. One advantage of using comments (rather than revision marks) is that they appear in context but are not integrated with the document's content. Each comment is numbered and identified by initials associated with the user who inserts it (using the initials specified on the General tab in the Word Options dialog box). You can move from comment to comment by using the Previous and Next buttons in the Comments group. Use the Delete command to remove a comment (or all comments at once) when a comment is no longer needed.

You can see comments in balloons and in the Reviewing pane.

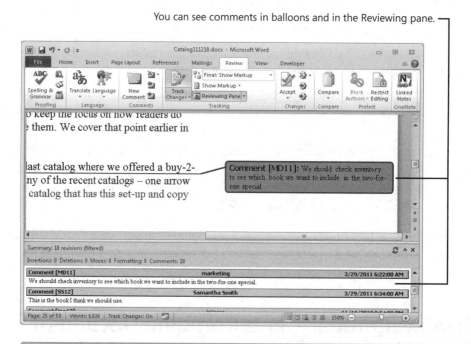

Tip To reply to a comment, place the cursor in a comment balloon and then click New Comment. Word identifies the new comment by adding R to the comment's ID. The R tells you that this comment is a reply to the comment that precedes it.

You can view comments in balloons in the Print Layout, Full Screen Reading, and Web Layout views. In Draft and Outline views, comments are displayed in ScreenTips when you rest the mouse pointer on the highlighted text. You can also view comments in the Reviewing pane. Other options for displaying comments are available in the Track Changes Options dialog box, which is covered in the next section.

➤ **To insert, review, and delete comments**

1. On the **Review** tab, in the **Comments** group, click **New Comment**, and then type the comment.

   Depending on which document view you are using, you will enter the comment in a balloon or in the Reviewing pane.

2. To move from comment to comment, click **Next** or **Previous** in the **Comments** group.

3. To delete a comment, select the comment and then click **Delete** in the **Comments** group.

   You can also delete all comments shown or all the comments in a document.

➤ **To reply to a comment**

1. Select the comment you want to reply to.

2. On the **Review** tab, click **New Comment**, and then type the reply.

Using Track Changes and Setting Track Changes Options

Tracking revisions that you or other users make to a document can be simple and straightforward. Click Track Changes on the Review tab, and then the insertions, deletions, and text moves you make in the document are highlighted, along with changes to formatting. You can then use the commands in the Changes group to find revisions and to accept or reject them.

You can also choose from a number of options for how revisions are tracked and displayed and how you view them. Many of these settings are controlled in the Track Changes Options dialog box.

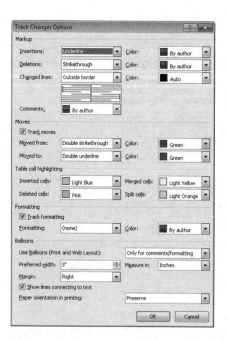

In the Track Changes Options dialog box, you can specify the following:

- Formatting that Word applies to insertions and deletions.
- Where Word places a line that indicates where a change was made.
- The color that identifies your changes or whether changes are specified by author.
- The background color for comment balloons.
- Whether and how Word tracks text that is moved.
- Highlighting for changes to table cells.
- Whether changes to formatting are tracked and how Word displays those changes.
- The size and position of comment balloons and whether Word displays a balloon for all types of changes, never uses balloons, or displays balloons only for comments and formatting changes. You can also specify whether Word shows a line that connects a balloon to the text it refers to.
- How Word orients the page when you print a document with revisions and comments.

> **Tip** Changes you make to a document are identified by the user name and initials entered in the Word Options dialog box. For some documents, you might want to be identified by your role or with a user name other than the one currently set. For example, you might want to associate revisions with the user name *Engineering* if you are reviewing a document on behalf of that department. You can change your identity from the Review tab by clicking Track Changes, Change User Name. Enter the user name and initials you want to use, and then click OK. Note, however, that any change you make is carried over to other documents. You should revert to your standard user name and initials as necessary.

Use the list of views available on the Display For Review menu (at the top of the Tracking group) to show or hide revisions:

- **Final: Show Markup** The default option, which shows the final document with insertions, deletions, and comments.

- **Final** Shows how the document appears if you accept all revisions.

- **Original: Show Mark** Shows the original document with insertions, deletions, and comments.

- **Original** Shows the original document without any revisions that have been made (as the document would appear if all revisions were rejected).

Because the Final and Original options let you see a document without its revision marks, you can use these options to read through passages of heavily revised text more easily.

The Show Markup menu lets you control the display of specific items. For example, in a document in which formatting changes have been tracked from start to finish, clear the check mark for Formatting to suppress the corresponding balloons or other highlighting. Word shows changes by all reviewers of a document by default. If you want to see the changes made by a specific reviewer or a particular set of reviewers, click Reviewers, click All Reviewers to remove the check mark, and then open the menu again and select the reviewer or reviewers whose work you want to inspect.

Display the Reviewing pane in horizontal or vertical layout so that you can see the collection of revisions made to a document. The Reviewing pane also shows a set of statistics about how many of each type of change the document contains.

> **See Also** For information about accepting or rejecting changes, see "Reviewing a Combined Document" later in this chapter.

➤ **To track changes and set track changes options**

1. On the **Review** tab, click **Track Changes** in the **Tracking** group.

   Word highlights the Track Changes command to indicate that the feature is active.

2. On the **Review** tab, click **Track Changes** and then click **Change Tracking Options**.

3. In the **Track Changes Options** dialog box, change the settings for how insertions and deletions should be marked, whether and how to track text moves and formatting changes, and which changes Word should display a balloon.

4. Use the **Display for Review** menu to choose whether to see the final or original document, with our without markup.

5. On the **Show Markup** menu, select or clear the check marks for which elements of the document markup you want to view (including comments, insertions and deletions, and formatting).

6. Click **Show Markup, Reviewers** to see only the changes made by a specific reviewer or set of reviewers.

Merging Documents

If you have two or more versions of a document that you want to compare or bring together, click Compare on the Review tab. Use the first option on the menu that Word displays to compare two versions of a document. (Word also calls this a *legal blackline*, a method of showing only what is different between two versions of the document.) In the Compare Documents dialog box, you point to the original document and the revised document, choose settings for the types of changes Word will mark, and specify whether Word will show the results of the comparison in the original document, the revised document, or a new document.

The second option on the Compare menu is Combine, which is more fully identified as Combine Revisions From Multiple Authors Into A Single Document. The Combine Documents dialog box is set up essentially the same as the Compare Documents dialog box.

When you click OK in the Combine Documents dialog box, Word is likely to display a message box telling you that only one set of formatting changes can be stored in the merged document. You need to choose between the changes in the original document and the revised document to continue merging the documents. Word displays the results of combining the documents in a set of windows that shows the combined document in a central pane and the original and revised documents in smaller panes at the right. Word also displays the Reviewing pane along the left side of the window.

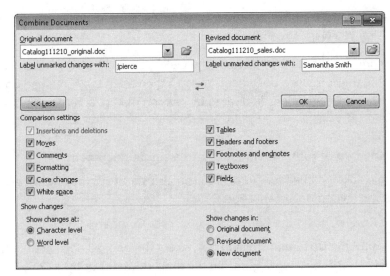

Clear check boxes in the Comparison Settings area for items Word can skip when it combines two documents.

The Character Level option shows changes in capitalization and other letter-by-letter changes.

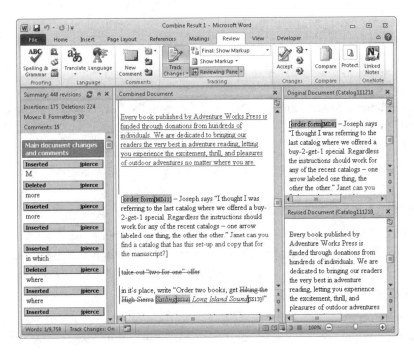

If you need to, you can merge another version of the document at this point by choosing Combine from the Compare menu again, pointing to the combined result document

(Combine Result 2 in the preceding screen shot) as the original document, and selecting the next version you want to combine.

To save the combined result, click Save on the Quick Access Toolbar (or click File, Save) and then name the combined document. You can then open the combined document and work through the variations (indicated by revision marks), accepting and rejecting them as necessary, to achieve a final document.

➤ **To combine two or more documents into a single document**

1. Open a blank document in Word. (You can also start with the original document or one of the revised documents open.)

2. On the **Review** tab, in the **Compare** group, click **Compare, Combine**.

3. In the **Combine Documents** dialog box, select the original document (if it isn't already selected) by choosing it from the drop-down list or by clicking the folder icon and browsing to the location where the document is saved.

4. Select the revised document you want to combine with the original document.

5. If necessary, click **More** to display the **Comparison settings** area and other options in the dialog box.

6. In the **Comparison settings** area, clear or select the check boxes to specify the document elements you want Word to use in its comparison.

7. In the **Show changes at** area, choose the option to show changes at the character level or the word level.

8. In the **Show changes in** area, choose an option for where Word will show changes: in the original document, the revised document, or a new document.

Reviewing a Combined Document

In the window that Word displays after you combine documents, you can scroll through the combined document and the original and revised documents at the same time. Your location in each document is synchronized, which lets you refer to any of the documents as you need to.

In the Reviewing pane, you can right-click an insertion or a deletion and then accept or reject it. Working in the Reviewing pane can be cumbersome. If you prefer to work in the document itself, close the Reviewing pane (by clicking the X in the pane's upper-right corner or clicking Reviewing Pane on the Review tab).

If you close the Reviewing pane, you can use commands in the Changes group to navigate from change to change (by clicking Previous or Next) and to accept or reject the changes showing in the combined document. The Accept and Reject menus have similar sets of commands: Accept and Move To Next, Accept Change, Accept All Changes Shown, and Accept All Changes In Document. The Accept (or Reject) All Changes Shown command is active only when you select an option other than All Reviewers from the Show Markup, Reviewers menu.

> **Tip** You can also right-click a change in the combined document and then click Accept Change or Reject Change in the menu that appears.

➤ To review changes in a combined document

1. In the **Reviewing** pane, right-click in a heading marked Inserted or Deleted and then choose the **Accept** or **Reject** option from the menu that appears.

   Or follow these steps:

2. On the **Review** tab, in the **Changes** group, click **Next** to move to the next revision.

3. In the **Changes** group, click the arrow under **Accept** (or under **Reject**) and then click **Accept Change** or **Reject Change**.

4. Click **Accept and Move to Next** to accept the revision and move directly to the next one. Click **Reject and Move to Next** to reject a revision and move to the next one.

5. To accept or reject all revisions at once, click the arrow under **Accept** (or **Reject**) and then click **Accept All Changes in Document** or **Reject All Changes in Document**.

➤ To accept or reject revisions made by a particular reviewer or set of reviewers

1. On the **Review** tab, in the **Tracking** group, click **Show Markup, Reviewers**.

2. Clear the check mark next to **All Reviewers**, and then repeat step 1 and select the first (or only) reviewer whose revisions you want to see. Repeat step 1 again to select any other reviewer.

3. In the **Changes** group, click the arrow under **Accept** (or **Reject**) and then click **Accept All Changes Shown** or **Reject All Changes Shown** to work with this group of revisions all at once.

   You can also move from revision to revision in the set that is shown and accept or reject revisions one at a time.

Practice Tasks

The practice files for these tasks are located in the practice files folder for Microsoft Word 2010. You can save the results of these exercises in the same folder. Change the file name so that you don't overwrite the sample files. When you are done, try performing the following tasks:

- Open the file SpringCatalog2012.docx, and make some revisions to this file and insert comments. For example, insert a table that you can use as the basis for an order form. Include columns such as Title, Price, and Quantity. Insert the titles of a few books or other publications you like as placeholders. Use the Save As command to save a new copy of this document.

- Create a new blank document in Word. Open the Combine Documents dialog box, and then point to the file SpringCatalog2012.docx as the original document. Merge the version of the document you created in the first step of this exercise to create a combined document.

- Open the Combine Documents dialog box again, and merge the document SpringCatalog2012_marketing.docx with the combined document you have already created.

- Save the combined document, open it in its own window, and then accept or reject one or more of the changes.

3.2 Create a Reference Page

Research and scholarly documents, and even many types of longer business documents, include citations to sources that the authors of the documents referred to in developing their ideas and performing their investigations and analyses. The References tab in Word 2010 provides tools that let you build a list of sources (using the information required by conventional authorities such as the Modern Language Association or the *Chicago Manual of Style*), manage these sources, and insert the citations where you need them in a document. When the citations are in place, you can easily create a bibliography or a list of works cited.

Word also provides a mechanism for creating and managing cross-references in a document. To aid navigation within a document, you can link a cross-reference to the element it refers to. Word also updates cross-references so that the information they refer to, such as section headings or page numbers, is kept up to date automatically.

Adding Citations to a Document

To add and define citations for a document, you work with the commands in the Citations & Bibliography group on the References tab. Word provides a number of built-in citation styles that you can choose from. These styles conform to conventions defined by organizations and in traditional style manuals. For example, the style list includes entries for the fifth edition of the American Psychological Association's style guide (APS Fifth Edition), the Modern Language Association (MLA Sixth Edition), and the fifteenth edition of the *Chicago Manual of Style*. The style you select here determines what information you enter for a citation.

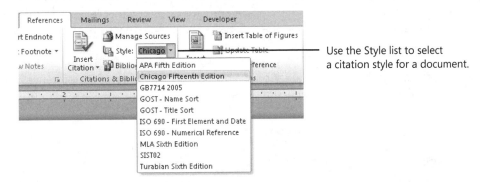

Use the Style list to select a citation style for a document.

You can use the Insert Citation command to add a citation that's already defined, to create a new source for a citation, or to enter a placeholder for a citation. You can return to a placeholder later when you need to fill in details for the source.

In the Create Source dialog box, first select the type of source (for example, book, conference proceedings, interview, or sound recording). The fields in the Create Source dialog box change to reflect the type of source you select. Word displays a simple example for each field when you select that field.

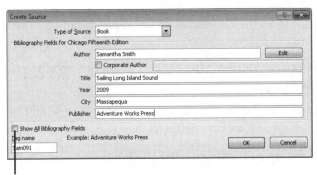

Select Show All Bibliography Fields to display fields for information such as volume, translator, and short title.

To create an entry with multiple authors, click Edit beside the Author field and then use the Edit Name dialog box to add each author name required for the citation. Word creates a tag name on the basis of the author name you enter.

Each citation you define is included in a gallery that appears when you click Insert Citation. Select a citation from that gallery when you need to insert it. To fill in the details for a placeholder, right-click the content control for the placeholder and click Edit Source. You can also use the Edit Source command to change the details of a citation inserted in the document.

To make changes to a citation itself, click the down arrow that appears on the citation's content control. The menu that appears provides options that let you edit the citation, edit the details for the source that is cited, convert the citation to static text, and update the citations and bibliography in the document.

When you work in the Edit Citation dialog box, you can add page references for the citation and choose to display the author, year, and title or suppress the display of one or more of these elements.

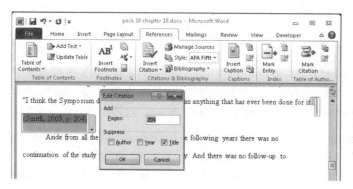

In the Edit Citation dialog box, you can specify the information that appears in the citation.

> **To insert a new citation**

1. On the **References** tab, in the **Citation & Bibliography** group, choose the style of citation you want to use.

2. Position the cursor where you want the citation to appear, and then click **Insert Citation, Add New Source.**

3. In the **Create Source** dialog box, select the type of source and then fill in the fields shown.

4. Select **Show All Bibliography Fields** if you need to enter additional details for the source.

➤ **To use a citation placeholder**

1. Position the cursor where you want the citation to appear, and then click **Insert Citation, Add New Placeholder.**

2. In the **Placeholder Name** dialog box, keep the default title provided or type a tag name for the source.

3. To fill in the source details, right-click the placeholder and then click **Edit Source.**

4. In the **Edit Source** dialog box, select the type of source and then fill in the fields required.

Managing Sources

When you define the details for a source in the Create Source dialog box, Word adds the reference to a master list of sources. To work with this list, you use Source Manager.

Use the Search and Sort boxes in Source Manager to quickly find a source or to arrange the sources by title instead of author.

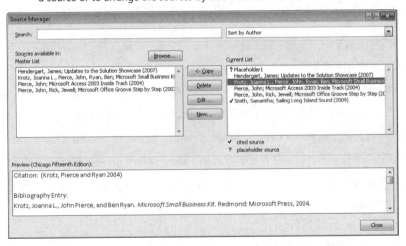

Tip Instead of providing details for each citation as you insert them, you can build a list of sources in Source Manager. Open Source Manager, and then use the Create Source dialog box (by clicking New in Source Manager) to provide the details for each source you need to cite. Then return to the document and place citations where you need them by using the entries in the Insert Citation gallery.

Source Manager shows two lists of sources: the master list and the list for the current document. You can copy sources from the master list when you need to cite them in the current document. (You can also copy a source in the list for the current document to the master list.) Use the other command buttons in Source Manager to edit source information or to delete a source. You cannot delete a cited source (indicated by a check mark) from the current list of sources.

Word stores the sources you define in a file named Sources.xml. To see this file, click the Browse button in Source Manager to display the Open Source List dialog box. You can copy this file and use it on another computer or share it with other users. To add sources from this file to Source Manager, display the Open Source List dialog box, select Sources. xml, and then click Open. But be warned that if you have sources defined on this computer (or if another user does), that source list is replaced by those defined in the copy of Sources.xml you open.

➤ **To manage sources for a document**

1. On the **References** tab, in the **Citation & Bibliography** group, click **Manage Sources**.

2. In the **Source Manager** dialog box, click **Copy** to move a source from the master list to the current list.

3. Select a source, and then click **Delete** to remove a source from a list.

4. Select a source, and then click **Edit** to update or revise details for the source.

5. Click **New** to open the **Create Source** dialog box and define a new source.

6. To change the sort order for the source lists, select an option from the **Sort** list.

7. To search for a particular source or set of sources, type the search string in the **Search** box.

Creating a Bibliography

To insert a bibliography that lists the sources cited in a document, click Bibliography in the Citations & Bibliography group. Word displays a gallery from which you can insert a list of sources that is labeled *Bibliography* or a list that uses the label *Works Cited*. Choose Insert Bibliography to insert a simply formatted bibliography.

Because bibliographies are a type of building block, you can change the formatting for the bibliography you insert, and then select it and save it to the Bibliography gallery to use in other documents.

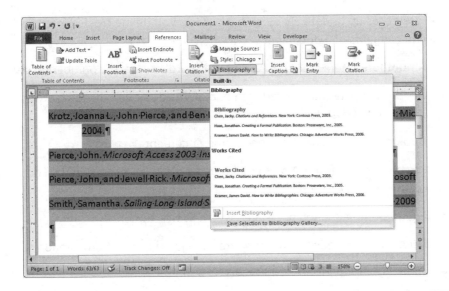

> **See Also** For more information about creating custom building blocks, see "Construct Reusable Content in a Document" in Chapter 2 in this part of the book.

➤ **To insert a bibliography or a list of works cited**

1. Position the cursor where you want the bibliography to appear.

2. On the **References** tab, in the **Citation & Bibliography** group, click **Bibliography**, and then choose the option you want from the gallery that appears.

➤ **To save a bibliography to the Bibliography gallery**

1. Insert the bibliography for the document.

2. Make any formatting changes you want to the bibliography entries.

3. Select the bibliography, and then click **Bibliography, Save Selection to Bibliography Gallery**.

4. In the **Create New Building Block** dialog box, type the name and description for this bibliography, specify its gallery and the template you want to save it in, and then click OK.

Using Cross-References in a Document

Cross-references let you easily locate specific content within the current document, and they also help keep numbered items (numbered tables and figures, for example) and page references up to date. By default, Word lets you define cross-references to the following elements of a document:

- **A numbered item** Paragraphs that use Word's automatic numbering styles

- **Heading** A paragraph styled with one of Word's built-in heading styles or a style based on those styles

- **Bookmark** A bookmark defined in the document

- **Footnote or endnote** Notes you insert by using commands in the Footnote group on the References tab

- **Equation** An equation associated with a Word caption

- **Figure** An illustration or other figure associated with a Word caption

- **Table** A table associated with a Word caption

Creating a Caption

Judging by the last three items in the preceding list, you shouldn't be surprised to find the Cross-Reference command in the Captions group on the References tab. (It also appears in the Links group on the Insert tab.) When you want to label an equation, a figure, or a table (or any other element you want to refer to in a document), select the object and then click Insert Caption.

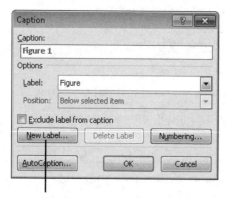

Click New Label to define a label
that you can assign to other elements
you want to cross-reference.

In the Caption dialog box, use the Label list to select the type of object you are adding a caption to. The default choices are equation, figure, and table. You can define other labels as you need them by clicking New Label. (You can delete custom labels when you no longer need them, but you cannot delete the default options.)

Type the text for the caption (making sure you include a space after the default label that's shown). Click the Numbering button to display the Caption Numbering dialog box, and then use this dialog box to switch to a different numbering format or to include a chapter number with a caption's label. (Chapters must be defined by using one of Word's built-in heading styles.)

AutoCaptions

If you need to insert a particular type of object repeatedly in a document and you want these objects to have a caption, click AutoCaption in the Caption dialog box. Select the object types (Bitmap Image or Microsoft Excel Worksheet, for example) for which you want Word to provide a caption automatically when you insert an object of this type. You can adjust the label that's used with a particular type of object and where Word positions the caption by default.

Inserting a Cross-Reference

With the cursor positioned where you want to add a cross-reference, type some text that introduces the object you are cross-referencing (for example, **For a summary of the amino acids analyzed, see**). Open the Cross-Reference dialog box, and then select the type of reference. For example, to reference a table, select that entry from the Reference Type list, and then Word displays a list of tables in the document (those tables labeled with a caption created in Word). With the type of reference selected, use the Insert Reference To list to choose the reference format—a page number, for example, or the text of a heading—and then choose the item you are referring to in the For Which Caption list.

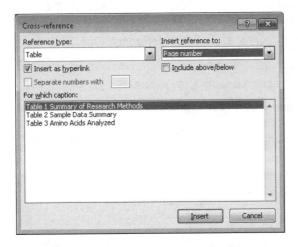

For some types of references (headings or bookmarks, for example), the Insert Reference To list includes two types of numbers: No Context and Full Context. These options are used with lists or outlines that use multiple levels. The Full Context option includes each element in a numbering scheme—for example, 4.1.1.a. The No Context alternative refers only to the last of the levels used.

Select the Include Above/Below option to insert a positional cross-reference that uses the word *above* or *below* depending on where the item you are referring to is located in relation to the reference.

Keep the Insert As Hyperlink check box selected if you want to create a hyperlink from the cross-reference to the reference's target. The hyperlinks you create in the Cross-Reference dialog box work in Word and in a browser if you save a document as a web page.

> **To create a caption for a document element**

1. Select the object you want to create a caption for.
2. On the **References** tab, in the **Captions** group, click **Insert Caption**.
3. In the **Caption** dialog box, in the **Label** list, select the type of object.
4. In the **Position** list, select an option for where you want the caption to appear.
5. Click **Numbering** to open the **Caption Numbering** dialog box, in which you can adjust number formatting for the caption.
6. Type the caption after the label in the **Caption** box, and then click **OK**.

> **To insert a cross-reference**

1. Type the text you want to use to introduce the item you are referencing.
2. On the **References** tab, in the **Captions** group, click **Cross-reference**.
3. In the **Cross-reference** dialog box, select the reference type.
4. In the **Insert reference to** list, select which option you want to use as the reference (page number, caption, section heading, for example).
5. In the **For which caption** list, select the target for the cross-reference.
6. Click **Insert**.

Practice Tasks

The practice files for these tasks are located in the practice files folder for Microsoft Word 2010. You can save the results of these exercises in the same folder. Change the file name so that you don't overwrite the sample files. When you are done, try performing the following tasks:

- Use the sources listed in the file PracticeSources.docx to create a list of six or seven sources in Source Manager.

- Open the file Citations.docx, and insert citations to the sources you defined. Insert several placeholders for citations as well.

- Open Source Manager, and edit information for three of the sources listed. Choose one or more of the entries for the placeholders you inserted, and then use the file PracticeSources.docx to enter details for those placeholders.

- Insert a bibliography for the file Citations.docx.

- Open the file X-refs.docx, which contains several tables and figures, along with section headings. Create captions for the tables and figures, and then insert cross-references to several of the elements in the file.

3.3 Create a Table of Authorities in a Document

Tables of authorities are used in legal documents as a reference to the cases, statutes, rulings, regulations, and other citations included in a document. Word can generate a table of authorities on the basis of the citations you mark and define in a document. Word's table of authorities feature provides several built-in categories that you use to classify citations, but you can modify this list or add categories of your own. Word also lets you choose options for formatting a table of authorities and for how the table displays the citations.

Marking Citations

To start building a table of authorities, select the text of a citation in the document and then click Mark Citation in the Table Of Authorities group on the References tab. The text you select appears in the Selected Text box and the Short Citation box in the Mark

Citation dialog box. You can edit the citation's text in the Selected Text box or in the Short Citation box. To change the formatting of the text, right-click in the Selected Text box and then choose Font.

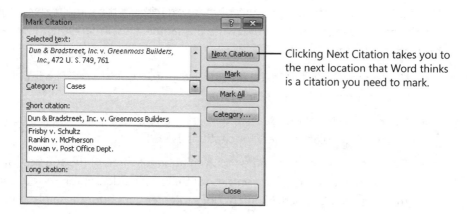

Clicking Next Citation takes you to the next location that Word thinks is a citation you need to mark.

Word provides seven named categories by default (cases, statutes, other authorities, rules, treatises, regulations, and constitutional provisions), along with unspecified categories numbered 8 through 16. You can replace a named category or assign a name to a numbered category to modify what Word provides.

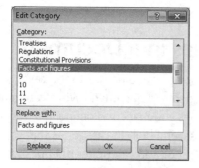

When you click Mark in the Mark Citation dialog box, Word adds the citation to a list. Click Mark All, and Word inserts a "table of authorities" field (identified by the characters TA) for each instance in the document that matches the text in the long and short forms you define. You can keep the Mark Citation dialog box open as you navigate through a document to mark other citations. The Next Citation button moves to the next likely citation in the document—Word uses clues such as "v." or dates in parentheses—for example, (2001)—to identify citations.

Formatting and Aligning a Table of Authorities

When you are ready to build your table of authorities, click Insert Table Of Authorities on the References tab.

In the Table Of Authorities dialog box, you can set the following options:

- **Category** Select which category of authorities you want to include, or choose All. You cannot choose more than one option in this list.

- **Use Passim** Keep this check box selected if you want to use the term *passim* to indicate that information the citation refers to is scattered throughout the source. Clear this check box to list specific pages.

- **Keep Original Formatting** Use this option to specify whether the citations listed in the table of authorities appear in the table as they are formatted in the document.

- **Tab Leader** Choose the type of tab leader to use (which helps align page numbers), or choose None from this list.

- **Formats** Choose a style for the table of authorities, or use the styles and formatting that is defined in the current template.

To change formatting for the table of authorities entries and the table heading, use the From Template setting in the Formats list, and then click Modify to open the Style dialog box. Select the element you want to change, click Modify in the Style dialog box, and then revise the formatting in the Modify Style dialog box.

➤ **To mark table of authorities citations**

1. In the document, select the text for a citation.

2. On the **References** tab, in the **Table of Authorities** group, click **Mark Citation**.

3. In the **Mark Citation** dialog box, edit the text for the citation in the **Selected text** box.

4. Edit the short form for the citation in the **Short citation** box.

5. In the **Category** list, select a category for the citation.

6. Click **Mark**, or click **Mark All**, to insert a table of authorities reference for each instance of this citation as you have defined it in the **Mark Citation** dialog box.

7. Click **Next Citation**, and repeat steps 3 through 6.

➤ **To format and generate a table of authorities**

1. Position the cursor where you want the table of authorities to appear in the document.

2. On the **References** tab, in the **Table of Authorities** group, click **Insert Table of Authorities**.

3. In the **Table of Authorities** dialog box, do the following:

   ○ Select the category of citation you want to create a table for, or select **All**.

   ○ Select or clear the **Use Passim** check box to use the term *passim* for short-form references or to show specific page numbers referred to in the citation.

   ○ Select or clear the **Use original formatting** option to maintain the formatting defined for the citation in the **Mark Citation** dialog box.

   ○ Select a tab leader to use to align page numbers.

   ○ Select a format for the table, or choose **From template**.

4. Click **OK**.

➤ **To replace a category for a table of authorities**

1. On the **References** tab, click **Mark Citation**.

2. In the **Mark Citation** dialog box, click **Category**.

3. In the **Edit Category** dialog box, select the category you want to change.

4. In the **Replace with** box, modify the category name.

5. Click **Replace**.

6. Make changes to other categories as necessary, and then click **OK**.

➤ **To modify styles for table of authorities entries**

1. In the **Table of Authorities** dialog box, select **From template** in the **Formats** list.

2. Click **Modify**.

3. In the **Style** dialog box, select the element you want to change—**Table of Authorities** (for entries) or **TOA Heading**.

4. In the **Style** dialog box, click **Modify**.

5. In the **Modify Style** dialog box, make changes to the style and then click **OK**.

6. Click **OK** to close the **Style** dialog box.

Practice Tasks

Tables of authorities are used specifically in legal documents. No special practice files have been included with this book, but you can use one of your own to build a table of authorities in Word by using the techniques you learned in this section.

3.4 Mark and Compile an Index for a Document

To create an index in a document, you need to complete two general steps: mark index entries in the file, and set options for how Word generates the index. You can find details about specifying index options in "Setting Index Options" later in this section. In the next section, you'll learn the mechanics of marking index entries.

Marking Index Entries

You can follow any of several approaches for marking index entries. You can select text in a document to use as an entry, insert an entry of your own where you want the index marker to appear, or insert index markers by importing a list of terms set up in an AutoMark file.

To mark entries in the file, begin by clicking Mark Entry in the Index group on the References tab to open the Mark Index Entry dialog box.

In the file, select a word or phrase you want to add as a main index entry and then click the dialog box to make it active. The text you select appears in the Main Entry field. You do not need to select text in the document to use as the main entry. You can also place the cursor where you want an index entry to appear and then type the main entry as a starting point.

You can edit the text for the entry and type a subentry if applicable. To include a third-level entry, type the subentry text followed by a colon (:), and then type the text of the third-level entry. In the Options area, select Cross-Reference and then type a reference to other index entries as applicable.

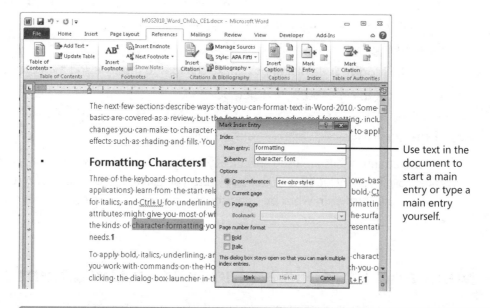

Use text in the document to start a main entry or type a main entry yourself.

> **Tip** To format the text for the index, select the text in the Main entry or Subentry box, right-click, and then click Font. Select the formatting options you want to use.

If this entry relates to the specific instance of this text on the current page, keep the Current Page option selected. To specify a page range for an entry, you first need to create a bookmark. Select the paragraphs in the range you want to use, and then use the Bookmark dialog box (which you can open by clicking Bookmark in the Links group on the Insert tab) to define the bookmark. In the Mark Index Entry dialog box, choose Page Range and then select the bookmark you defined for that range.

Use the options provided for formatting the page number in bold or italic, and when the entry is complete, click Mark to define it. Click Mark All to insert an index field for each occurrence of the main entry you defined in the document.

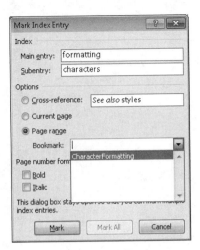

When you select text and mark it as an index entry, Word adds an index entry field. The field is identified by the characters XE and encloses all the information for an entry in curly braces. If you don't see the index fields in your document, click Show/Hide (the paragraph icon) in the Paragraph group on the Home tab. Here is an example of the information you might see for an index field:

{ XE "formatting:characters: font" \t See also styles" }

Another method for identifying the terms for an index is to list main entries in a separate file that Word uses to mark your document. You can set up the entries in a two-column table—with the terms you want to search for in the left column and the corresponding entries in the right column—or use a single list. The entries in this list are case sensitive. For example, if you are searching for the term *text effects*, Word won't insert an index field if the AutoMark file includes only an entry *Text effects*. To insert the entries, click Insert Index on the References tab, click AutoMark in the Index dialog box, and then select the file that lists the terms in the Open Index AutoMark File dialog box.

Setting Index Options

After you mark all the index entries, you use the Index dialog box to choose an index design and select other options.

For example, Word supports two types of indexes: indented and run-in.

In a run-in index, main entries and subentries are formatted as follows:

Styles: applying, 211; creating, 209; updating
    in template, 212. *See also* character formatting

In an indented index, the entries are listed in this format:

Styles
    applying, 211
    creating, 209
    updating in template, 212
    See also character formatting

When the length of an index is a factor, you save space by using a run-in index. When you select an option for the type of index, Word displays an example in the Print Preview area of the Index dialog box.

By default, Word creates a two-column index. You can choose the Auto setting or set the number of columns from 1 to 4. Choose the language you want to use as necessary. If you are setting up an indented index, you can change the alignment of page numbers by selecting the Right Align Page Numbers check box. Word previews this format when you select the option, and you can then select the type of tab leader you want to include (or select None from this list). The Formats list provide several options for the fonts, line spacing, and other styles Word applies when you generate the index.

If you keep From Template selected in the Formats list, click Modify in the Index dialog box to open the Style dialog box, which lists the styles for index levels 1 through 9.

Select an index level, and then click Modify to open the Modify Style dialog box and make changes to formatting attributes for that style.

> **See Also** For more information about modifying styles, see "Apply Advanced Font and Paragraph Attributes" in Chapter 2 in this section of the book.

When you finish defining options for the index, place the cursor where you want the index to appear, and click OK. Word sorts the entries alphabetically, adds page number references, and removes duplicate entries that occur on the same page.

Editing and Updating an Index

If you need to edit an index entry, you should edit the specific index marker and not the index that Word generates. Locate the field, and then edit and format the text within the quotation marks inside the curly braces that define the field. (Click Show/Hide on the Home tab if you don't see the fields in the document.)

To delete an index marker, select the field (including the braces) and press Delete.

When you need to edit an index, open the Find And Replace dialog box (by clicking Find, Advanced Find in the Editing group on the Home tab). Click Special (or first click More if you don't see the Special button), and then select Field. Click Find Next to move to the first field. To continue from field to field, click Find Next again, or close the dialog box and press Shift+F4.

After you revise the index entries, click F9 or click Update Index on the References tab.

> ➤ **To mark index entries**
>
> 1. On the **References** tab, in the **Index** group, click **Mark Entry**.
>
> 2. In the document, select the text for a main entry, and then click the **Mark Index Entry** dialog box to make it active. You can also position the cursor where you want an entry to appear, and then type the entry in the **Main Entry** box.
>
> 3. In the **Subentry** box, type a subentry (if needed). To define a third-level entry, add a colon to the end of the subentry, and then type the third-level entry.
>
> 4. To add a **See** or **See Also** reference, select **Cross-reference** and then type the text for the reference.
>
> 5. To specify a page range for an entry, click **Page Range** and then choose the bookmark for the range. (See the next procedure for the steps you follow to create a bookmark.)

6. In the **Page number format** area, select bold and italic formatting as required.

7. Click **Mark**. Click **Mark All** to mark all instances of this entry in the document.

➤ To define a bookmark for a page range

1. Select the paragraphs you want to include in the page range.

2. On the **Insert** tab, in the **Links** group, click **Bookmark**.

3. In the **Bookmark** dialog box, type a name for the bookmark and then click **Add**.

➤ To create an index from an AutoMark file

1. Create the AutoMark file using a two-column table. Specify the terms you want Word to search for in the left column. Add the corresponding index term to the right column.

2. On the **References** tab, in the **Index** group, click **Insert Index**.

3. In the **Index** dialog box, click **AutoMark**.

4. In the **Open AutoMark File** dialog box, select the file and then click **Open**.

➤ To specify index formatting options and generate the index

1. On the **References** tab, in the Index group, click **Insert Index**.

2. In the **Index** dialog box, set the following options. Refer to the **Print Preview** area of the dialog box to see the effects of your selections.

   ○ Select a type of index: indented or run-in.

   ○ Specify the number of columns.

   ○ Choose a language if you are using a language other than the default language on your system.

   ○ If you are using an indented index, click **Right align page numbers** (an optional choice) and then select the style of tab leader you want to use.

   ○ Select a format for the index, or keep **From template** selected.

3. In the document, place your cursor where you want the index to appear, and then click **OK** in the **Index** dialog box.

➤ To modify index styles

1. In the **Index** dialog box, select **From template** in the **Formats** list.

2. Click **Modify**.

3. In the **Style** dialog box, select the index level whose style you want to change and then click **Modify**.

4. In the **Modify Style** dialog box, make changes to the style and then click **OK**.

5. Click **OK** in the **Style** dialog box.

➤ **To edit and update an index**

1. In the document, click **Show/Hide** if the index fields are not displayed.

2. Select the text in the index field, and revise and format it as you need to.

3. Press F9 or click **Update Index** on the **References** tab.

Practice Tasks

The practice files for these tasks are located in the practice files folder for Microsoft Word 2010. You can save the results of these exercises in the same folder. Change the file name so that you don't overwrite the sample files. When you are done, try performing the following tasks:

- Open the file Chapter02.docx, which is an abbreviated version of the Word file for Chapter 2 in this section of the book. Work through three or four pages of the file, and add index entries for terms such as *formatting*, *styles*, *text effects*, and others. Add any applicable subentries, and define page ranges using bookmarks. Use the Index dialog box to set formatting options for the index, and then generate the index in Word. Edit a handful of entries using the field tags, and then update the index to reflect your changes.

Objective Review

Before finishing this chapter, be sure that you have mastered the following skills:

3.1 Review, compare, and combine documents

3.2 Create a reference page

3.3 Create a table of authorities in a document

3.4 Mark and compile an index for a document

4 Performing Mail Merge Operations

The skills tested in this section of the Microsoft Office Expert exam for Microsoft Word 2010 relate to mail merge operations, including how to use external data sources and merge rules and how to prepare and print envelopes and labels. Specifically, the following objectives are associated with this set of skills:

4.1 Execute a mail merge operation

4.2 Create a mail merge by using other data sources

4.3 Create labels and envelopes

Seeing the results of a successful mail merge operation can be very satisfying. After some preliminary work on your part—primarily creating the document you want to send and assembling or identifying information about the document's recipients—Word takes over, merges the content and information you supply, and produces each document you need. You can incorporate a number of options to control how Word produces the documents, and you aren't limited to producing paper mailings—you can also send a personal e-mail message to each recipient in a group by using the mail merge features in Word.

4.1 Execute a Mail Merge Operation

The Mailings tab on the Word 2010 ribbon provides the commands and options you need to set up and run a mail merge operation.

Setting up and running a mail merge operation entails six basic steps, as you move left to right across the Mailings tab (leaving the Create group alone for the moment):

1. Open the document you want to use in the mail merge, or start with a blank document and add text, illustrations, and other content. You can create the document later in the process, but you must have at least a blank document open to enable the commands you need on the Mailings tab.

2. Click Start Mail Merge, and select the option for the type of mail merge you want to run—Letters, E-Mail Messages, Envelopes, Labels, Directory, or Normal Word Document.

> **Tip** A directory is like a catalog. It includes the same type of information about a group of items (for example, the name of each item, a description, and a price), but the information is distinct for each item.

3. Click Select Recipients, and choose an option for the source of your recipient list. Use the Edit Recipient List command to select a subset from the recipient list and to update information. In the dialog box Word displays, you can sort and filter the list to organize and find particular entries.

4. Use the commands in the Write & Insert Fields group to insert an address block, a greeting line, and other merge fields, which are placeholders for information contained in the recipient list. Word inserts the details for each recipient's record when it runs the mail merge.

5. Preview the results. You can find a particular recipient or move from record to record in the list. Word can also check for errors in advance and compile those errors in a separate document.

6. Click Finish & Merge. The menu you see when you click this command lets you edit and save individual documents, print the documents all at once, or send the document as an e-mail message.

In the following sections, we'll expand on some of these basic steps.

> **Tip** The last option listed on the Start Mail Merge menu is Step By Step Mail Merge Wizard. The wizard opens a task pane and then leads you through the six mail merge steps.

> **See Also** To learn how to use an external data source to provide information about recipients and how to edit a recipient list, see "Create a Mail Merge by Using Other Data Sources" later in this chapter.

Building a Recipient List in Word

The Type New List option on the Select Recipients menu opens the New Address List dialog box. Enter information for the first recipient, and then click New Entry to add the next row. When you finish compiling the list and click OK, Word saves the list in the .mdb format. You can select the list and use it for other mail merge operations in the future.

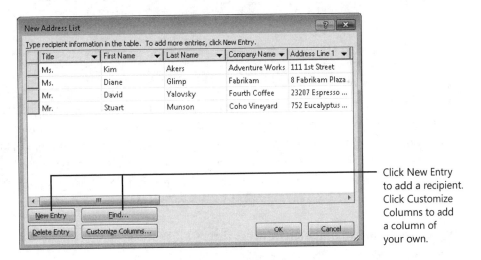

Click New Entry to add a recipient. Click Customize Columns to add a column of your own.

Scroll to the right in this dialog box to see the group of fields available by default. You can use the Customize Columns button to open a dialog box in which you can add fields of your own, delete fields you don't need, rename fields, and change the order in which the fields appear. By creating a custom field, you can expand the type of information the address list contains. For example, you could create a field named Donation and list the amount a recipient donated to your organization. You could create a field named Auction Item and use it to describe what someone purchased at an auction. You might create a field named Sales and use it to record the total dollar amount ordered by each of your customers. (The amount of information you can store in a custom field is limited to 254 characters, including spaces.)

Click a column heading to sort the list by that column, or click the arrow beside a column heading to open a menu that lets you sort and filter the list in other ways. You can filter for a particular value, filter for blank values to fill in missing information, or use the Advanced option to open the Filter And Sort dialog box. On the Sort Records tab, you can specify as many as three fields to sort by. On the Filter Records tab, you can set up a simple, single-field filter to find all records that equal (or do not equal) a particular value, for example, or you can define multifield filters by using the OR and AND operators. Use the OR operator when you want to select records that match any of the conditions you define. Use the AND operator to select records that match each condition you define.

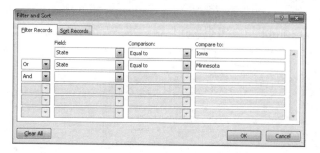

The Comparison list includes the Less Than, Greater Than, Less Than Or Equal, Greater Than Or Equal, and other operators. You might use these operators to find records with specific numeric values in a custom field you create. For example, for a mail merge operation related to a fund-raising campaign, you could create a custom field named Pledge (or Donation) and then filter on the values for that field (pledges above $1,000, for example) to send a document only to those recipients.

➤ To create and manage an address list

1. On the **Mailings** tab, click **Select Recipients**, and then click **Type New List**.

2. In the **New Address List** dialog box, type the information for the first recipient and then click **New Entry**.

3. Repeat step 2 to add all the recipients you need in this list.

4. To delete an entry, select the row, and then click **Delete Entry**.

5. To locate a specific recipient in the list, click **Find**.

   ○ In the **Find Entry** dialog box, type the text string you want Word to find. This might be a first name, a last name, a city name, or a value related to a different field.

   ○ To search for this text in a specific field, click **This Field** and then choose the field you want to search.

   ○ Click **Find Next**. Click **Cancel** when you locate the field you are looking for.

6. In the **New Address List** dialog box, click **OK**.

7. In the **Save Address List** dialog box, open the folder where you want to save this address list and then click **Save**.

➤ **To customize address list fields**

1. In the **New Address List** dialog box, click **Customize Columns**.

   Word displays the **Customize Address List** dialog box.

2. To define a new field, click **Add**, type the name of the field in the **Add Field** dialog box, and then click **OK**.

3. To delete a field, select the field and then click **Delete**.

4. To rename a field, select the field and click **Rename**. In the **Rename Field** dialog box, type the name you want to use in the **To** box and then click **OK**.

5. To change the order of the fields, select the field you want to move and then click **Move Up** or **Move Down**.

Adding Merge Fields

Merge fields correspond to the columns of information in a recipient list. To add the information stored in a recipient list to a document, you insert merge fields where you want the information to appear. You can place the information at the start of the document to define an address block or a greeting and also within the body of the document, where you want to include a company name, for example, or other information.

Word provides composite merge fields for an address block and a greeting line. The Address Block command in the Write & Insert Fields group inserts standard information such as title, first and last names, mailing address, city, state, country, and postal code. In the Insert Address Block dialog box, you can tailor the address block so that it fits the needs of the mail merge you have underway.

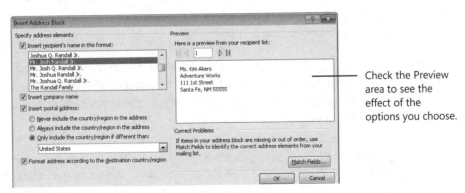

Check the Preview area to see the effect of the options you choose.

Here are some of the ways you can modify the standard address block:

- Choose a format for recipient names (first name only, first and last names, first and last names with title, and others).

- Clear the check box for the Insert Company Name option if you don't want to include that information. (The check box is selected by default.)

- Clear the check box for Insert Postal Address. For example, you might want only names to appear in the document and use address information for labels or envelopes. You can also specify under what conditions you want the country name to appear in the address block.

The Greeting Line command presents similar kinds of options. You can alter the salutation from Dear to To, for example, and specify how recipient names appear. Use the Greeting Line For Invalid Recipient Names list to choose a greeting that Word applies when information in the recipient list doesn't match the format you choose for a name.

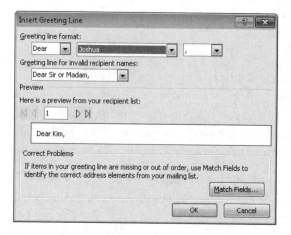

To insert individual merge fields, including any custom fields you define when building a recipient list, choose the fields from the Insert Merge Field list or use the Insert Merge Field dialog box. In the dialog box, select the Address Fields option to see an extended list of fields.

Keep in mind that you can insert these fields at any place in the document that makes sense. For example, in the final paragraph of a letter, you might repeat the recipient's first name for emphasis—"In closing, I want to thank you again <<First_Name>> for your support of Adventure Works."

> **Tip** You don't need to complete a mail merge operation in one sitting. You can save a document you are preparing for a mail merge operation, and Word maintains the association with the data source for recipients and any merge fields you insert. When you open the document to begin work again, click Yes in the message box that appears to confirm that you want to open the document and run an SQL command.

> **See Also** For more information about using the Match Fields button in the Insert Address Block or Insert Greeting Line dialog box, see the sidebar "Matching Fields" later in this chapter.

➤ To insert an address block

1. In the document, place the cursor where you want the address block to appear.

2. In the **Write & Insert Fields** group, click **Address Block**.

3. In the **Insert Address Block** dialog box, do the following:

   ○ Choose a format for recipient names, or clear the **Insert Recipient's Name In This Format** option to exclude names from the address block.

   ○ Specify whether you want to include a company name and postal address.

   ○ Select an option for when to include the country name in the address block.

   ○ Specify whether to format the address block using conventions for the destination country or region.

4. Use the **Preview** area to check how your choices affect the display of addresses.

➤ To insert a greeting line

1. In the document, place the cursor where you want the greeting line to appear.

2. In the **Write & Insert Fields** group, click **Greeting Line**.

3. In the **Insert Greeting Line** dialog box, do the following:

   ○ Specify a format for the elements of the greeting line, including the salutation and name format.

   ○ Choose a format for invalid recipient names.

4. Use the **Preview** area to see how your choices affect how the greeting line will appear.

➤ To insert a merge field

1. In the document, place the cursor where you want the merge field to appear.

2. In the **Write & Merge Fields** group, click **Insert Merge Field,** and then select the field you want to use, or open the **Insert Merge Field** dialog box, select the field, and then click **Insert**.

Using Merge Rules

Mail merge rules let you add conditions to the processing of your mail merge. The rules are listed on the Rules menu in the Write & Insert Fields group.

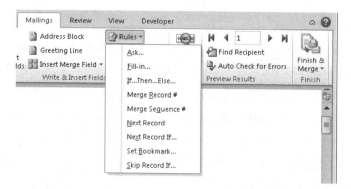

One helpful rule is the If Then Else rule. In the dialog box you use to set up this rule, you first specify an IF condition (for example, "If the Country field is equal to Canada"). In the Insert This Text box, type the text you want Word to insert when the condition you define is true. In the Otherwise Insert This Text box, type the text you want Word to insert when the IF condition is false. (Place your cursor where you want to insert the conditional text block before you define the rule.)

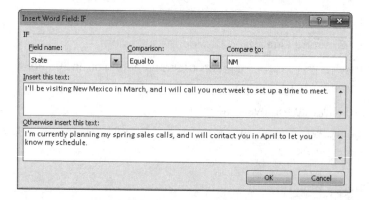

Two other rules you might make use of are Ask and Fill In. These rules can prompt you as each mail merge document is produced so that you can change information on the fly. To set up an Ask rule, position the cursor where you want to insert specific text, and then click Ask on the Rules menu. In the Insert Word Field: Ask dialog box, type a name for a bookmark. For example, create a bookmark named Discount where you want to specify the discount that a customer is going to receive. In the Prompt box, type a prompt that lets you or another user know what text to enter. In the Default Bookmark Text box, type the text you want to appear by default.

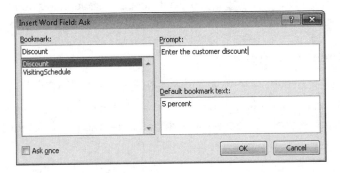

The Ask mail merge rule prompts you for information on the basis of a bookmark you define. Add custom text or accept the default text.

Select the Ask Once check box if you want to be prompted only at the start of the final mail merge. Keep the check box clear if you want the prompt to appear for each record. Click OK in the Insert Word Field: Ask dialog box, and then click OK again in the dialog box showing the default text. At this point, you'll see only a marker indicating that you've inserted the bookmark.

Now switch to the Insert tab on the ribbon, click Quick Parts, and then click Field. In the Field dialog box, scroll down in the Field Names list and select the Ref field. In the Field Properties area of the dialog box, select the name of the bookmark you created. You'll see now that the default text appears. When you start merging documents, you'll be prompted to accept the default text or insert an alternative for the particular document then being produced.

The Fill-In rule works similarly. Position your cursor where you want to be prompted to fill in certain information. Click Fill-In on the Rules menu, and then enter a prompt and default text in the Insert Word Field: Fill-in dialog box.

To associate a specific value with a bookmark, use the Set Bookmark rule. In the dialog box Word displays, type a name for the bookmark and then enter the value you want to associate with the bookmark. You can place the bookmark in multiple locations in the document (wherever the value you associate with it needs to appear). If you need to update the value later, you can edit the field's value once rather than update every instance.

➤ To define an If Then Else merge rule

1. In the **Write & Insert Fields** group, click **Rules** and then click **If Then Else**.

2. In the **Insert Word Field: If** dialog box, select the field you want to use in an IF condition, select a comparison operator and then enter the text or other value you want to match.

3. In the **Insert This Text** box, type the text that Word inserts when the IF condition is true.

4. In the **Otherwise Insert This Text** box, type the text that will appear when the condition you define is false.

Preview Mail Merge Results

On the Mailings tab, click Preview Results to toggle the display of merge fields so that they show recipient records. Click Find Recipient if you need to locate a specific recipient, or use the preview arrows to move from record to record in the recipient list.

Word can check for errors before you print documents or run your mail merge via e-mail. Click Auto Check For Errors. The dialog box that Word displays provides three options: simulating the merge and reporting errors in a new document, running the merge and pausing if Word encounters an error, and completing the merge and reporting errors in a separate document. The types of errors Word checks for include missing information in the recipient list.

Sending a Personal E-Mail Message to a Group of Recipients

As long as you have a compatible e-mail program (Microsoft Outlook, for example) and are using the same version of Word and Outlook, you can set up a mail merge operation to send an e-mail message to a list of recipients. Each message is a single item addressed to a single recipient—the message isn't sent to the group as a whole—and you can personalize each message as you might a mail merge document, by using, for example, only a first name.

Choosing E-Mail Messages from the Start Mail Merge menu switches the view of the open document to Web Layout. You can work in a different view if you want to. You won't create the e-mail messages until you merge recipient records and the document in the final step.

Select or build a recipient list. All the regular choices are available, but one key is that your data source should include a column labeled E-Mail Address in the header row. Set up the document with an address block, greeting line, and other merge fields as you would for a printed letter. You can then preview the results of each message you plan to send.

When you are ready to send the messages, click Finish & Merge, and then click Send E-Mail Messages. In the Merge To E-Mail dialog box, select the field you want to use for the message's To line (most likely, E-Mail Address), enter a subject line, and then select a format for the message (Attachment, HTML, or Plain Text). In the Send Records area of the dialog box, you can specify whether to send the message to all recipients, the current recipient, or a subset of recipient records. When you click OK, Outlook (or another compatible e-mail program) works behind the scenes to send the messages.

> ➤ **To send a personal e-mail message as a mail merge document**

1. Create the document you want to send as an e-mail message.

2. Select or build the recipient list, insert merge fields, and define merge rules as necessary.

3. On the **Mailings** tab, in the **Finish** group, click **Finish & Merge** and then click **Send E-Mail Messages**.

4. In the **Merge to E-mail** dialog box, select the field to use for the message's **To** line.

5. Enter a subject line for the message, and then select a message format.

6. Select which recipient records you want to send the message to, and then click **OK**.

Practice Tasks

The practice files for these tasks are located in the practice files folder for Microsoft Word 2010. You can save the results of these exercises in the same folder. Change the file name so that you don't overwrite the sample files. When you are done, try performing the following tasks:

- Open the sample file Job_prospects.docx, and then choose the option to create an e-mail message mail merge.

- Using the list of names on page 2 of Job_prospects.docx, create an address list in Word. Also, create a custom address list field named Position.

- Edit the recipient list, adding a contact of your own. Add your e-mail address to the E-Mail Address field for a handful of recipients.

- Insert an address block, and then insert the Position field in the highlighted area of the document.

- Create an If Then Else merge rule for the Position field that inserts the text "I am interested in your writer position" for the records in which Position equals Writer. For other records, use the text "I am interested in your recently announced position."

- Preview records, and then run the e-mail merge.

4.2   Create a Mail Merge by Using Other Data Sources

Names, addresses, and other information you want to include about recipients in your mail merge documents can come from a variety of sources. You can create an address list as a step in a mail merge operation (as discussed in "Building a Recipient List in Word" earlier in this chapter) or use a list that is stored in a Microsoft Excel worksheet, a Microsoft Access database, your contacts list in Microsoft Outlook, or one of a number of other formats.

To be of best use in a mail merge, the information in an external data source should be organized more or less as you need to use it for recipient information. For example, if you are compiling an address list in Excel, it's best to include a header row with column names that correspond to the fields Word uses for addresses in a mail merge.

Matching Fields

If the fields in an Excel worksheet or other data source you are using for recipient information don't correspond one-to-one with the fields in Word, use the Match Fields command in the Write & Insert Fields group to open a dialog box in which you can set up the field relationships you need. (You can also open this dialog box by clicking the Match Fields button in the Insert Address Block or Insert Greeting Line dialog box.)

If a field in your data source doesn't match a field in Word, Word displays Not Matched. To match fields in Word (listed at the left), select a field from the list to its right. Keep in mind that you cannot include any unmatched fields in the mail merge document. You can save the configuration of matching fields if you expect to use this data source for other mail merge operations on the computer you are using.

Selecting an External Data Source

When you choose Use Existing List from the Select Recipients menu, Word displays the Select Data Source dialog box. (The dialog box opens to the folder Program Files\Microsoft Office\Office14\Queries by default. You can browse to a different folder as you need to.)

Open the Files Of Type list at the lower-right corner of the dialog box (which displays All Data Sources by default) to reveal the variety of file formats you can choose from.

The All Data Sources entry includes, for example, the file types for Access databases and Excel workbooks and several other types. Use the specific options in the Files Of Type list (for example, Excel Files) to filter the types of files the dialog box displays.

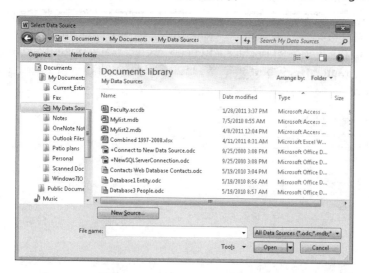

You can choose from a wide variety of file formats as the data source for a recipient list.

If you choose an Excel workbook or an Access database file, for example, Word displays the Select Table dialog box. This dialog box lists each worksheet and named range in an Excel workbook or the tables and queries defined in an Access database. Select the worksheet, range, or database object you want to use. The option First Row Of Data Contains Column Headers is selected by default. Clear this check box if the data source you select isn't set up that way.

You can set an option in Word to work more effectively with an Excel workbook that contains numeric data formatted as currency or percentages, which Word might not recognize correctly. On the Advanced page of the Word Options dialog box, scroll down to the General area, and then select the option Confirm File Format Conversion On Open. When you select an Excel workbook as a data source for a mail merge operation, Word displays the Confirm Data Source dialog box. Select MS Excel Worksheet Via DDE (click Show All if you don't see this item in the Open Data Source list), and then click OK. You can then select a cell range in the worksheet that you want to use.

A Word document that contains nothing but a table is also a valid source of data for a recipient list. Set up a table with the column headings you want to use for fields in the mail merge, type the recipient data in table rows, and then save the table as a separate document. When you click Use Existing List to open the Select Data Source dialog box, select Word Documents or All Word Documents from the Files Of Type list.

Creating a New Source

The Select Data Source dialog box might not provide access to the data source you want to use in your mail merge. For example, you might have this information stored in a Microsoft SQL Server database or in a database from Oracle. To create a data source, click New Source to open the Data Connection Wizard. On the first page, select the type of data source you want to connect to. As you step through the wizard, you need to provide information such as the server name and the user name and password required to gain access to the server. The Other/Advanced option in the list of data source types leads you to the Data Link Properties dialog box. In this dialog box, you can select a data source provider and then specify the information required to make a connection as well as information related to permissions and other initialization properties. You might need to obtain some of this information from a network or server administrator. Use the Help button in the Data Link Properties dialog box to obtain detailed information about each field.

➤ **To select an external data source**

1. In the **Start Mail Merge** group, click **Select Recipients** and then click **Use Existing List**.
2. In the **Select Data Source** dialog box, open the folder that contains the data source file you want to use.
3. If necessary, open the **Files Of Type** list and select the file format you need.
4. Select the data source file, and then click **Open**.
5. Depending on the type of data source you select, use the **Select Table** dialog box to choose the worksheet, cells range, or database object that contains the recipient information you want to use.

Using the Outlook Contacts List

You can maintain an array of information in a contact item in Outlook—much more than a contact's name and e-mail address. If you maintain and manage a detailed contacts list in Outlook by entering and updating company names, phone numbers, mailing and physical addresses, and other details, you can make productive use of your efforts by selecting the contacts folder as the data source for a mail merge. After you make that selection, you can work with the list of contacts and tailor it for your mail merge operation. All the contacts in the folder you choose are selected for the mail merge by default. Clear the check box beside any contact that you don't want to correspond with this time.

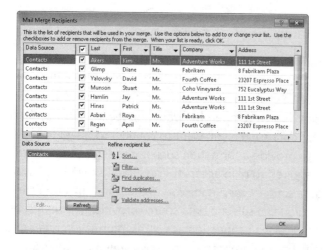

Tip If you make changes to your Outlook contact list, click Refresh to update the list of recipients for the mail merge. Keep in mind that you cannot edit Outlook contact information while working in the Mail Merge Recipients dialog box.

See Also For more information about using the links in the Refine Recipient List area of the Mail Merge Recipients dialog box, see the next section.

➤ To use an Outlook contact folder as a recipient list

1. In the **Start Mail Merge** group, click **Select Recipients** and then click **Select From Outlook Contacts**.

2. If prompted, choose the Outlook profile that is associated with the contacts folder you want to use.

3. In the **Select Contacts** dialog box, select the contacts folder and then click **OK**.

4. In the **Mail Merge Recipients** dialog box, clear the check box beside the name of any contact you don't want to include in this mail merge.

5. To refresh the list so that it shows recent changes made in Outlook, select **Contacts** in the **Data Source** area and then click **Refresh**.

Modifying the Recipient List

When you click Edit Recipient List in the Start Mail Merge group, Word displays the Mail Merge Recipients dialog box, which is shown in the previous section. To exclude a recipient from the mail merge operation underway, clear the check box beside the recipient's name.

You can scroll through a list of reasonable size, but for larger lists use the arrows beside a column name to sort or filter the list or use the links listed under Refine Recipient List. For example, you might want to sort by city or by company for a mailing you are preparing for contacts at particular clients or in particular locales.

The Sort and Filter commands under Refine Recipient List open the Sort And Filter dialog box. (You can also open this dialog box by choosing Advanced from the menu that appears when you click the arrow next to a column heading.)

> **See Also** For more information about using the Filter And Sort dialog box, see "Building a Recipient List in Word" earlier in this chapter.

The Find Duplicates command displays a dialog box that lists what Word believes are duplicate entries. Clear the check box for entries you don't want to include.

To locate a specific contact, click Find Recipient. Enter the text you are looking for (which might be a first or last name, a company name, or part of the address block), and choose to search in all fields or select the This Field option and then specify the field to use.

Validating Addresses

You can use software from vendors such as CorrectAddress and Stamps.com to validate mailing addresses. If you don't have such software installed, you'll see a message box when you click Validate Addresses. Click Yes in the message box to open a Microsoft web page where you can read about the services available.

For certain types of data sources (Excel workbooks and Access databases, for example, but not for Outlook contact lists), you can edit detailed information about recipients. In the Mail Merge Recipients dialog box, select the data source (under Data Source) and then click Edit.

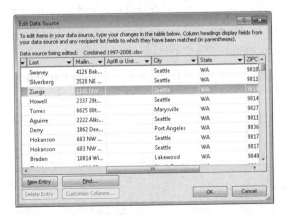

You can change information in the fields from your data source (by first clicking in a field to select it), or click New Entry to add a recipient record. When you click OK in the Edit Data Source dialog box, Word displays a message box that asks whether you want to update the recipient list and save the changes you make to the original data source file.

➤ **To edit a recipient list**

1. In the **Start Mail Merge** group, click **Edit Recipient List**.

2. In the **Mail Merge Recipients** dialog box, select the recipient list in the **Data Source** area, and then click **Edit**.

3. In the **Edit Data Source** dialog box, update the values for fields, or click **New Entry** to add a recipient record.

4. In the **Edit Data Source** dialog box, click **OK**. In the message box Word displays, click **Yes** to update the recipient list and save the changes to the original data source.

➤ **To refine a recipient list**

1. In the **Start Mail Merge** group, click **Edit Recipient List**.

2. In the **Mail Merge Recipients** dialog box, use the arrows beside column headings to sort the list by that field (in ascending or descending order) or to filter the list by values in that field or for blank or nonblank fields.

3. For more advanced sorts, in the **Refine Recipient List** area, click **Sort** to open the **Sort and Filter** dialog box. On the **Sort Records** tab, you can sort by up to three fields.

4. To define an advanced filter, in the **Refine Recipient List** area, click **Filter**.

   ○ On the **Filter Records** tab, select the field you want to filter by. Select a comparison operator, and then enter the text you want to use for the filter.

   ○ In the far left column, select the AND or OR operator, and then add another field to the filter. Repeat this step to define other conditions for the filter.

5. To check for duplicate recipients, click **Find Duplicates**. In the **Find Duplicates** dialog box, clear the check box beside the duplicate entries you don't want to include.

6. To locate a specific recipient, click **Find Recipient**. In the **Find Entry** dialog box, type the text you want Word to search for. To search in a particular field, select **This Field** and then select the field you want to use.

Practice Tasks

The practice files for these tasks are located in the practice files folder for Microsoft Word 2010. You can save the results of these exercises in the same folder. Change the file name so that you don't overwrite the sample files. When you are done, try performing the following tasks:

- Open the document Current_Promotions.docx, and then choose the option to use an existing list as the recipient list. Select the file Contacts.xlsx.

- Use the Match Fields command so that the merge fields for addresses in Word match fields listed in Contacts.xlsx.

- Edit the recipient list by adding an entry of your own and changing the values in some of the fields.

4.3   Create Labels and Envelopes

The Mailings tab in Word 2010 provides a couple of ways to create and print labels and envelopes. You can use the Envelopes or Labels option on the Start Mail Merge menu to merge information from your recipient list to produce the envelopes or labels you need. You can use the Envelopes and Labels commands in the Create group (at the far left of the Mailings tab) to prepare and print these items without setting up a full mail merge operation.

Setting Up Labels or Envelopes for a Mail Merge

When you are preparing to print labels or envelopes as part of a mail merge operation, start with a blank document. If you have a document open when you select either option from the Start Mail Merge menu and then click OK in the Envelope Options or Label Options dialog box, Word displays a warning that to continue, it must delete the contents of the open document and discard any changes.

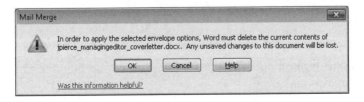

> **See Also** For detailed information about the Envelope Options and Label Options dialog boxes, see "Preparing and Printing Envelopes and Labels" later in this section.

Depending on the options you select for envelopes or labels (envelope size, for example, or label vendor and product number), Word displays a document with an area in which you insert merge fields. Type or select a recipient list, and then add the merge fields you want to include on the envelope or labels. You can use the Address Block command, for example, or add individual merge fields. You can also add merge rules. For example, you might add the Merge Record # rule as a way to determine how many labels or envelopes you print.

With merge fields in place, you can preview the results and then use the Finish & Merge menu to print the labels or envelopes.

➤ **To set up envelopes for mail merge**

1. Create a blank document.
2. On the **Start Mail Merge** menu, click **Envelopes**.
3. In the **Envelope Options** dialog box, select the envelope size.
4. Change the font formatting for the addresses as needed.
5. On the **Printing Options** tab, check that the settings are correct for the printer you are using.
6. Click **OK**.
7. Click **Select Recipients**, and then choose an option for the recipient list you want to use.
8. Add merge fields to the envelope to create an address block.
9. Preview the results, and check for any errors.
10. Click **Finish & Merge**, and then click **Print Documents**.

➤ **To set up labels for mail merge**

1. Create a blank document.
2. On the **Start Mail Merge** menu, click **Labels**.
3. In the **Label Options** dialog box, select the type of printer you are using.
4. In the **Label Information** area, select the label vendor and then the product number for the label you are using.
5. Click **OK**.

6. Click **Select Recipients**, and then choose an option for the recipient list you want to use.

7. Add merge fields to the document to create an address block.

8. Preview the results, and check for any errors.

9. Click **Finish & Merge**, and then click **Print Documents**.

Preparing and Printing Envelopes and Labels

The Envelopes and Labels commands in the Create group open the same dialog box, which displays a tab that corresponds to the command you clicked. You use these commands to produce a single envelope, a single label, or a sheet of the same label—in other words, the Envelopes and Labels commands don't provide access to the type of data source you use in a mail merge operation.

The Envelopes tab includes text boxes in which you enter the delivery address and return address. (Select the Omit check box if you don't want to include a return address.) You can type an address or click the address book icon to open your default e-mail program so that you can select an entry from the address book.

The Preview area shows the placement of the delivery address and the return address. Refer to the Feed diagram to see how you should position envelopes for your printer.

Tip If the return address you enter is new, Word offers to save the address as the default return address when you click Print.

If you are preparing labels, enter the address or choose it from your address book. Select the Use Return Address check box to enter the default return address for the label. The Print area lets you choose to print a full page of the same label or a single label. If you are printing a single label, you can set options for the row and column.

Adding Electronic Postage

If you have electronic postage software installed, you can add it to an envelope and set properties for the postage as necessary. If you don't have such software installed, Word presents a message box when you select the Add Electronic Postage check box or click the E-Postage Properties button and prompts you to visit a website on Office.com for more information. The website includes a link to Stamps.com, a provider of e-postage software, and it describes the services and features available. The site also includes a link to a help topic that lists the steps you follow to add e-postage to an envelope or a label.

If you are preparing an envelope, click the Options button on the Envelopes tab to open the Envelope Options dialog box. Here you can select an envelope size (the default is a size 10 envelope (which measures 4 1/8 x 9 1/2 inches). A number of other sizes are available. You can define a custom size if you scroll to the bottom of the list, click Custom Size, and then enter the dimensions in the Envelope Size dialog box.

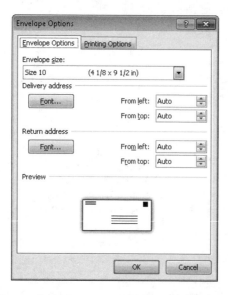

Click the Font button to change formatting properties for the delivery address or return address. You can also use the Delivery Address and Return Address areas to change the position of the addresses (aligned from the left and the top). Check the Preview area to see the effect of the adjustments you make.

> **See Also** For more information about font formatting attributes, including advance formatting, see "Apply Advanced Font and Paragraph Attributes" in Chapter 2 in this section of the book.

In the Label Options dialog box, select the type of printer you are using (a continuous-feed printer or a page printer) and select which tray to use if you are using a page printer. The type of printer you choose affects the options available in the Label Vendors and Product Numbers lists. For page printers, Microsoft is the default vendor, and the list includes a number of other vendors, including Avery and Staples. If you are using a continuous-feed printer, Avery A4/A5 is listed as the default label vendor. A small list of alternative vendors is available as well. After you select a type of printer and vendor, choose the type of label you are using from the Product Number list. Most of the product numbers listed here match an item number on the package the labels come in.

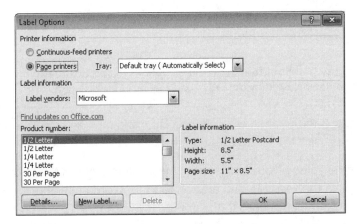

The Label Information options determine the list of label vendors. Choose a vendor, and then choose a product number.

If you want to design your own label or specify details for a label that isn't listed, use the Product Number list to select a label you want to base your label on and then click New Label. The dialog box that opens (called Label Details) displays a diagram of the label, listing its dimensions, its position in relation to page margins, the paper size, the number of labels across and down the page, and the label's pitch. Vertical pitch measures the height of the label plus the gap around it. Horizontal pitch is the width of the label plus the gap between labels across the page. For some labels, the settings for pitch will match the label's height and width. For others—especially for smaller labels that appear many to a page—the pitch settings are used to slightly space the labels.

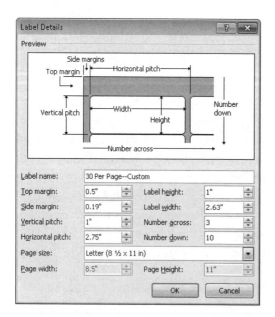

Use the settings in the Label Details dialog box to define a label of your own. Use the Vertical Pitch and Horizontal Pitch settings to determine the spacing between labels on the page.

> **Tip** You can click the Details button in the Label Options dialog box to explore and change settings for labels listed by default.

After you have address information entered for a label and have selected the kind of label you want to use, click the Print button on the Labels tab to produce the labels.

Before you print an envelope, you should check the Printing Options tab in the Envelope Options dialog box. In the Feed Method area on this tab, Word highlights the way in which you should feed the envelopes to the printer. If you change the settings Word recommends for the printer that's selected, Word displays a message indicating that the changes you made might be incorrect. Click Reset to return to Word's recommendations.

➤ To prepare and print an envelope

1. On the **Mailings** tab, click **Envelopes** in the **Create** group.

2. Type the delivery address, or click the address book icon and select an entry from your address book.

3. Type a return address (if one is needed), or select an entry from your address book to insert the return address.

4. Click **Options**. In the **Envelope Options** dialog box, select the envelope size and apply font formatting to the addresses as needed. Click **OK**.

5. In the **Envelopes and Labels** dialog box, click **Print** when you are ready to print the envelope.

➤ **To prepare and print a label**

1. On the **Mailings** tab, click **Labels** in the **Create** group.

2. Type the address, or click the address book icon and select an entry from your address book.

3. Select **Use Return Address** to add a return address to the label (if one is needed).

4. Click **Options**, and then select the type of printer you are using, the label vendor, and the product number of the label.

5. Click **OK** in the **Label Options** dialog box, and then click **Print** in the **Envelopes and Labels** dialog box when you are ready to print your labels.

Practice Tasks

The practice files for these tasks are located in the practice files folder for Microsoft Word 2010. You can save the results of these exercises in the same folder. Change the file name so that you don't overwrite the sample files. When you are done, try performing the following task:

- Open a new blank document. Select the file Contacts.xlsx to use as the recipient list, and then print a practice sheet of labels for a mail merge operation. You can experiment with different label sizes.

Objective Review

Before finishing this chapter, be sure that you have mastered the following skills:

4.1   Execute a mail merge operation

4.2   Create a mail merge by using other data sources

4.3   Create labels and envelopes

5 Managing Macros and Forms

The skills tested in this section of the Microsoft Office Expert exam for Microsoft Word 2010 relate to using macros and forms, including how to record and run a macro, how to run a macro automatically when you open a document, and how to design forms using forms controls. Specifically, the following objectives are associated with this set of skills:

5.1 Apply and manipulate macros
5.2 Apply and manipulate macro options
5.3 Create forms
5.4 Manipulate forms

In this chapter, you will work with commands in the Code and Controls groups on the Developer tab. You will learn how to record and run a macro, which lets you automate the steps involved in repetitive and common tasks. You'll also learn how to work with controls such as list boxes and date pickers and how you can use them to create a form.

> **Important** If the Developer tab is not displayed on the ribbon, open the Word Options dialog box from the File tab, click Customize Ribbon, and then select Developer in the list of main tabs.

5.1 Apply and Manipulate Macros

A macro is a procedure written in the Microsoft Visual Basic for Applications programming language (also known as VBA). A procedure is a series of instructions that are saved as a unit and can then be performed as a single instruction. In Microsoft Word, for example, you can record a series of commands or keystrokes as a macro. You can run the macro when you need to complete the steps again later in the same document or in other documents you create.

Some of the operations you might use in a macro include the following:

- Applying styles
- Changing page layout settings
- Changing view or zoom settings
- Entering or deleting text
- Navigating a document
- Opening dialog boxes and setting dialog box options
- Resizing embedded images
- Saving or opening files
- Selecting text

Using the Macro Recorder

If you are familiar with the VBA programming language, you can write the code for a macro yourself. If you aren't a programmer or you want to get a start on a macro you are writing, you can record the steps you want a macro to perform. Word generates the code for you, and you can then run the macro when you need it.

Before you record a macro, it's helpful to rehearse. Follow the steps you want to capture in the macro so that you are sure of their order and any prerequisites. For example, if you are searching for a particular character in a text string, does that character always appear in the same place? If not, how does that affect how you navigate to or select text you want to work with? Will it make your macro more efficient if you move to the start of the line or the start of the next paragraph when the macro's work is complete? If you expect to use this macro in other documents, apply the steps again in a different context in another part of the document and see whether you observe any variations you should account for. For macros that involve more than a few steps, you might want to list the steps for reference.

You should also refresh your knowledge of how to select text and navigate a document with the keyboard. You cannot use the mouse to select text or reposition the cursor when you record a macro. You can, however, use the mouse to issue commands on the ribbon or to select options in a dialog box.

> **See Also** Refer to the Help topic "Keyboard Shortcuts for Microsoft Word" for information about navigating a document with the keyboard.

In the Record Macro dialog box, you specify several properties for a macro prior to recording it:

- In the Macro Name text box, be sure to use a meaningful name even for simple macros (not just the default Macro1 or Macro2 that Word provides). Use a name that succinctly states the purpose of the macro, something like InsertTableforRFPs, AddMyHeader, or CheckForEMSpaces.

- Specify where to store the macro by choosing an entry in the Store Macro In list. Use the setting All Documents (Normal.dotm) to add this macro to the Normal template, which makes the macro available in any document you create in Word. You can also store the macro in the current template (if the document is attached to a template other than Normal.dotm) or in the current document.

- Use the Description box to add more details about what the macro does and when to run it.

> **Important** If you choose to save the macro in the current template or in the current document, the file you choose must be saved using the macro-enabled file format (.dotm for templates or .docm for documents).

The Record Macro dialog box lets you assign the macro to a custom keyboard shortcut or to a button you can add to the Quick Access Toolbar. You do not have to make such an assignment, but doing so makes the macro more accessible if you plan to use it repeatedly.

> **See Also** For information about assigning a macro to a button, see "Adding a Custom Macro Button to the Quick Access Toolbar" later in this chapter.

If you choose to assign a macro to the keyboard, Word opens the Customize Keyboard dialog box. The Save Changes In list specifies where to store the keyboard shortcut. In most cases, you should choose the setting here that matches your choice in the Record Macro dialog box. In other words, if you are saving the macro in Normal.dotm, also save the keyboard shortcut in Normal.dotm.

You use the Press New Shortcut Key box to enter the sequence of keys you want to use. You need to press the Ctrl key or the Alt key plus the key you want to use. You can add the Shift key to the Ctrl or Alt key combination for a larger number of choices. Word displays the text "Currently assigned to:" when you enter a key combination. You might need to experiment with different combinations to find one that is not assigned to another function (Word assigns certain functions to keystrokes by default—Ctrl+B and Ctrl+I for formatting, for example), or you can override the current assignment with your own. Be sure to click Assign in the Customize Keyboard dialog box before you click Close.

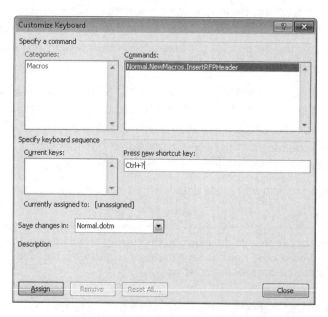

Press the Alt or Ctrl key (or both) to start defining a macro's keyboard shortcut.

When you click OK in the Record Macro dialog box (or click Close in the Customize Keyboard dialog box), you are recording. The cursor looks like a cassette tape to confirm this. Follow the steps you want to save in this macro. You can pause and resume recording if you need to. When you finish the steps, click Stop Recording in the Code group.

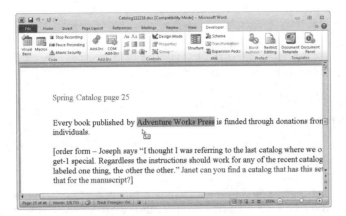

The cursor looks like a small cassette tape when you record the steps for a macro. Use the Pause Recording and Stop Recording commands in the Code group to control your recording.

> **Tip** You can also start and stop recording a macro by using buttons on the status bar. Right-click the status bar, and then make sure Macro Recording is selected to add this capability.

➤ To record a macro

1. In the **Code** group on the **Developer** tab, click **Record Macro**.

2. In the **Record Macro** dialog box, type a name and description for the macro.

3. In the **Store macro in** list, select the template or document in which you want to save the macro.

4. Click **OK**, and then follow the steps you want to record in the macro.

5. If necessary, in the **Code** group, click **Pause Recording,** and then click **Resume Recording** when you are ready to record again.

6. In the **Code** group, click **Stop Recording**.

➤ To assign a macro to the keyboard

1. In the **Record Macro** dialog box, click **Keyboard**.

2. In the **Customize Keyboard** dialog box, click in the **Press new shortcut key** box, press Alt or Ctrl (or both), and then press the key you want to assign the macro to.

3. In the **Save changes in** list, select the template or document in which you want to save this keyboard shortcut.

4. Click **Assign**, and then click **Close**.

Running a Macro

You can run a macro in several different ways:

- Use the Run button in the Macros dialog box.
- Assign the macro to the keyboard.
- Assign the macro to a command button.
- Assign the macro to a button that you can add to the Quick Access Toolbar.

> **See Also** For detailed information about the third and fourth options in this list, see "Running a Macro from a Command Button" and "Adding a Custom Macro Button to the Quick Access Toolbar" later in this chapter.

If you expect to run a macro only infrequently, using the Run button in the Macros dialog box is a simple approach. Click Macros in the Code group to open this dialog box, which lists each macro contained in the active templates and document. Click the macro you want to run, and then click Run.

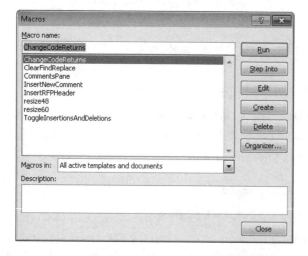

If you assigned the macro to the keyboard when you recorded the macro, position the cursor where you want to start running the macro, and then press the key combination you assigned.

> **See Also** To learn how to assign a macro to the keyboard, see "Using the Macro Recorder" earlier in this chapter.

➤ **To run a macro from the Macros dialog box**

1. Position your cursor where you want to start running the macro.

2. In the **Code** group, click **Macros**.

3. In the **Macros** dialog box, select the macro you want to run and then click **Run**.

Applying Macro Security

Word provides four basic options related to macro security. You set these options in the Trust Center, which you can open by clicking Macro Security in the Code group.

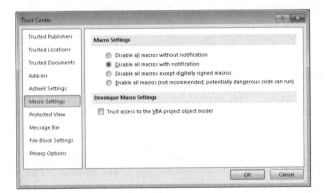

These settings control the level of macro security in documents that you receive in e-mail, for example, or that you might download from the Internet. As the text that accompanies the last of these options indicates, enabling all macros is not recommended because macros might contain code written with malicious intent. You might use this option on a computer that only you have access to—one dedicated for testing, for example, or that you use under circumstances that you control to a high degree.

The third option, Disable All Macros Except Digitally Signed Macros, lets you work with macros that are provided by trusted publishers. If a document contains a macro that is not from a trusted publisher, Word displays a security warning that lets you enable the macros.

> **See Also** For more information about security settings in Word 2010, including trusted publishers, see "Trust Center" in Chapter 1 in this part of the book.

If you keep the default choice, Disable All Macros With Notification, you need to enable content before you can run a macro. Word displays a security warning in the Message bar indicating that macros (or active content) have been disabled. If you know that the macros come from a source you trust, click Enable Content to gain access to the macros. When you enable macros, the document becomes a trusted document.

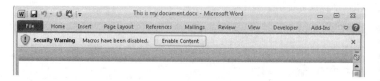 The default macro security setting causes Word to display a warning before macros are enabled.

> **Important** Word designates the default template location (Users*Username*\\AppData\\Roaming\\Microsoft\\Templates) as a trusted location. If you base documents on templates stored in this location, those documents are also trusted, and their active content is enabled when you open the document.

In documents that contain macros, you can also enable the macros by switching to Backstage view and clicking Enable Content in the Security Warning area of the Info tab. This approach provides some additional options. Choose the option Enable All Content to always enable the document's active content, which makes the document a trusted document. If you choose Enable Content, Advanced Options, Word displays a Security Options dialog box. Select the option Enable Content For This Session to activate macros while you have the document open. The next time you open the document, you will need to enable content again.

Practice Tasks

The practice files for these tasks are located in the practice files folder for Microsoft Word 2010. You can save the results of these exercises in the same folder. Change the file name so that you don't overwrite the sample files. When you are done, try performing the following tasks:

- Open the document MacroExamples.docx. Use the Save As command to save the document so that it is enabled for macros.

- Look over the numbered list at the start of the document, which is formatted using the built-in Normal style. Record a macro that does the following:
  - Applies the style Numbered List
  - Inserts a tab character before the number
  - Searches for the next period (.)
  - Repositions the cursor one character to the right, and then inserts a tab character
  - Repositions the cursor at the start of the next paragraph

- Record a macro that switches the document to Outline view and displays the first three outline levels. Assign this macro to the keyboard.

5.2   Apply and Manipulate Macro Options

Word provides a number of options for how to run a macro, including built-in macros you can use if you want to run a macro when you open or close a document. In the following sections, you'll learn how to use the AutoOpen macro, how to assign a macro to a command button, and how you can add a button that runs a macro to the Quick Access Toolbar.

Running a Macro When You Open a Document

You can define a macro that runs automatically when you open a document or when you create a document that's based on a template. To do this, you need to name the macro AutoOpen (in the first case) or AutoNew, and you must save the macro in a macro-enabled document, using the .docm (for documents) or .dotm (for templates) file name extension.

For example, you might want to display a document in a particular view and at a certain zoom percentage each time you open it. In the Record Macro dialog box, name the macro AutoOpen, and then switch to the view and zoom settings you want to use as you record the macro.

You can test your macro by making a small edit to the document (for example, type your name or something similar). Now switch to a different view, change the zoom setting, and then save and close the document. Open it again, and you'll see that the document is restored to the settings you specified in the macro.

In addition to AutoOpen, you can use the following Auto macros in Word:

- **AutoExec** This macro runs when you start Word, before Word opens any document. You should save the AutoExec macro in the default template (Normal.dotm).

- **AutoNew** The AutoNew macro runs when you create a new document based on the template in which the macro is defined. You might use the AutoNew macro to update fields in the document or to add information such as the document's creation date to the header or footer.

- **AutoClose** The AutoClose macro runs when you close a document. This macro should be saved in the current template.

- **AutoExit** The AutoExit macro runs when you quit Word. Save the AutoExit macro in the default Normal.dotm template.

➤ **To run a macro when a document opens**

1. Open the document in which you want to define the macro.
2. In the **Code** group on the **Developer** tab, click **Record Macro**.
3. In the **Record Macro** dialog box, name the macro **AutoOpen**.
4. Click **OK**, and follow the steps you want to record for the macro.
5. Click **Stop Recording** when you finish, and then save and close the document.
6. Open the document to test the macro you recorded.

Running a Macro from a Command Button

In the section "Create Forms" later in this chapter, you will learn about the types of form controls you can use in Word 2010. One of the controls you can add to a document is a command button (a type of ActiveX control), which is included in the group of legacy controls you can find in the Controls group on the Developer tab. You can assign a macro to a command button that runs when you click the button.

For the most part, ActiveX controls need to be programmed to carry out their function. However, if you want to assign a macro to a command button and are unfamiliar with

VBA, record the macro first. You can then refer to the macro by its name when you set up the command button.

> **See Also** For information about creating a macro, see "Using the Macro Recorder" earlier in this chapter.

To display the legacy tools in the Controls group, click the icon in the bottom-right corner. Click the command button icon, and Word adds a button to the document. Right-click the button, and then click View Code, which opens the Visual Basic editor with a click event procedure set up for the button.

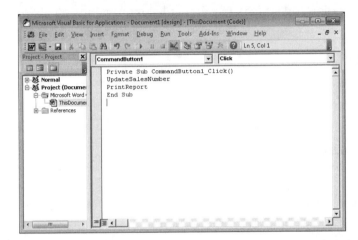

You can assign a macro to a command button in the Visual Basic editor. Record a macro first, and then enter the name of the macro in the button's click event.

To associate a macro with the command button, type the macro's name between *Private Sub CommandButton1_Click()* and *End Sub*. Use this approach if you want to assign a macro you recorded to the command button. Notice in the previous screen shot that the names of two macros appear (UpdateSalesNumber and PrintReport). A command button is a convenient way to run more than one macro with a single click. When you set up the command button, type the name of each macro you want to run in the order you want to run them.

You can also copy code from a macro you recorded (or wrote) and paste the code between these lines. Of course, you can write the macro code yourself if you know enough about VBA.

> ➤ **To assign a macro to a command button**

1. On the **Developer** tab, in the **Controls** group, open the menu of legacy commands and then click the icon for the command button.

2. Right-click the command button, and then click **View Code**.

3. In the Visual Basic editor, type the name of a macro or add the code you want to run when you click the button.

4. Close the Visual Basic editor, and then test the button.

More About VBA and the Visual Basic Editor

The information in this chapter is only the start of what you can do with macros, especially if you learn the essentials of VBA and start to write your own macros or edit and modify the macros you record. Recording a macro and then opening it in the Visual Basic editor can teach you a lot about what the VBA code does. For example, the following code is for a macro that helps format the numbered lists in the Word documents used to write the chapters of this book.

```
Sub NumListStyle()
'
' NumListStyle Macro
'
'
    Selection.Style = ActiveDocument.Styles("Num List")
    Selection.TypeText Text:=vbTab
    Selection.Find.ClearFormatting
    With Selection.Find
        .Text = "."
        .Replacement.Text = ""
        .Forward = True
        .Wrap = wdFindContinue
        .Format = False
        .MatchCase = False
        .MatchWholeWord = False
        .MatchWildcards = False
        .MatchSoundsLike = False
        .MatchAllWordForms = False
    End With
    Selection.Find.Execute
    Selection.MoveRight Unit:=wdCharacter, Count:=1
    Selection.TypeText Text:=vbTab
End Sub
```

In essence, this macro starts by applying the Num List style to the paragraph. It then inserts a tab character (*Selection.TypeText Text:=vbTab*). Inside the indented lines that begin *With Selection.Find*, the macro searches for the next period (.). When the macro locates the period (which follows the number for the item in the list), it moves the cursor one character to the right and then inserts another tab character. This macro is a simple one, but it saves several trips to the ribbon or to the keyboard.

To view a macro you have recorded, click Macros in the Code group on the Developer tab in Word, select the macro in the Macros dialog box, and then click Edit. The Visual Basic editor provides a number of tools to help you start learning about VBA. When you write lines of code, the Visual Basic editor provides choices applicable to the type of Word object you are working with. For example, when you type **ActiveDocument** (an object shown in the sample macro) followed by a period, Word displays choices such as *AcceptAllRevisions*, *AddToFavorites*, *ApplyTheme*, *DeleteAllComments*, *GoTo*, *Save*, *ShowGrammaticalErrors*, and many others. If you select *ApplyTheme* from the list that appears for *ActiveDocument* and type an opening parenthesis, the Visual Basic editor indicates that to apply a theme, you need to add the theme's name.

Click Help, Microsoft Visual Basic For Applications Help in the Visual Basic editor to open an extensive help system with concepts, how-to examples, and a full reference.

Adding a Custom Macro Button to the Quick Access Toolbar

One of the most convenient ways to run a macro is to add a button for that macro to the Quick Access Toolbar. You can assign the macro to a button when you first record it (see "Using the Macro Recorder" earlier in this chapter) or customize the Quick Access Toolbar later by using the Word Options dialog box.

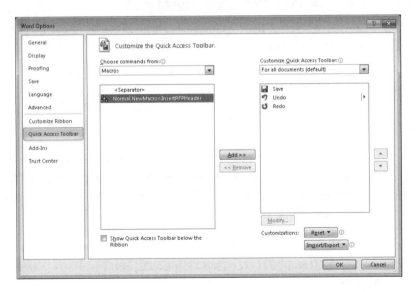

On the Customize The Quick Access Toolbar page, open the Choose Commands From list and select Macros. In the list of macros, select the one you want to add to the Quick Access Toolbar and then click Add. In the Customize Quick Access Toolbar list, select For All Documents if you want the button to appear on the Quick Access Toolbar for all documents you work on. You can also select the current document if you want to use the macro within that scope.

To rename the button or to change the icon associated with it, select it in the list of commands on the Quick Access Toolbar and then click Modify. Use the Modify Button dialog box to change the display name and to choose an icon. The display name appears in a ScreenTip when you point to the button with the mouse.

Use a friendly display name for macro buttons you add to the Quick Access Toolbar.

➤ To add a custom macro button to the Quick Access Toolbar

1. Click the arrow at the right end of the Quick Access Toolbar, and then click **More Commands**.

2. In the **Choose commands from** list, choose **Macros**.

3. In the list of macros, select the macro you want to place on the Quick Access Toolbar, and then click **Add**.

4. Click **Modify**, and then select the icon you want to use and change the display name for the button.

Practice Tasks

The practice files for these tasks are located in the practice files folder for Microsoft Word 2010. You can save the results of these exercises in the same folder. Change the file name so that you don't overwrite the sample files. When you are done, try performing the following tasks:

- Open the document RunMacros.docm.

- Use the Run button in the Macros dialog box to run the macro named InsertBoilerplate.

- Add a command button to the top-left corner of the document. Open the Visual Basic editor, and then assign the macros ApplyStyle and InsertDate to run when the command button is clicked.

- Add a button to the Quick Access Toolbar for the macro named CleanUp.

- As the last steps, click the command button to run its macros, and then run CleanUp from the Quick Access Toolbar.

5.3 Create Forms

Forms are more structured than many documents you create in Word. Forms are designed to collect specific information in particular formats and are often submitted to other people for processing or approval. Expense reports, invoices, order forms, and registration forms are among the types of forms you might create in Word.

Designing a Form

Although you can create a form for a single document, most forms are saved as a Word template so that they can be used more than once. Start with a blank template for a form you plan to design from scratch, or use one of the form templates available from Office.com as a starting point.

> **See Also** For more information about document templates, see "Apply a Template to a Document" in Chapter 1 in this section of the book.

To keep content controls aligned in a form, you can use a table, although this is not a requirement. Click Design Mode in the Controls group on the Developer tab before you start adding controls to your form. Design mode lets you see the tags that identify the content controls and lets you arrange and edit the content controls you add to the form.

Here's a quick rundown on the controls you can add to a form. Word displays a ScreenTip that identifies each control:

- **Rich text** Use this control for text fields in which you need to format text as bold or italic, for example, or if you need to include multiple paragraphs and add other content such as images and tables.

- **Plain text** Use the plain text control for simple text fields such as names, addresses, or job titles. The text added to a plain text control can be formatted only in limited ways.

- **Combo box** In a combo box, users can select from a list of defined choices or type their own information. If you select the Contents Cannot Be Edited check box in the properties for this control, users won't be able to add their own items to the list.

> **See Also** For more information about the Contents Cannot Be Edited option, see "Locking Controls" later in this chapter.

- **Drop-down list** In this control, users can select only from a list of defined options. A drop-down list might be used to display department names or meeting rooms (a list of specific items), whereas a combo box would be better suited for displaying a list of tasks, for example, so that users can select a task if it appears on the list or define one if it doesn't.

- **Building block** Use a building block control when you want users of the form to choose a specific block of text or a building block from another of the galleries in Word. In a proposal, for example, you might include a building block control that lets users choose text entries from the Quick Parts gallery to indicate the length of time for which the proposal is valid.

- **Picture** Use this control to embed an image file in a document. You could use a picture control to display a logo, for example, or pictures of project personnel.

- **Date picker** This control inserts a calendar control that lets you select or enter a date.

- **Check box** Use the check box control to provide a set of options—product sizes, for example, or options that indicate which events a user plans to attend.

You can add legacy controls available through the Controls group to your form if you are designing a form that will be used on computers on which earlier versions of Word are installed. The legacy controls available include those for a text box, a check box, and a drop-down list.

> **See Also** For more information about working with these controls, see "Adding and Removing Form Fields" later in this chapter.

You can also add one of many ActiveX controls to a form. For example, you can add a command button to a form and then assign a macro to the command button. To take full advantage of ActiveX controls on a form, you should know how to program the controls with VBA.

> **See Also** For more information, see "Running a Macro from a Command Button" earlier in this chapter.

Here's an example of a conference registration form that's being designed. The form uses (among other controls) plain text controls to gather personal information (name, address, city, and the like), date-picker controls for the arrival and departure dates, a combo box to list dietary preferences, a rich text control for the special requests area, and check boxes that users select to show which events they plan to attend.

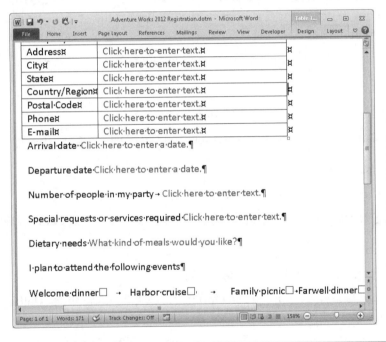

This form combines text labels and content controls of various types, including plain text controls, date pickers, and check boxes.

> **Tip** To group content controls, select the controls and then click Group in the Controls group. For example, if you want to keep the check boxes together as a unit so that they cannot be edited or deleted individually, select those controls and then click Group.

> **To add a text content control**

1. Click where you want to insert the control.

2. In the **Controls** group on the **Developer** tab, click **Rich Text Content Control** or **Plain Text Content Control**.

➤ **Insert a picture control**

1. Click where you want to insert the control.

2. In the **Controls** group on the **Developer** tab, click **Picture Content Control**.

➤ **Insert a combo box or a drop-down list**

1. Click where you want to insert the control.

2. In the **Controls** group on the **Developer** tab, click **Combo Box Content Control** or **Drop-Down List Content Control**.

3. Select the content control, and then click **Properties** in the **Controls** group.

4. In the **Drop-Down List Properties** area, click **Add**, and then use the **Add Choice** dialog box to define the first item for the list. Repeat this step to define each item required in the list.

5. Select options for other properties, and then click **OK**.

➤ **Insert a date picker**

1. Click where you want to insert the date picker control.

2. In the **Controls** group on the **Developer** tab, click **Date Picker Content Control**.

➤ **Insert a check box**

1. Click where you want to insert the check box control.

2. In the **Controls** group on the **Developer** tab, click **Check Box Content Control**.

➤ **Insert a building block**

1. Click where you want to insert the control.

2. In the **Controls** group on the **Developer** tab, click **Building Block Gallery Content Control**.

3. Click the content control to select it, and then click **Properties** in the **Controls** group.

4. Click the gallery and the category for the building blocks that you want to make available in the building block control, and then click **OK**.

➤ **To customize the text in a content control**

1. In the **Controls** group, click **Design Mode**.

2. Select the content control you want to edit.

3. Edit the placeholder text, and apply any formatting.

4. In the **Controls** group, click **Design Mode** again.

Working with Control Properties

Each control you add to a form has a set of properties. The most basic properties are Title and Tag. You can also choose how to format the contents of a control and set options for whether the control can be deleted and whether its content can be edited. Other properties depend on the type of control you are working with. For example, for a plain text control, you can set an option to allow multiple paragraphs. (If you keep the check box for this option clear, users can enter only a single paragraph in the control.) The date-picker control has a fairly extensive set of properties, including the date format, the locale, and the calendar type.

A title appears on the control to better identify it. The tag you define helps you locate a control and is involved if you link your form to a data source. Tags appear on either end of a control when you work in Design mode.

To open the Content Control Properties dialog box for a control, select the control and then click Properties in the Controls group.

The following sections provide more information on specific control properties.

Locking Controls

Two options you can apply to controls help you protect the design and content of your form. The first option (Content Control Cannot Be Deleted) prevents a user of a form from deleting that control. You should set this property on every control that is required in the form, but you should not set this property for controls that are optional. For example, you might design a form in which users need to select one of two text controls to display standardized text given specific conditions. The users need to delete the text control that doesn't apply. (Although a better approach in this case might be to include a building block content control and let users select the applicable text from the Quick Parts gallery.)

You can also set a property that prevents users from editing the content of a control. This option is suitable for titles, for example, or other controls whose content should remain static, such as text controls that display standardized text. But many controls require users to type text, choose an option, or select from a list. For controls of that nature, you should not set the option to prevent the content of a control from being edited.

> **See Also** For more information about restricting the editing of a form, see "Locking and Unlocking a Form" later in this chapter.

Formatting a Control

In the Content Control Properties dialog box, select the check box labeled Use A Style To Format Contents when you want to apply a style to the content in a control. You can choose a style from the Style list, or click New Style and use the Create New Style From Formatting dialog box to specify formatting attributes for the font and define other elements for the style.

> **See Also** For more information about creating styles, see "Apply Advanced Font and Paragraph Attributes" in Chapter 2 in this section of the book.

Building a List

If you are using a combo box or list box content control, the Content Control Properties dialog box includes fields that you use to define list items. In the dialog box, click Add to begin, and then specify the display name and value for the first list item in the Add Choice dialog box. By default, Word enters what you type in the Display Name box in the Value box (or vice versa, if you type a value first). You can change the value to be different (a numerical value to match the sequence of choices, for example). After you build the list, use the Modify, Remove, Move Up, and Move Down buttons to refine the list as you need to.

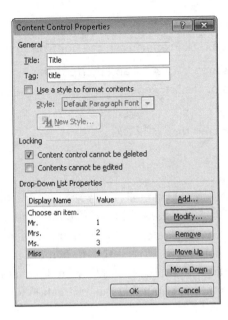

Click Add to add an item to the list. You can also modify or remove items or change the order of the list.

➤ **To lock a control**

1. Select the content control, and then click **Properties** in the **Controls** group.

2. In the **Content Control Properties** dialog box, in the **Locking** area, select one or both of the options that apply:

   ○ **Content Control Cannot Be Deleted**

   ○ **Contents Cannot Be Edited**

3. Click **OK**.

➤ **To format a control**

1. Select the content control, and then click **Properties** in the **Controls** group.

2. In the **Content Controls Properties** dialog box, select the **Use a style to format contents** check box.

3. Choose a style from the **Style** list, or click **New Style** and then define the attributes of the style in the **Create New Style From Formatting** dialog box.

4. Click **OK** in the **Create New Style From Formatting** dialog box, and then click **OK** in the **Content Controls Properties** dialog box.

➤ **To define a list**

1. Select the content control, and then click **Properties** in the **Controls** group.

2. In the **Drop-Down List Properties** area, click **Add**, and then use the **Add Choice** dialog box to define the first item for the list. Repeat this step to define each item required in the list.

3. Select options for other properties, and then click **OK**.

Adding Help to a Form

Content controls include a simple text statement that tells users what to do with the control. For example, text controls indicate "Click here to enter text," and the date-picker control prompts users with "Click here to enter a date." You can change this text so that it provides precise instructions and helps users work with a form more efficiently. Adding directions like this can also simplify a form. For example, with the addition of an introductory sentence, the contact information required in the reservation form under development can be reduced to a single column.

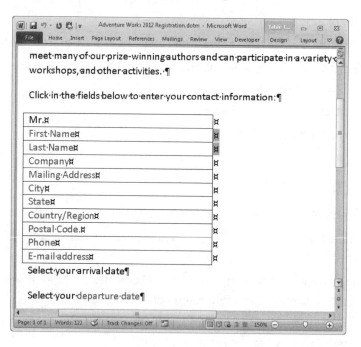

By changing the default text in a content control, you provide instructions to users and can simplify the layout of a form.

Changing the text is a simple operation. Click Design Mode in the Controls group on the Developer tab. Select the control whose text you want to change, select the text it contains, and then type the new text.

➤ **To customize the text in a content control**

1. In the **Controls** group, click **Design Mode**.

2. Select the content control you want to edit.

3. Edit the placeholder text, and apply any formatting.

4. In the **Controls** group, click **Design Mode** again.

Assigning XML Elements to Form Controls

An XML schema describes the structure of an XML document. A schema can, for example, define the elements required in an XML document, an element's attributes, and the default values for elements and attributes. When you associate an XML schema with a Word document that contains content controls, you can create a relationship between the control and an XML element defined in the schema. The relationships you create can serve as the basis for linking the form to a database. For example, users could enter data in a Word form that is attached to an XML schema, and then that data could be imported into a database table that is based on the same schema or on a compatible one.

> **See Also** If you want to learn more about XML and XML schemas, you can find additional information plus a number of tutorials at *www.w3schools.com/xml/default.asp*.

To set up this process, you first need to attach a schema to your form in Word. You can do this by clicking Schema in the XML group on the Developer tab. In the Templates And Add-Ins dialog box, click Add Schema, and then select the schema you want to apply. In the Schema Settings dialog box, you can add an alias for the schema if you want to. By assigning an alias, you can shorten the text string required to refer to the schema.

When you click OK in the Templates And Add-Ins dialog box, Word displays the XML Structure task pane. Before you assign specific elements to a content control, you need to add the root element to the document and any parent elements defined in the schema. To add the root element, select the entire document and then select the root element in the area at the bottom of the XML Structure task pane.

Use the XML Structure pane to apply an XML element to a content control. The question mark next to attendee indicates that information is missing—in this case, other elements need to be added to make the structure valid.

To associate an element with a content control, right-click the control, point to Apply XML Element on the menu that appears, and then choose the element you want to use. (Or you can select the control and then select the element you want to associate with it in the XML Structure task pane.)

A Form Without Content Controls

If you want to use XML to set up a relationship between a Word form and a database, you might be better off not using content controls and instead designing your form using simple text labels set up in a table or in some other structured and well-aligned format. Attach your schema to the Word document and then add the schema's elements to the document. (See the following procedure for details.) Before you save the document, click XML Options at the bottom of the XML Structure pane. In the XML Options dialog box, select the options Save Data Only and Ignore Mixed Content. The first of these options saves the XML tags and the data for each element but not information about the schema. The second option is useful for a form that likely contains standard text or other content in addition to XML data. When you save the document in Word, use the Word 2003 XML Document format (instead of Word XML Document). The Word 2003 XML Document format produces a simpler XML file. You could then import the XML file produced by Word into a Microsoft Access database or into a database designed with a different program.

> **Tip** The tags you define for a content control (and that Word displays when you click Design Mode) do not provide links to the XML, even if they match the name of an element, but entering a tag name for the control can help you understand the structure of the XML you are applying.

➤ **To assign an XML element to a content control**

1. On the **Developer** tab, click **Schema** in the **XML** group.

2. In the **Templates and Add-Ins** dialog box, click **Add Schema**.

3. In the **Add Schema** dialog box, select the schema and then click **Open**.

4. Click **OK** in the **Templates and Add-Ins** dialog box.

5. Select the entire document. At the bottom of the **XML Structure** pane, select the schema's root element in the **Choose an element to apply to your current selection** list.

6. Use the XML element list to add any parent elements.

7. Right-click the content control you want to assign an XML element to, point to **Apply XML Element**, and then select the element.

Practice Tasks

The practice files for these tasks are located in the practice files folder for Microsoft Word 2010. You can save the results of these exercises in the same folder. Change the file name so that you don't overwrite the sample files. When you are done, try performing the following tasks:

- Open the document StarterForm.docx. Using the content controls available in Word 2010, add the content controls referred to in the document and set the properties for the content controls as specified. This practice task will result in an order form in which users select products, specify the quantity and color they want for each item, and then specify selection options for shipping, along with special instructions, if needed. When you are finished, save the form using the name OrderForm.docx.

5.4 Manipulate Forms

In this section, you will learn about other steps you can take to protect a form from unexpected and unwanted changes. You will also learn how to add and remove form fields you want to use on a form.

Locking and Unlocking a Form

As you can with other types of documents, you can restrict the types of changes users can make to a form. After you have designed a form and set properties for the controls it contains, use the Restrict Editing command on the Developer tab to display the Restrict Formatting And Editing pane.

Choose the option to limit formatting if you want to maintain the look and feel of the form. Select the Editing Restrictions check box, and then choose Filling In Forms from the list. This option sets up the form so that users can edit controls as you designated, but users cannot change the design of the form or alter the text in titles or other labels.

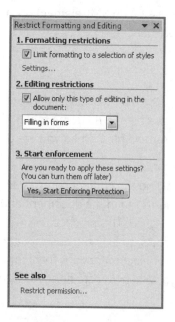

When you restrict editing in a form, users can edit the content in the controls but cannot change the design of the form.

See Also The option Filling In Forms does not let you specify groups or individuals who can make changes to the document. It just controls how users can work with the form. For more information on restricting editing to groups or individuals, see "Apply Protection to a Document" in Chapter 1 in this section of the book.

Click Yes, Start Enforcing Protection to apply your restrictions. You then need to define a password to protect the document.

> **Tip** To specify users who can bypass editing restrictions and work with the form while protection is applied, click Restrict Permission at the bottom of the Restrict Formatting And Editing task pane. In the Select User dialog box, select the user accounts to which you want to grant this privilege.

When a user bases a new document on the form template you've designed, he or she can fill in the required fields but cannot perform other types of edits. If a user clicks Restrict Editing, the task pane that Word displays describes this situation and presents the user with a Stop Protection button. To unlock the form and do work other than fill in its fields, a user must click Stop Protection and then type the password defined earlier.

➤ To lock a form

1. On the **Developer** tab, in the **Protect** group, click **Restrict Editing**.

2. In the **Restrict Formatting and Editing** task pane, select **Allow only this type of editing in the document** in the **Editing Restrictions** area, and then choose **Filling in Forms** from the list.

3. Click **Yes, Start Enforcing Protection**.

4. In the **Start Enforcing Protection** dialog box, type a password and then type the password again to confirm it.

5. Click **OK** in the **Start Enforcing Protection** dialog box.

Adding and Removing Form Fields

As mentioned earlier in the section "Designing a Form," you can use legacy form fields in addition to the Word 2010 content controls. You can add these fields from the Controls group or by adding the Form Field button to a custom group you create on the ribbon.

> **See Also** For detailed information about customizing the ribbon, see "Modifying the Display of the Ribbon" at the beginning of this book.

In the Form Field dialog box, which Word displays when you click the Form Field button, you first select the type of form field you want to add to the form in Word. The choices are Text, Check Box, and Drop-Down. After you make your choice, click Options.

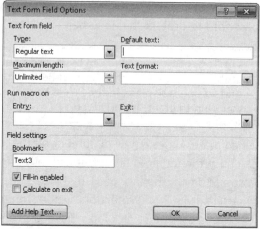

Select the type of form field, and then click Options. The options for a text form field are shown here.

Here is a summary of the options you can set for each type of form field:

- **Text** In the Type list, you can choose the type of data the text field will contain (including Regular Text, Number, and Date). The Type list also includes Calculation, which lets you define an expression that is evaluated when a user works with the form field.

  Use the Default Text box to define the text (or number or date) you want the field to show by default. In the Maximum Length box, Unlimited is the default option, but you can specify a certain number of characters. For example, a product ID might include exactly nine characters, and you can specify that under Maximum Length. The Text Format list changes depending on the choice you make in the Type list. Currency formatting options, for example, are available when you select Number in the Type list.

  Use the Run Macro On lists to select a macro that you want Word to run when a user enters or exits the field. Leave the Fill-In Enabled check box selected if you want users to be able to edit the contents of the field. Select Calculate On Exit if the form field is set up to calculate an expression.

- **Check box** For a check box form field, you can specify its size and whether it is selected or not selected by default. As you can with a text form field, you can specify a macro that runs when a user enters or exits the field.

- **Drop-down** Use the Options dialog box for a drop-down form field to define the items for the list. Type each item in the Drop-Down Item box, and then click Add. In the Run Macro On lists, choose a macro if you want to run one when a user enters or exits this field.

The Options dialog box for each type of form field includes the Add Help Text button. The Form Field Help Text dialog box contains two tabs: Status Bar and Help Key (F1). You can select AutoText entry and then choose an item from the list provided by Word, or select Type Your Own and then type the help text you want users to see on the status bar or in the Help window when a user presses F1.

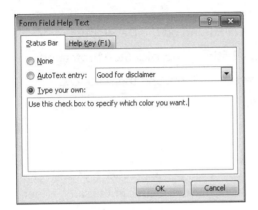

You can define help text that tells users how to use a form field.

Form fields do not become active unless you follow the steps outlined in the previous section ("Locking and Unlocking a Form") to apply editing restrictions for the form. When editing restrictions are enforced, you cannot change the properties of a form field. You must stop protection (by entering the specified password) before you can make any adjustments.

To remove a form field, remove protection from the form if necessary, select the field, and then press Delete.

➤ **To add a form field to a form**

1. Add the Form Field button to a custom group on the ribbon.

2. Click **Form Field**, and then select the type of form field you want to add (text, check box, or drop-down).

3. In the **Form Field** dialog box, click **Options**.

4. In the **Form Field** options dialog box, set properties for the form field (for example, define the list items for a drop-down field form, or specify the default value for a text form field).

5. Click **Add Help Text**, and then define the help text you want to appear on the status bar and in the Help window.

6. After you finish adding form fields and defining each field's properties, click **Restrict Editing** on the **Developer** tab.

7. In the **Formatting and Editing Restrictions** pane, select the check box under **Editing Restrictions**, and then select **Filling in forms** from the list.

8. Click **Yes, Start Enforcing Protection**, and then type the password you want to use to protect this form.

➤ **To remove a form field**

1. With the form open, click **Restrict Editing** on the **Developer** tab.

2. In the **Restrict Formatting and Editing** pane, click **Stop Protection**.

3. Type the password used to protect the form, and then click **OK**.

4. Select the form field you want to remove, and then press **Delete**.

Practice Tasks

The practice files for these tasks are located in the practice files folder for Microsoft Word 2010. You can save the results of these exercises in the same folder. Change the file name so that you don't overwrite the sample files. When you are done, try performing the following tasks:

- If you created the order form described in the practice task for the previous section, open that document (which should be named OrderForm.docx). If you did not create that form, open the file StarterForm.docx and work with it. You can ignore the instructions related to the previous practice task.

- Add the Form Field button to a custom group on the ribbon. Use the Form Field button to add a form field of each type to the form. Set the properties for each form following the instructions provided in the document.

- Protect the document using the Restrict Editing command. Remove protection, and then delete one or more of the form fields you added in the previous step.

Objective Review

Before finishing this chapter, be sure that you have mastered the following skills:

5.1   Apply and manipulate macros

5.2   Apply and manipulate macro options

5.3   Create forms

5.4   Manipulate forms

Microsoft Excel 2010 Expert

In the next four chapters, you'll build on the general skills required to create, edit, and format workbooks and worksheets in Microsoft Excel 2010. You'll learn more about the specific skills you need to be certified as a Microsoft Excel 2010 expert. The areas covered are the following:

- Sharing and maintaining workbooks
- Applying formulas and functions
- Presenting data visually
- Working with macros and forms

What You Need to Know

In creating the exercises for this part of the book, we assumed that you are proficient using many of the features in Microsoft Excel 2010. This level of proficiency includes familiarity with features such as conditional formatting, charts and graphs, data types, and data consolidation, as well as familiarity with tasks such as creating named ranges, locking cells, and inserting sparklines. The chapters that follow build on your knowledge of these features and also describe how to master others.

1 Sharing and Maintaining Workbooks

Many of the skills tested in this section of the Microsoft Office Expert exam for Microsoft Excel 2010 relate to using a workbook in a group, although many apply to work you do on your own as well. Specifically, the following objectives are associated with this set of skills:

1.1 Apply workbook settings, properties, and data options

1.2 Apply protection and sharing properties to workbooks and worksheets

1.3 Maintain shared workbooks

Setting up a workbook that will be used by more than one user often requires a number of steps. This work applies whether a workbook is used by multiple users separately or is set up to be shared and edited by a group of users simultaneously. You might start, for example, by creating a workbook and saving the workbook as a template on which other workbooks are based. You also often need to protect the structure of a workbook to prevent users from inserting or deleting worksheets or to define which operations users can perform when they work on individual worksheets.

For some workbooks, you might need to specify whether each member of a group has access to the workbook or tailor access so that some users can update the workbook but others only read it.

In this chapter, you learn how to set up and maintain a workbook that you plan to share. You learn how to save a workbook as a template, how to use workbook properties to help identify and organize workbooks, and how to formally share a workbook so that you can track and review multiple users' changes, handle conflicts, and merge changes into a single file. In addition, you learn about the steps involved in exchanging data that's defined using XML, because part of what's required to share workbooks is that you need to have access to data in a format that enables you to easily transfer it between different applications.

1.1 Apply Workbook Settings, Properties, and Data Options

The following sections describe how to save a workbook as a template, set advanced workbook properties—including properties that you define—and how to import and export data using XML documents and XML maps.

Saving a Workbook as a Template

A template lets you base a new workbook on a file with a set of column and row headings, formulas, formatting, and other workbook elements already in place. For example, organizations might build a budget from the bottom up by distributing workbooks to product managers, who work with their teams to forecast financial data and then forward the workbooks to group managers. Group managers summarize the data and pass the workbooks to department or division heads. In a process like this, using a workbook with a common structure supplied by a template greatly facilitates the consolidation, summary, and analysis of data.

The first step in designing a template is to set up a workbook with the formulas, formatting, and other elements you need. In a budget template, you might include worksheets for each month or each fiscal quarter and rows or columns that match budget categories. You can apply formatting for subtotal and total rows and font and other formatting attributes as need be.

> **See Also** For more information about working with formulas in Excel, see Chapter 2 in this section, "Applying Formulas and Functions."

To help prevent changes to a workbook template, you can assign a password to the template. You can assign one password for read access to the file and assign a different password that users must enter to modify the template.

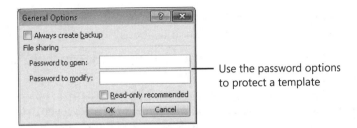

Use the password options to protect a template

> **See Also** For more information about steps you can take to protect a workbook and the worksheets it contains, see "Apply Protection and Sharing Properties to Workbooks and Worksheets" later in this chapter.

By default, Excel stores templates under a user's profile in the folder /Users/*UserName*/ AppData/Roaming/Microsoft/Templates. When you save a template in this location on a user's computer, Excel displays it in the Templates dialog box when the user selects My Templates on the New tab in Backstage view. You can also save a template to a network share where a group of users has access to it.

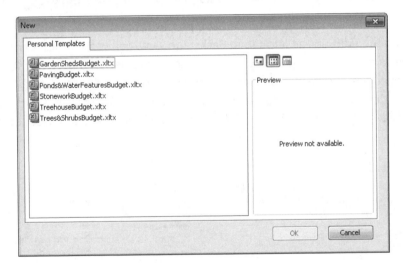

➤ To save a workbook as a template

1. Click **File**, and then click **Save As**.

2. In the **Save As** dialog box, open the **Save as type** list and select **Excel Template (*.xltx)**.

   If the file you are saving as a template includes macros, you need to select Excel Macro-Enabled Template (*.xltm). Choose Excel 97-2003 Template (*.xlt) if you are saving a template that will be used with earlier versions of Excel.

3. Click **Tools**, and then click **General Options**.

4. In the **General Options** dialog box, type a password that users enter to open the file and a separate password to control modifications.

5. Click **OK** in the **General Options** dialog box, and then click **Save** in the **Save As** dialog box.

> **See Also** For information about checking the compatibility of an Excel 2010 workbook with earlier versions of Excel, see "Preparing to Share a Workbook" later in this chapter. For information about creating and running macros, see Chapter 4 in this section, "Working with Macros and Forms."

Setting Workbook Properties

When you create, fill in, and then edit a workbook, Excel sets and tracks workbook properties such as the file's size, the dates on which the workbook was created and last modified, and the name of the workbook's author. Properties such as these are read-only. Other properties, including many advanced properties and any custom properties you define, can be set and updated by users to help identify and organize workbooks.

You might be familiar with some of the basic properties that Excel provides, which are listed along the right on the Info tab in Backstage view, below the thumbnail view of the active workbook, as shown here. You can see that values for a property such as Last Modified are displayed and cannot be overwritten. A label such as Add A Title appears beside the names of properties you can set on the Info tab. To see the full list of properties available on the Info tab, click Show All Properties at the bottom of the list.

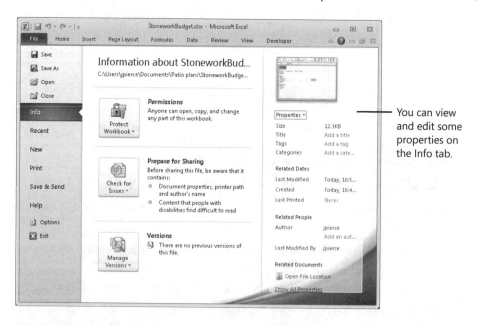

You can view and edit some properties on the Info tab.

To work with advanced properties, click Properties at the top of the list, and then click Advanced Properties. You'll see the Properties dialog box, two views of which are shown here.

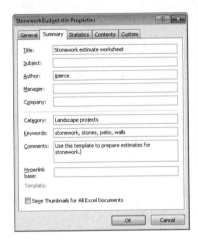 

The General, Statistics, and Contents tabs display information about the workbook. Many of these properties also appear in the list on the Info tab. On the Summary tab, you can type values for properties such as Title and Subject. The Custom tab shows a list of advanced properties—Checked By, Client, Project, and Typist among them—that let you identify additional attributes about the workbook. You can use the properties listed as a starting point for a custom property or define a custom property with a name that reflects specific information your company wants to collect or a property that records who approved an estimate for a new project, for example.

➤ **To set an advance property**

1. Click **File**, **Info**.
2. Click **Properties**, and then click **Advanced Properties**.
3. On the **Custom** tab, select the property from the list.
4. In the **Value** box, type the value for the property.
5. Click **Add**.

➤ **To define a custom property**

1. Click **File**, **Info**.
2. Click **Properties**, and then click **Advanced Properties**.
3. On the **Custom** tab, type the name of the property in the **Name** box.
4. From the **Type** list, select the data type for this property. You can choose from Text, Date, Number, and Yes/No.

5. In the **Value** box, type the value for the property.

6. Click **Add**.

➤ **To modify an advanced or custom property assigned to a workbook**

1. Click **File**, **Info**.

2. Click **Properties**, and then click **Advanced Properties**.

3. On the **Custom** tab, select the property in the **Properties** list at the bottom of the dialog box.

4. Change the name, type, or value of the property.

5. Click **Modify**.

6. Click **OK**.

Tip You can view and update some workbook properties while working on a worksheet. On the Info tab, click Properties, Show Document Panel.

Exchanging Data with XML

The type of information you work with in Excel—and might share with other users—can be stored in databases, text files, and other applications. External information such as this often exists as or can easily be converted to an XML data file. By mapping XML elements defined in an XML schema to the cells in a worksheet, you can import the data file into Excel, revise it, and then export the updated data for use in the original application or in other programs that can read and recognize the schema.

Working with XML in Excel has benefits such as these:

- You can import data into a workbook based on a template that is set up for the type of analysis or reporting you need to do. This cuts down on the number of workbooks you need to manage.

- You can use the calculation, data analysis, and formatting features you are familiar with in Excel to update and distribute data that is stored externally.

- You can export data to use it independently from other data in the workbook.

The process of importing and exporting XML involves several steps:

- Add an XML schema file to a workbook.
- Map XML schema elements to cells in your worksheet.
- Import an XML data file.
- Update data in Excel.
- Export data from your worksheet to an XML data file.

You can create the XML schema file yourself, or the schema you associate with your workbook can come from a different source—for example, an application developer or a database administrator who is familiar with the structure of the database you are importing data from.

> **Tip** The practice files included with this chapter include a simple XML schema that defines a collection of books. You can learn more about working with XML, including how to define elements and their attributes in an XML schema file, at *www.w3schools.com*.

The Excel user interface refers to a schema as an *XML map*. After you associate an XML map with a workbook, the map's elements appear in the XML Source pane. You can then drag the elements defined in the schema to the cells in the worksheet where you want the XML data to appear.

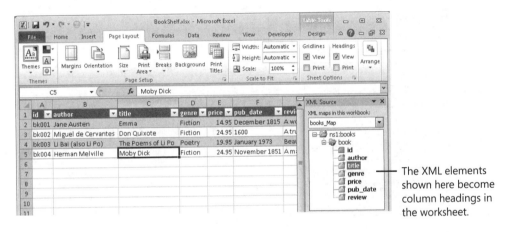

The XML elements shown here become column headings in the worksheet.

> **Tip** You use commands in the XML group on the Developer tab to import and export data and to control properties of the XML map you are using. The Developer tab is not shown on the ribbon by default. To display the Developer tab, click File, Options, and then click Customize Ribbon in the pane at the left. Under Main Tabs at the right side of the Excel Options dialog box, select Developer.

You can also import an XML file without specifying a schema or map. Excel analyzes the structure of the XML data file and creates a schema for you.

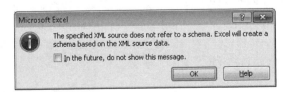

To set and modify options for an XML map, click Map Properties on the Developer tab. The XML Map Properties dialog box provides several options, including the following:

- **Validate Data Against Schema For Import And Export** Select this option if you want Excel to check that the structure of the XML data you import and export follows the structure specified in the XML schema file you used.

- **Overwrite Existing Data With New Data** Select this option if you want Excel to overwrite the data present in the workbook with current data from the XML file.

- **Append New Data To Existing XML Tables** Use this option to append new data to the data already in the workbook. For example, you can apply this option to workbooks into which you expect to import data from more than one XML file that conforms to the associated map.

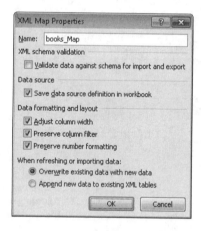

The other options in the XML Map Properties dialog box let you save a schema with the workbook and adjust the formatting and layout of column widths and other workbook features when you import data.

➤ To add an XML map to a workbook

1. In the **XML** group on the **Developer** tab, click **Source**.
2. In the **XML Source** pane, click **XML Maps**.
3. In the **XML Maps** dialog box, click **Add**.
4. In the **Select XML Source** dialog box, locate the XML data source file (.xsd or .xml), and then click **Open**.
5. In the **XML Maps** dialog box, click OK.

➤ **To set XML map properties**

1. In the **XML Source** pane, select the top element in the XML map.

2. In the **XML** group on the **Developer** tab, click **Map Properties**.

3. In the **XML Map Properties** dialog box, set the options you want to use and then click OK.

➤ **To import XML data**

1. In the **XML Source** pane, drag the XML elements to the area on the worksheet where you want the data to appear.

2. In the **XML** group on the **Developer** tab, click **Import**.

3. In the **Import XML** dialog box, locate the XML data file and then click **Open**.

➤ **To export XML data**

1. Make any changes to the XML data in the Excel worksheet, and then click **Save** in Excel.

2. In the **XML** group on the **Developer** tab, click **Export**.

3. In the **Export XML** dialog box, open the location where you want to save the XML file and then click **Export**.

Practice Tasks

The practice files for these tasks are located in the folder for Microsoft Excel 2010. You can save the results of these exercises in the same folder. Change the file name so that you don't overwrite the sample files. When you are done, try performing the following tasks:

- Open the file StoneworkBudget.xlsx, and then save the file as an Excel template.

- Create a workbook based on the StoneworkBudget template.

- In the new workbook, enter values for the **Department**, **Project**, and **Complete By** properties listed on the **Custom** tab of the **Properties** dialog box.

- Define a custom property named Estimator.

- Create a blank workbook. Add the XML schema file Books.xsd to the workbook as an XML map. Import the file Books.xml. Add new data to the worksheet or revise the data that you see, and then export the data to a new XML file. Open the XML file to see the changes you made.

1.2   Apply Protection and Sharing Properties to Workbooks and Worksheets

Only in rare cases can you share a workbook and let any other user work with it at will by changing the formatting, adding or deleting data, inserting worksheets, and the like. The majority of the time, you want at the very least to protect elements of important worksheets, and it's often the case that you want to share a worksheet only with certain users and to restrict what those users can do. Workbooks that contain important data or that you plan to use as the focus of a report, presentation, or analysis should be protected before you share them.

To apply permissions and protection to a workbook, you use commands on the Review tab or click Protect Workbook Structure under Permissions on the Info tab in Backstage view.

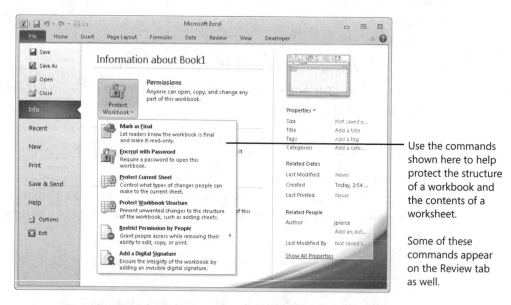

Use the commands shown here to help protect the structure of a workbook and the contents of a worksheet.

Some of these commands appear on the Review tab as well.

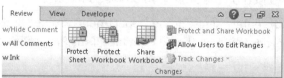

Protecting Worksheets and Workbooks

You can protect a workbook and specific worksheets in several ways:

- Protect a workbook's structure, including the workbook's worksheets and the size and position of windows. When you protect a workbook's structure, users cannot insert, delete, or rename worksheets or display worksheets that are hidden. When you protect a workbook's window, users can't change the size or position of windows.

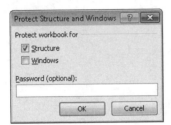

- Restrict the operations users can perform on specific worksheets—for example, worksheets that contain summary formulas that are referenced in other worksheets designed for entering data. You protect worksheets by selecting the specific operations users are allowed to perform. By keeping a check box clear, you prevent users from performing that task. The operations you can control include formatting cells, columns, and rows; inserting columns, rows, and hyperlinks; deleting columns and rows; sorting data; making use of automatic filters; using PivotTable reports; editing objects such as charts or illustrations; and editing scenarios, a feature related to the Excel Scenario Manager.

- In a protected worksheet, define worksheet ranges in which users can add and edit data after providing a password. In the Allow Users To Edit Ranges dialog box, you need to define cell ranges (by entering cell addresses or by dragging on the worksheet to define a range). You can also grant specific users permission to edit ranges without a password.

➤ To protect the structure of a workbook

1. On the **Info** tab, click **Protect Workbook**, and then click **Protect Workbook Structure**. Or click **Protect Workbook** in the **Changes** group on the **Review** tab.

2. In the **Protect Structure and Windows** dialog box, select the options you want and then enter an optional password.

➤ To protect the current worksheet

1. On the **Info** tab in Backstage view, click **Protect Workbook**, and then click **Protect Current Sheet**. Or, on the **Review** tab, click **Protect Sheet** in the **Changes** group.

2. In the **Protect Sheet** dialog box, select the operations you want to allow users to perform. **Select Locked Cells** and **Select Unlocked Cells** are selected by default.

3. Enter a password that allows you to remove sheet protection.

➤ To allow users to edit cell ranges in a protected sheet

1. On the **Changes** tab, click **Allow Users to Edit Ranges**.

2. In the **Allow Users to Edit Ranges** dialog box, click **New**.

3. In the **New Range** dialog box, enter a name for the cell range. (You can also accept the name Excel provides.) In the **Refers to cells** box, enter the cell range you want to protect.

4. In the **Range password** box, enter a password that a user must enter to edit data in this range.

5. To grant permission to specific users to edit a range without a password, click **Permission**, and then fill in the **Permission** dialog box.

Restricting User Access

Information rights management, a free service available from Microsoft, lets you restrict which users have access to a workbook (and other types of documents you create in Microsoft Office) and what those users can do to the data the workbook contains.

The first step in restricting user access is to set up information rights management on your computer. Microsoft Office takes care of this task the first time you click Protect Workbook, Restrict Permission By People on the Info tab. To use the free information rights management service from Microsoft, you must have a Windows Live ID.

> **Tip** You can sign up for a Windows Live ID by going to *live.com*. You can also register for a Live ID when you set up information rights management.

Setting Up Information Rights Management

If you want to use the information rights management service from Microsoft, you follow a few simple (and informative) steps. On the Info tab, when you click Protect Workbook, Restrict Permission By People, Restricted Access, you see a wizard page that introduces you to information rights management. To proceed, select the option Yes, I Want To Sign Up For This Free Service From Microsoft and then click Next. On the next page, you indicate whether you have a Windows Live ID, or you can choose the option to register for one if you do not. Click Next, and sign in with your Live ID. On the next page, specify whether you are using a private or public computer, review the licensing agreement and privacy statement, and click I Accept. After Office finishes setting up the information rights management service, click Finish.

You use the Permission dialog box to set up users with Read or Change permission. The dialog box describes the level of access each type of permission provides. Type e-mail addresses to identify users, or choose names from your address book. Click More Options, and Excel displays a version of the Permission dialog box in which you can fine-tune options for specific users—for example, you can grant users the additional permission to print content from the workbook and allow users with Read access to copy information in the workbook to use in other documents—and designate an individual (using an e-mail address again) that users can contact to request additional permissions.

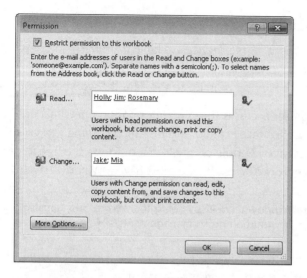

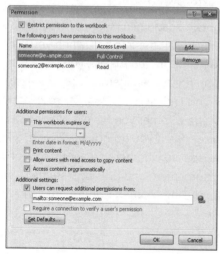

➤ **To restrict access to a worksheet**

1. On the **Info** tab, click **Protect Workbook**, and then click **Restrict Permission by People**.

2. Click **Restricted Access**.

   At this point, if you have not set up information rights management, you'll walk through the wizard.

3. In the **Permission** dialog box, click **Restrict permission to this workbook** to enable the **Read** and **Change** areas.

Read the descriptions below the text boxes for these areas to understand what permissions you restrict for the people you add to these lists.

4. Click **Read**, and then select the names of people you want to grant Read permissions to.

5. Click **Change**, and then select the names of people who need permission to read and edit the workbook.

6. Click **More Options**, and set the additional options you want to use.

Adding a Password to a Workbook

You can assign a password to a workbook that users need to enter to open the workbook or to modify it.

> **See Also** For information about entering a password, see "Saving a Workbook as a Template" earlier in this chapter.

On the Info tab, you can also apply a password that encrypts the contents of the workbook file, which means that the contents are protected from snooping unless a user enters the correct password.

➤ To encrypt a file with a password, follow these steps

1. Click **File**, **Info**.

2. On the **Info** tab, click **Protect Workbook** and then click **Encrypt with Password**.

3. In the **Encrypt Document** dialog box, type the password you want to use and then click **OK**.

4. Reenter the password.

   Take heed of the warning in the dialog box about lost passwords—lost passwords can't be recovered. Be sure to record the password in a safe place so that you can provide it to other users or refer to it yourself in the event you forget the password.

5. Click **OK**, and then save the workbook.

> **Tip** Not all file formats that Excel can read are compatible with passwords. For example, files stored in the .csv format do not accept a password.

Practice Tasks

The practice files for these tasks are located in the folder for Microsoft Excel 2010. You can save the results of these exercises in the same folder. Change the file name so that you don't overwrite the sample files. When you are done, try performing the following tasks:

- Open the file StoneworkBudget.xlsx, and then use commands on the Review tab to protect the workbook and the current worksheet.

- Define a range that requires a password to edit. Define a range password, and then try to edit a cell in that range.

1.3   Maintain Shared Workbooks

The following sections cover the basic tasks involved in preparing a workbook to be shared, the techniques you can use to share a workbook, and how you manage workbooks in which multiple users have made changes that you want to merge.

Preparing to Share a Workbook

The Prepare For Sharing area on the Info tab in Backstage view leads you to three tools you can use to ensure that workbooks you share are ready to go out into the world. Specifically, Prepare For Sharing lets you check a workbook's properties for any information that shouldn't be shared and to check a workbook's compatibility with accessibility standards and with earlier versions of Excel. The following list contains a description of these three tools:

- The Document Inspector checks a number of areas of a workbook to determine whether any information or settings in the workbook might cause problems when you share the workbook. For example, the Document Inspector checks whether the workbook contains any comments or annotations. In many cases, it is fine if the workbook does contain them. In fact, you might have added comments to point other users to areas of the workbook you want them to review. On the other hand, a workbook might contain a stray comment that would best be removed. Another example is hidden worksheets. If you hid any worksheets, did you do that intentionally? If so, should the hidden worksheets be revealed, or should they be deleted before you share the workbook?

Review the list of areas that the Document Inspector checks. If any area isn't relevant, clear the check box for that item. For example, if you are aware that the workbook has a header and a footer and you don't need to inspect that area, clear the check box for headers and footers. When you have set up the Document Inspector, click Inspect. When the inspection is complete, you see results something like those shown here. Click Remove All for areas that you want the Document Inspector to handle, and return to the worksheet to make adjustments (for example, remove comments or unhide hidden worksheets). When you finish with these adjustments, click Reinspect.

- The Accessibility Checker pane opens beside a workbook. In this window, Excel lists issues it detects that might make the workbook less accessible to people with disabilities. These items include the use of default sheet names (such as Sheet 1 and Sheet 2—use descriptive names instead) or the absence of column headings in a table. The Additional Information area at the bottom of the pane explains how to address the issues Excel detects.

- As a final step before sharing a workbook, you can run the Compatibility Checker. Here, Excel checks your workbook for formatting, features, and other attributes that are incompatible with earlier versions of Excel. If Excel uncovers compatibility issues, you can fix those issues or decide to leave them be.

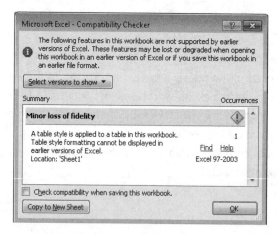

➤ **To inspect a workbook**

1. Click **File**, and then click **Info**.

2. On the **Info** tab, click **Check for Issues**, and then click **Inspect Document**.

3. In the **Document Inspector** dialog box, clear the check boxes for any content areas you don't want to inspect.

4. Click **Inspect**.

Excel inspects the document.

5. Review the inspection results that Excel displays. Click **Remove All** if you want Excel to clear up that area of the workbook for you. Otherwise, click **Close**, address the issues raised yourself, and then click **Reinspect**.

➤ **To check the accessibility features of a worksheet**

1. On the **Info** tab, click **Check for Issues**, and then click **Check Accessibility**.

2. In the **Accessibility Checker** pane, review the results that Excel displays. Click an entry in the list of issues, and then refer to the Additional Information section for steps to fix the issue.

3. Run the Accessibility Checker again to verify that the issues have been resolved.

➤ **To check compatibility**

1. On the **Info** tab, click **Check for Issues**, and then click **Check Compatibility**.

2. Review the information Excel provides in the **Microsoft Excel—Compatibility Checker** dialog box.

3. Click **Copy to New Sheet** to insert the information in the workbook.

4. Fix any issues that require your attention, and then click **OK**.

Sharing a Workbook and Tracking Changes

You share a workbook by using commands in the Change group on the Review tab. Excel provides several approaches for sharing a workbook, each of which is covered in this section.

The Share Workbook command opens a dialog box in which you can enable an option to let more than one user edit the workbook at the same time. On the Advanced tab in the Share Workbook dialog box, you can set the following options:

- **Track Changes** Set a period of time for which changes to the workbook are retained. The default time period is 30 days. You can also choose to not keep a history of changes.

- **Update Changes** Specify whether to update changes to the file when it is saved or at a time interval you set. Also choose whether to save your changes and see changes that other users made or to see only the changes made by other users.

- **Conflicting Changes Between Users** Specify whether Excel prompts you when a conflict occurs so that you can choose which change to save or whether to accept the set of changes being saved.

- **Include In Personal View** Retains your printer and filter settings in a shared workbook.

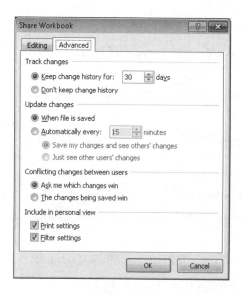

> **Tip** You cannot share a workbook that contains an Excel table or an XML map. You need to convert the table to a regular cell range or remove the XML map before you can share the workbook.

The Protect And Share Workbook command lets you protect change tracking and share the workbook in one step. Use this command when you want to be sure that Excel records all the changes users make while the workbook is shared. In the Protect Shared Workbook dialog box, select the Sharing With Track Changes option. This option shares the workbook and prevents users from removing change tracking. This step does not, however, prevent someone from removing sharing. You can address this situation by entering a password in the Protect Shared Workbook dialog box. Any user who tries to remove protection must enter the same password you define.

To turn on change tracking, click the Review tab, click Track Changes, and then click Highlight Changes. In the Highlight Changes dialog box, select the Track Changes While Editing option. This option shares the workbook and saves it.

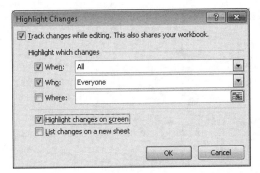

Excel provides options for the types of changes you want to track:

- **When** Specify whether you want to see all the changes since the workbook was first shared, only changes that haven't been reviewed, changes entered since the workbook was last saved, or changes made after a specific date.

- **Who** You can choose Everyone, Everyone But Me, or the names of individuals who have revised the workbook.

- **Where** Specify a cell or cell range where you want Excel to highlight changes.

The options at the bottom of the Highlight Changes dialog box let you control how you view changes. By default, Excel highlights changes on the screen by using cell borders and cell comments. You can view a specific change by resting your mouse pointer over a changed cell. The second option, List Changes On A New Sheet, instructs Excel to create a separate worksheet in the workbook (this worksheet is inserted after other worksheets in the workbook) on which it lists changes.

Reviewing Changes

To review changes made to a shared workbook, click Track Changes, Accept/Reject Changes. Excel saves the workbook and then displays the Select Changes To Accept Or Reject dialog box. This dialog box also contains When, Who, and Where lists. In the When list here, you can choose Not Yet Reviewed or Since Date. Set up this dialog box so that you can review the changes you need to see, and then click OK.

The Accept Or Reject Changes dialog box appears next. Excel highlights the first change for review on the worksheet. In the dialog box, you can read a description of the change under review, including the date and time of the change, who made the change, and details about changes to content. Use the buttons at the bottom of the dialog box to accept or reject each change or to accept or reject all changes at once.

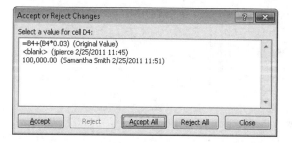

Merging Workbooks

If you need a group of people to review a common workbook, but that group doesn't have access to a shared storage location, you can save a workbook for sharing, distribute a copy of the workbook to each member of the group, collect the workbooks after changes are made, and then merge the changes into a single workbook.

> **Tip** When you distribute separate copies of a workbook to a group, base the workbook on a template. For more information, see "Saving a Workbook as a Template" earlier in this chapter.

One step you need to take before you compare and merge workbooks is to add the Compare And Merge Workbooks command to the Quick Access Toolbar or to the ribbon. If you work with shared workbooks frequently, you might add this command to a custom group on the Review tab.

> **See Also** For more information about customizing the ribbon and the Quick Access Toolbar, see "Modifying the Display of the Ribbon" at the beginning of this book.

After you enable the workbook for sharing, be sure to click the Advanced tab in the Share Workbook dialog box and check the value for the Keep Change History For option. If the period of time specified expires, you cannot merge the workbooks. If necessary, update the period of time that the change history is retained so that everyone who is reviewing the file has enough time finish his or her work.

When you click Compare And Merge Workbooks, Excel displays the Select Files To Merge Into Current Workbook dialog box. Select the first copy of the file you want to merge, click Open, and then repeat these steps for each version. You can also select all the versions you want to merge (use the Shift or Ctrl key to select multiple files) and incorporate those changes in one operation. You can now accept and reject changes and display the history worksheet as you do with shared workbooks.

> **See Also** For the steps you follow to review track changes, see "Reviewing Changes" earlier in this chapter.

➤ To share a workbook

1. On the **Review** tab, click **Share Workbook** in the **Changes** group.

2. In the **Share Workbook** dialog box, select **Allow changes by more than one user at the same time**.

3. Click the **Advanced** tab, and then set the advance sharing options you want to use.

4. Click **OK**.

   Excel displays a confirmation prompt and then saves the workbook. After you save the workbook, *Shared* appears in the title bar whenever anyone opens the workbook. This labels remains until the workbook is no longer shared.

➤ To turn on change tracking

1. On the **Review** tab, click **Track Changes** in the **Changes** group, and then click **Highlight Changes**.

2. Click **Track changes while editing**. Selecting this option also shares the workbook.

3. Click **OK**.

➤ To review changes to a shared workbook

1. On the **Review** tab, click **Track Changes** in the **Changes** group, and then click **Accept/Reject Changes**.

2. In the **Select Changes to Accept or Reject** dialog box, specify which changes you want to review, and then click **OK**.

3. In the **Accept or Reject Changes** dialog box, move from revision to revision and accept or reject each one. Click **Accept All** or **Reject All** to manage all revisions in one operation.

➤ To set up your workbooks for distribution and merging

1. Open the workbook you want to distribute.

2. Click the **Review** tab, and then click **Share Workbook**.

3. On the **Editing** tab in the **Share Workbook** dialog box, select the **Allow changes by more than one user at the same time** check box.

4. Click the **Advanced** tab. In the **Keep change history for** box, specify the time span that users have to review the file.

5. Click **OK** to save the shared workbook.

6. Click the **File** tab, and then click **Save As** to create copies of the workbook for each reviewer. Use the original workbook you shared as the master.

7. Pass out the copies to reviewers. Be sure to let them know when the files are expected back.

➤ **To merge changes**

1. Open the master shared workbook.

2. Click **Compare and Merge Workbooks** on the Quick Access Toolbar to display the **Select Files to Merge Into Current Workbook** dialog box.

3. Select the files you want to merge, and click **Open**.

4. On the **Review** tab, click **Track Changes** in the **Changes** group, and then click **Accept/Reject Changes**.

5. Accept or reject each change. See the steps under "To review changes to a shared workbook" for details.

Practice Tasks

The practice files for these tasks are located in the folder for Microsoft Excel 2010. You can save the results of these exercises in the same folder. Change the file name so that you don't overwrite the sample files. When you are done, try performing the following tasks:

- Open a workbook on your computer, and then use the Prepare For Sharing commands on the Info tab to inspect the document and check whether the file contains any accessibility or compatibility issues.

- Create a workbook based on the StoneworkBudget template you created earlier in this chapter. If possible, working with a small group of your coworkers, set up the workbook for sharing and practice the procedures for tracking changes, accepting and rejecting changes, and merging workbooks.

Objective Review

Before finishing this chapter, be sure you've mastered the following skills:

1.1   Apply workbook settings, properties, and data options
1.2   Apply protection and sharing properties to workbooks and worksheets
1.3   Maintain shared workbooks

2 Applying Formulas and Functions

The skills tested in this section of the Microsoft Office Expert exam for Microsoft Excel 2010 relate to working with formulas and functions. Specifically, the following objectives are associated with this set of skills:

2.1 Audit formulas
2.2 Manipulate formula options
2.3 Perform data summary tasks
2.4 Apply functions in formulas

2.1 Audit Formulas

In the following sections, you learn how you can trace and audit the formulas in a worksheet. The procedures you use let you see the relationships between formulas and the cells that feed values to a formula and those that depend on a formula's result. You'll learn as well how to identify and trace errors in formulas, locate invalid data, and how to correct formula errors.

Using Auditing Tools to Trace Formulas

Cell references in formulas on a worksheet and throughout a workbook can create a complex web of relationships. To understand the structure of these relationships, it helps to know which cells provide values to specific formulas (a worksheet's inputs) and which formulas depend on the values calculated by others (the results you see, or the outputs). The commands you use to track formulas—Trace Precedents and Trace Dependents—appear in the Formula Auditing group on the Formulas tab.

> **Tip** Click Show Formulas in the Formula Auditing group to switch between viewing the formulas underlying a worksheet and the worksheet's values.

Precedents are cells that provide a value for a formula in another cell. For example, if cell C3 includes the formula =A3 + B3, cells A3 and B3 are precedent cells for cell C3. And here, cell C3 is a dependent of cells A3 and B3 because it contains a formula that refers to (depends on) those cells.

When you use the Trace Precedents and Trace Dependents commands, Excel displays blue arrows that point to related cells. Clicking the command once lets you see direct precedent or dependent cells. If you keep clicking the command, Excel traces relationships to show all the other cells whose values or calculations are involved.

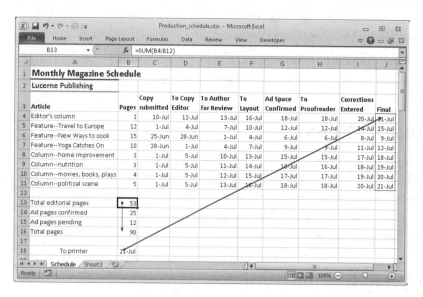

You can use the arrows to navigate. Click the arrow that points to the active cell, and the dependent or precedent cells become active. Use this technique to follow the trail of cell relationships.

> **Tip** You can also use the Go To Special dialog box to see precedents and dependents for a cell. First select the cell or range you want to examine. On the Home tab, click Find And Select, and then click Go To Special. In the Go To Special dialog box, select the Precedents or Dependents option, select Direct Only or All Levels, and then click OK. Excel highlights the applicable cells. This method of locating precedents and dependents does not show you the tracing arrows that the Trace Precedents or Trace Dependents commands do.

> ## Tracing Formulas in Separate Worksheets
>
> You can trace precedent and dependent cells for a formula that refers to cells in a separate worksheet or workbook. When you click the command to trace the cells you want to see, Excel displays a worksheet icon to indicate that the cells are in a different worksheet. Double-click the dotted line leading from the icon, and you see the Go To dialog box, which lists the cells.

➤ To track precedent cells

1. Select the cell whose precedents you want to trace.
2. Click the **Formulas** tab. In the **Formula Auditing** group, click **Trace Precedents**.
3. Click **Trace Precedents** again to see the next layer of relationships.

➤ To track dependent cells

1. Select the cell whose dependents you want to trace.
2. Click the **Formulas** tab. In the **Formula Auditing** group, click **Trace Dependents**.
3. Click **Trace Dependents** again to see the next layer of relationships.

➤ To remove the formula auditing arrows

1. In the **Formula Auditing** group, click the arrow beside **Remove Arrows**.
2. On the menu, click **Remove Arrows** to remove the arrows for precedent and dependent cells, or click **Remove Precedent Arrows** or **Remove Dependent Arrows** to remove a specific set of arrows.

Identifying Invalid Data and Formulas

Some cells or cell ranges require a specific type of data or specific values to be valid. You can set up data validation rules in Excel to restrict the type of data—to allow only dates or whole numbers, for example—or to define a range of valid values—for example, dates between July 1 and September 30 or the colors blue, cream, yellow, and black. Setting up data validation rules helps maintain the integrity of your data and can also make the process of entering data more accurate and convenient.

You define these rules in the Data Validation dialog box. In the dialog box, you can also create simple aids that appear on the screen to tell you and other users what data is valid and alert you when you enter data that's not valid.

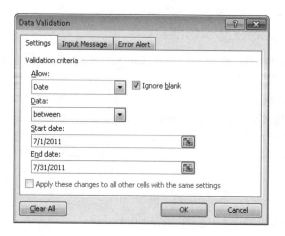

Define validation rules
for worksheets
in this dialog box.

The Input Message and
Error Alert tabs let you
define custom messages
and warnings.

The Allow drop-down list gives you several choices for the type of data that you define as valid:

- Any Value

- Whole Number

- Decimal

- List

- Date

- Time

- Text Length

- Custom

Based on the data type you select, the dialog box displays text boxes in which you specify other details. For example, if you select Text Length, you need to specify the minimum and maximum length (which might be the same). If you select List, you need to identify the valid items. You can do this by entering the items in the Source box and separating each item with a comma, or you can add the list to a worksheet and refer to the cell range where the list items appear. If you keep the In-Cell Dropdown check box selected when you create a list of valid values, Excel displays the items in a drop-down menu in the cell.

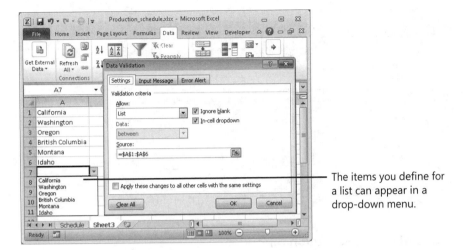

The items you define for a list can appear in a drop-down menu.

The Custom option lets you define a formula that Excel calculates to determine whether data is valid. For example, you might prevent someone from entering an expense item for entertainment unless the budget for entertainment (defined in a different cell) still has available funds.

> **Tip** If you open a worksheet you aren't thoroughly familiar with, you can check whether it contains data validation rules. Press Alt+E+G to open the Go To dialog box, and then click Special. In the Go To Special dialog box, select Data Validation and use the All option. Click OK, and Excel highlights the cell ranges subject to validation rules. You can then open the Data Validation dialog box to examine the rules that apply. You can also identify cells with data validation rules applied by clicking Find & Select on the Home tab, and then clicking Data Validation.

Use the Input Message tab to define the text for a ScreenTip that indicates what kind of data should be entered. On the Error Message tab, you can create a custom message box that Excel displays when invalid data is entered.

Validation rules let you control the data that is directly entered in a cell. If a user enters invalid data, Excel displays a generic message or the message you define, and the user must cancel the entry or try again. Excel does not display these messages when data is copied to a cell, when a value is entered by filling a cell range, when a formula calculates an invalid value, or when the data is entered by the operations of a macro.

In these cases, you can check whether a worksheet contains any invalid data. When you click Circle Invalid Data (in the Data Tools group on the Data tab), Excel marks the cells and ranges in which faulty data resides. With this information at hand, you can correct the data or (as necessary) relax the validation rules.

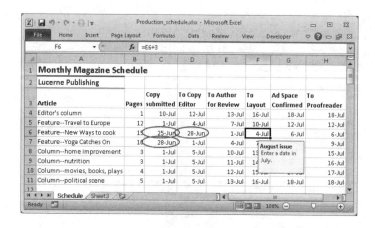

> ## To define data validation rules

1. On the worksheet, select the cell or cell range you want to work with.

2. Click the **Data** tab. In the **Data Tools** group, click **Data Validation**.

3. On the **Settings** tab of the **Data Validation** dialog box, select a data type from the **Allow** list.

4. Fill in the details for the type of data you selected in step 3.

5. On the **Input Message** tab, define the text for a ScreenTip that tells users what data is valid.

6. On the **Error Alert** tab, define the message that appears when invalid data is entered.

> ## To identify invalid data

1. Click the **Data** tab.

2. In the **Data Tools** group, click the arrow beside **Data Validation**, and then click **Circle Invalid Data**.

> ## To remove the data validation circles

1. Click the **Data** tab.

2. In the **Data Tools** group, click the arrow beside **Data Validation**, and then click **Clear Validation Circles**.

Correcting Formula Errors

A lot of formula errors occur very simply. For example, you might forget the required equal sign, misplace or omit an opening or closing parenthesis, define a cell range without using a colon, or try to divide by zero. Excel quickly spots these types of errors and displays a message that offers to fix them. Here, Excel has volunteered to add parentheses that were missing.

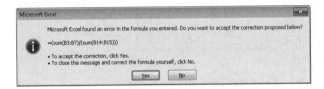

Error Checking Options

In Excel, error checking for specific types of formula errors is enabled by default. When Excel detects an error in a formula, it displays a small triangle in the cell's upper-left corner. You might also see this indicator when Excel detects that a formula is incomplete, contains a faulty reference, uses unacceptable syntax, or is otherwise wrong. Point to the arrow, and Excel displays an option button. Click this button, and you'll see a menu that tells you what error Excel discovered, leads you to help, offers a solution, or lets you ignore the error. If you choose to ignore the error at this point, you can come back and correct it later.

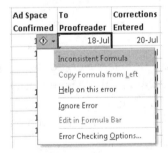

If you don't want Excel to check for certain types of errors as you work compiling and analyzing the data for a workbook, you can use the Formulas page of the Excel Options dialog box to turn off error checking altogether or to select the types of errors you want Excel to watch for.

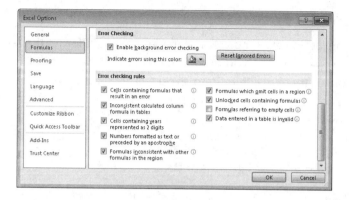

The Error Checking and Trace Error Commands

You can supplement the error checking that Excel performs in the background by using a couple of the commands in the Formula Auditing group on the Formulas tab. The Error Checking command opens a dialog box that identifies errors and lets you take one of several steps in response. In a worksheet that contains several formula errors, use the Previous and Next buttons in the Error Checking dialog box to navigate the worksheet.

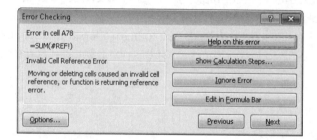

Clicking Show Calculation Steps opens the Evaluate Formula dialog box, which is the same dialog box you see when you click Evaluate Formula on the Formulas tab. Use this dialog box to follow the set of calculations a formula performs. Excel indicates at which step an error occurs. Use this information to troubleshoot the formula and make repairs.

The Trace Error command helps you identify a cell that is causing an error in a formula. Use this command in cells that display one of the following error values:

- **#DIV/0!** A divide-by-zero error, which occurs when you create a formula with a divisor that refers to a blank cell.

- **#NAME?** You used an invalid or nonexistent name. Excel also displays this error value when you fail to wrap a text string in quotation marks when you use it in a formula.

- **#VALUE** You referred to a text value in a mathematical formula.

- **#REF!** A formula refers to a range of cells that's been deleted.

- **#N/A** Excel displays this error value when a function or a formula can't find a value it needs.

- **#NUM!** You used an invalid numeric value in a formula or a function.

- **#NULL!** A formula includes a space between two ranges to indicate an intersection, but the ranges have no cells in common.

When you see a cell display one of these error values, click the arrow beside Error Checking in the Formula Auditing group, and then click Trace Error. Excel displays errors that point to the cells involved in the formula.

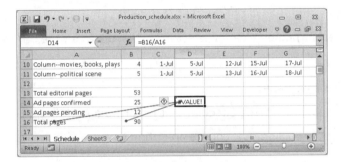

Using the Watch Window

The Watch Windows is not a troubleshooting tool per se, but using it lets you see how specific cells and formulas interact, especially in large worksheets in which the cells and formulas you are interested in might not be visible. Having this information in hand can often help you resolve errors or sort out results when they don't meet your expectations.

To open the Watch Window, click its command in the Formula Auditing group on the Formulas tab. You then select the cell or cells you want to keep an eye on. When you click Add Watch, Excel adds an entry to the Watch Window that lists the workbook, worksheet, cell reference, value, and any formula that's defined in that cell. As you update values and calculations in the workbook that affect the cells you are watching, the effect of those changes are reflected in real time in the Watch Window. You can also dock the Watch Window by dragging it to the top of the worksheet window.

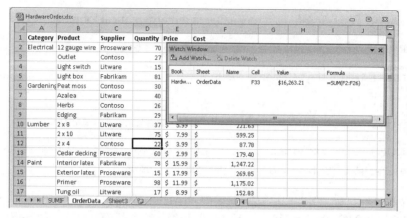

Cell F33 is not in sight, but you can watch how changes you make affect its value.

➤ To turn error checking options on or off

1. Click **File**, **Options**, and then click **Formulas** in the left pane.

2. Under **Error Checking Rules**, clear or select the check boxes for the rules you want to use.

➤ To check for errors manually

1. On the **Formulas** tab, click **Error Checking** in the **Formula Auditing** group.

2. In the **Error Checking** dialog box, choose an option to work with the formula.

➤ To trace an error

1. Select the cell that displays an error value.

2. On the **Formulas** tab, click the arrow beside **Error Checking** in the **Formula Auditing** group, and then click **Trace Error**.

➤ To add a cell to the Watch Window

1. On the **Formulas** tab, in the **Formula Auditing** group, click **Watch Window**.

2. In the worksheet, select the cell or cells you want to watch and then click **Add Watch** in the **Watch Window**.

Practice Tasks

The practice files for these tasks are located in the folder for Microsoft Excel 2010. You can save the results of these exercises in the same folder. Change the file name so that you don't overwrite the sample files. When you are done, try performing the following tasks:

- Open the file Production_schedule.xlsx. Select a cell in the Final column (column J), and use the Trace Precedent and Trace Dependent commands to track the cells that affect the formulas in this column.

- Using the file Production_schedule.xlsx, click Find & Select, Data Validation on the Home tab to identify which cells contain data validation rules. On the Data tab, click the arrow beside Data Validation and then click Circle Invalid Data to check whether any data is invalid. Using this worksheet, experiment with setting up other data validation rules.

- In the file Production_schedule.xlsx, click a cell in column H, and then open the error options menu. On the error options menu, click Copy Formula From The Left and see what effect it has on the schedule.

2.2   Manipulate Formula Options

Excel gives you a couple of options for managing how and when it calculates formulas in a workbook. Automatic calculation is the option Excel uses by default, but you can change this setting to improve performance or to update formulas manually. Another option lets you specify how many times Excel runs a calculation before it stops. This option is relevant when you need to resolve circular references in a worksheet or when you perform a what-if analysis.

> **Tip** For more information about what-if analyses, see "Apply Data Analysis," in Chapter 3 in this section of the book.

Using Automatic Workbook Calculation

Workbook calculation is the process Excel uses to compute formulas and display the results as values. The default setting for workbook calculation in Excel 2010 is Automatic. With the Automatic option set, Excel updates affected values in a workbook when you enter or revise applicable data. To avoid unnecessary calculations, Excel automatically recalculates formulas only when the cells that the formula depends on change.

In most cases, you have little reason not to retain the default setting, but you can control when and how Excel recalculates formulas. In lieu of using the standard Automatic setting, you can select one of two different options for workbook calculations: Automatic Except For Data Tables or Manual.

Updating calculations for a data table often takes a long time. That's why Excel gives you an option to retain automatic calculations except for table tables. Manual calculation comes in handy in situations when you are using a workbook with a large number of formulas or working with workbooks and worksheets that are linked to other workbooks and worksheets.

To change workbook calculation options, click File, Options, and then display the Formulas page of the Excel Options dialog box.

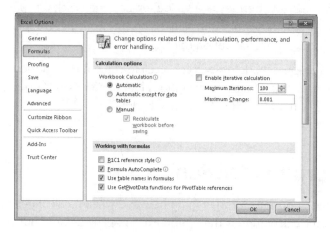

The Formulas tab on the ribbon also includes two commands you can use to perform manual calculation:

- Calculate Now calculates formulas in the whole workbook.
- Calculate Sheet updates the formulas in the current worksheet.

➤ **To change workbook calculation options**

1. Click **File, Options**.
2. In the **Excel Options** dialog box, click **Formulas**.
3. Under **Calculation options**, click one of the following options:
   - ○ **Automatic**
   - ○ **Automatic except for data tables**
   - ○ **Manual**

> **Tip** You can also change the way Excel calculates a workbook by using the Calculation Options button in the Calculation group on the Formulas tab. Click Calculation Options to see the three settings included in the Excel Options dialog box.

> ➤ **To calculate the current worksheet**

>   → Click the **Formulas** tab, and then click **Calculate Sheet**.

> ➤ **To calculate the current workbook**

>   → Click the **Formulas** tab, and then click **Calculate Now**.

Setting Options for Iterative Calculations

Most users of Excel have at one time or another entered a formula that creates a circular reference. A circular reference occurs when you refer to a cell in a formula that refers to that cell. The formula *=A1*B1* entered in cell B1 creates a circular reference.

The majority of the time, circular references need to be resolved by moving the formula to a different cell. Some calculations, however, depend on circular references. For example, IF statements that are used to specify conditions in a formula can result in circular references. To resolve these references, you need to change a default setting in Excel to enable iterative calculations.

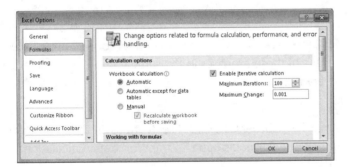

In an iterative calculation, Excel recalculates a worksheet until a specific numeric condition is met. If a formula refers back to one of its own cells, you must determine how many times the formula should be recalculated. Circular references can iterate indefinitely; however, you can control the maximum number of iterations (which affects how many times Excel calculates the worksheet) and the amount of acceptable change. Excel stops recalculating the worksheet if the maximum change from one iteration to the next is less than the value specified in the Maximum Change field (which is 0.001 by default). Reduce the Maximum Change setting to a smaller number (0.000001, for example) if you need to make calculations that require greater precision.

Iteration comes into play also when you use the Excel Solver or the Goal Seek command for performing a what-if analysis. Both commands use iterative calculations to obtain results that reflect criteria that you define. You can use the Excel Solver when you need to find the optimum value for a particular cell by adjusting the values of several cells or when you want to apply specific limitations to one or more of the values in the calculation. You can use the Goal Seek command when you know the result you want for a single formula but not the values the formula needs to get the result you want.

> **Tip** Both the Solver and Goal Seek commands are covered in detail in the section "Apply Data Analysis" in Chapter 3 in this section of the book.

➤ **To set the maximum number of iterations**

1. Click **File, Options**.

2. On the **Formulas** page, under **Calculation options**, select the **Enable iterative calculation** check box.

3. In the **Maximum Iterations** box, set the maximum number of times Excel should perform a recalculation.

4. In the **Maximum Change** box, specify the maximum amount of change to accept between recalculation results.

Practice Tasks

The practice files for these tasks are located in the folder for Microsoft Excel 2010. You can save the results of these exercises in the same folder. Change the file name so that you don't overwrite the sample files. When you are done, try performing the following tasks:

- Open the file HardwareOrder.xlsx. Click File, Options. In the Excel Options dialog box, display the Formulas page. In the Workbook Calculations area, select Manual.

- Display the worksheet named OrderData. In the Quantity column (column D) update the quantities for several items. Notice that Excel does not update the extend price in the Cost column. Click the Formulas tab on the ribbon. In the Calculation group, click Calculate Sheet, and you'll see the updated calculations under Cost.

2.3 Perform Data Summary Tasks

In this section, you'll learn how to summarize data in a worksheet based on criteria and conditions you define. You'll also learn how to work with array formulas.

Summing Data with the SUMIF and SUMIFS Functions

The straightforward addition that the SUM function performs in Excel can be extended when you use the SUMIF or SUMIFS function.

The SUMIF function adds values in a cell range that match criteria you define. The syntax of the SUMIF function is as follows:

```
SUMIF(range, criteria, [sum_range])
```

In a worksheet that lists products, categories, and prices, for example, you could use the SUMIF function to determine the total for a particular category or a particular product. The formula =SUMIF(Category,"Gardening",Cost) totals the costs for all cells listing products in the Gardening category.

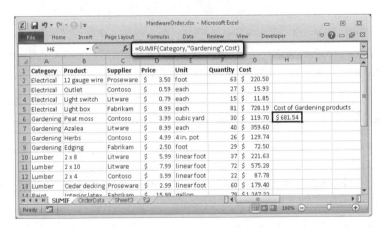

The SUMIFS function lets you add values in a cell range that match multiple criteria you define. The syntax of the SUMIFS function is as follows:

```
SUMIFS(sumrange,range1,criterion1,range2,criterion2,…,rangeN,criterionN)
```

SUMIFS sums up every entry in the *sumrange* that meets the different criteria you define.

For example, in a list of products that includes their cost, supplier, and category, you can use the SUMIFS function so that Excel adds only the costs of products of a specific type and that are available from a specific supplier. Here's an example of a formula that would make such a calculation:

=SUMIFS(Cost,Category,"Tools",Supplier,"Contoso",Product,"Hammer")

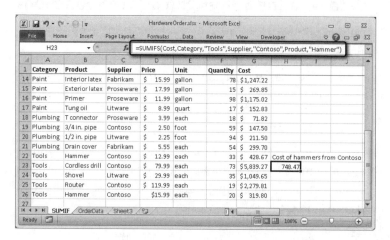

In the worksheet, each column is a named range. You could also specify Cost, for example, as the range G2:G26. Here, Cost is the range that Excel looks to for the values it adds. The criteria then spells out the specific data you want to summarize: hammers from the supplier Contoso.

Excel includes other functions similar to SUMIF and SUMIFS:

- **COUNTIF** Counts the number of cells that match criteria you define. The syntax for the COUNTIF function is =COUNTIF(range,criteria). You could use the COUNTIF function to find out how many student test scores are above 75 points, for example, or how many of your products are available in blue.

- **COUNTIFS** Counts the number of cells that match multiple criteria. The syntax for the COUNTIFS function is =COUNTIFS(criteria_range1, criteria1, criteria_range2, criteria2, ...). Use COUNTIFS to determine the number of products available in blue and still in stock.

- **AVERAGEIF** Averages the values in cells that match specified criteria. The syntax for AVERAGEIF is =AVERAGEIF(range, criteria,[average_range]). The average_range argument is optional.

- **AVERAGEIFS** Averages the values in cells that match multiple criteria. The syntax for AVERAGEIFS is =*AVERAGEIFS(average_range1, criteria1, average_range2, criteria2, ...).*

➤ **To use the SUMIF function**

→ Type the formula using the syntax **=SUMIF(range, criteria)**. For example, **=SUMIF(D12:D38,"cedar")**.

You can also use the Function Arguments dialog box, as follows:

1. On the **Formulas** tab, click **Math & Trig**.
2. Scroll down the list of functions, and click **SUMIF**.
3. In the **Function Arguments** dialog box, enter the range you want to summarize and the criteria you want to use, and then click **OK**.

➤ **To use the SUMIFS function**

→ Type the formula using the syntax **SUMIFS(sumrange,range1,criterion1, range2,criterion2,...,rangeN,criterionN)**.
For example, **=SUMIF(D12:D38,"Wood Type","Cedar","Size","10 x 10")**.

You can also use the Function Arguments dialog box, as follows:

1. On the **Formulas** tab, click **Math & Trig**.
2. Scroll down the list of functions, and click **SUMIFS**.
3. In the **Function Arguments** dialog box, enter the range you want to summarize and the criteria you want to use, and then click OK.

Understanding and Defining Array Formulas

An array is a group of items, and an array formula, which you can recognize because Excel encloses the formula with curly brackets, lets you use a single formula to make calculations on one or more items in a group of cells. A simple example of an array formula is {=D2:D26*E2:E26}, which multiples the values in the range D2:D26 by the corresponding range in column E.

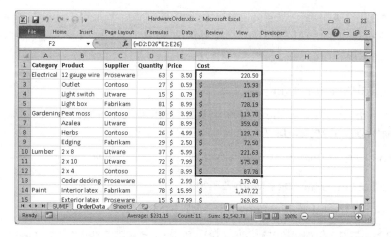

Array formulas operate on two or more sets of values. These sets of values are called *array arguments*. Each array argument must be the same size—that is, it must include the same number of rows and columns. An *array range* is the group of cells that use the same array formula. An array in Excel is considered one-dimensional if its items are contained in a single row or column. An array range that includes both rows and columns is considered a two-dimensional array. Also, array formulas can return their result in a single cell (for example, the aggregate sum of several rows of data) or in multiple cells (for example, a column or row of subtotals, as in the example shown in the preceding screen shot). A single-cell array formula that totals the individual items in the hardware order is *=SUM(D2:D26*E2:E26)*. In this case, Excel multiplies the values in the array (the cell range D2 through E26) and then uses the SUM function to add the totals together.

Working with Array Formulas

To enter an array formula, first select the range of cells where you want the results of the formula to appear. Enter the formula in the first cell of the range, and then press Ctrl+Shift+Enter. This keystroke combination tells Excel to create an array formula.

Excel imposes several restrictions on what you can and cannot do with an array formula:

- You cannot edit or delete individual cells in a cell range that contains results computed with an array formula. You need to work with the cells in the range as a whole. To change the formula in an array, select the entire array and then change the formula in the formula bar. You must press Ctrl+Shift+Enter again to confirm the change to the formula.

- You cannot paste an array formula into a cell range that includes blank cells and array formulas.

- You cannot cut, clear, or edit part of an array, but you can apply formats to individual cells in an array.
- You can copy cells from an array range and paste them in another area of your worksheet.

Defining Array Constants

Array constants are another element of array formulas. An array constant is a list of items that you enclose manually with curly braces. Here is an example:

={"January","February","March"}

Array constants can contain text (enclosed in quotation marks), as in this example, numerical values, or logical values.

You need to select the cell range that will contain the array items before you define the constant. After you select the range, use the formula bar to enter the list and add the braces, and then press Ctrl+Shift+Enter to create the constant—the same keystroke you use to enter an array formula. Excel surrounds the constant with another set of braces because you entered it as an array formula.

If you don't select a range of cells that matches the number of elements in your constant, you'll see the #N/A error (if you select too many cells) or be without a value you need (if you select too few.)

To create an array constant in a row, separate the items by using commas. Use semicolons to create a vertical array in a column. To create a two-dimensional array, separate the items in each row with commas and indicate each row of items by using a semicolon. The following example places the numbers 10, 20, 30 in row 1 and the numbers 40, 50, 60 in row 2:

={10,20,30;40,50,60}

Take care to use commas and semicolons in the correct place and for the type of array constant you want to create. You'll see a warning (or perhaps end up with a nonfunctioning constant) if you forget to insert a comma or semicolon or insert one in the wrong place.

Array constants cannot contain other arrays, formulas, or functions—they can contain only text or numbers that are separated by commas or semicolons. Numeric values you use in an array constant should not be formatted using percent signs, dollar signs, commas, or parentheses.

To facilitate the use of array constants in your formulas, you can name them. Use the same steps you use to name any other range. Select the range, click in the name box at the left end of the formula bar, and then type the name you want to use. You can also use the Define Name dialog box, which you open by clicking Define Name on the Formulas tab.

Examples of Array Functions and Formulas

Some of Excel's functions are designed to be applied to an array. The TRANSPOSE function is a straightforward example. The TRANSPOSE function lets you change the orientation of the columns and rows in an array so that the values in the columns are moved into rows and vice versa. When you use the TRANSPOSE function, you specify the array to convert, and you must enter the array formula in a range of the same size as the array you are transposing.

D1				{=TRANSPOSE(A1:B5)}				
	A	B	C	D	E	F	G	H
1	Students	Scores		Students	John	Mary	Betty	Fred
2	John	85		Scores	85	92	67	93
3	Mary	92						
4	Betty	67						
5	Fred	93						

The following examples demonstrate a few of the ways in which you can put array constants to use in array formulas. Some of the examples use the TRANSPOSE function to convert rows to columns and vice versa.

FREQUENCY is another array function. Use this function to calculate how often values occur within a range of values. In using the FREQUENCY function, you define the range that holds the values you want to analyze and a range (called the *bin range*) where you set up value ranges.

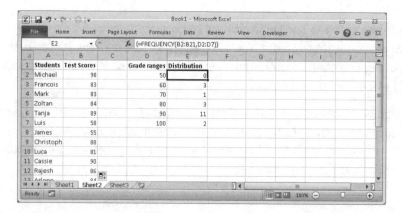

➤ **To enter an array formula**

   1. Select the range in which you want the formula to shows its results.

   2. Click in the formula bar, and enter the formula.

   3. Press Ctrl+Shift+Enter.

➤ **Create an array constant in a row**

   1. Select the number of cells you need in the row—for example, cells B1 through H1.

   2. In the formula bar, enter the formula (for example, ={1,2,3,4,5,6,7}), and then press Ctrl+Shift+Enter.

➤ **Create an array constant in a column**

   1. In your workbook, select the cells you need in a column—for example, C1 through C8.

   2. In the formula bar, enter the formula (for example, ={1;2;3;4;5;6;7;8}), and then press Ctrl+Shift+Enter.

➤ **Create a two-dimensional array constant**

   1. In your workbook, select a block of cells containing the number of columns and rows you need—for example, A1:D4.

   2. In the formula bar, enter the formula (for example, ={1,2, 3,4;5,6,7,8;9,10,11,12;13, 14,15,16}), and then press Ctrl+Shift+Enter.

➤ **Name an array constant**

   1. On the **Formulas** tab, in the **Defined Names** group, click **Define Name**.

   2. In the **Name** box, type the name for the constant.

   3. In the **Refers to** box, specify the cell range that defines the constant.

   4. Click **OK**.

➤ **To enter a formula using an array constant, follow these steps:**

   1. Select a range of cells in the size you need to contain the result.

   2. Enter an equal sign, a function name if you are using one, and an opening parenthesis.

   3. Type the values that define the constant. Enclose them in braces to indicate that the values make up an array constant. If you use a function, include the closing parenthesis.

   4. Press Ctrl+Shift+Enter.

Practice Tasks

The practice files for these tasks are located in the folder for Microsoft Excel 2010. You can save the results of these exercises in the same folder. Change the file name so that you don't overwrite the sample files. When you are done, try performing the following tasks:

* Open the file Arrays.xlsx. On the worksheet Arrays, enter an array formula using the AVERAGE function to find the average of the product of multiplying the values in column A by the values in column B.

* On the worksheet Arrays, use the TRANSPOSE function to transpose the values in row 1 so that they appear in a column. Transpose the values in column D so that they appear in a row.

* On the worksheet Frequency in the file Arrays.xlsx, use the COUNTIFS function to determine the number of test scores that are 80 and above.

2.4   Apply Functions in Formulas

This section describes how to locate and use Excel's built-in functions in your formulas. It also covers steps you can follow to ensure you enter a function correctly.

Using Built-in Functions

Many users of Excel have created formulas that include one or more of the most commonly used Excel functions, such as SUM, AVERAGE, COUNT, MAX, MIN, and others. Excel provides a large number of other functions that perform very specific operations. You can use these functions to calculate dates and time, perform statistical or financial analysis, work with text strings, look up values, and perform other such tasks. Commands in the Function Library group on the Formulas tab lead you to several of these groups of functions. The More Functions command takes you to the rest. Click Date & Time, for example, and Excel displays a list of functions you can use to display today's date (TODAY) or calculate the dates in a schedule using only workdays (WORKDAY).

When you select a function, Excel displays the Function Arguments dialog box, which you use to enter the information (called *arguments*) that the particular function needs to perform its calculation. The WORKDAY function, for example, requires two arguments—the start date and an interval of days—shown in bold, and one optional argument (Holidays) that lets you specify dates that you want the function to ignore in addition to weekend days.

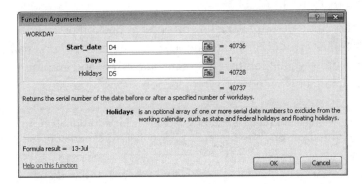

The Function Arguments dialog box provides a description of the function as well as a description of each of the function's arguments. As you fill in the arguments, the result of the formula is displayed near the bottom of the dialog box.

Another path to using a function is the Insert Function dialog box. (Click Insert Function in the Function Library group to display the dialog box.) If you know the category of function you need but not which specific function, select a category (such as Text). Then scroll through the list of functions to see a description for each one, or you might successfully zero in on the function you need by following the prompt and typing a brief description in the Search For A Function box.

Correcting Function Errors

You might see Excel's standard error values if you enter a function or its arguments incorrectly. The #NAME? error occurs, for example, if you enter the wrong name for a function. Excel provides several tools that help eliminate errors and ensure that you enter all the information a function needs to perform its operations successfully:

> **See Also** For error values and their definitions, as well as for additional information about correcting formula errors, see "Correcting Formula Errors" earlier in this chapter.

- Use the Function Arguments dialog box so that you are sure you enter each required argument in the correct format. The dialog box includes the link Help On This Function; click this link to read the full Help topic about how to use a particular function.

> **See Also** For more information about the Function Arguments dialog box, see the previous section, "Using Built-in Functions."

- When you are working with a function, highlight the function name and then press F1 to open the Excel help window and display the help topic for this function.

- Take advantage of the on-screen prompts that appear when you start entering a formula that contains a function. Excel first displays a list of functions that match the first few characters you type. After you select the function you need, press Tab to select the function. At this point, Excel displays the function name along with a list of its required and optional arguments. This information gives you a template to follow as you enter each argument.

A	B	C	D	E	F
Project Budget Stone Patio March 2, 2011					
BudgetItem	Quantity	Unit	Amount	Supplier	
Equipment	=LOOKUP(				
Rototiller	LOOKUP(**lookup_value**, lookup_vector, [result_vector]) LOOKUP(**lookup_value**, array)				

➤ To insert a function

1. Click the **Formulas** tab.

2. In the **Function Library** group, click the command for the category of function you want to use, or click **More Functions**.

3. In the list that appears, click the function you need.

4. In the **Function Arguments** dialog box, enter the arguments for the function. The dialog box provides a description of required arguments as well as optional arguments.

5. To learn more about the function you are using, click **Help on this function**.

➤ To find a function

1. In the **Function Library** group, click **Insert Function**.

2. In the **Insert Function** dialog box, type a description of the operation you want to perform in the **Search for a function** box.

3. To filter the list of functions, choose a category from the **Or select a category** list.

Practice Tasks

The practice files for these tasks are located in the folder for Microsoft Excel 2010. You can save the results of these exercises in the same folder. Change the file name so that you don't overwrite the sample files. When you are done, try performing the following tasks:

- To practice using a few of the functions in Excel, open the workbook Function_examples.xlsx.

    o In the PopulationData worksheet, use the VLOOKUP function to locate the world's seventy-third most populated city.

    o In the LoanData worksheet, use the PMT function to calculate the loan payments using the data that's shown.

    o In the TextStrings worksheet, use the LEFT function to capture the first three characters of each city's name.

Objective Review

Before finishing this chapter, be sure you've mastered the following skills:

2.1 Audit formulas

2.2 Manipulate formula options

2.3 Perform data summary tasks

2.4 Apply functions in formulas

3 Presenting Data Visually

The skills tested in this section of the Microsoft Office Expert exam for Microsoft Excel 2010 relate to working with charts, PivotTables, data analysis tools, and external sources of data. Specifically, the following objectives are associated with this set of skills:

3.1 Apply advanced chart features

3.2 Apply data analysis

3.3 Apply and manipulate PivotTables

3.4 Apply and manipulate PivotCharts

3.5 Use external data sources

3.1 Apply Advanced Chart Features

The data contained in a Microsoft Excel worksheet can often be presented as a chart for the purposes of analysis, reporting, and sharing. When you create a chart, you can choose from many options for the type of chart (pie, line, column, and others, for example) and for how you want to label and format the elements of a chart.

> **See Also** This section assumes you are familiar with techniques to create and format basic charts in Excel. If you need more information about creating charts, see the Excel Help topics listed under "Creating Charts" and "Formatting Charts."

In this section, you learn about specific features you can apply to charts to highlight trends in data, how to set up and apply a chart template, and how to use sparklines (a feature in Excel 2010 that lets you present a chart in a single cell). In the last part of this section, you'll learn about plotting chart data on more than one axis.

Adding Trendlines to Data

A trendline lets you see the general movement of the values in a set of data over time. A basic application of a trendline is to plot the course of revenue and expenses from month to month or year to year. Trendlines are used in regression analysis, a type of statistical analysis in which forecasts are made by estimating the relationship between variables so that the value of a given variable (the dependent variable) can be predicted on the basis of one or more other variables (independent variables).

> **Tip** Only specific types of charts work with trendlines. Area, bar, column, line, and other chart types work with trendlines, whereas pie and radar charts are some of the chart types that don't. If you change a chart or data series to a type of chart that does not support a trendline, Excel removes the trendline from the chart or series.

Excel provides six types of trendlines. The type and pattern of the data determines the type of trendline you should use. A trendline is most accurate in forecasting when its R-squared value—a number from 0 to 1 that reveals how closely the estimated values for the trendline correspond to the actual data—is at or near 1. When you fit a trendline to your data, Excel automatically calculates the R-squared value. If you want to, you can display this value on your chart.

The following list summarizes the types of trendlines available in Excel:

- **Linear** Data that is linear when its pattern increases or decreases at a fairly constant rate. A linear trendline fits a straight line to the data. You can also apply a linear forecast trendline that forecasts two periods ahead of the data set the trendline applies to.

- **Logarithmic** A logarithmic trendline is curved. It applies when data changes (increases or decreases) quickly and then levels off. A logarithmic trendline can use negative and positive values.

- **Polynomial** A polynomial trendline is a curved line used when data fluctuates. It is often applied to plot the ups and downs in large data sets. The order of the polynomial can be determined by the number of fluctuations in the data or by how many peaks and valleys occur in the curve. An Order 2 polynomial trendline usually has a single peak or valley. Order 3 has two peaks or valleys, and Order 4 has up to three peaks or valleys.

- **Power** A power trendline is a curved line that is used with data sets that compare measurements that increase at a specific rate—for example, a 2 percent increase in cost each month. You cannot create a power trendline if your data contains zero or negative values.

- **Exponential** An exponential trendline is a curved line that is used when data values rise or fall at constantly increasing rates. You cannot create an exponential trendline if your data contains zero or negative values.

- **Moving average** A moving average trendline smooths fluctuations in data to better show a pattern or trend. A moving average uses a specific number of data points (set by the Period option), averages them, and uses the average value as a point in the line. For example, if the period is set to 2, the average of the first two data points is used as the first point in the moving average trendline, if the period is set to 3, the average of the first three data points is used, and so on.

To apply a trendline, select the data set you want to use and then click Trendline on the Chart Tools Layout tab (in the Analysis group). The menu that Excel displays lists several types of trendlines. Select the type of trendline you want to apply, or click More Trendline Options to open the Format Trendline dialog box, where you can choose from all the types and set specific options.

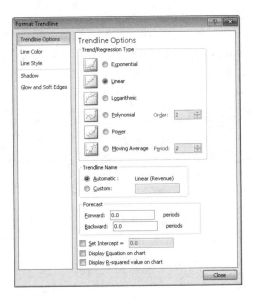

> **Tip** If the chart or a chart element other than the data series is selected when you click Trendline, Excel displays the Add Trendline dialog box. Use this dialog box to select the data set you want to use.

In the Trendline Name area of the Trendline Options page, Excel names the trendline by using the type of trendline and the data set label. To assign a different name, select the Custom option and then type the name you want to use.

In the Forecast area, you can specify the number of future or past periods you want the trendline to forecast based on the data. Use the check boxes at the bottom of this page to select options to set the intercept (the point at which the trendline crosses the vertical, or value, axis) and to display the trendline equation and the R-squared value on the chart.

Options in this last group do not apply to all types of trendlines. You can set the intercept only for an exponential, linear, or polynomial trendline. For a moving average trendline, you cannot display the trendline equation or the R-squared value.

> **Tip** Excel rounds the trendline equation to make it more readable. You can change the number of digits it displays by selecting the equation in the chart and then clicking the Format Selection button in the Current Selection group on the Chart Tools Format tab. In the Format Trendline Label dialog box, select the Number tab (and Number in the Category list, if necessary) and then specify how many digits you want to display by using the Decimal Places box.

The other pages in the Format Trendline dialog box let you apply formatting attributes to the trendline. The Automatic option on the Line Color page applies a solid black line style to the trendline. You can choose an option to show no line, a solid line (for which you choose the color and the degree of transparency), or a line with a gradient pattern (for which you can select preset options or apply attributes you define).

The Line Style page lets you set the width of the line, the style for a dashed line, and the type and size for arrows at the start and beginning of a line. The Compound Type option applies line styles with double or triple lines. Use the Cap Type option to apply a shape to each end of a line. Join type styles are used when two lines are joined. The options here are Round, Bevel, and Miter.

The Shadow page and the Glow And Soft Edges page provide formatting options that you can use to apply special visual effects to a trendline.

Adding Other Lines and Bars

The Analysis group on the Chart Tools Layout tab also includes the Lines and Up/Down Bars commands. Drop lines connect data points to the horizontal (category) axis. Applying drop lines can help clarify the location of data points. High-low lines extend from the highest value to the lowest value in each category. High-low lines appear by default in stock charts. Up-down bars show the difference between data points in a chart with more than one data series.

➤ **To add a trendline**

1. On the chart, click the data series you want to add a trendline to.

2. On the **Chart Tools Layout** tab, in the **Analysis** group, click **Trendline**.

3. Select the type of trendline, or click **More Trendline Options** and then select the type of trendline you want to use in the **Format Trendlines** dialog box.

➤ **To change the format of a trendline**

1. On the chart, click the trendline you want to change.

2. On the **Chart Tools Layout** tab, in the **Analysis** group, click **Trendline**, and then click **More Trendline Options**.

3. To change the color, style, or shadow options of the trendline, click the **Line Color**, **Line Style**, or **Shadow** category, and then select the options that you want.

➤ **To specify the number of periods to include in a forecast**

1. On the chart, select the trendline you want to work with.

2. On the **Chart Tools Layout** tab, in the **Analysis** group, click **Trendline**, and then click **More Trendline Options**.

3. In the **Forecast** area of the **Trendline Options** page, use the **Forward** and **Backward** boxes to specify the number of periods.

➤ **To set the intercept**

1. On the chart, select the trendline you want to work with.

2. On the **Chart Tools Layout** tab, in the **Analysis** group, click **Trendline**, and then click **More Trendline Options**.

3. Select the **Set Intercept** check box, and then type the value to specify the point on the vertical (value) axis where the trendline crosses the axis.

➤ **To display the trendline equation on the chart**

1. On the chart, select the trendline you want to work with.

2. On the **Chart Tools Layout** tab, in the **Analysis** group, click **Trendline**, and then click **More Trendline Options**.

3. Select the **Display Equation on chart** check box.

➤ **To display the R-squared value for a trendline**

1. On the chart, select the trendline you want to work with.

2. On the **Chart Tools Layout** tab, in the **Analysis** group, click **Trendline**, and then click **More Trendline Options**.

3. On the **Trendline Options** page, select **Display R-squared value on chart**.

➤ **To remove a trendline**

1. On the chart, select the trendline you want to remove.

2. On the **Chart Tools Layout** tab, in the **Analysis** group, click **Trendline**, and then click **None**, or simply press Delete.

Using a Chart Template

The special formatting and customizations you apply to a chart can be saved as a chart template. This template is then available for you to apply to other charts.

After you set up a chart with the styles, labels, and formatting you want, select the chart and click Save As Template in the Type group on the Chart Tools Design tab. By default, Excel saves the template in the Charts folder under \AppData\Roaming\Microsoft\ Templates, which is the default location for Office templates in your user profile. Chart templates use the .crtx file-name extension. Templates that you save in this folder appear in the Templates folder in the Insert Chart and Change Chart Type dialog boxes so that you can select the template when you create or update a chart.

To apply a chart template to a new chart, click a chart type in the Charts group on the Insert tab and then click All Chart Types at the bottom of the gallery. This command displays the Insert Chart dialog box. Open the Templates folder at the top of the list of chart types, and then select the template you want to use.

> **Tip** You can also open the Insert Chart dialog box by clicking the dialog box launcher in the Charts group.

To apply a template to a chart you have already designed, click Change Chart Type and then open the Templates folder in Change Chart Type dialog box and select the template you want to use.

If you save a template in a folder other than the Charts folder, click Manage Templates in the Insert Chart or Change Chart Type dialog box, locate the chart template, and then copy or move it to the Charts folder under Templates.

➤ **To save a chart as a chart template**

1. Select the chart you want to save as a template.

2. On the **Chart Tools Design** tab, in the **Type** group, click **Save As Template**.

3. In the **Save in** box, make sure that the **Charts** folder is selected.

4. In the **File name** box, type an appropriate name for the chart template.

➤ **To apply a chart template**

1. Select the data you want to plot in the chart.

2. On the **Insert** tab, in the **Charts** group, click any chart type, and then click **All Chart Types**.

3. In the **Insert Chart** dialog box, open the **Templates** folder, and then click the template you want to use.

➤ **To apply a chart template to an existing chart**

1. Select the chart.

2. On the **Chart Tools Design** tab, in the **Type** group, click **Change Chart Type**.

3. In the **Change Chart Type** dialog box, open the Templates folder, select the template you want to use, and then click **OK**.

➤ **To remove or delete a chart template**

1. On the **Insert** tab, in the **Charts** group, click any chart type, and then click **All Chart Types**.

2. In the **Insert Chart** dialog box, click **Manage Templates**.

3. In the dialog box that appears, select the chart and then press Delete or move the chart to a different folder if you no longer want it to be available in the Templates folder.

Visualizing the Data in a Cell by Using Sparklines

Sparklines (a new feature in Excel 2010) are in-cell charts that represent trends in data as a line chart or in column format. A third type of sparkline (called Win/Loss) lets you see positive and negative values. In a Win/Loss sparkline, negative values extend below the axis and positive values extend above it. You can use a Win/Loss sparkline to show which sale regions or time periods generated profit and which did not, for example, or to depict a sports team's won-lost record through the course of a season. Or you can use it with other data sets in which the outcome (positive or negative) is more important than the size of the values themselves.

You add a sparkline to a worksheet from the Insert tab, where the Sparklines group includes a command for each type of sparkline. In the Create Sparklines dialog box, specify the range of data you are plotting and the cell or cell range in which to place the sparkline. You can base a sparkline on a column or a row of data.

If you are working with a set of sparklines and want to expand the range of data the sparklines plot, format the range as a table. (Select the range and then press Ctrl+T to apply a table.) When you add columns to the right border of the table, the columns become part of the table, and formulas and charts (including sparklines) that refer to the table take account of the data in the new columns automatically.

When you select a cell that contains a sparkline, Excel displays the Sparkline Tools Design tab on the ribbon. You can use the ribbon to edit the data the sparkline refers to, to change the type of sparkline, to customize its appearance, and to apply a style.

> **Tip** If you add sparklines to adjacent cells, Excel groups the sparklines by default. You can ungroup the sparklines by selecting the group and then click Ungroup on the Sparklines Tools Design tab.

In the following sections, you'll learn more about how to work with each group of commands on the Sparklines Tools Design tab.

Sparkline Group

To change the data range for a sparkline or a group of sparklines, use the Edit Data command in the Sparkline group.

With a sparkline or sparkline group selected, click the Sparklines Tools Design tab, click Edit Data, and then choose Edit Group Location & Data to open the Edit Sparkline dialog box. This dialog box provides the same controls as the Create Sparklines dialog box shown earlier in this section. Use the Data Range box to change the cell range the sparkline or sparkline group refers to. Use the Location Range box to specify a new location for the sparkline or sparkline group.

The Edit Single Sparkline's Data command opens the Edit Sparkline Data dialog box and selects the cell range a specific sparkline refers to. You can then adjust the data range that this sparkline refers to.

Use the Hidden & Empty Cells command to set options for how sparklines treat empty and hidden cells. You can choose between showing empty cells as a gap in the sparkline or as the value zero (which is then plotted in the sparkline). For a line sparkline, you can also choose an option to connect data points with a line, which essentially removes the empty cell from being considered in how Excel shapes the sparkline. If the current worksheet includes hidden rows or columns, use the option provided in the Hidden And Empty Cell Settings dialog box to specify whether the data in those cells should be reflected in the sparkline.

Type Group

Use the Type group to switch between the different types of sparklines.

Show Group

Options in this group let you add markers to a sparkline to identify specific data points. For example, you can add a marker to identify the high point and low point in the data. Choose the Markers option (for a line sparkline) to add a marker for each data point plotted by the sparkline.

In a column sparkline, Excel shows the data points you select in the Show group by changing the color of the applicable column.

Style Group

Choose one of the built-in styles from the gallery available in this group to apply it to the sparklines. Use the Sparkline Color command to change the color of the sparklines. If you select options in the Show group (High Point and Low Point, for example) to mark details of a column sparkline, the color you choose from the Sparkline Color palette is applied to the columns between the high and low point. You can separately format the colors for particular markers by clicking Marker Color and then choosing the specific point from the menu.

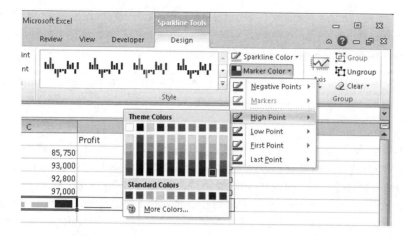

Use a color to call attention to specific points on a sparkline. Choose the data points you want to format from the Marker Color menu.

Group Group

You can group and ungroup sparklines by using commands in the Group group area of the Sparklines Tools Design tab. Use the Clear command to remove specific sparklines or a group of sparklines from the worksheet.

The Axis command provides a set of options for how to display the horizontal and vertical axes on sparklines. For the horizontal axis, you can choose Date Axis Type to see gaps in time periods being plotted by a sparkline. For example, when you apply the date axis type to a column sparkline that plots data points separated by unequal periods of time, the columns are resized and spaced to show the differences. In a line sparkline, the shape of the line and the location of the data points change to account for the irregular time periods.

> **Tip** Increase the height of the row that contains a sparkline to see the differences in values more clearly.

For a sparkline that plots positive and negative values, click Show Axis to display the axis line at zero. You can use the Plot Data Right-To-Left option to change the direction in which data is plotted in a sparkline or sparkline group.

Excel sets the scale for the vertical axis of a sparkline so that the minimum and maximum values fall just below and above the data range. These are the values Excel applies when you choose Automatic For Each Sparkline when setting options for the vertical axis. In cases when the minimum value in a data series plotted with a column sparkline results in a column that's barely visible within the cell, you can specify a custom value for the minimum (or maximum) value used in creating the axis's scale. Choose Custom Value and then enter the value you want to use.

➤ **To insert a sparkline**

1. Select the cell or cell range where you want to add sparklines.

2. On the **Insert** tab, in the **Sparklines** group, click **Line**, **Column,** or **Win/Loss,** depending on the type of sparkline you want to use.

3. In the **Create Sparklines** dialog box, specify the data range you want the sparklines to refer to, specify the location range, and then click **OK**.

➤ **To change the data range for an individual sparkline**

1. Select the sparkline.

2. On the **Sparkline Tools Design** tab, click **Edit Data, Edit Single Sparkline's Data**.

3. In the **Edit Sparkline Data** dialog box, specify a new data range and then click **OK**.

➤ **To change the location or data range for a group of sparklines**

1. Select the sparkline group or a sparkline in the group.

2. On the **Sparkline Tools Design** tab, click **Edit Data, Edit Group Location & Data**.

3. In the **Edit Sparklines** dialog box, specify a different data range for the sparkline group, a different location range for the group, or both.

➤ **To work with hidden and empty cells in the data range**

1. Select the sparkline or the sparkline group.

2. On the **Sparkline Tools Design** tab, click **Hidden & Empty Cells**.

3. In the **Hidden and Empty Cell Settings** dialog box, select an option for showing empty cells as gaps or as zero in the sparklines. (For line sparklines, you can also choose to connect the data points with a line.)

4. If you want the data in hidden rows and columns to be plotted in the sparkline, select this option.

➤ **To highlight data points in a sparkline**

1. Select the sparkline or group of sparklines.

2. On the **Sparkline Tools Design** tab, select the options in the **Show** group for the points you want to highlight. (The **Markers** option applies only to line sparklines.)

➤ **To format sparklines**

1. Select the sparkline or group of sparklines.

2. On the **Sparkline Tools Design** tab, select a style from the gallery in the **Style** group.

3. Click **Sparkline Color**, and then select the color you want to apply. (The color change applies only to sparklines in the middle range if the options to show the high and low or first and last points are selected in the **Show** group.)

4. Click **Marker Color** to apply a color to specific markers (such as the high point or the low point).

➤ **To set a maximum and minimum value for the vertical axis**

1. With the sparkline or sparkline group selected, in the **Group** group, click **Axis**.

2. Under **Vertical Axis Minimum Value Options** or **Vertical Axis Maximum Value Options**, click **Custom Value**.

3. In the **Sparkline Vertical Axis Setting** dialog box, set minimum or maximum values for the axis's scale.

➤ **To show the horizontal axis when your data has negative and positive values**

1. With the sparkline or sparkline group selected, in the **Group** group, click **Axis**.

2. Under **Horizontal Axis Options**, click **Show Axis**.

Creating Dual-Axes Charts

In some charts, the data that the chart represents is mixed (for example, one data set shows prices and the other shows volume). You might also need to create a chart from data sets with significantly different values (for example, a chart plotting revenue in the tens of thousands of dollars along with the number of active sales representatives, which is between 5 and 10).

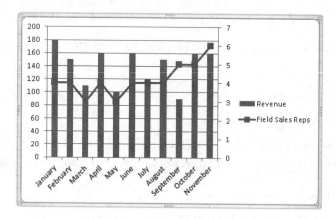

You can use a dual-axes chart to plot different data sets. In this chart, revenue is plotted on the primary axis in a column chart. The number of field sales representatives is shown on a secondary axis in a line chart.

To handle examples such as these in a chart, you can add a second value axis for one of the sets of data. With a secondary value axis in place, you can add a second category (horizontal) axis. You can also change the chart type for the data series plotted on the secondary axis—for example, you can plot one set of data in a column chart and then change the data series plotted with the secondary axis to a line chart.

> **Tip** You can apply a secondary axis only to a two-dimensional chart. You cannot apply secondary axes to three-dimensional charts.

To begin, in a chart with multiple data series, select the data series you want to plot on a secondary axis. On the Chart Tools Format tab, in the Current Selection group, click Format Selection to display the Format Data Series dialog box. In the Plot Series On area, click Secondary Axis.

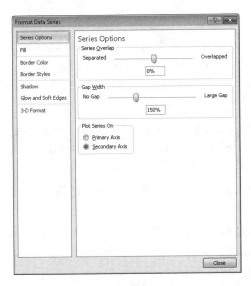

To add a secondary horizontal axis (after the secondary vertical axis is in place), select the data set and then click Axes on the Chart Tools Layout tab. Click Secondary Horizontal Axis, and then choose the option for how you want to display the axis.

To change the chart type for the secondary axis, right-click the data series plotted on that axis and choose Change Series Chart Type. In the Change Chart Type dialog box, select the type of chart you want to use.

➤ **To add a secondary vertical axis**

1. In the chart, select the data series you want to plot on a secondary axis.

2. On the **Chart Tools Format** tab, in the **Current Selection** group, click **Format Selection**.

3. In the **Format Data Series** dialog box, in the **Plot Series On** area, select **Secondary Axis**.

➤ **To change the chart type for the data set plotted on a secondary axis**

1. Right-click the data set and choose **Change Data Series Chart Type**.

2. In the **Change Chart Type** dialog box, select the chart type you want to use and then click **OK**.

Practice Tasks

The practice files for these tasks are located in the practice files folder for Microsoft Excel 2010. You can save the results of these exercises in the same folder. Change the file name so that you don't overwrite the sample files. When you are done, try performing the following tasks:

- Open the file ChartTechniques.xlsx. Use the data on Sheet1 to create a line, column, and x,y scatter chart so that you can see how different chart types affect the display of the data.

- Format the column chart using the Chart Tools Design and Format tabs, and then save the column chart as a template.

- Using the line chart, apply a linear trendline to the data series Income. Set options to display the R-squared value and the trendline equation. Specify a forecast two periods in the future.

- Create column sparklines for the line chart to plot the changes in Income. Based on the data, set a minimum value for the vertical axis so that the smallest column is clearly visible.

- In the column chart, apply a secondary axis to the data set for energy consumption and then change the chart type for that data set to a line chart.

3.2   Apply Data Analysis

Data analysis and business modeling are two of the main uses of Excel. By using built-in tools that appear on the What-If Analysis group on the Data tab, you can calculate a value for a variable that helps you meet a goal, define and run scenarios, and test a range of values for one or two variables by using a data table. When you load the Solver and the Analysis ToolPak add-ins, you gain access to analytical tools that help you manage complex data analysis needs. In the following sections, you'll learn more about these features in Excel 2010.

Performing a What-If Analysis

What-if analyses let you try out different sets of values in your formulas to examine a range of results. You might use a what-if analysis to see the effect of a 10 or 15 percent rise in product prices or the effect on your bottom line of price increases for various materials you use. Excel also lets you set goals or targets when you analyze data. For example, you can set a goal for product revenue, and Excel can calculate the number of units of that product you need to sell to meet that target.

To perform a what-if analysis in Excel, you can use the Goal Seek feature, data tables, or the Excel Scenario Manager. Scenarios and data tables take sets of input values and determine possible results. A data table can use only one or two variables, but it can accept many different values for those variables. A scenario you create with Scenario Manager can accept multiple variables, but it can use only up to 32 values. Goal Seek works differently from scenarios and data tables in that it takes a result and determines possible input values that produce that result. You can use only one variable with Goal Seek.

In addition to these three tools, you can install an add-in that helps you perform a what-if analysis. The Solver can take account of more than one variable and also apply constraints to come up with an optimal solution for the models you are analyzing.

> **Tip** If you work with what-if analysis tools, you'll find it helpful to name cells and cell ranges rather than use cell references (for example, Revenue instead of D12). Seeing names instead of cell references on the report that Scenario Manager produces makes the data easier to understand. To name a cell or cell range, select it and then type a name in the name box to the left of the formula bar. Names cannot include spaces and must be unique within a workbook. For more information, see the Excel Help article "Define and Use Names in Formulas."

Using Goal Seek

The Goal Seek feature helps you discover what value you need to obtain a specific result. (Remember that Goal Seek works with only one variable input value.) In the Goal Seek dialog box, you point to the cell with the formula (called the *set cell*), type the value for the goal you are seeking, and then specify the variable cell—the cell whose value Excel calculates so that the goal you define is met.

For example, to calculate the minimum price at which you can sell 6500 units of a product and reach a revenue goal of $85,000, you set up a worksheet with the number of units in one cell, keep the Price cell blank, and type the formula =*units*price* in the cell for revenue. Select the cell with the formula, and then click Goal Seek on the What-If Analysis menu on the Data tab. In the dialog box, Excel fills in the cell you selected as the set cell. In the To Value box, specify $85,000 (or whatever goal you are trying to reach), and then refer to the Price cell in the By Changing Cell box. When you click OK, Goal Seek calculates the value for the changing cell that is required to meet your goal.

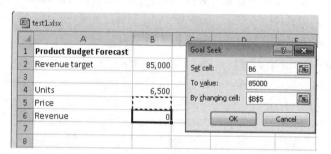

Set up the Goal Seek dialog box to set the target cell to a specific value by calculating the value for the changing cell.

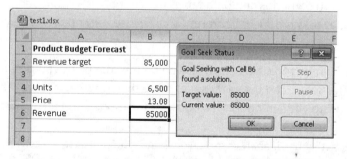

Goal Seek informs you when it finds a solution.

> **Tip** The Step and Pause buttons visible in the Goal Seek Status dialog box are enabled when Excel needs many iterations of the calculation to find the goal. Use the Pause button to pause the calculation, and click Step to see the results of the current iteration.

> **See Also** If you need to determine more than one input value, use the Solver add-in instead of Goal Seek. For more information about the Solver add-in, see "Using Solver" later in this chapter.

➤ **To identify a goal by using Goal Seek**

1. Set up your worksheet with the data you want to use in the formula Goal Seek will calculate.

2. Enter the formula that Goal Seek will use to derive your goal.

3. Select the cell with the formula. On the **Data** tab, in the **Data Tools** group, click **What-If Analysis** and then choose **Goal Seek.**

    The cell you selected appears in the Goal Seek dialog box as the set cell.

4. In the **Goal Seek** dialog box, type your goal in the **To value** box. In the **By changing cell** box, specify the cell whose value Goal Seek will calculate.

5. In the **Goal Seek** dialog box, click **OK**, and then click **OK** in the **Goal Seek Status** dialog box.

Using Data Tables

A data table is a range of cells you use to show the result (output) of changing one or two variables in a formula. For example, you could use a one-variable data table to see the effect that different interest rates have on a monthly payment or to see how a change in price affects your profitability. If you want to analyze how changes to interest rates and the amount of a down payment affect the monthly payment—or to test how changes to price and unit cost affect your profitability—you would use a two-variable data table.

To use a data table of either type, you need to set up a worksheet with the formula that Excel will evaluate—for example, you would use the PMT function to calculate loan payments or use a formula such as *=revenue-cost* to calculate profitability—and provide the values or references required for the calculations (loan amount, interest rate, the amount of revenue, and similar types of data).

> **See Also** For more information about Excel functions, see "Apply Functions in Formulas" in Chapter 2 in this section of the book.

You also need to enter the list of values for the variable (or variables) you want to analyze—for example, to test a range of prices, list each price in a single row or column—and the formulas for the output you want Excel to provide. For a one-variable data table, your worksheet might look something like the following:

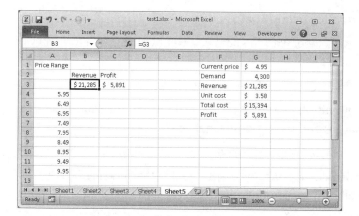

This one-variable data table lists variables for the current price in column A. The formula for Revenue is entered in cell B3, and the formula for Profit in cell C3.

When the worksheet is set up, select the cell range for the data table's output, including the row that contains the output formulas (which is row 3 in the preceding example). On the Data tab, in the Data Tools group, click What-If Analysis, Data Table. In the Data Table dialog box, specify the cell that contains the value you are testing (which is price, cell G1, in this example), and then click OK. Excel evaluates the formulas and fills in the data table by using the values you listed.

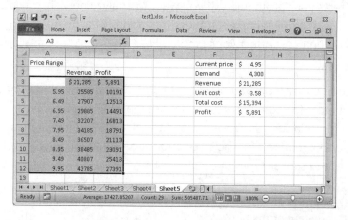

A two-variable data table includes the list of values for one variable in the table's first column and a list of values for the second variable in the table's first row. A two-variable data table can have only a single output cell, which contains the formula you want Excel to calculate by using the variables in the table. You must place that formula in the top-left cell of the table (above the column variable and to the left of the row variable).

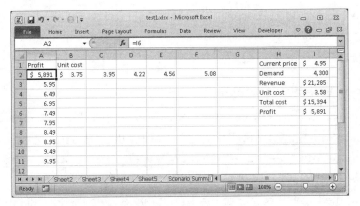

In a two-variable data table, the values for one variable are listed in the first column; the values for the second variable are in the first row. Place the formula for the output in the cell at the upper left (A2 here).

When you fill in the Data Table dialog box, enter both the row input cell (the cell containing the value you are testing by using the values in the table's top row) and the column input cell (the cell containing the value you are testing by using the values in the table's first column). When you click OK, Excel fills in the data table based on the values you provide.

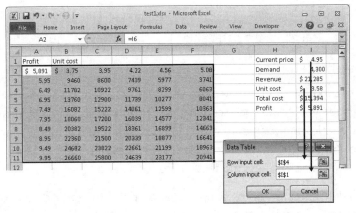

Provide references for both the row and column input cells in a two-variable data table. When you click OK, Excel creates the data table.

➤ **To set up a one-variable data table**

1. In the worksheet, enter the data required to calculate the data table's output.

2. In a single row or column, type the values for the variable you want to use as input for the data table.

3. In the top row of the data table, enter the formulas used for calculating the output.

4. Select the output range for the data table, including the row containing the output formulas.

5. On the **Data** tab, in the **Data Tools** group, click **What-If Analysis**, and then click **Data Table**.

6. In the **Data Table** dialog box, specify the row input cell or column input cell, depending on whether you listed the values for the variable in a row or column.

7. Click **OK**, and Excel fills in the data table.

➤ **To set up a two-variable data table**

1. In the worksheet, enter the data required to calculate the data table's output.

2. In a top row of the output range, list the values for the first variable you want to use. In the leftmost column of the output range, type the values for the second variable you want to use as input for the data table.

3. In the cell at the top-left corner of the output range, type the formula that will calculate the output for the data table.

4. Select the output range for the data table, including the row containing the output formula.

5. On the **Data** tab, in the **Data Tools** group, click **What-If Analysis**, and then click **Data Table**.

6. In the **Data Table** dialog box, specify the row input cell and the column input cell.

7. Click **OK**, and Excel fills in the data table.

Building What-If Scenarios

To handle what-if situations with many more variables, you can use Scenario Manager. In Scenario Manager, you name each scenario, point to the cells whose values you want to alter in that scenario, and then enter the values you want to use in the changing cells for that scenario. (You might use Scenario Manager to develop the best, most likely, and worst-case scenarios for a business model you are considering.)

In a worksheet in which you want to set up scenarios, enter the basic data and the formulas you use to make calculations. For example, in a worksheet used to evaluate budgets for books or other publishing projects, you would have data such as the expected price, the unit cost, the expected demand, the royalty percentages, and items related to expenses such as printing and binding, design, editing, marketing, and the like. You would have formulas that calculate gross revenue, summarize expenses, and calculate net profit.

Open Scenario Manager from the What-If Analysis menu on the Data tab, click Add, and then type a name for the scenario. In the Changing Cells box, specify each cell whose value you want to change in the scenarios. As the Add Scenario dialog box instructs you, press the Ctrl key and click a cell to add changing cells that are not adjacent to one another. When you click OK in the Add Scenario dialog box, Excel displays the Scenario Values dialog box, in which you type a value for this scenario for each of the changing cells you selected. Click Add in this dialog box to define another scenario, or click OK to return to the Scenario Manager dialog box, which lists each scenario you define.

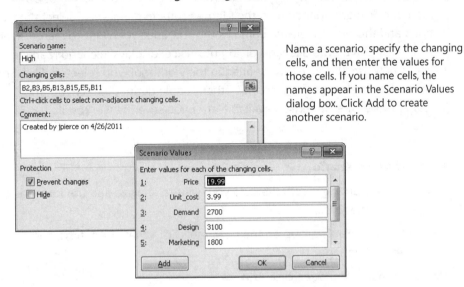

Name a scenario, specify the changing cells, and then enter the values for those cells. If you name cells, the names appear in the Scenario Values dialog box. Click Add to create another scenario.

Click the Show button in Scenario Manager to insert the values for the selected scenario in the worksheet and have Excel recalculate formulas. By working through the list of scenarios, you can see the results of each change in value.

To edit a scenario, click Edit in Scenario Manager and then make any changes to the changing cells or the values for that scenario.

To produce a scenario report (which you can also display as a PivotTable), click Summary. In the Scenario Summary dialog box, designate the result cells you want the summary to report on. Excel creates a fully formatted report in a separate worksheet in the workbook.

> **See Also** For more information about working with PivotTables, see the next section, "Apply and Manipulate PivotTables."

Merging Scenarios

If you need to collect information for scenarios from other people, you can distribute a workbook set up with the information you are analyzing, have other people define scenarios in their copies of the workbook, and then merge scenarios in a single workbook. With the workbooks that contain the scenarios open, click Merge in Scenario Manager. In the Merge Scenario dialog box, select the workbook and the worksheet that contains the scenarios you want to merge. When you click OK in the Merge Scenario dialog box, Excel displays Scenario Manager again, which now lists the scenarios defined in the workbook you selected. Click Show to see how the values in the scenarios other people defined affect your model. The scenarios you merge remain available after you save the workbook.

➤ To define a scenario

1. Set up a worksheet with the data you want to analyze and the formulas that evaluate that data.

2. In the **Data Tools** group on the **Data** tab, click **What-If Analysis**, and then click **Scenario Manager**.

3. In **Scenario Manager**, click **Add**.

4. In the **Add Scenario** dialog box, type a name for the scenario.

5. In the **Changing cells** box, specify each cell whose value you want to alter in this scenario.

6. Add a comment to describe the scenario, and then click **OK**.

7. In the **Scenario Values** dialog box, type the value you want to use in this scenario for each changing cell.

8. Click **Add** to define another scenario, or click **OK** to display Scenario Manager.

➤ To see the results of a scenario

1. In the **Data Tools** group on the **Data** tab, click **What-If Analysis**, and then click **Scenario Manager**.

2. In Scenario Manager, in the list of scenarios, select the scenario you want to examine, and then click **Show**.

➤ **To edit a scenario**

1. In the **Data Tools** group on the **Data** tab, click **What-If Analysis**, and then click **Scenario Manager**.

2. In **Scenario Manager**, in the list of scenarios, select the scenario you want to examine and then click **Edit**.

3. In the **Edit Scenario** dialog box, change the scenario name or alter the list of changing cells. Click **OK**.

4. In the **Scenario Values** dialog box, modify the values for any or all of the changing cells and then click **OK**.

➤ **To delete a scenario**

1. In the **Data Tools** group on the **Data** tab, click **What-If Analysis**, and then click **Scenario Manager**.

2. In **Scenario Manager**, in the list of scenarios, select the scenario you want to examine and then click **Delete**.

➤ **To create a scenario summary**

1. In the **Data Tools** group on the **Data** tab, click **What-If Analysis**, and then click **Scenario Manager**.

2. In **Scenario Manager**, click **Summary**.

3. In the **Scenario Summary** dialog box, select an option for the report type (either the summary report or a PivotTable report).

4. In the **Result cells** box, specify the cell or cells you want the report display.

Using Solver

Excel Solver is another tool for performing complex what-if analyses in Excel. Solver is designed to find the optimal value (either maximum or minimum) for data you are analyzing.

In a Solver model, you need to define three basic elements:

- An objective or target, which is the value you want to optimize.

- Changing cells, which are the values you can adjust to reach the objective.

- Constraints, which are conditions that must be met in evaluating the model. For example, you might set a constraint that a price must be at least a minimum amount or that demand cannot exceed a certain level because supplies required to produce the product are restricted.

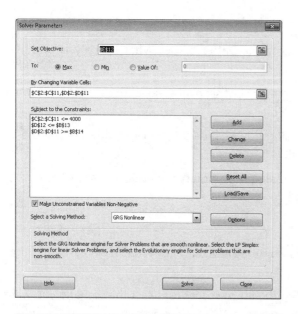

> **Important** Solver is an Excel add-in you have to load before you use it. To load Solver, click File, Options. In the Excel Options dialog box, click Add-Ins, and then in the Manage list (near the bottom of the Add-Ins page), select Excel Add-Ins (if necessary) and then click Go. In the Add-Ins dialog box, select Solver Add-In and then click OK. Excel adds a command to open Solver in a group named Analysis on the Data tab.

Click Solver on the Data tab to open the Solver Parameters dialog box. In the Set Objective box, specify the cell whose value you want to optimize (and choose Max or Min) or select the Value Of option and type the value you want to achieve. In the By Changing Variable Cells box, specify the cells or cell ranges of the variable cells. Separate nonadjacent cells with a comma. To define a constraint, click Add and then fill in the Add Constraint dialog box. You can apply a constraint to a cell range by selecting all the cells in that range.

When you set up constraints, you can specify that a cell or cell range must be a whole number by choosing it from the list of operators. Solver fills in the last box with the word *integer*. You can specify Bin (binary) as the constraint type to set up yes/no decisions.

Select Dif to specify a constraint to indicate that all the values in the constrained cell or cells are different.

When you are ready to solve the problem, click Solve. Solver displays the Solver Results dialog box to inform you whether it found a solution or encountered any problems. The options in the Solver Results dialog box are straightforward. Click one or more of the reports in the Reports area to have Solver add the report to a new worksheet in the workbook.

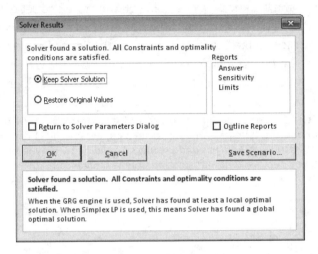

Solver Reports

Solver can produce three reports about the problems you apply it to. In brief, the Answer report shows the target cell, the changing cells, and the constraints and provides status information about the constraints. The Sensitivity report indicates how sensitive the target cell is to changes in constraints. The Limits report indicates how much you can change the values in the changing cells within the limits of the constraints.

Solver provides three options in the Select A Solving Method list in the Solver Parameters dialog box:

- **GRG Nonlinear** This is the default method, which applies to nonlinear problems whose points sit on a line that is curved.

- **Simplex LP** Use this method for straight-line problems.

- **Evolutionary** This method applies to problems whose elements do not fit on either a straight or curved line (that is, the elements are more random or discontinuous).

The Solver Options dialog box lets you set options for solving limits (maximum time and number of iterations), provides an option (Show Iteration Results) that lets you step through each iteration of Solver's calculations, and provides an option that controls the precision of values that are under constraints. The default value for precision is 0.000001. Changing the precision to a lower amount (closer to 1) might result in additional time being needed to solve a problem.

When you save a workbook in which you have defined a problem for Solver, Excel saves the Solver information with the workbook. By default, you can store one set of Solver parameters with each worksheet in a workbook; however, you can store additional sets of parameters (models) by clicking the Load/Save button in the Solver Parameters dialog box. Use the Load/Save dialog box to specify a cell range that holds a saved model and then click Load. To save a model, select the number of cells indicated and then click Save.

> **See Also** This section is a brief introduction to Solver. To learn more about the details of how to work with Solver and the type of problems it can analyze, see the chapters about Solver in *Microsoft Excel 2010 Data Analysis and Business Modeling* by Wayne Winston (Microsoft Press, 2010). You can also find information at *www.solver.com*.

➤ **To load the Solver add-in**

1. Click **File**, and then click **Options**.
2. In the **Excel Options** dialog box, click **Add-Ins**.
3. In the **Manage** list, select **Excel Add-ins** and then click **Go**.
4. In the **Add-ins** dialog box, select **Solver Add-in** and then click **OK**.

➤ **To set up Solver parameters**

1. On the **Data** tab, in the **Analysis** group, click **Solver**.
2. In the **Solver Parameters** dialog box, specify the **Set Objective** cell.
3. In the **To** area, select **Max**, **Min**, or **Value Of**. If you choose **Value Of**, type a value.
4. In the **By Changing Variable Cells** box, specify the cells whose values Solver can change when analyzing the data.
5. In the **Subject to the Constraints** area, click **Add**, and then define the constraint in the **Add Constraint** dialog box. Click **Add** in the **Add Constraint** dialog box to define another constraint. Click **OK** when you finish defining constraints.
6. Click **Solve**.

Using Automated Analysis Tools

Like the Solver, the Analysis ToolPak is an Excel add-in that is useful for performing complex data analysis, specifically for types of statistical analysis. For example, you can use the Analysis ToolPak to generate a set of descriptive statistics for a data sample.

> **Important** You need to load the Analysis ToolPak to use it. Open the Excel Options dialog box from the File menu, and then click Add-Ins in the list on the left. On the Add-Ins page, in the Manage list, choose Excel Add-Ins if that option isn't showing and then click Go. In the Add-Ins dialog box, select Analysis ToolPak and click OK. A Data Analysis command (in the Analysis group) now appears on the Data tab on the ribbon.
>
> The Analysis ToolPak—VBA add-in lets you work with the functions in the toolpak by using Microsoft Visual Basic. You don't need to load this add-in unless you plan to write a program for Excel.

The Data Analysis dialog box lists the variety of functions you can perform on a set of data with the Analysis ToolPak. Selecting an option in this dialog box opens a dialog box you fill in with information required for the analysis. The following sections provide additional information about some of the Analysis ToolPak's functions.

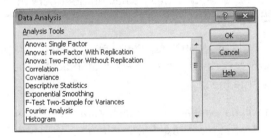

Generating Descriptive Statistics

Use the Descriptive Statistics option when you have a set of data that you want to analyze for values such as mean, standard deviation, median, count, largest, smallest, and others. In the Descriptive Statistics dialog box (which Excel displays when you choose the Descriptive Statistics option in the Data Analysis dialog box and click OK), you first specify the input range that contains the data set. If the data is listed in worksheet columns, select Columns for the Grouped By option. If the data is in rows, choose Rows. If you used the first row of the data range for labels, choose the Labels In First Row option. For the output option, specify a starting cell in the same worksheet or choose New Worksheet Ply (to add the output to a different worksheet in the current workbook) or New Workbook. Select Summary Statistics to include the set of statistics.

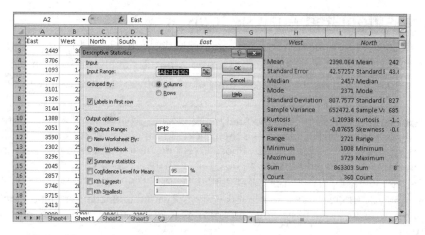

The Kth Largest and Kth Smallest options provide roughly the same information shown in the Minimum and Maximum rows in the statistics Excel generates. You can use the Minimum and Maximum values as a gauge in looking for outliers—individual entries in the set of data that are above or below what you would expect. If you see a value that is unexpectedly small or large, you might review the data set to see whether it was accurately recorded in Excel. An unexpectedly large or small number here might also mean that your data is not distributed normally.

You can choose the Confidence Level For Mean option (and enter a standard percentage, such as 90 or 95 percent) to have Excel provide an estimate that indicates the degree of uncertainty in the estimate of the true mean.

Not every statistic listed by Excel will have meaning for each data set you measure. Some of the statistics you'll want to consider in most cases include the mean, which is the average value in the data sample; the median, which indicates the value at the data set's midpoint; and mode, which tells you the value that appears most frequently among the items in the data set. The value for Skewness indicates the relative symmetry of the data set. A value between –1 and +1 indicates a generally symmetrical set.

Displaying a Histogram

A histogram lets you see the frequency with which items in a data set fall within certain intervals that you (or Excel) define.

To set up the intervals (or bins) that you want to use in your analysis, list them on the worksheet. For example, you might want to see how often daily sales totals fall between $1,000 and $3,750 in intervals of 250. You must list the bins in ascending order, but they don't need to be defined using an even interval. If you don't define the bins yourself, Excel creates evenly spaced intervals from the data set, using the minimum and maximum values in the data set as the starting and ending point for the bins.

In the Histogram dialog box, you specify the input range, the bin range (if you defined the bins), and the output range, which is the cell in which the upper-left corner of the output will appear. You can also place the output in a new worksheet or workbook.

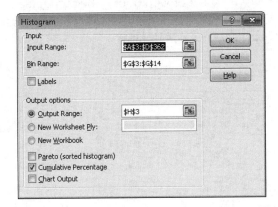

By selecting the Pareto option, you can sort the output in descending order of frequency. The Cumulative Percentage option adds a column to the output that shows the total percentage of items accounted for as you move up each level in the list of bins. Select the Chart Output option to include a chart as well as the distribution data.

	West	North	South		Bin	Frequency	Cumulative %	Bin	Frequency	Cumulative %
1										
2	West	North	South							
3	3076	3257	1629		1000	1	0.07%	1250	151	10.49%
4	2911	3223	2726		1250	151	10.56%	3750	150	20.90%
5	1433	1032	3568		1500	130	19.58%	3500	138	30.49%
6	2198	1272	2824		1750	128	28.47%	2750	131	39.58%
7	2202	2822	2722		2000	128	37.36%	1500	130	48.61%
8	2807	1801	3556		2250	113	45.21%	2500	130	57.64%
9	1412	1028	2109		2500	130	54.24%	1750	128	66.53%
10	2703	1029	3507		2750	131	63.33%	2000	128	75.42%
11	2488	1949	1832		3000	126	72.08%	3000	126	84.17%
12	3318	1005	3514		3250	114	80.00%	3250	114	92.08%
13	2527	3587	2603		3500	138	89.58%	2250	113	99.93%
14	1186	2412	2084		3750	150	100.00%	1000	1	100.00%
15	2207	3627	1856		More	0	100.00%	More	0	100.00%
16	1933	2921	2278							
17	2072	2200	1876							
18	1726	3230	2501							
19	2606	1539	2214							
20	2790	2046	2306							
21	2064	2505	3545							
22	1808	3559	1805							
23	3220	2093	1368							
24	1648	2686	2055							
25	2082	2730	1540							
26	3238	2511	1962							

Histogram

Frequency / Cumulative %

Using Rank And Percentile

By using the Rank And Percentile option, you can determine the relative order (rank) of each item in a data set and that item's percentile within the data set. You could use this option to organize a set of test scores, for example, or many other types of data. In the Rank And Percentile dialog box, you specify the input range (which can contain only numeric values), whether the data is in columns or rows, and the output range (or the option to place the output in a new worksheet or workbook). The output identifies each point (each item in the data set), its rank, and the percentile. Select the Labels In First Row option so that Excel uses that label in the output table.

	A	B	C	D	E	F	G	H
1	Daily sales							
2	2449		Point	Daily sales	Rank	Percent		
3	3706		15	3746	1	99.40%		
4	1093		31	3746	1	99.40%		
5	3247		138	3746	1	99.40%		
6	3101		16	3715	4	99.10%		
7	1326		2	3706	5	98.80%		
8	3144		42	3701	6	98.60%		
9	1388		193	3689	7	98.30%		
10	2051		19	3688	8	98.00%		
11	3590		246	3678	9	97.70%		
12	2302		125	3675	10	97.40%		
13	3296		50	3664	11	97.20%		
14	2045		88	3662	12	96.90%		
15	2857		244	3661	13	96.60%		

You can include more than one column (or row) in the input range. Excel creates columns in the output table for each column or row in the input range. To arrange the output table so that its records appear in the same order as the items in the input range, sort the output by the Point column.

Generating Random Numbers

To create number sets you can use for analytical models and other types of simulation, choose the Random Number Generation option in the Data Analysis dialog box. Use the Random Number Generation dialog box to specify the number of variables (the number of columns), the number of random numbers (how many numbers Excel will generate within each column), the type of distribution, and distribution parameters. (The parameters you need to enter change depending on the type of distribution.) As necessary, you can also specify a seed number to start from.

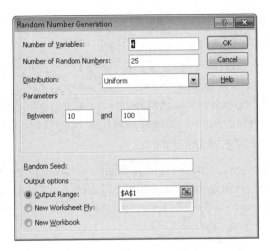

You can choose from seven options in the Distribution list.

- **Uniform** This option generates a set of evenly distributed numbers between the starting and ending numbers you specify. (The set includes the numbers you specify as well.)

- **Normal** For a normal distribution, you specify the mean and the standard deviation. In the set of numbers, the value you specify for the mean is more likely to occur than others. Values greater than or less than the mean are equally likely to occur, and numbers close to the mean are more likely to occur than numbers much smaller or larger. The standard deviation indicates the average of the difference between a random number and the mean you specify.

- **Bernoulli** This option generates in the output range either a 0 or a 1 based on the *p* (probability) value you enter as a parameter. Bernoulli distribution models are used in probability studies where they can be used to test the probable success of a specific number of trials.

- **Binomial** The Binomial option is another type of distribution used to model probability. You specify the *p* value and the number of trials. Based on the *p* value you enter, Excel generates a 0 or a 1 to reflect the number of trials that are likely to be successful given the parameters you define.

- **Poisson** The Poisson distribution option can be used to model the frequency with which a certain outcome occurs over a particular span of time. The value you specify for the parameter Lamba reflects the outcome you expect. For example, if on average you have 60 customers enter your store each day and want to know how often you can expect more customer visits than average over a 30-day period, type 30 in the Number Of Random Numbers box and 60 as the value for Lamba.

You can then count how many numbers generated exceed 60 (or use an Excel function to count the instances for you).

- **Patterned** The Patterned option creates one or more series of numbers that can be repeated individually and in sequence a specified number of times. The parameters for the Patterned option include values for the starting and ending number, the interval between numbers (or steps), and how often each number and each sequence of numbers should be repeated.

- **Discrete** Use this option with a two-column range in which you define possible outcomes in one column and probabilities in another. The probability values must be between 0 and 1 and the sum of these values must be 1. The range you define is the only input for this type of distribution.

Sampling Data

Use the Sampling option to extract a subset of items from a larger set of data. In the Sampling dialog box, you define the input range (select Labels if the top row includes a text label) and the sampling method. Use the Periodic method to pick out an item at every *n*th occurrence. Use the Random method to extract a specific number of samples from the data set. The output options in the Sampling dialog box are also an output range or a new worksheet or a new workbook.

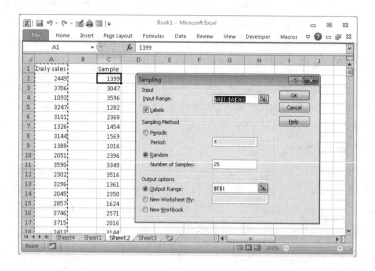

Using Other Analysis ToolPak Options

Among the other analysis functions available in the Data Analysis dialog box are options for performing Anova (variance) analysis and calculating correlation, covariance, and moving averages. You can learn more about these types of analysis in the Excel help topic "Perform statistical and engineering analysis with the Analysis ToolPak" and in the book *Microsoft Excel 2010: Data Analysis and Business Modeling* by Wayne Winston (Microsoft Press, 2010).

➤ **To load the Analysis ToolPak**

1. On the **File** menu, click **Options**.

2. In the **Excel Options** dialog box, click **Add-Ins**.

3. In the **Manage** list, select **Excel Add-Ins**, and then click **Go**.

4. In the **Add-Ins** dialog box, select **Analysis ToolPak** and then click **OK**.

➤ **To use an Analysis ToolPak option**

1. On the **Data** tab, click **Data Analysis**.

2. In the **Data Analysis** dialog box, select the option you want to use and then click **OK**.

3. In the dialog box for the option, specify the input range, parameters, and the option for output.

Practice Tasks

The practice files for these tasks are located in the practice files folder for Microsoft Excel 2010. You can save the results of these exercises in the same folder. Change the file name so that you don't overwrite the sample files. When you are done, try performing the following tasks:

- Open the file DataAnalysis.xlsx. This workbook contains a worksheet with data you can use to test your abilities with the tools you learned about in this section.

- On the GoalSeek worksheet, calculate the interest rate required to secure the loan listed according to the number of periods listed.

- On the DataTables worksheet, use the data and formulas provided to set up and fill in a two-variable data table that calculates the effect of changes in price in increments of 5 between 15 and 35, and changes to unit costs in increments of 2 between 12 and 32.

- On the ScenarioManager worksheet, define three scenarios (High, Medium, and Low) based on changing the cells for price, unit cost, royalty rate, and marketing. Set up the scenarios using the values listed on the worksheet.

- On the AnalysisToolPak worksheet, use the data provided to generate a set of descriptive statistics, a histogram, and a rank and percentile list.

3.3   Apply and Manipulate PivotTables

Arranging a large data set as a PivotTable report can help facilitate your analysis and presentation of the information it contains. In a PivotTable, you can apply filters, summarize and outline data, and quickly change how the data is organized to gain additional perspective on its makeup.

In this section, you learn how to set up and work with a PivotTable. You will also learn how to filter and organize data by applying a slicer, a feature introduced in Excel 2010.

Building a PivotTable

The PivotTable command appears on the Insert tab on the ribbon. To begin, click PivotTable, select the cell range that holds the data you want to include, and specify whether you want to create the PivotTable on the current worksheet or on a new worksheet.

> **See Also** The Create PivotTable dialog box includes an option to use an external data source for the PivotTable—for example, a Microsoft Access database or a web query you have saved. For more information about creating and working with external data sources, see "Use External Data Sources" later in this chapter.

When you click OK in the Create PivotTable dialog box, Excel displays the PivotTable Field list and marks the area where the PivotTable will appear. The ribbon displays the PivotTable Tools Options and Design tabs.

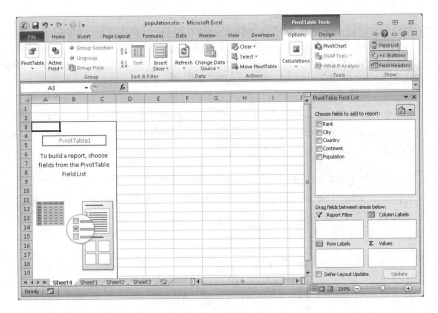

The PivotTable Field list shows the column headings for the data (the fields) as well as four areas to which you add fields as you build the PivotTable. From the field list, drag the field or fields you want to use for the PivotTable's columns to the Column Labels area. Similarly, drag the field or fields whose data you want to appear in the PivotTable's rows to the Row Labels area, and drag the field or fields with the data you want to summarize to the Values area. Add any fields you want to filter by to the Report Filter area.

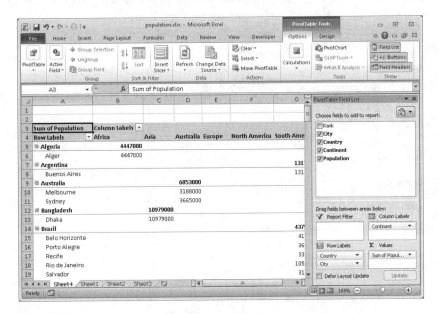

> **Tip** You can also select the check box beside a field's name in the PivotTable Field List area. Excel adds fields with numeric data to the Values area and fields that contain text to the Row Labels area. You can drag fields between the areas to organize the fields for the PivotTable. You do not need to include every field.

If you add more than one field to a PivotTable area, the order of the fields affects how the data is grouped. For example, in the world population example, placing Country above City in the Row Labels area groups cities within each country.

In the PivotTable Field List area, click the arrow beside a field name to display a menu that lets you change the order of the field (when more than one field appears in a specific area), move the field to a different area, remove the field, or open the Field Settings dialog box.

Use the Field Settings dialog box to provide a custom name for a field, to specify options for how the data is subtotaled and included in filters, and to specify options for the field's layout and how it appears if you print the PivotTable.

On the Subtotals & Filters tab, select Custom to specify that the field's values are subtotaled by the function or functions you select. Click None if you don't want to show a subtotal for the field, or leave the Automatic option selected if the behavior Excel provides fits your needs. On the dialog box's Layout & Print tab, you can select a tabular or outline format for item labels and set other options that affect the layout of this field in the PivotTable. This tab has one option related to printing a PivotTable. Select the option if you want to insert a page break after each item.

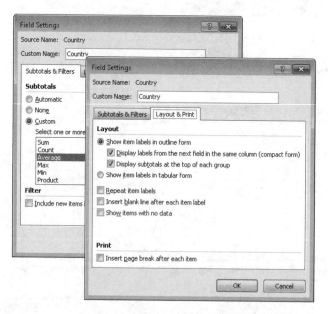

The Field Settings dialog box provides options for subtotals as well as for the layout of a field.

With the initial layout of the PivotTable established and the data in place, you can work with the commands on the PivotTable Tools tabs to refine the appearance of the PivotTable and to analyze and review the data it contains. For example, you can change the order or arrangement of the fields in the PivotTable field list to gain a different perspective on your data. In the city population example, you could add Continent to the Report Filter area and move Country to the Column Labels area. You could then filter the data to see populations in cities for a particular continent. By using the plus and minus buttons, you can expand or collapse groups of records in the PivotTable.

Formatting a PivotTable

The PivotTable Tools Design tab contains a gallery of styles you can apply to a PivotTable. The styles apply formatting to row and column headers and to grand total rows at the bottom of a PivotTable. As with other galleries, Excel applies a preview of the style to the PivotTable when you point to a style with your mouse. Click the style you want to apply. Click Clear at the bottom of the gallery to remove all formatting, and then you can begin again or work with a plain, unformatted PivotTable.

If you want to set up your own look and feel for a PivotTable, click New PivotTable Style in the PivotTable styles gallery. In the New PivotTable Quick Style dialog box, type a name for the style, select the table element you want to format, and then click Format. You then use the Format Cells dialog box to specify attributes for the font, border, and fills. You cannot choose a different font, but you can choose a font color and attributes such as bold or italic. Use the Stripe Size list in the New PivotTable Quick Style dialog box to apply a style to one or more rows or columns.

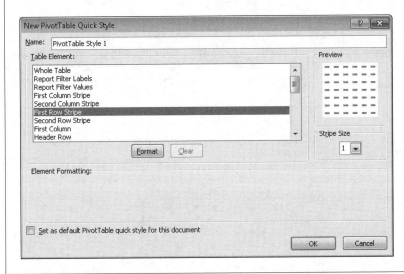

Select the check boxes beside the elements included in the PivotTable Style Options group on the PivotTable Tools Design tab to show or hide formatting for that element. For example, select the Banded Rows or Banded Columns check box to apply different formatting to alternating rows or columns. Clear the check box for Row Headers or Column Headers if you don't want special formatting applied to those elements.

In the Layout group on the PivotTable Tools Design tab, you can select options for showing or hiding subtotals and grand totals, for the report layout, and for whether to display blank rows between items in the PivotTable. You can choose between three standard report layouts—compact, outline, and tabular. The compact format places detail items under a row heading in the same column. In the outline format, these detail items appear in their own column, which expands the area of the PivotTable. The tabular format is similar to the outline format and displays gridlines at the borders of columns and rows.

Working with Data in a PivotTable

The PivotTable Tools Options tab lets you sort and filter data, refresh the data, choose a different data source, move the PivotTable to a different location or a different worksheet, and perform many other tasks.

Using Field Headers

The field headers (Row Labels and Column Labels) reveal a menu from which you can sort and filter the data in a PivotTable in a variety of ways.

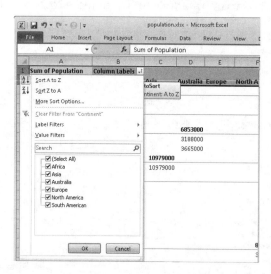

Use the field headers to sort and filter the data in a PivotTable. Use the search box to find an item in a lengthy list.

Choose one of the built-in sort options (ascending or descending), or click More Sort Options to open a dialog box that lets you sort manually (by dragging items), by the label field (Continent, for example), or by the value field. In the city population example, you could choose Sum Of Population (the value field) to sort the continents in ascending or descending order of population. Click More Options in the Sort dialog box to reach a dialog box that lets you set an option for automatic sorting when the data is updated or to choose to sort the PivotTable by the values in a selected row.

Label filters let you display a subset of records in the PivotTable on the basis of criteria you define. Select a built-in condition (such as equals, does not equal, contains, does not contain, and several others) and then specify the value to filter for.

> **Tip** If more than one field is included in an area of the PivotTable (as Country and City are in this example), be sure to use the Select Field box at the top of the field header menu to specify the field you want to use before sorting or filtering records.

Use a value filter to select a set of records on the basis of the value field. The options for value filters include an entry named Top 10. Choose this item, and then use the Top 10 Filter dialog box to specify criteria. The options are more extensive than a list of the top-10 records. You can choose Top or Bottom, specify the number of records (10 by default), and choose to see the group of items themselves or a percentage of the records.

Use the check boxes in the list of items under the search box to select one or more values to see. For example, to filter for a specific category or a set of categories, clear the Select All check box and then select the check boxes for the categories you want to see. You can use the search box to locate an item (which is helpful in a long list of countries, cities, or other items). As you type each character, Excel narrows the choices in the list that match what you have typed.

Managing the Data

In the Data group on the PivotTables Tools Options tab, click Refresh to update the data in the workbook. Click Refresh All to update all information from the data source. The Refresh menu also includes a command that shows you the refresh status (if any information in the PivotTable is not up to date), lets you cancel a refresh operation, or lets you change connection properties if the PivotTable is connected to an external data source.

Click Change Data Source to select a different range in the current data source (for example, if you want to work with only a subset of the initial data or expand the cell range you used initially). You can also use the Change Data Source command to view and update connection properties if you are working with an external data source.

If you need to relocate the PivotTable, in the Actions group, click Move PivotTable and then specify a different cell range in the current worksheet or click New Worksheet.

Changing Your View of the Data

In addition to applying filters with field headers, you can make a series of selections on the Options tab to change the way the data in a PivotTable is summarized and presented. The PivotTable used as an example in this section initially shows the names of continents as the column labels, countries and cities in the PivotTable's rows, and city populations in the PivotTable's data area, with subtotals for each country and a grand total for each continent in the PivotTable's last row.

To change the view of this data, you can select an item in the data area, click Calculations on the Options tab, click Summarize Values By, and choose Count (for example). Instead of showing the population figures, the PivotTable now shows how many cities in each country are among the world's most populous. Select a country name, and then click Collapse Entire Field in the Active Field group. This action hides the city names, condensing the view to show each country in a separate row.

You could pivot the data again by displaying the PivotTable Field list and dragging the Continent field from the Column Labels area to the Row Labels area, placing it above Country and City. By collapsing the detailed display again, you could see how many of the world's 100 most populous cities are in each continent.

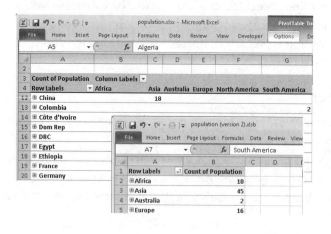

By changing the setting for how values are summarized and rearranging fields, you create new views of the data.

Using the Calculations Group

Using the commands in the Calculations group, you can summarize and show values in a variety of ways and make calculations on the basis of the data.

On the Summarize Value By menu, you can choose Sum (the default), Count, Average, Max, Min, Product, or More Options. By clicking More Options, you open the Value Field Settings dialog box. Choose from other options in the Summarize Value Field By list (the additional items include StdDev—for standard deviation—among others), and use the Custom Name box to name the value field.

Choose Show Value As to display a menu that provides various ways to show the summarized data. You can choose % Of Grand Total or % Of Column Total, for example. To show the percentage that each city's population represents of its country's total, you could use % Of Parent Total and then choose Country as the base field.

The Show Value As menu also includes a More Options command that opens the Value Field Settings dialog box. Provide a custom name for the field value, choose an option for how to show the values, and (as necessary) specify the base field when showing relationships between the detail values and the summary values.

Select Fields, Items, And Sets from the Calculations menu to define a calculated field, to define a calculated item, and to work with the formulas you define. A calculated field is derived from calculations performed on fields already in the PivotTable. Creating a calculated item adds an item to an existing field. The item is derived from calculations performed on other items that are already in the field.

To create a calculated item, for example, select the item where you want to include the calculated item (for example, a column heading); click Calculations, click Fields, Items, & Sets; and then click Calculated Item. In the Insert Calculated Item dialog box, type a name for the item and then use the Formula box to create the expression that calculates the item. To add an item or a field to the formula by using the lists in the dialog box, select the field or item and then click Insert Field or Insert Item. When you click OK in the dialog box, Excel adds the item to the PivotTable.

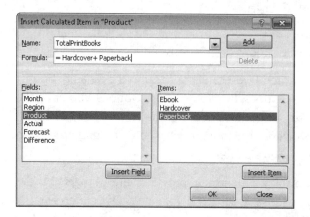

> **Tip** If you need to edit the formula for a calculated item or field, open the Insert Calculated Item or Insert Calculated Field dialog box, select the item or field you want to modify from the Name box, and then click Modify. Click Delete to remove the calculated item or field.

Using a Report Filter

In the population PivotTable, the Rank field is used as the report filter. You can apply a simple filter to the data by clicking the down arrow beside the field (which appears above the PivotTable). If necessary, click Select Multiple Items to display check boxes beside each item listed (in this example, numbers from 1 to 100, representing the rank of each city). To see the top 10 cities, for example, clear the check box beside All, and then select the check box for the ranks 1 through 10. To clear a filter and show all the details items again, click Clear, Clear Filters in the Actions group.

Slicing the Data in a PivotTable

Inserting a slicer is another way to filter a PivotTable and gain different views of the data it holds. In the Insert Slicers dialog box (which you access by clicking Insert Slicer in the Sort & Filter group on the PivotTable Tools Options tab), select the field or fields for which you want to create a slicer. Excel creates a slicer, which appears in a movable pane that displays the values for the field or fields you select.

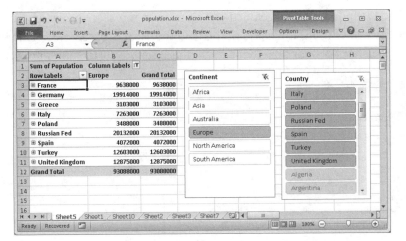

Select a button in a slicer to filter data. Making a selection in one filter changes the options in another.

To filter the data in the PivotTable by one or more of the values shown in the slicer, click the colored block for that value (or hold down the Ctrl key to select more than one). You can use multiple slicers together. Notice in the preceding illustration that selecting South America in the Continent slicer reorders the items in the Country slicer so that the countries in that continent are highlighted and appear at the top of the slicer. Items that don't apply appear dimmed. Click the Filter icon in the top-right corner of each slicer to return the view to an unfiltered status.

You work with slicers by using commands on the Slicer Tools Options tab, which appears on the ribbon when you select a slicer. Use the Slicer Styles gallery to apply formatting to a slicer. (Styles change the fill color and shading of selected and unselected items in a slicer.) In the Arrange group, use the Bring Forward, Send Backward, and Selection Pane commands to help locate and arrange slicers when you are working with more than one. You can align slicers, and you can group related slicers so that you can move them as a single unit. Use the Buttons and Size groups to specify the number of columns in a slicer, the dimensions of each button (item) in a slicer, and the size of the slicer itself.

> **Tip** Many of the commands in the Arrange and Size groups are also available if you right-click a slicer.

> **See Also** You can assign a macro that runs when you click a slicer. Right-click the slicer, and then choose Assign Macro. Click Record to start recording the macro, or click New to write the macro's code yourself in the Microsoft Visual Basic editor. For more information about recording macros in Excel, see Chapter 4, "Working with Macros and Forms" in this section of the book.

In the Slicer Settings dialog box, which you open from the Slicer group, you can rename the slicer (instead of using the name of the field the slicer is based on), change the caption, and set options for how the items in the slicer are sorted and filtered.

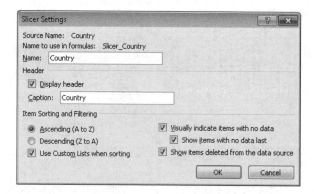

After you create a slicer, you can copy it to other worksheets in a workbook that contains a PivotTable.

➤ To create a PivotTable

1. On the **Insert** tab, click **PivotTable**.

2. In the **Create PivotTable** dialog box, select the data range for the PivotTable, or select the option to use an external data source. Specify whether to place the PivotTable on the current worksheet or on a new worksheet, and then click **OK**.

3. In the **PivotTable Field** list, drag the fields to the **Report Filter**, **Column Labels**, **Row Labels**, and **Values** areas.

➤ To sort data by using a field header

1. Click the arrow beside the **Column Labels** or **Row Labels** field header.

2. On the menu, choose **Sort A to Z** (ascending) or **Sort Z to A** (descending) or click **More Sort Options**.

3. If you click **More Sort Options**, use the **Sort** dialog box to specify the sort order, choose whether to sort by the label or by a value field, or choose to sort manually.

4. To specify options for automatic sorting or by values in a specific row, click **More Options** in the **Sort** dialog box and then set these options in the **More Sort Options** dialog box.

➤ To filter data by using a field header

1. Click the arrow beside the **Column Labels** or **Row Labels** field header.

2. To apply a label filter, click **Label Filters**, choose the filter condition, and then type the value to filter for in the **Label Filter** dialog box.

3. To apply a value filter, click **Value Filters**, choose the filter condition, and then type the value to filter for in the **Value Filter** dialog box.

4. To show a subset of the data, clear the check box for **Select All** and then select the check boxes for the items you want to see.

5. To search for a specific item you want to use for a filter, type the name of the item in the search box.

➤ **To change the data source for a PivotTable**

1. Select the **PivotTable**.

2. On the **PivotTable Tools Options** tab, click **Change Data Source**.

3. In the **Change PivotTable Data Source** dialog box, specify the new range you want to use.

➤ **To choose an option for summarizing values**

1. Select a value in the PivotTable.

2. On the **PivotTable Tools Options** tab, click **Calculations**, and then click **Summarize Values By**.

3. Choose an option from the menu, or click **More Options**.

4. If you select **More Options**, use the **Summarize Values By** tab on the **Value Field Settings** dialog box to specify a name for the option and to select the type of calculation.

5. To apply a different number format, click **Number Format** and then choose the format you want in the **Format Cells** dialog box.

➤ **To choose an option for showing values**

1. Select a value in the PivotTable.

2. On the **PivotTable Tools Options** tab, click **Calculations**, and then click **Show Values As**.

3. Choose an option from the menu, or click **More Options**.

4. If you select **More Options**, use the **Show Values As** tab on the **Value Field Settings** dialog box to specify a name for the option and to select the type of calculation. Specify a base field and base item as necessary.

5. To apply a different number format, click **Number Format** and then choose the format you want in the **Format Cells** dialog box.

➤ To create a calculated field

1. On the **PivotTable Tools Options** tab, click **Calculations**, click **Fields, Items, & Sets**, and then click **Calculated Field**.

2. In the **Insert Calculated Field** dialog box, type a name for the field.

3. In the **Formula** box, type the formula that calculates the field. To use an existing field in the formula, select the field and then click **Insert Field**.

4. Click **Add** to add the calculated field to the list of fields.

5. Click **OK** to add the field to the PivotTable.

➤ To create a calculated item

1. Select an item in the PivotTable.

2. On the **PivotTable Tools Options** tab, click **Calculations**, click **Fields, Items, & Sets**, and then click **Calculated Item**.

3. In the **Insert Calculated Item** dialog box, type a name for the field.

4. In the **Formula** box, type the formula that calculates the item. To use an existing field in the formula, select the field and then click **Insert Field**. To use an existing item in the formula, select the item and then click **Insert Item**.

5. Click **Add** to add the calculated item to the list of items.

6. Click **OK** to add the field to the PivotTable.

➤ To insert a slicer

1. Select the PivotTable.

2. On the **PivotTable Tools Options** tab, click **Insert Slicer**.

3. In the **Insert Slicers** dialog box, select the check box for each field for which you want to set up a slicer.

➤ To filter data with a slicer

1. In the slicer, click the item you want to apply as a filter. To select more than one item, press Ctrl and click each item.

2. To clear the filters from a slicer, click the **Clear Filter** icon in the top-right corner of the slicer.

➤ To format a slicer

1. Select the slicer or a group of slicers.

2. On the **Slicer Tools Options** tab, apply a style from the **Slicer Styles** group.

3. To change the dimensions and arrangements of the buttons in a slicer, use the **Button** group to specify the number of columns and the height and width of the buttons.

4. To change the dimensions of the slicer, specify the height and width in the boxes in the **Size** group.

Practice Tasks

The practice files for these tasks are located in the practice files folder for Microsoft Excel 2010. You can save the results of these exercises in the same folder. Change the file name so that you don't overwrite the sample files. When you are done, try performing the following task:

* Open the file Weather.xlsx, and create a PivotTable using the data it contains.

3.4 Apply and Manipulate PivotCharts

PivotCharts are a graphical tool that you can create to accompany a PivotTable. You work with PivotCharts in many of the same ways you work with PivotTables. You should review the previous section, "Apply and Manipulate PivotTables," to learn how to work with data in a PivotTable.

Creating a PivotChart

The Create PivotTable With PivotChart dialog box opens when you select PivotChart from the PivotTable menu on the Insert tab. In this dialog box, you specify the cell range that contains the data you are working with (you can select the cell range before opening the dialog box) or choose the option Use An External Data Source to set up data from a source outside the workbook. You also need to choose whether to add the PivotChart to a new worksheet or to a location on the current worksheet.

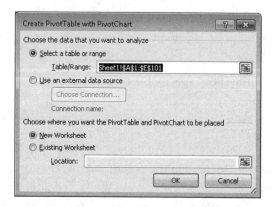

After Excel creates the placeholders for the PivotTable and the PivotChart, use the PivotTable Field list to add the fields you want to use in the different areas of the PivotChart: Report Filter, Legend Fields (the data series), Axis Fields (the categories), and the values. Drag a field from the list at the top to the area where you want to use it. If you select the field's check box, Excel adds it to an applicable area. (A field with numerical values is added to the Value area, for example.) You can modify the organization of the chart by moving fields to different areas—by dragging the fields or by right-clicking the field and using commands on the short-cut menu.

> **Tip** You can insert an associated PivotChart after you create a PivotTable by clicking PivotChart in the Tools group on the PivotTable Tools Options tab.

After you build the initial PivotChart, you work with the data it presents by using the following four PivotChart Tools tabs:

- **Design** Use the Design tab to change the chart type, save the chart as a template, switch the row and column orientation, modify the data range for the chart, apply a chart layout and chart style, and move the chart. You can place a PivotChart on its own worksheet (which Excel names Chart1 by default). This provides more room to display the chart, but you have to switch to the worksheet that contains the PivotTable if you want to work with the data by using the PivotTable Tools tabs. These tabs are not available on the worksheet that contains the chart.

- **Layout** Use the Layout tab to specify display options for different chart elements, including the axes, legend, title, and data labels. For example, you can reposition the chart's label or add a chart title. Use the Format Selection command in the Current Selection group to open dialog boxes that let you apply advanced formatting and display options. You also use this tab to add a trendline to a chart.

> **See Also** You can find details about working with many of the commands on the Design tab and the Layout tab in the Excel Help topics "Creating a Chart" and "Formatting a Chart." For information about working with trendlines, see "Adding Trendlines to Data" earlier in this chapter.

- **Format** The Format tab also includes the Format Selection command, which you can use to open formatting dialog boxes. The Format tab also lets you apply shape styles (to the columns in a column chart, for example) and text effects and specify dimensions for a chart. The Arrange group helps you locate and align shapes and group and ungroup shapes.

- **Analyze** Use the Active Field group on this tab to show or hide details for the field. From the Data group, you can insert a slicer to filter the chart's data, refresh the data, and clear filters applied to the data. Use the Show/Hide group to control whether the PivotTable Field list and field buttons are displayed.

Changing the View for a PivotChart

Keep in mind that the data and view for a PivotChart depends in part on how you organize and change the PivotTable the chart is based on. For example, when you apply a filter to the PivotTable, that filter also affects the data displayed in the PivotChart. The same holds true when you filter the data shown in the PivotChart. A filter you apply to the chart changes the display of the PivotTable.

To show or hide the PivotTable Field list and the field buttons on the chart, use the commands in the Show/Hide group on the Analyze tab. You should display the field list when you want to reposition fields or to add or remove a field from the PivotChart (and PivotTable). For example, switch the axis and the legend fields or combine fields in these areas to alter the data in the chart.

Use the field buttons as you do the field headers in a PivotTable to apply a filter directly to the chart. Use the menu that is displayed to sort the data in the chart, to apply a label or a value filter, to search for a specific item, or to select a subset of the data.

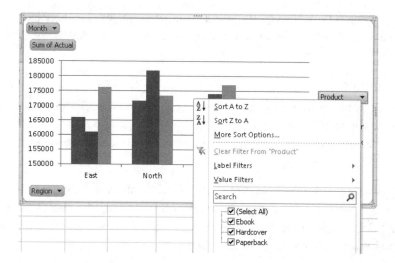

Use a field button in a PivotChart to display a menu that lets you sort and filter the data in the chart.

Insert a slicer from the PivotChart Tools Analyze tab to filter the data in a PivotChart. When you make a selection in the slicer, the filter is applied to the chart and to the PivotTable. If you move the PivotChart to its own worksheet (so that it is not an object on the worksheet that contains the PivotTable), you cannot insert a slicer when you view the PivotChart. You must return to the worksheet that contains the PivotTable to insert a slicer.

> **See Also** For details about working with slicers, see "Slicing the Data in a PivotTable" earlier in this chapter.

To analyze the data in a PivotChart in other ways, select the PivotTable that's associated with the PivotChart and then use the commands on the PivotTable Tools Options tab to create a different view. For example, use the Summarize Values By and Show Values As commands in the Calculations group to show the maximum value for a category or to show values as a percentage of the grand total. You can add a calculated item or a calculated field to the PivotTable that you can use in the PivotChart.

> **See Also** See "Using the Calculations Group" earlier in this chapter for more information.

➤ To create a PivotChart

1. On the **Insert** tab, click **PivotTable**, and then click **PivotChart**.

2. In the **Create PivotTable with PivotChart** dialog box, specify the data range to use or click the option to use an external data source.

3. Choose the option to place the PivotTable and PivotChart in a new worksheet or in a location on the current worksheet.

4. Click **OK**.

5. In the **PivotTable Field** list, drag the fields to the areas where you want them to appear in the chart: **Report Filter**, **Legend Fields (Series)**, **Axis Fields (Categories)**, or **Values**.

➤ **To rearrange a PivotChart and sort and filter data**

1. To change the view of the data in a PivotChart, use the **PivotTable Field** list to place a field in a different area or to combine fields.

2. To sort the data shown in a PivotChart, click the arrow beside a field button and then choose a sort option.

3. To filter the data shown in a PivotChart, click the arrow beside a field button and then define a label filter or a value filter or use the check boxes to select a subset of the data.

Practice Tasks

The practice files for these tasks are located in the practice files folder for Microsoft Excel 2010. You can save the results of these exercises in the same folder. Change the file name so that you don't overwrite the sample files. When you are done, try performing the following task:

- Create a PivotChart based on the PivotTable you created in the Practice Tasks section for PivotTables.

3.5   Use External Data Sources

In this section, you learn how to create data connections in Excel that let you work with information from a Microsoft Access database, a website, a text file, or other sources, including a Microsoft SQL Server database. When you connect to an external data source, Excel provides options to import the data into a PivotTable, a PivotTable with a PivotChart, or a table. When you set up the external data as a PivotTable (with or without a PivotChart), you can use tools such as a slicer to analyze the data.

> **See Also** For more information about creating and working with PivotTables and PivotCharts, including how to apply a slicer to a PivotTable, see "Apply and Manipulate PivotTables" and "Apply and Manipulate PivotCharts" earlier in this chapter.

Creating a Data Connection

You work with two groups of commands on the Data tab to create and manage connections to data sources outside an Excel workbook. Use the Connections group to manage the connections you create. The Get External Data group includes the following commands that let you create connections:

- From Access
- From Web
- From Text
- From Other Sources
    - From SQL Server
    - From Analysis Services
    - From XML Data Import
    - From Data Connection Wizard
    - From Microsoft Query

For each type of data connection, you need to know specific information. The following sections contain details for the four main choices in the Get External Data group.

From Access

You need to provide the name and location of the database, select which database object you want to connect to (a table or a query defined in the database), and specify how you want the data to be presented in Excel—as a table, as a PivotTable, or as both a PivotTable and a PivotChart report. You also need to specify whether you want to import the data to the current worksheet or to a new worksheet.

You can also set properties for the connection. In the Connection Properties dialog box, you can name the connection and provide a description to identify the purpose of the connection. You should also specify whether you want the connection to be refreshed in the background, at a set interval of time, or when you open the file. (These options are not mutually exclusive; you can choose all three.)

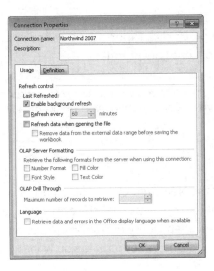

> **Tip** The Connection Properties dialog box is used for more than one type of connection. The options available in the dialog box are applicable to the type of connection you are creating.

The Definition tab of the Connection Properties dialog box provides more advanced options. You can use the controls on this tab to change the connection file, to view or edit the connection string, and to change the command type and command text (for example, you can select SQL in the Command Type list and then use SQL commands to retrieve the data you want).

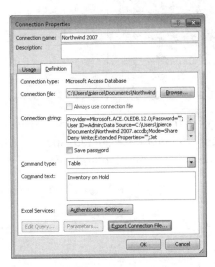

If you plan to make this worksheet available via Excel Services, click Authentication Settings and then specify the type of authentication required for users to access this data.

To use this connection on a different computer, click Export Connection File and then save the file in the Office Database Connections (.odc) format.

> **Tip** Excel Services is a service application that lets you work with Excel workbooks on Microsoft SharePoint. Through Excel Services, you can share workbooks on a SharePoint site or on a dashboard.

From Web

When you click From Web, Excel displays the New Web Query dialog box. Use the address bar to open the website you want to work with. (Use the arrow to open a list of sites you visited recently.) Resize the New Web Query dialog box to see more of the page it displays, click the arrow icons to select the tables of data you want to use, and then click Import.

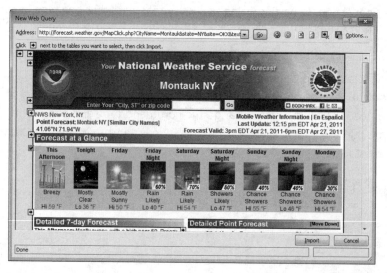

Click the arrow icons to a table on the web page. The icons appear as check marks on the tables you select.

To set properties for web queries, you work in the External Data Range Properties dialog box. By default, the option to save the query definition is selected. Specify options for how you want to refresh the data and options for formatting and layout properties.

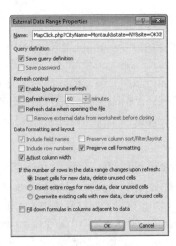

The set of options at the bottom of the dialog box control how Excel handles the data if the number of rows change when the data is refreshed. By default, Excel inserts cells for new data and deletes cells that are not being used. You can also direct Excel to insert entire rows and clear the data from cells that aren't used or to overwrite cells that currently contain data.

From Text

When you create a connection to a text file (a file that uses the .txt, .csv, or .prn file name extension), Excel starts the Text Import Wizard, which is a three-step wizard that helps you specify criteria for how Excel will import the data in the file:

- In the first step, you indicate whether a specific character separates (delimits) the fields of data in the text file or whether the data is aligned in fixed-width columns. You can also choose which row to use as the starting point for your import.

- The information you provide in the second step depends on whether the file is delimited or uses fixed-width columns. For the first option, you need to specify which character to use as a delimiter. For fixed-width files, you indicate where column breaks should occur.

- In step 3, you can apply different formats to the data. The General format converts numeric values to numbers, date values to dates, and remaining values to text. You can apply the Text or Date format to a specific column or specify which columns to skip. The Advanced button on this page of the wizard lets you specify how to separate values in numeric fields (for example, to use a comma to separate thousands).

  In the Import dialog box for a text file, click Properties to specify settings for properties similar to those available for a website.

From Other Sources

Among the other data sources you can connect to from Excel are a SQL Server database and an XML file. In addition, you can connect to a SQL Server Analysis Services cube file (a file type related to online analytical processing, or OLAP), to a query defined in Microsoft Query, or to other data sources that support Microsoft OLE DB providers, including the OLE DB provider for Oracle. The following list provides additional details about several of the other connection types:

- To connect to a SQL Server database, you work with the Data Connection Wizard. You need to know the server name, and (depending on how the server is config-ured) a user name and password might be required to log on. After you connect to SQL Server, you select the database you want to work with. You can also set an option to connect to a specific table. On the last page of the wizard, you name the connection file and type a description. You can also provide a friendly name and keywords that can be used to search for the connection. If you expect to use the current worksheet with Excel Services, click Authentication Settings and then specify the settings that are applied when the worksheet is accessed through Excel Services.

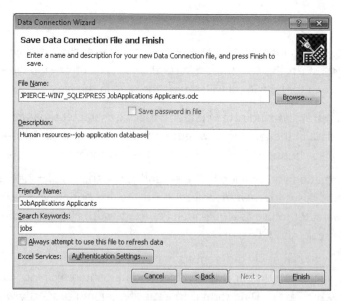

When you finish with the wizard, you see the Import Data dialog box and can choose how and where you want to view the data in the workbook.

- To use an XML file, click From XML Data Import on the From Other Sources menu and then select the file in the Select Data Source dialog box. If the XML file you choose does not refer to a schema, Excel displays a message box indicating that

Excel will create a schema on the basis of the XML file. When you click OK in this message, Excel displays the Import Data dialog box, where you can specify where to place the data and set properties for how the data will be refreshed and how it will be formatted. If the XML does reference a schema, Excel displays the Import Data dialog box directly. To see the structure of the XML file, switch to the Developer tab and then click Source in the XML group.

> **Tip** If the Developer tab is not displayed on the ribbon, click File, Options. In the Excel Options dialog box, click Customize Ribbon and then select the check box for Developer in the list of main tabs.

> **See Also** For more information about working with XML data in Excel, see "Exchanging Data with XML" in Chapter 1 in this section of the book.

- The From Data Connection Wizard option under From Other Sources opens the same wizard you use for connecting to a SQL Server database. On the Welcome page, click the type of data source you want to connect to—for example, if you work with Oracle databases, click Microsoft Data Access—OLE DB Provider for Oracle. The Other/Advanced item in the list of data sources leads to the Data Link Properties dialog box, where you can select from among a large group of OLE DB providers. You can also use the From Data Connection Wizard option to connect to SQL Server or to SQL Server Analysis Services.

  In general, you need to know the server name, log-on information, and other information similar to what is required for a SQL Server database.

- From Microsoft Query you can define or choose a data source defined in Microsoft Query, which is a program designed for importing external data into Office applications. You can use Microsoft Query to connect to an Access database, a SQL Server database, an OLAP cube, or another Excel file.

  You can also use Microsoft Query to define a new data source. For example, in the Choose Data Source dialog box, under Databases, select New Data Source. In the Create New Data Source dialog box, type a name for the connection and then select the driver for the type of database you want to use. The list of drivers includes entries for Access, Excel, text files, Microsoft Visual FoxPro, Oracle, and SQL Server. If you set up a connection to Access, for example, you need to select the database and a default table before you reach the Query Wizard. In this wizard, you choose which columns (fields) you want to include in your query, and you can then apply a filter to the data and sort it. On the wizard's final page, keep the default option to return the data to Excel selected or choose to view the data or edit the query in Microsoft Query.

➤ To get data from an Access database

1. On the **Data** tab, in the **Get External Data** group, click **From Access**.

2. In the **Select Data Source** dialog box, locate the database you want to connect to and then click **Open**.

3. In the **Select Table** dialog box, select the database object (table or query) that contains the data you need and then click **OK**.

4. In the **Import Data** dialog box, select the option for how you want to display the data in Excel (Table, PivotTable Report, or PivotChart and PivotTable Report). Specify where in the current worksheet the data should be placed, or click **New worksheet**.

5. In the **Import Data** dialog box, click **Properties**.

6. In the **Connection Properties** dialog box, type a name for the connection, enter a description, and set the refresh control and other properties. Click **OK**.

7. In the **Import Data** dialog box, click **OK**.

➤ To get data from the web

1. On the **Data** tab, in the **Get External Data** group, click **From Web**.

2. In the **New Web Query** dialog box, use the **Address** box to open the website that contains the data you need.

3. Click the arrow icons beside the tables you want to select on the web page, and then click **Import**.

4. In the **Import Data** dialog box, specify where in the current worksheet to place the data or click **New worksheet**.

5. In the **Import Data** dialog box, click **Properties**.

6. In the **External Data Range Properties** dialog box, type a name of the connection and set options for refresh control and data formatting and layout. Click **OK**.

7. In the **Import Data** dialog box, click **OK**.

➤ **To get data from a text file**

1. On the **Data** tab, in the **Get External Data** group, click **From Text**.

2. In the **Import Text** file dialog box, select the file you want to import and then click **Import**.

3. In step 1 of the Text Import Wizard, choose **Delimited** or **Fixed width** depending on how the data is organized in the text file. Click **Next**.

4. In step 2 of the Text Import Wizard, specify the delimiting character (if you chose Delimited in the previous step) or specify column breaks if you selected Fixed width.

5. In step 3 of the Text Import Wizard, change the data format for any columns (if required) and select any columns you want to skip. Click **Finish**.

6. In the **Import Data** dialog box, specify where in the current worksheet to place the data or click **New worksheet**.

7. In the **Import Data** dialog box, click **Properties**.

8. In the **External Data Range Properties** dialog box, type a name of the connection and set options for refresh control and data formatting and layout. Click **OK**.

9. In the **Import Data** dialog box, click **OK**.

Using Existing Connections

The Existing Connections command leads you to a dialog box that lists connections defined in the current workbook, on your computer, and on your network. Select a connection in this list and then click Open to add that connection to the current workbook. Excel displays the Import Data dialog box as it does when you import data from a new source.

Click Connections in the Connections group to work with the Workbook Connections dialog box. In this dialog box, you can add connections to the workbook, remove a connection, set connection properties, and refresh the data in a specific connection or in all connections. Follow the directions at the bottom of the dialog box to "see where the connections are used."

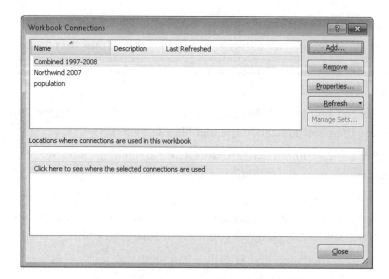

To manage external connections, open the Workbook Connections dialog box, where you can add a new connection, delete those you don't need, set properties, and refresh the data.

➤ To open an existing connection

1. On the **Data** tab, in the **Get External Data** group, click **Existing Connections**.

2. In the **Existing Connections** dialog box, select a connection and then click **Open**.

➤ To manage workbook connections

1. On the **Data** tab, in the **Connections** group, click **Connections**.

2. In the **Workbook Connections** dialog box, use the command buttons provided to add or remove a connection, set connection properties, and refresh connections.

Editing Links

When managing the data in a set of related workbooks, you might use external references in your formulas. For example, in a workbook named SalesForecast.xlsx, you could use a formula such as *=[budget_FY2012.xlsx]!Total* to refer to the cell named Total in the workbook Budget_FY2012.xlsx. Using external references keeps the data in related workbooks current without anyone needing to manually change the values.

To manage external references, select the cell that includes the reference and then click the Edit Links command in the Connections group to open the Edit Links dialog box.

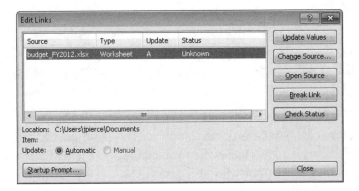

In the Edit Links dialog box, you can update the value for an external reference, change the source of the reference (by referring to a different cell or cell range or to a different workbook entirely), open the workbook that is the source of the link, break the link if it's no longer needed, and check the status of the link to be sure the values are up to date.

The Startup Prompt button displays a dialog box in which you specify whether Excel notifies you about the link when you open the workbook (you can then update the link or not), whether Excel updates links automatically with notification, or whether Excel displays no notification and does not update the links. (If you specify the last option, you can update the link later in the Edit Links dialog box.)

When you choose the option to display a startup prompt, you'll see this message when you open a workbook that contains external links.

➤ To manage external references

1. In the **Connections** group on the **Data tab**, click **Edit Links**.

2. In the **Edit Links** dialog box, use the command buttons provided to update values in the workbook, change the data source for a link, open the source workbook, break the link, and check the status of the link.

3. Click **Startup Prompt** to specify an option for whether Excel displays an alert when it opens the workbook, does not show the alert and updates the links automatically, or does not show the alert and does not update the links.

Practice Tasks

The practice files for these tasks are located in the practice files folder for Microsoft Excel 2010. You can save the results of these exercises in the same folder. Change the file name so that you don't overwrite the sample files. When you are done, try performing the following tasks:

- Open the file ExternalData.xlsx, and create a connection to Employees.accdb (a Microsoft Access database) and to Employees.txt (a simple text file). Choose the option to create a PivotTable when you connect to the text file, and then practice creating a PivotTable with this data.

- Create a web query by using a table that appears on one of your favorite websites.

Objective Review

Before finishing this chapter, be sure you have mastered the following skills:

3.1   Apply advanced chart features

3.2   Apply data analysis

3.3   Apply and manipulate PivotTables

3.4   Apply and manipulate PivotCharts

3.5   Use external data sources

4 Working with Macros and Forms

The skills tested in this section of the Microsoft Office Expert exam for Microsoft Excel 2010 relate to using macros and forms, including how to record and run a macro and how to insert controls to build a form. Specifically, the following objectives are associated with this set of skills:

4.1 Create and manipulate macros

4.2 Insert and manipulate form controls

> **Important** The topics and procedures in this chapter refer to command groups on the Developer tab. If the Developer tab is not displayed on the ribbon, click Options on the File tab, click Customize Ribbon in the Excel Options dialog box, and then select Developer in the list of main tabs.

4.1 Create and Manipulate Macros

A macro in Excel can perform an operation as routine as adding your company address to a worksheet or printing a worksheet with specific settings. You could record a macro that enters a series of dates, months, or other periods of time in a worksheet row, aligns the cell data, and then applies formatting to the cells. Macros can, of course, be used to do many other tasks, especially once you learn how to enhance the operations of a macro you record or write macros from scratch by using Microsoft Visual Basic for Applications (VBA).

When working with macros in Excel, keep in mind that the default file format—Excel Workbook (.xlsx)—does not support macros. If you record or write a macro in a workbook and try to save the workbook as an .xlsx file, Excel displays a message indicating that you can't include the macro. To include macros in a workbook, you must save the workbook in the Excel Macro-Enabled Workbook (.xlsm) format or as a macro-enabled template (.xltm). You can also use the Excel 97–2003 Workbook (.xls) format, but that format does not support many of the features in Excel 2010.

You'll see this message if you try to save a macro in a macro-free file format. Use the macro-enabled workbook format (.xlsb) instead.

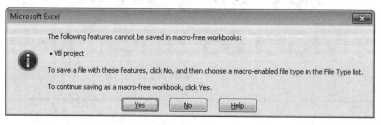

> **Tip** You can change the default file format in which workbooks are saved to a format that supports macros by opening the Excel Options dialog box from the File tab, displaying the Save page, and then selecting the format you want in the Save Files In This Format list.

You can run the macros in a workbook in a variety of ways, which lets you choose the option that fits the situation at hand. For a macro you want to apply to every workbook, you can add a button that runs the macro to the Quick Access Toolbar or to a custom group on the ribbon. You can also define a macro that runs whenever a workbook is opened or run a macro by using a keystroke.

> **See Also** For general information about customizing the ribbon, see "Modifying the Display of the Ribbon" at the beginning of this book.

In the following sections, you'll learn details about recording a macro and about different ways you can run a macro.

> **See Also** For information about assigning a macro to a command button that you add to an Excel worksheet, see "Inserting Form Controls" later in this chapter.

Recording and Storing a Macro

In the Record Macro dialog box, you should first provide a name for the macro you're recording. (You can accept the default name that Excel displays, but providing your own descriptive name is more useful.) You must begin a macro name with a letter; you can include numbers later in a macro's name. Macro names cannot include spaces. Use an underscore character to separate words or use interior capitalization (for example, My_new_macro or MyNewMacro).

> **See Also** For more information about assigning a shortcut key, see "Assigning a Keystroke to a Macro" later in this chapter.

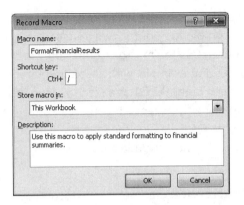

Use the Store Macro In list to specify whether you want access to the macro globally or only in the current workbook.

By default, Excel first displays This Workbook in the Store Macro In list. Keep this option if you want the macro to be available only in this workbook. Choose Personal Macro Workbook to make a macro available throughout Excel. The Personal Macro Workbook (Personal.xlsb) is a file Excel creates when you first choose to save a macro in it. (Excel prompts you to save Personal.xlsb when you save a macro in the Personal Macro Workbook and when you add macros to it after that.) Excel opens Personal.xlsb when you run Excel but hides the workbook by default. You can view it by choosing Unhide in the Window group on the View tab.

> **Tip** The option you choose in the Store Macro In list is retained by Excel. If you choose Personal Macro Workbook in this list, that option appears in the list the next time you open the Record Macro dialog box. Check this setting to be sure that you are saving a macro where you want to.

Using the XLStart Folder

Excel by default saves Personal.xlsb in a folder named XLStart, which it creates under your user profile. In Windows 7 or Windows Vista, the XLStart folder is located at Users*username*\\AppData\\Roaming\\Microsoft\\Excel. In Windows XP, the folder is located at \\Documents and Settings*username*\\Application Data\\Microsoft\\Excel. If you want Excel to open a specific workbook each time you run Excel, add that workbook to the XLStart folder. If you want each workbook you create to contain specific information—a custom header, for example—create a workbook named Book.xlsx and save it in the XLStart folder. Excel opens this workbook when it starts. Add the details you need to the workbook, and then save it with its own name.

Before you record a macro, you should also determine whether to use absolute or relative cell references. (You can use a combination of the two as necessary). If you keep absolute references (which uses the format C3), the macro operates only in the specific cells you use when you record the macro. For example, with absolute references, if you insert a series of dates or names in the cell range A1:G1 as a step in recording a macro, that macro works only in that cell range when you run it. If you use relative references (by clicking Use Relative References in the Code group), the macro will insert the data in any comparable range of cells. Relative references include a dollar sign ($) to denote the relative cells.

You can alternate between absolute and relative references while recording a macro by turning on or off the Use Relative References command. The command appears highlighted when it is enabled.

> **Tip** The View tab also provides a Macros group. If the Developer tab is not displayed, you can use this group to view available macros, record a macro, and turn on or off relative references when recording a macro.

Macro Security Settings

The default security setting for macros in Excel is Disable All Macros With Notification. With this option selected, when you open a workbook that contains macros, Excel displays a security warning indicating that macros are disabled. Click Enable Macros if you trust the workbook and need access to the macros. You can change security settings by clicking the Macro Security command in the Code group on the Developer tab. Use the Macros Settings page of the Trust Center dialog box to select a different option. For example, if you are experimenting with macros during a work session, select Enable All Macros (Not Recommended) as a temporary measure and then reset the default option (or choose one of the other options that disable macros) when you are done. The other options available are Disable All Macros Without Notification and Disable All Macros Except Digitally Signed Macros.

If you select the most restrictive setting (Disable All Macros Without Notification), you can still gain access to macros in a workbook by saving that workbook in a trusted location. (The Trust Center does not check files stored in a trusted location.) You can view default trusted locations and add a new location by using the Trusted Locations page in the Trust Center dialog box (the same dialog box that Excel displays when you click Macro Security in the Code group).

Digital signatures are used to verify the source of a macro and to confirm that a macro (or a Visual Basic project that contains a macro) has not been modified since it was signed. If you select the option Disable All Macros Except Digitally Signed Macros, Excel enables macros automatically if the macros are signed and originate from a source (a publisher) you have trusted. Excel displays a security warning and the Enable Macros button when you open a workbook from a source that is not a trusted publisher. Unsigned macros are disabled if you select this option.

➤ **To record a macro**

1. On the **Developer** tab, click **Record Macro**.

2. In the **Record Macro** dialog box, type a name for the macro.

3. Enter a shortcut key if you want to run the macro from the keyboard.

4. In the **Store macro in** list, specify whether to store this macro in the current workbook, the Personal Macro Workbook, or a new workbook.

5. Type a description of the macro, and then click **OK**.

6. To turn on relative references, click **Use Relative References** in the **Code** group.

7. Follow the steps you want to record in the macro.

   Click the **Use Relative References** command to control the use of relative references as you record the macro.

8. When you complete the steps, click **Stop Recording**.

Modifying a Macro

When you record a macro in Excel, Excel stores the macro in a module that you can work with in the Visual Basic editor. To open the Visual Basic editor, click Visual Basic in the Code group. To work with a specific macro, first click Macros on the Developer tab (or click Macros, View Macros on the View tab). In the Macro dialog box, select the macro you want to modify and then click Edit. You'll see the modules for the current workbook listed in the pane at the left (called the Project Explorer). The code for the macros in that module appears in the Code window.

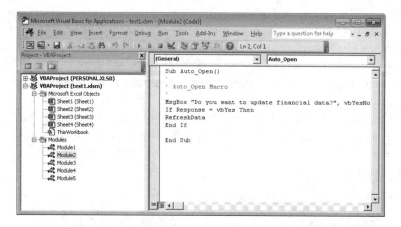

If you are familiar with VBA, you can modify code directly. If you are working with macros you recorded, you can expand and change the operations of a macro by adding code for one macro to another macro or by calling one macro from another.

For example, as part of recording a macro that inserts your company's address or another block of text, you might apply formatting to the cells by using a specific font and font size, bold text, a light-colored fill, and a centered alignment. Excel would generate code something like the following to apply that formatting (you would see this code within the code that performs the macro's other operations):

```
With Selection.Font
    .Name = "Arial"
    .FontStyle = "Bold"
    .Size = 11
    .Strikethrough = False
    .Superscript = False
    .Subscript = False
    .OutlineFont = False
    .Shadow = False
    .Underline = xlUnderlineStyleNone
    .ThemeColor = xlThemeColorLight1
    .TintAndShade = 0
    .ThemeFont = xlThemeFontNone
End With
With Selection
    .HorizontalAlignment = xlCenter
    .VerticalAlignment = xlBottom
    .WrapText = False
    .Orientation = 0
    .AddIndent = False
    .IndentLevel = 0
    .ShrinkToFit = False
    .ReadingOrder = xlContext
    .MergeCells = False
End With
```

```
With Selection.Interior
    .Pattern = xlSolid
    .PatternColorIndex = xlAutomatic
    .ThemeColor = xlThemeColorLight2
    .TintAndShade = 0.799981688894314
    .PatternTintAndShade = 0
End With
```

If you want to use this formatting code in another macro, you can copy the code and paste it into the code from another macro. You can also save this code as a separate subprocedure in a module and run it on its own when you want to apply the same formatting to a selection of cells.

A subprocedure is a set of code statements enclosed by *Sub* and *End Sub* statements. You can see these statements in the preceding screen shot. When you record a macro in Excel, the macro is defined in a subprocedure. You can call one macro from another by referring to the name of the macro you want to run in the subprocedure for the second macro. In the following code, for example, the RefreshData macro is run from the Auto_Open macro:

```
Sub Auto_Open()
'
' Auto_Open Macro
'

    MsgBox "Do you want to update financial data?", vbYesNo
        If Response = vbYes Then
        RefreshData
        End If

End Sub
```

To save code as its own subprocedure, click Visual Basic on the Developer tab. In the Visual Basic editor, in the Project Explorer, open the module that contains the macro with the code you want to copy. Select that code, and copy it to the Clipboard.

On the Insert menu in the Visual Basic editor, click Procedure. Type a name and keep the default settings in the Type and Scope sections. The Sub option creates a subprocedure, and the Public option makes the code available to macros in other modules.

When you click OK in the Add Procedure dialog box, the Visual Basic editor inserts the lines *Public Sub* (which includes the name you provided) and *End Sub*. Paste the code you copied between these lines.

Even though you didn't specifically record a macro with this name, you'll find an entry for it in the Macro dialog box in Excel. You can now run the macro as you would any other, including by calling the macro from another macro. To do this, you add the macro's name to the macro you want to call it from. Here's an example in which the FormatStandard macro is called at the end of the AddressBlock macro.

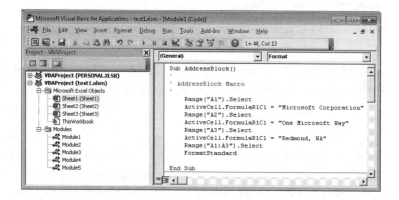

> ➤ **To open the Visual Basic editor to work with a macro**

→ Click **Visual Basic** in the **Code** group on the **Developer** tab.

> ➤ **To modify a macro**

1. In the **Code** group, click **Macros**.

2. In the **Macro** dialog box, select the macro you want to modify and then click **Edit**.

3. Revise the macro by using the Visual Basic editor, and then click **Save** on the Visual Basic editor toolbar.

> ➤ **To insert a subprocedure in the Visual Basic editor**

1. In Excel, click **Visual Basic** in the **Code** group on the **Developer** tab.

2. In the Visual Basic editor, on the **Insert** menu, click **Procedure**.

3. In the **Add Procedure** dialog box, type a name for the procedure.

4. In the **Type** group, keep **Sub** selected. In the **Scope** group, keep **Public** selected, and then click **OK**.

5. In the Code window, write or copy code for the new subprocedure.

6. On the Visual Basic editor toolbar, click **Save**.

Run a Macro from the Macro Dialog Box

You can run a macro directly from the Macro dialog box, which Excel displays when you click Macros in the Code group on the Developer tab. Use the Macros In list to select from the macros available only in the current workbook, in all open workbooks, in Personal.xlsb (which contains global macros), or other choices.

Before you open the Macro dialog box, be sure you place the cursor in the cell where the macro should begin its operations (if necessary). When you've done this, click Macros, select the macro you want to run, and then click Run.

When you run a macro from the Macro dialog box, use the Macros In list to select which macros you want to see.

> ➤ **To run a macro from the Macro dialog box**

1. Position your cursor where you want to start running the macro.

2. In the **Code** group, click **Macros**.

3. In the **Macro** dialog box, choose an option from the **Macros in** list to display the available macros.

4. Select the macro you want to run, and then click **Run**.

Assigning a Keystroke to a Macro

In the Record Macro dialog box, you can assign a shortcut key to a macro before you start recording. The shortcut key must be used in combination with the Ctrl key. You can also press the Shift key to use uppercase characters or a special character you access with the Shift key, but you cannot use an Alt key combination. To specify this shortcut when you record a macro, just type the key in the Short Key area of the Record Macro dialog box.

If you don't assign a shortcut key when you record a macro, you can assign one later through the Macro dialog box. Click Macros on the Developer tab, select the macro in the list of macros, and then click Options. Use the Shortcut Key area of the Macro Options dialog box to assign the keystroke combination you want to use.

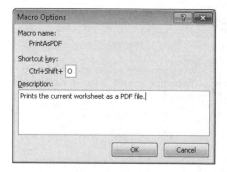

➤ **To assign a shortcut key to a macro**

➜ When you record the macro, enter the shortcut key you want to use in the **Shortcut key** area of the **Record Macro** dialog box.

or

1. On the **Developer** tab, click **Macros**.

2. In the **Macro** dialog box, select the macro you want to work with and then click **Options**.

3. In the **Macro Options** dialog box, enter the shortcut key in the **Shortcut key** area and then click **OK**.

Running a Macro When You Open a Workbook

By naming a macro Auto_Open, you define the macro so that it runs whenever you open a workbook. You will probably save an Auto_Open macro in a specific workbook (you might use an Auto_Open macro to set properties for your view of a workbook, for example), but you can save an Auto_Open macro in your Personal Macro Workbook (Personal.xlsb) so that it is applied to more than one workbook. However, keep in mind that an Auto_Open macro runs before other workbooks are opened, so storing it in

Personal.xlsb is often problematic. If you record actions that you want Excel to perform on the default Book.xlsx workbook or on another workbook that is opened from the XLStart folder, the Auto_Open macro fails when you start Excel because the macro runs before the workbooks stored in XLStart are opened.

> **See Also** For more information about the XLStart folder, see "Using the XLStart Folder" earlier in this chapter.

Another approach to automatically running a macro when you open a workbook is to use the workbook's *Open* event, which you can add code to in the Visual Basic editor. (Events are part of Visual Basic for Applications. The default event for a command button is the *Click* event, for example. In addition to the *Open* event, you can control workbooks by using the *BeforeClose* or *AfterClose* events, for example.)

To use a workbook's *Open* event, click Visual Basic in the Code group to open the Visual Basic editor. In the Project Explorer (the pane at the left), right-click This Worksheet and choose View Code. In the Code window, open the list on the left (the Object list) and choose Workbook (if Workbook is not displayed). Open the list at the right (the Procedure list), and choose Open. In the Code window, you'll see the following lines of code:

```
Private Sub Workbook_Open()

End Sub
```

Insert the code for the macro you want to run when Excel opens the workbook. You can write this code yourself, insert the name of a macro you recorded or wrote already, or copy code from another macro and paste it between *Private Sub Workbook_Open()* and *End Sub*. The code shown in the following screen shot updates an external connection to a text file when the workbook opens.

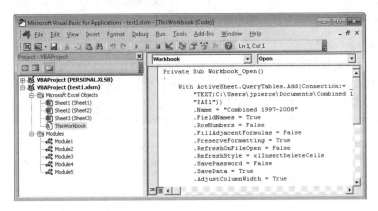

> **See Also** For more information about working with macros in the Visual Basic editor, see "Modifying a Macro" earlier in this chapter. For information about managing external connections in Excel, see "Use External Data Sources" in Chapter 3 in this section of the book.

➤ **To create an Auto_Open macro**

1. On the **Developer** tab, click **Record Macro**.

2. In the **Macro** dialog box, name the macro Auto_Open.

3. Click **OK**, and then record the steps you want the macro to perform.

4. Click **Stop Recording**, and then save the workbook.

   The macro runs the next time you open the workbook.

➤ **To run a macro from a workbook's *Open* event**

1. On the **Developer** tab, click **Visual Basic** in the **Code** group.

2. In the Visual Basic editor, right-click **This Workbook** in the Project Explorer and choose **View Code**.

3. In the Code window, choose **Workbook** from the Object list and **Open** from the Procedure list.

4. Insert the code for the macro between the lines of code Private Sub Workbook_Open() and End Sub.

5. On the Visual Basic editor's toolbar, click **Save**.

Adding a Macro Button to the Ribbon

To run a macro from the ribbon, you need to add the macro to a custom group. You can create a custom group for one of the built-in tabs or create a tab of your own and add the macro to a group on your custom tab.

To start, open the Excel Options dialog box from the File tab and then click Customize Ribbon in the list on the left. If you are adding a custom group to one of the main tabs, consider the purpose of the macro in deciding where to place it. If you use the macro to format a workbook, you might add the group to the Page Layout tab. If the macro is designed for working with data, it might be useful to place it on the Data tab. If you have several macros and want to collect them on a tab of their own, create a custom tab that holds all your macros.

You can run a macro from the ribbon by adding it to a custom group on a built-in tab or by creating a custom tab and group to hold the macro.

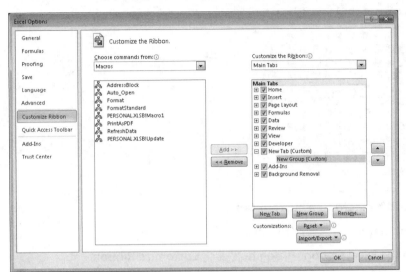

If you are adding a macro to a built-in tab, use the New Group button to create a custom group on that tab. To create a custom tab, click New Tab. Excel creates an entry for the tab and creates a new group for that tab as well. To name the tab (to something more meaningful than New Tab), select the entry for the custom tab, click Rename, and then type a display name for the tab. Do the same for the new group Excel creates by default for a custom tab. If you are adding several macros to a custom tab, use more than one group and name them so that they reflect the type of macros you are adding (Formatting, Analysis, and so on).

In the Choose Commands From list, select Macros. In the Main Tabs list, select the group where you want to place the macro, select the macro in the list at the left, and then click Add. If you want to provide a different display name for the macro or change the icon Excel uses to display it, click Rename and then make the modifications you want in the Rename dialog box.

➤ To add a macro to a custom tab

1. On the **File** tab, click **Options**.

2. In the **Excel Options** dialog box, click **Customize Ribbon**.

3. Under the **Main Tabs** list, click **New Tab**.

4. In the **Main Tabs** list, click **New Tab (Custom)**, and then click the **Rename** button.

5. In the **Rename** dialog box, type a display name for the custom tab and click **OK**.

6. In the **Main Tabs** list, click **New Group (Custom)** under the tab you created, and then click **Rename**.

7. Type a display name for the group, and select a symbol if you don't want to use the default icon Excel provides.

8. In the **Choose commands from** list, select **Macros**.

9. Select the macro you want to add, and then click **Add**.

➤ To add a macro to a built-in tab

1. On the **File** tab, click **Options**.

2. In the **Excel Options** dialog box, click **Customize Ribbon**.

3. In the **Main Tabs** list, select the tab where you want to add the macro and then click **New Group**.

4. In the **Main Tabs** list, click **New Group (Custom)**, and then click **Rename**.

5. Type a display name for the group, and select a symbol if you don't want to use the default icon Excel provides.

6. In the **Choose commands from** list, select **Macros**.

7. Select the macro you want to add, and then click **Add**.

Adding a Macro Button to the Quick Access Toolbar

One of the most convenient ways to run a macro is to add a button for that macro to the Quick Access Toolbar. You assign the macro to a button by using the Excel Options dialog box.

On the Customize The Quick Access Toolbar page, open the Choose Commands From list and select Macros. In the list of macros, select the one you want to add to the Quick Access Toolbar and then click Add. In the Customize Quick Access Toolbar list, select For All Documents if you want the button to appear on the Quick Access Toolbar for all workbooks. You can also select the current workbook if you want to use the macro within that scope.

To rename the button or to change the icon associated with it, select it in the list of commands on the Quick Access Toolbar and then click Modify. Use the Modify Button dialog box to change the display name and to choose an icon. The display name appears in a ScreenTip when you point to the button with the mouse.

For macros you run frequently, add a button for that macro to the Quick Access Toolbar. Excel displays the name you provide in a ScreenTip.

> ➤ **To add a custom macro button to the Quick Access Toolbar**

1. Click the arrow at the right end of the Quick Access Toolbar, and then click **More Commands**.

2. In the **Choose commands from list**, choose **Macros**.

3. In the list of macros, select the macro you want to place on the Quick Access Toolbar and then click **Add**.

4. Click **Modify**, and then select the icon you want to use and change the display name for the button.

Creating an Action Macro

In a worksheet that includes graphical objects—an image, for example, or clip art or a shape—you can assign a macro to all or a portion of the object and run that macro when you click the object (or a particular spot on the object). For example, in a worksheet to which you've added several shapes (using the Shapes gallery on the Insert tab) to illustrate a process or a decision path, you can assign a macro to one or more of the shapes. You can assign a macro to a diagram you insert using SmartArt (but not to the individual shapes in the diagram). You can also place an object on a picture, assign a macro to that object, and then apply formatting that hides the object. Using these steps, you effectively create a hidden hot spot on the picture that runs a macro when you click it.

To run a macro from an object, right-click the object and choose Assign Macro. In the Assign Macro dialog box, Excel provides a default name for the macro by appending *Click* to the type of object (for example, Rectangle2_Click). Use the default name, or type one of your own. You can select a macro from the list of available macros (by using the Macros In list to display macros from your Personal Macro Workbook or from other open workbooks), click Record to record a new macro, or click New to open the Visual Basic editor and write a macro using VBA. You can also edit an existing macro by selecting it and clicking Edit.

In the Assign Macro dialog box, you can select a macro, click New to write a macro yourself, or click Record to record a macro you want to run from an object.

You'll know that a macro is assigned to an object because the cursor appears as a hand with a pointing finger (the same icon you see when you point to a hyperlink). Click the object to run the macro.

To hide a shape or other object to which you've assigned a macro, right-click the shape and choose Format Shape. In the Format Shape dialog box, choose No Fill on the File page and No Line on the Line Color page.

> **Tip** If you are applying this formatting to a picture or another object, the Format command and dialog box will be named with the type of object.

➤ **To assign a macro to a shape or other object**

1. Right-click the shape or object and choose **Assign Macro**.

2. In the **Assign Macro** dialog box, use the **Macros in** list to select the macros you want to see (This Workbook, All Open Workbooks, or another option).

3. Select the macro you want to assign to the shape and click **OK**, or click **Record** to record the macro, or click **New** to write the macro in the Visual Basic editor.

➤ **To hide a shape or other object to which a macro is assigned**

1. Right-click the shape and choose **Format Shape**.

2. In the **Format Shape** dialog box, on the **Fill** page, click **No Fill**.

3. On the **Line Color** page, click **No Line**.

Practice Tasks

The practice files for these tasks are located in the folder for Microsoft Excel 2010. You can save the results of these exercises in the same folder. Change the file name so that you don't overwrite the sample files. When you are done, try performing the following tasks:

- Open a blank worksheet. Record a macro named GetResults that performs the following operations:

   ○ Uses the From Text command in the Get External Data group (on the Data tab) to import the text file Results.txt (which is included in the sample files folder). Click Next in the Text Import Wizard's first step. In the second step, select comma as the delimiting character and then click Finish.

   ○ Select the top row of the data, and apply bold formatting.

   ○ Select the cells containing the data, and format them as currency.

   ○ Stop recording the macro at this point. Delete the data you imported, and then run the macro from the Macro dialog box to test it.

- Open the workbook SampleMacros.xlsm. Using the macros in this workbook, practice running the macros from the ribbon, from the Quick Access Toolbar, and from an object you add to the workbook.

4.2   Insert and Manipulate Form Controls

One way in which you can collect and present data in Excel is through the use of form controls you add to a worksheet. Controls such as list boxes, check boxes, and command buttons help structure a worksheet and manage its data, and they allow you and other users to work with data and objects on a worksheet in specific ways. The sections that follow describe how to add controls, define their behavior and values, and set properties for the controls.

Inserting Form Controls

Excel displays two groups of controls when you click Insert in the Controls group on the Developer tab—form controls and ActiveX controls. You can set up a form control, such as a list box, by using data on a worksheet. ActiveX controls are often handled programmatically by using Visual Basic for Applications, although you can set properties for ActiveX controls and use them without writing any code. The focus in this section is on form controls. You'll learn more about ActiveX controls in the section "Making Use of ActiveX Controls" later in this chapter.

Excel provides nine types of form controls:

- **Command button** Use a command button to run a macro when a user clicks the button.

- **Combo box** A combo box creates a drop-down list that lets users select an item from a set of items you define or enter an item in the list.

- **Check box** Use a check box to let users make selections from a series of options. A user selects the check box to indicate yes (or true). A user clears a check box to indicate no (or false). You can place a set of check boxes in a group box to present them as a single element. Users can select more than one check box in a group to indicate a range of choices. (For example, on an order form, users could select each of the product categories they want to review.)

- **Spin button** Add a spin button to increase or decrease the value (within a minimum and maximum value that you define) in a specific cell. When you click the up or down arrow on the spin button, the value in the cell that the button is linked to changes, and you can see how these changes affect the results of formulas, for example.

- **List box** Use a list box to display a set of items from which users can choose (a set of nine colors, for example). You can define a list box so that users can select only a single item, multiple items that are adjacent, or multiple items that are not adjacent.

- **Option button** An option button marks one in a set of exclusive options. For example, Update Manually or Update Automatically. As you do with check boxes, you often present option buttons within a group box.

- **Group box** A group box organizes a set of controls into a single element. You usually use a group box with check boxes or option buttons.

- **Label** Use a label to identify or describe the function of a cell, cell range, or another control. You can use a label as you would a caption.

- **Scroll bar** The scroll bar control is similar to the spin button. As you change the position of the scroll bar, you change a value in the cell the scroll bar is linked to.

To add any of these controls to a worksheet, click Insert in the Controls group, click the icon for the type of control you want to add (ScreenTips identify each control), and then click the cell on the worksheet where you want to place the control. Your next step is usually to right-click the control and choose Format Control. You use the Format Control dialog box to specify a cell range for a list, for example, or to specify whether a check box is selected by default, or to set up the maximum and minimum values for a spin button or a scroll bar. In the sections that follow, you'll learn more details about setting up each type of control.

> **Important** The text field, combo list edit control, and combo drop-down edit controls do not apply in Excel 2010, nor does the Run Dialog button. These controls are used in Excel 5.0 dialog sheets.

Inserting a Command Button

Form control command buttons are designed to run macros. When you add a command button to a worksheet, Excel displays the Assign Macro dialog box and assigns a default name to the macro it will associate with the button. To assign a macro that you already recorded or developed in VBA, use the Macros In list to specify the list of macros you want to choose from (All Open Workbooks or Personal.xslb, for example). Then select the macro and click OK. (If you want to make changes to a macro after you select it, click Edit.)

To work with a new macro, click New to write the macro in the Visual Basic editor or click Record to open the Record Macro dialog box, where you can name and describe the macro and then record it.

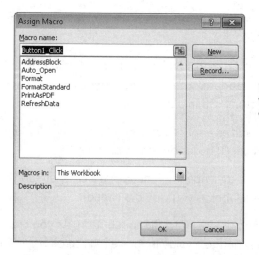

Excel opens the Assign Macro dialog box when you add a command button form control to a worksheet.

To change the label on a command button, click Design Mode in the Controls group, right-click the control, and choose Edit Text. The cursor is positioned at the start of the default text (something like Button 1). Select that text, delete it, and then type a label that describes the button's operation.

Setting Up a Combo Box or a List Box

You define the items that appear in a combo box or list box control by entering them in a cell range. You can list the items on the same worksheet or on a different worksheet in the workbook. (The source of the items can come from a cell range in a separate workbook, but that workbook must be open to populate the list in the control.)

Click the combo box icon in the group of form controls, and then drag across the worksheet to position the combo box and set its initial size. You can resize the control by dragging one of the handles on its borders and at the corners. To reposition the control, point to the border (you'll see the cursor appear as a four-way arrow) and then drag it to a new location.

Right-click the control and choose Format Control to open the dialog box in which you specify properties for the control. On the Control tab of the Format Control dialog box, click in the Input Range box and then specify the cell range for the list. You can type the range or drag through it on the worksheet where the list appears.

In the Cell Link box, specify a cell (or a cell range) in which you want to capture the value that reflects which item a user selects in the list. The items are numbered sequentially. You might use this value in a formula, for example, or to control other aspects of the form.

For a combo box and a list box control, you specify the input range for the list and the linked cell that shows which option is selected in the control. For a list box, you also specify a selection type.

You follow the same steps for defining an input range and a linked cell for a list box. On the Controls tab for a list box, you also need to specify an option in the Selection Type area. The options in this area are Single, Multi, and Extended. Use Single if you want a user to select only one item from the list. The Multi option enables users to select multiple adjacent items, and Extended lets users select items that are not adjacent.

> **See Also** You can learn more about the options on the other tabs of the Format Controls dialog box in the section "Defining Form Control Properties" later in this chapter.

Inserting Check Boxes and Option Buttons

After you insert a check box or an option button control (or a set of these controls), right-click the control and choose Format Control. On the Controls tab for these controls, use the Value area to specify whether the control should be selected or deselected as its default state. A Mixed value applies to multiple selections. Also specify the linked cell. When a check box is selected, the linked cell displays the value True. You can use this condition to affect the results of formulas. For example, you could refer to the linked cell in an IF statement that inserts a value in the cell with the IF formula depending on the state of the check box.

When you add a set of options buttons to a group control, right-click one of the option buttons and then specify the linked cell in the Cell Link box on the Control tab. You need to set the linked cell only once. Each option button enclosed in the group control uses the same linked cell.

To change the label for a check box, option button, or group control, right-click the control (be sure you have Design Mode enabled) and choose Edit Text. The cursor appears at the start of the default text. Select that text, delete it, and then type a label that identifies the control.

Using Spin Buttons and Scroll Bars

Add a spin button or a scroll bar to a worksheet when you need a control with which you can increase or decrease the value (within a range that you define) in a specific cell. On the Control tab for a spin button, you specify the current value (which you can leave blank or at the default value 0), the minimum and maximum value, and the interval for incremental changes. You might specify a range of 1,000 to 10,000 with incremental changes of 500, for example. You also need to specify the cell (in the Cell Link box) where the value set by the control appears. Here again, you can use this value in calculations as you need to. For example, if the value in the linked cell equals or exceeds a certain amount, you can use an IF statement to set the value in another cell accordingly.

> **Tip** If you want to use a spin button to change a cell's value as a percentage instead of as a set increment, enter a formula in another cell that divides the value in the linked cell by 100.

A scroll bar control also adjusts the value in a cell as you move the scroll bar up or down. You can use a scroll bar to continuously change the value of the linked cell as you scroll. On the Controls tab, set the values for the current value, the minimum and maximum values, and the value for incremental change. The Page Change field affects the speed at which the scroll bar changes values. Scroll up to move toward the minimum value; scroll down to move incrementally toward the maximum value for the control.

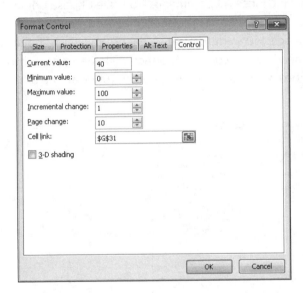

Spin buttons and scroll bars change the value in the linked cell when you interact with the control. Specify the maximum and minimum values you want to use.

Adding a Label

Use a label control to identify controls (or other items on a worksheet) that don't have labels of their own. You probably won't add a label for a command button or a check box, for example, but you might use a label for a combo box or a list box. To enter the text for a label, right-click the control and choose Edit Text.

Creating a Data Form

Excel can create a data form from the column headings in a table or a cell range. A data form is especially useful for entering and updating information in a worksheet in which you frequently scroll to enter data in many columns. A data form presents the columns in a single dialog box that also includes command buttons that let you delete a row or add a new row.

The first step in creating a data form is to add the Forms button to the Quick Access Toolbar. Click the arrow at the right end of the Quick Access Toolbar, click More Commands, and then choose All Commands from the Choose Commands From list. Scroll down to the Forms button, select it, click Add, and then click OK. Open the workbook in which you want to create a data form (which should be organized with column headings, of course), and then click the Forms button. Excel creates the dialog box, which you can then use to work with the data in the workbook.

> **To insert a command button**

1. On the **Developer** tab, click **Insert** in the **Controls** group.

2. In the **Form Controls** group, click the command button icon, and then click on the worksheet where you want to place the button.

   Excel displays the Assign Macro dialog box.

3. In the dialog box, type a name for the button's macro (or use the default name Excel provides.)

4. Select the macro you want the button to run, or click **New** to write a macro in the Visual Basic editor, or click **Record** to record a new macro.

➤ To insert a combo box or list box control

1. On the **Developer** tab, click **Insert** in the **Controls** group.

2. In the **Form Controls** group, click the combo box or list box icon, and then click on the worksheet where you want to place the control.

3. Right-click the control and choose **Format Control**.

4. On the **Control** tab of the **Format Control** dialog box, specify the input range and the linked cell for the control.

5. For a list box, choose the selection type (**Single**, **Multi**, or **Extended**).

➤ To insert a check box or option button control

1. On the **Developer** tab, click **Insert** in the **Controls** group.

2. In the **Form Controls** group, click the check box or option button icon, and then click on the worksheet where you want to place the control.

3. Right-click the control and choose **Format Control**.

4. On the **Control** tab of the **Format Control** dialog box, use the Value area to specify whether the control should be selected or deselected by default.

5. In the **Cell link** box, specify the cell that you want to link to the control.

6. To create a group of check boxes or option buttons, click **Insert** in the **Controls** group, click the group box icon, and then click on the worksheet where you want to add the group.

7. Drag the check box or option button controls into the group control.

➤ To insert a spin button or scroll bar control

1. On the **Developer** tab, click **Insert** in the **Controls** group.

2. In the **Form Controls** group, click the spin button or scroll bar icon, and then click on the worksheet where you want to place the control.

3. Right-click the control and choose **Format Control**.

4. On the **Control** tab of the **Format Control** dialog box, enter values in the **Current value**, **Minimum value**, **Maximum value**, and **Incremental change** boxes. For a scroll bar, also enter a value for the **Page change** box.

5. In the **Cell link** box, specify the cell that you want to link to the control.

➤ **To insert a label control**

1. On the **Developer** tab, click **Insert** in the **Controls** group.

2. In the **Form Controls** group, click the label icon, and then click on the worksheet where you want to place the control.

3. Right-click the control and choose **Edit Text**.

4. Delete the default text, and then type the text you want to use.

➤ **To change the default label for a command button, option button, or check box**

1. Right-click the control and choose **Edit Text**.

2. Delete the default text, and then type the text you want to use.

Defining Form Control Properties

The Format Controls dialog box contains several other tabs that you work with to manage the size, display, and behavior of form controls:

- **Size tab** On the Size tab, you can adjust the height and width of controls (and the proportional scale). Use the Lock Aspect Ratio option to keep the height and width of the control proportionate.

- **Protection tab** The Protection tab lets you lock a control (and the text contained in some controls), but as information on the Protection tab explains, the options you set on this tab "have no effect unless the sheet is protected." To protect the worksheet, click Protect Sheet on the Review tab, or click Format on the Home tab and choose Protect Sheet.

> **See Also** For more information about applying protection to a worksheet, see "Protecting Worksheets and Workbooks" in Chapter 1 in this section of the book.

- **Properties tab** Options on the Properties tab affect the positioning of a control and whether the control appears when you print the worksheet. The positioning options are Move And Size With Cells, Move But Don't Size With Cells, and Don't Move Or Size With Cells. These settings affect the behavior of the control when you resize or move cells that appear behind them.

The default settings for the options on the Properties tab depend on the type of control. For example, the Print Object option is not selected for a command button, but this option is set by default for a check box. The Move And Size With Cells option is enabled for a command button, but this option is not available for many other types of controls.

● **Alt Text tab** The Alt Text tab lets you provide text that is displayed while a form is loading in a web browser. Alt text is also used in search engines and can provide people with disabilities with information about a control.

Some types of controls include other tabs. For example, the Format Control dialog box for check boxes and option buttons includes the Colors And Lines tab. Use this tab to specify a fill color and degree of transparency, as well as a line color, style, and weight. (The options for arrow styles are not available.)

You can apply additional formatting to a command button control by using the Font, Alignment, and Margins tabs in the Format Control dialog box. The settings on the Margins tab affect the positioning of the button's label.

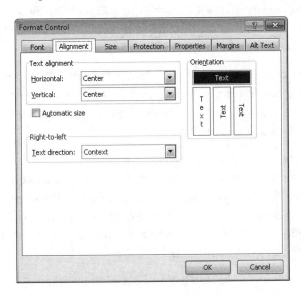

For a command button control, use the Font and Alignment tabs to modify how the button is displayed.

➤ **To set properties for form controls**

1. Right-click the control and choose **Format Control**.

2. Use the **Size**, **Protection**, **Properties**, and **Alt Text** tabs in the **Format Control** dialog box to specify options for the control's behavior.

3. For a command button control, use the **Font**, **Alignment**, and **Margins** tabs to apply additional formatting to the button and its label.

4. For check boxes and option button controls, use the **Colors and Lines** tab to apply line styles and fill colors.

Making Use of ActiveX Controls

The types of basic ActiveX controls you can insert on a worksheet form are similar to the types of form controls. You can insert a command button, a combo box, a list box, a check box—all the same types of controls except for a group box. You can also insert an ActiveX text box control, an image control, and a toggle button control.

- In a text box, you can type, edit, or display data that is linked to a cell.
- Use a toggle button control to signify Yes/No or On/Off. A toggle button changes its appearance when it is enabled and when it is not.
- Use an image control to embed an image on a form.

When you click More Controls in the ActiveX Controls group, Excel displays a dialog box that lists numerous ActiveX controls that are installed with Excel. These are generally advanced controls that require programming.

To insert an ActiveX control, click the icon for the control in the ActiveX Controls group (click Insert in the Controls group to display the menu of controls), and then click the spot where you want to place the control on the worksheet. The steps you take at this point depend on the type of control you are inserting.

When you add an ActiveX command button control, for example, you won't see the Assign Macro dialog box. To provide the code you want the button to execute, right-click the button and choose View Code to open the Visual Basic editor. In the Code window, you will see the opening and closing lines of a subprocedure for the button's *Click* event. If you aren't familiar with VBA, you can enter the name of a macro you recorded here or copy and paste the code for a macro you recorded.

You can set properties for a command button (such as BackColor, Locked, Height, Width, and others) and for other controls by clicking Design Mode, right-clicking the button, and then choosing Properties. (You can also click Properties in the Controls group.) The Properties pane that's displayed lets you view a control's properties alphabetically or by category.

One advantage of using ActiveX controls is the extensive list of properties you can use to affect how the control is displayed and behaves.

Some properties are the same as for form controls. For example, ActiveX controls have a LinkedCell property that serves the same purpose as the Linked Cell box on the Format Control dialog box you use with form controls. The Placement property is comparable to the options that control moving and sizing a control that you can select on the Properties tab of the Format Controls dialog box.

You can use the Font property for an ActiveX list box control, for example, to change the font and font formatting applied to the list items. Other properties you can set for a list box include BorderColor, BorderStyle, TextAlign, and Visible (which lets you hide the control if you want to). Other types of controls have the same or similar properties.

Two important properties to keep in mind are the Name property and the Caption property. The Name property identifies the control (such as CommandButton1). The Caption property, which does not apply to all control types, sets the text displayed in a control. For a check box or a command button, for example, type the text you want the control to display in the Caption property.

Here are some of the other important properties you work with in setting up different types of ActiveX controls:

- **Check box** Set the Value property to True to select the check box; set this property to False if you want the check box to be cleared. Among the formatting properties for a check box are BackColor, Shadow, SpecialEffect, and TextAlign.

- **Combo box** Use the ListFillRange property to specify the cell range that includes the items you want the combo box to display. (You need to type the cell range here; you can't drag through the worksheet as you can for a form control.) To set up a two-column combo box, specify 2 for the ColumnCount property, set the ColumnHeads property to True, and set the ColumnWidths property so that each column is displayed at the size you want it. The BoundColumn property controls which column (in a multicolumn combo box) provides a value. The ListRows property sets the maximum number of rows to display.

- **List box** As you do for a combo box, use the ListFillRange property to specify the input range. The MultiSelect property controls whether users can select one or more items in the list box. Use fmMultiSelectSingle for selecting a single item. Use fmMultiSelectMulti to allow selection of multiple adjacent items. The fmMultiSelectExtended option is the value to choose if you want users to be able to select multiple nonadjacent items.

- **Option button** Set the Value property to True or False to specify whether the option button is selected by default.

- **Scroll bar** Use the Max and Min properties to set the range of values controlled by the scroll bar. The SmallChange property specifies the increment in which the value changes when you click the up or down arrow. The LargeChange property specifies the increment of change when you click the area of the scroll bar between the arrows.

- **Spin button** Use the Max, Min, and SmallChange properties to specify the maximum value, minimum value, and increment of change. Here, as with other controls, the LinkedCell property specifies the cell in which the value associated with the spin button appears.

Security Settings for ActiveX Controls

As it does for macros, the Trust Center provides a page in which you can review and change security settings for ActiveX controls. With the default setting, Excel notifies you that a workbook contains active content. You need to click Enable Content in the message bar to let ActiveX controls run. You can also choose an option to disable all ActiveX controls or to enable all controls without restrictions (this option is not recommended because some ActiveX controls could run code that harms your computer). Or you can choose an option to be prompted to enable controls that are marked by a developer as Safe for Initialization (SFI). If a control is not marked, it is not considered safe (making it a UFI—Unsafe for Initialization—control) and is not enabled.

To change these settings, click Options on the File menu. In the Excel Options dialog box, click Trust Center. Click Trust Center Settings, and then click the ActiveX Settings page.

➤ **To insert and set properties for an ActiveX control**

1. On the **Developer** tab, click **Insert** in the **Controls** group.

2. In the **ActiveX Controls** group, click the icon for the control you want to add, and then click on the worksheet where you want to place the control.

3. In the **Controls** group, click **Design Mode**.

4. Right-click the control, and then click **Properties**.

5. Use the properties pane to specify values for the control's properties.

> **Tip** For a summary of ActiveX control properties, see the previous section. See the Excel help topics under Forms and Controls for extensive lists of properties you set for specific ActiveX controls.

A Simple Order Form

Combining form controls and ActiveX controls with formulas and functions is what makes forms most useful. For example, here are some steps you could follow to create a simple order form that uses several combo boxes, matching spin buttons, a group of option buttons, and a command button (all form controls), together with the INDEX, IF, and SUM functions.

1. Add four combo boxes (or some appropriate number of them) to a worksheet. Stack the combo boxes in the same column. You can size them so that they fit in a single row. The input range for these combo boxes will be the same and refer to the cell range where you list your products. (In this example, the list is included in a cell range on a separate worksheet.) Set the Cell Link box in the Format Controls dialog box to point to the cell adjacent to the combo box in the next column (column C here, the product ID).

2. Add matching spin buttons with which users can specify a quantity. Set the minimum and maximum range and the incremental change to appropriate values (1 to 25 with an increment of 1). Set the Cell Link box for each spin button to the cell adjacent to the control (column E in this example).

3. In the sample order form, prices for each product are listed on a separate worksheet next to the corresponding product. Products are identified in the linked cell for the combo box by the number of their order in the list. By using the INDEX function and a reference to the linked cell, the product price is entered in column G. The full formula (for row 5) is =(INDEX(Sheet2!B1:B10,C5)). The first argument for the INDEX is the cell range with the prices. The second argument (C5) is the linked cell for the combo box. When a user selects a different product from the combo box, the value in cell C5 (or cells C7, C9, and C11) changes and the INDEX function returns the price for that product.

4. The value for each entry in the Total column is calculated by multiplying the quantity (column E) with the price in column G. The total in cell I13 is just the sum of the item totals.

5. The shipping amount is also determined by the INDEX function in conjunction with the group of option buttons that identify shipping options. The amount charged for each option is listed on a separate worksheet. The linked cell for the option button group is F14. When a user selects a shipping option, the value in the linked cell reflects that choice. The formula in cell I14 uses the INDEX function to look up shipping charges: =(INDEX(Sheet2!E1:E3,F14)).

6. An IF statement in cell I16 determines whether the order is large enough to receive a 10 percent discount. The formula is =IF(I13>=100,I13*.1,0). If the value of the order (in cell I13) is greater than or equal to 100, a discount of 10 percent of that amount is entered in cell I16. If the order is less than 100, the formula enters 0.

7. To finish off the order form, the command button runs a macro that saves the form as a PDF file.

Practice Tasks

The practice files for these tasks are located in the folder for Microsoft Excel 2010. You can save the results of these exercises in the same folder. Change the file name so that you don't overwrite the sample files. When you are done, try performing the following tasks:

- Open the file LoanCalculator.xlsx. Sheet1 identifies the cells whose input is required for the PMT function, which you can use to calculate loan payments based on interest rate, loan amount, and number of payments.

- Insert form controls to automate the formula by using the named cells as the linked cells for various controls. Add a spin button control that changes the interest rate between 3 and 9 percent. (You need to divide the value by 100 to insert a percentage in the formula.) Add a scroll bar that changes the amount of a loan between $5,000 and $30,000 in $1,000 increments.

- Create a list for the possible number of payments (12 through 60). In the adjoining column, number these options 1 through 5. Add a list box control to your form, and use the cell range that contains the list of payment options as the input range. Specify the Number of Payments cell as the linked cell.

- Now use the LOOKUP function to equate the output from the list box with the number of payments. The syntax for the LOOKUP function is =*LOOKUP (lookup_value,lookup_vector,[result_vector])*. Here, you look up the value in the Number of Payments cell, compare it to the numbered list 1–5, and return the matching result from the list of payment options to the PMT formula.

Objective Review

Before finishing this chapter, be sure you have mastered the following skills:

4.1   Create and manipulate macros

4.2   Insert and manipulate form controls

Exam 77-885

Microsoft Access 2010 Specialist

In the next five chapters, you'll build on the general skills required to create and manage databases in Microsoft Access 2010. You'll learn more about the specific skills you need to be certified as a Microsoft Access Specialist. The areas covered are the following:

- Using the Access workspace
- Building tables
- Building forms
- Creating and managing queries
- Designing reports

What You Need to Know

The exercises in this part of the book are designed primarily for users who are learning to design and build Access databases. We assume that you have some familiarity with Access features, know how to enter and edit data, and understand the basic definition and function of relational databases and database objects such as tables and forms. To provide context and an opportunity for review, the following lists provides brief explanations of five important terms:

- **Tables** Tables define the data stored in a database. Tables are composed of fields, and each field is defined as a particular data type (text, number, date, or another data type). Each field also has certain properties. For example, you can specify that a field is required. You can also define the size of a field (such as the maximum number of characters a field can contain). Users of a database fill in fields (and must fill in required fields) with values to create a record in the database. In most tables, each record is identified by a unique value called a *primary key*, which might be a single field (such as ID) or a combination of fields. You'll learn the details of designing tables in Chapter 2, "Building Tables."

- **Forms** Forms are used to enter and edit data. Forms are often bound to tables (or to queries) as a record source. Forms use controls such as text boxes, check boxes, and list boxes to provide a user interface for a database. Forms can also be used to confirm and execute database operations and to navigate from one database object to another. As you'll learn in Chapter 3, "Building Forms," Access provides a number of built-in form designs, a gallery of form controls, and tools you use to design and lay out a form.

- **Queries** Queries are used to select records that meet specified criteria and to perform specific actions. To build a select query, you add fields from one or more tables and then specify criteria that Access uses to select records. For example, you might want to see only records with a certain value in a date field (all records created after 1/1/2012, for example) or only records associated with a specific project. Using criteria, you can also create and run action queries that insert, update, or delete selected records. You'll learn more details about queries in Chapter 4, "Creating and Managing Queries."

- **Reports** Reports are often used to summarize data in various ways and then present the data. You might print reports for a meeting or distribute them electronically as a PDF file or in e-mail. You'll learn about the ways in which you work with reports in Chapter 5, "Designing Reports."

- **Relationships** Relationships help maintain the integrity of the information in a database and also reduce data redundancy. You can create several different types of relationships between tables in an Access database. In a one-to-many relationship, a record in one table can be related to one or many records in another. You can also create one-to-one relationships and many-to-many relation-ships. Relationships are created by linking a table's foreign key (a customer ID field in an order table) with another table's primary key (the customer ID field in the cus-tomer table). Relationships protect data integrity by preventing you from creating orphan records (for example, an order with no customer). Relationships help reduce data redundancy by letting you store information in separate tables that you can link together. For example, you can create a customer table and then relate each order in an order table to the record for a particular customer. This prevents you from having to enter a custom record for each separate order.

1 Using the Access Workspace

The skills tested in this section of the Microsoft Office Specialist exam for Microsoft Access 2010 relate to using the Access workspace. Specifically, the following objectives are associated with this set of skills:

1.1 Create and manage a database

1.2 Configure the navigation pane

1.3 Use application parts

In this chapter, you'll learn about many of the commands and features available in Backstage view, which you can open from the File tab on the Microsoft Access 2010 ribbon. From Backstage view, you create, open, and save databases, and you can also perform actions that help maintain and secure a database. You'll also learn how to work with the navigation pane, which lists the tables, forms, queries, reports, and other objects that define the structure and operations of a database. In the chapter's last section, you'll learn about application parts, which are building blocks you can use to add features and functionality to a database. You can define your own application parts when you save a database as a template.

1.1 Create and Manage a Database

You perform many of the operations and tasks involved in setting up and maintaining a database from Backstage view. Among the standard commands you use in Backstage view are Save, Open, New, and Print. You can use the Save & Publish page in Backstage view to save a database in a specific format, to back up a database, or to make a database available on a Microsoft SharePoint site. The Info page provides commands you use to help maintain and secure a database.

The following sections provide details about the work you do in Backstage view to create and manage a database.

Creating a Database by Using a Template

When you run Access (assuming you don't open a database from the Recent list or double-click a database file), the program opens in Backstage view and displays options for creating a database. These options include a blank database and a blank web database, as well as several paths to database templates.

> **See Also** You'll see examples of creating a blank database in Chapter 2, "Building Tables," later in this part of the book.

You can base a database on a template by choosing an option on the New page in Backstage view. To find more templates on Office.com, use the search box.

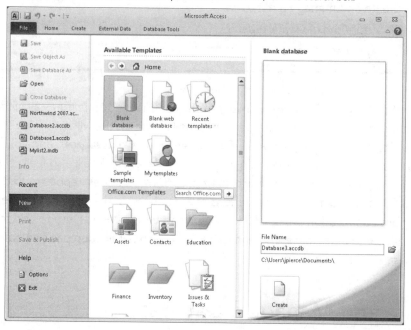

Templates come with database objects already in place, including one or more tables, data entry forms, and basic reports. Click Recent Templates to see any templates you've worked with lately. Sample Templates displays a window in which you can select from templates for different types of databases, including those you use to track and manage events, assets, contacts, and marketing templates. My Templates displays the templates stored in the default templates folder for Access. In Windows 7 or Windows Vista, this folder is located in your user profile at Users*UserName*\AppData\Roaming\Microsoft\Templates\Access. In Windows XP, this folder is located under Documents and Settings*UserName*\Application Data\Microsoft\Templates.

> **Tip** The sample templates that come with Access 2010 include the Northwind database, which has been part of Access for many versions of the program. The Northwind database provides examples for how to design a database in Access, including details like a log-in dialog box, sample macros, and Microsoft Visual Basic for Application modules. Refer to the Northwind database when you are looking for a particular solution, or just work with it from time to time to gain an understanding and appreciation of the extent of the work you can do in Access.

After you click Recent Templates, Samples Templates, or My Templates, select the template you want to work with and type a name for the database in the File Name box. Click the folder icon to browse to a location other than the default location for saving a database. When you click Create, Access prepares the template and opens the new database. Depending on your security settings, you might need to click Enable Content in the message bar to start working with the database. In most cases, you'll see a default table or form open for data input. Display the navigation pane by clicking the double-arrow button at the top of the pane to see the other database objects included in this template.

Access templates provide tables, forms, and other objects that you can use as is or modify. Open the navigation pane to see the database objects the template provides.

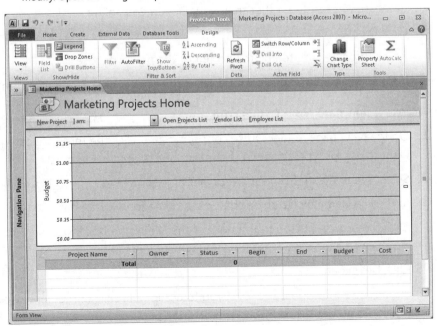

> **See Also** For more information about how to view objects on the navigation pane, see "Configure the Navigation Pane" later in this chapter.

You can find many other templates on Office.com. Use the search box to help locate a template you can use for a specific purpose, or click a category listed under Office.com Templates and then select one of the templates that Access displays. The preview area on the right side of the New page provides information about the template's size, how other users have rated it, and who provided the template. Type a name for the database in the File Name box, click the browse button if you want to save the database in a location other than the default Documents folder, and then click Download. You might need to accept a license agreement associated with the template. Click I Accept if you see this message box. You'll see a progress window as the template is downloaded. Access then displays a default form or other database object, and for some templates Access opens the Help window and displays an article that describes more about the template. To learn more about the types of database objects the template provides, open the navigation pane.

➤ **To create a database from a recent, sample, or user template**

1. On the **New** tab, click **Recent Templates**, **Sample Templates**, or **My Templates**.

2. In the **File Name** box at the right, type a name for the database.

   Click the browse button to the right of the File Name box if you want to store the database in a location other than your Documents folder.

3. Click **Create**.

   Access prepares the template and opens the new database.

4. If the message bar appears with a security warning, click **Enable Content**.

➤ **To use a template from Office.com**

1. On the **New** page, under Office.com Templates, click the template category you want to use, or type a term in the search box to locate a template.

2. Select the template from the list of available templates.

3. In the File Name box at the right, type a name for the database.

   Click the browse button to the right of the File Name box if you want to store the database in a location other than your Documents folder.

4. Click Download.

5. If you see a message box asking you to accept a license agreement, click **I Accept** (if you do accept the terms).

   Access prepares the template and opens the new database.

Using the Save Object As Command

As you fill out the structure of a database, you might find that a query you design returns a set of records that you want to save as a table. Similarly, as you build forms for data input, the fields you add to a form could serve as the basis for a report you want to use for analysis. You can use the Save Object As command on the File tab to save an object as a different type.

> **Tip** Another use for the Save Object As command is to create a copy of a database object. For example, you might use this command to save a copy of a form with a new name and then modify that form.

When you choose this command, Access opens a simple Save As dialog box and displays Copy Of *ObjectName* in the Save box. Type the name you want to assign to the new object, and then choose the type of object you want to use from the As list.

> **Tip** You can also choose Save Object As on the Save & Publish page in Backstage view to perform this operation. You'll learn more about the Save & Publish page later in this section.

▶ **To save a database object as another type of object**

  1. In the navigation pane, select the object you want to save.
  2. Click **File, Save Object As**.
  3. In the **Save As** dialog box, type a name for the new object.
  4. In the **As** list, select the type of object, and then click **OK**.

Using Open Dialog Box Options

Most of the time, you will use the standard Open option in the Open dialog box to open a database so that you and other users can enter, update, and edit data. However, the Open dialog box provides options you can apply in situations when you need to open a database exclusively or open a database as a read-only file.

Click Open on the File tab, and then click the arrow beside the Open button in the Open dialog box. In addition to Open, the options available are the following:

- **Open Read-Only**   Use this option when you want only to view data but not enter or update data. Choosing this option does not prevent other users of the database from opening the database to enter or edit data or make changes to the database.

- **Open Exclusive**   Use this option when you want exclusive access to the database. You need to choose this option before you can encrypt a database. You should also use this option when you need to make changes to the design of the database. (You'll learn more about encrypting a database later in this chapter.)

- **Open Exclusive Read-Only**   Use this option to open the database in read-only mode. Other users can open the database, but they can open it only in read-only mode.

- **Show Previous Versions**   If you have set up the feature to maintain previous versions, choose this option to display them.

➤ **To open a database**

1. Click **File, Open**.

2. In the **Open** dialog box, select the database you want to open.

3. Click **Open**, or click the arrow beside the **Open** button and select an option to open the database as read-only, exclusively, or exclusively read-only.

Working on the Save & Publish Page

The Save & Publish command on the File tab opens a page in Backstage view that presents options for saving a database in a particular format, saving a database object, and publishing a database to Access Services, which makes the database available in a web browser. When you save a database, you can also choose an option to package the database, create an executable file, back up the database, or save the database to a SharePoint site.

The Save & Publish page provides options for how you can save a database. You can also use this page to back up a database and to store a database on a SharePoint site.

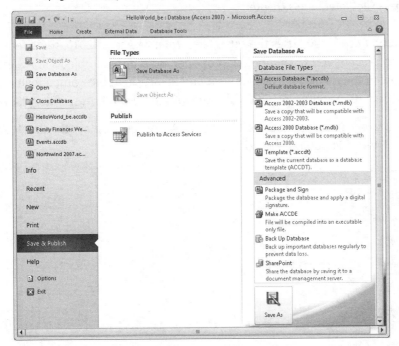

Using the Save Database As Option

With Save Database As selected, the options listed under Database File Types are the default format (.accdb) or the format used in Access 2002–2003 or Access 2000. You should select the Access 2002–2003 or Access 2000 format when you need to share a database with users who are working with those versions of the program. Choose Template from this list to save the database you're working with as a template.

If you select any of the first three options, Access displays the standard Save As dialog box, with the format you selected as the only option available in the Save As Type list.

Keep in mind, however, that Access 2010 comes with features that can keep you from saving a database to an earlier file format. For example, the encryption mechanism used with .accdb files is different from the format used in earlier versions of Access. You need to remove a password from an Access 2010 database before you can save it in an earlier file format. A database that includes new data types or property settings cannot be saved in an earlier format. For example, using the Attachment data type (which is new to Access 2010) or calculated fields in tables prevents you from saving an .accdb file in an earlier file format.

> **See Also** For information about encrypting and decrypting a database, see "Encrypting a Database File" later in this chapter.

Even though Access 2007 uses the same file format as Access 2010, some features in Access can prevent you from modifying or opening database objects in Access 2007 or from opening the database itself. You can find an article about compatibility issues between Access 2010 and Access 2007 at *msdn.microsoft.com/en-us/office/cc907897.aspx*.

When you select Template and then click Save As, Access displays the Create New Template From This Database dialog box.

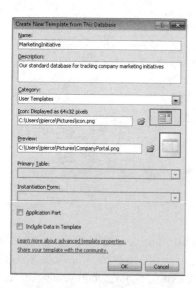

In this dialog box, type a name and description for the template. Under Category, User Templates is selected by default, but you can type a category of your own if you prefer. If you plan to share this template with other users or just want to add a professional touch to a template you're creating for yourself, you can specify image files to use as an icon for the template (this icon replaces the standard Access icon in the program's application window) and as the thumbnail preview of the template that appears in Backstage view. If you select the Application Part check box, you should specify a primary table. Select the Include Data In Template option to keep the data already stored in the database as part of the template.

> **Important** Use the Instantiation Form option when you want to display a splash screen or a form that performs a startup routine. Access displays the form you select in this option only once and then deletes the form. You should be careful not to confuse this option with a startup form, which you can specify for the current database by using the Access Options dialog box.

> **See Also** For detailed information about application parts, see "Use Application Parts" later in this chapter.

With Save As Database selected in the File Type list, four options appear in the Advanced area: Package And Sign, Make ACCDE, Back Up Database, and SharePoint. (The first two of these options are used primarily by database developers or administrators as a means to distribute a database to its users.)

- **Packaging and Signing a Database** If you need to distribute and deploy an Access database to a group of users, you can use the Package And Sign option to create an Access deployment file (.accdc) that includes a digital signature identifying the source of the database. You can place the package in a location where users can retrieve the file. Users extract the database file from the package and then start working with the database.

> **Tip** You can apply the Package And Sign option only to databases saved in the newer formats, including .accdb and .accde.

Before you can digitally sign a database, you need a digital certificate. (See the following sidebar for information on how to obtain one.) When you select Package And Sign and click Save As, Access displays a Windows Security dialog box. Select the certificate you want to use to sign the database and then click OK. In the Create Microsoft Access Signed Package dialog box, provide a name for the database package (Access provides a default name by appending the current date to the name of the database), open the location where you want to store the package, and then click Create.

When a user double-clicks the package file to extract the database, Access displays a security notice if the database comes from a source that is not among the user's trusted publishers. A user can view the details of the digital certificate from the dialog box to identify the source of the database. When a user clicks Open in the Microsoft Access Security Notice dialog box, Access displays the Extract Database To dialog box, in which a user specifies where to save the database file.

Obtaining a Digital Certificate

You can obtain a digital certificate from a certificate authority such as VeriSign (*www.verisign.com*) or create a self-signed digital certificate by using a tool that comes with Office. To create a self-signed certificate, open the Start menu, click Microsoft Office, and then click Microsoft Office 2010 Tools. (If this feature is not installed, you can install it from the installation media for Office.) Under Microsoft Office 2010 Tools, click Digital Certificate For VBA Projects. In the Create Digital Certificate dialog box, type a name for the certificate, click OK, and then click OK in the confirmation dialog box.

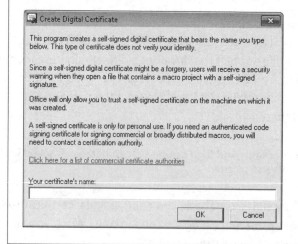

Use this dialog box to create a certificate you can use to digitally sign a database.

- **Creating an Executable File**   When you create an executable file (which uses the .accde file name extension), Access compiles any Visual Basic for Application (VBA) code the database includes. The operations defined by the code are still available in the database, but users can't view or modify the code. Also in an .accde database, users can't open forms or reports in Layout or Design view to modify them.

And creating an executable file helps maintain a small file size in a database that contains a significant amount of VBA code.

When you choose the Make ACCDE option, Access displays the Save As dialog box. Use this dialog box to specify the file's name and choose a location in which to save it. (Depending on a user's security settings, the user might see a Microsoft Access Security Notice dialog box when he or she opens the .accde file. Click Open in this dialog box to run the database file.)

- **Backing Up a Database** By double-clicking the Back Up Database option (or selecting it and clicking Save As), you can create a copy of your database. Access opens the Save As dialog box with the database's name and the current date entered in the File Name box. Click Save to create the backup.

- **Adding a Database to a SharePoint Site** When you select the SharePoint option and click Save As, Access displays the Save To SharePoint dialog box. Use the address box to open the site you want to use, and then supply your user name and password if they are required. Open the document library where you want to place the database file and then click Save. Access displays a progress message as it retrieves the file and saves it to the SharePoint site.

> **Tip** When you open a database that's saved to a SharePoint site, Access prompts you to save a local copy. You'll also see a message bar beneath the ribbon with a button that you use to save changes you make to the SharePoint site.

➤ To save a database file in a different format

1. Click **File**, **Save & Publish**, and then click **Save Database As**.
2. Under **Database File Types**, select the format you want to use and then click **Save As**.
3. In the **Save As** dialog box, type a name for the database, open the location where you want to save the file, and then click **Save**.

➤ To package and sign a database

1. Click **File**, **Save & Publish**, and then click **Save Database As**.
2. Under **Advanced**, select **Package and Sign** and then click **Save As**.
3. In the **Windows Security** dialog box, select the certificate you want to use to sign the database and then click **OK**.
4. In the **Create Microsoft Access Signed Package** dialog box, type a name for the database, open the location where you want to save the file, and then click **Create**.

➤ **To create an executable-only database**

1. Click **File**, **Save & Publish**, and then click **Save Database As**.

2. Under Advanced, select **Make ACCDE** and then click **Save As**.

3. In the **Save As** dialog box, type a name for the database, open the location where you want to save the file, and then click **Save**.

➤ **To back up a database**

1. Click **File**, **Save & Publish**, and then click **Save Database As**.

2. Under **Advanced**, select **Back Up Database** and then click **Save As**.

3. In the **Save As** dialog box, type a name for the database (or use the default name Access provides), open the location where you want to save the file, and then click **Save**.

➤ **To save a database to a SharePoint site**

1. Click **File**, **Save & Publish**, and then click **Save Database As**.

2. Under **Advanced**, select **SharePoint** and then click **Save As**.

3. In the **Save to SharePoint** dialog box, type the URL for the site in the address box.

4. In the **Windows Security** dialog box, type your user name and password for the site.

5. In the **Save to SharePoint** dialog box, open the document library where you want to save the file.

6. Type a name for the database, and then click **Save**.

Using the Save Object As Option

The Save Object As option on the Save & Publish page becomes available when a database object is open or an object is selected in the navigation pane. Under Database File Types, double-click Save Object As to open a Save As dialog box that you can use to make a copy of the object or save it as a different type.

> **See Also** For more details about saving an object as a different type, see "Using the Save Object As Command" earlier in this chapter.

You can also publish the current object as a PDF or XPS file. You can select any type of object to save in these formats, but not all objects are efficiently presented as an XPS or a PDF file. A plain table in PDF format, for example, shows its fields, values, and gridlines.

Creating an XPS or PDF file for a table might be useful when you need to discuss the table's structure. You will probably work with reports most often. The formatting and organization of reports makes their presentation in these formats more useful.

Select the PDF Or XPS option, click Save As, and then type a file name in the Publish As PDF Or XPS dialog box. In the Save As Type list, select the format you want to use. Specify whether you want to open the file after it is published, and specify an option for optimization (which affects the file's size). Click the Options button to open a dialog box in which you can specify a page range and other options.

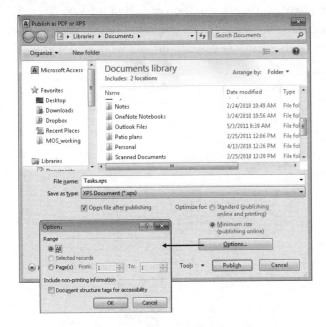

You can save a report or a different type of database object in PDF or XPS format. Use the Options dialog box to specify a page range and other options.

> **Tip** You can use the Save As Client Object option under Advanced to save an object from a web database for use in a client (desktop) Access database.

➤ **To publish a database object as a PDF or XPS file**

1. Open the database object you want to work with, or select it in the navigation pane.

2. Click **File**, **Save & Publish**, and then click **Save Object As**.

3. Under **Database File Types**, select **PDF or XPS** and then click **Save As**.

4. In the **Publish as PDF or XPS** dialog box, select the format you want to use, type a name for the file, and open the location where you want to save the file.

5. To specify a page range and other options, click **Options**, specify the settings in the **Options** dialog box, and then click **OK**.

6. In the **Publish as PDF or XPS** dialog box, click **Publish**.

Publishing a Database to Access Services

When you are working with a database designed for the web (a database that you designed by using the Blank Web Database option or one of the web database templates), you can publish the database to a SharePoint site that supports Access Services (which is a component of SharePoint Server) and work with it in a web browser.

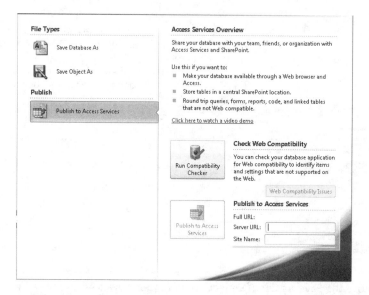

On the Save & Publish page, select Publish To Access Services. You can click Run Compatibility Checker to be sure that the database is fully compatible for the web. If Access detects any errors, it adds them to a table in the database. You can open the table to review the problems by clicking Web Compatibility Issues. Of course, you should correct these issues before you publish the database.

In the Server URL box, type the name of the server with SharePoint Server and Access Services. Use the Site Name box to identify the site. The information you enter is combined and shown in the Full URL string. After you click the Publish To Access Services button, you might be prompted to enter a user name and password for the site. Access checks the database for compatibility with the web, runs through a series of routines that prepares the database, and then displays a message when the database is successfully published.

To view and work with the database on the web, type the site's URL in your browser's address box and enter the user name and password (if required).

If a default form is specified for the database, you'll see that form displayed on the SharePoint site. You won't see the Access navigation bar or the ribbon. From the Options menu that's displayed in SharePoint, choose Settings to open a page where you can select a database object to modify or add fields. The Site Permissions command on the Options menu opens a page where you can update permissions for database users. Choose Open In Access to display the database in Access, where you can make changes to the database using the full range of the program's features.

➤ **To publish a database to use with Access Services**

1. Open the web database you want to work with.

2. Click **File**, **Save & Publish**, and then click **Publish to Access Services**.

3. Click **Run Compatibility Checker**. If Access detects any problems, click **Web Compatibility Issues** to review the issues before continuing.

4. In the **Server URL** box, type the URL for the SharePoint Server where Access Services is available.

5. In the **Site Name** box, type a name for the site.

6. Click **Publish to Access Services**.

Compacting and Repairing a Database

As you and other users work with a database, the file grows larger and can also become corrupt. A database file grows larger as you add more data and also because Access creates and uses hidden objects to perform the work it does. Although a file doesn't always become corrupt as it is used, frequent use—especially by multiple users working on the database over a network—can result in a corrupted file, which can in some cases result in data loss or affect the ease with which you can change the database's design.

One step you can take to keep ahead of these potential problems is to run the Compact & Repair Database command, which appears on the Info tab in Backstage view. You might run this command as part of your regular backup routine. If Access encounters no problems when you run this command, you'll simply see that Access is occupied for a few minutes (the cursor shows that the program is working). If the database is open as read-only, however, Access can't run this command, and it displays a message informing you of this. If more than one person has the database open when you run Compact &

Repair Database, Access also displays a message telling you that you attempted to open a database that is already open. Before you compact a multiuser database, you should be sure no one has the database open and then open the database for exclusive access.

> **See Also** For more information about opening a database for exclusive access, see "Using Open Dialog Box Options" earlier in this chapter.

> **Tip** Select the Compact On Close option on the Current Database page of the Access Options dialog box to compact a database each time you close it.

If you want to compact a database other than the one that is currently open, close the current database and then click Compact And Repair Database on the Database Tools tab. In the Database To Compact From dialog box, select the database and then click Compact. Access now displays the Compact Database Into dialog box and displays a temporary name for the compacted database in the File Name box. You can use the original name or type a new name. If you use the original name, Access prompts you to replace the original database. Click Yes in this message box to complete the operation.

➤ **To compact and repair the current database**

1. If you have the database open in read-only mode, click **File, Open**, and then use the **Open** dialog box to open the database using the **Open Exclusive** option. If more than one person has the database open, ask them to close the database. Use the **Open** dialog box to open the database by using the **Open Exclusive** option.

2. Click **File, Info**.

3. Click **Compact & Repair Database**.

➤ **To compact and repair a database that isn't currently open**

1. Close any open databases.

2. On the **Database Tools** tab, in the **Tools** group, click **Compact and Repair Database**.

3. In the **Database to Compact From** dialog box, select the database you want to compact, and then click **Compact**.

4. In the **Compact Database Into** dialog box, specify a name for the compacted database, and then click **Save**.

5. If you specified the current name of the database, click **Yes** in the message box Access displays to confirm that Access should replace the current database file.

Encrypting a Database File

When you define a password for a database, any user who wants to work with the database must provide the password. You can use this process to restrict who can open a database that is stored in a location that many users share.

A database must be open for exclusive use before you can encrypt the database with a password. To open the database for exclusive use, click Open on the File tab. In the Open dialog box, click the arrow beside Open, and then click Open Exclusive. (If you are encrypting the current database, you don't need to close it before you open it for exclusive use.)

On the Info tab, click Encrypt With Password. In the Set Database Password dialog box, type a password and then enter it again to verify it.

> **Tip** If any properties of the database are incompatible with encryption, Access displays a message box telling you that the feature (such as row-level locking) will be ignored. You can safely dismiss this message and proceed with encryption.

To remove a password from a database, first open it for exclusive use. (You'll need to provide the password to complete this step.) On the Info tab, click Decrypt Database. Enter the password in the prompt, and then click OK.

➤ To encrypt a database with a password

1. On the **File** tab, click **Open**.
2. In the **Open** dialog box, click the arrow beside the **Open** button and then click **Open Exclusive**.
3. Click **File, Info**, and then click **Encrypt With Password**.
4. In the **Set Database Password** dialog box, type a database password and then type the password again in the **Verify** box.
5. Click **OK**.

➤ To remove a database password

1. On the **File** tab, click **Open**.

2. In the **Open** dialog box, click the arrow beside the **Open** button and then click **Open Exclusive**.

3. Type the password for the database.

4. Click **File, Info**, and then click **Decrypt Database**.

5. In the **Unset Database Password** dialog box, type the password applied to the database, and then click **OK**.

Setting Access Options

To manage settings for how you interact with Access and how Access interacts with and manages data and databases, you use the Access Options dialog box. (Click Options on the File tab to open it.) Select a category listed along the left side of the dialog box to work with the options it provides.

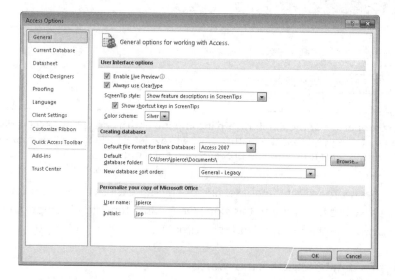

> **See Also** For information about the Customize Ribbon and Quick Access Toolbar pages in the Access Options dialog box, see "Modifying the Display of the Ribbon" at the beginning of this book.

The following sections describe some of the options available in each category.

General

By using options on the General tab, you can turn off Live Preview (the feature in Office 2010 that shows previews of formatting and other visual effects), specify a style for ScreenTips, and choose a color scheme. In the Creating Databases section, choose a default file format for blank databases (the Access 2007 format also applies to Access 2010), the folder in which databases are saved by default, and the default sort order for new databases. You can also provide a user name and initials that identify you in Office applications.

Current Database

The list of options in the Current Database category apply to the open database. The options are divided into six sections:

- **Application Options** In the Application Title and Application Icon boxes, you can provide text and point to an image file to customize the Access application window. Instead of the default Access logo, the icon you specify appears in the window's top-left corner. The text you enter appears in the window's title bar instead of the default text, which includes the file name and format and "Microsoft Access." In the Display Form list, select a form you want Access to display when you open the database. You can use this option to display your own navigation form or a log-in form, for example. Use the other options to turn on or off various features, such as Layout view or the status bar. You'll learn more about some of these options in the following chapters.

- **Navigation** Use the check box in this area to show or hide the navigation pane. Click Navigation Options to open a dialog box in which you can set up groups for organizing how the database objects are displayed in the navigation pane.

> **See Also** For more information about working with the navigation pane and setting navigation pane options, see "Configure the Navigation Pane" later in this chapter.

- **Ribbon And Toolbar Options** The Ribbon Name and Shortcut Menu Bar lists let you select a custom tab or menu bar developed in an earlier version of Access. By clearing the Allow Full Menus and Allow Default Shortcut Menus options, you re-strict the commands available to users when they work in a database. For example, users will see only the File and Home tabs on the ribbon, and these tabs will include only a subset of the commands available for designing and managing a database.

- **Name AutoCorrect Options** For information about the options in this section, see "Renaming Objects" later in this chapter.

- **Filter Lookup Options** Use these options to manage how Access displays values in lists used in filters. For tables or queries that store or retrieve thousands of records, you can prevent these lists from appearing by specifying a number for the option Don't Display Lists When More Than This Number Of Records Is Read.

- **Caching Web Service And SharePoint Tables** These options pertain to web databases, which cache data locally for easier retrieval when you use the data in a table. Select the option Use The Cache Format That Is Compatible With Microsoft Access 2010 And Later to enable the options to clear the cache when you close the database or to never cache data.

Datasheet

Use options in this category to control the display of gridlines in datasheet view, to set a visual effect for cells, the default column width, and font properties.

Object Designers

In the next four chapters, you'll learn details about building tables, forms, queries, and reports. The options in the Option Designers category let you specify default settings for the tools you use to build these database objects. For example, you can specify the default field type for tables and the default setting for data type for number fields. For queries, you can choose whether to display table names when you design a query. For forms and reports, you can set an option for how Access recognizes when multiple objects are selected—whether you need to drag to fully enclose all the objects or partially enclose the objects you want to select. Use the options under Error Checking In Form And Report Design View to specify which types of errors you want Access to check for. For example, Access can check for any labels on a report or a form that are not associated with a control (such as a text box) that is linked to a database field.

Proofing

Use this page to specify which corrections Access makes automatically when you enter text and to set options for how spelling is corrected throughout Microsoft Office. The AutoCorrect dialog box includes an option to have Access always capitalize the first word of a sentence, for example (an option you might be familiar with in working with Microsoft Word). Some of these options apply less often in Access than they do in Word (for example) because you generally don't type as much text. Experiment with these options and fine-tune them as you continue working in Access.

Language

Use this page to set options to specify language-specific options for dictionaries, grammar checking, and sorting. You can also choose a language for the display and Help system.

Client Settings

The options on this page control the behavior of the Access client (a desktop database rather than a web database) when you enter and edit data. For example, you can choose whether Access should display a message to confirm changes to database records and whether Access should select the entire field when you select that field. You can also control whether the arrow key moves to the next field or the next character, specify margins for printing, and specify whether Access opens the database that was used last when it starts.

Add-Ins

On the Add-Ins page, you can see which (if any) add-ins are installed with your copy of Access. Use the Manage list at the bottom of this page to load an add-in you want to use.

Trust Center

The Trust Center page provides links to privacy statements and security information on Microsoft's website. Click Trust Center Settings on this page to open the Trust Center dialog box, in which you can set options for how Access responds when you open a database containing macros, add-ins, or ActiveX controls. For most users, the default settings for macros and ActiveX controls are suitable. (Access prompts or notifies you before enabling the controls or macros.) For add-ins, you can require that add-ins are signed by a trusted publisher or choose the option Disable All Application Add-Ins. As the Add-Ins page indicates, choosing the Disable All Application Add-Ins option can keep you from taking advantage of the features an add-in is designed to provide.

The Trust Center also provides pages that let you designate trusted locations, trusted documents, and trusted publishers. The following list describes each of these designations:

- A trusted location is a folder on your computer (or possibly on your network, although creating a trusted location on a network is not recommended) from which a database can be opened without Access applying Trust Center settings. Databases in these locations do not open in Protected Mode. When Access opens a database in Protected Mode, you see a security warning that requires you to click Enable Content before you can fully work with the database or run macros, for example. Access lists one trusted location by default. You can also add, modify, and remove trusted locations by using command buttons on the Trusted Locations pages.

- A trusted document is one for which you have enabled content. After you click Enable Content in the security warning, you won't see the warning the next time you open the database.

- A publisher is an individual or a company that develops a database that contains content such as a macro or an ActiveX control. As a step you take in enabling the content in these databases, you can designate the person or organization as a trusted publisher so that Access trusts the databases sent by this source in the future.

➤ **To set Access options**

1. Click File, Options.

2. In the **Access Options** dialog box, click the category you want to work with, and then specify the options you want to use.

Practice Tasks

The practice files for these tasks are located in the practice files folder for Microsoft Access 2010. You can save the results of these exercises in the same folder. Change the file name so that you don't overwrite the sample files. When you are done, try performing the following tasks:

- Create a database by using the Marketing Projects sample template that comes with Access 2010. Open the navigation pane, and browse through the objects provided by the template. Open several of the objects (double-click the object) to review the types of controls and layouts used in the objects.

- Open the database for exclusive use, and define a password for the database.

- Open the Access Options dialog box, and work with several of the options on the Current Database page. Enter an application title, for example. Specify a display form, and then close and reopen the database to see that Access displays this form automatically.

- Experiment with the editing options on the Client Settings page of the Access Options dialog box. Change these options and then see the effect of the changes on how you navigate in one of the template's tables.

- Run the Compact & Repair Database command.

- Save the database as a different template in the default location. Create your own category for the template as a step in saving it.

1.2 Configure the Navigation Pane

The navigation pane, which Access displays by default when you open a database, lists the tables, forms, queries, reports, and other objects that define the structure and operations of a database. To show or hide the navigation pane, click the arrow button at the top-right corner of the pane. (The ScreenTip that Access displays identifies this button as the Shutter Bar Open/Close Button.)

When you right-click an object in the navigation pane, the menu that appears lets you rename an object, delete an object, or take a number of other actions. In the navigation pane, you can group objects and also apply a filter to view the objects in a variety of ways—by type of object or by creation date, for example, or by using a category and group that you define.

> **See Also** The shortcut menu that appears when you right-click an object in the navigation pane includes commands such as Open, Design View, and Layout View (depending on the type of object). You'll learn more about opening database objects in different views in Chapters 2 through 5.

In the following sections, you'll learn about some of the steps you can perform from the navigation pane and how to set navigation pane options.

Renaming Objects

Consistency in the names you give to database objects can bring a professional touch to your database, but establishing and following naming guidelines also helps you and other users remain clear about the function of each object. As part of planning a database, you should settle on a convention for naming objects. You might use a set of prefixes, for example, to identify the type of database object (something like *tbl* for tables, *rpt* for reports, and *frm* for forms).

If you need to rename a database object, right-click the object in the navigation pane and choose Rename from the shortcut menu. Access highlights the object you select. Simply type the name you now want to use.

Keep in mind, however, that renaming a database object can affect a database in ways you don't intend. For example, if a form named EmployeeRatings uses a table named Employees as the source of its records, changing the name of the Employees table breaks the EmployeesRatings form because Access can't locate the object that provides the source of the form's records. To help manage this situation, Access provides a feature known as name AutoCorrect. With this feature enabled, when you rename an object that other objects depend on, Access can update the references to that object where they occur.

You enable and control options for name AutoCorrect for each database you create. For example, you can set an option so that name AutoCorrect creates a log of the changes it makes. To set these options, open the Access Options dialog box from the File tab, click the Current Database category, and then scroll down to the Name AutoCorrect Options area.

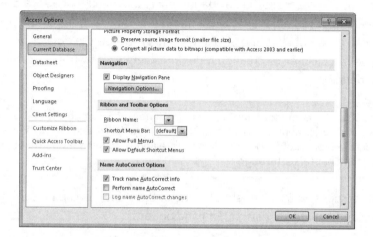

When you select the check box for Track Name AutoCorrect Info, Access displays a message that tells you it needs to generate name maps and that this operation might take several minutes. To continue enabling name AutoCorrect, click OK.

With the name AutoCorrect enabled, you can select the option Perform Name AutoCorrect to have Access use the name maps to update the name of an object when the object is renamed. Choose the Log Name AutoCorrect Changes option if you want Access to create a log showing the changes it makes. Access keeps track of the changes in a table it creates called Name AutoCorrect Log.

Viewing Object Dependencies

With name AutoCorrect enabled, Access creates and maintains maps showing the dependencies between database objects. You can view these dependencies by clicking Object Dependencies in the Relationships group on the Database Tools tab. In the pane that appears, you can view the objects that depend on the object selected in the navigation pane and the objects it depends on.

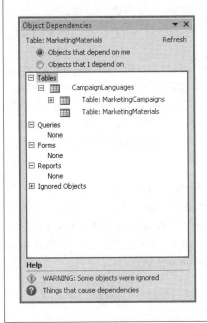

After Access creates the name maps, you can see which objects depend on others by choosing Object Dependencies on the Database Tools tab.

Tip Name AutoCorrect is not suitable for every situation because the feature does affect database performance to some degree and can also increase the size of a database. You might want to keep the option turned off for a database whose structure is unlikely to change or when you need to maintain a smaller file size.

Tip Name AutoCorrect also works at the level of fields and controls (such as text boxes).

➤ **To rename an object**

1. Display the navigation pane.

2. Right-click the object you need to rename, and then click **Rename**.

3. Type a new name for the object, and then click **OK**.

➤ **To enable and use name AutoCorrect**

1. Click **File**, **Options**.
2. In the **Access Options** dialog box, click **Current Database**, and then scroll to the **Name AutoCorrect Options** section.
3. Select the **Track name AutoCorrect Info** check box.
4. Select the **Perform Name AutoCorrect** check box.
5. Select the **Log name AutoCorrect changes** check box to maintain a log of changes.

Deleting Objects

In a database, especially in a relational database system such as Access, you need to take care before you delete an object. In fact, Access won't let you delete some objects without taking prior steps. For example, you can't delete a table that has a relationship with another table before you remove the relationship. Access prevents this action because deleting a table can produce orphan records—a book with no author, for example, or orders with no customer.

When you right-click an object in the navigation pane and choose Delete, Access displays a message prompting you to confirm that you want to delete the object. If you click Yes in this message, you'll see another message if the object you are deleting is related to another. In this message, Access prompts you to confirm that Access should delete the relationship and then delete the object.

Importing and Exporting Data from the Navigation Pane

Two of the other operations you can perform from the navigation pane are importing and exporting data. When you choose Import or Export from the shortcut menu, Access displays a list showing data formats such as XML File, SharePoint List, Text File, and others. When you import many formats, Access displays a Get External Data dialog box that contains fields in which you specify required information, such as the file name and location, whether you want to import the data to a new table or append records to the select object, or the name of a SharePoint site. In the Export dialog box, Access requires the destination where you want to save the data you are exporting, export options that control formatting and layout, and similar types of information. You can also use the commands on the External Data tab to import and export data.

> **See Also** For more information about importing data, see "Import Data from a Single Data File" in Chapter 2 in this part of the book.

Setting Options for the Navigation Pane

To change how database objects are grouped in the navigation pane, click the down arrow at the top of the pane to display a menu from which you can choose a built-in category (such as Object Type, Tables And Related Views, Created Date, and Modified Date). For each category, the Filter By Group area of the menu shows options you can apply to see a specific subset of objects. For example, if you select Modified Date under Navigate To Category, you can then choose Three Weeks Ago, Yesterday, Older, All Dates, or another option. For the Object Type category, you can view all objects or only objects of a specific type.

The Tables And Related Views category displays each table in the database together with the other database objects that depend on it. Use this view when you are making changes to a table's design. By choosing the Tables And Related Views category and then choosing a single table in the Filter By Group list, you can see which objects depend on the table, and you can review the design of those objects to be sure that any changes you make to the table don't affect the other objects in ways you don't intend.

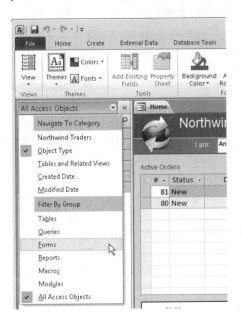

Use the Navigate To Category and Filter By Group lists in the navigation pane to organize and filter your view of objects. The Object Type category lets you see all objects or only objects of a single type.

> **Tip** If you right-click the title bar in the navigation pane, you display a menu from which you can choose a category, a sort order, and the view options Details, Icon, and List. The Details option shows each object's created and modified dates (which the List option does not). Icon view uses icons that represent each object type. You can use the search box at the top of the navigation pane to locate a particular object (or group of objects) by name. As you type a text string, Access filters the list of objects and displays those that match. Click the Clear Search String button at the right side of the search box to return the navigation pane to its full view.

In new databases you create, Access also provides a category called Custom. You can use this category to begin setting up categories and groups of your own and then assign objects to those groups.

> **Tip** Some of the database templates that come with Access also provide additional categories for viewing database objects in the navigation pane. For example, the Marketing Projects template provides a category called Marketing Projects Navigation, which lets you filter by groups such as Projects, Deliverables, Vendors, and Employees.

To set up categories and groups of your own, right-click the navigation pane's title bar and choose Navigation Options. (You can open the same dialog box from the Current Database page of the Access Options dialog box.)

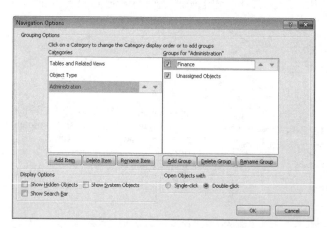

Select a category to see which groups it contains. Clear the check box for a group to hide it. You can begin to define a new category by renaming the built-in Custom entry.

The categories defined for the database appear in the list at the left, and each group defined for a category appears in the list at the right. If you want to hide a group from being displayed in the navigation pane, clear the check box for that group. Use the check boxes in the Display Options area of the dialog box to indicate whether you want to show hidden and system objects in the navigation pane and to show or hide the search bar. The options under Open Objects With let you control whether an object opens when it is single-clicked (like a hyperlink) or double-clicked in the navigation pane.

To modify the built-in Custom category, select it in the Categories list, click Rename Item, and then type a name for the category. In the Groups For "Custom" list, you'll see two groups—Custom Group 1 (a built-in group that contains no database objects) and Unassigned Objects, which is a built-in group that contains all objects in the database. To create your first group for the renamed Custom category, select Custom Group 1, click Rename Group, and then type a name for the group. To create additional groups for this category, click Add Group. When you finish defining categories and groups, click OK in the Navigation Options dialog box.

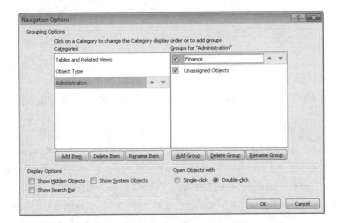

This view of the Navigation Options dialog box shows a new category (Administration) and a new group (Finance) for that category.

> **Tip** You can reposition a custom category or group by using the up and down arrows that appear beside an item's name. You can also delete or rename custom categories and groups. You cannot place a custom category above the two built-in categories or place a custom group below the built-in group Unassigned Objects.

To add database objects to a group in a custom category, select the category from the Navigate To Category list in the navigation pane menu. In the Unassigned Objects list, right-click an object you want to add to a new group (use the Ctrl key to select more than one object), choose Add To Group from the shortcut menu, and then select the group you want to add the object or objects to.

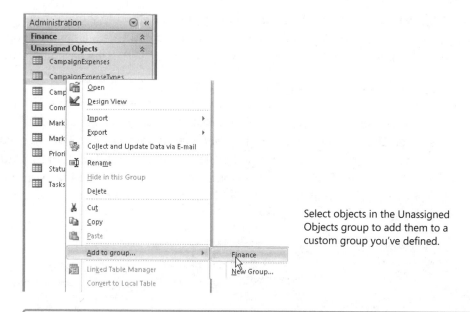

Select objects in the Unassigned Objects group to add them to a custom group you've defined.

> **Tip** You can also drag an object from the Unassigned Objects group to the group where you want to place it.

When you add a database object to a custom group, you add only a shortcut to that object, not the object itself. (This means that you can delete a shortcut from a custom group without deleting the database object itself.) When you right-click an object in a custom group, you can use the Rename Shortcut command to assign a different name to the shortcut. Use the Hide In This Group command to hide the object, and use the Remove command to remove the object from the group. After you have assigned all the unassigned objects to a navigation pane group, you can return to the Navigation Options dialog box and clear the check box for Unassigned Objects to hide it. You can also right-click the Unassigned Objects heading in the navigation pane and choose Hide.

Practice Tasks

The practice files for these tasks are located in the practice files folder for Microsoft Access 2010. You can save the results of these exercises in the same folder. Change the file name so that you don't overwrite the sample files. When you are done, try performing the following tasks:

- Open the database file Hello_World.accdb from the practice files folder.
- Open the Access Options dialog box, and enable name AutoCorrect. Select the option to have Access log changes.

- Display the Object Dependencies pane to view the dependencies for one or more of the database objects. Rename the table RenameTest to Events. Open the log table and see that Access updated the table's name in the forms that depend on it.
- Practice filtering, sorting, and changing the view of the database objects in the navigation pane.
- Use the Navigation Options dialog box to create a new category called Administration and a new group called Finance. Add the CampaignExpenses and CampaignExpenseTypes tables to the Finance group.

1.3 Use Application Parts

One of the ways in which you can incorporate features into a database is by adding an application part. An application part can be a single form (which is not yet bound to the records in any table or query) or a set of database objects (a table or two and related forms and reports, for example). You can also create and save one or more database objects as an application part to make them available in other databases. For example, you might format a form in a way that you want to use in other databases. By saving this form as an application part, you can insert it in any database where you need it.

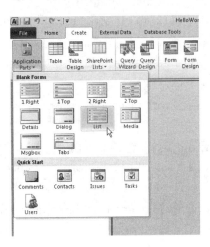

Use the Application Parts gallery to insert a blank form or a collection of objects (listed under Quick Start) to a database.

Insert a Blank Form

The blank forms that Access provides as application parts serve as a starting point for designing a form. Each form comes with basic command button controls and design elements (a title, for example, and placeholders for fields and labels) that you build on to complete the design and layout of the form. The command buttons that appear on application part forms are already programmed to perform certain actions. For example, the Dialog form you can insert from the Application Parts gallery comes with a Save button and a Save & Close button. By default, the Save button is designed to save a database record you add by using the form. The Save & Close button saves a record and then closes the form. (You can replace the default action performed by a command button by assigning a different macro to the button's OnClick event.)

> **See Also** For detailed information about creating a form, including how to work in Design view and Layout view, see Chapter 3, "Building Forms," later in this section of the book.

You can choose from 10 types of built-in blank forms. (Access displays a ScreenTip that briefly describes each blank form's layout and design).

- Single-column forms (with labels to the right of the field names or above the field names).

- Two-column forms (with labels to the right of the field names or above the field names).

- A details form, which is a single record form with a subform that shows detailed records related to the record displayed in the main form.

- A dialog form you can design as a dialog box that can be used to confirm operations (such as saving a record) and perform other database operations.

- List form, which displays multiple items in a list format. The command buttons that come with this form are set up to let you create a new record, edit a record, and delete a record.

- Media form, which displays a single record with placeholders for media objects such as images or videos.

- MsgBox form, which is used to display messages to users of a database. This form comes with Yes, No, and Cancel buttons. You can use this form to let users confirm actions.

- Tab form, which presents a form on which you define tabs (or pages) to present and manage a set of related data.

When you click the type of form you want to insert in a database, Access prepares the template and then adds an entry for the form to the navigation pane. (If the navigation pane is filtered so that forms are not displayed, you need to change the filter to see the form Access inserted.) To view the form, right-click the entry for the form in the navigation pane and choose Open. This lets you see what the basic form looks like, but the form is not operational at this point.

This example shows the basic layout and command buttons that come with a form inserted as an application part.

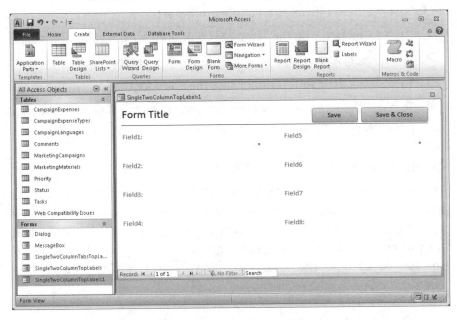

> **Tip** Application part forms that you add to a database use a control layout so that all the controls move and resize together. You'll learn more about working with a control layout in Chapter 3.

To start designing the form, right-click the entry and choose Layout View or Design View. To specify a record source for the form (the table or query that includes the records you want to display and work with in the form), click Property Sheet in the Tools group on the Form Design Tools Design tab. On the Property Sheet's Data tab, open the list for the Record Source property, and then choose a table or query. To add fields to the form, click Add Existing Fields in the Tools group and then click Show All Tables in the Field list. (Of course, you can't assign a record source to a form until you have defined at least one table in the database.)

> **See Also** For more details about defining a record source for a form and adding fields, see Chapter 3.

> **See Also** When you click the ellipsis beside the Record Source property, you launch the Query Builder. You'll learn more about building queries in Chapter 4, "Creating and Managing Queries" later in this section of the book.

> ### To insert a blank form as an application part

1. On the **Create** tab, in the **Templates** group, click **Application Parts**.
2. In the **Application Parts** gallery, click the type of form you want to add.
3. To view the basic form, double-click the entry for the form in the navigation pane.
4. To name the form, right-click the entry for the form in the navigation pane, choose **Rename**, and then type a name for the form.

Using Quick Start Elements

The Quick Start group in the Application Parts gallery provides a comments table and four compound application parts for managing contacts, issues, tasks, and users. You can apply these application parts to many types of databases. The ScreenTip that Access displays when you point to an item in this group tells you which objects the application part contains. For example, the Issues application part inserts a table (named Issues) plus two forms (Issue Details and Issues New).

Quick Start application parts provide objects such as tables and forms.

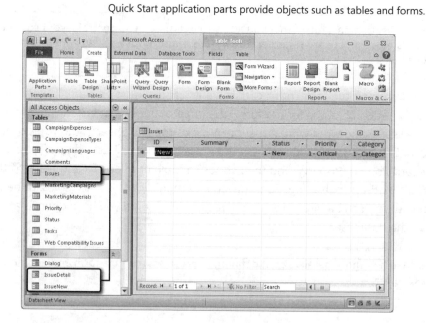

When you add a Quick Start application part to a database that already includes tables, Access displays the Create Relationship Wizard. The first page in the wizard displays two options for creating a relationship and a third option to insert the table without creating a relationship with another table in the database. (You can choose the option There Is No Relationship in the wizard and set up a relationship later as necessary.)

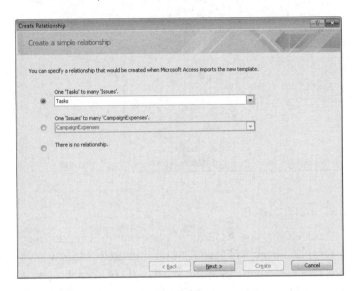

The first two options let you set up a one-to-many relationship between a table already in the database (One 'Tasks' To Many 'Issues') or a one-to-many relationship between the table you are adding (Issues in this example) and an existing table. A one-to-many relationship occurs when a record in one table can be related to many records in another table. The classic example is the relationship between customers and orders. Each customer record in a database is unique, but each customer record can be related to all the orders placed by the customer (the many side of the relationship). In this example, many issues can be related to one task.

When you click Next, the Create Relationship Wizard displays a page on which you specify the field from the table on the "one side" of the relationship that Access uses to create a relationship with the table on the "many side." In the issues and tasks example, you would select a field such as TaskID so that you could associate each issue with a task in the Issues table. Access adds the field you specify to the table on the many side of the relationship, creating a lookup column in that table. In the text box labeled What Name Would You Like For Your Lookup Column, type a name for that column. When you click Create in the wizard, Access adds the table and other objects defined by the application part.

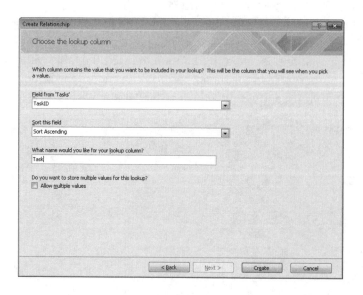

Applying a User Template

The section "Using the Save Database As Option" earlier in this chapter describes how to save a database as a template from the Save & Publish page in Backstage view. As a step in creating a template, you can create an application part. The objects you save appear in the Application Parts gallery under the heading User Templates by default. You can define a different category when you save the template.

To begin, you need to design the tables, queries, forms, reports, and supporting objects that you want to include in the application part. You'll learn the details for designing each type of object in Chapters 2 through 5 in this section of the book.

When you have set up the objects (you can include data in the tables if you want to), click Save & Publish on the File tab. Click Save Database As, and then double-click Template in the Database File Types area. Access opens the Create New Template From This Database dialog box.

Type a name and description for the template. In the Category list, leave User Templates selected or type the name for a category you want to create. If you want to include an icon for the template, select the image file by using the browse button. To associate a preview image with the template, click the browse button and locate the image file you want to use.

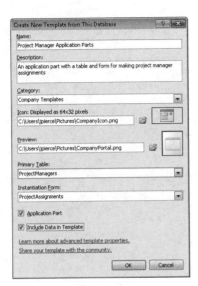

If you have at least one table in the application part, Access displays the Create Relationship Wizard when you add the application part to an existing database. Use the Primary Table option, which is enabled when you select Application Part, to specify which table to use as the default option in the Create Relationship Wizard.

> **Important** Use the Instantiation Form option when you want to display a splash screen or a form that performs a startup routine. Access displays the form you select in this option only once and then deletes the form. You should be careful not to confuse this option with a startup form, which you can specify for the current database by using the Access Options dialog box.

Select Include Data In Template to keep any data already stored in the database. (The Include Data In Template option might be useful if you are creating your own Contacts application part, for example, in which you define a Contacts table that identifies individuals or organizations who will act as contacts for more than one database.) When you click OK in the dialog box, Access displays a message telling you where the template has been saved.

Now, when you or another user displays the Application Parts gallery, the templates you saved are available to insert in other databases.

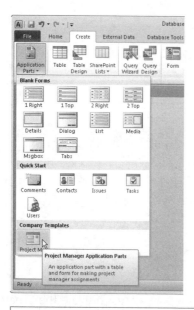

You can save a form or a small database as an application part and define your own category. These application parts appear at the bottom of the Application Parts gallery.

Practice Tasks

No practice files are required for this set of practice tasks. Open Access 2010 on your computer, and then follow these steps:

- On the New page in Backstage view, create a new blank database. Name the database ApplicationPartsTest.accdb.

- Using the Application Parts gallery, insert a blank dialog form and a blank message box (MsgBox) form. Also insert the Comments table from the Quick Start section of the gallery.

- Open the forms and table to review their basic layout and design.

- Save this combination of database objects as your own application part. When you create the application part, define a category called My App Parts to contain the application parts you design.

Objective Review

Before finishing this chapter, be sure you have mastered the following skills:

1.1   Create and manage a database

1.2   Configure the navigation pane

1.3   Use application parts

2 Building Tables

The skills tested in this section of the Microsoft Office Specialist exam for Microsoft Access 2010 relate to building tables. Specifically, the following objectives are associated with this set of skills:

2.1 Create tables in Design view

2.2 Create and modify fields

2.3 Sort and filter records

2.4 Set relationships

2.5 Import data from a single data file

2.1 Create Tables in Design View

When you create a blank database, Microsoft Access 2010 inserts a table (named Table1 by default) and displays that table in Datasheet view. Datasheet view resembles a worksheet in Microsoft Excel by presenting a grid of cells in columns and rows. Each column represents a field, and each row represents a record in the table. Access also adds a default ID field and inserts a unique number when you enter data in a row to identify that record. To refine the design of the table as you work in Datasheet view, you can enter field names, and on the basis of the type of data you add to a column, Access assigns a data type to that field.

By building a table in Datasheet view, you begin to identify the structure of a database as you compile the data you want to store and manage. A different approach is to define the structure of a table as your starting point, and to accomplish this you work with a table in Design view.

In this section, you'll learn about the steps you take to create a table in Design view and about working with commands on the Table Tools Design tab.

> **See Also** For information about using an application part to insert a table in a database, see "Using Quick Start Elements" in Chapter 1, "Using the Access Workspace," in this part of the book.

Getting Started

With a database open, click the Create tab and then click Table Design to open a new table in Design view. In this view, you work with three main columns: Field Name, Data Type, and Description. For each field you define, you must provide information in the first two columns. Adding information to the Description column is optional, but describing each field in a table is an effective way to start documenting your database. Adding a concise explanation in the Description column also assists users of the database because Access displays this description in the status bar when the field is selected in Datasheet view or in a form.

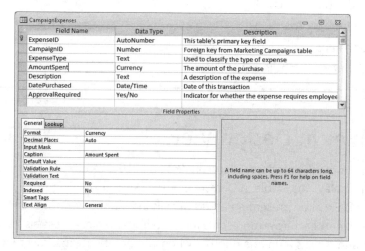

When you work in Design view, refer to the explanatory text that Access provides in the lower-right corner of the window.

To start defining a field, click in a row in the Field Name column and type the field's name. You can press Tab to move the cursor to the Data Type column, or click in that column to display a drop-down arrow that displays the list of data types. Use one of the items in this list to assign a data type to the fields in the table:

- **Text** Use the Text data type for simple text fields such as contact or project names or for fields such as street addresses and postal codes, which include numbers that aren't used in mathematical operations. You can store as many as 255 characters in a text field, but you can also set the Field Size property to specify a length shorter than the limit.

> **See Also** For more information about field properties, see "Setting and Updating Field Properties" later in this chapter.

- **Memo** The Memo data type is designed for fields in which you want to store large blocks of text. You can store approximately 1 gigabyte of alphanumeric data in a memo field, but not all that data will be displayed on a form or in a control on a report.

- **Number** Use the Number field to store numeric data. You can choose between various field sizes, including Byte, Integer, Long Integer, and Decimal. You should choose a field size according to the size and kind of numbers you will store in the field:

  - **Byte** A 1-byte integer containing values from 0 through 255.

  - **Integer** A 2-byte integer containing values from −32,768 through 32,767.

  - **Long Integer** A 4-byte integer containing values from −2,147,483,648 through 2,147,483,647.

  - **Single** A 4-byte, floating-point number containing values from -3.4×10^{38} through 3.4×10^{38} and up to seven significant digits.

  - **Double** An 8-byte, floating-point number containing values from -1.797×10^{308} through 1.797×10^{308} and up to 15 significant digits.

  - **Replication ID** A 16-byte globally unique identifier (GUID).

  - **Decimal** A 12-byte integer with a specified decimal precision that can contain values from approximately -9.999×10^{27} through 9.999×10^{27}. The default precision (number of decimal places) is 0, and the default scale is 18.

- **Date/Time** Designed to store dates and times. You can choose formats such as Short Date (3/08/2012) and Long Date (Monday, May 23, 2011). You can perform calculations on the data in date/time fields to determine the interval between two dates, for example.

- **Currency** Use this data type for monetary values. You can specify formats that include up to four decimal places.

- **AutoNumber** Use AutoNumber for fields for which you want Access to generate a unique identifying number. A table can have only one AutoNumber field. An AutoNumber field is often used as a table's primary key, which is a field or combination of fields that uniquely identifies each record in a table.

> **See Also** For information about setting a table's primary key, see "Specifying a Primary Key" later in this chapter.

- **Yes/No** Designed for fields whose value is true or false. In yes/no fields, Access stores a 1 for true (yes) or a 0 for false (no).

- **OLE Object** An OLE object field is used to store objects such as pictures or charts created in another Microsoft Windows–based application.

- **Hyperlink** Use the Hyperlink data type for fields in which you want to store the address for a site on the web or an intranet or the path to a file on a network or the local computer.

- **Attachment** By applying the Attachment data type, you create a field in which you can store documents, spreadsheets, presentations, and other file types. You can include an unlimited number of attachments per record, although you are restricted by the limitation on the overall size of an Access database, which cannot exceed 2 gigabytes.

- **Calculated** Use the Calculated data type for a field in which you define an expression that uses data from one or more other fields. Calculated fields include a Result Type property that lets you specify the data type for the result of the calculation.

- **Lookup Wizard** Use the Lookup Wizard entry in the Data Type list to create a lookup field. A lookup field uses values from a related table or from a list you define. You can create a complex lookup field to store more than one value of the same data type in each record. (See the next section for more information.)

> **Important** You cannot use the Attachment or Calculated data types in Access databases stored in the .mdb format. These data types are available only in the .accdb format.

> **See Also** To learn more about working with fields, see "Inserting, Deleting, and Renaming Fields" later in this chapter.

➤ **To create a table in Design view**

1. On the **Create** tab, click **Table Design**.
2. In the **Field Name** column, type the name for the table's first field.
3. In the **Data Type** column, select the data type for the field.
4. In the **Description** column, type a description for the field.
5. On the Quick Access Toolbar, click **Save**.
6. In the **Save As** dialog box, type a name for the table.
7. In the message box about the table's primary key, click **Yes** to have Access create a primary key, or click **No** to save the table without creating a primary key.

Creating a Lookup Field

You use a lookup field in a table to get values from another table or a query or from a list that you define. When you select Lookup Wizard in the Data Type list, Access starts the wizard, and your first decision is to specify the source of the lookup field's values.

If you choose the option to get values from another table or a query, you specify the object and then select the field or fields that contain the values you want to use. The wizard next provides a page in which you can specify a sort order, and on the next page you are given the option to hide the key field from the lookup table. On the last page of the wizard, you name the field and click Finish. Access adds the field to the table and creates a relationship between the table you are working with and the source table for the lookup field.

The process is similar when you specify a list yourself. Select that option when Access displays the wizard, and then specify the number of columns and the values you want to use. Name the field, and click Finish.

You can make adjustments to a lookup field and set lookup properties when a table is open in Design view. In the Field Properties area, click the Lookup tab. In the Display Control property, you can choose between using a text box, a list box, or a combo box control. For list boxes and combo boxes, the Row Source Type property determines the source of the lookup—a table or query, field list, or list of values that you provide. The Row Source property shows the table or query you are using. If you are building a list of your own, you can enter the values here (or when you use the Lookup Wizard).

Among the other properties you can set for a combo box lookup field is Limit To List. If you set this to No, users of the database can enter new values in the field. Set the Allow Multiple Values property to Yes if you want users to be able to specify more than one value for the lookup field. Use the Allow Value List Edits property to control whether users can make changes to the list of values defined for the lookup field.

➤ To create a lookup field from another table or query

1. Open the table in Design view.
2. Type the field name in the **Field Name** column, and then click **Lookup Wizard** in the **Data Type** list.
3. In the Lookup Wizard, select the option to get values from another table or query.
4. Click **Next**, and then select the table or query you want to use.
5. On the next page, select the field or fields to use in the lookup field.
6. On the next page, specify a sorting order. (This step is optional.)

7. On the next page, specify how you want the columns in the field to appear. Keep the option to hide the key column if doing so is appropriate.

8. Click **Next**, type a name for the field, and then click **Finish**.

➤ To create a lookup field from a list

1. Open the table in Design view.

2. Type the field name in the **Field Name** column, and then click **Lookup Wizard** in the **Data Type** list.

3. In the Lookup Wizard, select the option **I will type in the values that I want**.

4. Click **Next**, and then enter the values for the lookup list.

5. Click **Next**, type a name for the field, and then click **Finish**.

Setting Table Properties

As you can with fields, you can set properties for tables. For example, you can use table properties to describe the table, specify a default view, apply a filter or a sort order, or define a validation rule. Click Property Sheet in the Show/Hide group on the Table Tools Design tab to work with table properties.

Use the Description property to document the purpose of the table. In the Default View property, you can select Datasheet, PivotTable, or PivotChart. Use the Filter property to define criteria that filters the display of the data. Set the Filter On Load property to Yes to apply this filter when you open the table in Datasheet view. Set the Order By On Load property to Yes to sort records when you display the table in Datasheet view.

> **See Also** The Filter and Order By properties are set for tables when you apply a sort order or a filter in Datasheet view and then save the table. You'll learn more details later in this chapter in "Sort and Filter Records."

The Orientation property specifies whether data is read left to right (the default setting for most versions of Access) or right to left (the setting used in languages that are read right to left). The Read Only When Disconnected property (not shown in the preceding screen shot) relates to working with data from a Microsoft SharePoint site. If this property is set to No, you can still insert and update records in a table linked to a site when you are working offline.

> **Tip** You can set the Order By, Filter By, Orientation, and Read Only When Disconnected properties for a table that is open in Datasheet view by clicking Table Properties on the Table Tools Table tab.

Creating a Table Validation Rule

You can use a table validation rule to compare values in fields. Access checks table validation rules when you save a record or insert a new row. You can also use the Test Validation Rules command on the Table Tools Design tab to check valid data.

> **See Also** As Access indicates in the message it displays when you click Test Validation Rules, this command tests table and field validation rules as well as the field properties Required and AllowZeroLength. You'll learn more about field validation rules and field properties in "Setting and Updating Field Properties" later in this chapter.

To specify a validation rule for a table, click in the Validation Rule box in the table's property sheet and then write the expression for the rule. For example, the expression *[EndDate]>=([LaunchDate]+30)* compares the values in the EndDate and LaunchDate fields and requires that the value for EndDate be at least 30 days later than the value for LaunchDate.

With this validation rule in place, Access displays an error message if an invalid date has been entered in the EndDate field when you save the record. You can customize the information displayed in the error message by typing your own message in the Validation Text property.

Introducing Expressions

You use expressions in many areas of Access—to define validation rules, to specify query or filter criteria, to define a calculated field, to calculate values, and as part of other operations. An expression includes elements such as a function (for example, *Sum()* or *Now()*), operators (such as +, *, and >=), constants (a city name, for example, or a numerical constant), and identifiers, which point to database objects and fields. Identifiers include a reference to the type of object, the object itself, and a field—for example, *Forms![Tasks]![TaskDescription]*. In Chapter 4, "Creating and Managing Queries," you can learn more about working with expressions and with the Expression Builder.

Inserting a Subdatasheet

Several table properties are related to the use of subdatasheets. A subdatasheet is a feature that lets you see information from a related table while you are viewing a main table in Datasheet view. For example, in a Customers table you could insert a subdatasheet that shows records from the Orders table.

Use the plus and minus signs to expand and collapse the subdatasheet's records.

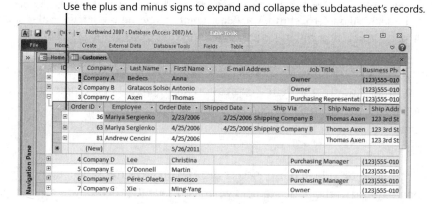

To set up a subdatasheet, specify the related table properties as follows:

- **Subdatasheet Name** The Auto setting specifies a subdatasheet using the first table with which this table has a "many" relationship—for example, many orders are associated with one customer. Specify None to include no subdatasheet, or choose a table or query from the list displayed in the property sheet to insert a subdatasheet from a specific table or query.

> **See Also** For more information about the types of table relationships, see "Setting Relationships" later in this chapter.

- **Link Child Fields** Identifies the field or fields in the subdatasheet that are used to create a relationship with the main table.

- **Link Master Fields** Identifies the field or fields in the main table that are used to create a relationship with the subdatasheet table.

- **Subdatasheet Height** Set this property to zero inches (0") to show all related records from the subdatasheet. Set the property to a particular height in inches to control the subdatasheet display.

- **Subdatasheet Expanded** Set this property to Yes to expand the subdatasheet records for all records in the main table when you open the main table in Datasheet view.

➤ To set table properties

1. In the navigation pane, right-click the table and choose **Design View**.
2. On the **Table Tools Design** tab, in the **Show/Hide** group, click **Property Sheet** (if the property sheet is not already displayed).
3. Click in the box for the property you want to set, and then type the setting for the property or choose a setting from the list Access provides.

➤ To define a table validation rule

1. In the navigation pane, right-click the table and choose **Design View**.
2. On the **Table Tools Design** tab, in the **Show/Hide** group, click **Property Sheet** (if the property sheet is not already displayed).
3. In the property sheet, click in the **Validation Rule** property.
4. Type the expression for the validation rule, or click the ellipsis button to open the Expression Builder.
5. After you define the expression, click in the **Validation Text** property and type the text for the message Access displays when it detects invalid data.

➤ To set up a subdatasheet

1. In the navigation pane, right-click the table and choose **Design View**.
2. On the **Table Tools Design** tab, in the **Show/Hide** group, click **Property Sheet** (if the property sheet is not already displayed).
3. Click in the **Subdatasheet Name** property, and then choose the table whose records you want to display in the subdatasheet.
4. In the **Link Child Fields** property, choose the field that links the subdatasheet to the main table.
5. In the **Link Master Fields** property, choose the field that links the main table to the subdatasheet.
6. In the **Subdatasheet Height** property, specify the height for the subdatasheet records (or keep the default value of 0").
7. In the **Subdatasheet Expanded** property, select **Yes** if you want to expand all the records in the subdatasheet when you open the main table in Datasheet view.

Defining Indexes

Indexes help Access efficiently search through the records in a database. When an index is set up, Access searches an internal table that stores values for indexed fields with a pointer to the location of the record where those values are stored. Access uses the index to find a record you need without having to search all the records in the database.

You should index fields that you expect to use regularly to specify criteria in queries, for example—fields such as LastName or Company for contacts or the ProductName field in a database that tracks orders. You can create an index for a single field by setting the Indexed property on the General tab of the Field Properties area when a table is open in Design view. Choose Yes (Duplicates OK) to create an index for a field that can include duplicate values (a field such as City, Country, or LastName, for example). The other choice, Yes (No Duplicates), applies to fields like a primary key field in which only unique values can be stored.

> **Tip** Access automatically creates an index for a table's primary key field.

You can also create indexes based on multiple fields. You should consider creating a multiple-field index when you search frequently using criteria for more than one field—for example, product name and store location. To create a multiple-field index, open the table in Design view and then click Indexes in the Show/Hide group on the Table Tools Design tab. In the Indexes window, type a name for the index in the first blank row. In the Field Name column, select the fields you want to include in that index. Use the Sort Order column to specify how you want Access to sort the records in this index.

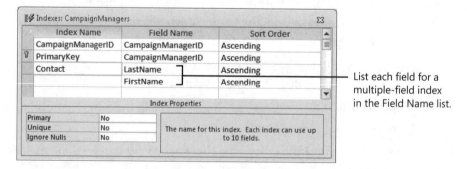

List each field for a multiple-field index in the Field Name list.

When you set up an index, Access displays the Index Properties area of the window. Unless you are creating an index for the primary key, keep the Primary property set to No. In the Unique property, choose Yes or No depending on whether each value in the fields in this index must be unique. In most cases, you can keep the Unique property set to No. For the Ignore Nulls property, choose Yes if you want Access to exclude records with a null value from this index. (A null value indicates that data is missing in a field because it hasn't been entered or doesn't apply. A null value is not the same as the value zero or a zero-length string—a text string with zero characters.)

➤ **To create a single-field index**

1. In the navigation pane, right-click the table and choose **Design View**.

2. Select the field you want to create an index for.

3. In the **Field Properties** area, set the **Indexed** property to **Yes (No Duplicates)** or **Yes (Duplicates OK)**.

➤ **To create a multiple-field index**

1. In the navigation pane, right-click the table and choose **Design View**.

2. In the **Show/Hide** group on the **Table Tools Design** tab, click **Indexes**.

3. In the **Indexes** window, in the first blank row, type a name for the index in the **Index Name** column.

4. In the **Field Name** column, select the first field to include in the index.

5. In the next blank row in the **Field Name** column, select the next field to include in the index.

6. In the **Index Properties** area, set the **Primary**, **Unique**, and **Ignore Nulls** properties to the values required for this index.

7. In the **Sort Order** column, specify whether to sort a field in ascending or descending order.

Creating a Data Macro

You can use macros throughout Access to help automate and maintain your database. After you become familiar with Access, you might want to define a data macro (a feature new in Access 2010) that is linked to an event such as inserting, updating, or deleting a record in a table. On the Create Data Macros menu, you can choose from the events After Insert, After Update, After Delete, Before Delete, and Before Change.

When you create a macro, you specify one or more actions that the macro executes. For a data macro, you can choose from actions such as CreateRecord, EditRecord, LogEvent, and SendEmail. For example, you could use the SendEmail action with the After Update event to notify users of a database that the value in a specific field has changed.

To create such a macro, open the table in Design view, click Create Data Macros, and then select After Update. Access Opens the macro designer and displays the Macro Tools Design tab. From the Add New Action list, select SendEmail. Use the To, Cc, Bcc, Subject, and Body fields that Access displays to specify the recipients of the e-mail message, add a subject line, and provide any elaboration or instructions required in the message's body. Right-click in the area that defines the action (where the e-mail message fields are displayed), and choose Make If Block.

In the macro designer, use an If block to specify conditions.
Define macro actions by using the Add New Action list.

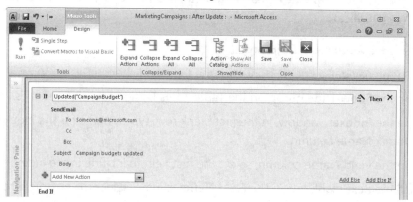

To fine-tune this macro so that it runs only if the value of a certain field is updated, in the If box, type **Updated** (one of the functions built in to Access) and then the field's name within parentheses and enclosed in quotation marks—*Updated("CampaignBudget")* in this example. Click Save, and then click Close to return to table Design view. You can test this data macro by addressing the e-mail message to yourself, opening the table in Datasheet view, and then making a change to the field you specified. If the macro is set up correctly, you might see a message indicating that a program is trying to send an e-mail message and prompting you to allow the operation.

> **Tip** You can define a data macro for a table when the table is open in Datasheet view by using the event commands on the Table Tools Table tab.

> ### To create a data macro for a table
>
> 1. In the navigation pane, right-click the table and choose **Design View**.
> 2. In the **Field**, **Record & Table Events** group on the **Table Tools Design** tab, click **Create Data Macros**, and then select the event you want to use.

3. In the macro designer, select a macro action from the **Add New Action** list.

4. To add an If block in which to specify a condition, right-click the shaded action area and choose **Make If Block**.

5. Define an expression for the If condition.

6. Save the macro, and then click **Close** to return to table Design view.

Practice Tasks

The practice files for these tasks are located in the practice files folder for Microsoft Access 2010. You can save the results of these exercises in the same folder. Change the file name so that you don't overwrite the sample files. When you are done, try performing the following tasks:

- Open the file Hello_World_ch2.accdb. In Design view, create a table named Tasks with the following fields:

Field	Data Type
TaskID	AutoNumber
TaskName	Text
Description	Memo
Status	Number
StartDate	Date/Time
DueDate	Date/Time
DateCompleted	Date/Time
AssignedBy	Number
AssignedTo	Number

Create a table validation rule that requires the DueDate field to be greater than the StartDate field.

- Use the Lookup Wizard to create a lookup field that links the Status field to the Status table.

- Create a multiple-field index for the fields DueDate and DateCompleted.

2.2   Create and Modify Fields

In the previous section, you learned about table Design view and the different areas of the Design view window that you work with to create a table. You also learned some of what you can do using commands on the Table Tools Design tab. In this section, you'll learn details about managing and viewing fields in a table. You'll also learn more about setting and updating field properties.

You can accomplish many of the tasks described in this section with the table open in Design view or in Datasheet view. We'll cover how to perform the tasks in both views.

Inserting, Deleting, and Renaming Fields

As a step in creating a database—before actually creating tables, forms, and other database objects in Access—you should define which tables you need, how those tables are related, which fields each table requires, and the names of fields. Knowing details such as these makes the process of building database objects more efficient. However, when you need to make adjustments when you are designing a table or after a table contains data, you can work with ribbon commands and shortcut menus to insert new fields or modify ones already defined in a table.

Working with Fields in Datasheet View

When a table is open in Datasheet view, you can work with commands in the Add & Delete group on the Table Tools Fields tab to insert and delete fields. A field you insert is added to the right of the field selected in the table.

The Add & Delete group provides commands that correspond to Access field data types. The Text, Number, Currency, Date/Time, and Yes/No data types appear on their own command buttons. You can insert a field and apply a specific data type by clicking one of these commands. Click the More Fields button to open a menu from which you can choose from other data types—including Attachment, Hyperlink, and Memo—and a variety of formats for number and date and time data types.

Near the bottom of the More Fields list is a group of Quick Start items. These Quick Start items contain one or more fields that are assigned appropriate data types. You can add Quick Start items (also known as *data type application parts*) to a table to start defining the fields the table should contain.

Quick Start data types provide more than field names. Many field properties are already set so that you can start using the fields to capture data without doing additional work.

For example, choose the Address Quick Start to add the fields Address, City, State Province, ZIP Postal, and Country Region. (You can rename the fields to fit them to your particular database.) The Payment Type Quick Start inserts a lookup field that includes the list Cash, Credit Card, Check, and In-Kind.

You can create your own Quick Start data types by selecting the field or fields you want to use and then choosing Save Selection As New Data Type at the bottom of the More Fields list. In the Create New Data Types From Fields dialog box, type a name and a description for the new data type and then choose a category (or enter a new category name).

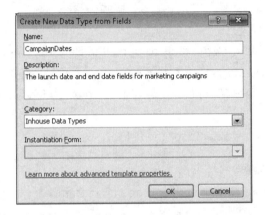

> **Tip** Data types you create are stored in the default location for Access database templates, using the file name extension .accft. You can share these files so that colleagues and coworkers can also work with the data types you create.

Another way to insert and manage fields in Datasheet view is with the shortcut menu that appears when you right-click one of the table's column headings. This menu includes an Insert Field command, and when you choose Insert Field, Access adds a column to the table to the left of the column heading you clicked. To define the data type for a field you insert from the shortcut menu, you can type a value in the field that Access uses to apply a data type, or you can use the Data Type list in the Formatting group on the Table Tools Fields tab to select the data type and format you want to apply to this field. The controls that are available in this group depend on the data type you select.

> **Tip** You can also insert a field in a table that's open in Datasheet view by clicking in the Click To Add column, which is displayed after all the columns already defined for the table.

To rename a field, double-click the column heading for the field, or right-click the heading and then choose Rename Field.

> **See Also** For information about the name AutoCorrect feature and renaming database objects, see "Renaming Objects" in Chapter 1 in this section of the book.

To delete a field from a table in Datasheet view, click the Delete button in the Add & Delete group, or right-click a field's column heading and choose Delete Field. Keep in mind that Access prevents you from deleting a field that is part of a relationship and displays a message box informing you that you must delete the relationship first.

➤ To insert a field in Datasheet view

1. In the navigation pane, double-click the table to open it in Datasheet view.

2. On the **Table Tools Fields** tab, in the **Add & Delete** group, click the data type for the field you want to insert. Click **More Fields** to display an extended list of data types.

3. In the column heading row, type a name for the field.

➤ To insert a Quick Start data type

1. In the navigation pane, double-click the table to open it in Datasheet view.

2. On the **Table Tools Fields** tab, in the **Add & Delete** group, click **More Fields** and then scroll down to display the **Quick Start** group.

3. Select the **Quick Start** data type you want to insert.

➤ To define a custom data type

1. In the navigation pane, double-click the table to open it in Datasheet view.

2. In the datasheet, select the field or fields you want to include in the custom data type.

3. On the **Table Tools Fields** tab, in the **Add & Delete** group, click **More Fields** and then click **Save Selection as New Data Type**.

4. In the **Create New Data Type from Fields** dialog box, type a name and description for the custom data type. Select an entry from the **Category** list, or type the name for a new category.

➤ **To rename a field in Datasheet view**

1. In the navigation pane, double-click the table to open it in Datasheet view.

2. Right-click the column heading for the field and choose **Rename Field**.

3. In the highlighted area, type the new name for the field.

➤ **To delete a field in Datasheet view**

1. In the navigation pane, double-click the table to open it in Datasheet view.

2. Right-click the column heading for the field and choose **Delete Field**.

3. Click **Yes** in the prompt Access displays to confirm that you want to delete the field.

Working with Fields in Design View

With a table in Design view, you work in the Field Name column when you need to rename a field. Simply select the field's name, and then type the new name.

You can add a field to the table by using the first blank row. To insert a field between fields you've already defined, click in the row above which you want to insert the field and then click Insert Rows in the Table Tools Design tab's Tools group. You can also right-click the row above which you want to insert a field and click Insert Fields on the shortcut menu. To delete a field, click in the row and then choose Delete Rows in the Tools group, or right-click in the row for the field you want to delete and then choose Delete Rows. If you choose the Delete Rows command for a field that is part of a relationship, Access prevents you from deleting the field.

➤ **To insert, rename, and delete fields in Design view**

1. In the navigation pane, right-click the table and choose **Design View**.

2. In the **Field Name** column, modify a field's name to rename the field.

3. To insert a row between two fields, select the row above which you want to insert the field, and then click **Insert Rows** in the **Tools** group on the **Table Tools Design** tab.

4. To delete a field, select the field and then click **Delete Rows** in the **Tools** group.

Hiding and Freezing Fields

When a table includes more than ten or so fields, you can't easily view all the fields with the table open in Datasheet view. You might need to scroll left or right to locate the field you need. Access provides two features that let you view a table with a large number of fields more efficiently. You can temporarily hide fields you don't need to refer to, and you can freeze fields so that the field or fields you freeze remain in view as you scroll.

To hide or freeze fields, you use commands on the shortcut menu that appears when you right-click a column heading in Datasheet view.

Right-click the column heading for a field you want to hide and then choose Hide Fields. You can drag through two or more column headings to hide multiple fields. (You can also hold down the Shift key and click column headings to select more than one adjacent column.)

To show hidden fields again, right-click a column heading and choose Unhide Fields. In the Unhide Columns dialog box, select the check box for each field you want to show.

> **Tip** You can use the Unhide Columns dialog box to hide fields as well. Display the dialog box by choosing Unhide Fields from the shortcut menu, and then clear the check boxes for any fields you want to hide.

To freeze a field or a set of fields (use the Shift key or drag to select more than one adjacent field), right-click the column heading for the field and then choose Freeze Fields. You'll see no visual indicator that a field is frozen until you start moving the horizontal scroll bar to the right. The field or fields you freeze remain in view as a reference as you enter or update data. You can freeze a field whose column is at any position in the datasheet. When you do this, Access moves the column or columns to the far left of the datasheet, placing the column or columns before any others.

To unfreeze fields, right-click a column heading and choose Unfreeze All Fields. If Access moved a field to the first position in the table, unfreezing all fields does not return this column (or columns) to its original position in the table. You need to drag the column heading to place the column where you want it in the table.

➤ To hide and unhide fields

1. In the navigation pane, double-click the table to open it in Datasheet view.
2. Right-click the column heading for a field, and choose **Hide Fields**.
3. To show hidden fields, right-click a column heading and choose **Unhide Fields**.
4. In the **Unhide Columns** dialog box, select the check boxes for the fields you want to show.

➤ To freeze and unfreeze fields

1. In the navigation pane, double-click the table to open it in Datasheet view.
2. Right-click the column heading of the field you want to freeze, and choose **Freeze Fields**.
3. To unfreeze fields, right-click a column heading and choose **Unfreeze Fields**.

Setting and Updating Field Properties

You can set many different properties for the fields in a table. In previous sections, you've seen examples of working with the Indexed property, for example, and the Field Size property. You can set some field properties when working in Datasheet view, including the Name, Caption, Description, Default Value, and Field Size properties. To work with the full range of field properties, you need to open the table in Design view. In the next section, you'll learn about working with the Field Properties area of the Design view window. After you examine how you work with properties in Design view, you'll learn how to set and update properties in a table that's open in Datasheet view.

Setting Field Properties in Design View

When you have a table open in Design view, select a field to display the current settings for its properties in the Field Properties area. In the area to the right of the list of properties, Access provides a brief description of each property and, in some cases, notes some restrictions or qualifications (such as a text field can contain a maximum of 255 characters). You'll see the following properties for a text field. In many cases, you don't need to set all of a field's properties.

- **Field Size** The maximum number of characters that can be entered in the field. For example, let's say your company uses a six-character product code (with a combination of letters and numbers). You could set the Field Size property to 6 to ensure that no one entered more characters than are allowed.

- **Format** Specifies how the value in a field is displayed. You often set this property for number and date/time fields.

- **Input Mask** The specific pattern in which data in the field is entered. You can use an input mask that Access provides or define one of your own. Some of the built-in input masks are for phone numbers, U.S. Social Security numbers, ZIP codes, passwords, and various date formats. To set up an input mask, click in the Input Mask property box and then click the ellipsis to run the Input Mask Wizard.

- **Caption** The Caption property determines the text that appears in a label when the field is added to a form or a report. The field name is used by default.

- **Default Value** A value that Access enters automatically for a field. For example, you might use the built-in function *Now()* in an order date field to automatically fill in today's date when a new order is entered.

- **Validation Rule** Use this property to set up a field validation rule. Simple validation rules often compare the value of a field to one or more constants. For example, you could enter the expression *<1000* as a field validation rule to ensure that the field contains no values greater than 1,000. You can also use this property to specify a short list of valid values—for example, to specify the valid values for a product size field, you could use the expression "Large" OR "Medium" OR "Small". Be sure to enclose text strings in quotation marks. Dates should be enclosed with pound signs (#), as in #03/31/2012#. You can use the LIKE operator and wildcard characters to specify a valid pattern. For example, for a five-digit U.S. ZIP code, use the expression LIKE "#####".

> **Tip** Use the ? wildcard character as a placeholder for any character. The # symbol refers to any single digit. The asterisk (*) can be used to note zero or more characters. For example, use the expression LIKE "*south*" to find any value that contains the text string "south".

- **Validation Text** Enter text in this property to define the error message Access displays when invalid data is entered in the field.

- **Required** Set this property to Yes to require users to enter a value in the field before they can save the record.

- **Allow Zero Length** Set this property to Yes or No depending on whether you want to allow zero-length strings in this field. A zero-length string is essentially a known empty value, which you might use to indicate that a user has no preference about the value in the field or that the value does not apply. (By contrast, a null value indicates an unknown empty value.)

- **Indexed** Indicates whether the field is indexed. Choose Yes (No Duplicates) or Yes (Duplicates OK).

> **See Also** For more information about indexes, see "Defining Indexes" earlier in this chapter.

- **Unicode Compression** When you set this property to Yes, Access stores compressed characters using fewer bytes, which saves space in the database.

- **IME Mode and IME Sentence Mode** These properties apply to computers that run Windows using Asian languages.

- **Smart Tags** Use this property to specify actions a user can take from a shortcut menu when the field is displayed in Datasheet view or on a form.

- **Text Align** Specifies how text is aligned in the field. You can choose from General (the default), Left, Center, Right, and Distribute. The Distribute option spreads the data evenly over the field.

Other field properties include the following:

- For fields using the Date/Time data type, you'll see the property Show Date Picker. Use the For Dates option to show a date picker for a field, or choose Never to hide it.

- For Memo fields, use the Text Format property to specify Plain Text or Rich Text. The Rich Text option provides more formatting.

- For Memo and Hyperlink fields, set the Append Only property to Yes if you want to retain the history of changes to these fields.

- For a calculated field, you can use the Expression property to compose the expression that performs the calculation and then choose a data type for the result in the Result Type property.

> **To set and update field properties in Design view**

1. In the navigation pane, right-click the table and choose **Design View**.

2. Select the field whose properties you want to set.

3. In the **Field Properties** area, specify the value for the properties or choose an option from the list Access provides.

Setting Field Properties in Datasheet View

On the Table Tools Fields tab, you can set and update field properties by using a variety of commands. You need to select a field in the datasheet before you can set or modify the field's properties.

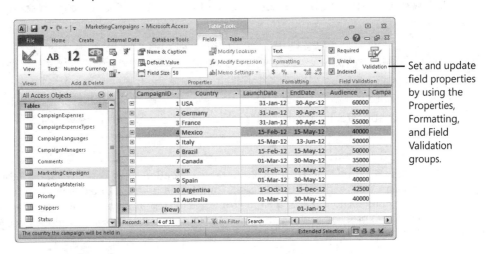

Set and update field properties by using the Properties, Formatting, and Field Validation groups.

The Properties group includes the following commands for setting and updating properties:

- Click Name & Caption to modify the Name, Caption, and Description properties for a field.

- Click Default Value to open the Expression Builder, where you can enter a value that is used in the field by default.

- Type a value in the Field Size box to set this property.

- For memo fields, click Memo Settings in the Properties group to choose the Append Only or Rich Text option. (See the previous section for more information about these options for a memo field.)

- When you select a calculated field, Access enables the Modify Expression command, which you can use to open the Expression Builder and revise the expression that defines the field.

- When you select a lookup field, Access enables the Modify Lookups command. Use this command to open the Lookup Wizard and define or modify the fields used to create the lookup relationship.

The Formatting group on the Table Tools Fields tab provides controls with which you can set or modify the data type and format for a field. Some of the controls in this group are available only when you select a field with a specific data type. (You can't increase or decrease decimal points for a text field, for example.)

In the Field Validation group, select the check boxes for the Required, Unique, and Indexed properties if these properties should be set to Yes for a field. To set up a field or record (table) validation rule, click Validation and then select Field Validation or Record Validation Rule. Choosing either command opens the Expression Builder, where you can define the validation rule you want to use. Choose the Field Validation Message and Record Validation Message options to define the message Access displays when it detects invalid data. (Using the Validation Message options is the same as entering text in the Validation Text property for a table or a field when you are working in Design view.)

> **See Also** For more information about table validation rules, see "Creating a Table Validation Rule" earlier in this chapter. For information about field validation rules, see the previous section, "Setting Field Properties in Design View." For information about using the Expression Builder, see "Getting Help with the Expression Builder" in Chapter 4 in this part of the book.

➤ **To set and update field properties in Datasheet view**

1. In the navigation pane, double-click the table to open it in Datasheet view.

2. Click the **Table Tools Fields** tab.

3. Select the field whose properties you want to work with.

4. Use the commands in the **Properties** group to set or update the field's Name, Caption, Description, Default Value, and Field Size properties.

5. For lookup fields, click **Modify Lookups** to change the properties of the lookup field.

6. For calculated fields, click **Modify Expression** to revise the field's expression.

7. For memo fields, click **Memo Settings** to set the Append Only and Text Format properties.

8. Use the **Formatting** group to update a field's data type and formatting properties.

9. Use the **Field Validation** group to set the Required, Unique, and Index properties and to set up a field or record (table) validation rule.

Practice Tasks

The practice files for these tasks are located in the practice files folder for Microsoft Access 2010. You can save the results of these exercises in the same folder. Change the file name so that you don't overwrite the sample files. When you are done, try performing the following tasks:

- Open the file Hello_World_ch2.accdb.

- Open the Tasks table you created in the practice tasks for section 2.1 in Datasheet view, and insert the fields DependentTasks and TimeSpent. Set the data types for both fields to Number.

- Select the fields StartDate, DueDate, and DateCompleted, and create a Quick Start data type called TaskDates.

- Apply the Hide Fields and Freeze Fields commands to the Tasks table.

- For the TimeSpent field, set the Required property to Yes.

- Use the Name & Caption command to update the Caption property for the DateCompleted field so that it reads "Completion Date."

2.3   Sort and Filter Records

Over time, even a relatively small Access database can grow to include thousands of records. Locating a specific record by scrolling through a table's datasheet or by using a form becomes inefficient in circumstances like this. To locate a single record or a group of records that have specific criteria in common, you can use commands to find, sort, and filter records when you are working with a table in Datasheet view.

Finding Records

To find records in a table, you work with the Find And Replace dialog box and with a few other commands in the Find group on the Home tab. To open the dialog box, click Find on the Home tab, or right-click a column heading in the datasheet and choose Find.

Type the value you are looking for in the Find What box (or select an item you entered previously by using the drop-down list). Use the Look In list to specify whether Access should search the current field or the entire table (the Current Document option). The Match list provides three options: Any Part Of Field, Whole Field, and Start Of Field. The Whole Field option is the default setting. When this option is selected, Access finds only records with values that match the entire text string you type in the Find What box. For example, if you type **Blue** in the Find What box, Access does not find records whose value is Light Blue, Dark Blue, or Navy Blue. Choose the Any Part Of Field option from the Match list if you want to locate all four of these records (or those like them). Use Start Of Field to locate records that begin with a specific string of characters—all records whose Description field starts with "Spa," for example, to find the records for Spanish olive oil, spaghetti, and sparkling water. The Search list lets you specify whether Access should search down, up, or all (both directions). Select the Match Case check box to implement a case-sensitive search. The Search Fields As Formatted option is enabled when you are searching a field that has a particular format or an input mask. With this option selected, Access searches the data as it is displayed instead of how Access stores it. This option is particularly useful in date and time fields.

Use the Replace tab in the Find And Replace dialog box if you want to insert new data for the data Access finds. You can replace all instances of the data (Replace All) or a single instance (Replace).

The Go To command in the Find group lets you move from record to record in a table or to the first or last record. You can also use this command to insert a row at the end of the datasheet to enter a new record.

The Select command lets you select the current record (the record where the cursor is inserted) or all records in the table.

➤ To find records

1. In the navigation pane, double-click the table to open it in Datasheet view.
2. On the **Home** tab, click **Find**.
3. In the **Find and Replace** dialog box, type the text you want to find in the **Find What** box.
4. In the **Look In** list, select **Current field** or **Current document** (the entire table).
5. In the **Match** list, select **Whole Field**, **Any Part of Field**, or **Start of Field**.
6. In the **Search** list, select **All**, **Up**, or **Down**.
7. Select **Match Case** to perform a case-sensitive search.
8. Select **Search Fields As Formatted** if you want to search the data as it is formatted in the datasheet.
9. Click **Find Next**.

Sorting Records

On the Home tab, in the Sort & Filter group, you can use the Ascending and Descending commands to sort a table's records by a field you select. Click the column heading in the datasheet (or click a cell in that column), and then click the command for the sort order you want to apply. To return a table to the default sort order, click Remove Sort.

You can sort a table by multiple columns as well. For example, you could sort the CampaignBudget field in descending order and the LaunchDate field in ascending order to see how budgets compare for each campaign scheduled to launch on a specific date. When you sort by multiple fields, apply the second, or *inner*, sort first (in this case, budgets in descending order).

You can sort by multiple fields to create a view that lets you quickly compare a set of values.

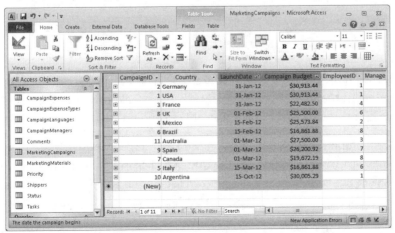

You can also click the Filter button to display sorting options or sort by using commands on a shortcut menu. Click in the column for the field you want to sort by, click Filter, and then choose Sort A To Z or Sort Z To A for a text field. You'll see the commands Sort Smallest To Largest or Sort Largest To Smallest for number fields, or Sort Oldest To Newest and Sort Newest To Oldest for date fields. You see the same sorting options when you right-click in a column or when you click the down arrow that appears to the right of a field's name.

For more advanced sorts, click Advanced in the Sort & Filter group and then click Advanced Filter/Sort. Access displays a window with a list of the table's fields in the top pane and a grid at the bottom. If you open this window when a sort order is applied, you'll see the field and sort criteria specified in the grid.

> **See Also** The Advanced Filter/Sort window is very much like the query design window you'll learn about in Chapter 4.

In the Advanced Filter/Sort window, create multiple-field sorts by selecting fields in the Field row.

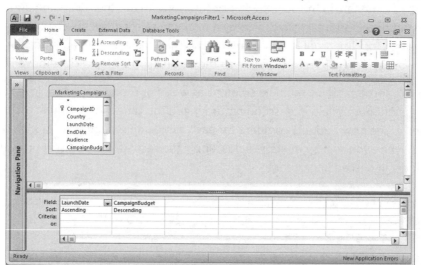

To specify a field to sort by, drag the field to the Field row in the grid, or simply select a field from the list that appears when you click in the Field row and then click the down arrow. In the Sort row, specify Ascending or Descending.

To create a multiple-field sort in the Advanced Filter/Sort window, drag a second field from the field list to the Field row in the grid. (Or click in the next blank cell in that row and select the field from the drop-down list.) In the Sort row, select Ascending or Descending. After you arrange the fields you want to sort by, click the Toggle Filter button in the Sort & Filter group, and Access displays the table in datasheet view sorted as you specified. Click Remove Sort to return the table to its default sort order.

➤ **To sort records from the Home tab**

1. In the navigation pane, double-click the table to open it in Datasheet view.

2. Select the field you want to sort by.

3. On the **Home** tab, in the **Sort & Filter** group, click **Ascending** or **Descending**.

➤ **To sort records by using a shortcut menu**

1. In the navigation pane, double-click the table to open it in Datasheet view.

2. Right-click the field you want to sort by, and then choose the command for the sort order you want to use. (The command names depend on the field's data type.)

➤ **To set up an advanced sort**

1. In the navigation pane, double-click the table to open it in Datasheet view.

2. On the **Home** tab, in the **Sort & Filter** group, click **Advanced** and then click **Advanced Filter/Sort**.

3. In the **Advanced Filter/Sort** window, in the **Field** row in the grid, select the fields you want to sort by.

4. In the **Sort** row, select the sort order you want to use.

5. In the **Sort & Filter** group, click **Toggle Filter** to sort the records.

6. Click **Remove Sort** to return the table to its default sort order.

Filtering Records

By applying a filter to a table in datasheet view, you can select the specific set of records you want to review, such as all orders placed on or after a specific date or all amounts less than or greater than a target.

Access provides many ways to filter records. For example, click in the column for the field you want to filter and then click the Filter button in the Sort & Filter group. Access displays a menu with the values in that field. Clear the Select All check box, select the check box for each record you want to see, and then click OK to apply the filter. Click the Toggle Filter button to display all the records in the table again.

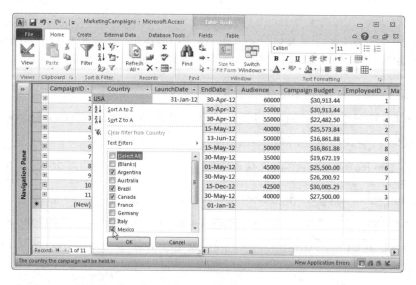

Another way to filter is to filter by selection. Select a value or a portion of a value to use as the filter criterion. In the Sort & Filter group, click Filter By Selection and then choose one of the expressions Access provides. For text fields, you'll see expressions such as Equals *"Value"*, Does Not Equal *"Value"*, and Contains *"Value"*. For date fields, the expressions include Equals Date, Does Not Equal Date, On Or Before Date, On Or After Date, and Between, which lets you specify a date range to use as the filter. For number fields, Less Than Or Equal To and Greater Than Or Equal To options are included along with Equals and Does Not Equal.

> **Tip** You can filter by selection progressively to hone in on a particular set of records. For example, the first time you apply a filter, the criteria you use reduces 200 records to 75. Apply filter by selection using different criteria to those 75 records to review a smaller subset.

You'll see similar filtering expressions on the menu that appears when you right-click in a column. The shortcut menu also includes a command that leads to additional filters based on the field's data type. The Text Filters command displays the Equals and Does Not Equal options and also Begins With, Does Not Begin With, Ends With, and Does Not End With. Choose an option, and then specify the criteria in the Custom Filter dialog box that Access displays.

The Date Filters commands includes options such as Before, After, and Between, as well as Next Week, Last Week, Year To Date, and many others. You can also choose All Dates In Period and then choose a period such as Quarter 1 or a specific month of the year.

The Advanced button in the Sort & Filter group provides other options for applying a filter, including Filter By Form and Advanced Filter/Sort. When you click Filter By Form, Access opens a blank datasheet with the names of the table's fields at the top of each column. On the Look For tab, click in the highlighted row and then choose the value from the field you want to use as the filter's criterion. You can choose a value in more than one field to create an AND condition. For example, a filter that displays records for which product size equals Large and product color equals Blue. Click the Or tab at the bottom of the window to set up additional values for the filter. If you specify filter criteria on the Or tab, Access returns records that match either the criteria you specify on the Look For tab or the criteria defined on the Or tab.

In the Advanced Filter/Sort window, you use the grid below the list of table fields to build filter criteria. Select a field in the Field row in the grid (or drag a field from the field list to the grid), and then define the criteria you want to apply. To define the criteria, you write an expression such as =*"France"* for a text value, or *>#2/1/2004#* for a date field.

Filters are similar to Access queries in that they define criteria through which a subset of a table's records are displayed. (Queries can use more than one table.) You can see the similarity between filters and queries by experimenting with two other commands on the Advanced Filter/Sort menu: Load From Query and Save As Query.

To use a query you've defined as criteria for a filter, click Advanced in the Sort & Filter group and then click Load From Query. In the Applicable Filter dialog box, select a query and then click OK. Access shows the query's fields and criteria in the design grid area of the Advanced Filter/Sort window. Click Toggle Filter to apply the filter to the table.

You can use the Save As Query command to save the criteria you specified for a filter as a query that you can run on the table or include in other queries. Click this command and then type a name for the query in the Save Query As dialog box.

> **Tip** Use the Clear Grid command to remove any criteria from the grid.

➤ To filter a field

1. In the navigation pane, double-click the table to open it in Datasheet view.
2. Select the field you want to filter by, and then click **Filter** in the **Sort & Filter** group on the **Home** tab.
3. In the menu that Access displays, clear the check box for **Select All**.
4. Select the check box for each record you want to see, and then click **OK**.

➤ To filter by selection

1. In the navigation pane, double-click the table to open it in Datasheet view.

2. Select the value or the portion of a value you want to use as the filter.

3. In the **Sort & Filter** group on the **Home** tab, click the **Filter by Selection** button.

4. In the menu Access displays, select the expression for the filter (**Equals**, **Does Not Equal**, or another option).

5. Click **Toggle Filter** to remove the filter from the table.

➤ To filter by form

1. In the navigation pane, double-click the table to open it in Datasheet view.

2. In the **Sort & Filter** group on the **Home** tab, click **Advanced** and then click **Filter By Form**.

3. In the **Filter by Form** window, on the **Look for** tab, select the value from the field you want to use as the filter.

   If you select a value for more than one field on the **Look for** tab, you create AND conditions—only records that meet both conditions are selected.

4. Click the **Or** tab to set up OR conditions.

   In an OR condition, Access displays records that meet either the condition on the **Look for** tab or the condition on the **Or** tab.

5. In the **Sort & Filter** group, click **Toggle Filter** to apply the filter. Click **Toggle Filter** again to remove the filter.

➤ To create an advanced filter

1. In the navigation pane, double-click the table to open it in Datasheet view.

2. On the **Home** tab, in the **Sort & Filter** group, click **Advanced** and then click **Advanced Filter/Sort**.

3. In the **Advanced Filter/Sort** window, in the **Field** row in the grid, select the fields you want to use in the filter.

4. In the **Criteria** row, specify the expression to use in the filter.

5. In the **Sort & Filter** group, click **Toggle Filter** to apply the filter. Click **Toggle Filter** again to remove the filter.

➤ To use a query as a filter

1. In the navigation pane, double-click the table to open it in Datasheet view.

   2. On the **Home** tab, in the **Sort & Filter** group, click **Advanced** and then click **Advanced Filter/Sort**.

   3. Click **Advanced Filer/Sort** again, and then choose **Load from Query**.

   4. In the **Applicable Filter** dialog box, select the query you want to use as a filter and then click **OK**.

   5. In the **Sort & Filter** group, click **Toggle Filter** to apply the filter. Click **Toggle Filter** again to remove the filter.

➤ **To save a filter as a query**

   1. In the navigation pane, double-click the table to open it in Datasheet view.

   2. On the **Home** tab, in the **Sort & Filter** group, click **Advanced** and then click **Advanced Filter/Sort**.

   3. In the **Advanced Filter/Sort** window, in the **Field** row in the grid, select the fields you want to use in the filter.

   4. In the **Criteria** row, specify the expression to use in the filter.

   5. Click **Advanced Filer/Sort**, and then choose **Save As Query**.

   6. Type a name for the query in the Save As Query dialog box, and then click OK.

Practice Tasks

The practice files for these tasks are located in the practice files folder for Microsoft Access 2010. You can save the results of these exercises in the same folder. Change the file name so that you don't overwrite the sample files. When you are done, try performing the following tasks:

- Open the file Hello_World_ch2.accdb, and then open the CampaignExpenses table in Datasheet view.

- Sort the table's records in ascending order by using the Description field, and then remove the sort.

- Sort the Description field in descending order and the AmountSpent field in ascending order.

- Filter the ExpenseType field to show only records that equal the value "Travel".

- Create an advance filter using criteria that filters for expense types equal to Production and the amount spent is greater than $800.

2.4   Set Relationships

In this section, you'll learn the details of how you set up a primary key field for a table. You'll also learn more about table relationships—the different types of relationships, how to create them, and how to edit relationships.

Specifying a Primary Key

A table's primary key uniquely identifies each record in a table. You can use a single field (for example, a unique product or customer code or an ID field that is set to the AutoNumber data type that Access provides) or a combination of fields as a table's primary key. (A multifield primary key is called a *composite key*.) If you don't use the AutoNumber data type but instead use a field whose value you enter, be sure that you set the field's Required property to Yes and that you use a field or a combination of fields whose values change infrequently or not at all.

> **See Also** For information about setting field properties, see "Setting and Updating Field Properties" earlier in this chapter.

> **Tip** When you create a new table in Datasheet view by clicking Table on the Create tab, Access includes an ID field in the table and sets this field to be the table's primary key.

In Access, primary keys are also used to establish table relationships. For example, if you have a table named ProjectManagers whose primary key is the ProjectManagerID field, you can add the ProjectManagerID field to the Projects table to identify the manager for each project. In the Projects table, the ProjectManagerID field is referred to as a *foreign key*. Primary keys and foreign keys can also be used in queries to join tables so that Access can use that relationship to retrieve the set of records you want.

> **See Also** For more information about queries, see Chapter 4.

To set the primary key for a table, you must first open the table in Design view. (Select Design View from the View menu on the Table Tools Design tab or the Table Tools Fields tab, or right-click the table in the navigation pane and choose Design View.) Click the row selector for the field or fields you want to designate as the primary key (press the Ctrl key and click to select multiple fields), and then click Primary Key in the Tools group on the Table Tools Design tab. Access adds a small key icon to the row selector area to indicate that a field is a primary key field.

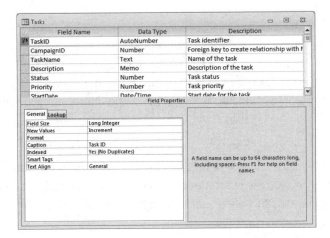

If you need to remove the primary key designation from a field, select the field in Design view and then click Primary Key in the Tools group. To change a table's primary key, remove the current primary key and then specify the field or fields you want to use.

If a table already contains data, any fields you designate for the primary key must have unique values. Also, if a primary key is part of any table relationships, you must remove the relationships before you can change the primary key.

> **See Also** You'll learn more about adding and deleting relationships in the next section.

➤ To set a primary key

1. In the navigation pane, right-click the table and choose **Design View**.

2. Select the field or fields you want to designate as the table's primary key.

   To select multiple fields, press Ctrl and select the fields.

3. On the **Table Tools Design** tab, click **Primary Key**.

➤ To remove the primary key designation from a field

1. In the navigation pane, right-click the table and choose **Design View**.

2. Select the field or fields from which you want to remove the primary key designation.

3. On the **Table Tools Design** tab, click **Primary Key**.

Setting Relationships

To help maintain the integrity of your data and to reduce the need to store redundant data, you can create relationships between tables. Table relationships can also be used when you want to include records from more than one table in a query, form, or report. You define a different type of relationship depending on the data that each table contains:

- Between most tables, you will create a *one-to-many relationship*. In this relationship, any one record in the first table can be related to many records in the second table (for example, one customer can place many orders), but any record in the second table is related to only one record in the first table (for example, each order is placed by only one customer).

- You can also create a *one-to-one relationship*, in which each record in the first table is related to one record in the second table. You can use this type of relationship when you want to use a separate table to define and store fields for data you don't refer to as often or that you want to keep more confidential. For example, in an Employees table you could store general employee information such as first and last name, department, job title, and building and office location. In a separate EmployeesRating or EmployeeWages table, you could store performance ratings and salaries—information that you want only certain people or groups to use. Each record in the Employees table would have a single matching record in the table for ratings or wages.

- Some tables have a *many-to-many relationship*. For example, an orders table and a products table have a many-to-many relationship. Each record in the orders table can have many matching records in the products table, and each record in the products table can have many matching order records. You can't define this type of relationship directly. Instead, you create a linking table (also called a *junction table*) to create two one-to-many relationships. The linking table includes the primary key fields from both the other tables. In the Northwind sample database that comes with Access, the Order Details table is a linking table.

To view and define relationships between tables, click the Database Tools tab and then click Relationships. Access displays the Relationships window and the Relationship Tools Design tab.

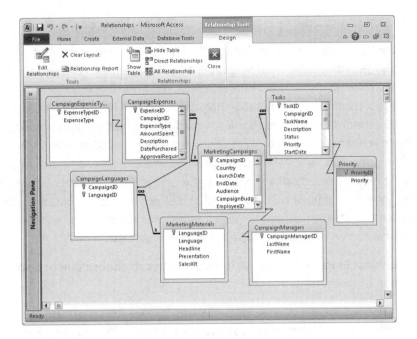

To create a relationship, drag the linking field in the first table (the "one" table in a one-to-many relationship) to the second table (the "many" table). When you release the mouse, Access displays the Edit Relationships dialog box. In the dialog box, if Access detects matching fields, you'll see the fields selected in the Table/Query and Related Table/Query lists. If you need to select a different field in the Related Table/Query list, select that field and then click Create New to establish the relationship. The relationship type is indicated at the bottom of the dialog box.

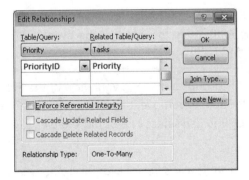

See Also You'll learn more about join types in Chapter 4.

You can choose several options in the Edit Relationships dialog box:

- **Enforce Referential Integrity** Referential integrity is used to prevent orphan records (records with no matching record) and to maintain references between related tables. By using referential integrity, you ensure that no record in one table refers to a record in another table that doesn't exist—for example, a record for a book cannot refer to an author if a record for that author does not exist. If you enforce referential integrity, Access does not allow operations that violate referential integrity rules for that relationship. For example, Access does not allow you to update records that modify the target of a reference. You can't enter a customer ID in the orders table if that customer ID does not exist in the customer table. Also, you can't delete records that remove a target. For example, you can't delete a customer record if order records for that customer exist.

- **If you select Enforce Referential Integrity, you can choose one or both of the Cascade options:**

  - Choose Cascade Update Related Fields to have Access update the foreign key for all related fields when you make a change to the primary record.

  - Choose Cascade Delete Related Records to have Access delete all related records when you delete a primary record. (If you deleted a customer, Access would also delete all order records for that customer.)

To modify a relationship, right-click the line between the tables and choose Edit Relationship. (Or select the line and click Edit Relationships in the Tools group on the Relationship Tools Design tab.) To delete a relationship, right-click the relationship line and choose Delete.

> **Tip** Click Relationship Report in the Tools group to reproduce the layout in the Relationship window in a format you can print.

Use the commands in the Relationships group to manage your view of the Relationships window. Select a table, and click Hide Table to remove it from the window. Click Show Tables to display a dialog box in which you can select one or more tables to add to the tables already shown.

To see the relationships for a particular table, click Clear Layout to remove all the tables from the Relationships window, click Show Tables, and then select the table whose relationships you want to examine. Click Direct Relationships to display the tables directly related to the table you selected.

When you close the Relationships window, Access prompts you to save the current layout. Click Yes or No depending on your preference.

➤ **To create a table relationship**

1. On the **Database Tools** tab, click **Relationships**.

2. If the tables you need aren't displayed, click **Show Table** in the **Relationships** group, select the tables in the **Show Table** dialog box, and then click **Add**.

3. Drag the linking field in the first table (the "one" table in a one-to-many relationship) to the second table (the "many" table).

    Access displays the Edit Relationships dialog box.

4. In the dialog box, be sure the linking fields are selected in the **Table/Query** and **Related Table/Query** lists and then click **Create**.

5. Select **Enforce Referential Integrity** if you want to enable this feature for this relationship. If you enable referential integrity, select one or both of the Cascade options.

➤ **To modify a relationship**

1. On the **Database Tools** tab, click **Relationships**.

2. In the **Relationships** window, right-click the relationship line between two tables and choose **Edit Relationship**.

3. In the **Edit Relationships** dialog box, make changes to the relationship (for example, select Enforce Referential Integrity if that option is not yet selected) and then click **OK**.

Practice Tasks

The practice files for these tasks are located in the practice files folder for Microsoft Access 2010. You can save the results of these exercises in the same folder. Change the file name so that you don't overwrite the sample files. When you are done, try performing the following tasks:

*   Open the file Hello_World_ch2.accdb.

*   Open the Tasks table, and designate the TaskID field as the table's primary key.

*   Open the Relationships window, and create a relationship between the Tasks table and the Priority table. Base the relationship on the PriorityID and Priority fields.

2.5   Import Data from a Single Data File

One way to add data to new tables or tables you've defined is to import data. Access 2010 can import data from a variety of formats, including Microsoft Excel workbooks, text files, XML files, Microsoft SharePoint lists, and Microsoft Outlook folders. You'll find the commands for importing data in these formats and others in the Import & Link group on the External Data tab.

When you import data, you generally have three options: importing the source data into a new table, appending the data, or linking to the data source to create a linked table. You specify the information that Access requires to import data in the Get External Data dialog box. The title bar in the dialog box reflects the source format.

> **Tip** You can save the settings you use to import data and then run the import operation when you need to later by using the saved settings.

Importing Data into a New Table

When you have data in an Excel worksheet, a text file, an XML file, or another compatible format, you can import that data into Access and create a table. Access can use column headings in the source data as field names, and Access often displays a wizard that helps you provide the information Access requires to import data from a particular format.

Importing Data from Excel

Click Excel in the Import & Link group to display the Get External Data dialog box, which you use to select the import option and identify the source file. Choose the option Import The Source Data Into A New Table In The Current Database. When you click OK, Access display the Import Spreadsheet Wizard.

In the wizard, select the worksheet with the data you want to import, or select the Show Named Ranges option and then select a range. You can scroll through the sample data that is displayed in the wizard, but you cannot modify it here.

The wizard's second page prompts you to confirm whether the first row of the data contains column headings that Access can use as field names. Select the First Row Contains Column Headings check box if this option matches the organization of the worksheet.

On the next page, you can specify each field's data type and whether Access should index the field. Select a field in the preview area and then specify the settings you want in the Field Options area. You can also select the option to skip the selected field.

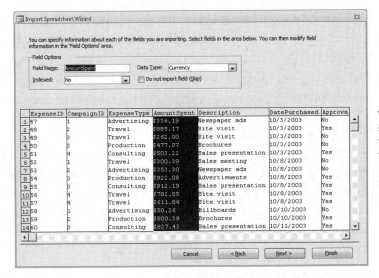

When you import a spreadsheet or a text file as a new table, the import wizard lets you specify field names and data types.

On the wizard's fourth page, you can set the table's primary key. Choose the option for Access to create an ID field to use as the primary key, choose your own primary key, or specify no primary key.

On the wizard's next page, type a name for the table (or accept the default title the wizard provides). When you click Finish, Access again displays the Get External Data dialog box and provides an option for you to save the import steps. Select this option if you expect to import this data frequently. If you select Save Import Steps, Access displays text boxes in the Get External Data dialog box that you use to name and describe the import steps. You are also presented with an option to set up a task in Microsoft Outlook to remind you to run this import operation again.

> **Tip** After you import the table, you can modify and update the data and table and field properties by opening the table in Datasheet or Design view.

➤ To import data from Excel into a new table

1. On the **External Data** tab, click **Excel** in the **Import & Link** group.

2. In the **Get External Data** dialog box, select the option **Import the source data into a new table in the current database**, use the **Browse** button to locate the source file, and then click **OK**.

3. In the **Import Spreadsheet Wizard**, select the worksheet or named range with the data you want to import.

4. Click **Next** to work through the wizard to specify whether the first column of the data includes column headings, set field options, designate a primary key, and name the table.

5. Click **Finish** in the wizard, and then select the option **Save import steps** in the **Get External Data** dialog box if you want to save the steps in this operation.

Importing Data from Another Access Database

If another Access database contains data you need, click the Access option in the Import & Link group. Use the Get External Data dialog box to point to the database that contains the source data. Choose the option Import Tables, Queries, Forms, Reports, Macros, And Modules Into The Current Database. When you click OK, Access displays the Import Objects dialog box, which lists the objects in the source database on separate tabs.

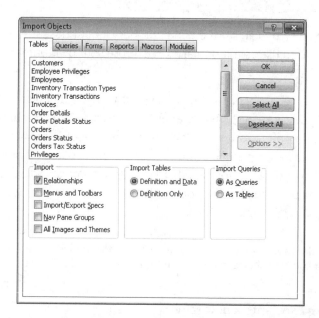

To bring data into your database, work with the Tables tab. (You can use the Import Objects dialog box to add other types of objects to a database, but you cannot open a form or run a query that you import unless you also import that object's record source.) Click the Options button to display the Import, Import Tables, and Import Queries areas of the dialog box.

- **Import** If you are importing more than one related table and want to preserve the tables' relationship, select the Relationships option. Use the Menus And Toolbars option to import any custom menus and toolbars from databases created in versions of Access prior to Access 2007. Use the Import/Export Specs option to include any import or export specifications defined in the source database. (See the sidebar "Creating an Import Spec" in the following section.) Select Nav Pane Groups to import any custom navigation pane groups set up in the source database, and select All Images And Themes to include these elements with the import.

- **Import Tables** Use the Definition And Data option to import the data along with the table's structure. Select Definition Only if you want to import only the framework for the table (field and field and table property definitions) but not the data the table contains.

- **Import Queries** Use the options in this area to import a query as a table or as a query.

> **To import data from another Access database**

1. On the **External Data** tab, click **Access** in the **Import & Link** group.

2. In the **Get External Data** dialog box, use the **Browse** button to locate the source database.

3. Select the option **Import tables, queries, forms, reports, macros, and modules into the current database**, and then click **OK**.

4. In the **Import Objects** dialog box, select the table or tables (or other objects) you want to import. Click the **Options** button to set options for the import operation.

5. In the **Get External Data** dialog box, select **Save import steps** if you want to save the steps in this operation.

Importing a Text File

When you select Text File in the Import & Link group, you can import a file with the .txt, .csv, .tab, or .asc file name extension. After you select a file and click OK in the Get External Data dialog box, Access displays the Import Text Wizard. On the first page, indicate whether a specific character separates (delimits) the fields of data in the text file or whether the data is aligned in fixed-width columns. The information you provide on the second page depends on whether the file is delimited or uses fixed-width columns. For the first option, you need to specify which character to use as a delimiter. For fixed-width files, you indicate where column breaks should occur.

The final pages of the Import Text Wizard are like those you work with in the Import Spreadsheet Wizard. The wizard lets you rename fields, specify a data type, indicate whether the field should be indexed, and skip a particular field. The wizard also prompts you to set up a primary key for the table.

Creating an Import Spec

When you click the Advanced button in the Import Text Wizard, Access displays the Import Specification dialog box. You can specify settings in this dialog box and save those settings in an import specification file that you can apply to the text file the next time you import it. Among the settings you make in this dialog box are file format (delimited or fixed-width), field delimiter, date format information, and field names and data types. Click Save As to save the specification. When you need to use it again, click Advanced in the Import Text Wizard, click Specs in the Import Specification dialog box, select the specification you need, and then click Open. The settings are applied in the wizard, so you simply need to click Finish to import the text file.

➤ **To import data from a text file into a new table**

1. On the **External Data** tab, click **Text File** in the **Import & Link** group.

2. In the **Get External Data** dialog box, select the option **Import the source data into a new table in the current database**, use the **Browse** button to locate the source file, and then click **OK**.

3. In the **Import Text Wizard**, specify the format for the file you are importing: **Delimited** or **Fixed Width**.

4. Click **Next** in the wizard, and then choose the delimiting character or specify column breaks (depending on the format). Select **First Row Contains Field Names** if this option applies.

5. Click **Next** in the wizard, and then work through the remaining pages to specify whether the first column of the data includes column headings, set field options, designate a primary key, and name the table.

6. Click **Finish** in the wizard, and then select the option **Save import steps** in the **Get External Data** dialog box if you want to save the steps in this operation.

Tip To work with import steps you saved, click Saved Import in the Import & Link group. Select the operation you want to run, and then click Run. You can use the Manage Data Tasks dialog box to run saved exports as well and to set up a task in Outlook to remind you when next to run the import or export operation.

Importing Data from Other Formats

You can also import data from an XML file or a SharePoint list. The steps you follow to import data from these formats are essentially the same as for text files or an Excel worksheet. For a SharePoint list, for example, type the address for the SharePoint site in the Get External Data dialog box. Select the option to import the data into a new table. After you click OK, you might need to provide your user name and password to gain access to the SharePoint site. If Access connects to the site successfully, you'll see the lists available on the site. Use the check boxes to select the list or lists you want to import. If you select more than one list, each list is imported as a separate table.

Importing a contacts or tasks folder from Microsoft Outlook is an effective way to add this information to a database. Select Outlook Folder from the More list in the Import & Link group. Choose the folder you want to import, and then click Next; Access displays the Import Exchange/Outlook Wizard. Use the wizard to provide field names, specify data types, set up indexes, and skip fields when necessary. Also choose whether you want Access to generate a primary key. After you name the table and click Finish, you'll see the standard prompt letting you save the import steps. Select this option if you want to before you complete the import operation.

Appending Records

When you choose the import option to append records (which reads Append A Copy Of The Records To The Table), Access adds the records in the source data to the table you choose in the Get External Data dialog box. The steps for importing the data are essentially the same as when you import data into a new table.

See Also For detailed steps for various import formats, see the procedures in the previous sections.

To avoid errors when you append data, the organization of the external data source should match the structure of the table you are appending records to. For example, in an Excel worksheet that does not contain column headings, the position and the type of data need to match the field order and data types in the destination table. When column headings are present, the name and data type for each column must match the corresponding fields (although the order of the columns and fields do not need to match). Also check whether the source data contains any fields not included in the table. If the source data does contain other fields, you should add these fields to the destination table or specify to skip them for the import process. The destination table can include extra fields provided those fields have their Required property set to No and the fields do not contain any validation rules that prohibit null values.

The source data must include data that is compatible with the table's primary key. The data in that column must be unique. You'll receive an import error message if a primary key value in the source data matches one already defined in the destination table. Also, if the Indexed property of any field in the destination table is set to Yes (No Duplicates), the source data must include unique values for that field.

> **Important** You cannot choose the option to append records for all the formats Access can import. You can choose this option for Excel, for a text file, or for an Outlook folder, for example. The option is not available for an XML file or for a SharePoint list.

➤ **To append records to a table in the current database**

1. On the **External Data** tab, click the command for the data source you want to import.

2. In the **Get External Data** dialog box, select the option **Append a copy of the records to the table** and then select the table you want to append records to.

3. Click **Browse** to locate the file with the source data, and then click **OK**.

4. Follow the steps in the import wizard (if Access provides one) to import and append the data.

5. In the **Get External Data** dialog box, select the option **Save import steps** if you want to save the steps in this operation.

Using Linked Tables

Linked tables let you refer to and use information from an external data source. You can create a linked table that is based on an Excel worksheet, a text file, or one of the other external data formats that Access 2010 supports. Linking to an Excel worksheet or a text file, for example, creates a one-way link—you can read the data in Access, but you cannot insert or update records; the data is maintained only in the external data source. However, you can link to tables in another Access database and work with those tables as you do other tables.

> **Tip** You can link to tables in other Access databases to work around the 2-gigabyte restriction on the size of a single Access database file.

If you link to an Access database or another external data source that is protected with a password, you need to provide the password to link successfully. Access can save the password so that you do not need to provide it each time you open the external table. Because Access saves this information, you might want to take the steps to encrypt your database.

> **See Also** For more information, see "Encrypting a Database File" in Chapter 1 in this section of the book.

Linking to a Table in Another Access Database

In the Get External Data dialog box that appears when you click Access in the Import & Link group, select the option Link To The Data Source By Creating A Linked Table. Browse to the database you want to link to, and then click OK. In the Link Tables dialog box, select the table or tables you want to link to. Access adds an entry for the linked table to the navigation pane. The icon that Access uses to mark the entry shows the type of data source and includes a small arrow to indicate that the table is a linked table.

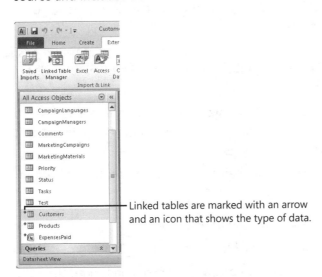

Linked tables are marked with an arrow and an icon that shows the type of data.

➤ **To link to a table in another Access database**

1. On the **External Data** tab, click **Access** in the **Import & Link** group.

2. In the **Get External Data** dialog box, select the option **Link to the data source by creating a linked table**.

3. Click **Browse** to locate the source database, and then click **OK**.

4. In the **Link Tables** dialog box, select the table or tables you want to link to and then click **OK**.

Linking to an Excel Worksheet or a Text File

Click the Excel or Text File command in the Import & Link group as the first step in linking to a worksheet or a text file. In the Get External Data dialog box, choose the option Link To The Data Source By Creating A Linked Table and browse to the file you want to link to. When you click OK, Access displays a wizard much like the wizard you follow to import data into a new table. Provide the information requested by the wizard to create the linked table.

➤ **To link to a text file**

1. On the **External Data** tab, click **Text File** in the **Import & Link** group.

2. In the **Get External Data** dialog box, select the option **Link to the data source by creating a linked table**, use the **Browse** button to locate the source file, and then click **OK**.

3. In the **Link Text Wizard**, specify the format for the file you are importing: **Delimited** or **Fixed Width**.

4. Click **Next** in the wizard, and then choose the delimiting character or specify column breaks (depending on the format). Select **First Row Contains Field Names** if this option applies.

5. Click **Next** in the wizard, and then work through the remaining pages to specify whether the first column of the data includes column headings, set field options, designate a primary key, and name the table.

6. Click **Finish** in the wizard, and then click **OK** in the **Link Text Wizard** message that confirms the table was linked.

➤ **To link to an Excel worksheet or named range**

1. On the **External Data** tab, click **Excel** in the **Import & Link** group.

2. In the **Get External Data** dialog box, select the option **Link to the data source by creating a linked table**, use the **Browse** button to locate the source file, and then click **OK**.

3. In the **Link Spreadsheet Wizard**, select the worksheet or named range with the data you want to import.

4. Click **Next** to specify whether the first column of the data includes column headings.

5. Click **Next**, and then type a name for the linked table.

6. Click **Finish** in the wizard, and then click **OK** in the **Link Spreadsheet Wizard** message that confirms the table was linked.

Managing Linked Tables

If a source file you have linked to is moved to a different location, you can update the link by using the Linked Table Manager command in the Import & Link group. Click this command to display the Linked Table Manager dialog box, which lists each table you have linked to in the current database. Select the check box for the link you want to update, and then click OK. Access then displays the Select New Location dialog box, where you can locate the file in its new location. Select the Always Prompt For New Location option if you want Access to prompt you when a linked file has been moved.

➤ **To manage linked tables**

1. On the **External Data** tab, click **Linked Table Manager** in the **Import & Link** group.

2. In the **Linked Table Manager** dialog box, select the check box for the table or table whose link you want to update and then click **OK**.

   If the source file is not in the original location, Access displays the **Select New Location** dialog box.

3. In the **Select New Location** dialog box, open the new location for the file, select the file, and then click **Open**.

4. Click **OK** in the **Linked Table Manager** message box.

Practice Tasks

The practice files for these tasks are located in the practice files folder for Microsoft Access 2010. You can save the results of these exercises in the same folder. Change the file name so that you don't overwrite the sample files. When you are done, try performing the following tasks:

- Open the file Hello_World_ch2.accdb.
- Import the file CampaignExpenses.xlsx as a new table.
- Link to the Products table in the Access database Import_Test.accdb.
- Import the tables Customers and Orders from the file Import_Test.accdb.

Objective Review

Before finishing this chapter, be sure you have mastered the following skills:

2.1   Create tables in Design view

2.2   Create and modify fields

2.3   Sort and filter records

2.4   Set relationships

2.5   Import data from a single data file

3 Building Forms

The skills tested in this section of the Microsoft Office Specialist exam for Microsoft Access 2010 relate to building forms. Specifically, the following objectives are associated with this set of skills:

3.1 Create forms

3.2 Apply form design options

3.3 Arrange fields and objects on a form

3.4 Format forms

Forms serve as the user interface for an Access database, simplifying how you navigate between the objects and features you define in your database and organizing the work of inserting, updating, and deleting data. In this chapter's first section, you'll learn about the various ways you can create a form by using options on the Create tab, including the Form Wizard. You'll also be introduced to working with a form in Layout view and Design view. In the chapter's three other sections, you'll examine in more detail how to work with the commands on the Form Layout (or Design) Tools tabs: Design, Arrange, and Format. (The context tab is named *Form Layout Tools* when a form is open in Layout view and *Form Design Tools* when a form is open in Design view).

> **See Also** In Access databases, forms and reports have a number of characteristics in common. In Chapter 5, "Designing Reports," you'll learn about the details of Access reports, but you will apply many of the skills you learn in this chapter when you create reports as well as forms.

> **Important** The options and tools for creating forms in web databases are somewhat different from the options and tools available for desktop, or client, databases. For example, Design view is not available for creating forms in web databases. Also, web forms must be created in Layout view by using a layout to contain the form's controls. You can apply the same general procedures to create a web form or a client form.

3.1   Create Forms

Access can create a form for you in a single step, or you can start with a blank form in Layout view or Design view and place and define each control yourself. Access also provides other options for creating forms that use one of several form layouts, including layouts for a navigation form. To begin building a form, you use one of the commands in the Forms group on the Create tab.

In desktop (client) databases, you can create and modify forms in Layout view or Design view. In web databases, you can use only Layout view to create and modify forms. In Layout view, you can view the form's data while you work on the form, which lets you resize the form's controls (a text box, for example) to fit the data. Layout view also provides more visual guidance about how the final form will appear. (Layout view was introduced in Access 2007. In previous versions of Access, you had to switch between Design view and Form view to see data in the form.)

When you work with a form in Design view, you cannot see live data as you create the form, but Design view can often provide a better sense of the form's structure because you can see each section of a form. (Forms include a Header, Detail, and Footer section.) Design view also offers more types of form controls and access to specific properties (such as the form's Default View property) that aren't available in Layout view. Later in this section, you'll learn more details about the steps you follow to create a form in Layout view and Design view.

> **Tip** You can open a form in a specific view by right-clicking the form in the navigation pane and then selecting the view you want. In the Form Layout (or Design) Tools Design tab, you can click View in the Views group to switch between views. You can also use the View buttons at the bottom-right corner of the Access window to switch between views.

Building a Form with the Form Wizard

The fastest way to create a client form in Access is to select a table or a query in the navigation pane and then click Form in the Forms group on the Create tab. Access uses all the fields included in the record source (the table or query) to create the form, which you can use to work with data a single record at a time. After you define the fields in a table, you can use this approach to assemble a form that you use to enter data. You can modify the forms you create this way in Layout view or Design view to add additional controls and features.

You can build a form almost as quickly—and gain options for selecting fields and a form layout—by using the Form Wizard. The Form Wizard steps you through the selection of a form's record source, the fields to include on the form, and the form's layout.

The wizard uses the table or query you select in the navigation pane as the default choice for the form's record source. On the wizard's first page, you can choose a different object when necessary. Move the fields you want to include on the form from the Available Fields list to the Selected Fields list. Use the double-arrow button to move all the fields to the form.

The wizard offers four options for a form's layout: Columnar, Tabular, Datasheet, and Justified. When you select an option, the wizard shows a preview of how the general layout will appear.

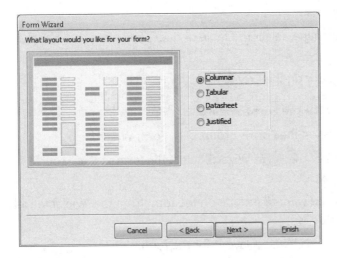

Select a Layout option offered in the Form Wizard. A preview of the layout is shown to the left of the list.

On the wizard's final page, the wizard assigns a default form name that matches the name of the object you selected as the form's record source. You can use this name, add a prefix (such as *frm*) to indicate the type of object, or type a different name. As the final step, specify whether to open the form to work with data or open the form in Design view to modify it.

> **See Also** For information about working in Design view, see "Creating and Modifying a Form with Form Design Tools" later in this chapter.

Create a Main Form and a Subform with the Form Wizard

Subforms let you work with records from another table or query in a main form. To create a main form and subform by using the Form Wizard, choose the table or query for the main form and add the fields you want to use. Then, still on the wizard's first page, select the table or query on which to base the subform and add the fields you want to include in the subform. When you click Next in the wizard, it lets you choose between creating a form with a subform or linked forms. Choose the option to create a subform, click Next, and then complete the steps in the wizard.

➤ **To create a quick form**

1. In the navigation pane, select the table or query you want to use as the form's record source.

2. In the **Forms** groups on the **Create** tab, click **Form**.

➤ **To create a form with the Form Wizard**

1. On the **Create** tab, in the **Forms** group, click **Form Wizard**.

2. On the first page of the **Form Wizard**, select the form's record source from the **Tables/Queries** list.

3. Move the fields you want to include on the form from the **Available Fields** list to the **Selected Fields** list.

4. Click **Next**, and then choose a layout for the form.

   Use the previews that the wizard displays when you select an option to see how the form's general layout will appear.

5. Click **Next**. Type a name for the form (or accept the default name), and then specify whether you want to open the form to view and update data or open the form in Design view to modify it. Click **Finish** to create the form.

Creating a Blank Form

When you want to build a form from scratch starting out in Layout view, click Blank Form in the Forms group on the Create tab. Access displays a form window and the Field list.

Tip Double-click the Field list's title bar to dock the list at the right side of the Access window.

In the Field list, click Show All Tables (if necessary) and then click the plus sign (+) beside the table you want to use as the form's record source. Clicking the plus sign displays a list of the table's fields, and you can then drag a field from the list (or double-click the field) to place it on the form.

After you add a field from a specific table to the form, Access updates the view in the Field list, dividing the list into three areas:

- **Fields Available For This View** This area shows the fields from the table you are using as the record source.

- **Fields Available In Related Tables** This area lists the tables related to the table that's serving as the record source.

- **Fields Available In Other Tables** This area lists the other tables in the database. (If all the tables in the database are related to the table you are using, Access does not display this group.)

> **See Also** For more information about creating table relationships, see "Set Relationships" in Chapter 2, "Building Tables," in this section of the book.

Drag fields from the Field list to insert them on the form. In Layout view, the fields are added to the form in the stacked layout.

When you drag a field to the form, Access displays an orange bar that indicates where the control will appear in the column of fields. This bar appears at the bottom of the stack at first, but you can drag it up to insert the field within the current group. To add a new column in which to place controls, right-click a control on the form, point to Insert, and then choose Insert Left or Insert Right. To insert a row, right-click a control, point to Insert, and then choose Insert Above or Insert Below.

> **See Also** For more information about arranging fields on a form in Layout view, see "Working with Control Layouts in Layout View" later in this chapter.

You can click the link Show Only Fields In The Current Record Source to remove the lists of related tables and other tables from the Field list. When you click this link, the Field list shows only those fields you have added to the form. Click the Edit Table link to open the table in Datasheet view, where you can insert or update the table's data while you are designing the form.

Use the Property Sheet command in the Tools group on the Form Layout Tools Design tab to view default values for the form's properties and the controls you add to the form. (When you display the property sheet, Access hides the Field list. Click Add Existing Fields in the Tools group to open the Field list again.)

To view the form's Record Source property, for example, select Form from the selection list at the top of the property sheet (under Selection Type). On the property sheet's Data tab, click in the Record Source property box and then press Shift+F2 to open the Zoom dialog box. Access uses a SELECT statement (an element of the Structured Query Language) to identify the table and the fields you've added to the form. For example, the following SELECT statement identifies four fields from the table named MarketingCampaigns:

```
SELECT MarketingCampaigns.Country, MarketingCampaigns.LaunchDate,
MarketingCampaigns.EndDate, MarketingCampaigns.Audience FROM MarketingCampaigns
```

> **See Also** For more information about form properties, see "Updating Forms from the Tools Group" later in this chapter.

When you add a field to a form, Access uses the field's data type to determine which type of form control to associate with the field. In many cases (for text and number fields, for example), Access creates a text box control and an associated label. For lookup fields, Access creates a combo box control, and for yes/no fields, Access inserts a check box control. You can add other types of controls—a command button, for example, or a label control—by using the options in the Controls group. Select the type of control you want to add, and then click on the form where you want the control to appear.

> **See Also** For more information about adding controls and setting control properties, see "Adding Form Controls" later in this chapter.

You can also use the commands in the Header/Footer group on the Design tab to add a title, logo, or date and time to the form. The Title command adds a label you can update to the form's header. Click Logo to open the Insert Picture dialog box, which you can use to select the image file for the logo you want to include. The Date And Time command opens a dialog box that lets you select the date and time format you want to include.

> ➤ **To create a blank form using Layout view**

1. On the **Create** tab, in the **Forms** group, click **Blank Form**.
2. In the **Field** list, click **Show All Tables** (if no tables are shown) and then click the plus (+) sign beside the table you want to use as the form's record source.

   If you don't see the **Field** list, click **Add Existing Fields** on the **Form Layout Tools Design** tab.
3. From the **Field** list, drag the fields you want to include on the form and place them in the form window.

   You can align and reposition fields after you place them.
4. To add a logo, title, or date and time to the form, use the commands in the **Header/Footer** group.
5. On the **Form Layout Tools Design** tab, click **Property Sheet**.
6. In the property sheet, you can specify properties for the form and the form's controls.

Creating and Modifying a Form with Form Design Tools

The Form Design command in the Create tab's Forms group opens a blank form window in Design view. Use the Add Existing Fields command in the Tools group (on the Form Design Tools Design tab) to open the Field list. You can then expand the list of fields for the table you want to use as the form's record source and drag fields to place them on the form. When you add the first field to the form, Access changes the organization of the Field list as it does in Layout view. (For more details, see the previous section.)

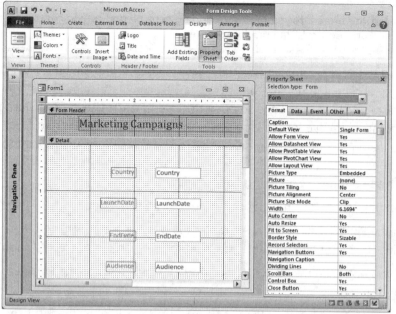

In Design view, you can see each section in a form, such as the Form Header and Detail sections shown here. Use the property sheet to set form properties. Drag controls to position and align them.

Using a Query as a Form's Record Source

If you want to use a query as a form's record source, use the Form Wizard to create the form, select the query you want to use, and then modify the form as necessary in Layout view or Design view. You can also click the ellipsis button in the Record Source property box to open the Query Builder. In the Show Table dialog box, select the Query you want to use, click Add, and then use the Field list in the design grid to select the fields you want to include on the form. Close the Query Builder to return to form Design view.

See Also For more information about working with the Query Builder, see Chapter 4, "Creating and Managing Queries" in this section of the book.

As you add fields to the form, Access starts defining the form's Record Source property. Click Property Sheet in the Tools group on the Form Design Tools Design tab to display the property sheet. Use the selection list to select the form, control, or form section (Detail, for example) whose properties you want to update or view. (You can find an example of the expression Access uses to create a form's record source in the previous section.)

> **See Also** For more information about form properties, see "Updating Forms from the Tools Group" later in this chapter.

To align and position fields when you work in Design view, you can use the grid marks and the ruler. Access highlights the ruler when you drag a control so that you can see its relative position. By right-clicking a control, you can work with the options for the Align, Size, and Position commands to adjust the layout of the form. For example, to align a group of labels, select the group by holding down the Ctrl key and clicking each label (or drag to select the group), right-click the selection, point to Align, and then choose the Left or Right option.

> **See Also** You'll learn more about arranging controls on a form later in this chapter in "Arrange Fields and Objects on a Form."

When you first create a blank form in Design view, the form contains only the Detail section. You locate most of the form's controls in its Detail section, but a form can also include Header and Footer sections. You can use the Header section, for example, for the form's title, to include a logo, or to show the date and time. You might use the Footer section to show a Totals field that is calculated from the values of other fields on the form.

To insert the Header and Footer sections, right-click in the Detail section and choose Form Header/Footer. You can also use the commands in the Header/Footer group on the Design tab to add the Header and Footer sections and insert a form element. The Title command adds a label to the Header section. Click Logo to open the Insert Picture dialog box, which you can use to select the image file for the logo you want to include. The Date And Time command opens a dialog box that lets you select the date and time format you want to use. Access adds the date, time, or both to the form's Header section.

When you work in Design view, you'll often add one or more controls to a form to supplement the controls Access creates when you insert fields. For example, you might add option buttons, check boxes, and a list box that provide a set of choices related to the form. Or you might include a subform control that displays data from a related table or query.

> **See Also** For information about using a subform control, see "Adding a Subform" later in this chapter.

To add a control, select the type of control you want to add in the Controls group and then click on the form where you want to place the control. For text box, combo box, and list box controls, Access displays a wizard by default that helps you set up the properties and functionality of the control.

> **See Also** For more information about adding form controls and setting control properties, see "Adding Form Controls" later in this chapter.

➤ To create a form in Design view

1. On the **Create** tab, in the **Forms** group, click **Form Design**.

2. To display the **Field** list, click **Add Existing Fields** in the **Tools** group on the **Form Design Tools Design** tab.

3. In the **Field** list, click **Show All Tables** (if no tables are shown) and then click the plus (+) sign beside the table you want to use as the form's record source.

4. From the **Field** list, drag the fields you want to include on the form and place them in the form window.

   You can align and reposition fields after you place them.

5. To add a logo, title, or date and time to the form, use the commands in the **Header/Footer** group.

6. On the **Format Layout Tools Design** tab, click **Property Sheet**.

7. In the property sheet, you can specify properties for the form and the form's controls.

Building a Navigation Form

To augment or replace the Access navigation pane, you can build a form for navigation. (Navigation forms make use of a navigation control that's new in Access 2010.) By using this control, you build a form with which you can switch between other forms and reports in the database.

> **Tip** Navigation forms are especially useful in web databases because web browsers do not display the Access navigation pane.

As a starting point, select one of the layouts provided on the menu that appears when you click Navigation in the Forms group on the Create tab. Each of the built-in layouts provides tabs (in various locations and orientations) that you click to switch to the object you want to use.

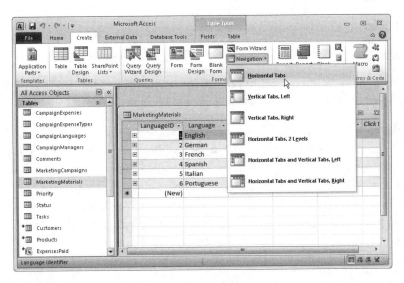

Choose an option from this menu to start building a navigation form.

After you select a layout, Access opens the new form in Layout view. You add forms and reports to the navigation form by dragging them from the navigation pane to the Add New tab in the navigation form.

Build a navigation form by dragging forms and reports to the Add New button. You can use your own navigation form in place of the Access navigation pane.

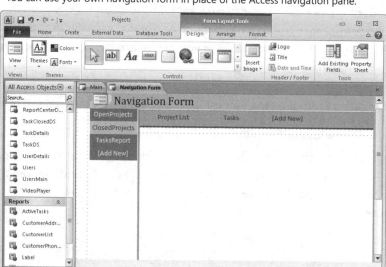

You can then fill in the Detail section of the form by adding fields from the Field list or inserting form controls from the Controls group.

After you create the navigation form, you can select it as the default form that Access displays when you open the database. You should be sure to take this step if you are using the navigation form in a web database (because the navigation pane is not displayed in a browser). Open the Access Options dialog box by clicking Options on the File tab. On the Current Database page, in the Application Options section, select the navigation form in the Display Form list; for a web database, select the form from the Web Display Form list.

The Client Forms and More Forms Commands

In web databases, the Forms group on the Create tab includes the Client Forms command. The options under Client Forms include Form Wizard, Form Design, Form, and others. You can use these commands to create client forms for the database. Other form layouts are also available. For example, the Split Form option sets up a form that shows the same data in two views—a main section at the top of the form and a datasheet below that. Use the Datasheet option to create a form that opens in Datasheet view by default. With the Modal Dialog option, you can create a form that functions like a dialog box, with OK and Cancel buttons.

In desktop or client databases, the More Forms command appears instead of Client Forms. This menu includes Split Form, Datasheet, and other options. The Multiple Items option (which is also available on the Client Forms menu) creates a form in which multiple records appear on each page. (The formal name of the view for this type of form is Continuous Forms.)

➤ **To create a navigation form**

1. On the **Create** tab, in the **Forms** group, click **Navigation**, and then choose the layout you want to use.

2. Display the navigation pane if necessary.

3. In the navigation pane, select a form or report, and then drag the object to the **Add New** button in the navigation form.

4. Use the **Controls** group and the **Field** list to add other controls and fields to the body of the form.

Practice Tasks

The practice files for these tasks are located in the practice files folder for Microsoft Access 2010. You can save the results of these exercises in the same folder. Change the file name so that you don't overwrite the sample files. When you are done, try performing the following tasks:

- Open the file Hello_World_ch3.accdb. Use the database's tables and queries to create forms by using two or three of the options on the Create tab. For example, use the Form command to create a form for the Tasks table. Use the Form Wizard to create a form based on the MarketingCampaigns table.

- Create a navigation form for the Hello World database. Add the forms you created in the first practice task to the navigation form.

- Open the database ProjectsWeb.accdb. Use the Blank Form option on the Create tab to create a form based on the Projects table.

3.2   Apply Form Design Options

In the following sections, you'll learn about other commands and options on the Form Layout (or Design) Tools Design tab. You can use these commands to modify the way a form looks and to add controls to the form (such as text boxes and list boxes). The Design tab also includes the Header/Footer group. You can use a form's header or footer to include a logo, for example, the form's title, and other information.

Applying Themes to a Form

Themes are used throughout Microsoft Office 2010 to provide a standardized look to documents, spreadsheets, presentations, and database objects. In Access, themes control colors and fonts. For forms, themes affect the color and font used in the form header and the font used in labels and text box controls.

You apply a theme to a form by using the Themes gallery, which Access displays when you click Themes on the Form Layout (or Design) Tools Design tab. If the Live Preview featured is enabled, you see a preview of a theme as you hover your mouse pointer over the options in the gallery.

> **Tip** If Live Preview is not enabled, click Options on the File tab. On the General page of the Access Options dialog box, select Enable Live Preview.

The Themes gallery is divided into two groups. The group labeled In This Database shows the default database theme and any other theme applied to a database object. The Built-In group lists the themes that Access provides by default.

> **Tip** Click Browse For Themes at the bottom of the Themes gallery to locate other theme files (which use the .thmx file name extension) that are available on your network or in a different folder on your local computer.

When you apply a theme to a form, that theme is inherited by other objects in the database. Applying a theme to all the objects in your database in a single step saves lots of time, but you can also apply a theme to a single object or to all objects that share the same theme. Click Themes to open the Themes gallery, right-click a theme, and then choose one of the following options:

- Apply Theme To All Matching Objects
- Apply Theme To This Object Only
- Make This Theme The Database Default

> **Tip** If you expect to apply a theme frequently (to objects in more than one database, for example), choose Add Gallery To Quick Access Toolbar.

When you apply a theme to a specific object, Access lists this theme in the In This Database group in the Theme gallery. A ScreenTip identifies which object the theme applies to or whether the theme applies to the database.

You aren't bound by the formatting in a theme. To apply a different color scheme to a form, click Colors in the Themes group and then select the option you want to use. If you want to update objects that use the same theme, right-click an option in the built-in colors list and then choose Apply Color Scheme To All Matching Objects.

You can also modify the font used in a form by clicking the Fonts command in the Themes group and then applying one of the options that Access displays.

If you specify a different color scheme or font for a form, you can save those settings as a new theme. Open the form that includes the formatting you want to save. Click Themes on the Design tab, and then click Save Current Theme. In the Save Current Theme dialog box, type a name for the theme and then click Save. The themes you define and save are displayed in the Themes gallery in their own group, named Custom.

➤ To apply a theme to a form

1. In the navigation pane, right-click on the form and then choose **Design View** or **Layout View**.

2. On the **Form Design** (or **Layout**) **Tools Design** tab, click **Themes**, and then select the theme you want to apply to the form.

➤ To modify the color scheme for a theme

1. In the navigation pane, right-click on the form and then choose **Design View** or **Layout View**.

2. On the **Form Design** (or **Layout**) **Tools Design** tab, click **Colors** in the **Theme** group and then select the color scheme you want to use.

➤ To define and apply your own color scheme

1. On the **Form Design** (or **Layout**) **Tools Design** tab, click **Colors** in the **Theme** group and then click **Create New Theme Colors**.

2. In the **Create New Theme Colors** dialog box, specify the colors for the theme elements (such as Text/Background—Dark 1).

3. Type a name for the custom color scheme, and then click **Save**.

4. In the **Themes** group, click **Colors**, and then select the custom color scheme you want to apply.

➤ To modify the font scheme for a theme

1. In the navigation pane, right-click on the form and then choose **Design View** or **Layout View**.

2. On the **Form Design** (or **Layout**) **Tools Design** tab, click **Fonts** in the **Theme** group and then select the font scheme you want to use.

➤ To define and apply your own font scheme

1. On the **Form Design** (or **Layout**) **Tools Design** tab, click **Fonts** in the **Theme** group and then click **Create New Theme Fonts**.

2. In the **Create New Theme Fonts** dialog box, specify the heading font and the body font.

3. Type a name for the custom font scheme, and then click **Save**.

4. In the **Themes** group, click **Fonts**, and then select the custom font scheme you want to apply.

Adding Form Controls

When you have a form open in Layout view or Design view, you can add controls (a text box, command button, or check box, for example) to the form. To add a control, click the icon for the control you want to include, and then click on the form where you want to place the control. For some types of controls, Access displays a wizard or a dialog box that you use to specify the information required to set up the control.

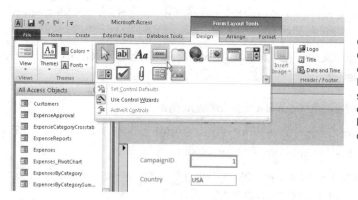

Click a control in the Controls group and then click the form to insert it. Keep Use Control Wizards selected to set up command buttons, list boxes, and combo boxes.

After controls are in place, you can modify the form's layout by resizing and aligning controls, for example. You do this by using the handles on a control, by using commands on the Form Design (or Layout) Tools Arrange tab, or by setting control properties in the property sheet, which you display by clicking the Property Sheet command.

> **See Also** For more information about working with the Arrange tab, see "Arrange Fields and Objects on a Form" later in this chapter.

Working with Control Properties

In the property sheet, properties are arranged in five tabs: Format, Data, Event, Other, and All. Properties vary depending on the type of control, but controls also have many properties in common. Here is a description of the tabs and the properties they contain:

- The Format tab for many types of controls includes properties such as Caption, Height, Width, and Text Align. The Visible property is also included on the Format tab. You can use a control's Visible property to show or hide the control under conditions you define.

- The Data tab is where you find the Control Source property. This property specifies the field or the expression from which the control gets its data. Not all types of controls have a Control Source property. *Bound controls* (controls that are linked to a field) include text boxes; option groups (which contain option buttons or check boxes); combo boxes and list boxes; charts; and subforms and subreports. Unbound controls include labels, command and toggle buttons, tab controls, hyperlinks, the web browser control, lines, and images.

  The Data tab also includes properties such as Default Value, Validation Rule, and Validation Text.

> **See Also** For more information about validation rules, see "Setting Field Properties in Design View" in Chapter 2 in this section of the book.

- The Event tab lists properties such as On Click, Before Update, On Enter, and On Exit. You can associate a macro or a subprocedure written in Microsoft Visual Basic for Applications (VBA) with an event to automate the operations of a form.

- The Other tab contains miscellaneous properties. Among these is the Name property. You use the Name property to refer to a control in VBA code, for example, and in an expression. (The Name property is not the same as the Caption property, which controls the display text associated with the control.) Access creates a default value for the Name property (such as Text 10 or List6) when you add a control.

You can use the ControlTip Text property to define the text for a ScreenTip that appears when you point to the control with your mouse.

- The All tab displays all properties associated with a control.

The following list describes the purpose of each control and lists additional control properties.

- **Text box** Displays text fields, general number and currency fields, and memo fields. In addition to using the Width and Height properties, you can format a text field by setting properties such as Back Color, Border Style, Border Width, Font Name, and Font Size. For a field that uses the Memo data type, you could set the Scroll Bars property to Vertical to more easily review the text that's displayed.

- **Label** Identifies fields and controls on the form. Label formatting properties include Font Name, Font Size, and Font Weight and Border Style, Border Width, and Border Color. In client forms, you can use the Special Effect property to give the label a sunken or raised look. (This property isn't available in forms for web databases.)

- **Button** Button controls are generally used to perform an action such as opening another form, navigating to records, or running macros or other Visual Basic code. In web forms and client forms, you can set a variety of formatting properties for buttons. For example, you can add a picture to a button. You can use the Hover Color and Pressed Color properties to specify the color of the button and its text when you hover over or press the button.

- **Tab control** You can use tab controls to set up tab pages on which you can organize a set of data. In a projects database, for example, you could use one page of a tab control for schedule information, a second for budget fields, and a third for displaying data about contacts. You can set properties for the tab control and for each page. You can add text boxes, list boxes, buttons, and other types of controls to a tab page to define and interact with the data it displays.

- **Hyperlink** Use a hyperlink control to link to a file, a web page, or an e-mail address. In a client database, you can also use a hyperlink to open another object in the database. When you add a hyperlink control to a form, Access displays the Insert Hyperlink dialog box. In the Link To list, select a category. If you select Existing File Or Web Page, you can use the Browse The Web or the Browse For File button to locate the page or file. Use the Address box to specify the URL or path, and enter the text you want to display on the form in the Text To Display box. For e-mail addresses, you need to provide the e-mail address and text for the message's Subject line.

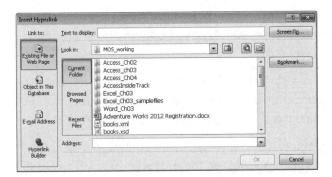

- **Web browser control** Lets you display a file or a web page on a form. When you add a browser control to a form, Access opens the Insert Hyperlink dialog box and displays the Hyperlink Builder option. In the dialog box, type or browse to the page you want to display. Access adds the URL to the Base URL box. For example, you could use http://bing.com as the base URL. By typing **/search?q=** in the Paths area and defining a parameter named **Term** with the value **Microsoft + Office** in the Parameters area, the control returns search results related to Microsoft Office. Of course, you could substitute other text to search for or use an expression to provide a value from a control on your form.

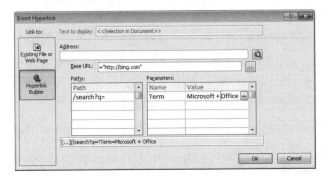

- **Navigation control** A navigation control provides buttons to which you can assign forms or reports. For more information about using the navigation control, see "Building a Navigation Form" earlier in this chapter.

- **Combo box** A combo box lets users select an item from a list or specify a new item (assuming that the Limit To List property is set to No). You can format a combo box by setting font and border properties, for example. A combo box's data properties include the Row Source property, which specifies the list's values; and Row Source Type, which indicates whether the list comes from a table or a query or a value list that you define. For client forms, Access provides a wizard you can use to set up a combo box.

- **List box** A list box displays a list of values from a table or a query or from a list that you define. Like a combo box, you use the Row Source and Row Source Type properties to set up the list.

- **Check box** Use a check box to specify yes/no or true/false choices. A check box has fewer formatting properties than other types of controls. Use the Control Source property to bind the control to a field.

- **Attachment** You can bind an attachment control to a field with the Attachment data type. Use the properties on the property sheet's Format tab to specify border styles, height, width, and any special effects.

- **Subform/Subreport** This control lets you embed another form or report within the form. For more information, see "Adding a Subform" later in this section.

- **Image** Use an image control to display a logo or another type of image on a form.

When you are working in Design view, the following controls are also available:

- **Option group** Use this control to create an option group that contains check boxes, option buttons, or toggle buttons. When you bind an option group to a field, the value of that field can be determined by which option button or check box a user selects in the group. For example, you could bind an option group to the field ProductSize and include option buttons for Small, Medium, and Large.

- **Option button** An option button is also used to capture yes/no or true/false information. You can add a set of option button controls to an option group to set the value for the field bound to the option group.

- **Page Break** Inserts a page break between pages of a multipage form.

- **Chart** Use this control to insert a chart on a form. When you insert a chart control, Access starts the Chart Wizard, which you use to set up the chart.

- **Line** Use the line control to add a line to visually separate controls, for example.

- **Toggle button** You can use a toggle button control to capture yes/no information. When a toggle button is clicked (appears pressed in), its value is yes or true. When the button is not pressed, its value is false.

- **Rectangle** Use this control to add a filled or empty rectangle to a form. You can enclose controls in a rectangle to help format the form.

- **Unbound object frame** Use an unbound object frame to add an object from another application to your form. The application needs to support object linking and embedding (OLE). You can add pictures, sounds, charts, or slides to your form, for example.

- **Bound object frame** A bound object frame is used to display and edit an OLE object field from the form's record source. You can display pictures and graphs on a form. For other types of objects, Access displays the icon for the object's application.

Using Control Wizards

By default, Access enables the option Use Control Wizards and displays a wizard when you insert a button, combo box, or list box on a client form. Here are brief summaries of the steps you follow when you work with the wizards.

- **Command Button Wizard** On the wizard's first page, select a category and then select an action for the button to perform. In the Record Navigation category, for example, you can specify that the button goes to the next or previous record or finds a specific record. In the Form Operations category, the actions include Close Form, Print A Form, and Refresh Form Data (among others). You can choose an option to include a picture or a text label on a button. In the last step, you provide a name for the button. You use this name to refer to the button in expressions or macros.

- **Combo Box Wizard and List Box Wizards** In these wizards, you first specify whether the list will come from a table or a query or from a list that you define. Work through the wizard to select the table and fields, or type the values in the list. Before you complete the steps in the wizard, you need to specify whether Access should remember the value selected in the list (you might use this value in an expression) or save the value in a particular field.

Adding a Subform

By setting up a main form and a subform, you can view the data from related tables. You can define a main form and a subform when you create a form with the Form Wizard, but if you want to add a subform to a form you have already created, you can use the subform wizard, which appears when you insert a subform/subreport control on a form.

> **See also** For more information about the Form Wizard, see "Building a Form with the Form Wizard" earlier in this chapter.

To use the Subform Wizard, be sure the Use Controls Wizard option is selected in the Controls group. Click the subform/subreport control, and add it to the form.

You can base the subform on a table, query, or form you've already defined. If you select the option Use An Existing Form, select the form in the list, click Next, type a name for the subform, and click Finish. When you choose the Use Existing Tables And Queries option, the wizard next displays a page on which you choose fields from one or more tables to include on the subform. On the wizard's next page, you need to define which field links the subform and the main form. If the table or query you selected has a relationship to the main form's record source, Access shows a list of fields you can choose from. If Access cannot determine the linking fields, it selects the Define My Own option on this page. You then need to select the linking fields you want to use. On the wizard's last page, you type a name for the subform.

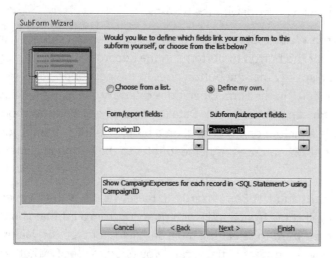

On this page of the SubForm Wizard you need to identify the field or fields that link the main form and the subform.

If you want to fine-tune the work the wizard performed, open the property sheet, select the subform control, and then adjust the Height and Width properties, for example, or reposition the control by setting the Top and Left properties, or type a message in the Status Bar Text property (on the property sheet's Other tab) to describe the purpose of the subform.

➤ **To insert controls and set control properties**

1. In the navigation pane, right-click the form and then choose **Design View** or **Layout View**.

2. On the **Form Design** (or **Layout**) **Tools Design** tab, in the **Controls** group, click the control you want to add to the form.

3. Click on the form where you want to place the control.

Depending on the type of control, Access displays a wizard or a dialog box you use to specify information required to set up the control.

4. On the **Form Design** (or **Layout**) **Tool Design** tab, in the **Tools** group, click **Property Sheet**.

5. In the property sheet, specify the values for the control properties you want to set.

Using a Form Header and Footer

As you learned in the sections "Creating a Blank Form" and "Creating and Modifying a Form with Form Design Tools" earlier in this chapter, a form includes three sections: Detail, Header, and Footer. You can use the Header/Foot group on the Form Layout (or Design) Tools Design tab to insert a logo, a title, and the date and time in your form.

The commands in the Header/Footer group insert built-in elements, but you can add other controls to a form's header or footer by dragging the appropriate control to that section of the form. For example, you can add button controls to the header or footer section to save room for text boxes and other controls in the Detail section.

➤ **To insert information in a form header or footer**

1. In the navigation pane, right-click the form and then choose **Design View** or **Layout View**.

2. On the **Form Design** (or **Layout**) **Tools Design** tab, in the **Header/Footer** group, click the option for the element you want to add to the form:

- **Logo** Select the image file from the **Insert Picture** dialog box.
- **Title** Type a title for the form in the label control Access provides.
- **Date and Time** Specify the date and time format you want to use in the **Date and Time** dialog box.

Updating Forms from the Tools Group

The Design tab's Tools group includes two commands in Layout view: Add Existing Fields, which opens the Field list for a form, and Property Sheet, which opens the property sheet pane in which you can specify properties for the form and its controls. In the section "Create Forms" earlier in this chapter, you can see examples of how to work with both the Field list and the property sheet. The section "Adding Form Controls" provides detailed information about many control properties. You should review those sections for the details of how to use the Field list and the property sheet to add fields to a form and to set control properties.

In Design view, the Tools group includes four additional commands:

- Tab Order, which is covered later in this section.

- Subform In New Window, which you can use to display a subform in its own window.

- View Code, which opens the Microsoft Visual Basic for Applications editor.

- Convert Form's Macros To Visual Basic, which opens the Convert Form Macros dialog box. You can use this dialog box to specify settings for converting macros.

> **Important** This chapter does not cover the details of using macros or Visual Basic for Applications code in a form. For more information about macros, see the help topic "Introduction to the Macro Builder." For help using the Visual Basic editor, click Visual Basic on the Database Tools tab, and then click Help, Microsoft Visual Basic for Applications Help.

Setting Form Properties

A form and its sections (Detail, Header, and Footer) also have a number of properties you can set and modify in the property sheet. With the property sheet open, select Detail, Form Header, or Form Footer from the selection list to view and set properties for a section. Select Form to work with the properties for the form itself.

For a form, you might work with one or more of the following properties on the property sheet's Format tab:

- **Default View** In Design view, you can choose the option to open the form in Datasheet view, for example. Choose Single Form to view a single record on the form. Choose Continuous Forms to view multiple records.

- **Allow Form View, Allow Datasheet View, Allow Layout View** Use these properties to control the views in which you can display the form.

- **Navigation Buttons, Navigation Caption, Scroll Bars, Record Selectors** Set the Navigation buttons property to No if the record navigation buttons aren't required on the form. If you do show the navigation buttons, you can type text in the Navigation Caption property to replace the default caption "Record." The Scroll Bars property gives you options for showing only the vertical scroll bar, only the horizontal scroll bar, both, or neither. The Record Selectors property controls whether the record selector is displayed on the form.

- **Close Button, Min Max Buttons** Set these properties to Yes or No depending on whether you want the form to include the Close button, the Minimize button, and the Maximize button in the upper-right corner of the form.

On property sheet's Data tab, you can view and set properties that affect how a user works with the form's data:

- **Data Entry** Set this property to Yes (the default setting is No) if you want Access to display a blank record when you open the form.

- **Allow Additions, Allow Deletions, Allow Edits** These properties control whether a user can use this form to insert records, delete records, and change the values in form controls.

- **Allow Filters** Set this property to No if you don't want users to be able to filter the records shown in this form.

Setting the Tab Order for a Form

When you work with a form in Design view, the Tools group on the Form Design Tools Design tab includes the Tab Order command. Setting the tab order for a form can help users enter data efficiently because they can use the Tab key to move from field to field on the form following the order you specify. The Tab Order dialog box lists each section of the form and the fields and controls within that section. The fields are listed in the current tab order. As the dialog box explains, select a row (or multiple rows) and then drag the row or rows to the position where you want it. The Auto Order button in the dialog box arranges the tab order so that it corresponds to how the form's controls are placed left to right and top to bottom on the form.

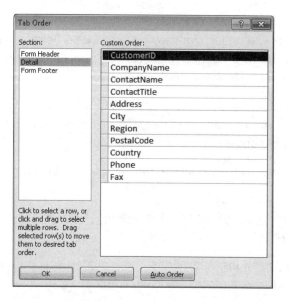

> **Tip** You can also specify the tab order by setting the Tab Index property, which appears on the Other tab in the property sheet. Set the Tab Index property for the first control in the tab order to 0, the second to 1, and so on.

➤ To set properties for a form and form sections

1. In the navigation pane, right-click the form and then choose **Design View** or **Layout View**.

2. On the **Form Design** (or **Layout**) **Tools Design** tab, in the **Tools** group, click **Property Sheet**.

3. In the selection list, select **Form**, **Detail**, **Form Header**, or **Form Footer**.

4. In the property sheet, type values for the properties or choose from options Access provides.

➤ To set the tab order for a form

1. In the navigation pane, right-click the form and then choose **Design View** or **Layout View**.

2. On the **Form Design** (or **Layout**) **Tools Design** tab, in the **Tools** group, click **Tab Order**.

3. In the **Tab Order** dialog box, select the field or fields whose tab order you want to set, and then drag the field or fields to the position you want them.

4. Click **Auto Order** to arrange the tab order to match the order of the fields on the form.

5. Click **OK**.

Practice Tasks

The practice files for these tasks are located in the practice files folder for Microsoft Access 2010. You can save the results of these exercises in the same folder. Change the file name so that you don't overwrite the sample files. When you are done, try performing the following tasks:

- Open the file Hello_World_ch3.accdb.

- Open the Tasks form in Design view, and apply the Equity theme to the form. Use the Colors and Fonts commands to modify the elements of the theme, and then save the modified theme as a custom theme.

- Use the Form Design command to open a blank form in Design view. Using the Field list, add the fields from the MarketingCampaigns table to the form.

  - Display the form's Detail section. Use the Header/Footer group to add a title to the form. Give the form the title Marketing Campaign Summary.

  - Add a command button control to the form. Using the control wizard, set up the button so that it opens the Task form.

  - Add a hyperlink control to the form. Set up the hyperlink so that it sends a message to your e-mail address.

  - Add a subform control to the form that displays the CampaignExpenses table.

  - Open the Tab Order dialog box, and modify the form's tab order.

3.3 Arrange Fields and Objects on a Form

Access provides a number of tools and techniques you can use to arrange the controls and other objects (like images) that you include on forms. In Design view, for example, you can simply drag fields and their labels to arrange them. You can precisely specify the size and position of controls by setting the Height, Width, Top, and Left properties.

Sizing and Ordering Controls in Design View

In Design view, the Form Design Tools Arrange tab includes the Sizing & Ordering group. This group provides commands you can apply to controls to modify their size, the spacing between controls, and their alignment. For example, if you want two or more text boxes to have the same size, select the text box controls, click Size/Space, and then choose one of the options in the Size group. You can also use the Size/Space menu to control the spacing between controls and to group controls so that you can reposition the controls as a unit.

In Design view, use the Size/Space menu to resize controls and to adjust the spacing between controls.

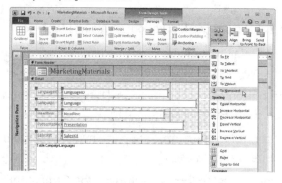

> **Tip** In the Grid section of the Size/Space menu, click Grid to show or hide the design grid. Temporarily hiding the grid helps you see the form's background. Click Ruler to hide or show the ruler. Keep Snap To Grid enabled to make positioning controls easier.

Use the Align command in the Sizing & Ordering group to align a group of controls. The Bring To Front and Send To Back commands change the relationship of objects that overlap on a form.

➤ **To size and space controls in Design view**

1. In the navigation pane, right-click the form and then choose **Design View**.

2. Select the control or controls you want to work with.

3. On the **Form Design Tools Arrange** tab, in the **Sizing & Ordering** group, click **Size/Space**, and then choose the option you want to apply to the controls.

➤ **To align controls in Design view**

1. In the navigation pane, right-click the form and then choose **Design View**.

2. Select the control or controls you want to work with.

3. On the **Form Design Tools Arrange** tab, in the **Sizing & Ordering** group, click **Align**, and then choose the option you want to apply to the controls.

➤ **To change the order of controls**

1. In the navigation pane, right-click the form and then choose **Design View**.

2. Select the control or controls you want to work with.

3. On the **Form Design Tools Arrange** tab, in the **Sizing & Ordering** group, click **Send to Back or Bring to Front**.

Working with Control Layouts in Layout View

When you create a form in Layout view, the form's controls are contained within a layout, which helps manage the alignment and arrangement of controls. For client forms, using a layout is optional, but Access requires a layout for forms created in a web database or in a database you publish to Access Services.

> **See Also** For more information, see "Publishing a Database to Access Services" in Chapter 1, "Using the Access Workspace," in this section of the book.

For client forms, Access provides two default layouts. In the *tabular* layout, controls are arranged in columns and rows (something like a spreadsheet or a table). Labels are displayed in the form's Header section (like column headings) above the text box controls, which Access places in the form's Detail section. In the *stacked* layout, controls appear in two columns, with labels in the left column and text boxes controls to the right. All controls in the stacked layout are included in a single form section. Access uses the stacked layout for forms created with the Form tool and for blank forms you create in Layout view by clicking Blank Form on the Create tab. You can switch between the tabular and stacked layouts by clicking the button for the layout you want to apply in the Table group on the Form Layout Tools Arrange tab.

> **Tip** In Design view, you can remove a layout by selecting the controls on the form and clicking the Remove Layout command in the Table group on the Form Layout Tools Arrange tab. If you are creating a form in Layout view, you can right-click a control, point to Layout, and then click Remove Layout. (In Layout view, the Remove Layout command does not appear in the Table group.)

Adding Gridlines

You can also use the Table group to display gridlines on a form. The options are Both, Horizontal, Vertical, Top, Bottom, or None. None is the default selection, but adding gridlines can help highlight certain controls and other information. Use the Color, Width, and Border options at the bottom of the Gridlines menu to change how the gridlines you add appear.

You work with the commands in the Rows & Columns group when you need to expand the area of a layout by inserting rows or columns. To add a row to a layout, first select an adjacent cell and then click Insert Above or Insert Below. Similarly, select an adjacent cell, and then click Insert Left or Insert Right in the Rows & Columns group to insert a column. (To delete a row or column, right-click a cell in that row or column and choose Delete Row or Delete Column.)

Another way to alter the arrangement of a layout is to merge or split cells. By merging cells, you can have one control span two columns or rows. After selecting the cells you want to merge, click Merge in the Merge/Split group. In contrast, when you split a cell in a layout, you can place two controls in that cell. Use the Split Horizontally or Split Vertically command to split cells.

By using the Move Up and Move Down commands (in the Move group), you can reposition the rows or a single cell in a layout. Click a cell in the row you want to move, click Select Row in the Rows & Columns group, and then click Move Up or Move Down.

The three commands in the Arrange tab's Position group control spacing between controls, the margins around the text a control displays, and how controls are anchored within the layout. Each setting in the Control Margins menu (None, Narrow, Medium, and Wide) progressively increases the space between the upper-left corner of a control and the position where the control's text appears. The Wide setting can obscure text in a text box that is anything less than approximately .3 inches in height (assuming the font size you are using is the default 11 points).

Settings under Control Padding (also None, Narrow, Medium, and Wide) control the space between controls in the layout. Click Select Layout in the Rows & Columns group, click Control Padding, and then choose the padding option you want to apply.

Resizing the form's window can affect how controls are arranged. By using one of the anchoring options that Access provides, you can fasten controls to the top left (the default position), top right, bottom left, or one of the other anchoring positions. After you select an option from the Anchoring menu, resize the form window to see the effect. You can anchor the entire layout or specific elements on a form. For example, if you add a line to mark a section of a form, you can apply the Stretch Across Top anchoring option so that the line stretches across the top of the form when the form window is resized.

➤ **To work with control layouts in Layout view**

1. In the navigation pane, right-click the form and then choose **Layout View**.

2. Click the **Form Layout Tools Arrange** tab.

3. To apply a different default layout to the form, click **Stacked** or **Tabular** in the **Table** group.

4. To insert a row or column in the layout, click a cell in the adjacent row or column, click **Select Row** or **Select Column** in the **Rows & Columns** group, and then click **Insert Above** or **Insert Below** (for rows) or **Insert Left** or **Insert Right** (for columns).

5. To merge two cells in the layout, select the cells and then click **Merge** in the **Merge/Split** group.

6. To reposition a row in the layout, click a cell in the row, click **Select Row** in the **Rows & Columns** group, and then click **Move Up** or **Move Down in the Move group**.

7. To specify margins for a control or the layout, select the control or click **Select Layout** in the **Rows & Columns** group. In the **Position** group, click **Control Margins**, and then choose the option you want to apply.

8. To insert padding for a control or the layout, select the control or click **Select Layout** in the **Rows & Columns** group. In the **Position** group, click **Control Padding**, and then choose the option you want to apply.

9. To apply an anchoring option to the layout, click **Select Layout** in the **Rows &
Columns** group. In the **Position** group, click **Anchoring**, and then choose the
option you want to apply.

Practice Tasks

The practice files for these tasks are located in the practice files folder for Microsoft
Access 2010. You can save the results of these exercises in the same folder. Change
the file name so that you don't overwrite the sample files. When you are done, try
performing the following tasks:

- Open the file Hello_World_ch3.accdb.

- Open the Campaign Information form in Design view. Use the commands
  in the Sizing & Ordering group to align the labels to the left and to resize
  the text boxes so that they match the size of narrowest one. Use the Spacing
  options on the Size/Space menu to apply equal vertical space between the
  controls.

- Open the Marketing Materials form in Layout view. Insert a new column to
  the right, and then add the fields Headline, Presentation, and Sales Kit. Adjust
  the margins and the control padding so that both are set to Medium.

3.4   Format Forms

You can format a form (and other objects in a database) by applying a theme from the
Themes gallery. Themes include built-in settings for fonts and color schemes, and you
can adjust these elements to define your own theme.

> **See Also** For details about applying and defining themes, see "Applying Themes to a
> Form" earlier in this chapter.

For additional formatting options, you can turn to the Form Layout (or Design) Tools
Format tab, which provides commands for specifying font properties and number
formatting and for changing the background for a form. The Format tab also includes
the Control Formatting group. With the commands in this group, you can apply a style
to a control, add special visual effects, and define conditional formatting that lets you
highlight data that matches criteria you define.

> **Tip** When you are formatting controls on a form, you can use the list in the Selection group at the far left of the Format tab to select the control.

Modifying a Form's Background

The Background group on the Format tab includes two commands: Background Image and Alternate Row Color.

To use an image as the background for a form, click Background Image, click Browse, and then open the location where the image file you want to use is stored. After you add the image, you can set properties for the image to modify how Access displays it.

Click Property Sheet on the Format Layout (or Design) Tools Design tab. In the property sheet, click the Format tab. The properties you use to control the display of a background image include the following. (Settings in one or more of these properties affect the options for others.)

- **Picture Type** This property can use one of three settings. Use the Embedded option if you want Access to add a copy of the image to the form. With this option, you know the image is available whenever you load the form, but adding a copy of the image increases the size of the form and the database. If you choose Link, Access uses the path and file name specified in the Picture property to locate the image file each time you open the form. If the file is moved, Access can't display it until you update the path. If you use the Shared option, Access adds a copy of the image to a system table. You can then select the image from the Picture property list to display it as a background in other database objects.

- **Picture** Specifies the image file used as the background. Choose an image from the list, or click the ellipsis button if you want to select a different image file.

- **Picture Tiling** If you set the Picture Size Mode property to Clip or Zoom and the image you are using is smaller than the form's dimensions, set this property to Yes to display multiple copies of the image on the form.

- **Picture Alignment** When the Picture Size Mode property is set to Clip or Zoom, you can choose an option in the Picture Alignment property to center the image or place it in a corner of the form.

- **Picture Size Mode** This property controls the size at which Access displays the image. The options include the following:

  - **Clip** Access trims the borders of the image so that it fits the size of the form.

- ○ **Zoom** Access increases or decreases the size of the image to fit the size of the form. With this option, Access retains the proportions of the image.

- ○ **Stretch, Stretch Horizontal, Stretch Vertical** When you choose one of these options, Access resizes the image to fit the size of the form, but the image's proportions can be distorted.

You can use the Alternate Row Color button with a form open in Datasheet view to apply a color you specify (a theme color, standard color, or color you define) to alternating rows of the table. Generally, you will see a form in Datasheet view only if you select Datasheet in the Default View property for the form or you select Datasheet as the layout option when you use the Form Wizard. When you open the form, you'll see the Alternate Row Color command on the Form Tools Datasheet tab.

➤ **To add an image to the form's background**

1. Open the form in Layout view or Design view.

2. Click the **Form Design Tools Format** tab.

3. In the **Background** group, click **Background Image**.

4. Select an image from the Image gallery, or click **Browse** to locate the image file you want to use.

5. Select the image file in the **Insert Picture** dialog box, and then click **OK**.

➤ **To set properties for a background image**

1. Open the form in Layout view or Design view.

2. On the **Form Layout (or Design) Tools Design** tab, click **Property Sheet**.

3. In the property sheet, select **Form** from the **Select type** list.

4. Set the values you want to use for the following properties: **Picture Type**, **Picture**, **Picture Tiling**, **Picture Alignment**, and **Picture Size Mode**.

➤ **To use an alternating row color**

1. Open the form in Datasheet view.

2. On the **Form Tools Datasheet** tab, click **Alternate Row Color**, and then choose the color you want to apply.

Formatting Form Controls

By working with the commands in the Font group on the Format tab, you can make changes to font properties for labels and other controls on the form.

> **Tip** The Font group includes the Format Painter button. Apply the changes you want to the font in one control, click that control, and then use the Format Painter to apply those changes to other controls.

For example, click a label on a form and then choose the font you want to use from the Font list. You can also change the size of the font, choose a different font color, or apply a background color to a control. Use the alignment buttons to position the text flush left, flush right, or centered.

In the Number group, you can apply a format to fields that use the Number, Currency, or Date/Time data type. For example, select a date field in a form, and then choose a format from the list of formats provided. The format you choose here affects how the date is displayed, but it doesn't change the date format specified for the field in table Design view.

Commands in the Control Formatting group let you format controls in other ways, although these commands don't apply to all types of controls. Use the Shape Fill command to add a background color to a control. The Shape Outline command lets you modify the color and style of a control's borders. For a command button, you can use options on the Shape Effects menu to apply a shadow, a glow effect, or softened or beveled edges. Access enables the Change Shape command when you select a command button, tab control, or navigation button, for example. Use the options to display the button as an oval or another of the available shapes.

Formatting Controls in the Property Sheet

Each control on a form has a group of properties on the Format tab of the property sheet. (Click Property Sheet on the Form Layout (or Design) Tools Design tab to display the property sheet.) You can use these properties to review the formatting for a control and to make changes. For a text box, you can set properties such as Width, Height, Back Color, Border Style, Border Color, Font Name, Font Size, Text Align, and many others. For detailed formatting requirements, use the property sheet together with or in place of the commands available on the ribbon.

> **See Also** For more information, see "Working with Control Properties" earlier in this chapter.

➤ **To format form controls**

1. Open the form in Layout view or Design view.

2. Click the **Form Design (or Layout) Tools Format** tab.

3. In the **Selection** group, choose the control you want to format or click **Select All**. (You can also click to select a control on the form.)

4. In the **Font** group, choose a new font, font size, or font color; apply bold, italic, or underline formatting; add a background fill color; and align the text.

5. For number, currency, and date and time fields, use the **Number** group to apply number, date/time, and currency formatting to the field.

6. In the **Control Formatting** group, do the following:

- Use the **Quick Style** and **Change Shape** commands to format a button.

- Use the **Shape Fill** command to add a background fill color to a control.

- Use the **Shape Outline** command to apply line styles and colors to the control's borders.

- Use the **Shape Effects** command to add a shadow or glow effect to a button control.

Applying Conditional Formatting

Conditional formatting rules let you apply specific formatting to data that matches criteria you define. You can set up conditional formatting rules for text boxes and combo boxes, but not for other types of controls.

For example, you could set up a rule that applies to a field named ExpirationDate. In the rule, you could define special formatting that Access applies to the field when the expiration date is 30 days or sooner from today. You might also use conditional formatting for a field that tracks the number of units in inventory for each product. When the value of the QuantityOnHand field reaches the level you specify, Access applies the conditional formatting. By highlighting data in this way, you can see important information at a glance.

Click Conditional Formatting in the Control Formatting group to open the Conditional Formatting Rules Manager dialog box. In the Show Formatting Rules For list, select the field you want to work with. (The control that's selected when you click Conditional Formatting is shown by default.)

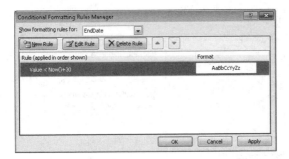

Click New Rule to open the New Formatting Rule dialog box. The Select A Rule Type list has two options:

- **Check Values In The Current Record Or Use An Expression** Use this option when you want to write an expression (such as *=Now()+30* for the ExpirationDate field example mentioned earlier) or set up a rule that applies when the value of a field is, for example, between two other values or equal to, greater than, or less than a value you specify.

- **Compare To Other Records** Choose this option if you want to set up data bars that show the value of one field in comparison to others.

> **Tip** You can define up to 50 conditional formatting rules for a control.

Checking Values in the Current Record or Using an Expression

With the first choice (Check Values In The Current Record Or Use An Expression), you start defining the rule by specifying criteria in the Edit The Rule Description area. In the first list in this area, choose Field Value Is, Expression Is, or Field Has Focus.

- **Field Value Is** With this option, you next select a comparison operator (Between, Equal To, Less Than, or others). Depending on which operator you select, you then enter values you want Access to use for comparison. You can enter a constant or define an expression.

- **Expression Is** Use the text box Access provides to define the expression you want to use to set up the rule.

- **Field Has Focus** If you select this option, Access applies the conditional formatting when a user selects the field.

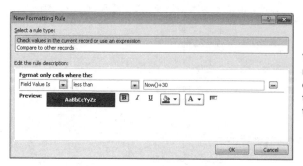

You define the conditional formatting rule for field values by choosing an operator (Less Than is used here) and then typing a value or an expression that Access uses for comparison.

> **See Also** For more information about creating expressions and using the Expression Builder, see "Getting Help with the Expression Builder" in Chapter 4 in this section of the book.

You then define the formatting you want Access to apply when the conditions you define are true. You can apply bold, italic, or underlining; specify a fill color; or use a different font color. Click the Enable button if you want Access to disable the control when the rule is true.

Using Data Bars

Data bars are used most effectively in continuous forms, split forms, or forms open in Datasheet view. When you set up data bars, you specify options in the Type and Value lists to determine how the shortest and longest bars are displayed. The default values for Type are Lowest Value and Highest Value (where the data bar for the highest value covers the entire control). You can also choose Number or Percent in the Type list. If you select either of these options, you enter a constant or an expression in the Value list.

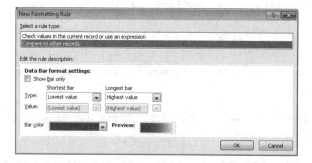

Access shows both the field value and the data bar by default. Select Show Bar Only if you don't need to see the field value. Choose the color you want for the color bar, and use the Preview area to see how the data bar will appear. Of course, you will also see the effects of the conditional formatting in the form.

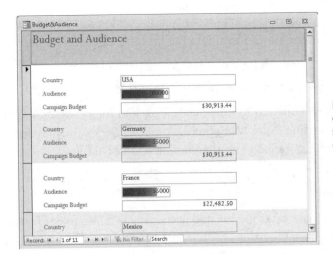

By applying data bars with conditional formatting, you can see how values compare to each other on a form.

> **To set up conditional formatting that checks values or uses an expression**

1. Open the form in Layout view or Design view.

2. Select the text box or combo box you want to apply conditional formatting to.

3. On the **Form Design Tools Format** tab (or the **Form Tools Datasheet** tab), click **Conditional Formatting** in the **Control Formatting** group.

4. In the **Conditional Formatting Rules Manager** dialog box, click **New Rule**.

5. In the **New Formatting Rule** dialog box, in the **Select a rule type** list, select **Check values in the current record or use an expression**.

6. In the **Edit the rule description** area, specify the criteria for the conditional formatting rule.

7. Use the formatting controls to specify the formatting Access applies when the criteria you define is true.

8. Click **OK** in the **New Formatting Rule** dialog box, and then click **OK** in the **Conditional Formatting Rules Manager** dialog box. (Click **Apply** if you want to apply the rule you just defined and then define additional rules.)

> **To set up conditional formatting using data bars**

1. Open the form in Layout view or Design view.

2. Select the text box or combo box you want to apply conditional formatting to.

3. On the **Form Design Tools Format** tab, click **Conditional Formatting** in the **Control Formatting** group.

4. In the **Conditional Formatting Rules Manager** dialog box, click **New Rule**.

5. In the **New Formatting Rule** dialog box, in the **Select a rule type** list, select **Compare to other records**.

6. In the **Edit the rule description** area, specify the settings you want to use in the **Type** and Value lists for the shortest data bar and the longest data bar.

7. If you want to see only the data bar, select **Show Bar only**.

8. Select the color you want to use in the **Bar color** list.

9. Click **OK** in the **New Formatting Rule** dialog box, and then click **OK** in the **Conditional Formatting Rules Manager** dialog box. (Click **Apply** if you want to apply the rule you just defined and then define additional rules.)

Practice Tasks

The practice files for these tasks are located in the practice files folder for Microsoft Access 2010. You can save the results of these exercises in the same folder. Change the file name so that you don't overwrite the sample files. When you are done, try performing the following tasks:

- Open the file Hello_World_ch3.accdb, and then open the Tasks form in Layout view or Design view.

- Change the font for the text box controls to Calibri. Apply bold formatting to the Description field.

- Apply the Short Date format to the Start Date and Due Date fields.

- Add a background image to the form by using one of the sample pictures available on your computer.

- Select the New Task command button and then use the Quick Styles and Change Shape commands to format the button.

- Create a conditional formatting rule that applies bold formatting and a red fill when the Start Date field is earlier than January 1, 2012.

- Create a conditional formatting rule that applies bold formatting and a green fill when the Due Date field is less than 30 days from January 1, 2012.

Objective Review

Before finishing this chapter, be sure you have mastered the following skills:

3.1   Create forms

3.2   Apply form design options

3.3   Arrange fields and objects on a form

3.4   Format forms

4 Creating and Managing Queries

The skills tested in this section of the Microsoft Office Specialist exam for Microsoft Access 2010 relate to using queries. Specifically, the following objectives are associated with this set of skills:

4.1 Construct queries

4.2 Manage source tables and relationships

4.3 Manipulate fields

4.4 Calculate totals

4.5 Generate calculated fields

You'll learn how to create different types of queries in the first section of this chapter. As you'll see, you can use queries to help maintain database records and to analyze data. For example, you can use a make-table or an append query to create archives of your records. With a select query, you can retrieve records that match specific criteria—for example, all orders above a certain dollar amount or all customers in a specific city who have not placed an order in the last 60 days. In this chapter's other sections, you'll learn how to manage tables and relationships in queries, how to sort records and manage fields, how to calculate summary values in a query, and how to work with expressions and calculated fields.

4.1 Construct Queries

The Create tab on the Microsoft Access 2010 ribbon includes two commands in its Queries group: Query Wizard and Query Design. The Query Wizard command leads you to a choice of wizards. You'll learn about the Simple Query Wizard and the Crosstab Query Wizard in this section. The Query Design command opens the Query Designer.

In the Query Designer, you specify the fields to include in the query, define criteria you want Access to apply when it runs the query, and work with commands on the Query Tools Design tab to create a specific type of query.

You build select and action queries in the Query Designer by using the Show Table dialog box and the Query Tools Design tab.

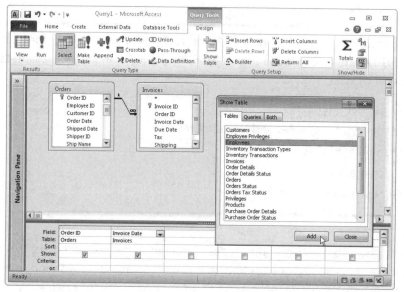

Selecting Records with a Query

You can use a select query to return all or a subset of the records stored in one or more tables. In a select query, you specify which fields you want to use, and you can then define criteria to return the set of records you want to see. To create a select query, you can use the Simple Query Wizard or build the query yourself by using the Query Designer.

Using the Simple Query Wizard

To start the Simple Query Wizard, click the Query Wizard command in the Queries group on the Create tab. In the New Query dialog box, select Simple Query Wizard (the default choice) and then click OK. You can then use the wizard to add fields from one or more tables (or queries) to the query you are creating.

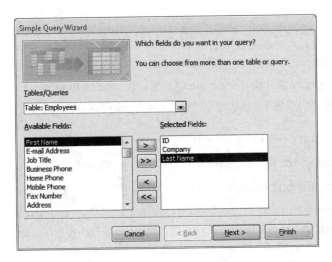

In the Simple Query Wizard, use the Tables/Queries list to choose each table or query you want to use in a select query.

If you add fields from only one table and those fields store only text data (not numeric data), the second and last step in the wizard is to provide a name for the query and then specify whether to open the query to see the records it returns or open the query in Design view.

If you include numeric fields or fields from more than one table, the wizard also prompts you to specify whether you want to create a detail query or a summary query. A detail query shows each individual record for the query. In a summary query, you can calculate the total of the values in a field or determine the average, minimum, or maximum value in a field. When date fields are present in a summary query, the wizard also prompts you to choose an option for how you want to group dates in the query. For example, you can group dates by quarter or by year.

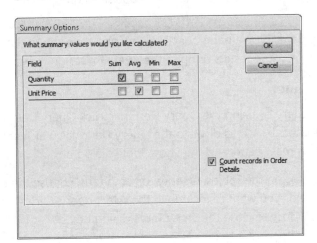

When you create a summary query by using the Simple Query Wizard, you select the function to apply to a field in this dialog box.

> **See Also** For more information about summary queries and grouping records in a query, see "Calculate Totals" later in this chapter.

On the wizard's last page, type a name for the query and choose between the options to open the query and view the records it returns or open the query in Design view.

➤ **To create a select query with the Simple Query Wizard**

1. On the **Create** tab, in the **Queries** group, click **Query Wizard**.

2. In the **New Query** dialog box, select **Simple Query Wizard**, and then click **OK**.

3. In the **Simple Query Wizard**, in the **Tables/Queries** list, select the first table or query you want to use for the query. In the **Available Fields** list, select the fields you want to include, and then click the arrow button to move the fields to the **Selected Fields** list. Use the double-arrow button to move all the fields to the **Selected Fields** list.

4. Repeat step 3 to specify other tables or queries to use in the query and the fields you want to include.

5. Click **Next**. If you included any numeric fields or fields from more than one table, the wizard prompts you to select the option to create a detail query or a summary query.

   If you select the **Summary** option, click the **Summary Options** button and then select the summary function you want to apply to the fields that Access lists. Click **OK** in the **Summary Options** dialog box.

6. Click **Next**. If prompted by the wizard, choose an option to group dates in the query.

7. On the wizard's last page, type a name for the query and then choose whether to open the query to review the results or open the query in Design view.

Using the Query Designer

To start building a select query by using the Query Designer, click Query Design in the Queries group on the Create tab. Access displays the Query Designer, which shows the query design grid below its main pane, and the Show Table dialog box.

In the Show Table dialog box, on the Tables, Queries, or Both tabs, choose the tables or queries that contain the fields you want to include in the select query. Click Add to insert the objects, and then click Close to close the Show Table dialog box.

> **Tip** Hold down the Ctrl key and click to select more than one nonadjacent item in the Show Table dialog box. To select a group of adjacent objects, hold down the Shift key, click the first object, and then click the last object in the group.

You can drag the lists of fields in the Query Designer's main pane to reposition the lists and to see relationship lines that link two tables. To add fields to the query, select a field you want to use in the field list in the Query Designer's main pane, and then drag the field to the Field row in a blank column in the design grid. (You can use the Ctrl and Shift keys to select multiple fields.) You can also work directly in the design grid by selecting fields from the list of fields displayed when you click in the Field row. To add all the fields in a table to the query design grid, double-click the asterisk (*) at the top of the field list.

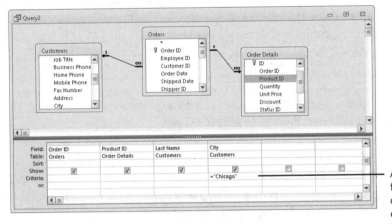

After you add fields to the query design grid, you can use the Criteria row to specify conditions for the records the query returns.

> **Tip** You can toggle on and off the display of table names in the query design grid by clicking Table Names in the Show/Hide group on the Query Tools Design tab.

To run a query, click the Run command in the Results group on the Query Tools Design tab. When you run the query, Access displays the results in Datasheet view. With the query in Datasheet view, you can use commands in the Sort & Filter group on the Home tab. To return to Design view, you can click View, Design View in the Views group on the Home tab, right-click the tab showing the query's name and choose Design view, or click the Design View button in the group of view buttons in the bottom-right corner of the Access window.

In select queries, you'll often define criteria that Access applies to select a specific set of records. For example, to find records for customers in a specific city, add the City field to the query and then type ="**CityName**" (where "*CityName*" is the city you want to examine) in the Criteria row for that field. You must enclose text values in quotation marks.

To specify criteria for a date field, enclose the date (or dates) with the pound sign (#). For example, to find records for orders placed in April 2012, you could use the criteria expression *Between #4/1/2012# and #4/30/2012#.*

In the query design grid, when you define criteria for more than one field, the query selects only the records that match the criteria for both fields—for example, records that have a value in the Order Date field greater than 3/15/2012 *and* a value for the Company Name field of Fabrikam. If you want to set up OR criteria (to find records with a value in the City field of Las Vegas *or* Chicago), use the Or row below the Criteria row to specify the second criteria.

> **See Also** You'll learn more about building expressions you can use in queries later in this chapter in "Generate Calculated Fields." You'll learn about sorting records in the Query Designer in "Specifying the Sort Order for a Query."

You can also create a parameter for a select query and then provide a value for the parameter when you run the query. Access uses the value you enter as criteria to return specific records. A parameter provides flexibility in applying criteria because you can use the same query to retrieve a different set of records.

To define a parameter, click in the Criteria row for the field you want to work with and then type a prompt enclosed in square brackets. For example, to create a parameter for the City field, type something like **[Enter a city name]**. When you run the query, Access displays the Enter Parameter Value dialog box, which shows the prompt you defined. Type the value you want to use as criteria (for example, Chicago or Montreal for the city parameter), and then click OK. Access returns the set of records that match the criteria you provide.

> **Tip** You can use parameters in select queries as well as crosstab, append, make-table, and update queries.

As the final step in defining a query parameter, you should define the parameter's data type. Click Parameters in the Show/Hide group on the Query Tools Design tab. In the Query Parameters dialog box, type the parameter name (including the brackets) just as it appears in the design grid. In the Data Type column, select the data type (such as Text or Date/Time) that matches the field for which you defined the parameter.

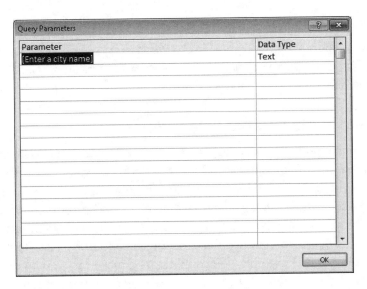

In the Query Setup group, use the Return (or Top Value) list to specify whether you want to see only some of the records that match your criteria. You can select one of the preset values (5, 25, or 100, for example) or a percentage or type in the list box to specify how many records you want to see. After you sort the records in a query (see "Specifying the Sort Order for a Query" later in the chapter for details), you can use the Top Values list to show, for example, the top 20 orders customers have placed this month.

➤ To create a select query in Design view

1. On the **Create** tab, in the **Queries** group, click **Query Design**.

2. In the **Show Table** dialog box, select the tables or queries you want to use in the query. Click **Add** to add the tables to the Query Designer, and then click **Close**.

3. From the table field lists, drag the fields you want to include in the query. (You can also select fields from the list Access displays when you click in the **Field** row in the query design grid.)

4. Define any selection criteria for the query in the **Criteria** row.

5. In the **Results** group on the **Query Tools Design** tab, click **Run** to see the records returned by the query.

➤ To define a parameter for a query

1. In the navigation pane, right-click the query and then choose **Design View**.

2. Type the parameter in the **Criteria** row, and enclose the parameter in square brackets.

3. In the **Show/Hide** group, click **Parameters**.

4. In the **Query Parameters** dialog box, in the **Parameter** column, type the parameter exactly as it appears in the design grid. In the **Data Type** column, select the data type for the parameter, and then click **OK**.

Using a Make-Table Query

When you run a make-table query, Access creates a table (in the current database or in another database you designate) that includes the fields you specified for the query. You can use a make-table query to improve performance when you find yourself fre-quently running a select query that involves several tables whose data doesn't change. Access can run the select query more quickly if it is based on a single table (created by the make-table query) instead of multiple tables. You can also use a make-table query to build your data archives. For example, you could create a make-table query to store all the orders for the past year and use the Orders table only for current orders.

To be sure that Access creates a table that includes the correct records, you can base a make-table query on a select query, run the select query to review the records, and then create the make-table query.

> **See Also** For details about creating a select query, see the previous section.

When the select query is set up to return the records you want in a table, display the query in Design view and click Make Table in the Query Type group. In the Make Table dialog box that Access displays, type a name for the new table and also specify whether you want to include the table in the current database or in a different database. If you choose Another Database, type the file name for the database or click Browse to select the database file.

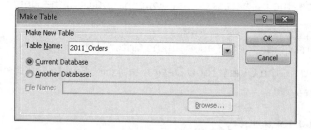

By clicking OK in the Make Table dialog box, you set up the query. To create the table, double-click the make-table query in the navigation pane or click Run in the Results group on the Query Tools Design tab. Click Yes in each of the message boxes Access displays to complete the operation.

> **Tip** When you create a table by using a make-table query, Access includes the field names and data types in the new table but not the settings specified for other field properties. Also, the new table does not include a primary key. You need to open the new table in Design view to update field properties and assign a primary key.

➤ **To create and run a make-table query**

1. Create a select query on which to base the make-table query.

> **See Also** See "Selecting Records with a Query" earlier in this chapter for details about how to create a select query.

2. With the select query open in Design view, click **Run** in the **Results** group.

3. Review the records returned by the select query, and then click **View**, **Design View** in the **Views** group to return the query to Design view.

4. On the **Query Tools Design** tab, click **Make Table** in the **Query Type** group.

5. In the **Make Table** dialog box, type a name for the table and specify whether Access should create the table in the current database or in another database. If you select **Another Database**, type the file name or use the **Browse** button to locate the file.

6. Click **OK** in the **Make Table** dialog box.

7. In the **Results** group, click **Run**.

8. Click **Yes** in the message boxes Access displays to confirm the operation.

Appending Records with a Query

Another operation you can perform by using a query is to append records to a table. (An append query is similar to a make-table query, but instead of creating a table, as a make-table query does, an append query inserts records into a table that's already defined.) Append queries are useful tools for archiving records. For example, you could create a table named Completed Orders and then design a query based on the Orders table to select the records for completed orders. By running this query periodically as an append query, you create an archive of completed orders.

> **Important** The data you insert by using an append query must conform to the design of the destination table. For example, the data must conform to any validation rules defined for the destination table or the fields it contains.

As with make-table queries, you can start to build an append query by defining and testing a select query that returns the records you need. After setting up the select query, click Run in the Results group on the Query Tools Design tab to review the records the query returns. If the results are correct, display the query in Design view again and then click Append in the Query Type group. In the Append dialog box, use the Table Name list to select the table you want to append records to in the current database. If you want to append records to a table in a different database, select Another Database and then use the Browse button to locate the file. Access refreshes the Table Name list to show items from the database you specify. Select the table, and then click OK. Save the query, and then run it by double-clicking the query in the navigation pane or by opening the query in Design view and clicking Run in the Results group on the Query Tools Design tab. When you run the query, Access displays a message box asking you to confirm the operation. Click Yes to proceed. You can open the table to which the records were appended to verify that the records were inserted correctly.

> **To create and run an append query**

1. Create a select query on which to base the append query.

> **See Also** See "Selecting Records with a Query" earlier in this chapter for details about how to create a select query.

2. With the select query open in Design view, click **Run** in the **Results** group.

3. Review the records returned by the select query, and then click **View, Design View** in the **Views** group to return the query to Design view.

4. On the **Query Tools Design** tab, click **Append** in the **Query Type** group.

5. In the **Append** dialog box, type a name for the table and specify whether Access should create the table in the current database or in another database. If you select **Another Database**, type the file name or use the **Browse** button to locate the file.

6. Click **OK** in the **Append** dialog box.

7. In the **Results** group, click **Run**.

8. Click **Yes** in the message box Access displays to confirm the operation.

Updating and Deleting Records with a Query

The Query Type group on the Query Tools Design tab includes options for creating update queries and delete queries. These types of action queries are also helpful tools for maintaining records in your database.

To create either an update query or a delete query, click Query Design in the Queries group on the Create tab. Add the table or tables you want to use in the query and then insert the query's fields in the design grid, just as you do when you create a standard select query.

> **See Also** For information about building a select query, see "Selecting Records with a Query" earlier in this chapter.

After the select query is set up as you want it, click Update in the Query Type group. Access adds the Update To row to the design grid. In the Update To row for the field or fields you want to update, enter the expression that will update the field's current values. For example, to apply a 3 percent increase to the list price of your products, you could enter the expression **[List Price]*1.03** in the Update To row. When you run the update query, Access displays a message box telling you how many rows (records) will be updated. Click Yes to complete the operation.

> **Important** You cannot undo the changes made by an update query. Before you run the query, you should make a backup copy of the table whose records will be updated. Also, you can check which records will be updated before you run the query by switching the query to Datasheet view (click View, Datasheet View in the Results group) before you run the query.

You can use a delete query to delete selected records from a table. After setting up a select query with the fields you need to work with, click Delete in the Query Type group. Access adds the Delete row to the query grid and removes the Show and Sort rows. In the Delete row, the keyword Where appears. You need to specify criteria in the Criteria row that selects the records Access will delete. For example, you might delete all records where the Discontinued field equals Yes or delete all records for which the order date is later than a year from today.

When you work with delete queries, you should keep in mind that you might delete some records you were not expecting to. This occurs if the table you are deleting records from is related to another table and the tables' relationship is defined to use the Cascade Delete Related Records option. (For more information about the Cascade Delete Related Records option, see "Set Relationships" in Chapter 2, "Building Tables.") You can turn off this option if necessary by clicking Relationships on the Database Tools tab and then right-clicking the relationship line linking the tables whose relationship you want to modify. Choose Edit Relationship, and then clear the check box for the Cascade Delete option. Of course, you should also create a backup of your database before you run the delete query.

When you run the delete query, Access displays a warning indicating the number of records that it will delete. Click Yes to complete the operation, noting that you cannot use the Undo command to reverse this action.

➤ **To create and run an update query**

1. On the **Create** tab, in the **Queries** group, click **Query Design**.

2. In the **Show Table** dialog box, select the table you want to use in the query. Click **Add** to add the table to the Query Designer, and then click **Close**.

3. From the table field list, drag the fields you want to include in the query. (You can also select fields from the list Access displays when you click in the **Field** row in the query design grid.)

4. Define any selection criteria for the query in the **Criteria** row.

5. In the **Query Type** group, click **Update**.

6. In the **Update To** row for the field or fields you want to update, enter an expression that calculates the updated values.

7. In the **Results** group on the **Query Tools Design** tab, click **Run**. Click **Yes** in the warning Access displays to complete the operation.

➤ **To create and run a delete query**

1. On the **Create** tab, in the **Queries** group, click **Query Design**.

2. In the **Show Table** dialog box, select the table you want to use in the query. Click **Add** to add the tables to the Query Designer, and then click **Close**.

3. From the table field list, drag the fields you want to include in the query. (You can also select fields from the list Access displays when you click in the **Field** row in the query design grid.)

4. In the **Query Type** group, click **Delete**.

5. In the **Criteria** row, specify the criteria for selecting the records you want to delete.

6. In the **Results** group on the **Query Tools Design** tab, click **Run**. Click **Yes** in the message box Access displays to complete the operation.

Viewing Data in a Crosstab Query

With a crosstab query (which is a type of select query), you can perform calculations using summary functions such as Sum, Avg, and Count and organize data for analysis. Access provides a wizard you can use to create a crosstab query, or you can use the Query Designer to specify the fields for the query and to define the calculations you want the query to perform.

The results of a crosstab query are displayed in a datasheet whose structure is different from datasheets for simple select queries and tables. The query's data is grouped by two sets of values. One set appears down the left side of the datasheet, and the other appears across the top.

Crosstab queries are something like a PivotTable. When you add fields to a crosstab query, you specify which fields to use as row headings (you can use as many as three fields), which field appears in the columns across the top, and which field is used for the summary values.

Using the Crosstab Query Wizard

The Crosstab Query Wizard is a good starting point for creating a crosstab query. You can use the wizard to set up the basic query and then open the query in Design view to modify it. You can select fields from only one table when you use the Crosstab Query Wizard. To work around this limitation, create a select query that includes fields from the tables you need to use and then choose the select query as the record source when you work in the Crosstab Query Wizard.

In the New Query dialog box that appears when you click Query Wizard on the Create tab, select Crosstab Query Wizard and then click OK to start the Crosstab Query Wizard. In the wizard, you identify the following information:

- The table or query on which to base the crosstab query.
- The field or fields (up to three fields) you want to use as row headings. If you use more than one field, Access sorts the query's records in the order in which you select the fields. Keep in mind that using more than one field makes the query more difficult to read.
- The field you want to use for the column headings. It's generally good practice to choose a field that includes only a few values for the column heading field.
- The interval for grouping date/time information in the column headings (if you choose a date/time field for the column heading). You can choose Year, Quarter, Month, Date, or Date/Time.

- The field whose value you want to summarize and the function you want to apply. You will see different functions depending on the field's data type. This page of the wizard also includes the option Yes, Include Row Sums. Select this check box to insert a row heading in the query that uses the same field and function as the field value. A row sum also inserts a column that summarizes the remaining columns.

- The name you want to assign to the query.

When you click Finish in the Crosstab Query Wizard, Access opens the query in Datasheet view.

Crosstab queries are useful for analyzing data. The query shows field values in row and column headings and summarizes the values in the field you choose.

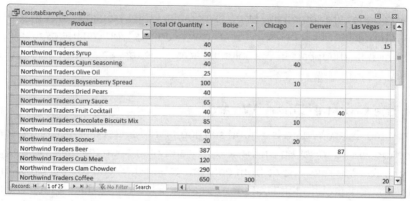

Product	Total Of Quantity	Boise	Chicago	Denver	Las Vegas
Northwind Traders Chai	40				15
Northwind Traders Syrup	50				
Northwind Traders Cajun Seasoning	40		40		
Northwind Traders Olive Oil	25				
Northwind Traders Boysenberry Spread	100		10		
Northwind Traders Dried Pears	40				
Northwind Traders Curry Sauce	65				
Northwind Traders Fruit Cocktail	40			40	
Northwind Traders Chocolate Biscuits Mix	85		10		
Northwind Traders Marmalade	40				
Northwind Traders Scones	20		20		
Northwind Traders Beer	387			87	
Northwind Traders Crab Meat	120				
Northwind Traders Clam Chowder	290				
Northwind Traders Coffee	650	300			20

Record: 1 of 25 — No Filter | Search

Creating a Crosstab Query in Design View

As mentioned earlier, when you use the wizard to create a crosstab query, you can base the query only on a single table or a single query. When you work in Design view, you can include multiple tables or queries as the crosstab query's record source. You can also first create a select query that returns the records you want and use that query as the single record source for the crosstab query.

> **See Also** For information about creating select queries, see "Selecting Records with a Query" earlier in this chapter.

To set up a crosstab query in Design view, click Query Design on the Create tab, and then use the Show Table dialog box to add the tables and queries you want to use as the record source for the crosstab query. In the Query Type group, click Crosstab.

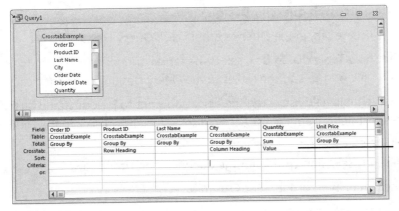

When you build a crosstab query in Design view, specify the row, column, and value fields in the Crosstab row.

The design grid for a crosstab query contains a Total row and a Crosstab row (as well as the Sort and Criteria rows you work with in other types of queries). You use the Crosstab row to specify which field or fields to use as row headings, which field to use for the query's column headings, and which field to summarize for the query's values. You use the Total row to specify the summary function the query applies.

➤ To create a crosstab query with the Crosstab Query Wizard

1. On the **Create** tab, in the **Queries** group, click **Query Wizard**.

2. In the **New Query** dialog box, select **Crosstab Query Wizard** and then click **OK**.

3. On the wizard's first page, select the table or query on which to base the crosstab query.

4. Click **Next**. On the wizard's second page, specify the field or fields (up to three fields) you want to use as row headings.

5. Click **Next**, and then select the field you want to use for the column headings.

6. Click **Next**. If you chose a date/time field for the column heading in step 5, on the wizard's next page, specify the interval for grouping date/time information in the column headings.

7. Click **Next**, and then select the field whose value you want to summarize and the function you want to apply.

8. Click **Next**, type a name for the query, and then click **Finish**.

➤ **To create a crosstab query in Design view.**

1. On the **Create** tab, in the **Queries** group, click **Query Design**.

2. In the **Show Table** dialog box, select the tables or queries you want to use in the query. Click **Add** to add the tables to the Query Designer, and then click **Close**.

3. From the table field lists, drag the fields you want to include in the query. (You can also select fields from the list Access displays when you click in the **Field** row in the query design grid.)

4. Define any selection criteria for the query in the **Criteria** row.

5. In the **Query Type** group, click **Crosstab**.

6. In the **Crosstab** row, specify the field or fields you want to use for row headings, column headings, and the query's values.

7. In the **Total** row for the value field, select the summary function you want to apply.

8. In the **Results** group, click **Run** to see the query's results.

Union, Pass-Through, and Data Definition Queries

The Query Type group also includes options for creating Union, Pass-Through, and Data Definition queries. You need to define these types of queries by using the Structured Query Language (SQL). You can find more information about SQL queries by reading the Access Help topic "Introduction to Access SQL."

Practice Tasks

The practice files for these tasks are located in the practice files folder for Microsoft Access 2010. You can save the results of these exercises in the same folder. Change the file name so that you don't overwrite the sample files. When you are done, try performing the following tasks:

- Open the file Hello_World_Ch4.accdb.

- Use the Simple Query Wizard to create a query using all the fields in the Campaign Expenses table. In the wizard, choose the option to view information so that you can examine the query's results.

- Open the Campaign Expenses query in Design view. Define criteria in the AmountSpent field to view only records for which the value of this field is greater than 500.

- Using the Query Designer, create a query based on the Marketing Campaigns table. Add the fields Campaign ID, Country, and CampaignBudget. Create an update query to increase campaign budgets by 5 percent.

- Create a select query based on the CampaignExpenses, CampaignExpenseTypes, and MarketingCampaigns tables. Add the CampaignID and Country fields from the Marketing Campaign table, the ExpenseType field from the CampaignExpenseTypes table, and the AmountSpent field from the CampaignExpenses table. Run the query to see the records the select query returns. Now convert this query to a crosstab query. Use the AmountSpent field as the value field. Try using the Country and ExpenseType fields as the row headings and column headings fields to see different views of the data.

4.2 Manage Source Tables and Relationships

In this section, you'll learn more about managing tables and relationships in a query. As you saw in examples in the previous section, you manage which tables and other queries are included as the record source for a query by using the Show Table dialog box. To display this dialog box, you need to first open a query in Design view. You can then use the dialog box to add other objects to the query. You can also remove a table from the Query Designer when it's no longer needed.

The tables you include in a query are often already related. If that's the case, you'll see a relationship line linking the tables when you display the query in Design view. You can also create relationships when you work in the Query Designer by joining tables for the purposes of the query.

> **See Also** For more information about table relationships, see "Set Relationships" in Chapter 2.

Adding and Removing Data Sources for a Query

When you start a new query in Design view, Access displays the Show Table dialog box, which you use to add the tables and other queries on which to base the new query. If you need to add tables to a query later, open the table in Design view and then click Show Table in the Query Setup group on the Query Tools Design tab. You can also right-click in the Query Design's main pane (but not on a field list) and choose Show Table from the shortcut menu.

If you need to remove a table from the Query Designer, right-click the table's field list and choose Remove Table.

➤ To add tables to the Query Designer

1. Open the query in Design view.
2. On the **Query Tools Design** tab, in the **Query Setup** group, click **Show Table**.
3. In the **Show Table** dialog box, select the tables or queries you want to add, click **Add**, and then click **Close**.

➤ To remove a table from the Query Designer

1. Open the query in Design view.
2. Right-click the field list for the table and choose **Remove Table**.

Working with Joins and Relationships in a Query

In queries, you need to define the link between the tables, called a *join*, to return the set of records you need. Access automatically joins related tables by using the fields the table's relationship is based on. You can change the join type when necessary and also define or edit relationships when you work in the Query Designer.

You can control whether Access automatically creates joins by using the Enable AutoJoin option (which is enabled by default) in the Query Design area on the Object Designers page of the Access Options dialog box. (Click File, Options to open this dialog box.) With this option enabled, when you create a query based on two tables that aren't directly related, Access attempts to join the tables by trying to match the primary key for one of the tables with a field with the same name and data type in the other table. If Access doesn't find a match, you can link the tables by selecting the linking field in one table and dragging it to the field you want to link to in the second table. By joining the tables in this way, you link them for the purposes of designing and running the query. You don't, however, create a permanent relationship that you can view and edit in the Relationships window.

By default, Access uses an *inner join*, a type of join that returns only matching records. With an inner join, a query that uses the Customers and Orders tables joined on the CustomerID field returns each customer record with a matching order record, but the query does not return records for customers who have not placed an order (because no record matches that customer record in the Orders table).

You can also create an *outer join*. By using an outer join, you can return all rows from one of the tables along with matching records from the other. With this type of join, you can create a query that returns all the records from the Customers table, including records for customers who haven't placed an order. You can create a "left" outer join or a "right" outer join to retrieve all the records from one of the tables. *Left* and *right* refer to how the tables are identified in the Join Properties dialog box, which you open by right-clicking the line linking two tables in the Query Designer and choosing Join Properties. To use an outer join to return all records from one table and matching records from another, choose option 2 or 3, depending on which table's records you want to view.

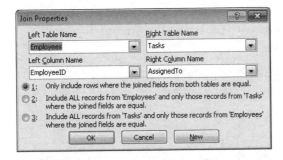

> **Tip** You can also specify the join type that related tables use when you have the Relationships window open. Click the relationship line for the tables you want to work with, and then click Edit Relationships in the Tools group on the Relationship Tools Design tab. Click the Join Type button in the Edit Relationships dialog box, and then select the type of join you want to use.

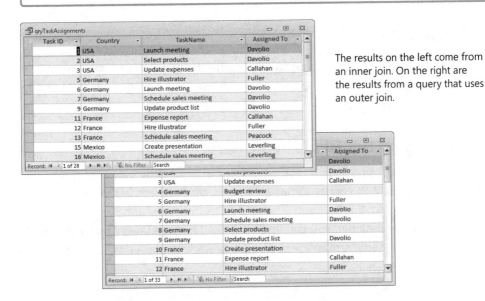

The results on the left come from an inner join. On the right are the results from a query that uses an outer join.

Practice Tasks

The practice files for these tasks are located in the practice files folder for Microsoft Access 2010. You can save the results of these exercises in the same folder. Change the file name so that you don't overwrite the sample files. When you are done, try performing the following tasks:

- Open the file Hello_World_Ch4.accdb.
- From the navigation pane, open the Tasks query in Design view.
- Display the Show Table dialog box, and add the MarketingCampaigns table to the query.
- From the MarketingCampaigns table, add the Country field to the query, and then run the query to see the results.
- Display the Show Table dialog box again, and add the Employees table to the query. Remove the MarketingCampaigns table from the Query Designer.
- Link the Tasks and the Employees table by using the EmployeeID and AssignedTo fields.
- Add the AssignedTo field to the query, and then run the query to review the results. Now use the Join Properties dialog box to create an outer join that shows all the records from the Tasks table. Run the query again to see how the outer join changes the query's results.

4.3   Manipulate Fields

After you set up a query, you can work with the query's fields and the records it returns by changing or rearranging the fields, showing and hiding query fields, and sorting the query's results.

Changing the Fields in a Query

You can add, remove, and rearrange fields in a query by using the mouse. To insert a field, first open the query in Design view. In the field lists in the top pane of the Query Designer, select the field you want to add to the query and drag the field to a blank row in the query designer. You can insert the field between two other fields by dragging it to the column in the query grid where you want to place the field. Access moves the other fields in the query to the right. You can also add a field by selecting it from the drop-down list in the Field row in the query design grid.

> **See Also** If you need to add a field from a table or a query that isn't already part of the query, use the Show Table dialog box to add the table or the query. For more information, see "Adding and Removing Data Sources for a Query" earlier in this chapter.

To remove a field, click at the top of the field's column in the design grid to select the field and then press Delete. You cannot use the Undo command to reverse this action.

If you want to change the order of the fields in the grid, first click at the top of the column of the field you want to move. (Hold down the Shift key to select more than one adjacent column.) Next drag the field or fields to the new position. Access displays a black bar to indicate the new position.

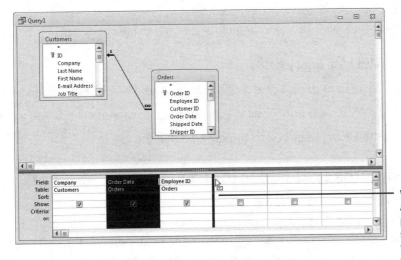

When you drag a field to a new position, Access shows a black bar to indicate where the field will appear.

> **To add, remove, and rearrange fields in a query**

1. In the navigation pane, right-click the query and then choose **Design View**.

2. To insert a field, select the field in the field list in the top pane of the Query Designer and then drag the field to the query design grid.

3. To delete a field, click at the top of the field's column and then press **Delete**.

4. To change the order of the fields, click at the top of the column for the field you want to move (hold down the Shift key to select more than one column), and then drag the column or columns to the new location.

Showing and Hiding Query Fields

In the query design grid for select queries and other types of queries, you can use the Show check box to show or hide a field in the datasheet in which Access displays the query's results. By default, the Show check box is selected for each field you add to a query.

For example, you might add an ID field or a date field to a query and then use that field to define query criteria or to sort the query. For the ID field, you might specify a particular customer's ID. You could use the date field to return all the records for orders placed since the start of your current fiscal year. You could use the City or State field in a contacts table to define criteria in a query that returns records in only one or two cities or states.

These fields are essential to defining the query, but you don't always need to show them in the query's results. If you want to hide a field in the results datasheet, clear the Show check box for that field. To show the field again, select the check box.

➤ **To show and hide query fields**

1. In the navigation pane, right-click the query and then choose **Design View**.
2. In the query design grid, clear the **Show** check box for any fields you want to hide.
3. Select the **Show** check box to display a field in the results.

Specifying the Sort Order for a Query

The Sort row in the query design grid lets you choose how Access sorts the records the query returns. In the Sort list, you can select Ascending, Descending, or Not Sorted. You can sort by a single field or by more than one field. When you specify a sort order for more than one field, Access sorts records according to the order in which the fields appear left to right in the query design grid.

> **Tip** If you add all the fields from a table or query to the query design grid by dragging the asterisk, you cannot use the Sort row to sort records.

To specify a sort order, click in the Sort row for a field, and then select the sort order you want to apply. Be sure to reposition fields as necessary when you are sorting records by more than one field. (See "Changing the Fields in a Query" earlier in the chapter for details on how to rearrange field order.)

> **Tip** If you want to sort by multiple fields in a particular sequence but also display one of these fields later in the order of the fields, add a second instance of the field, set the sort order for the field, and then clear the Show check box so that the second instance of the field doesn't appear in the query's results.

➤ To use the Sort row in a query

1. In the navigation pane, right-click the query and then choose **Design View**.

2. In the query design grid, click in the **Sort** row for the field you want to sort by, and then select **Ascending**, **Descending**, or **Not Sorted**.

3. To sort by more than one field, specify the sort order for the additional fields. In the query design grid, arrange the fields left to right in the order in which you want Access to use these fields to sort records.

Practice Tasks

The practice files for these tasks are located in the practice files folder for Microsoft Access 2010. You can save the results of these exercises in the same folder. Change the file name so that you don't overwrite the sample files. When you are done, try performing the following tasks:

- Open the file Hello_World_Ch4.accdb.

- Open the TaskAssignments query in Design view, and make the following changes. Run the query after each change so that you can see how the change affects the query's results.

    ○ From the Tasks table, add the fields TaskName, Description, Start Date, and Due Date.

    ○ Hide the field Task ID.

    ○ Sort the query on the Start Date field.

4.4   Calculate Totals

Queries let you select specific records and perform operations such as updating, deleting, or appending records. You can also use queries to summarize data. For example, you can use a query to show the average value in a field or to count the number of records that meet specific criteria.

To perform these operations in a query, you use the Total row. The Total row does not appear in the Query Designer by default. To display the Total row, click Totals in the Show/Hide group on the Query Tools Design tab.

Grouping Query Records

The Group By option is selected in the Total row when you insert the row. On its own, the Group By option returns records that have unique values in each field in the query. However, you can use the Group By option together with a summary function to summariz.

For example, to see how many orders were placed on each day of a particular month, you could create a query that uses the Order Date field and the Order ID field. If you run this select query without any settings in the Total row, you'll see a record for each order. Now display the Total row by clicking Totals in the Show/Hide group. In the Order Date field, leave Group By selected and in the Order ID field select Count in the Total row. When you run this query again, you'll see the records grouped by each order date and also the number of orders placed that day.

➤ **To group records in a query**

1. In the navigation pane, right-click the query and then click **Design View**.
2. On the **Query Tools Design** tab, in the **Show/Hide** group, click **Totals**.

Summarizing Data in a Query

The options in the Total row include several functions you might be familiar with, including Sum, which calculates the total of the values in the field, and Avg, which calculates the average value. The Total row provides the following options as well:

- **Min** Identifies the smallest value in the field.
- **Max** Identifies the highest value in the field.
- **Count** Counts the number of values in a field, but ignores Null (blank) values.
- **StDev** Shows you the standard deviation for the values in the field.
- **Var** Calculates the variance of the values in the field.
- **First** Returns the value for the field from the first row encountered in the group.
- **Last** Returns the value for the field from the last row encountered in the group.

- **Expression** Select this option when you want to create an expression in the Total row that uses one or more of the aggregate functions Access provides.

- **Where** Use this setting to specify a filter that is applied to the records in the query.

> **See Also** You can also use reports to summarize the data in a table or the results returned in a query. For more information about reports, see Chapter 5, "Designing Reports."

To calculate a summary value, add the fields you want to use to the query and then click Totals in the Show/Hide group. In the Total row for the field whose values you want to summarize, select the function you want to use. To see several summary values for a specific field at one time, add several instances of the field to the query and choose a different summary function for each instance. For example, you could add three instances of the Quantity field to see the total quantity ordered as well as the minimum and maximum quantities.

By adding more than one instance of a field to a totals query, you can apply different functions to the field to gain perspective on your data.

Creating Custom Field Names

When you create a totals query, Access appends the name of the summary function to the field name and comes up with labels such as SumOfQuantity. You can create your own labels in the Query Designer by typing the text you want to use in front of the field name in the Field row followed by a colon. For example, instead of seeing SumOfQuantity, you can type **Total Quantity:** in front of the field name Quantity. Access uses this label when you display the query's results in Datasheet view.

You can apply criteria in a totals query as you can in a select or other type of query. For example, when you use the Sum function in the Total row, enter a value in the Criteria row to select values that are above or below a certain threshold—total quantities greater than 250, for example (*>250*). To apply a filter to a total query, select Where in the Total row and then type the criteria for the filter in the Criteria row.

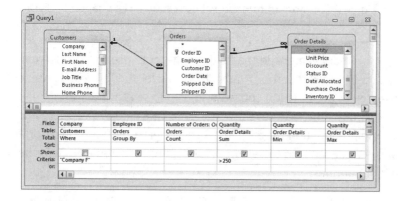

> ➤ **To view summary data in a query**

1. In the navigation pane, right-click the query and then click **Design View**.

2. On the **Query Tools Design** tab, in the **Show/Hide** group, click **Totals**.

3. In the **Total** row, select the summary function you want to apply to a field.

4. Use the **Criteria** row to define criteria you want to apply to the totals query.

5. To apply a filter to the query, select **Where** in the **Total** row and then specify the filter criteria in the **Criteria** row.

6. On the **Query Tools Design** tab, click **Run** to see the query's results.

Practice Tasks

The practice files for these tasks are located in the practice files folder for Microsoft Access 2010. You can save the results of these exercises in the same folder. Change the file name so that you don't overwrite the sample files. When you are done, try performing the following tasks:

- Open the file Hello_World_Ch4.accdb, and then open the query CampaignExpenseSummary in Design view.

- Add the Total row, and summarize the AmountSpent field by using the Sum function, Min function, and Max function.

4.5   Generate Calculated Fields

In this section, you'll learn about creating a calculated field in a query. You'll also learn more about the types of expressions you use throughout Access databases and the tools Access provides to help you create the expressions you need.

Adding an Expression to a Query

You use expressions in many areas of Access—in validation rules, for example, and in the Control Source property on forms. Queries are another area where you often need to use an expression to work with the data as you need to.

Expressions contain several elements, including functions, operators, constants, and identifiers (which refer to the names of fields or tables, for example). In a query, you can use an expression to create a calculated field. For example, in a query that summarizes orders, you can create a calculated field defined by an expression that shows the period of time between the order date and a shipped date. This expression would look like the following:

```
[OrderDate]-[ShippedDate]
```

> **Tip** When you use an expression to create a calculated field, Access provides the default label Expr1 (for the first expression in a query) as a column heading in the results datasheet. To rename the calculated field, type the field name you want to use followed by a colon and then type the expression—for example, **Fulfillment Time:[OrderDate]-[ShippedDate]**.

You can also use expressions to combine the values in two or more text fields. For example, the expression *[City] & ", " & [State/Province]* combines these two fields in a single text string. The ampersand (&) is the operator you use to combine the values.

As you can see in these examples, you enclose identifiers such as field names in square brackets. The operators you can use in an expression include mathematical operators (+, -, /, and *); the ampersand (&) for combining text fields; logical operators, such as Or, And, and Not; and comparison operators such as < (less than), > (greater than), Between, and Like.

To create a calculated field in a query, open the query in Design view and then click in the Field row in a blank column. (To insert a blank column between two fields already in the query, select the column at the right and then click Insert Columns in the Query Setup group.) You can type the expression directly in the Field row or use one of the methods described in the following sections—entering the expression in the Zoom dialog box or using the Expression Builder.

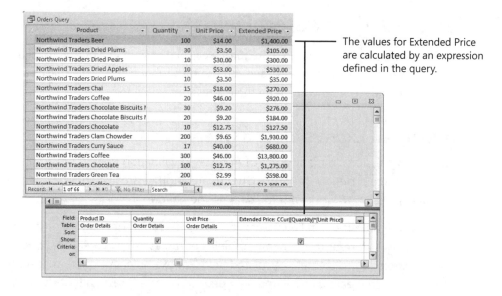

The values for Extended Price are calculated by an expression defined in the query.

➤ **To create a calculated field**

1. Open the query in Design view.

2. In the Query Designer, click in the **Field** row in the column in which you want to insert the calculated field.

3. Type the expression that performs the calculation.

   To provide a custom label for the calculated field, type the label you want to use before the expression followed by a colon.

   To open the **Zoom** dialog box to write the expression, press Shift+F2.

   To open the Expression Builder for help writing the expression, click **Builder** in the **Query Setup** group.

Entering an Expression in the Zoom Dialog Box

When you need to write an expression to create a calculated field in a query (or to define criteria), you can open the Zoom dialog box to give yourself some extra space in which to write the expression or to edit an expression that is already defined.

To open the Zoom dialog box, click in the design grid where you want to create the expression—in the Criteria row, for example, or in the Field row—and then press Shift+F2.

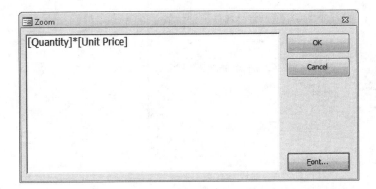

The Zoom dialog box provides a large text box in which you can compose an expression. Click the Font button in the Zoom dialog box to display the Font dialog box. You can then select a different font, font style, font size, and other attributes. You won't see this formatting in the Query Designer, but it might improve the readability of the expression while you are working with it in the Zoom dialog box.

➤ **To display the Zoom dialog box to write or review an expression**

1. In the query design grid, click in the cell where you want to write an expression.
2. Press Shift+F2.
3. Click the **Font** button in the **Zoom** dialog box to format the text you enter there.

Getting Help with the Expression Builder

When you want help creating an expression, you can use the Expression Builder. To open the Expression Builder when you are working on a query in Design view, right-click in the Field or Criteria row and choose Build. You can also click Builder in the Query Setup group.

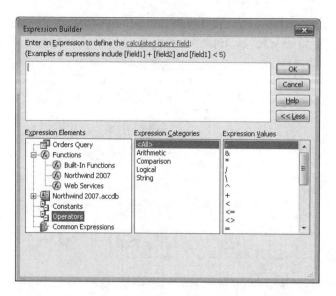

You work in four panes in the Expression Builder. You create the expression in the top pane by typing or by selecting options in the Expression Elements, Expression Categories, and Expression Values panes. The Expression Values pane is blank until you choose an option other than the current object—Orders Query in the preceding screen shot—in the Expression Elements pane. You can hide the three bottom panes by clicking the Less button. Click More to show them again.

When you build an expression by selecting items in the three bottom panes, you generally move left to right. When you select an element in the Expression Elements list, the categories for that element appear in the Expression Categories pane. When you select a category, the Expression Builder lists the values related to that category in the Expression Values pane. Double-click an item in the Expression Values pane to add it to the expression.

For example, to create an expression that multiplies the value of one field by the value of another field (for example, Quantity by Unit Price), select the query name in the Expression Elements list and then double-click Quantity in the Expression Categories list. In the Expression Elements list, select Operators; in the Expression Categories list, select Arithmetic, and then double-click the multiplication operator (*) in the Expression Value list. Now select the query again in the Expression Elements list, and then double-click on Unit Price in the Expression Categories list. In the top pane, you'll see the expression that you defined.

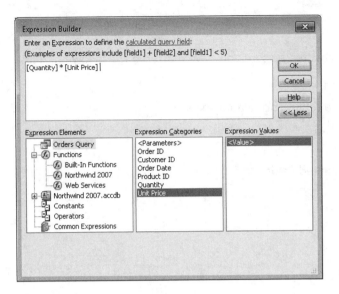

When you type in the Expression Builder's main pane, Access uses IntelliSense to display a list of items that match the characters you type. You can choose a function name or a field name from this list to include it in the expression. As you continue typing, Access adjusts the list on the basis of each character you type. Access also displays a description of the items in the IntelliSense list. When you select a function from the IntelliSense list or start typing a function's name, Access also provides information about the function's syntax, showing required and optional arguments.

Practice Tasks

The practice files for these tasks are located in the practice files folder for Microsoft Access 2010. You can save the results of these exercises in the same folder. Change the file name so that you don't overwrite the sample files. When you are done, try performing the following tasks:

- Open the file Hello_World_Ch4.accdb, open the ExpenseReport query to view its records, and then open the query in Design view.

- Create a field that calculates how much of each campaign budget remains. Hint: You must use the Sum function in the expression to calculate the total of the AmountSpent field. Also, choose Expression in the Total row.

- Create a field that calculates the percentage of the budget spent to date.

Objective Review

Before finishing this chapter, be sure you have mastered the following skills:

4.1 Construct queries

4.2 Manage source tables and relationships

4.3 Manipulate fields

4.4 Calculate totals

4.5 Generate calculated fields

5 Designing Reports

The skills tested in this section of the Microsoft Office Specialist exam for Microsoft Access 2010 relate to using reports. Specifically, the following objectives are associated with this set of skills:

5.1 Create reports

5.2 Apply report Design tab options

5.3 Apply report Arrange tab options

5.4 Apply report Format tab options

5.5 Apply report Page Setup tab options

5.6 Sort and filter records for reporting

When you need to create a particular view of your data or want to group or summarize data and provide it in a format that's suitable for a presentation or a meeting, you often use reports. As with forms, you can build reports by using fields from one or more tables or queries. You can also format reports to emphasize data and enhance their appearance by defining conditional formatting rules and adding elements such as graphics or logos, titles, and descriptive labels.

An important step in setting up a report is knowing how you want Access to group records. Access uses the grouping instructions you specify to organize the report's records. For example, in a report based on fields from the Products and Suppliers tables and grouped by supplier, Access inserts a group header for each supplier's name and can then list and sort that supplier's products within that group.

Like forms, reports contain different sections, including Page Header, Detail, and Page Footer. You can also add the Report Header and Report Footer sections to show the report's title and possibly for a logo. In the Page Footer section, you might display page numbers and similar types of information. In the Report Footer section, you can add a grand total field for values on the report.

You can view completed reports in Report view or Print Preview. Report view allows you to interact with the report through controls such as a command button or hyperlink. You can also filter a report's records when you display it in Report view. In Print Preview, you can specify page settings or choose an option to distribute the report. For example, on the Print Preview tab, Access provides commands you can use to export a report to PDF or XPS format or send it to recipients in e-mail.

In this chapter, you'll first learn about the options Access provides for creating reports. In the later sections, you'll learn how to organize and format reports, how to specify page setup and layout options for reports, and how to sort and filter the data in reports.

> **Important** Forms and reports have many characteristics in common, and a number of the tools you use to modify the design and formatting of reports are the same as you use for forms. You should be sure to review Chapter 3, "Building Forms," for detailed information about topics such as working in Layout view, using the field list, and creating custom themes. Throughout this chapter, you'll find references that point you to discussions of features described in more detail in Chapter 3.

5.1   Create Reports

The options for creating reports on the ribbon's Create tab are Report, Report Design, Blank Report, Report Wizard, and Labels. The Report command creates a simple report that includes all the fields in the table or query you select in the navigation pane. You can take this step to build a basic report or as a starting point for a report that you refine and modify in Layout view or Design view.

> **See Also** Details about using the Labels command are not included in this chapter. For information, read the Access Help topic "Create mailing labels in Access."

The Report Wizard provides several options for the layout of a report and for how the report's data is grouped, sorted, and summarized. You can view the report the wizard creates as is or open it in Design view to make modifications. If you want to create a report from scratch, choose the Blank Report command to work in Layout view, or choose Report Design to create the report in Design view.

Running the Report Wizard

Use the Report Wizard when you want help creating a report that includes fields from more than one table or query. When you move fields to the Selected Fields list on the wizard's first page, add the fields in the order you want them to appear in the report. By inserting the fields in order, you don't have to rearrange them later if you modify the report.

If you add fields from at least two tables or queries, the wizard prompts you to specify how you want to view the records in the report. The answer you give to this prompt specifies the first grouping level Access uses for the report. For example, you can choose By Suppliers or By Products for a report that includes fields from the tables that store that data. When you choose an option on this page, the wizard displays a preview showing how the report's records will be organized.

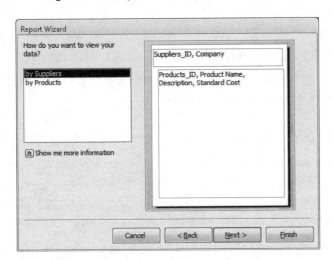

When you select fields from more than one table in the Report Wizard, you need to specify how you want to group the data.

> **Tip** Click the Show Me More Information button in the Report Wizard to display pages that provide additional examples and explanations.

You can select additional fields to use as grouping levels as well. When you choose a field to group by, click Grouping Options to open a dialog box in which you set the grouping interval. Grouping intervals depend on a field's data type. For a date/time field, you can use an interval such as year or quarter. For a numeric field, you can specify an incremental value such as 1,000.

The wizard lets you choose as many as four fields to sort by. For numeric fields, click the Summary Options button in the wizard to select a function such as Sum or Average, which Access uses to summarize report data. For the layout for the report, you can choose Stepped, Block, or Outline. You can also select portrait or landscape orientation and specify whether the wizard should adjust the width of each field so that fields fit on the page.

On the wizard's last page, you type a name for the report and indicate whether you want to open the report in Print Preview or Design view, where you can modify the report.

➤ **To create a report with the Report Wizard**

1. On the **Create** tab, in the **Reports** group, click **Report Wizard**.

2. Use the **Tables/Queries** list to choose an object, and then add the fields you want to use in the report to the **Selected Fields** list.

3. Click **Next**, and then specify the field or fields by which you want to group records in the report.

4. Click **Next**, and then choose the field or fields you want to use to sort records.

5. Click **Next**, and then choose a report layout and a page orientation.

6. Click **Next**. Type a name for the report, choose whether to preview the report or open the report in Design view, and then click **Finish**.

Building a Report in Layout View

The Blank Report command opens an empty page in Layout view and displays the Field list. (Click Show All Tables in the Field list if no tables are shown.) When you work in Layout view, under Report Layout Tools, you'll see the Design, Arrange, Format, and Page Setup tabs. (You also see these tabs when you work on a report in Design view.)

To add a field to the report, expand the list of fields for a table in the Field list and then drag the field to the report page or double-click the field. When you add the field, you see live data. You'll also see an option button (identified with a lightning bolt). Click this button to use a command that lets you switch the report to a stacked layout instead of the tabular layout, which is the layout Access uses for reports by default. (In the tabular layout, labels for fields appear across the top of the page as column headings, with text boxes that show the field's values arranged below the labels. The stacked layout places labels to the left of the field's text boxes.)

> **See Also** You can also change the layout for a report by displaying the Report Layout Tools Arrange tab, clicking Select Layout in the Rows & Columns group, and then clicking Stacked or Tabular in the Table group. You'll learn more about working with the Arrange tab later in this chapter.

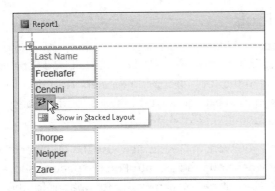

When you add the first field to a blank report in Layout view, Access displays an option button you can use to switch to the stacked layout.

As you add fields and after you have the report's fields in place, you can use options on the Report Layout Tools Design, Arrange, and Format tabs to refine the report's layout and appearance. For example, you can apply a theme to change the font and color scheme for the report or use commands on the Format tab to format controls with details such as colored fills or outlines.

> **See Also** For details about working with themes, the Grouping & Totals group, report controls, headers and footers, and the property sheet, see "Apply Report Design Tab Options" later in this chapter. For more information about commands on the Arrange and Format tabs, see "Apply Report Arrange Tab Options" and "Apply Report Format Tab Options."

➤ **To create a report using Layout view**

  1. On the **Create** tab, in the **Reports** group, click **Blank Report**.

  2. In the **Field** list, click **Show All Tables** (if no tables are shown) and then click the plus (+) sign beside the table you want to use as the form's record source.

   If you don't see the **Field** list, click **Add Existing Fields** on the **Report Layout Tools Design** tab.

  3. From the **Field** list, drag the fields you want to include on the form and place them in the form window.

   You can align and reposition fields after you place them.

  4. To add a logo, title, or date and time to the form, use the commands in the **Header/Footer** group.

  5. On the **Report Layout Tools Design** tab, click **Property Sheet**.

  6. In the property sheet, you can specify properties for the report and the report's controls.

Using Report Design Tools

The Report Design command opens a blank report page in Design view. The page shows three of the sections you can use in a report—Page Header, Detail, and Page Footer. Use the Add Existing Fields command in the Tools group (on the Report Design Tools Design tab) to open the Field list. You can then expand the list of fields for the table you want to use as the report's record source and add fields to the report.

To align and position fields when you work in Design view, use the grid marks and the ruler. Access highlights the ruler when you drag a control on the page to show you its relative position. By right-clicking a control, you can work with options for the Align, Size, and Position commands to adjust the placement and dimensions of controls. For example, to align a group of labels or text box controls, select the group by holding down the Ctrl key and clicking each control (or drag to select the group), right-click the selection, point to Align, and then choose the Left or Right option.

> **See Also** You'll learn more about arranging controls on a report later in this chapter in "Apply Report Arrange Tab Options."

You will locate many of the report's controls in its Detail section, including labels and text boxes related to the report's data. The Page Header section displays information at the top of each page of a report. You might use this section to show a date for a report or a heading you want on each page. Information in the Page Footer section—page numbers, for example—appears at the bottom of each page. Information in the Report Header and Report Footer sections appears only once—at the top of the report's first page and at the bottom of the report's last page, respectively. You can use the Report Header section to display the report's title or to include a logo.

To display the Report Header and Report Footer sections, right-click in the Detail section and choose Report Header/Footer. You can also use the commands in the Header/Footer group on the Design tab to add information to these sections by inserting an element such as a title, a logo, a date, and page numbers.

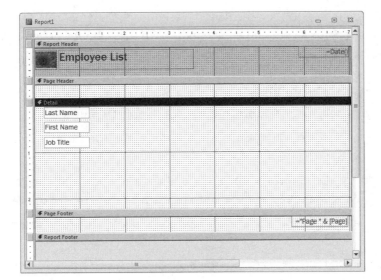

In Design view, you can display and work in each of a report's sections.

> **Tip** If you don't need to use the Report Footer section in a report, for example, click Property Sheet on the Report Design Tools Design tab, and then set the Height property for the section to 0".

When you work in Design view (or in Layout view), you'll often add one or more controls to a report to supplement the controls Access creates when you insert fields. For example, you might add additional labels or an image or include a subreport control that displays data from a related table or query.

> **See Also** For information about using subreports, see "Adding a Subreport" later in this chapter.

To add a control, select the type of control you want to add in the Controls group and then click on the page where you want to place the control.

> **See Also** For more information about working with controls and setting control properties, see "Adding Form Controls" in Chapter 3 and "Working with Controls on a Report" later in this chapter.

In Design view, you use options on the Report Design Tools Design, Arrange, and Format tabs to refine the report's layout and appearance. For details about working with the commands on these tabs, see the remaining sections in this chapter.

➤ **To create a report in Design view**

1. On the **Create** tab, in the **Reports** group, click **Report Design**.

2. To display the **Field** list, click **Add Existing Fields** in the **Tools** group on the **Report Design Tools Design** tab.

3. In the **Field** list, click **Show All Tables** (if no tables are shown) and then click the plus (+) sign beside the table you want to use as the form's record source.

4. From the **Field** list, drag the fields you want to include on the form and place them in the form window.

   You can align and reposition fields after you place them.

5. To add a logo, title, or date and time to the form, use the commands in the **Header/Footer** group.

6. On the **Format Layout Tools Design** tab, click **Property Sheet**.

7. In the property sheet, you can specify properties for the report and the report's controls.

Practice Tasks

The practice files for these tasks are located in the practice files folder for Microsoft Access 2010. You can save the results of these exercises in the same folder. Change the file name so that you don't overwrite the sample files. When you are done, try performing the following tasks:

- Open the file Hello_World_ch5.accdb.

- Use the Report tool to create a report based on the Expense Report query (qryExpenseReport). Save this report with the name **Expense Summary**.

- Use the Report Wizard to create a report using the Marketing Campaigns and the Tasks tables. Group the report by the field Country.

- Create a report in Layout view that includes fields from the Marketing Campaigns and Campaign Expenses tables. Apply the stacked layout to the report. Switch the report to Design view, and insert the Report Header and Report Footer sections. Add a title and the date to the Report Header section.

5.2   Apply Report Design Tab Options

In this section, you'll learn how to refine the design of a report by applying options on the Report Design (or Layout) Tools Design tab. These options include the Themes gallery, which you can use to help format a report, as well as the Controls group. By adding controls to a report, you can enhance both its appearance and its function. You'll also learn how to create groups and totals for a report and about some of the report properties you can set in the property sheet.

Applying a Theme to a Report

In Access reports, themes provide font and color schemes. You can apply a built-in theme by choosing one from the Themes gallery, which Access displays when you click Themes on the Report Layout (or Design) Tools Design tab. If Live Preview is enabled, you see a preview of the theme as you hover your mouse pointer over the options in the gallery.

> **Tip** If Live Preview is not enabled, click Options on the File tab. On the General page of the Access Options dialog box, select Enable Live Preview.

When you apply a theme to a report (or to a form), that theme is inherited by other objects in the database. You can apply a theme to a specific report (or apply a different theme to all reports and other objects that use the same theme) by right-clicking a theme in the gallery and choosing one of the following options:

- Apply Theme To All Matching Objects
- Apply Theme To This Object Only
- Make This Theme The Database Default

When you apply a theme to a specific object, Access lists this theme in the In This Database group in the Themes gallery. A ScreenTip identifies which object a theme applies to or whether a theme applies to the database.

> **See Also** For information about modifying the font and color schemes for a theme and the steps you follow to create a custom theme, see "Applying Themes to a Form" in Chapter 3.

➤ **To apply a theme to a report**

1. In the navigation pane, right-click on the report and then choose **Layout View** or **Design View**.

2. On the **Report Layout** (or **Design**) **Tools Design** tab, click **Themes**, and then select the theme you want to apply to the form.

Grouping Report Fields and Calculating Totals

Specifying how records are grouped in a report is an important aspect of the report's design. You can set grouping levels when you use the Report Wizard. When you build or modify a report in Layout view or Design view, you can use the Group & Sort command in the Grouping & Totals group. The Grouping & Totals group also includes the Totals command, which you use to summarize field values in a report.

When you click Group & Sort, Access displays the Group, Sort, And Total pane at the bottom of the report window. Click Add A Group, and then select the field you want to use for grouping. Access adds a group header section that uses the name of the field you select.

> **Tip** If you work in Layout view, you'll see more clearly how the selections you make in the Group, Sort, And Total pane affect the report's organization. You won't see this level of detail in Design view.

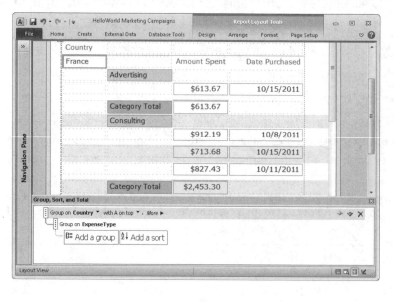

This report is grouped on two fields—Country and Expense Type. It also includes a group total.

To add another grouping level, click Add A Group again and select another field. When you click More in the Group, Sort, And Total pane, you'll see options you can set for the grouping field:

- **Sort Order** Changes the sort order.

- **Group Interval** Specifies how records are grouped. You can group a text field on the first letter, for example (which groups all A items together and so on). Date fields can be grouped by day, week, month, quarter, or an interval you define.

- **Totals** You can add totals for multiple fields and apply different summary functions (Sum and Avg or Min and Max, for example) to the same field. Use the Total On list to select a field, use the Type list to select the function, and then select the options you want to use to show the totals.

- **Title** Use this option to change the title of the field being summarized. The title is used for the column heading and for labeling summary fields in headers and footers. Click the field link, and then type the new title in the Zoom dialog box.

- **With/Without A Header Section** Use this setting to add or remove the header section for each group. Access moves the grouping field to the header when you add the header section. Access prompts you to remove any controls (other than the grouping field) from the header when you remove it.

- **With/Without A Footer Section** Use this setting to add or remove the footer section that follows each group. When you remove a footer section that contains controls, Access asks for confirmation to delete the controls.

- **Keep Group Together** The settings for this option determine how groups are laid out on the page when the report is printed.

To summarize the values in a field and add a text box that displays the summary value, click in the field you want to summarize and then click Totals in the Grouping & Totals group. The options available depend on the data type of the field you select. For numeric fields, the range of options include Sum, Average, Count, Max, Min, and others. For text and date/time fields, the Count options are available.

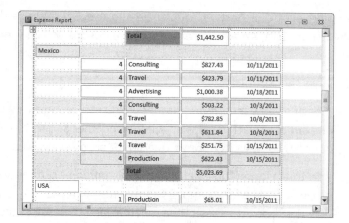

Use the Totals command to provide a summary value for values in a report.

Tip After you create a summary report, click Hide Details in the Grouping & Totals group to show only the summary fields.

➤ To group records in a report

1. Open the report in Layout view or Design view.

2. On the **Report Layout** (or **Design**) **Tools Design** tab, click **Group & Sort**.

3. In the **Group, Sort, and Total** pane, click **Add a group**, and then select the field to group by.

4. In the **Group, Sort, and Total** pane, click **More**, and then specify settings for sorting, grouping intervals, totals, title, header and footer sections, and how to keep groups together on the page.

➤ To summarize values on a report

1. Open the report in Layout view or Design view.

2. In the report, select the field you want to summarize.

3. On the **Report Layout** (or **Design**) **Tools Design** tab, in the **Grouping & Totals** group, click **Totals**, and then choose the summary function you want to apply.

Working with Controls on a Report

Reports are designed primarily to present data—unlike forms or tables, which you use to enter, update, and delete data. Given this, you often work only with label and text box controls to identify and present data in report. For example, you might add a label to identify a summary field in a group header section or to provide a title in the Report Header section. You can add an image control to enhance the appearance of a report.

> **See Also** For more information about how to work with specific controls, see "Adding Form Controls" in Chapter 3.

Although the data in a report is more static than in a form or a table, you can use a command button on a report to perform an action related to the report or add a hyperlink control to display a website or an e-mail address. In Report view, a command button or a hyperlink is operational, but keep in mind that controls like these are not active when you view the report in Print Preview. You won't see a command button in Print Preview, and a hyperlink appears only as static text.

> **See Also** You'll find more information about report views in "Using Report View Types" later in this chapter.

➤ To add controls to a report

1. Open the report in Layout view or Design view.

2. On the **Report Layout** (or **Design**) **Tools** tab, in the **Controls** group, click the type of control you want to add and then click on the report page where you want to add the control.

> **Tip** For some types of controls, Access displays a control wizard you can use to set up the control.

Using a Subreport

You can insert a subreport into a main report to provide related information. You can create the subreport first by using the Report Wizard or Layout or Design view, or you can define the subreport as you work in the Subreport Wizard. In either case, the subreport must contain a field you can use to link it to the main report.

To add a subreport, follow the steps in the Subreport Wizard, which appears when you add a subreport control to the report page. In the wizard, you can first select the report you want to use as the subreport or choose the option to base the subreport on an existing table or query. If you choose to work with a table or query, the wizard's next page lets you select the table or query and add the fields you want to use. You then need to either select the set of linking fields that Access detects or define your own. After you name the subreport, click Finish in the wizard to add it to the main report.

➤ **To insert a subreport control**

1. Open the main report in Design view or Layout view.

2. On the **Report Design** (or **Layout**) **Tools Design** tab, select the Subform/Subreport control in the **Controls** group, and then click in the main report where you want to place the subreport.

3. Follow the steps in the **Subreport Wizard** to choose the report, table, or query on which to base the subreport, select fields for the subreport, and specify the field that links the subreport and the main report.

Adding Information to a Report's Header and Footer

You can use commands in the Design tab's Header/Footer group to insert standard elements in a report's header and footer sections. The Logo, Title, and Date And Time commands add information to the report's header. The Page Numbers command opens a dialog box in which you select a format for the page number, the position (page numbers can appear in the report's header or its footer), and the alignment (centered, right, or left). Clear the check box for the Show Number On First Page option to start pagination on the report's second page.

You can add page numbers to a header or a footer and align them at the right or left or in the center.

> **Tip** You can add other controls to a report's header or footer by dragging the appropriate control to that section of the form.

➤ **To insert information in a form header or footer**

1. In the navigation pane, right-click the report and then choose **Design View** or **Layout View**.

2. On the **Report Design** (or **Layout**) **Tools Design** tab, in the **Header/Footer** group, click the option for the element you want to add to the form:

   ○ **Logo** Select the image file from the **Insert Picture** dialog box.

   ○ **Title** Type a title for the form in the label control Access provides.

- ○ **Date and Time** Specify the date and time format you want to use in the **Date and Time** dialog box.

- ○ **Page Numbers** Specify the format, location (in the header or footer section), and alignment for report page numbers.

Managing Report Fields and Properties

Each control on a report, each report section, and the report itself has a group of properties that you can work with on the property sheet. To see them, click Property Sheet on the Report Layout (or Design) Tools Design tab to display the property sheet. For example, you can set properties on the property sheet's format tab to fine-tune the formatting for a control. For a text box, you can set properties such as Width, Height, Back Color, Border Style, Border Color, Font Name, Font Size, Text Align, and many others.

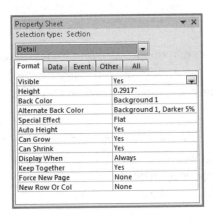

In the property sheet, you can fine-tune formatting for report sections and controls. Use the list at the top to select the item whose properties you want to view and set.

For report sections (such as Detail, Page Header, and Page Footer), you can set the Height property to 0" to hide the section. For the Detail section, set the Can Grow and Can Shrink properties to Yes if you want the size of the Detail section to increase and decrease depending on the amount of information it displays for a particular record. The Report Header and Report Footer sections also have the Can Grow and Can Shrink properties. For these sections and for the Page Header and Page Footer sections, you can also set the Display When property to Always, Print Only, or Screen Only. For example, if you add page numbers to the Page Footer section, set Display When to Print Only to show the page numbers only when you print the report.

Report properties include the Default View property, which controls whether the report opens in Print Preview or Report view by default. The report opens in the view you specify for the Default View property when you right-click a report in the navigation pane and choose Open. The Grid Y and Grid X properties control the number and spacing of the dots in the design grid in Design view. If you use Design view frequently, you might want to set the values for Grid Y and Grid X to 10 or 12 to more easily align controls on the grid. You can view and alter the Record Source property for a report by displaying the property sheet's Data tab, clicking in the Record Source property box, and then pressing Shift+F2 to open the Zoom dialog box or clicking the ellipsis to view the record source in the Query Builder.

➤ **To display the property sheet to set control and report properties**

1. Open the report in the Design view or Layout view.

2. On the **Report Design** (or **Layout**) **Tools Design** tab, click **Property Sheet** in the **Tools** group.

3. Click in the box for the property you want to set, and then select an option Access provides or type the value you want to use.

Practice Tasks

The practice files for these tasks are located in the practice files folder for Microsoft Access 2010. You can save the results of these exercises in the same folder. Change the file name so that you don't overwrite the sample files. When you are done, try performing the following tasks:

- Open the file Hello_World_ch05.accdb, and then open the Expense Summary report you created in the practice tasks for section 5.1 in Layout view. (If you did not create this report, open the report named Expense Summary_2 from the navigation pane.)

- Apply the Aspect theme to the report.

- Group the report on the Country field. Use the Totals button to sum the Amount Spent field, and add the Summary field to the group footer.

- Open the property sheet. Select the Auto_Header control, and change its Caption property to **Expense Summary**.

- Open the Campaign Summary report, and add the Campaign Expenses subreport to the main report. Position the subreport to the left of the Tasks subreport.

5.3   Apply Report Arrange Tab Options

You can use a variety of tools and techniques to arrange the controls and other objects (like images) that you include on reports. In this section, you'll first learn about some of the ways you arrange report controls when have the report open in Design view. You'll then learn about arranging fields when you work with report layouts.

Arranging Reports in Design View

When you have a report open in Design view, the Report Design Tools Arrange tab includes the Sizing & Ordering group. This group provides commands you can apply to controls to modify their size, the spacing between controls, and their alignment. For example, if you want two or more text boxes to have the same size, select the text box controls, click Size/Space, and then choose one of the options in the Size group. You can also use the Size/Space menu to control the spacing between controls and to group controls so that you can reposition the controls as a unit. Use the Align command in the Sizing & Ordering group to align a group of controls. The Bring To Front and Send To Back commands change the relationship of objects that overlap on a form.

> ➤ **To arrange controls in Design view**

1. In the navigation pane, right-click the form and then choose **Design View**.

2. Select the control or controls you want to work with.

3. On the **Report Design Tools Arrange** tab, in the **Sizing & Ordering** group, do the following:

   ○ Click **Size/Space**, and then choose the option you want to apply to the controls.

   ○ Click **Align**, and then choose the option you want to apply to the controls.

   ○ Click **Send to Back** or **Bring to Front**.

Working with Report Layouts

When you create a report in Layout view, the report's controls are contained within a layout that helps manage the alignment and arrangement of controls. For reports, Access provides two default layouts: tabular and stacked.

In the *tabular* layout, controls are arranged in columns and rows (something like a spreadsheet or a table). Labels are displayed in the report's Page Header section (like column headings). Text box controls that display a field's data are included in the report's Detail section.

In the *stacked* layout, controls appear in two columns, with labels in the left column and field controls to the right. All controls in the stacked layout are included in a report's Detail section.

By default, Access uses the tabular layout for reports it creates with the Report tool and for blank forms you create in Layout view. You can switch between the tabular and stacked layouts by choosing the layout you want to apply from the Table group on the Report Layout Tools Arrange tab.

> **Tip** When a report is open in Design view, you can remove a layout by selecting the controls on the form and clicking the Remove Layout command in the Table group on the Report Design Tools Arrange tab. If you are creating a form in Layout view, you can right-click a control, point to Layout, and then click Remove Layout. (In Layout view, the Remove Layout command does not appear in the Table group.)

You work with the commands in the Rows & Columns group when you need to expand the area of a layout by inserting rows or columns. To add a row to a layout, first select an adjacent cell and then click Insert Above or Insert Below. Similarly, select an adjacent cell, and then click Insert Left or Insert Right in the Rows & Columns group to insert a column. (To delete a row or column, right-click a cell in that row or column and choose Delete Row or Delete Column.)

Another way to alter the arrangement of a layout is to merge or split cells. By merging cells, you can have one control span two columns or rows. After selecting the cells you want to merge, click Merge in the Merge/Split group. In contrast, when you split a cell in a layout, you can place two controls in that cell. Use the Split Horizontally or Split Vertically command to split cells.

By using the Move Up and Move Down commands in the Move group, you can reposition the rows or a single cell in a layout. Click a cell in the row you want to move, click Select Row in the Rows & Columns group, and then click Move Up or Move Down.

The two commands in the Arrange tab's Position group control spacing between controls and the margins around the text a control displays. Each setting in the Control Margins menu (None, Narrow, Medium, and Wide) progressively increases the space between the upper-left corner of a control and the position where the control's text appears. The Wide setting can obscure text in a text box that is anything less than approximately .3 inches in height (assuming the font size you are using is the default 11 points).

Settings under Control Padding (also None, Narrow, Medium, and Wide) control the space between controls in the layout. Click Select Layout in the Rows & Columns group, click Control Padding, and then choose the padding option you want to apply.

➤ **To work with control layouts in Layout view**

1. In the navigation pane, right-click the form and then choose **Layout View**.

2. Click the **Report Layout Tools Arrange** tab.

3. To apply a different default layout to the form, click **Stacked** or **Tabular** in the **Table** group.

4. To insert a row or column in the layout, click a cell in the adjacent row or column, click **Select Row** or **Select Column** in the **Rows & Columns** group, and then click **Insert Above** or **Insert Below** (for rows) or **Insert Left** or **Insert Right** (for columns).

5. To merge two cells in the layout, select the cells and then click **Merge** in the **Merge/Split** group.

6. To reposition a row in the layout, click a cell in the row, click **Select Row** in the **Rows & Columns** group, and then click **Move Up** or **Move Down in the Move group**.

7. To specify margins for a control or the layout, select the control or click **Select Layout** in the **Rows & Columns** group. In the **Position** group, click **Control Margins**, and then choose the option you want to apply.

8. To insert padding for a control or the layout, select the control or click **Select Layout** in the **Rows & Columns** group. In the **Position** group, click **Control Padding**, and then choose the option you want to apply.

Practice Tasks

The practice files for these tasks are located in the practice files folder for Microsoft Access 2010. You can save the results of these exercises in the same folder. Change the file name so that you don't overwrite the sample files. When you are done, try performing the following tasks:

- Open the file Hello_World_ch05.accdb, and then open the Task Summary report in Layout view.

- Switch the report from the tabular layout to the stacked layout.

- Set the control margins to None and the control padding to Narrow.

- Select the Priority row, and move it above the Status row.

5.4   Apply Report Format Tab Options

You can format a report by adding a background image or by adding color elements to a report. You can use the Conditional Formatting command in the Control Formatting group to specify conditions under which Access applies special formatting to information in a report.

> **Tip** When you are formatting controls on a report, use the list in the Selection group at the far left of the Format tab to select the control.

Adding a Background Image to a Report

To use an image as the background for a report, click Background Image on the Report Layout (or Design) Tools Format tab. Click Browse, and then open the location where the image file you want to use is stored. After you add the image, you can set properties for the image to modify how Access displays it. Right-click the report and choose Report Properties. In the property sheet, click the Format tab. The properties you use to control the display of a background image include the following: Picture Type, Picture, Picture Tiling, Picture Alignment, and Picture Size Mode.

> **See Also** For descriptions of these properties and their settings, see Chapter 3.

➤ **To add an image to the form's background**

1. Open the report in Layout view or Design view.
2. Click the **Report Layout** (or **Design**) **Tools Format** tab.
3. In the **Background** group, click **Background Image**.
4. Select an image from the **Image** gallery, or click **Browse** to locate the image file you want to use.
5. Select the image file in the **Insert Picture** dialog box, and then click **OK**.

Formatting Report Controls

By working with the commands in the Font group on the Format tab, you can make changes to font properties for labels and other controls on a report.

> **Tip** The Font group includes the Format Painter button. Apply the changes you want to the font in one control, click that control, and then use the Format Painter to apply those changes to other controls.

For example, click a label on a report and then choose the font you want to use from the Font list. You can also change the size of the font, choose a different font color, or apply a background color to a control. Use the alignment buttons to position the text flush left, flush right, or centered.

In the Number group, you can apply a format to fields that use the Number, Currency, or Date/Time data type. For example, select a date field in a form, and then choose a format from the list of formats provided. The format you choose here affects how the date is displayed, but it doesn't change the date format specified for the field in the table.

Commands in the Control Formatting group let you format controls in other ways. Use the Shape Fill command to add a background color to a control such as the report's title. The Shape Outline command lets you modify the color and style of a control's borders.

➤ **To format report controls**

1. Open the form in Layout view or Design view.

2. Click the **Report Layout** (or **Design**) **Tools Format** tab.

3. In the **Selection** group, choose the control you want to format or click **Select All**. (You can also click to select a control on the form.)

4. In the **Font** group, choose a new font, font size, or font color; apply bold, italic, or underline formatting; add a background fill color; and align the text.

5. For number, currency, and date and time fields, use the **Number** group to apply number, date/time, and currency formatting to the field.

6. In the **Control Formatting** group, do the following:
   - Use the **Shape Fill** command to add a background fill color to a control.
   - Use the **Shape Outline** command to apply line styles and colors to the control's borders.

Highlighting Report Data with Conditional Formatting

Conditional formatting rules let you apply specific formatting to data that matches criteria you define. As you can with forms, you can define rules for forms that fall into two categories:

- **Check Values In The Current Record Or Use An Expression** Use this option when you want to write an expression or set up a rule that applies when the value of a field is, for example, between two other values or equal to, greater than, or less than a value you specify.

- **Compare To Other Records** Choose this option if you want to set up data bars that show the value of one field in comparison to others.

> **See Also** For detailed steps for how to set up conditional formatting rules, see "Applying Conditional Formatting" in Chapter 3.

Practice Tasks

The practice files for these tasks are located in the practice files folder for Microsoft Access 2010. You can save the results of these exercises in the same folder. Change the file name so that you don't overwrite the sample files. When you are done, try performing the following tasks:

- Open the file Hello_World_ch05.accdb, and then open the Campaign Expenses report in Layout view.

- Add a light color fill to the report's title, and change the font to Calibri, with a font size of 20.

- Create a conditional formatting rule that applies bold and a red font color to values in the Amount Spent field that are greater than $300.

5.5   Apply Report Page Setup Tab Options

When a report is open in Design view or Layout view, the ribbon displays the Page Setup tab, which contains commands in two groups: Page Size and Page Layout.

Specifying the Page Size for a Report

The options for a report's page size include standard sizes, such as Letter (8.5 by 11 inches), A4 (8.27 by 11.69 inches), or Legal (8.5 by 14 inches). Choose the size you want to apply to the report from the options displayed on the Size menu.

To adjust the margins for a report, click Margins in the Page Size group and then choose one of the three options Access provides: Normal, Wide, and Narrow. You can refer to the dimensions Access lists and the simple preview to gauge how the margins affect the space provided for the data the report presents.

> **Tip** The Live Preview feature doesn't apply to margin settings here, but if you display the report in Layout view, you can see the effect of each option on the report, as long as you select the Show Margins check box in the Page Size group.

Select the Print Data Only option if you want to print the report's data without the formatting applied to the report.

Changing the Page Layout for a Report

In the Page Layout group, use the Portrait and Landscape options to set the page orientation for the report. If you want to set up a columnar report, click Columns and then specify settings on the Columns tab in the Page Set Up dialog box. You need to consider the number of fields, the width of report controls, and the page size and settings when you set up a report in columns. Columnar reports are best used for lists, directories, or other types of reports that include only a few fields. Stacking the fields (by using the stacked layout, for example) saves space as well.

Columnar reports should include only a few fields. If the report's data doesn't fit, Access displays a warning.

The Page Setup dialog box also includes the Print Options and Page tabs. You can set specific dimensions for a report's margins on the Print Options tab (if the Normal, Wide, and Narrow options provided in the Page Size group don't give you what you need). The Print Options tab also includes the Print Data Only check box.

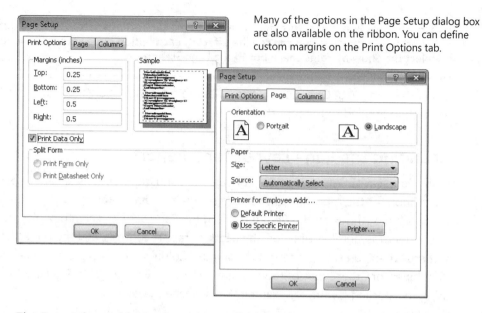

Many of the options in the Page Setup dialog box are also available on the ribbon. You can define custom margins on the Print Options tab.

The Page tab provides options also available in the Page Layout and Page Size groups, including Portrait and Landscape options for the report's page orientation, page size settings, and options that let you select which printer to use if you want to produce a hard copy of the report.

> ► **To specify page size settings for a report**

1. In the navigation pane, right-click the report and then choose **Design View** or **Layout view**.

2. Click the **Report Layout** (or **Design**) **Tools Page Setup** tab.

3. In the **Page Size** group, click **Size** and then choose an option for the report's page size.

4. Click **Margins**, and then choose one of the default options for page margins.

   To specify particular dimensions for page margins, click **Page Setup** in the **Page Layout** group and then set the margins on the **Page Options** tab in the **Page Setup** dialog box.

5. Select **Print Data Only** to print the report's data without the report's formatting.

➤ **To specify page layout settings for a report**

1. In the navigation pane, right-click the report and then choose **Design View** or **Layout view**.

2. Click the **Report Layout** (or **Design**) **Tools Page Setup** tab.

3. In the **Page Layout** group, click **Portrait** or **Landscape** to set the page orientation.

4. Click **Page Setup** to open the **Page Setup** dialog box. Use the tabs in the dialog box to specify the following settings:

   ○ **Print Options tab** Set the page margins, and select **Print Data Only** if you want to apply this option.

   ○ **Page tab** Choose **Portrait** or **Landscape** for the page orientation, choose a paper size, and specify the printer to use to produce the report.

➤ **To specify column settings for a report**

1. In the navigation pane, right-click the report and then choose **Design View** or **Layout view**.

2. Click the **Report Layout** (or **Design**) **Tools Page Setup** tab.

3. In the **Page Layout** group, click **Columns**.

4. On the **Columns** tab in the **Page Setup** dialog box, specify the number of columns, the row and column spacing, the column size, and the column layout option.

5. Click **OK** in the **Page Setup** dialog box, and then open the report in Print Preview to test the settings.

Practice Tasks

The practice files for these tasks are located in the practice files folder for Microsoft Access 2010. You can save the results of these exercises in the same folder. Change the file name so that you don't overwrite the sample files. When you are done, try performing the following tasks:

- Open the file Hello_World_ch5.accdb. Open the Campaign Summary report in Layout view.

- Work with the options in the Page Size and Page Layout groups to change the report's page orientation and the settings for its margins.

5.6   Sort and Filter Records for Reporting

In this section, you'll learn more about working in the different views for a report and about filtering and sorting report records in Report view.

Using Report View Types

At the far left of the Report Layout (or Design) Tools Design tab (and on the Home tab), the View menu lets you open a report in one of four views: Report view, Print Preview, Layout view, and Design view. As you learned earlier in this chapter, you use Layout view and Design view to create and modify reports. Print Preview is a static view (meaning you can't interact with data in this view) that lets you see how the report's printed pages will appear—for example, whether the margins are set correctly, whether formatting is in place, and whether all the information you want in the report's header and footer sections is included. The Print Preview tab that Access displays in this view includes a Print button, the Page Size and Page Layout groups (see the previous section for details about these groups), the Zoom group, and the Data group. You can use options in the Data group to export a report to Microsoft Excel, to a text file, as a PDF or XPS document, in e-mail, and in other formats. When you click E-Mail, you then select the form in which to send the report.

Report view is a more interactive view. In Report view, hyperlinks are active, for example, and you can also apply a filter to a report. After you apply a filter, you can print the filtered report to show only that subset of data.

> **See Also**   For more information about working with controls in Report view, see "Working with Controls on a Report" earlier in this chapter.

Filtering Records in Report View

To filter a report that's open in Report view, right-click in the field you want to filter by to display a menu that includes filtering options. For example, to filter values in a text field right-click an instance of the value you want to filter for and then choose Equals *"field name"*. You can also choose Does Not Equal, Contains, and Does Not Contain or use options on the Text Filters menu.

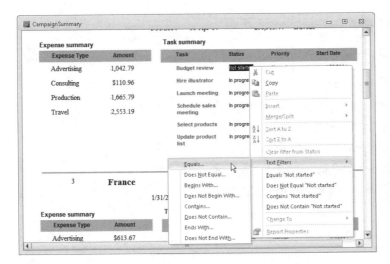

Right-click in a field when a report is open in Report view and then filter the report.

For other data types, you'll see options such as Greater Than, Between, and On Or Before. To remove a filter, click the Toggle Filter button in the Sort & Filter group on the Home tab.

> **See Also** The Advanced Filter/Sort button is also available in Report view. Use this button to open a window in which you can define a sort order by using more than one field and also specify filter criteria using AND and OR conditions. For more information about setting up advanced filters and sorts and using the Find And Replace dialog box to locate records, see "Sort and Filter Records" in Chapter 2, "Building Tables."

Practice Tasks

The practice files for these tasks are located in the practice files folder for Microsoft Access 2010. You can save the results of these exercises in the same folder. Change the file name so that you don't overwrite the sample files. When you are done, try performing the following tasks:

- Open the file Hello_World_ch05.accdb, and then open the Campaign Summary report in Print Preview. On the Print Preview tab, adjust the margins by using the Margins command in the Page Size group. Export the report as a PDF file.

- Right-click the report window's title bar, and open the report in Report view. Filter the report so that it shows only tasks that have the status In Progress.

Objective Review

Before finishing this chapter, be sure you have mastered the following skills:

5.1 Create reports

5.2 Apply report Design tab options

5.3 Apply report Arrange tab options

5.4 Apply report Format tab options

5.5 Apply report Page Setup tab options

5.6 Sort and filter records for reporting

Microsoft SharePoint 2010 Specialist

In the next five chapters, you'll build on the general skills required to create, edit, and manage content on a Microsoft SharePoint team site. You'll learn about the specific skills you need to be certified as a SharePoint 2010 specialist.

This section has been constructed so that you can follow a path from the basics of building a SharePoint site to adding site components and features. Also, you'll learn SharePoint 2010 administration of a team site so that you can configure components that enable integration with Microsoft Office applications. This section teaches the skills necessary for an individual to collaborate frequently with other users on a team and throughout an enterprise by using SharePoint. The following chapters also help you understand how to best use SharePoint 2010 productively by centralizing content for your team and how to administer a SharePoint 2010 site.

What You Need

To work through this section, you need full access to a SharePoint 2010 team site. Because SharePoint 2010 is a server-based platform rather than a desktop application, you need access to a server or an online environment where SharePoint 2010 is installed or hosted.

Obtain SharePoint Through a SharePoint 2010 Host Provider

SharePoint 2010 host services are becoming popular with organizations that do not have the in-house technical expertise to deploy and manage the service installation. There are a large number of consultant organizations specializing in providing hosted solutions that include SharePoint 2010. Some provide access to SharePoint 2010 Foundation, and others provide access to both SharePoint 2010 Foundation and SharePoint 2010 Server. Visit *www.microsoft.com/hosting/en/us/default.aspx* for more information.

Install SharePoint in a Virtual or Server Environment

If you have access to a virtual or server environment, you can download the Microsoft SharePoint 2010 trial edition and install it. This trial edition is valid for 180 days and provides all the features and areas covered in this guide. Visit *technet.microsoft.com/en-us/evalcenter/ee388573.aspx* for more information about the trial edition.

SharePoint 2010 Server 2010 Enterprise is required for use with this study guide.

1 Creating and Formatting Content

The skills tested in this section of the Microsoft Office Specialist exam for SharePoint 2010 cover creating and formatting content in SharePoint 2010. Specifically, the following objectives are associated with this set of skills:

1.1 Navigate the SharePoint hierarchy

1.2 Manage lists and document libraries

1.3 Manage list items

1.4 Work with document sets

Understanding what makes up a SharePoint site and how to create, store, and manage content for a site are critical skills required by certification candidates. This chapter describes the tasks required to create SharePoint content that you need to store on a SharePoint site by designing SharePoint repositories such as document libraries and lists, as well as structuring navigation of the site so that users can access the content.

> **Important** This chapter examines both lists and document libraries. The term *repository* when used in this chapter relates to either a list or a document library in the SharePoint site.

> **Important** To complete the tasks in this chapter, you need your own SharePoint site that has no restrictions applied. The SharePoint site must be based on a default SharePoint Team Site template.

1.1   Navigate the SharePoint Hierarchy

The objective in this section is to learn the basics concerning the structure of a SharePoint site. This section will cover the following topics:

- Using the Quick Launch bar
- Adding content to the Quick Launch bar
- Using the All Site Content page
- Using the SharePoint breadcrumb trails feature
- Using the top link bar to navigate the content and structure of a site

To figure out where to store your data on a SharePoint site, you need to understand the navigation features provided in the site. And, as you create content on the SharePoint site, you need to learn how to make navigating to content easier by manipulating and customizing the navigational aids.

We'll begin by looking at the basic hierarchy of SharePoint. At the top of the tree is a *site collection*. A site collection is known as a *top-level* site. Any sites within the site collection are called *subsites*. If doing so is more convenient, you can access your SharePoint site directly through a subsite that's more specific to your needs.

For example, suppose that a team site has the URL *http://fabrikam.com* and is accessed by three departments in the company: Human Resources, Project Management, and Communications. The Human Resources site is called *HR*, Project Management's site is called *PM*, and Communications has its own site called *Comms*. These sites are internally accessed through *http://fabrikam*. The URL for each department's subsite is as follows:

- Human Resources: *http://fabrikam.com/hr*
- Project Management: *http://fabrikam/pm*
- Communications: *http://fabrikam/comms*

> **Tip** For a subsite, you can type a starting / (forward slash) plus the remaining part of the URL instead of typing the full URL. For example, if the target is a subsite called **pm** with a location of http://fabrikam/pm, all you need to type is **/pm** because the parent site is *http://fabrikam.com* and *pm* is the subsite.

All SharePoint sites provide the following navigation options:

- Access to an external website's content
- Access to internal content
- Connection to internal content areas
- Connection to documents

A SharePoint site's hierarchy is structured through navigation elements at the top and sides of pages within the site. The navigation performed from the top of the site is called *global navigation*, and it is accessed in an area called the top link bar. *Current navigation* refers to accessing content internal to the site, which you do by using elements located on the left side of the site, in an area called the *Quick Launch bar*.

To control aspects of site navigation, structure, and content, you use the SharePoint ribbon. The ribbon allows you to do the following:

- Administer the SharePoint site.
- Navigate the SharePoint site hierarchy.
- Save changes to the current page.
- Access the top link bar and the site's breadcrumbs (which are described later in this chapter).
- Manage the current page and its library.
- Carry out editing tasks on the current page.

The ribbon is positioned at the top of the page. The ribbon consists of a number of tabs that provide commands. For example, when the Browse tab is clicked (as you can see in the following screen shot), you see the icon and title for the site, as well as links on the top link bar allowing access to any subsites. At the top right of the page, you see the name of the person who is currently logged on.

The ribbon contains the following items:

- **Breadcrumb trail icon** Allows navigation within the SharePoint site hierarchy. For example, if you are visiting a SharePoint subsite, clicking this icon displays links to the parent and the child of the current site (if there is one).
- **Edit page icon** Allows editing to take place on the current page.
- **Browse** Displays the current page title with its icon and the top link bar.
- **Page** Provides access to relevant page editing tools, management tools, sharing tools, page library features, and settings.

The Site Actions menu provides links to administrative pages and editing features. The list of options depends on the template the SharePoint site is based on. For example, if the site template is of a Publishing type, the commands listed are related to publishing pages. The Site Settings option displays a page with links to administrative pages for the site.

When you click the arrow next to Site Actions, the following drop-down menu is displayed (which relates to the SharePoint Team Site template):

> **Important** You must be at least a member of the Site Members group in SharePoint Server 2010 or the Site Owners group in SharePoint Foundation 2010 to see the Site Actions menu.

Using the Quick Launch Bar

The Quick Launch bar provides access to content created on the site and can also provide links to external content. You can add, modify, delete, and reorder the links that appear on the Quick Launch bar.

The Quick Launch bar is located on the left side of a SharePoint site. By default, it displays links to the site's repositories, and these links are categorized into headings. For example, when a team site is created, a link to Shared Documents is displayed on the Quick Launch bar.

Headings are used to categorize links. For example, the Libraries heading includes all document libraries, and the Lists heading includes all list repositories. By default, you can click a heading to display all the items within that heading. For example, if you click the Libraries heading, all document library titles are displayed on the All Site Content page.

For the Lists heading, all repositories of the list type (for example, calendar, tasks, and announcements) are displayed on the All Site Content page.

> **Note** You can easily customize the Quick Launch bar so that the headings are not links. (You will be shown later how to do this.)

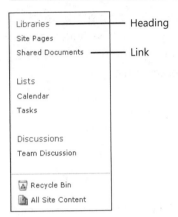

> **Tip** Recycle Bin appears on the Quick Launch bar if you are a site administrator.

➤ **To view the contents of the Shared Documents library**

1. Open your SharePoint site.
2. Click **Shared Documents** on the Quick Launch bar.

   The **Shared Documents** library contents are displayed.

➤ **To see all lists in a SharePoint site**

1. Open your SharePoint site.
2. Click **Lists** on the Quick Launch bar.

   All lists are displayed on the **All Site Contents** page.

➤ **To display all the libraries in a SharePoint site**

1. Open your SharePoint site.
2. Click **Libraries** on the Quick Launch bar.

   All document libraries in your SharePoint site are displayed.

Adding Content to the Quick Launch Bar

This section teaches you how to add, edit, and remove links and headings on the Quick Launch bar. To accomplish these tasks, you need to configure the Quick Launch bar's navigational settings, located on the Site Settings page of the SharePoint site. On the ribbon, click Site Actions, Site Settings to access these settings.

The Site Settings page is where all administrative options are shown for the SharePoint site. The page is divided into sections, and those sections have links that you can click to display a page of configuration options. The option you need in this case is Quick Launch, which you can find in the Look And Feel section.

Specify whether a tree view should be displayed to aid navigation. The tree view displays site content in a physical manner.

> **Important** The Quick Launch option is available to a SharePoint team site that has not had the Publishing feature enabled. If the Publishing feature was enabled on the site, or the site was based on the Publishing template, the option is called Navigation and provides additional features.

Here is an example of a default Quick Launch configuration page:

There are three options at the head of this section as shown on the screen shot:

- **New Navigation Link** Click this link to create a new link in the Quick Launch bar and to specify the heading area in which it should appear.

- **New Heading** Click this link to create a new heading in the Quick Launch bar.

- **Change Order** Click Change Order to modify the position of links.

➤ **To add a new link and heading to the Quick Launch bar**

1. Click **New Navigation Link**.

2. In the URL prompt, type the URL of the web address (for example, **http://www.microsoft.com**).

3. In the **Description** field, type a description of the link.

4. Use the **Heading** drop-down list to select the area of the Quick Launch bar where you want to place the link. For example, select **Libraries**.

5. Click **OK**.

   The new navigational link is placed at the bottom of the **Libraries** section of the Quick Launch bar.

   Create a new heading called **Links**, and put this new link into that section. (See the next procedure.)

6. To create a new heading, click **New Heading**.

7. Delete the default value of http://, and then type a period (.) in the URL prompt. This ensures that if the heading is clicked the site home page is redisplayed.

8. Type **Links** in the **Description** field.

9. Click **OK**.

➤ **To edit a link or heading from the Quick Launch bar**

1. Click the icon next to the link or heading you want to delete.

   The **Edit Navigation Link** page is displayed.

2. Make modifications to the **Web Address** and **Description** fields, and select the relevant heading if you are editing a link. Otherwise, alter the heading title.

➤ **To delete a link or heading from the Quick Launch bar**

1. Click the icon next to the link or heading you want to delete.

   The **Edit Navigation Link** page is displayed.

2. Click **Delete**.

> **Tip** If you delete a heading, all links within that heading are also deleted.

Using All Site Content

All SharePoint content is structured into lists, libraries, and subsites and can be viewed on a special page called All Site Content. This section describes the All Site Content page in SharePoint and teaches you how to access it and view the lists, document libraries, surveys, sites, workspaces, and subsites that have been created in a SharePoint team site. You can access the All Site Content page in any of the following ways:

- On the ribbon, click Site Actions. From the drop-down menu that is displayed, choose the View All Site Content option.

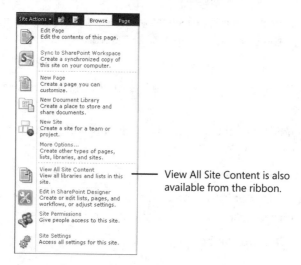

View All Site Content is also available from the ribbon.

- Click the All Site Content link on the Quick Launch bar.

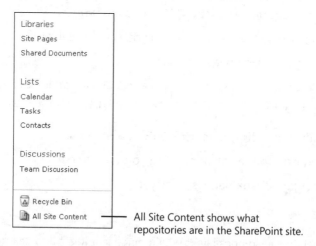

All Site Content shows what repositories are in the SharePoint site.

Tip You can also use the All Site Content link to create a new list, document library, workspace, or subsite.

This is what a default All Site Content page looks like:

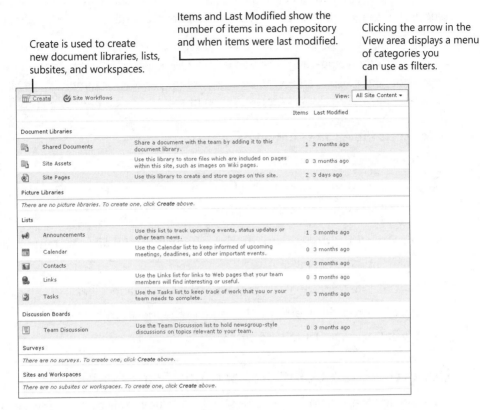

Create is used to create new document libraries, lists, subsites, and workspaces.

Items and Last Modified show the number of items in each repository and when items were last modified.

Clicking the arrow in the View area displays a menu of categories you can use as filters.

The All Site Content page is divided into five sections of repositories, plus a few other elements:

- Document Libraries
- Picture Libraries
- Lists
- Discussion Boards
- Surveys
- Sites and Workspaces
- Recycle Bin

When a team site is created, a document library called Shared Documents is automatically created. This library is displayed in the Document Libraries section on the All Site Content page.

On the right side of the All Site Content page, you'll see the View box with the All Site Content option chosen. Click the arrow on the right side to select a filter for the repositories that are displayed on the All Site Content page.

The option you choose in the View area also applies to the default headings in the Quick Launch bar. When a heading is clicked on the Quick Launch bar, the repositories under that heading are displayed on the All Site Content page. For example, if the Sites heading is clicked, the Sites And Workspaces section of the All Site Content page is displayed.

➤ **To access the All Site Content page**

1. Open your SharePoint Site.
2. Click **Site Actions, View All Site Content**.

   The **All Site Content** page is displayed.

➤ **To display all the document libraries while on the All Site Contents page**

1. Open your SharePoint site.
2. Click **All Site Content** at the bottom of the Quick Launch bar.
3. Click the drop-down arrow to the right of the **View** box.
4. Select **Document Libraries** from the drop-down list.

Using the SharePoint Breadcrumb Trails Feature

In this section, we'll explore how to use the breadcrumb trails feature. If a Human Resources subsite, Project Management Office subsite, and Building Management Facilities subsite existed within a parent company site portal (and the company was called Fabrikam Inc.), the SharePoint hierarchy might look like this:

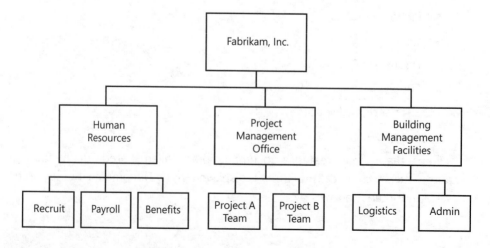

As you can see, each of the three departments in the Fabrikam portal (the top-level site) have subsections, which are structured as subsites for each department. The Project Management Office has two subsites, created for two project teams. Those project teams then manage their own projects as subsites in their own project team subsite. All of these project team sites are managed by the Project Management Office. So, as SharePoint sites grow in this model, so will the SharePoint hierarchy. For example, the next diagram shows that the Project A team is running three projects, and each of those projects is structured as a separate subsite.

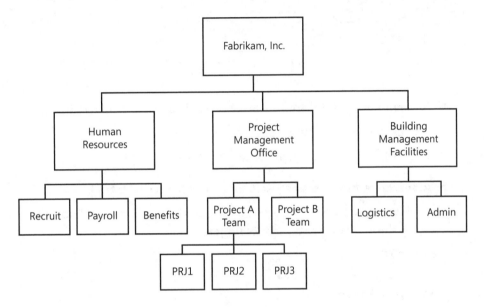

Imagine that a user who is working in subsite PRJ1 wants to go back to the Project Management Office parent site, and that another user needs to go to the top-level site (the Fabrikam Inc. portal). This is where the breadcrumb trail option comes in handy.

At the top of the ribbon, the breadcrumb trail shows the path to the current page within the site. The trail helps you keep track of where the current page is located within the site. Components on the breadcrumb trail are links that take you to the corresponding page. Note that the last item on the breadcrumb trail is not a link; rather, the item shows the title of the current page.

The breadcrumb trail shows the structure of the site in graphical format. Here is an example of the breadcrumb trail for the Project Management Office site, where the user is working in the Project Team A subsite:

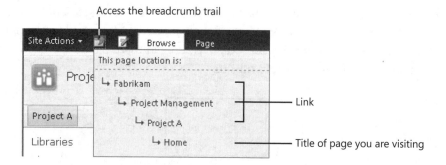

Access the breadcrumb trail

Link

Title of page you are visiting

> **To navigate back to the top-level site using the breadcrumb trail**

1. Click the breadcrumb trail icon to display the site structure.

2. Click the top site name in the site structure list.

> **To navigate back up one site using the breadcrumb trail**

1. Move the mouse cursor over the breadcrumb trail icon, and hover it there until you see the ScreenTip that reads **Navigate Up**.

2. Click the icon.

Practice Tasks

Practice the skills you learned in this section by performing the following tasks on your site:

- Display the contents of the Shared Documents library using the Quick Launch bar.

- Add a heading to the Quick Launch bar called Links. Make sure the heading displays the home page of the site when it is clicked.

- Add a new link to the Quick Launch bar called Microsoft. Set the URL to *http://microsoft.com* and position the link under the heading Links.

- Display only the document libraries in the All Site Content page.

1.2   Manage Lists and Document Libraries

The most important aspect of a SharePoint site is the management of the content contained on that site in various lists and document libraries. This section teaches you aspects of managing lists and document libraries, including how to create lists and libraries, edit list and document library properties, view formats using the standard and datasheet views, manage views, and create columns.

> **Important** To progress through this section, you need to be an administrator on the SharePoint site you have access to.

A SharePoint list can be thought of as a spreadsheet that is split into columns and rows of information. Each column can be set to hold specific information, or it can hold automatically created information. A list can also be construed as holding *structured* information because each column describes an element of a row of information in a list. There are various list templates available, ranging from Announcements to Project Task lists.

A SharePoint document library is a specialized form of list used to store documents. A document library is created to store a collection of documents or files that you want to share. Document libraries support features such as subfolders, file versioning, and check-in/check-out.

Creating Lists and Libraries

There are three ways to create a repository. The first way is to use *site actions*. The second method is to start by clicking the All Site Content link on the Quick Launch bar. The third way is to use one of the repository headings displayed on the Quick Launch bar.

When you click All Site Content, you'll see all existing lists and document libraries in the site on the All Site Content page. If you use the repository heading, you'll see the repositories that are related to that heading. For example, if the heading is Libraries, all the library type repositories are displayed.

➤ **To create an announcements list**

1. On the Quick Launch bar, click **All Site Content**. The **All Site Content** page is displayed.

2. Click **Create**.

3. In the **Filter By** section, click **List** so that all the list templates are displayed.

4. Click **Announcements**, which is the first list template shown.

5. On the right side of this page, enter the name of the list.

The **Create** button in this area creates the list when you click it. The **More Options** button provides an option to enter a description and an option to choose whether the Quick Launch bar is updated with a link to the list.

6. Click **Create**.

The list is created and displayed. The ribbon displays the **List Tools** tabs that provide options to configure the list.

Editing List and Document Library Properties

Lists and document libraries have features that allow further customization and that further define their operational aspects. You can alter what is displayed in a repository, how it is displayed, and its format. You can be alerted about changes in the repository made by colleagues or changes made through an automated event. You can integrate the repository with Microsoft applications such as Microsoft Word and Microsoft Excel. You can also further customize the look and feel of the repository, including creating columns, sorting data, adding workflows, and more.

> **Important** The options available are based on the permissions applied. The following text assumes you have complete control of the list (that is, you have Full Control permissions for the site).

When you first create a library, the ribbon displays the Library Tools tab. For lists, the ribbon provides the List Tools tabs, which provides access to commands you use to customize and edit features of the list. If you are working with an existing list or library, access it using the Quick Launch bar or the All Site Content option.

Viewing Formats Using the Standard and Datasheet View

Lists provide two types of views: a standard view and a datasheet view. A standard view provides the information as SharePoint columns and is based on a default view.

The datasheet view is akin to a Microsoft Excel worksheet and provides you with the ability to copy and paste data into a repository. This view makes adding, editing, and deleting multiple list items and files easier. You can create list items by copying data from

Microsoft Excel. You can also edit properties of list items or files by copying cells, and you can even delete many files.

If you want to use the datasheet view, your computer needs to meet certain requirements. The datasheet component must be installed on your machine, and this component is part of Microsoft Office 2010. Also, the browser you use must be compatible with the datasheet view and provide the ability to show ActiveX controls.

➤ **To switch to the datasheet view**

1. On the Quick Launch bar, click the link related to the list you want to show in datasheet view.

2. On the ribbon, click the **List** tab under **List Tools**.

3. In the **View Format** section, click **Datasheet View**.

Creating, Modifying, and Deleting Views

A SharePoint view is simply a display of content from a SharePoint repository. A view controls what content is displayed and how the content should be displayed. Views can be created by the user or the repository administrator.

A view lists columns that you want to display. Views also support grouping, sorting, and filtering and can be used to aggregate content within a repository. Aggregation options include summing up values in a column, averaging values, or performing calculations with other aggregation functions.

A repository can support multiple views, allowing users to create custom views. And views can be further personalized, meaning that each user can maintain unique views not available to anyone else.

All repositories have a default view, depending on the type of repository being used. For example, the default view for an announcements list is called All Items. For document libraries, the default view is called All Documents. Each of these views has been config-ured to show specific columns, displayed in a format related to the type of repository being used.

> **Tip** The permutations of the types of views you can create is limited only by your imagination. Therefore, this section describes only the basics of view features.

You should create a view when you need to see the content of a repository in a certain way. When you create a view, it is added to the View menu of the repository. If you're going to create the view in a list repository, use the Create View option in the List tab under List Tools.

> **See Also** If you are unsure of how to display the Create View option, review the section "Editing List and Document Library Properties" earlier in this chapter.

> **Important** If the Create View button is disabled, you might not have the relevant permissions to create a view. This section assumes you have Full Control permissions on the SharePoint site where you are going to create views.

When the Create View button is clicked, the Choose A View Format options are displayed. These options allow you to choose from several types of views, or you can start from a view that already exists (such as the All Items or All Documents view). The view formats available are listed in Table 1-1.

Table 1-1 View Types

View Format	View Description
Standard View	View data on a web page. You can choose from a list of display styles.
Datasheet View	View data in an editable spreadsheet format that is convenient for bulk editing and quick customization.
Calendar View	View data as a daily, weekly, or monthly calendar.
Gantt View	View list items in a Gantt chart to see a graphical representation of how a team's tasks are scheduled over time.
Access View	Start Microsoft Access to create forms and reports that are based on this list.
Custom View in SharePoint Designer	Start SharePoint Designer to create a new view for this list, with capabilities such as conditional formatting.

> **Note** SharePoint Designer is a tool that you can use to design SharePoint applications and customize SharePoint. For more information and details about how to obtain this tool, visit this link *www.microsoft.com/DOWNLOADS/en/details.aspx?FamilyID =d88a1505-849b-4587-b854-a7054ee28d66&displaylang=en.*

If you create a standard view, for example, the Create View page is displayed with the sections you need to fill out, as described in Table 1-2.

Table 1-2 **Create View Page Options**

Section	Description
Name	Type a name for the view. The name should be descriptive so that site visitors will know what to expect. You can also set the view to be the default so that all site visitors will see this view when visiting the repository.
Audience	This is where you can select whether the view is available to all site visitors (public view) or available as a private view (personal view) so that only you can see and use the view.
Columns	Select the columns of the list you want to see, and place them in the order in which they should be displayed (from the left side of the page to the right).
Sort	Select up to two columns to determine the order in which the items in the view are displayed.
Filter	Show all of the items in this view or a subset of the items by using filters. To filter on a column based on the current date or the current user of the site, type **[Today]** or **[Me]** as the column value. Use indexed columns in the first clause to speed up your view. Filters are particularly important for lists containing five thousand or more items because they allow you to work with large lists more efficiently.
Inline Editing	Choose whether to include an edit button on each row. This button allows users to edit the current row in the current view without navigating to the form. Inline editing is available only on views that have their style set to Default.
Tabular View	Choose whether to provide individual check boxes for each row. These check boxes allow users to select multiple list items to perform bulk operations.
Group By	Select up to two columns to determine what type of group and subgroup the items in the view will be displayed in.
Totals	Select one or more totals to display. The column functions available are Count, Average, Maximum, and Minimum. These functions are available based on the type of column.
Style	Depending on the repository, the following styles are available: In a document library: Basic Table; Document Details; Newsletter; Newsletter, No Lines; Shaded; Preview Pane; and Default. In a list: Basic Table; Boxed, No Labels; Boxed; Newsletter; Newsletter, No Lines; Shaded; Preview Pane; and Default.

Section	Description
Folders	Specify whether to navigate through folders to view items or to view all items at once. If the repository is structured by items or files within folders, you can provide a view whereby the items or files are displayed without the folders. This is useful if you want to show all the items or files at once to the user without the user having to traverse folders to view items and folders.
Item Limit	Use an item limit to limit the amount of data returned to users of this view. You can make this an absolute limit or allow users to view all the items in the document library in batches of the specified size.
	By default, the number of items available for display in a document library is 30 per batch. You can limit the total number of items to a specified amount. For example, you might want to display only the five most recently updated documents in a library. You can do this by using the Sort option to place the most recently modified documents at the top of the list and then set the item limit to 5.
Mobile	Adjust mobile settings for this view by enabling it for mobile access, making this view the default view for mobile access, and adjusting the number of items to display in the List View Web part for this view. You can additionally set the field to be displayed in a mobile list simple view.

> **Tip** You do not need to use all the sections on the Create View page. You can revisit the page as many times as you want to further customize and refine the view.

Here are some additional notes on a few of the sections:

- In the columns section, some columns have additional options, which are displayed to the right of the column in brackets:

  - **(Icon Linked To Document)** Choosing this option displays a small picture indicating the type of a particular document. When this option is selected, clicking the document launches the application associated with the document. The document will then be loaded into the application.

  - **(Linked To Document With Edit Menu)** Choosing this option displays the document as a link. When the link is clicked, the document will be opened in its associated application. Additionally, a drop-down menu is displayed providing options on the right of the document.

  - **(Link To Edit Menu)** Displays a drop-down menu.

  - **(For Use In Forms)** The column will be available in a datasheet.

- You can use the inline editing feature to edit repository items in the view without having to open each item to edit it. Note that this feature does not apply to editing files in a document library. They must be edited in the applicable program, such as Microsoft Word. When inline editing is enabled by selecting its check box, this feature inserts an icon to the left of the selected item in the repository. When the icon is clicked, the row selected becomes editable and two icons are displayed at the beginning of the row: a Save icon and a Cancel icon.

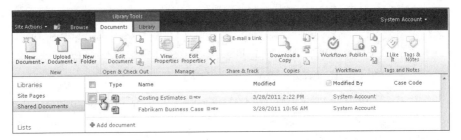

- The Totals section on the Create View page provides options for making calculations on selected columns in a repository. For example, you might want to display the number of items meeting a filter applied to a list. When you expand the Totals section, SharePoint lists the columns in the view where calculations can be carried out. Use the menu to select a calculation option based on the type of column. If the column type is text based, the only option is Count. If the column type is numerical, the options are Count, Average, Maximum, Minimum, Sum, Std Deviation, and Variance.

> **Tip** To take advantage of the advanced functionality that is provided by SharePoint Designer 2010 to modify a view, point to Modify This View, select the down arrow, and then click Modify In Designer (Advanced). SharePoint Designer 2010 must be installed on the local computer to use this option. If you select this option and it is not installed, you'll be prompted to install it. SharePoint Designer 2010 is a free download and available from this link: *www.microsoft.com/DOWNLOADS/en/details.aspx?FamilyID= d88a1505-849b-4587-b854-a7054ee28d66&displaylang=en*.

➤ To modify a view

1. On the Quick Launch bar, click the name of the repository that contains the view you want to modify.

   If the repository is not on the Quick Launch bar, click **Site Actions**, click **View All Site Content**, and then click the name of the repository.

2. On the ribbon, click the **Library** or **List** tab.

3. Select the view you want to modify from the **Current View** list in the **Manage Views** group.

4. Click **Modify View**.

> **Tip** If Modify View is disabled, you might not have the necessary permissions to modify the current view. You can, however, modify your personal views. You can also modify public views if you have the design permission level for the repository.

➤ **To delete a view**

1. On the Quick Launch bar, click the name of the repository that contains the view you want to delete.

   If the repository is not on the Quick Launch bar, click **Site Actions**, click **View All Site Content**, and then click the name of the repository.

2. On the ribbon, click the **Library or List** tab.

3. Select the view you want to delete from the **Current View** list in the **Manage Views** group.

4. Click **Modify View**.

   > **Tip** If Modify View is disabled, you do not have the necessary permissions to modify the current view. You can, however, modify your personal views. You can modify public views if you have the design permission level for the repository.

5. In the top area of the view, click **Delete**.

6. When prompted, click **OK**.

➤ **To switch views**

1. On the Quick Launch bar, click the name of the repository that you want to switch views in.

   If the repository is not on the Quick Launch bar, click **Site Actions**, click **View All Site Content**, and then click the name of the repository.

2. On the ribbon, click the **Library or List** tab.

3. Select the view you want to switch to from the **Current View** list in the **Manage Views** group.

Creating Columns

A SharePoint repository consists of columns that store content. When you select the Create Column option, the Create Column dialog box is displayed. Here you enter the name of the column, select the type of column you want to add, and apply validation features to that column.

Each column type offers various configuration options. For example, a Single Line Of Text column type has a Maximum Number Of Characters setting, whereas a Multiple Lines Of Text column type has a configuration option for how many lines it should allow. When you choose the type of column, additional settings are made available to further configure that column.

When you choose Choice (Menu To Choose From) as the column type, you can select the Allow Fill-In Choices option, which allows users editing the contents of this column to enter their own values, as well as the ability to choose from the defined choices. This option is generally set to No.

Column names must be unique in the list—that is, you can't have two columns with the same name. Also, be mindful of the column name length because this can alter the width of the column in a SharePoint view. There are several types of columns listed by default, and SharePoint developers can add to those types. Be sure to describe the column in the Description field so that other users know what kind of information is displayed in the column.

In the Additional Column Settings section, several options are available that are designed to protect the integrity of the information entered into the column. You can choose Yes for the Require That This Column Contains Information option to force the user to enter information into the column. You can choose Yes for Enforce Unique Values to ensure that the column does not contain duplicate information. You can enter a value in the Maximum number of characters field so that the length of the information entered into the column does not exceed that value. You can also enter a default value that aids the user entering the correct information into the column.

> **Important** Care should be taken when using the Enforce Unique Values option. This option should be set to Yes only on columns where there is a clear indication that an item is being duplicated. Also, only indexed columns can have the Enforce Unique Values option applied to them.

You can take further steps to provide a column with methods to enforce the integrity of the content it provides. The Column Validation section allows you to specify the formula that you want to use to validate the data in the column when new items are saved to the list. The formula must evaluate to True for validation to pass. For example, if your column is called "Company Name," a valid formula would be [Company Name]="My Company".

➤ **To create a column**

1. On the Quick Launch bar, click the name of the repository you want to add a column to.

    If the repository is not on the Quick Launch bar, click **Site Actions**, click **View All Site Content**, and then click the name of the repository.

2. On the ribbon, click the **Library** or **List** tab.

3. In the **Manage Views** group of the **Library** or **List** tab, click **Create Column**.

    > **Tip** Only the Create Column icon is displayed if the screen is not wide enough to display the Create Columns label.

4. In the **Column Name** text box, type the name of the column.

5. From the **Type of information in this column is** list, choose the field type you want to apply to the column.

6. In the **Additional Column Settings** area, in the **Description** text box type a description of what kind of content the column will hold.

7. Select **Yes** for **Require that this column contains information** if you want to ensure that the column stores a value when it is used. This option is set to No by default.

8. Select **Yes** for **Enforce unique values** if you want to ensure the column will not store duplicated information. This option is set to No by default.

9. In the **Maximum number of characters** text box, type a numerical value indicating how many characters can be entered into the column.

10. In the **Default value** area, select the **Text** option, or if you want the column to show a calculated value, select **Calculated Value**. Use the text box to type the default text or a formula.

11. Clear the check box for **Add to all content types** if you have a number of content types associated with the library and want to be able to choose which content type includes the new column. This option defaults to Yes.

12. Clear the check box for **Add to default view** if you do not want the column to be displayed on the view that all users will see when visiting the list or library. This option defaults to Yes.

13. Expand the **Column Validation** section by clicking the plus sign to its left.

14. In the **Formula** text box, type a formula if required to enforce validation.

15. In the **User message** text box (if you enter a formula), type a descriptive message to inform users what is required for the column data to be considered valid.

1.3   Manage List Items

A crucial aspect of maintaining user content in a SharePoint site is the management of list information (called *items*). Items are akin to rows of information in a Microsoft Excel spreadsheet. This section will teach you the basics of managing list items.

Creating Items

When you're working in a list, you create a new list item by using the New Item button on the Items tab or by using the Add New Item link that might be shown under the view displaying the existing list items.

However, unlike with documents, using the New Item button does not open another application; rather, it opens a dialog box that enables you to fill in the properties or columns for the new list item.

The ribbon at the top of the New Item dialog box displays different options based on the type of information being entered into the column. For example, if the column supports Rich Text information, the ribbon displays three tabs: Edit, Format, and Insert. Because each list can have different properties (or columns) in different orders, the screen can look totally different in each list. For example, the Announcements list has properties such as Title and Body, whereas the Contacts list has properties such as First Name, Last Name, and Business Phone.

Tip Like document libraries, lists can support multiple content types. This means that the New Item button on the Items tab might also offer a drop-down menu of options from which you choose the type of list item you want to create.

➤ **To create a new item in a SharePoint list**

1. Access the list where the item is to be created.

2. On the ribbon, click **Item** on the **List Tools** tab.

3. In the **Items** group, click the **New Item** button.

   The **New Item** dialog box is displayed.

4. Complete the form, and click **Save** to create the new list item, or click **Close** to cancel the action.

Editing Item Properties

You can customize lists and document libraries in SharePoint by adding extra columns. These columns are also known as *properties*. For example, every file in a document library has a Name property. The Name property is the physical name of the document.

There is also a Title property, and this can hold the title of the document. To edit the properties of a file, locate it in the folder where it is saved and highlight it by selecting the check box that appears to the left of the file when you hover the cursor over the row for that file. When you select the file in this way, the ribbon switches to the Documents tab. If you have permissions to edit the file or item's properties, the Edit Properties button is available on the ribbon.

Edit Properties button

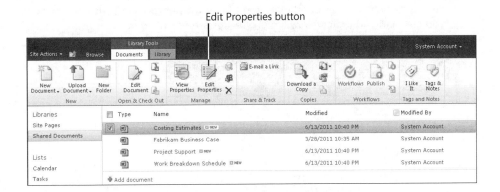

> **Note** It is easy to confuse the Edit Document button with the Edit Properties button. The Edit Document button opens a document for editing, whereas the Edit Properties button opens the document's properties page.

Alternatively, you can hover the cursor over the link to the file and then open the drop-down menu of actions for that file. If you have permissions to edit that file's properties, you see the Edit Properties option in this menu. Also, the Edit Properties menu option appears when you have permissions to edit a document or a list item's properties.

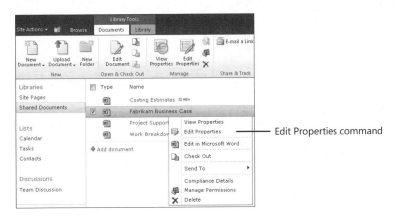

Edit Properties command

With list items, the procedure is slightly easier than with files. Simply click the title of the list item to open the dialog box that shows the item's properties and then choose Edit Item on the ribbon. Clicking this button switches the dialog box to one where you can modify the current properties of the file or list item.

> **Note** When you're editing the properties of a file or a list item, properties that are mandatory are marked with a red asterisk (*), and you must fill in those properties before you can save your changes. If you don't fill in those properties, SharePoint does not let you click OK and indicates which properties are not filled in.

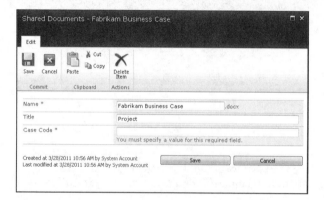

File and list item properties can be of different types, and each type has a different way of capturing data. For example, a text property displays a text box for you to enter data. A date property can appear as a text box (for the date) with a button next to it that looks like a calendar that enables you to choose a date, and it can even have two drop-down menus for selecting a time. A yes/no field appears as one check box; if the check box is selected, that means Yes.

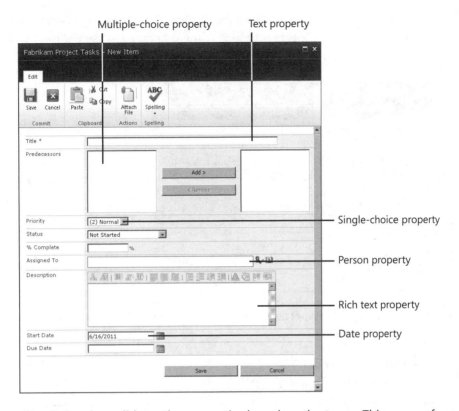

SharePoint also validates the properties based on the types. This means, for example, that you cannot write text in a date field or in a numeric property. If you do so, SharePoint shows you a red error message under that field and prevents you from saving the properties until the problem is corrected.

In addition, the document library or list manager might choose to impose additional conditions on some of the properties. For example, a condition might state that the title of a file should be fewer than 43 characters. SharePoint also alerts you if you try to save properties when one of those conditions is not met, and it tells you what field is not set correctly and what limitations are configured for that field.

An important action when creating a new file in some document libraries is choosing the content type for the file. Different content types require different properties, so it is recommended that before you enter the other properties you select the content type first.

This should not be a problem because the Content Type property is always the first one to appear in the list of properties if the document library was configured to use more than one content type.

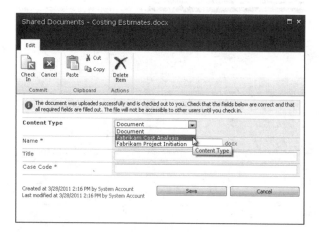

After you fill in all the properties you want, click Save at the bottom or the top of the page to save the changes.

If the document library is set up to require you to check in and check out files, you must check in the file after changing its properties.

> **See Also** To edit the properties of multiple list items or files, you can also use the datasheet view.

➤ To edit item properties

1. On the Quick Launch bar, click the name of the repository you want to add a column to.

   If the repository is not on the Quick Launch bar, click **Site Actions**, click **View All Site Content**, and then click the name of the repository.

2. On the ribbon, click the **Documents** or **Items** tab.

3. Select a document or item by clicking on its row, or click the check box to the left. When a document or item is selected, the Edit Properties icon can be clicked.

4. Click **Edit Properties**.

5. Edit the data as required.

6. Click **Save** to update the properties for the document or list item.

Using the Inline Editing Feature

Some views support an option called *inline editing*. When you select this option, you can edit the properties for a file or a list item without opening the properties page. When this option is enabled, a new icon appears next to the check box of each row. This icon, when clicked, switches the row to editing mode, where you can change which columns are visible in the view. In editing mode, you can also cancel your changes by clicking the Cancel button or save the changes by clicking the Save button.

➤ To use the inline editing feature

> **Note** To use Inline editing, the feature needs to be enabled on the repository's view. To enable inline editing, review the section "Creating, Modifying, and Deleting Views" earlier in this chapter. The following assumes inline editing has been enabled on the view.

1. On the Quick Launch bar, click the name of the repository you want to add a column to.

   If the repository is not on the Quick Launch bar, click **Site Actions**, click **View All Site Content**, and then click the name of the repository.

2. On the ribbon, click the **Documents** or **Items** tab.

3. Move your mouse over the row that you want to edit, and then click the icon displayed to the right of the selection check box on the far left of the row. (The icon has a ScreenTip that displays Edit when the mouse is positioned over it.)

4. Columns that are not managed by SharePoint (for example, Modified and Modified By are managed by SharePoint) are then displayed in Edit mode.

5. Modify the information in the columns as required.

6. Click the **Save** icon displayed to the right of the row selection check box, or click the **Cancel** icon to cancel any changes.

Deleting Items

You can delete items from a list by using one of several methods.

Delete a Single File or List Item Using the Delete Button

To delete a single file or list item, highlight that file or list item by selecting the check box that appears to the left of the file or item when you hover the cursor on the row for that file or list item. This causes the row to be highlighted and the ribbon to switch to the Documents tab or the Items tab. On the ribbon, click Delete Document or Delete Item. You are prompted to confirm the deletion.

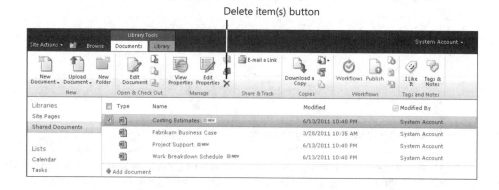

Delete item(s) button

> **Tip** Deleting files requires a different set of permissions than editing, so you might not see the Delete option on the ribbon. In that case, you should ask the manager of that list to delete the item.

➤ To delete a single file or list item by using the delete button

1. On the Quick Launch bar, click the name of the repository from which you want to delete a document or list item.

2. On the ribbon, click the **Documents** or **Items** tab.

3. Select the documents or list item that you want to delete by clicking the row selection check box located to the far left of the document or list item.

4. Click the **Delete** button in the **Manage** section on the ribbon.

5. Confirm that the file can be sent to the site Recycle Bin by clicking **OK**.

Delete a Single File or List Item by Using the Drop-Down Menu

An alternative way to delete a single file or list item is to hover the cursor over the item's title or the file's file name and then open the drop-down menu that becomes available. From this menu, choose Delete Item or Delete.

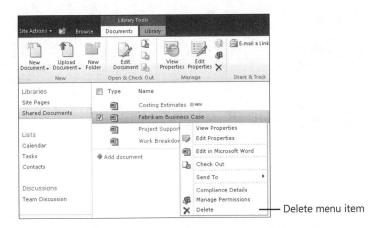

Delete menu item

> **➤ To delete a single file or list item using the drop-down menu**

1. On the Quick Launch bar, click the name of the repository from which you want to delete a document or list item.

2. On the ribbon, click the **Documents** or **Items** tab.

3. Select the document or list item that you want to delete by clicking the row selection check box located to the far left of the document or list item.

4. Right-click the selected row so that the context menu is displayed.

5. Click the **Delete** option in the menu.

6. Confirm that the file can be sent to the site Recycle Bin by clicking **OK**.

Delete Several Files or Items by Using the Delete Button

You can also delete several files or items at once by selecting those files or items using the check boxes that are shown on the left of the view. The check boxes become visible if you hover your mouse's cursor over the row for an item or a file. After you select several files or items, click the Delete Document button on the Documents tab or the Delete Item button on the Item tab to delete them all at the same time.

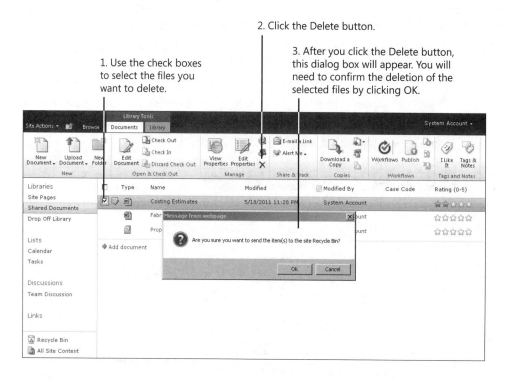

2. Click the Delete button.

1. Use the check boxes to select the files you want to delete.

3. After you click the Delete button, this dialog box will appear. You will need to confirm the deletion of the selected files by clicking OK.

➤ **To delete several files or list items using the Delete button**

1. On the Quick Launch bar, click the name of the repository from which you want to delete documents or list items.

2. On the ribbon, click the **Documents** or **Items** tab.

3. Select the documents or list items you want to delete by clicking the row selection check box located to the far left of the document or list item.

4. Click the **Delete** button in the Manage section of the ribbon.

5. Confirm that the files can be sent to the site Recycle Bin by clicking **OK**.

Delete Several Files or List Items by Using Datasheet View

Another method for deleting multiple files or list items is to use datasheet view. After you switch to datasheet view, highlight a row or more than one row, and then right-click the left-most column of that row. A special drop-down menu is displayed that appears only in datasheet view. From this menu, select the Delete option.

> **See Also** More information on switching views is given in section "Viewing Formats Using the Standard and Datasheet View" earlier in this chapter.

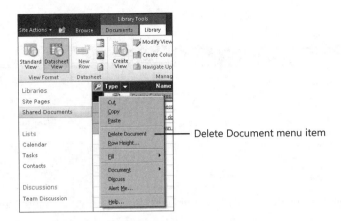

Delete Document menu item

> **To delete several files or list items using datasheet view**

1. On the Quick Launch bar, click the name of the repository from which you want to delete documents or list items.

2. On the ribbon, click the **Library** or **List** tab.

3. Click **Datasheet View** in the **View Format** group.

4. Click the left-most column of the row you want to delete.

5. Press the Shift key, and click the left-most column of other rows you also want to delete.

6. Right-click the left-most column and click the **Delete** option.

7. Confirm that the files can be sent to the site Recycle Bin by clicking **OK**.

Delete Files in a Document Library by Using the Open With Explorer Option

In document libraries, you can also use the Open With Explorer option on the Library tab. Clicking this icon opens the document library in Windows Explorer, just as it would any folder on your computer. From this view, you can select the files you want to delete and press the Delete key on the keyboard or right-click the files and choose Delete from the shortcut menu.

> **Note** Use this option with caution. If you delete files using the Open With Explorer option, the files will be permanently deleted. They will not go to the Recycle Bin.

Open With Explorer

Note If the window is wider, the label is included with the Open With Explorer command.

➤ **To delete files in a document library by using the Open With Explorer option**

1. On the Quick Launch bar, click the name of the library from which you want to delete a document.

2. On the ribbon, click the **Library**.

3. In the **Connect & Export** group, click **Open with Explorer**.

4. Highlight the files you want to delete.

5. Press the Delete key.

Enabling Version Control

This section demonstrates how to enable and configure version history and how to limit the number of saved versions. Version control is an essential need in content management. In SharePoint, version control helps users to track the changes made to content by saving a copy of each iteration. This provides a way of rolling back to a previous saved version if needed.

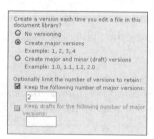

In the preceding screen shot, the Create Major Versions option is selected. This option creates versions like 1.0, 2.0, or 3.0. You can control the number of the versions you want to keep by selecting the Keep The Following Number Of Major Versions check box and specifying a number. When using this feature, the number you enter shows how many versions are saved in addition to the current version. If you enter 2, you have access to the current version plus the most recent two versions.

> **Important** Versions are complete copies of the document.

By default, version control is not enabled. When opening an item's menu (the drop-down list for an item), you won't see the Version History option.

➤ To enable versioning

1. Navigate to the document library by clicking on its title.
2. In the document library, click the **Library** tab.
3. Click **Library Settings** in the **Settings** section.
4. Under **General Settings**, click **Versioning Settings**.
5. On the **Versioning Settings** page, select the options required under **Document Version History**.

Managing Workflows

A SharePoint workflow allows automation of a human process associated with a document. Workflows help teams share documents and manage tasks by applying processes to documents and items in a SharePoint site. Workflows can help organizations adhere to consistent processes. They also improve organizational efficiency and productivity by managing the tasks and steps involved in those processes. This enables people who perform these tasks to concentrate on performing the work rather than on managing the workflow.

Table 1-3 lists the workflows available in SharePoint.

Table 1-3 **Available Workflows in SharePoint**

Title	Description
Approval	This workflow routes a document or item to a group of people for approval. By default, the Approval workflow is associated with the Document content type; thus, it is automatically available in document libraries. A version of the Approval workflow is also associated by default with the Pages library in a publishing site, and it can be used to manage the approval process for the publication of Web pages.
Collect Feedback	This workflow routes a document or item to a group of people for feedback. Reviewers can provide feedback, which is then compiled and sent to the person who initiated the workflow. By default, the Collect Feedback workflow is associated with the Document content type; thus, it is automatically available in document libraries.
Collect Signatures	This workflow routes a Microsoft Office document to a group of people to collect their digital signatures. This workflow must be started in a client program that is part of the 2007 or 2010 Office release. Participants must complete their signature tasks by adding their digital signature to the document in the relevant Microsoft Office program. By default, the Collect Signatures workflow is associated with the Document content type; thus, it is automatically available in document libraries. However, the Collect Signatures workflow appears for a document in the document library only if that document contains one or more Microsoft Office Signature Lines.
Disposition Approval	This workflow, which supports records management processes, manages document expiration and retention by allowing participants to decide whether to retain or delete expired documents. The Disposition Approval workflow is intended for use primarily within a Records Center site.
Three-State	This workflow can be used to manage business processes that require organizations to track a high volume of issues or items, such as customer support issues, sales leads, or project tasks.

Table 1-4 lists the components of a workflow.

Table 1-4 **Components of a Workflow**

Title	Description
Content Type	A workflow can be associated with the list or with a list content type. This means that the workflow can run against all items in the list or on the content types associated with that list. For documents, the default content type is Document. When more content types are associated with a list, they too can be associated with a workflow.
Workflow Template	A workflow template is needed to add to the content type chosen. Workflow templates (Disposition Approval, Three-State, Collect Feedback, Collect Signatures, and Approval) are described in Table 1-3.
Workflow Name	Used to name the workflow. Users need to know the name of the workflow associated with the content type.

Title	Description
Task List	When workflow tasks run, these tasks need to be saved somewhere so that those assigned to the task can carry them out and update status, which in turn updates the state of the workflow.
History List	When a workflow is started, is in progress, or has been completed, the history list captures the relevant information. This is used for audit purposes, for example.
Start Options	Start Options defines who can start a workflow and in what circumstances the workflow can be started. The workflow start options allow a site visitor who has Edit Item permissions to work in a manual state, as well as those who have Manage List permissions. The workflow can also be started automatically based on an event, for example, when an item is added into the list or when an item is changed in the list.

The process to create a workflow is as follows:

1. Select the content type associated with the workflow.

2. Specify the kind of workflow, the workflow progress lists, when the workflow starts, and who can start the workflow.

3. Select who is assigned to carry out the workflow tasks, the timeframe of when those tasks should be carried out, and what happens to the document if the workflow is successful or the document has changed during the process.

> **Note** The Remove Workflows page can also be used to alter the status of the workflow. For example, instead of removing the workflow, you might simply want to stop the workflow from running. To do this, select the No New Instances option on the Remove Workflows page. This will prevent the workflow from running.

> **Important** Before performing the following steps, you should create a new document library in your SharePoint site.

> **To create an approval workflow**

1. Access the repository by clicking its title in the Quick Launch bar (or by using the **All Site Content** option and clicking on repository title).

2. On the ribbon, click the **Library** tab or the **List** tab.

3. In the **Settings** section, click the **Workflow Settings** button.

   After you've clicked the **Workflow Settings** button, the **Workflow Settings** page is displayed.

4. In the **These workflows are configured to run on items of this type** list, select **Document**. Wait a moment while the page updates.

5. Click the **Add a workflow** link. Doing this loads the workflow settings page that you use to configure the workflow against the selected content type.

6. From the **Content Type list**, select **Document**.

7. In the **Workflow area**, select **Approval – SharePoint 2010** from the **Select a workflow template** list.

8. In the **Name** prompt, type a name for the workflow.

9. In the **Task List area**, select **New task list** from the **Select a task list** list.

10. In the **History List** area, select **Workflow History (new)** from the **Select a history list** drop-down list.

11. In the **Start Options** area, select the check box for **Allow this workflow to be manually started by an authenticated user with Edit Item permissions**. Select the check box **Start this workflow when a new item is created**. You do this so that if the document requires approval after being rejected, the user submitting the document into the document library can again invoke the workflow manually. Also, you need the workflow to immediately start when a user saves a new document into the documents library.

12. Click **Next** at the bottom of the page to display the final workflow configuration page.

13. In the **Approvers** prompt, enter the approvers or the owners of the SharePoint site, or the Approvers group if you have one. Do this by clicking the **Book** icon and searching for the group and/or user accounts.

14. In the **Request** prompt, type **Please approve the document**.

15. On the **End on Document change** prompt, select the **Automatically reject the document if it is changed before the workflow is completed** check box.

16. On the **Enable Content Approval** prompt, select the **Update the approval status after the workflow is completed (use this workflow to control content approval)** check box.

17. Click **Save** at the bottom of this page to save the workflow and redisplay the workflow settings page. The name of the workflow you just created is displayed at the top of the page, along with the number of workflows in progress (which will be 0 because no documents have yet been submitted for approval).

➤ To access workflow settings in a repository

1. Access the repository by clicking its title in the **Quick Launch** bar (or by choosing the **All Site Content** option and clicking on the repository title).

2. On the ribbon, click the **Library** tab or the **List** tab.

3. In the **Settings** section, click **Library Settings** or **List Settings**.

4. The **Library Settings** or **List Settings** information screen is displayed. In the **Permissions and Management** area, click **Workflow Settings**.

➤ To delete a workflow

1. Access the repository by clicking its title in the **Quick Launch** bar (or by choosing the **All Site Content** option and clicking on repository title).

2. On the ribbon, click the **Library** tab or the **List** tab.

3. In the **Settings** section, click the **Workflow Settings** button.

4. From the **These workflows are configured to run on items of this type** drop-down list, select **Document** if necessary. (You might need to do this when a workflow is associated with the Document content type.)

   When you select **Document**, the page is updated.

5. Click the **Remove a workflow** link to display the **Remove Workflows** page.

6. Click the **Remove** option on this page.

7. Click **OK** to complete the process of removing the workflow.

Uploading Documents

You can upload a single document or upload multiple documents in one step. To do this, first access the document library where you want to upload documents.

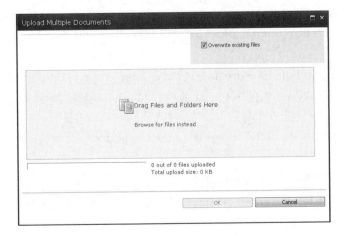

If you do not want to use a drag-and-drop approach, you can click the Browse For Files Instead link to access a page that allows you to select a check box for the files and folders you want to upload.

> **Note** Drag and drop is available if you have Microsoft Office 2010 installed on your computer. If you do not have Microsoft Office 2010 installed, a Windows Explorer–type dialog box is displayed and you have to select files by selecting the check box next to the files you want to upload.

➤ **To upload a single document**

1. On the **Quick Launch** bar, click the name of the document library you want to upload a document to.

   If the document library is not on the **Quick Launch** bar, click **Site Actions**, click **View All Site Content**, and then click the name of the document library.

2. Click **Documents** on the **Library Tools** tab.

3. Click **Upload Document**. The **Upload Document** dialog box appears. Click the **Browse** button to locate the document you want to upload.

4. Click **OK**.

➤ **To upload multiple documents**

1. On the right side of the **Upload Document** button, click the drop-down arrow to display the following two options: **Upload Document** and **Upload Multiple Documents**.

2. Choose **Upload Multiple Documents**. The **Upload Multiple Documents** dialog box is displayed.

3. If the **Drag Files and Folders Here** box is displayed in the **Upload Multiple Documents** dialog box, open a folder on your computer and drag files into that area.

4. If the **Drag Files and Folders Here** area is not displayed in the **Upload Multiple Documents** dialog box, the Windows Explorer dialog box is displayed. Select the files you want to upload by selecting the check box next to each file.

5. Click **OK** when you have all the files you want to be added to the document library.

Creating and Saving Documents

In this section, you'll see how to create a Microsoft Word 2010 document from within a SharePoint document library. To complete this exercise, you need access to a document library in your SharePoint site.

If there are columns assigned to the document library, they are displayed at the top of the document. For example, if the document library includes a column called Case Code, you'll be promoted to enter information into that column within the application. The following screenshot shows the two columns from a SharePoint document library within Microsoft Word.

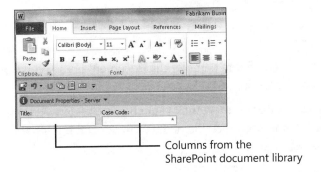

Columns from the
SharePoint document library

When you are saving the document, the application displays the document library where you started from. Click Save to save the document.

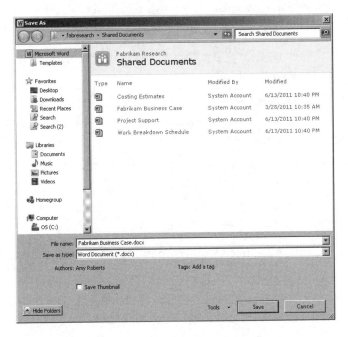

If the columns displayed at the top of the document are not populated with information and are set as mandatory columns (indicated by a red asterisk), you'll be informed of the issue. The message box appears also if columns do not have valid content. You can correct the issues by clicking on the Go To Document Information Panel button

➤ **To create a document**

1. On the **Quick Launch** bar, click the name of the document library you want the new document to be created in.

   If the document library is not on the **Quick Launch** bar, click **Site Actions**, click **View All Site Content**, and then click the name of the document library.

2. Click **Documents** on the **Library Tools** tab.

3. Click **New Document** to launch Microsoft Word 2010 using the template assigned, which by default is named **template.docx**.

> **Note** If the document library template is not a Microsoft Word document and is, for example, a Microsoft Excel workbook, Microsoft Excel will be launched, not Microsoft Word.

4. Enter the content for your document.

5. Click **File, Save** to save the document.

6. The document library in which you originated the document is displayed. Enter the name of the document and click **Save**.

7. If there are columns associated with the document, a page is displayed in which you enter information for those columns.

Practice Tasks

Practice the skills you learned in this section by performing the following tasks on your site:

- Create a new list called Events. Add a column called Event Type that uses the column type Choice, with three entries: Party, Conference, and Meeting.

- Add a new item into the Events list. Set the Event Type column entry to Conference. Save the item.

- Go back into the item and edit its properties. Change the Event Type column entry to Meeting.

- Modify the default view of the Events list to include the inline editing feature.

- Go back into the Events list and add more items to the list. Experiment with the inline editing feature, and alter values in the Event Type column for multiple items.

- Delete two items using the Delete option in the ribbon.

- Delete another two items using the drop-down menu.

- Enable version control for the Events list, and set the number of retained versions to 30.

- Create an approval workflow, and ensure it operates for any new items on the list.

- Carry out these exercises for a document library. Call this document library *Events1*, and create the same column called *Event Type*. Use the Windows Explorer option to delete files.

1.4 Work with Document Sets

A document set enables users to group multiple documents that support a single project or task into a single entity. All documents in a document set share metadata, and the entire set can also be versioned. A document set is a site collection feature that must first be activated.

The following list gives examples of situations in which a document set might be useful:

- When creating a request for proposal (RFP) response Using document sets in this case enables you to manage content across multiple documents—such as the actual proposal (.docx), the presentation (.pptx), and estimates and pricing (.xlsx)— that are part of the response to an RFP.

- When creating product documentation In this case, document sets can be used to create multiple related documents such as a technical decision maker/business decision maker brochure (.docx/.pdf), evaluation guides (.docx), various presentations (.pptx), feature comparison sheets (.xlsx), and other documents that need to be created as part of product release.

> **Important** The document set feature is not available in SharePoint Foundation 2010. Document sets are built on content types, and you can create multiple unique document set content types as part of your implementation.

Users interact with document sets in much the same way as they interact with regular SharePoint folders. There are some differences, however, that make them very useful in some scenarios. Here is a summary of some differences that add to their usefulness:

- A document set content type can be used as is, customized by modifying its settings in the site content gallery or when the document set is added to the document library, or used as the basis for creating a custom document set content type.

- A *Welcome page* welcomes and orients users of a document set by displaying the contents of the set and its properties. You can use the default Welcome page, shown next, or create your own.

- You can use the default New page or create your own.

- You can restrict the content types allowed in the document set by selecting from a list of available site content types.

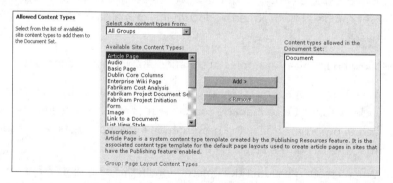

- You can include specific items or documents that you want to include in all document sets created from the content type. There is also an option to prefix each file name with the name of the document set.

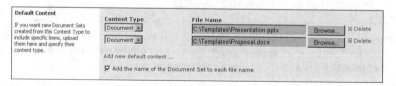

- ○ Document sets include a list of metadata used to synchronize all items in the document set.
- ○ Document sets include versioning capabilities.
- ○ Document sets include new activities that can be used to create workflows.

This is how the command group for a document set appears:

Following are some of the important considerations you should be aware of when planning a solution with document sets:

- There is no limit to the number of documents that can exist in a document set. However, load times might be slowed down if you increase the list view threshold, which by default is set at five thousand items.
- Folders are not allowed in document sets.
- Metadata navigation cannot be used in a document set.
- When you use the Send To feature with a document set, the sum of the size for all the documents in a document set cannot be larger than 50 MB. So, for a collection or work product with a very large number of items, a folder structure in a document library might be a better solution.
- There is no limit to the number of document sets that can exist in a document library. However, the number of document sets that can appear in lists is limited by the list view threshold.

➤ **To activate the document set site collection feature**

1. Go to **Site Settings**, and open the **Site Collection Features** page from the **Site Collection Administration** list.
2. Click **Activate** in the **Document Sets** area.

Defining the Document Set Content Type and Creating a Document Set

A document set is a site content type, so you must define the new document set at the site settings level. After you define the document set, you can select it for use in the relevant document library.

➤ **To define a document set content type**

1. Go to **Site Settings,** and click **Site Content Types** in the **Galleries** section.

2. Click **Create** to display the new site content type page.

3. In the **Name and Description** prompt, type **Fabrikam Projects Document Set** in the **Name** text box and **Project Documentation** in the **Description** text box.

4. From the **Select parent content type from** drop-down list, select **Document Set Content Types** to specify the parent content type. Because you have selected a Document Set Content Type, the **Parent Content Type** drop-down list will display **Document Set**.

5. In the **Group** section, select **Existing Group Document Set Content Types** to make finding the document set easier in the future.

6. Click **OK**.

> **Note** If the Document Set Content Types option is not available, the Document Set feature has not been enabled.

➤ **To create a document set**

1. Open the document library in which you want to enable document sets.

2. Go to the **Document Library Settings, Advanced Settings** page for the library.

3. Change the **Allow management of content types** setting to **Yes**. The setting for **Allow management of content types** defaults to **No**. You need to set this to **Yes** so that you can add the document set content type to the document library.

4. On the **Document Library Settings** page, click the **Add from existing site content types** link.

5. Select the document set content type (or any custom content type you created based on it) from the **Available Site Content Types** options list.

Adding Documents to a Document Set

When you create a document set, you need to put documents into it and update it. The procedures in this section show you how to accomplish those tasks.

➤ To add documents to a document set

1. Open the document library in which the document set is enabled.

2. Click the down arrow next to the **New Document** button to display the document sets enabled in the document library.

3. Click the document set from the drop-down menu.

4. Type the name of the set and a description of the document set.

5. Click **OK**.

   The document set page is displayed, allowing you to add documents into that document set by using the Upload and Create Document options.

> **See Also** For more information on how to create documents, review the section "Creating and Saving Documents" earlier in this chapter.

About Setting Document Set Versioning

Document set versioning is additive, which means it does not replace versioning for individual items but provides an additional layer of support designed specifically for viewing and managing the document set's life cycle. This means that individual items inside a set can have versions and the set itself can have versions.

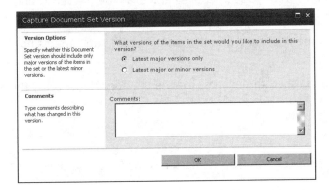

A document set version is simply a set of metadata associated with the document set, including a Check In Comments text field, a summary view of document set properties, and a summary view of changes to properties of document sets. A document set has a Version History page where users can see a chronological list of changes and act on a previous version of a document set.

You can also delete or restore a version. One thing to remember is that when you delete a document set version, it does not delete the versions of the items in the document set.

Practice Tasks

Practice the skills you learned in this section by performing the following tasks on your site:

- Create a new document library called *Projects*.
- Create a document set content type called *Project Fabrikam*.
- Associate the Project Fabrikam document set with the Projects document library.
- Remove the default Document content type from the Projects document library.
- Set versioning on the Projects document library.
- Create a new document using the Project Fabrikam content type in the Projects document library. Name this document *ProjectEvents*.
- Upload documents to the document set, and examine the version history on the documents in the document set.
- Delete the document set, and practice creating more documents based on the document set.
- When you have finished this exercise, delete the document library Projects.

Objective Review

Before finishing this chapter, be sure you've mastered the following skills:

1.1 Navigate the SharePoint hierarchy

1.2 Manage lists and document libraries

1.3 Manage list items

1.4 Work with document sets

2 Managing SharePoint Sites

The skills tested in this section of the Microsoft Office Specialist exam for SharePoint 2010 include managing pages and the Web Parts on a page and analyzing site activity. Specifically, the following skills are described:

2.1 Manage pages

2.2 Administer sites

2.3 Manage Web Parts on a page

2.4 Manage content types

2.5 Manage users and groups

2.6 Create SharePoint workspace sites

2.7 Analyze site activity

> **Important** To work through the practice tasks in this chapter, you need your own Microsoft SharePoint site that has no restrictions applied. The SharePoint site must be based on a default SharePoint Team Site template.

2.1 Manage Pages

All SharePoint sites are made up of pages. These pages can be static or dynamic. Dynamic pages are those defined by SharePoint. SharePoint builds these pages based on various content repositories. Static pages are created by users and hold information that does not change as often. When information does change, the user carries out the modifications.

SharePoint provides a number of page templates, and their availability depends on the site template the site is based on. For a Publishing site, for example, you can create the page types shown in Table 2-1.

Table 2-1 Possible page types for a publishing site

Page Template	Purpose
Article	Body only
Article	Image on left
Article	Summary links
Redirect	Redirect
Enterprise Wiki	Basic
Welcome	Advanced search
Welcome	Blank web page
Welcome	People search results
Welcome	Search box
Welcome	Search results
Welcome	Site Directory home
Welcome	Splash
Welcome	Summary
Welcome	Table of contents

As with page templates, there are SharePoint site templates. For example, a SharePoint Team Site is one of the available site templates. With the exception of Web Database sites (which integrate with Microsoft Access 2010), all site templates allow you to create a basic page and a Web Part page. Basic pages and Web Part pages can contain Web Parts.

> **See Also** For more information about Web Parts, see "Manage Web Parts on a Page" later in this chapter. For more information about SharePoint site templates, read the section "SharePoint 2010 Starts at Site Templates" in the Appendix.

When a site is created, SharePoint 2010 creates a special wiki page library called Site Pages. By default, all new pages you create in the site are stored in the Site Pages library. You use the Site Pages library to manage these pages.

Creating a SharePoint Page

To create a basic page, you can use the New Page option on the Site Actions menu.

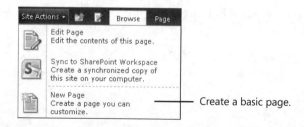 Create a basic page.

The first step to creating a new page is to enter the name of the page in the Name box in the New Page dialog box. If you enter spaces in the name of the page, the spaces are converted to the characters *%20* when you click the Create button. For example, a page named *Events Information Page* becomes *Events%20Information%20Page*.

When the new page is created, it is displayed in Edit mode. The ribbon changes to display the editing options for the new page.

> ➤ **To create a page**

1. On the ribbon, click **Site Actions**.

2. On the **Site Actions** menu, click **New Page**.

3. In the **New Page** dialog box, type a name for the new page.

4. Click **Create**.

Editing Pages

If you need to make changes to a page that is displayed, you can quickly edit the page by using the Site Actions, Edit Page option to put the page in Edit mode. (You can also click the Page tab displayed on the ribbon bar.) If the Site Pages library or a document library is displayed, click the page you want to edit to display it, and then use the Site Actions menu or the Page option to edit the page.

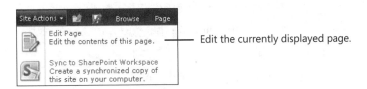

Edit the currently displayed page.

When you choose Edit Page, the ribbon switches to a Page Edit mode layout, providing many features that enable you to modify the layout of the page, add content, alter the styles, and much more.

Managing Pages from a Library

Another method you can use to create, edit, or delete pages is to visit the library where a page is stored. If you display the Site Pages library, for example, you can create pages using the same procedure as for creating a document. You can edit the page properties by displaying the drop-down menu associated with the page. You can delete pages by using the Delete option, which is also displayed in the drop-down menu associated with the page. To make changes to the page itself, however, the page must be displayed—meaning that you must click on the page in the Site Pages library to display it and then use the Site Actions menu and choose the Edit Page command.

Tip You can also change the title and description and set an icon for the page when in Edit Page mode by using the Title Bar Properties option.

➤ To edit the home page of the SharePoint site

1. Navigate to the home page of your SharePoint site.
2. From the ribbon, click **Site Actions** to display the **Site Actions** menu.
3. Click the **Edit Page** option.

    The page is placed into Edit mode, and the ribbon displays editing features.

4. Make changes to the page as required.
5. To save, click the **Save & Close** button at the left side of the ribbon.

➤ To set a page as the home page of the SharePoint site

1. Navigate to the page on the SharePoint site that you want to set as the home page.
2. Click the **Page** tab on the ribbon.
3. Click the **Make Homepage** button in the **Page Actions** group.
4. You will be asked to confirm the action. Click **OK** to set the page as the home page.

Deleting Pages

To delete a page (other than a page designated as the Home page) from a SharePoint site, start by displaying the page. At the top of the ribbon, you'll see the Page, Format Text, and Insert tabs. Click Delete Page on the Page tab.

Note that you cannot delete a site's Home page. You can only delete the current Home page if you have already designated another page as the Home page. (See the procedure in the preceding section for details.)

Delete Page on the Page tab

When you delete a page, the page is removed from the SharePoint site and placed in the Recycle Bin. To restore the page, you can visit the Recycle Bin and recover it.

> **See Also** For more information about recovering data, see "Recovering Data" later in this chapter.

➤ **To delete a page from a SharePoint site**

1. Navigate to the page that you want to delete in your SharePoint site.

2. Click the **Page** tab on the ribbon.

3. Click **Delete Page**.

Practice Tasks

Practice the skills you learned in this section by performing the following tasks on your site:

- Create a new page called Events, and then set that page as the home page.
- Create a new page called About My Site, and then set that page as the home page.
- Change the title of the Events page to My Site Events.
- Edit the About My Site page, and add content to that page.
- Set the Home page as the home page.
- Delete the Events page.
- Delete the About My Site page.

2.2   Administer Sites

This section teaches you the basics of site administration in a SharePoint site. You will learn how to create and configure a SharePoint site, organize site content, view user alerts, modify site appearance, and recover data.

Creating and Configuring a SharePoint Site

You might at some point need to create a new SharePoint site. Reasons for creating a site might be any of the following:

- You have a group of people who need to share specific information that is apart from the content already stored on a site.

- Specific information needs to be protected and managed by individuals, and they require more than just document library features.

To help meet user requirements for the structure, format, and functionality that users want on their site, you can create sites from various site templates provided with SharePoint.

> **See Also** For more information about site templates, see "SharePoint 2010 Starts at Site Templates" in the Appendix.

To create a site, you should first gather information about the site. Three pieces of information are especially important:

- The title of the site

- The people who will own the site (that is, those who will be able to add content to the site)

- How access to the site should be displayed

You can create a SharePoint site by clicking New Site on the Site Actions menu on the ribbon or by clicking the All Site Content link on the Quick Launch bar. If you don't see the Site Actions menu or the option to create a site does not appear on the menu, you might not have permission to create a site.

When setting permissions, you can give permissions to the new site to the same users who have access to the parent site, or you can give permissions to a unique set of users. When specifying navigation options, you can choose whether this site will have its own top link bar or use the one from its parent site.

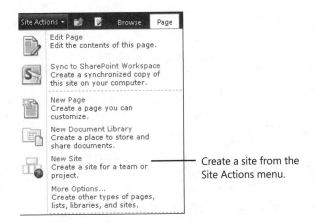

Create a site from the
Site Actions menu.

➤ **To create a SharePoint site**

1. Click **Site Actions**, and then click **New Site**.

2. In the **Create** dialog box, type a title and URL for the site.

3. In the center of the dialog box, SharePoint displays the available site templates. Click the site template you want to apply.

4. Choose any permission and the navigation options that you want to specify, and then click **Create**.

Organizing Site Content

Site administrators need to be able to easily organize the layout of a site and potentially any subsites. SharePoint provides the Content And Structure page, which allows you to manipulate a tree view of sites and manage them and their content.

The Content And Structure page is accessible from the Administration section of the Site Settings page, but it is available only when the SharePoint Server Publishing Infrastructure feature is activated. You can take steps to confirm that Content And Structure is available and enable the page if necessary by activating the SharePoint Server Publishing Infrastructure feature. (See the "To activate the Content And Structure option" procedure later in this chapter to learn how to do this.)

To assist you in configuring a site, the Content And Structure page provides you with the ability to copy content from one place to another. You can also configure site properties on the Content And Structure page. This option is useful when you need to alter settings for many subsites because it allows you to do so without having to access each site individually.

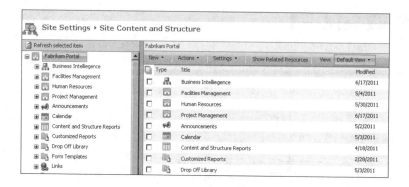

➤ To confirm the Content And Structure page is available

1. On the ribbon, click **Site Actions** to display the **Site Actions** menu.

2. Click **Site Settings** to display the **Site Settings** page.

   Under **Site Administration**, you should see the option **Content and Structure**. If that option is not displayed, the Publishing Infrastructure feature has not been enabled.

➤ To activate the Content And Structure option

1. On the ribbon, click **Site Actions** to display the **Site Actions** menu.

2. Click **Site Settings** to display the **Site Settings** page.

3. In the **Site Collection Administration** section, click **Site collection features**.

4. Next to **SharePoint Server Publishing Infrastructure**, click the **Activate** button to enable that feature.

5. In the **Site Administration** section on the **Site Settings** page, check that the **Content and Structure** option is displayed.

➤ To copy content using the Content And Structure page

> **Important** The following procedure is based on copying documents from one document library to another.

1. On the ribbon, click **Site Actions** to display the **Site Actions** menu.

2. Click **Site Settings** to display the **Site Settings** page.

3. In the **Site Administration** section, click **Content and Structure** to display the **Content and Structure** page.

4. Click the title of the document library that you want to copy documents from.

5. At the left of the document you want to copy, select the check box.

6. Click **Actions** on the menu bar, and then click **Copy**. The **Copy** dialog box is displayed.

7. Click the destination document library that you want to copy the document to.

8. Click **OK** at the foot of the dialog box.

SharePoint copies the document to the destination document library.

➤ **To alter site properties using the Content And Structure page**

1. On the ribbon, click Site Actions to display the **Site Actions** menu.

2. Click Site Settings to display the Site Settings page.

3. In the **Site Administration** section, click **Content and Structure**.

4. On the left, click the drop-down arrow to the right of the site title in the Explorer window to display additional options.

These options can be applied to help you manage the site. For example, if you click the drop-down arrow to the right of a site, you see options for quickly accessing site settings, permissions, and general settings.

Using the Content Organizer

The Content Organizer allows you to create metadata-based rules that move content submitted to the site to the correct library or folder. In other words, when a user uploads a file to any of the document libraries in the site and the user tags the file, based on how the file is tagged it is automatically moved to the correct location. This feature helps site administrators preserve the organization of site file content.

The Content Organizer is a site feature and works only on document content types. Additionally, the Content Organizer allows you to specify the maximum number of items a container (for example, a folder) can hold before a new container is created. For example, you might specify that a folder can contain 5,000 files. When file 5,001 is placed in the folder, a new folder is created (based on a naming convention you specify), and the file is moved to that folder.

To use the Content Organizer, you must ensure that the feature is enabled and then configure it. After you enable the Content Organizer, you see two new options in the Site Settings page in the Site Administration section, called Content Organizer Settings and Content Organizer Rules. You will also see a new document library called Drop Off Library. This library is where you need to upload content that is subject to the rules defined in the Content Organizer.

Use the Drop Off Library to test new rules by uploading documents into that library and seeing whether the content is redirected to the target locations and configured according to the Content Organizer settings.

This Content Organizer Settings page is quite detailed, with options for redirection, sending to other sites, folder partitioning, and more. Table 2-2 provides a basic description for each of the sections in the Content Organizer settings page.

Table 2-2 Content organizer settings page options

Section	Purpose
Redirect Users to the Drop Off Library	When this setting is enabled, users are redirected to the Drop Off Library when they try to upload content to libraries in this site that have one or more content organizer rules pointing to them.
	If this setting is disabled, users can always bypass the organizer and upload files directly to a library or folder.
	Users will never be redirected to the Drop Off Library when organizing pages.
Sending to Another Site	If there are too many items to fit into one site collection, enable this setting to distribute content to other sites that also have content organizers.
Folder Partitioning	The organizer can automatically create subfolders when a target location exceeds a certain size.
Duplicate Submissions	Specify what should occur when a file with the same name already exists in a target location.
	If versioning is not enabled in a target library, the organizer appends unique characters to duplicate submissions regardless of the setting selected.
Preserving Context	The organizer can save the original audit logs and properties if they are included with submissions. The saved logs and properties are stored in an audit entry on the submitted document.
Rule Managers	Specify the users who manage the rules and can respond when incoming content doesn't match any rule. Rule Managers must have the Manage Web Site permission to access the content organizer rules list from the site settings page.

➤ **To enable the Content Organizer**

1. On the ribbon, click **Site Actions** and then click **Site Settings**.

2. Click **Manage Site Features** in the **Site Actions** section. This displays the **Site Features** page.

3. You will see the Content Organizer displayed along with a description of its purpose, and an **Activate** button to the right of that. Click the **Activate** button.

➤ **To configure the Content Organizer**

1. On the ribbon, click **Site Actions** and then click **Site Settings**.

2. Click **Content Organizer Settings** in the **Site Administration** section.

   This displays the **Content Organizer Settings** page. Work through the page by setting the entries you might require.

3. Click **OK** at the foot of the **Content Organizer Settings** page.

4. Click **Content Organizer Rules** in the **Site Administration** section.

   This displays the **Content Organizer Rules** page. Rules are displayed on this page along with their priority and a description of where files will be redirected when the rule runs.

5. To add a new rule, click **Add new item**.

6. In the **New Rule** dialog box, fill in the **Rule Name**, **Rule Status and Priority**, **Submissions Content Type**, **Conditions**, and **Target Location** fields.

7. Click **OK** to save the new rule.

Viewing User Alerts

In this section, you learn how an administrator can remove an alert for a user. Users can manage their own alerts and delete alerts they no longer require. In some cases, a user might not be able to remove an alert, perhaps because the alert has been set up for that user and he or she does not generally use SharePoint. In those cases, a site administrator can remove the alert for the user.

The User Alerts feature lets you manage user alerts and is available on the Site Settings page in the Site Administration section.

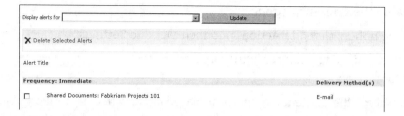

➤ To remove an alert for a user

1. On the ribbon, click **Site Actions** and then click **Site Settings**.

2. In the **Site Administration** section of the **Site Settings** page, click the **User alerts** link to display the **User Alerts** page.

3. From the **Display alerts for** list, select the user whose alerts you want to view.

4. Click the **Update** button to the right of the **Display alerts for** list to display any existing alerts set for the selected user.

5. If any alerts are displayed, select the check box to the left of the alert you want to remove and then click **Delete Selected Alerts**.

Modifying Site Appearance

A site administrator can alter the appearance of the SharePoint site under his or her control. Options to do this are available from the Site Settings page of the SharePoint site and displayed in the Look And Feel section. Two of these options, for the Quick Launch bar and the top link bar, are covered in Chapter 1, "Creating and Formatting Content," in the section "Using the Quick Launch Bar." This section covers the remaining features in the Look And Feel section of the Site Settings page. You will learn how to add a tree view to the site and how to set a site theme.

Using a SharePoint Tree View

Consider this scenario: You are the owner of the Fabrikam SharePoint site. This parent site has three subsites (Human Resources, Project Management, and Building Management). These sites have content in the form of lists, document libraries, calendars, discussions, and more. You have been asked to provide users with the ability to view the site and gain access to any part of that site from the parent site. You are aware that users can use Windows Explorer to traverse folders to manage their files.

To fulfill this request, you can provide a tree view. A tree view displays site content in a manner akin to viewing the site hierarchically.

Applying a SharePoint Site Theme

SharePoint themes represent a collection of graphics and cascading style sheets that can modify how a SharePoint site looks. SharePoint 2010 provides 20 themes; each of these has properties whose color can be altered to your choosing. Additionally, the heading font and body font can be altered. Themes can also be customized by using SharePoint Designer 2010 or Microsoft Visual Studio 2010.

➤ **To enable the SharePoint tree view in a SharePoint site**

1. Navigate to the home page of your SharePoint site.

2. On the ribbon, click **Site Actions**, and then click **Site Settings**.

3. In the **Look and Feel** section of the **Site Settings** page, click **Tree View**.

   The Tree View page is displayed.

➤ **To apply a theme to a site**

1. Navigate to the home page of your SharePoint site.

2. On the ribbon, click **Site Actions** and then click **Site Settings**.

3. In the **Look and Feel** section of the **Site Settings** page, click **Site Theme**.

   The Site Theme page is displayed.

4. From the **Select a Theme** section on this page, click the theme you want to adopt on the site.

5. In the **Customize Theme** section, click the **Select a color** link beside the property you want to further customize. Choose the relevant color from the palette displayed, and click **OK** to confirm the color selection.

6. Below the properties that allow a color alteration, alter the heading and body fonts.

7. Click **Preview** so that SharePoint displays the home page of the site based on the choices you made. Note that to preview themes, you can close the preview window and repeat steps 4 and 5.

8. Click the **Apply** button displayed at the foot of the **Site Theme** page to apply the theme to the site.

   Wait for the new theme to be applied. When the theme is applied, the screen will display the Site Settings page.

Recovering Data

The Recycle Bin is a holding area for anything that is deleted from a SharePoint site using the delete options available, whether the content deleted is a list item, a list, a document, a document library, or a site.

The Recycle Bin in SharePoint 2010 is a two-stage feature with which a user can delete content and then restore that content to its original location within a configurable amount of time. That is the first-stage Recycle Bin. The first-stage Recycle Bin is located at the bottom left of the SharePoint site within the Quick Launch bar.

Recycle Bin in Quick Launch bar

To recover deleted content from the first-stage recycle bin, the user first needs to access the Recycle Bin. The following illustration shows an example of a first-stage Recycle Bin listing content that has been deleted.

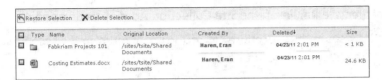

As a SharePoint administrator, you can also access the second-stage Recycle Bin, which is at the site-collection level and is also known as the *Site Collection Recycle Bin*. If a deleted item is not in the first-stage Recycle Bin, an administrator can restore the file from the second-stage Recycle Bin—if the file was deleted within the configurable timeframe set for the second-stage Recycle Bin. The SharePoint administrator can access the second-stage Recycle Bin from the first-stage Recycle Bin page or from the Site Settings page in the Site Collection Administration section.

In this section, you will learn about the Recycle Bin for the site (the first-stage Recycle Bin) and the Recycle Bin that can be accessed by a SharePoint administrator (the second-stage Recycle Bin). You will learn how to recover content from both of these Recycle Bins.

> **Important** To access the second-level Recycle Bin, you must be a site collection administrator.

> **Important** If you are working with a new site, you might need to delete some content from the site before you work with these procedures.

➤ To recover data from the first-stage Recycle Bin

1. Navigate to the home page of your SharePoint site.

2. Click the **Recycle Bin** link displayed at the bottom left of the site.

   The first-stage Recycle Bin is displayed, listing content that has been deleted. A check box is displayed to the left of each item.

3. Select the check box associated with the content item you want to restore.

4. Click the **Restore Selection** link. You will be prompted to confirm that you want to restore the item or selected items.

5. Click **OK** to restore the selected items.

➤ **To access the second-stage Recycle Bin from Site Actions menu**

1. Navigate to the home page of your SharePoint site.

2. On the ribbon, click **Site Actions** and then click **Site Settings**.

3. Click the **Recycle Bin** link in the **Site Collection Administration** section.

4. Follow the steps in the procedure "To recover content from the second-stage Recycle Bin" later in this section.

➤ **To access the second-stage Recycle Bin from the first-stage Recycle Bin**

1. Navigate to the home page of your SharePoint site.

2. Click the **Recycle Bin** link displayed at the bottom left of the site.

   The first-stage Recycle Bin page is displayed.

3. In the description at the head of the page, click the link **Site Collection Recycle Bin**.

4. Follow the steps in the next procedure.

➤ **To recover content from the second-stage Recycle Bin**

1. In the second-stage Recycle Bin, select the check box associated with the content you want to restore.

2. Click the **Restore Selection** link. You are prompted to confirm that you want to restore the item or selected items.

3. Click **OK** to restore the selected items.

Practice Tasks

Practice the skills you learned in this section by performing the following tasks on your site:

- Create a new subsite called Project Management based on the Team Site template. Set the navigation options so that the Project Management site has its own top link bar.

- Create a new subsite called Human Resources based on the Enterprise Wiki. Set the permissions option so that the Human Resources site will have its own set of permissions.

- Access the top-level site; using Content and Structure, go to the site settings for the Project Management subsite.

- Set up the Content Organizer so that files that begin with *Project* go to the Shared Documents library of the Project Management subsite.

- Preview the site theme called Laminate.

- Apply the site theme Ricasso to the Human Resources subsite.

- Delete a document from the SharePoint site, and recover the document from the first-stage Recycle Bin.

2.3 Manage Web Parts on a Page

Web Parts are reusable components that can contain any type of web-based information. This includes collaborative, analytical, and database information. Unlike Web Part pages, wiki pages contain a mixture of free-format static text and images. However, they can also include Web Parts. SharePoint provides methods for storing static information on a Web Part page by using special Web Parts designed to hold this type of information.

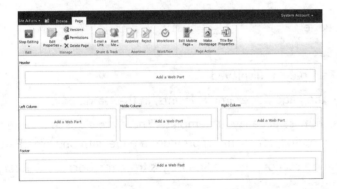

There are many built-in Web Part categories and types. Web Parts can display data from sources such as the following:

- Lists

- Search results

- Forms

- Other web pages

Creating a Web Part Page

Let's say you have been asked to display an Announcements list on a page called Events. This is not the only list that will be displayed on that page, and the requirement is for people to be able to see what events are available and be informed about forthcoming events via the Announcements list information. The page will also display a calendar and pictures at some point, all related to events.

As you can see from this scenario, it's not required that you add Web Parts to the home page. You can display the Web Parts on their own Web Part page. This is a good route to follow because you can build the page and then provide links to access it from the Quick Launch bar.

➤ **To create a Web Part page**

1. Navigate to the home page of your SharePoint site.

2. Click **Site Actions**, **More Options** to display the **Create** dialog box.

3. On the **Filter By** menu on the left, click **Page** to display page types that can be created.

4. Click **Web Part Page**.

5. Click **Create**.

   The **New Web Part** page is displayed.

6. Type a name for the page (for example, Events) in the **Name** box.

7. In the **Layout** section, select a layout template. There are eight to choose from. The Full Page, Vertical option, for example, provides a page with one Web Part zone.

8. In the **Save Location** section, choose **Site Pages** from the document library drop-down menu.

9. Click **Create** to create the page.

Adding and Configuring a Web Part

Adding a Web Part to a SharePoint site requires that you make a decision about the purpose of the Web Part you want to display, how it will be used by the site's users, and the functionality you want to display on the website.

You can configure a Web Part by accessing the Web Part options for the Web Part. If the Web Part is a list or document library type, you can also configure what the user sees by accessing the Web Part, going to the settings for the relevant list or document library, and updating the view options.

There are a large number of properties that you can set on a Web Part. Specific properties depend on the type of Web Part. Each Web Part has properties that are unique to that Web Part as well as properties that are common to many Web Parts, which include properties that affect the appearance of the Web Part.

➤ **To add a Web Part**

1. Open a page from the **Site Pages** document library. (If you created the Events page in the previous procedure, use it.)

2. Click the **Page** tab on the ribbon, and then click **Edit Page**.

   The Web Part zones are displayed. (For the Events page used in the previous example, there will be one Web Part zone titled Full Page.)

3. Click the **Add a Web Part** link in the center of the displayed Web Part zone.

4. Below the ribbon, the Web Parts that can be used are displayed. In the **Categories** section, click the **Lists and Libraries** category.

5. In the **Web Parts** section, the Announcements Web Part is displayed. Click the **Announcements Web Part**.

6. In the **About the Web Part** section, you'll see the **Add Web Part To** drop-down list. For a full page Web Part, you'll see only Full Page. If there are multiple Web Part zones, you will be able to select the Web Part zone you want to add the Web Part to.

7. Click **Add** at the bottom of the About the Web Part section.

8. The Announcements Web Part is displayed in the bottom of the Web Part zone.

9. On the **Page** tab, click **Stop Editing**.

➤ **To configure a Web Part**

1. Open a page from the **Site Pages** document library. (You can use the Events page if you created it in the procedure "To create a Web Part page" earlier in this section.)

2. Click the **Page** tab on the ribbon, and then click **Edit Page**.

   The page's Web Part zones are displayed. (For the Events page, there is one Web Part zone titled Full Page.)

3. All Web parts within the Web Part zones have titles. Double-click the title bar for the Web Part you want to modify to display the **Web Part Tools** tabs on the ribbon.

4. Click the **Options** tab under **Web Part Tools** to display the options for the selected Web Part.

5. Click the **Web Part Properties** button. A pane is displayed at the far right of the page, showing the available options for the Web Part.

6. To change the title of the Web Part, for example, expand the **Appearance** section of the Web Part properties pane by clicking the plus (+) sign.

Once expanded, the Appearance section shows properties of the Web Part that can be modified.

7. In the **Title** field, type a new title for the Web Part.

8. Scroll to the bottom of the Web Part properties pane, and click **OK**.

Hiding and Removing a Web Part

In some cases, you might want to hide or remove a Web Part that is being displayed on a SharePoint site. Both hiding and removing a Web Part ensures that the Web Part is not displayed on the site; however, there are differences between these actions.

Consider the following scenario.

The management of Fabrikam decides that the display of announcement information on the Fabrikam home page of the company's SharePoint site is no longer required. However, while the confirmation for this change of policy is being sought, the site administrator wants to ensure that nobody can see the Web Part.

The solution to the problem in this scenario is to *hide* the Web Part. This solution allows the Web Part to be re-displayed if required.

Hiding a Web Part keeps the Web Part stored in the site but not displayed to visitors, and it can be seen only by a person with the ability to edit the page where the Web Part has been hidden.

Removing a Web Part means the Web Part is not displayed on the page. You can either remove it from the page or permanently delete it from the site. Now consider the following scenario.

A review of the Fabrikam site has been performed. An announcement list is no longer required. This list is also displayed as a Web Part on the front page of the site.

The solution to the problem in this scenario is to remove the Web Part by permanently deleting it because the list associated with it is no longer required. Removing a Web Part includes two options. One is to *close* the Web Part, which moves the Web Part into a special maintenance page. The other option is to *delete* the Web Part, which permanently removes the Web Part from the site.

The reason for having these two options is related to maintenance. As a site grows, closed Web Parts end up on a special maintenance page, located on the Site Settings page of the site. If you close too many Web Parts, the maintenance page for Web Parts eventually becomes cluttered and difficult to manage.

However, if you delete a Web Part, the Web Part is permanently deleted and therefore will not end up on the maintenance page.

> **Tip** You will know that a Web Part is hidden because the title is prefixed with the term *(Hidden)*.

> **Important** To complete this procedure, you should have a Web Part page and a Web Part displayed on that page.

➤ To hide a Web Part

1. Open the page with the Web Part from the **Site Pages** document library.

2. Click the **Page** tab on the ribbon, and then click **Edit Page**.

3. Double-click the Web Part's title bar to display the **Web Part Tools** tabs on the ribbon.

4. Click on the **Options** tab below **Web Part Tools**.

5. Click the **Web Part Properties** button.

   A pane is displayed at the far right of the page showing the available options for the Web Part.

6. Expand the **Layout** section of the Web Part properties pane by clicking the plus (+) sign.

7. Select the check box for the **Hidden** option.

8. Scroll to the bottom of the Web Part properties pane, and click **OK**.

➤ To remove a Web Part

1. From the **Site Pages** document library, open the page with the Web Part you want to remove.

2. Click on the **Page** tab on the ribbon, and then click **Edit Page**.

   The Web Part zones are displayed.

3. Double-click the Web Part's title bar to display the **Web Part Tools** tabs on the ribbon.

4. Click on the **Options** tab below **Web Part Tools** to display the options for the selected Web Part.

5. Click the **Delete** button.

You will be prompted to confirm the deletion of the Web Part because this will permanently remove the Web Part from the site.

6. Click **OK** when asked to confirm that you want the Web Part to be deleted.

Export and Import a Web Part

As you continue to configure Web Parts in your SharePoint site, you will find that certain Web Parts have many configuration options set. If you need to move these Web Parts to another environment, the last thing you want to do is start configuring all the options again in the Web Part in the new site. Most Web Parts that you add and configure can be exported and then imported to another SharePoint site collection for reuse.

When exported, a Web Part is known as a *Web Parts Control Description file* and has a .dwp extension. This file contains information about the Web Part and the current state of Web Part properties.

To export the Web Part, you need to edit the page and then use the Options menu for the Web Part you want to export. When you choose the Export option, you are prompted to save the file locally to your machine. (You should save the file with the .dwp file extension.)

> **Tip** The Web Parts Control Description file contains XML that describes the Web Part class and assembly to use and the default values of the Web Part properties. After you have saved this file, you can use any text editing tool, such as Notepad or Visual Studio 2010, to change the values of the properties.

If you have a Web Parts Control Description file that you created yourself or received from someone else, or if you want to import a preconfigured Web Part, you can upload the .dwp file to the Web Part Gallery. After the .dwp file has been successfully installed, you can add the Web Part to a SharePoint site page.

> **Important** This uploaded Web Part configuration is only temporarily available in the gallery to the user editing the specific page and will not be available after the user exits Edit mode.

➤ **To export a Web Part**

1. Edit the page that displays the Web Part you want to export.

2. Click the drop-down arrow to the right of the Web Part's title bar.

3. Click **Export**.

4. In the dialog box that is displayed, click **Save** to save the Web Part.

➤ **To import a Web Part**

1. Choose the page to which you want to import the Web Part.

2. Select **Edit Page** from the **Site Actions** menu on that page.

3. Click an **Add a Web Part** button on the page.

4. Click the drop-down arrow to the right of **Upload a Web Part** (located beneath the **Categories** section displaying available Web Parts).

5. Click **Browse** to display a dialog box in which you select the Web Part file you want to import.

6. Click **Upload** to import the Web Part into the Web Part Gallery on the site. It is included in the listing of available Web Parts.

Practice Tasks

Practice the skills you learned in this section by performing the following tasks on your site:

- Create a Web Part page called Events. Create a document library and an announcements list, and display their Web Parts on the Events page.

- Add a Content Editor Web Part to the Events page. Modify the Web Part, and add content to the Rich Text Editor of the Web Part.

- Hide the Announcements Web Part.

- Export the Content Editor Web Part, and then permanently delete the Content Editor Web Part.

- Import the Content Editor Web Part. Create another page called Announcements, and add the Content Editor Web Part to that page.

2.4   Manage Content Types

Suppose that a colleague walks over to you and says, "Hey, I just e-mailed you a Word document." You respond, "Okay, what is it?" If your colleague replies, "I just told you, it's a Word document," you are liable to get a little annoyed. "I know it's a Word document, but what kind of document is it, actually?"

SharePoint has the same problem. When you upload content into SharePoint, what are you uploading? Are you just uploading documents?

At the simplest, most abstract level, SharePoint is a place to upload your content. SharePoint lists and libraries hold your information and hold your documents. But you do not think about your content in this way. You do not think in terms of documents. You think in terms of business plans, project schedules, or even things like menus and posters. You can go from the generic (document) to the specific (business plan) by defining a content type.

> **Tip** You can control workflow on content types, auditing them and setting expiration policies. All of these features in SharePoint can be based on the content type. If you have documents relating to a menu for Friday at the cafeteria, the lifetime of that document and the way it should be treated are different from a document containing company tax records.

Content types are not the same as file types. One file type can be associated with multiple content types. A Word document could be a legal contract, policy document, or business plan content type. The reverse is also true—a content type can be more than one file type. If you have a business plan content type, it can be associated with a Microsoft Excel workbook, PowerPoint presentation, Word document, or OneNote notebook.

Because of the relationship between a file type and a content type, you can have content types that represent different types of documents stored in the same document library. Content types are composed of columns that are collectively called *metadata* (information about information). Metadata further defines and explains the purpose of the content (for example), and it allows users to categorize and refine the nature of the content.

For example, a business plan document content type could hold, say, a code indicating the project and customer it is related to. A project schedule content type could hold the name of the project manager, approvers, and stakeholders for the schedule in several columns all assigned to the business plan document content type.

Using content types, you upload content in the usual manner. However, you can indicate data relevant for the content type, which allows the content to be further controlled and for the other features, such as auditing and expiration, to be applied to content types.

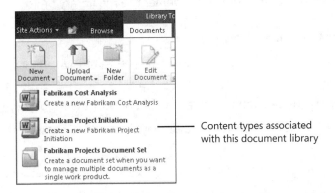 Content types associated with this document library

The preceding screen shot shows three content types. Two are based on Microsoft Word templates that are customized for the purpose of the document (Cost Analysis and Project Initiation). The third is a document set content type, which allows you to group different types of document.

> **See Also** Document sets are covered in "Work with Document Sets" in Chapter 1 in this part of the book.

In this section, you learn how to perform content type management for a document library or list, assign a content type to a document library list, and add columns to a content type.

Assigning Content Type Management

A content type is a collection of settings that can be applied to content. A content type is reusable because it is independent of sites and lists. Content types are designed to give users the ability to organize SharePoint content in a centralized and meaningful manner. Site columns (metadata) can be encapsulated within a content type to enable reusable structure or can be independently added to sites and lists.

For example, the Task content type includes site columns for Task status, Start Date, and Due Date; the Schedule content type includes site columns for Location, Start Time, and End Time.

Using content types as a template when a new task or event list needs to be created is much more efficient than rebuilding separate lists from site columns.

Assigning content type management to a library or list allows control and customization of content types associated with that repository. To expand the functionality of a library or list to store different types of content, including the metadata associated with that content, you need to assign content type management to the library or list.

➤ **To assign content type management**

1. Navigate to the document library or list to which you want to assign a content type.

2. Click on the **Library** (or **List**) tab to display the options for the repository.

3. Click **Library Settings** (or **List Settings**) to display the settings page for the repository.

4. In the **General Settings** section of settings page, click **Advanced Settings**.

5. On the **Advanced Settings** page, in the **Content Types** section, select **Yes** for the **Allow management of content types** option.

   Doing this allows the management of content types on the document library or list. Each content type appears on the new button and can have a unique set of columns, workflows, and other behaviors.

6. On the **Advanced Settings** page, click **OK**.

   A new section titled Content Types appears on the settings page.

Assigning a Content Type to a Document Library or List

After you have enabled content types for a repository, you use the Library Settings or List Settings page to specify the content types you want to use. When content types are defined for a document library or list, you can use a particular content type by clicking the drop-down arrow to the right of the New Item button and selecting the content type.

> **Important** Before you can assign a content type to a document library or list, you must assign content management to the document library or list. Follow the steps in the previous section if you have not already done this.

➤ **To assign a content type**

1. Navigate to the document library or list to which you want to assign a content type.

2. Click on the **Library** (or **List**) tab on the ribbon to display the options for the repository.

3. Click **Library Settings** (or **List Settings**) to display the repository's settings page.

4. In the **Content Types** section, click **Add from existing site content types** to display the Add Content Types page.

5. On the **Add Content Types** page, you will see a list of all available content types. Use the **Select site content types from** list to apply a filter.

6. Select a content type you want to assign to the document library or list, and click **Add** to add the content type to the **Content types to add** list box. (You can also double-click the content type to add it to the list.) You can remove a selected content type by double-clicking on the content type in the **Content Types to add** list or by highlighting the content type in the list and clicking **Remove**.

7. When you finish selecting the content types you want to include, scroll to the foot of the **Add Content Types** page and click **OK**.

Adding a Column to a Content Type

Adding a column to a content type allows you to extend its functionality. An additional column lets you record more information about a type of document or a list item. For example, SharePoint includes a content type called Phone Call Memo. This content type is useful if you want to record information from a caller. This content type has three columns: Title, Phone Number, and a text box allowing you to record notes. You might, however, want to add a choice column to record the kind of call (for example, whether it is a sales inquiry or business call). If so, you can name this column Call Type.

You can add a column that is part of the document library or list, or you can choose from the columns defined at the site level.

> **Important** The following procedure assumes you have created a column in the repository you are using or can use a site column to assign a content type. You should already have assigned content management to the document library or list. If you have not yet done this, follow the procedure in the section "Assigning Content Type Management" earlier in this chapter.

➤ **To add a column to a content type**

1. Navigate to the document library or list that contains the content type you want to work with.

2. Click on the **Library** (or **List**) tab on the ribbon to display the options for the repository.

3. Click **Library Settings** (or **List Settings**) to display the repository's settings page.

4. In the **Content Types** section, click the title of the content type you want to assign a column to.

This displays the **List Content Type Information** page for the content type you selected. The columns already assigned to this content type are displayed.

5. To add an existing column or a site column to the content type, click **Add from existing site or list columns** at the bottom of the **Columns** section.

You will see the Add Columns To Content Type page.

6. By default, list columns (if any) are displayed. These are columns that can be assigned to the content type. You can select site columns by selecting a group from the **Select columns from** list. Click the **Add** button to add the column to the **Columns to add** list (or double-click the column to add the column to the list). You can remove selected columns by double-clicking on the column in the **Columns to add** list or by highlighting the column and clicking the **Remove** button.

7. When you finish selecting the columns you want to add to the content type, scroll to the foot of the page and click **OK**.

Practice Tasks

Practice the skills you learned in this section by performing the following tasks on your site:

- Create a new list, and assign content management to that list.
- Add two content types to that list.
- Add a column to one of the content types.
- Delete a content type from the list.

2.5 Manage Users and Groups

For site administrators, the crucial aspect of site content control is managing access. A SharePoint site is made up of items, documents, lists, document libraries, and subsites. Subsites, in turn, can be made up of the same types of content again. The key aspects of managing access to this content are understanding the roles and permissions that can be applied, where they can be applied, and who they should be applied to.

Defining User and Group Accounts

Three SharePoint site security groups are provided by default: Owner, Members, and Visitors. Owners have Full Control permissions, Members have Contribute permissions, and Visitors have Read permissions. You can customize these groups by assigning a permission level to them, and you can also create new SharePoint groups with relevant permission levels. For example, you might want to create an additional SharePoint group or groups and assign those groups to specific document libraries or lists, with explicit permissions set for that group.

You work with the Permission Tools Edit tab to manage users and groups.

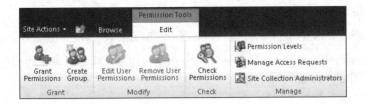

➤ To define a group

> **Important** The following procedure is performed in the context of setting site permissions only.

1. Navigate to the home page of your SharePoint site.
2. Click **Site Actions**, **Site Permissions** to display the **Site Permissions** page.
3. On the **Edit** tab, click **Create Group**.
4. In the **Name and About Me Description** section, enter a title for the group.
5. The **Owner** section will be populated with the user account that is creating the group. You can alter this to any other user who has access to this site, or enter the name of an existing SharePoint group.
6. The **Group Settings** section contains options for specifying who has the permissions to view members of the list and who has the permission to add and remove members from the group.
7. The **Membership Requests** section allows members to request membership in the group and have these requests sent to a particular e-mail address. If you select Yes for **Allow requests to join/leave this group**, you can select **Auto-accept requests** or have the requests sent to an e-mail address to be dealt with later.
8. In the **Give Group Permission to this Site** section, set the permissions for the group. For more details, see the following section.
9. Click **Create**.

➤ **To add users to a group**

> **Important** The following procedure assumes you have already created a SharePoint group or want to add users to an existing SharePoint group.

1. Navigate to the home page of your SharePoint site.

2. Click **Site Actions**, **Site Settings** to display the **Site Settings** page.

3. Click **People and Groups** in the **Users and Permissions** section.

4. On the Quick Launch bar, click the name of the group you want to add users to.

    The page now reflects the members of the group (if any users have already been added into the group).

5. Click **New**.

6. On the **Grant Permissions** page, enter the user account you want to add to the group. You can click the **Check Names** button to check the validity of the user account you enter. Click the **Browse** button to display a People Picker dialog box in which you can find the user account.

7. When you have specified the user you want to add to the group, click **OK** in the **Grant Permissions** dialog box.

Setting User and Group Permissions

If the purpose of your SharePoint site is for members of a particular workgroup to share documents and information, you can add members of that workgroup (that is, their Windows user accounts or Windows groups) to an appropriate SharePoint group on your site. For example, you can add workgroup members to which you want to assign Contribute permissions to the Members group. This way, they can add documents and update lists. You can also add other members of the workgroup to the Visitors group so that they can read documents and view lists but not contribute to the site. You might also want help managing the site, so you can assign some members to the Owners group.

You can also append permissions to accounts. For example, if you have already assigned Full Control to the user account and then later assign Design to the same user account, the user account permissions will be Full Control, Design.

> **Tip** To edit a user's permission, select the check box next to the user account on the Site Permissions page and then click Edit User Permissions to display the Edit Permissions page.

➤ **To set user permissions**

1. Navigate to the home page of your SharePoint site.

2. Click Site Actions, Site Permissions.

3. On the **Permission Tools Edit** tab, click Grant Permissions.

4. In the **Grant Permissions** dialog box, in the **Select Users** section, enter the user account (or accounts) you want to set permission for.

5. In the **Grant Permissions** section, select the group from the drop-down list. Add users to the SharePoint group that you want the user to join.

   Another option available in the Grant Permissions section is **Grant users permission directly**. Choosing this option displays all the available permissions for the SharePoint site and allows you to directly grant the permission to the user without the user joining any group. This approach is not recommended because managing many persons having the same permission creates an administrative overhead. Creating a group and then adding users to those groups is cleaner and easier to manage.

6. Click one (or more) of the permissions you want to assign to the user account (or accounts).

7. Click **OK**.

➤ **To set group permissions**

1. Navigate to the home page of your SharePoint site.

2. Click Site Actions, Site Permissions to display the **Site Permissions** page.

3. Click **Grant Permissions**.

4. Enter the name of the group in the **Select Users** section. Click the **Check Names** button below the **Select Users** section text box to check the validity of the group.

5. In the **Grant Permissions** section, select the option **Grant users permission directly**. Doing this displays all the available permissions for the SharePoint site.

6. Choose the permission you want to associate with the group.

7. Click **OK**.

➤ **To modify permissions for an existing group**

1. Navigate to the home page of your SharePoint site.

2. Click Site Actions, Site Permissions to display the **Site Permissions** page.

3. Select the check box next to the group account.

4. On the ribbon, click **Edit User Permissions**.

The Edit Permissions page is displayed. The name of the group is displayed in the Users or Groups section.

5. In the **Choose Permissions** section, alter the permissions for the group.

6. Click **OK**.

Practice Tasks

Practice the skills you learned in this section by performing the following tasks on your site:

- Create a group called Event Contributors, and set their permission level to Contribute.

- Add a user to that group,

- Alter the permissions for that new group to Reader, and change the title of the group to Event Visitors.

2.6 Create SharePoint Workspace Sites

A document workspace enables you to collaborate on documents with one or more colleagues. To easily manage content related to a specific meeting, you can create a meeting workspace.

You can create a workspace from within a document library, an Office application, or the home page of a site. In this section, you will learn how to set up and use a document workspace and how to set up and use a meeting workspace.

The following screen shot shows the Create site page, on which you can choose the Document Workspace template or the Basic, Blank, Decision, Social, and Multipage Meeting workspace templates.

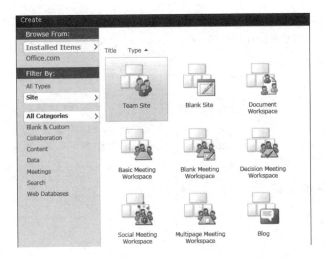

You can also create a meeting workspace directly from a Calendar list.

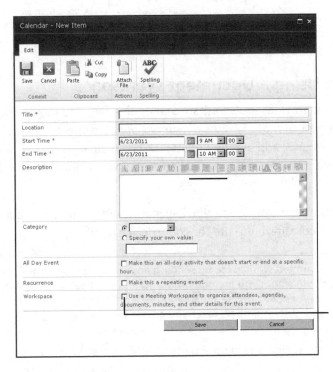

A meeting workspace can be created by selecting this check box.

You can create a document workspace from a Word document by choosing Create Document Workspace from the Send To menu.

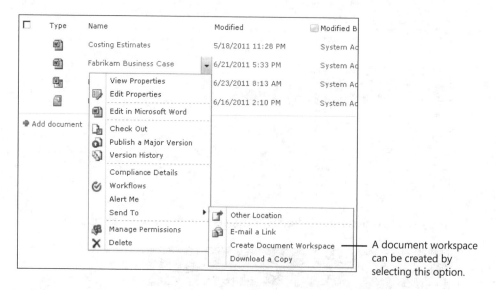

A document workspace can be created by selecting this option.

Setting Up and Using a Document Workspace

A document workspace provides tools to share and update files and to keep people informed about the status of those files. As a member of a document workspace, you can add and edit documents, add and edit related tasks, create e-mail alerts for yourself or other workspace members, add announcements, and provide links to related information.

When you create a document workspace, you can start using it right away, add other lists or libraries to it, or customize the site for your specific needs.

> **Tip** If you set up a document workspace by sending an e-mail message from Microsoft Outlook 2010, the people whom you include on the To and Cc lines of the message are automatically added as members of the site. If you use a different procedure to create a workspace, you can add other members after you create the site.

You can create a document workspace directly from a Microsoft Word document. When doing this, a site is created using the Document Workspace template. The site's title reflects the name of the document, and the URL for the site is the title of the document. Additionally, a copy of the document is placed into the Shared Documents library of the document workspace.

Using a document workspace is no different from using a normal team site except the templates provided are geared to making collaboration on a document easy to do. That means you can introduce any further documents into the document workspace and add any further functionality to the document workspace.

> **See Also** For more information on the types of document workspaces available in SharePoint, refer to "SharePoint 2010 Starts at Site Templates" in the Appendix.

➤ To create a document workspace by using the New Site command

1. Navigate to the home page of your SharePoint site.

2. Click **Site Actions**, **New Site** to display the **Create** dialog box.

3. In the **Filter By** section on the left side of the dialog box, click **Site** to display all available site templates.

4. Click **Document Workspace**.

5. At the lower right of the **Create** dialog box, click **More Options**.

6. Type a title for the document workspace, a description, and a URL, and choose the navigation options available on the **Create** dialog box.

7. Click **Create**.

➤ To create a document workspace from a document

1. Navigate to the document library or list that holds the document you want to create a document workspace for.

2. Highlight the document, and from its drop-down menu select **Send To**, **Create a Document Workspace**.

3. You will be asked to confirm the name of the document workspace and its location. Click **OK** to create the workspace.

Setting Up and Using a Meeting Workspace

A meeting workspace is simply another site template. You can create one as a new site using the procedure described in the previous section, except you select Meeting Workspace as the template instead of Document Workspace.

> **See Also** For more information on the types of meeting workspaces available in SharePoint, refer to "SharePoint 2010 Starts at Site Templates" in the Appendix.

You can also create a meeting workspace from a Calendar list in SharePoint. Using this approach, a meeting workspace is associated with the relevant calendar. While you are working in the meeting workspace, you can go back to the calendar entry by clicking the Go To Calendar link displayed at the top of the site under the site title and date of the meeting.

➤ **To create a meeting workspace from a Calendar list**

1. Navigate to the Calendar list, and then click the **Events** tab under **Calendar Tools**.

2. Click **New Event**.

3. Enter the information required for the calendar item.

4. In the **Workspace** area of the **New Item** dialog box, select the **Use a Meeting Workspace to organize attendees, agendas, documents, minutes, and other details for this event** check box.

5. Click **Save**.

6. On the New **Meeting Workspace** page, enter the title for the meeting workspace (or use the title of the calendar item), a description, and a URL (which, by default, uses the name of the calendar item as well). Choose the navigation options you want to use.

7. Click **OK**.

   The Template Selection page is displayed.

8. On the **Template Selection** page, select the Meeting Workspace template you want to apply (Basic, Blank, Decision, Social, or Multipage). You can also select a custom template (if one is available).

9. Click **OK**.

Practice Tasks

Practice the skills you learned in this section by performing the following tasks on your site:

- Create a document workspace.
- Create a meeting workspace from a new calendar entry.

2.7   Analyze Site Activity

As a site administrator, you need to know how to track site usage, growth, and trends. All of these kinds of site activity are collected in SharePoint Web Analytics. There are three categories of SharePoint Web Analytics reports: Traffic, Search, and Inventory. The reports are aggregated for various SharePoint entities such as site, site collection, and Web application for each SharePoint farm. Further, reports are also aggregated per search service application. By default, the reports show the data for a period of 30 days, but you can change the time period to view data for up to 25 months by using the Analyze tab on the ribbon.

Visually, metrics are shown in one of two ways: in trend reports and rank reports. A trend report shows how a particular metric is doing over a period of time. A rank report shows the top 2000 results for a particular metric.

> **Important** To view site analytics, data collection must be enabled for your SharePoint site. You can do this by using the Central Administration facility.

When you view summary information for traffic and inventory, you see the following site analytics:

- Total number of page views
- Average number of page views per day
- Total number of daily unique visitors
- Average number of unique visitors per day
- Total number of referrers
- Average number of referrers per day
- Total number of sites

> **Tip** The Web Analytics Web Part, which is located in the Content Rollup category, is a useful Web Part. It can be configured to poll the most popular pages or the content that is searched most often on the site.

To look at detailed reports concerning site activity, you can select any of the report icons on the Site Web Analytics Reports page and then click Change Settings. This displays a number of options on the ribbon, allowing you to customize the report, export the report to a spreadsheet, schedule reports, filter reports, and more.

➤ **To view summary information concerning traffic and inventory**

1. Navigate to the home page of your SharePoint site.

2. Click **Site Actions**, **Site Settings** to display the **Site Settings** page.

3. Click **Site Web Analytics reports** in the **Site Actions** section.

4. Click **Summary** at the left side of the page.

➤ **To view site detailed reports**

1. Navigate to the home page of your SharePoint site.

2. Click **Site Actions**, **Site Settings** to display the **Site Settings** page.

3. Click **Site Web Analytics Reports** in the **Site Actions** section.

4. Click **Change Settings** at the top of the relevant report.

5. Use the options available to further detail the report.

Practice Tasks

Practice the skills you learned in this section by performing the following tasks on your site:

- Analyze the preceding seven days using the Top Pages report.
- Show a Number Of Sites report.
- Analyze the preceding 30 days on the Number Of Daily Unique Visitors report.

Objective Review

Before finishing this chapter, be sure you have mastered the following skills:

2.1 Manage pages

2.2 Administer sites

2.3 Manage Web Parts on a page

2.4 Manage content types

2.5 Manage users and groups

2.6 Create SharePoint workspace sites

2.7 Analyze site activity

3 Participating in User Communities

Many of the skills tested in this section of the Microsoft Office Specialist exam for Microsoft SharePoint 2010 focus on the features and benefits of SharePoint 2010 My Site. Specifically, the following objectives are associated with this set of skills:

3.1 Configure My Site

3.2 Collaborate through My Site

3.3 Tag and note content

There are two types of SharePoint sites. One is a collaborative site that allows users to share information with other users within a department, company, or other functional area. The other is a personal site provided for each user, with which the user can share content with others. Personal sites are provided through a site collection known as My Site. Each personal site (called My Content) provides the user with all the key features of a SharePoint site. Users can create and manage documents libraries, picture libraries, calendars, surveys, and links. And because the user is the owner of the site, he or she can choose what content to share with other employees and what information is private.

My Site is where users can see user profiles for other users and manage their own user profile. Name, e-mail address, and department are just a few of the pieces of information stored in the user profile. Users can personalize My Site with the profile information they choose to include, provide other users with the ability to link content to the site (called *tagging*), link users to other users (identify users as *colleagues*), and provide a mechanism for content to be commented on dynamically through *note content* commenting.

In this chapter, you learn how to work with the SharePoint My Site and relevant areas. For you to work through this section, your administrator needs to ensure that My Sites are available. You also need to have full access to your own SharePoint My Site within the My Site page.

Throughout this chapter, the procedural steps direct you to "Access My Site." When you are instructed to do so, carry out the following steps:

1. Access your SharePoint site.

2. Click the drop-down arrow to the right of your name, which is displayed on the top right portion of the page.

3. Click My Site in the menu that's displayed to open the My Site home page.

When you access the My Site home page, SharePoint provides a top-level menu with links back to the My Site home page, the user newsfeed, the personal site, and the user profile.

3.1   Configure My Site

This section will teach you the basics of configuring My Site features. In the first part, you will learn how to complete four tasks:

- **Adding keywords** You can enter keywords to identify areas of expertise in the Ask Me About section of a My Site, and you can use social tagging with the Tags And Notes and I Like It features on the My Profile page of a My Site.

- **Adding colleagues** Listing colleagues on your My Site is a way to build a social community of employees, which helps you search for people and connect them to one another.

- **Selecting a theme** You can change the look and feel of your My Site and the personal sites of others. You can use the same procedure to set a theme for your My Site as you used for setting a theme for a team site, but SharePoint provides more options for site themes for a team site. For example, you can select colors and fonts to customize a team site. The only options available for My Site are the theme choices displayed.

- **Configuring the Colleague Tracker Web Part** The role of the Colleague Tracker Web Part is to alert you of changes made to colleagues' profiles and changes in user memberships. The Colleague Tracker also issues alerts that display colleagues' upcoming birthdays (if the colleague birthdate profile field has been populated), notify you when new blog posts have been added by colleagues, send out-of-office messages, and alert you of upcoming anniversaries. You can modify what you want to be notified about by setting the properties of the Web Part.

> **See Also** For more information about how to add a Web Part to a Web Part page, follow the instructions given in "Manage Web Parts on a Page" in Chapter 2, "Managing SharePoint Sites." The Colleague Tracker Web Part is located in the Recommended Items category of the Web Parts list and is called Colleagues.

The final two parts of this section describe how to configure personal settings on My Site and how to complete two further objectives:

- **Configure RSS feeds** Display changes in libraries, calendars, and lists on other SharePoint sites, including sources of information on the Internet.

- **Configure user profiles** Modify user profile information.

> **Note** Before you proceed, you need to be sure you have full access to your My Site.

Setting Up My Site

A key feature of My Site is the ability it gives you to find and connect with other people through the public views of their personal sites. When a user name appears in the portal site, it acts as a link you can click to see the public view of that person's personal site. Everything that a person chooses to share is available to see. You can also provide information to identify what you have in common with other people by setting keywords to describe skills and by identifying colleagues.

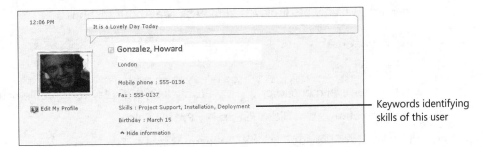

Keywords identifying skills of this user

The look and feel of My Site can be modified by using site themes. There are two places to set site themes on My Site. As a SharePoint administrator, you can set up a theme that affects the display for anyone accessing My Site using the My Site, My Newsfeed, or My Profile links or the Find People option. Themes can also be set by using the My Content link, which displays the user's personal site.

Change the theme of My Site. The same option is available in My Content.

➤ To add keywords

1. Access My Site.

2. On the top-level menu, click **My Profile** to display your profile page.

3. Below the photo area, click the **Edit My Profile** link.

   The properties of the profile are now displayed in Edit mode.

4. Scroll to the **Details** section.

5. The **Skills** property is displayed in Edit mode. Enter the keywords you want to associate with the profile, separated by semicolons (;).

6. Do not alter the drop-down list to the right that shows the privacy options. (The option displayed defaults to Everyone.)

> **See Also** For more information on privacy options, read the section "Configuring Profiles" later in this chapter.

7. Scroll to the bottom or top of the page, and click the **Save and Close** link to update the profile and return to the **My Profile** page.

   Keywords will now be displayed in the **Ask Me About** section.

➤ To add colleagues

1. Access My Site.

2. On the top-level menu, click the **My Profile** link to display your profile page.

3. Below the photo area, click the **Edit My Profile** link.

4. In the **My Profile** page, click the **Colleagues** tab.

   The Colleagues management page is displayed.

5. Click **Add Colleagues** to display the **Add Colleagues** dialog box.

6. In the **Colleagues** prompt, enter the names of the colleagues you want to add. If you are adding more than one colleague in this prompt, separate each name by a semicolon (;).

7. In the **Add to Group** section, click the **Yes** option if you want to add the colleague to My Team. If you click **Yes**, the information in your profile that has its privacy level set to My Team will be visible to the colleagues you selected in the previous step. Click **No** if you do not want to add the selected colleagues to My Team.

8. In the **Add to Group** section, for the **Add to a Group** drop-down list, select an existing group to display the colleagues in or put them in a new group of your choosing by using the **New Group** prompt.

   The default group displayed in the **Add to a Group** list is General, and the other option available is **Peers**.

9. In the **Show To** section, select an option from the **Show these colleagues to** drop-down list. These are the privacy levels that determine how the colleague is displayed to others visiting your My Site.

   The default privacy level displayed in the **Show these colleagues to** list is Everyone. For more information about privacy levels, read the section "Configuring Profiles" later in this chapter.

10. Click **OK** to save the selection of colleagues and display them in the **Colleagues** section of the **My Profile** page.

> **Note** You can also use the Colleagues section to edit information for colleagues or delete colleagues from your list. Select the check box to the left of the name of the colleague whose status you want to change and then click the Edit Colleagues or Remove Colleagues link.

The colleagues you added using this procedure will also be displayed in the Colleague Tracker Web Part.

➤ **To configure the Colleague Tracker Web Part**

1. Access My Site.

2. On the top-level menu, click the **My Profile** link to display your profile page.

3. Click **Site Actions, Edit Page**.

4. Add the Colleague Tracker Web Part to the page.

5. Click the **drop-down arrow** to the right of the Colleague Tracker Web Part, and then select the **Edit Web Part** option.

➤ **To select a theme**

> **Important** The following procedure assumes you want to set the theme for your My Site.

1. Access My Site.

2. On the top-level menu, click the **My Profile** link to display your profile page.

3. Click **Site Actions**, **Site Settings** to display the **Site Settings** page.

4. In the **Look and Feel** section, click the **Site Theme** link to display the **Select a theme** page.

5. Select the theme you want to apply, and then click the **Apply** button.

Setting Up RSS Feeds

Really Simple Syndication (RSS) is a widely used technology for transmitting information across the Internet and intranets. Many websites offer RSS feeds you can subscribe to so that you can get the latest information from the source automatically.

You can also subscribe to RSS feeds from SharePoint libraries, lists, and other elements. For example, when you subscribe to a document library RSS feed you can see when someone adds a document.

You can also use RSS feeds on the My Site profile page. This allows the My Site user to display information from the Internet (such as news and weather reports) and results from document libraries or lists. To see the results of an RSS feed, you can use the RSS Viewer Web Part. RSS feeds and the RSS Viewer Web Part provide you with a convenient way to view information from many sources on a single page.

You follow different steps to obtain the URL for your RSS feed, depending on whether the feed is coming from a website or from a location on a SharePoint site.

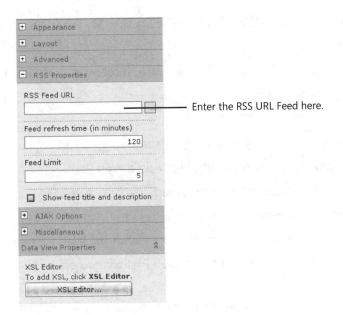

Enter the RSS URL Feed here.

➤ To obtain the URL for an Internet RSS feed

1. Go to the website for which you want to add an RSS feed.

2. On the page or on the Internet Explorer toolbar, click the RSS logo. The RSS feed appears in the browser.

3. Right-click the **Subscribe to this feed** link, and then click **Properties**.

4. Copy the address (URL). Be sure to copy the entire address.

5. Paste this address into Notepad.

➤ To obtain the URL for an RSS feed from a SharePoint document library or list

1. Open the SharePoint document library or list for which you want to set up an RSS feed.

2. Click **Library** or **List** on the **Library Tools** or **List Tools** tab on the ribbon.

3. Click the **RSS Feed** icon in the **Share & Track** section.

4. Copy the URL from the Internet Explorer **Address** prompt. Make sure you copy the entire address.

5. Paste this address into Notepad.

➤ **To configure the RSS Viewer Web Part on the My Site My Profile page**

1. Access My Site.

2. On the top-level menu, click the **My Profile** link to display your profile page.

3. On the ribbon, click **Site Actions**.

4. Click **Edit Page**.

   The page will now be displayed in Edit mode, showing Web Part zones.

5. In the Web Part zone labeled **Top Zone**, click **Add a Web Part**.

6. In the **Categories** section, click **Content Rollup**.

7. Click **RSS Viewer** in the **Web Parts** section

8. Click the **Add** button in the bottom right of the **About the Web Part area.**

   The Add Web Part zone will default to the Web Part zone where you clicked Add A Web Part in step 5.

   When you click the Add button, the RSS Viewer Web Part is added to the Web Part Zone labeled Top Zone.

9. Click the drop-down arrow to the right of the RSS Viewer Web Part to display a context menu. Click **Edit Web Part**.

10. Paste the URL for the feed into the **RSS Feed URL** prompt.

11. Alter the **Feed Refresh Time** to a value in seconds.

12. Alter the **Feed Limit** to a numerical value that limits the number of items being displayed in the RSS Viewer Web Part.

13. Click **OK**.

Configuring Profiles

The My Site profile page contains rich information about employees, including a photo, a short biography, job title, location, contact information, and lists of previous projects, skills, and interests. This information makes it easier to find the right people and subject matter experts across the company.

On an employee profile page, you can view an employee's areas of expertise in their Ask Me About section. You can see what the employee has been working on recently in that person's Recent Activities feed and see his or her position in an organization.

Employees can easily edit their profile information by using a Rich Text Editor, and the ribbon menu includes many formatting options. Employees can also choose what to display by setting privacy levels on that information.

> **Tip** Some fields in the profile can be imported from a corporate directory system, such as Active Directory.

> **Note** User profiles are managed in a special area for SharePoint administrators. SharePoint administrators can modify what properties are displayed in what sections, how those properties are configured, and what sections can be displayed. For more information on this (from an administrative perspective), refer to the article "Add, edit, or delete custom properties for a user profile (SharePoint Server 2010)" at *technet.microsoft.com/en-us/library/cc262327.aspx*.

You can manage privacy settings for your user profile by using the menu that appears to the right of some of the properties you can edit. The menu provides the following options:

- Everyone
- Only Me
- My Manager
- My Team
- My Colleagues

By using privacy settings on My Site, you can enable SharePoint to display information to only specific categories of people. You can use privacy settings on some of the details of the profile page, such as skills, interests, birthdays, mobile phone numbers, and fax. You can also use privacy settings on membership lists, links, and your colleagues list.

For example, for a property called Birthday, you might want only your team to see the date your birthday falls on, so you can alter the drop-down list to show My Team when editing the Birthday property on the profile page. Table 3-1 summarizes the options for privacy settings.

Table 3-1 **Explanation of Privacy Settings**

Category	Allows these people to view the content
Everyone	Everyone with permissions to view your My Site.
My Colleagues	Anyone listed on your My Colleagues page. By default, this category includes your manager, your peers, and your direct reports.
My Team	Your manager, your peers, and your direct reports. This includes colleagues who have been added to your team.
My Manager	Your direct manager.
Only Me	Yourself.

➤ **To configure your user profile**

1. Access My Site.

2. On the top-level menu, click the **My Profile** link to display your profile page.

3. Below the photo area, click the **Edit My Profile** link.

   Properties of the user profile are now displayed in Edit mode. Some of these properties are disabled because they might be linked to an external source or protected from modification.

4. Modify the properties of the profile as required.

5. Click **Save and Close** to update the changes and return to the **My Profile** page.

Practice Tasks

Practice the skills you learned in this section by performing the following tasks on your site:

- Access your My Site, and change the theme to Municipal.

- Edit the Mobile Phone property of your profile, and set the privacy level for the Mobile Phone property to Only Me.

- Add an RSS Viewer Web Part to the Overview section of your My Site. Obtain an RSS feed URL from a SharePoint list you have access to, and apply that URL to the RSS Viewer Web Part.

- Add two colleagues to your My Profile page. Assign one of those colleagues to the Peers group and the other to the General group.

- Add a new keyword to your profile.

3.2   Collaborate Through My Site

In this section, you learn how to build content and share content on My Site. You will learn how to extend My Site by using My Site management and customization features on the My Profile page of My Site. The following areas are covered:

- Updating the profile status
- Sharing pictures and documents in My Site
- Managing personal documents
- Browsing the organization hierarchy
- Adding Web Parts to My Site

This section also covers other basic operations of the My Profile page:

- Setting a status message on your profile that is displayed to others who visit your profile
- Editing the My Profile page and modifying through Web Parts what content you display to visitors of your profile page

Updating the Profile Status

To update your profile status, you need to enter a status message. The status message is shown in a caption displayed at the top right of the profile picture frame, as shown in the following screenshot.

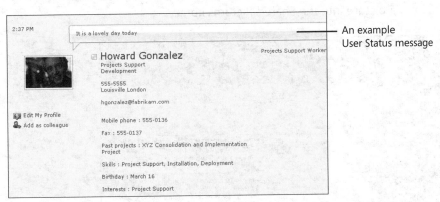

Tip If you use Microsoft Office Live Communicator in your organization and SharePoint is integrated with Active Directory, SharePoint can display a presence status icon to the left of the user account name displayed in the My Profiles page. This icon shows a color, which is determined by your presence status. For example, if your presence status is Available, the icon is green; if your presence status is Busy, the icon is red.

> **See Also** For more information about Microsoft Office Live Communicator (now known as Lync 2010), see the article at *office.microsoft.com/en-us/communicator-help/*.

➤ **To update your profile status message**

1. Access your SharePoint site.

2. Click the drop-down arrow to the right of your name at the top right of the page.

3. Click the **My Profile** link.

4. On the **My Profile** page, type the status message you want to display.

Sharing Pictures and Documents in My Site

The My Site page includes access to a special site called My Content. This site is where you can store and manage personal content and make that content accessible to visitors of the profile page.

Clicking My Content the first time creates and sets up the personal site by populating the site with default libraries and lists. By default, this site contains document libraries for private and shared documents, a pictures list library, and a blog subsite. The Personal Documents library is visible only to you and administrators. The content you place in Shared Documents is displayed on your public home page in the Content section.

To share documents with visitors of your public home page, upload a document into the Shared Documents library. To share pictures with visitors of your public home page, upload a picture into the Shared Pictures library.

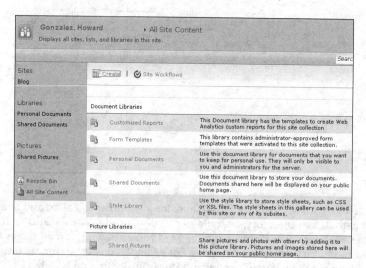

> **Important** The following procedure assumes you have a personal My Site and are familiar with accessing document libraries and lists and uploading content to them.

➤ To share documents and pictures

1. Access My Site.
2. Click **My Content**.
3. Access the **Shared Documents** library.

   If you are sharing pictures, use the Shared Pictures library instead.
4. Upload a document or a picture.
5. Click **My Profile** to display your public home page.
6. Click the **Content** tab displayed in the center of the page.

   When you complete these steps, you see the document or picture you uploaded, with information that shows the type of document it is, the name of the document, when the document was last modified, and where the document is located. Clicking the Properties button to the far right displays additional information about the document.

Managing Personal Documents

You can manage personal documents within your personal SharePoint My Site, which is accessible from the My Content link. To manage documents on the site, you need to understand which repositories the site contains, how to integrate the site with Microsoft Office, how to add documents, how to save documents to My Site from Microsoft Office, and how to upload content and organize the document libraries by adding folders. This section describes the steps necessary to carry out these tasks. First, let's look in more detail at the basics of the My Content area:

- **My Content has Personal and Shared Document libraries** By default, your My Content area contains libraries for personal documents, shared documents, and shared pictures. By default, personal documents are visible only to you, and shared documents and pictures are visible to other individuals you choose.

- **Microsoft Office can connect to your My Site** When you first access your My Content area, you might be asked to let Microsoft Office remember your site. If you are using your own computer, you can safely allow this. Doing so links your Microsoft Office applications directly to your My Site for easy integration.

- **There are various methods for adding documents to your My Site** You can add items to your My Site by uploading them via your browser or by saving them directly from a Microsoft Office application such as Microsoft Word. You can also map a network drive to SharePoint to drag and drop files and folders. Mac OS X users can access SharePoint files via the Microsoft Document Connection application in Office 2011.

> **Important** To save files directly from Microsoft Office, you must first set a default My Site.

You can set Personal Documents as a location if you want to reuse a specific document library in a SharePoint site without having to enter its URL each time. In doing so, you save the location so that the next time you want to use it you can select that location in the Save To SharePoint panel instead of having to find or paste the URL using the Save As dialog box.

> **Note** Save To SharePoint is available from all Microsoft Office 2010 applications. For a list of instructions for each application, visit this link: *office.microsoft.com/en-us/word-help/save-a-file-to-a-sharepoint-library-HA010370482.aspx.*

➤ **To upload a document via your browser to a document library in My Content**

1. Access your My Site.
2. On the top-level menu, click **My Content** to display your **My Content** area.
3. Click **Personal Documents** or **Shared Documents**.
4. Click **Add document**.
5. Browse to locate the document for uploading.
6. Click the file name to select it.
7. Click **OK**.

➤ **To set Personal Documents as a Microsoft Word 2010 location**

1. Copy the URL of the document library (in this case, the URL of Personal Documents in the My Site My Content Personal Documents library).
2. Open Microsoft Word 2010.
3. Click **File** on the ribbon.
4. Click **Save and Send**.

5. Click **Save to SharePoint**.

6. Double-click **Browse for a location** in the **Save to SharePoint** panel to display the **Save As** dialog box.

7. Paste the URL of the document library into the **File name** prompt.

8. Click **Save**.

➤ **To save a document to My Site from Microsoft Word 2010**

> **Note** This procedure assumes you have visited the location called Personal Documents when last saving a document in Microsoft Word 2010. If that is not the case, follow the preceding procedure.

1. Open Microsoft Word 2010.

2. Open the document you want to save, or create a new document.

3. In Microsoft Word, click **File, Save and Send**.

4. In the **Save & Send** section, double-click **Save to SharePoint**.

5. Under **Locations**, select **Personal Documents** and then click **Save As**.

6. In the **Save As** dialog box, type a file name and then click **Save**.

➤ **Add a folder to the Personal or Shared Document Library**

1. From the **Personal** or **Shared Documents** library, under **Library Tools**, select **Documents**.

2. On the ribbon, click **New Folder**.

3. Enter a folder name, and then click **Save**.

➤ **Delete a document from the Personal or Shared Document library**

1. From your personal or shared document library, click the file to delete it.

2. On the ribbon, click **Delete Document**.

3. When prompted to confirm, click **OK**.

> **See Also** For detailed steps for deleting and restoring documents, see "Deleting Items" in Chapter 1, "Creating and Formatting Content."

Browsing the Organization Hierarchy

A number of fields make up a user profile. One of these fields is used to provide information about where the user is situated in an organization's tree.

The Organization Browser Web Part uses the Manager field from SharePoint's user profiles to build an organizational hierarchy. The Organization Browser is interactive in that you can navigate up and down the hierarchy as well as left to right to see the colleagues who share your manager. The Web Part is displayed by default on each user's My Profile site under the Organization tab and is also included as a tree view on the My Profile page.

> **See Also** This procedure directs you to add a Web Part if the Web Part is not already displayed. If you do not know how to add Web Parts, see "Adding Web Parts to My Site" (the next section) or "Manage Web Parts on a Page" in Chapter 2 in this section of the book.

➤ **To access the Organization Browser and modify the Web Part to display a tree or graphical view**

1. Access your My Site.

2. On the top-level menu, click **My Profile** to display the **My Profile** area.

3. Click the **Overview** tab.

4. Edit the page, add the Organization Browser Web Part.

5. Edit the Organization Browser Web Part to display the Web Part configuration options on the right of the screen.

6. Scroll to the **Default Options Values** section at the bottom of the Web Part configuration options. Expand this section.

7. You will see one option here, **Only Show HTML View**. Select the check box if you want to display a tree view, or clear the check box if you want a graphical display.

8. Click OK to save the changes to the Web Part.

Adding Web Parts to My Site

The My Site home page can also display Web Parts. Displaying Web Parts on the My Site home page is extremely useful. For example, you can use a Web Part to display content you want everyone to see on the home page, or you can use a functional Web Part such as the RSS Feeds Viewer or the Organization Browser. You can also display content that is stored in My Site. For example, an announcements list might be stored in My Site, and you could display the content of that list in a Web Part on the My Site home page.

> **Note** You need administrator (Site Collection Administrator role) rights to My Site to modify the shared view of the private view of the My Site home page. These modifications affect the private view for the personal pages of all users. If you modify the personal view of the home page, the changes are made only to the private view of your personal site. If you don't have administrator rights, you cannot modify the shared view of the My Site home page.

> **See Also** For more information about adding Web Parts, see "Manage Web Parts on a Page" in Chapter 2 in this section of the book.

➤ **To add a My Links Web Part to the My Site home page**

1. Access My Site.
2. On the **Site Actions** menu, click **Edit Page**.
3. Click **Add a Web Part** on the **Top Web Part Zone**.
4. Click **Insert** on the **Page Tools** tab on the ribbon to display the **Insert** section.
5. Click the **Web Part** button in the **Insert** section to display available Web Parts.
6. In the **Categories** section, click **Recommended Items**.
7. Click the **My Links** Web Part.
8. In the **Add Web Part to** drop-down menu, select **Middle Left Zone**.
9. Click the **Add** button at the right of the screen.

Practice Tasks

Practice the skills you learned in this section by performing the following tasks on your site:

- Alter your profile status message to read "Learning SharePoint."
- Share a document and a picture by uploading them into your My Site in the applicable document and picture library.
- Open Microsoft Office, and save a document to your Personal Documents library.
- Configure the Organization Browser on your My Profile page to show a tree view.
- Add another Organization Browser Web Part on your My Profile page, and configure it to show a graphical view.
- Add the Colleagues Web Part to the home page of My Site.

3.3   Tag and Note Content

SharePoint provides social feedback features such as the ability for users to add tags and notes to content as part of the managed metadata service. This increases the classification of content and the overall ability to find specific content. My Site includes features such as the Activity Feed and the Tag Cloud to help bring to the surface some of the information captured by tags and notes. Documents, list items, SharePoint pages, and external pages can be tagged.

Adding Notes on the Note Board for a List or Library

The Note Board helps users express thoughts in their immediate context rather than having to move to e-mail, instant messaging, or the phone. For example, users can make comments about a web page while they are viewing the page. Other users can then see the comment and a link to the web page, which they can visit if they are interested in the subject. This helps My Site websites and My Profile pages become centralized places to manage public conversations. Notes can be used on a page, a document, or an external site. When notes are created, they appear in the Note Board related to the content and under the user profile for easy retrieval. Other people can also view the notes posted.

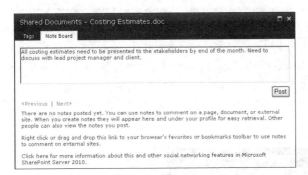

When posted, notes appear under the Note Board text box and in the Tags And Notes section of your My Profile page. You can, at any point, go back to any note and edit or update the note. You can also review notes made by colleagues by clicking on the View Related Activities link displayed in the Tags And Notes section. Other people can see the notes you post.

> **Tip** You can use the Notes facility at any time by copying the link that is displayed at the foot of the Note Board text box and adding that link to your Internet browser favorites list.

➤ **To add notes for a list or a library**

1. Access the document library or list where you want to add notes.

2. Click a list item or document that you want to add notes to.

3. On the ribbon, in the **Tag and Notes** section, click the **Tags & Notes** button to display the **Tags and Notes** dialog box.

4. The dialog box displays two tabs at the top under the title of the item or document that you select in step 2. Click on the **Note Board** tab to display the **Note Board** section.

5. In the **Note Board** text box, type the notes you want to make about the document and then click **Post**.

Adding Tags for a List or Library

A *tag* in SharePoint is a term that you want to assign to content. For example, a document titled "Project Schedule for Fabrikam XYZ Project" could have three tags: *project*, *XYZ*, and *schedule*. It could also include terms related to who is running the project, the departments involved, and other tags. Tagging allows people to locate documents more easily and enhances searches when you enter common terms. All terms are centrally stored so that they can be reused. When you save terms, you also see a list of suggested tags users can apply to content. If you click any of those suggested tags, a page is displayed showing links to all the content that has been tagged using that term. Tags you set are also displayed in the Tag Cloud and listed. Both the Tag Cloud and the list are located in the Tags And Notes section of the My Profile page. For more information on tag clouds, see the section "Using and Reviewing Tags and Tag Clouds" later in this chapter.

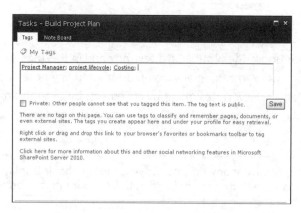

➤ **To add tags to a list or library**

1. Access the document library or list where you want to add tags.

2. Select a list item or document that you want to tag.

3. On the ribbon, in the **Tag and Notes** section, click the **Tags & Notes** button to display the **Tags and Notes** dialog box.

4. Click on the **Tags** tab, and then use the **Tags** text box to add the terms you want to assign to the selected list item or document. Separate multiple terms by using a semicolon (;).

5. Click **Save**.

Rating an Item

A rating in SharePoint Server 2010 is an assessment or classification of content on a scale that indicates how well the content meets specific criteria. Ratings show an average score that can range from 1 to 100, and a pop-up window displays additional information about the score. Users can rate items in a SharePoint list or document library and for individual web pages. Users do not need Write permission on an item to rate it. Users rate individual list items by using a graphical star system. When ratings are enabled, users can hover over the rating stars and then select the rating. The ratings field uses a five-star system to display the average score from all users who have rated that individual item.

Type	Name	Modified	Modified By	Rating (0-5)	Number of Ratings
📄	Costing Estimates	5/24/2011 5:02 PM	Mahood. Justin	★★★★☆	1
📄	Fabrikam Business Case	5/3/2011 1:38 PM	Mahood. Justin	★★★★☆	1
📄	Fabrikam Case Analysis	5/3/2011 1:39 PM	Mahood. Justin	★☆☆☆☆	1
📄	Fabrikam Projects 101	5/3/2011 1:38 PM	Mahood. Justin	★★☆☆☆	1

Hover the mouse over the stars to set a rating.

> **Important** Rating needs to be enabled as a feature before it can be used, and it is not enabled by default. You can enable the feature from the List or Library Settings page by selecting the Rating Settings option. On the Rating Settings page is the option Allow Items In This List To Be Rated. Click Yes to turn it on. After Rating is enabled, you will see two new columns attached to your list: Rating 0-5 and Number Of Ratings.

➤ **To rate an item**

1. Access the document library or list that contains the item you want to rate.

2. Select a list item or document that you want to rate.

3. Hover your mouse cursor over the stars to select the rating.

Using and Reviewing Tags and Tag Clouds

SharePoint 2010 includes a Tag Cloud Web Part that provides a visual representation of the metadata associated with the content inside a repository. Additionally, tag profile pages contain lists of items such as sites, documents, or people that are tagged with a particular term, as well as a list of community members and discussions, which facilitates information retrieval.

A SharePoint 2010 tag cloud is a Web Part that appears by default on My Site. Administrators and users can filter the tag cloud to display tags that are used by the owner of the My Site, specific groups, or everyone who can view the My Site.

The tags displayed can also be filtered based on date and language. Frequently used tags are displayed in large, bold text, whereas tags that are less often used appear in smaller text. Each tag can display an associated number that indicates how many times the tag has been applied.

> Costing database administration Estimations
>
> field support I like it Need to read this urgently
>
> project lifecycle project
>
> management: installation Project
> Manager Project Notes quality control SharePoint
> strategic planning systems development This is cool
> vendor management

You might want to delete tags (or notes) from content when they are no longer required. You might also want to set tags as private so that other people cannot see that you tagged an item. And you might also need to see what content has been tagged and what content has had notes assigned to it and view any activity related to the tagged or noted content. For all of these operations, you use the Tags And Notes section in the My Profile page.

➤ **To view the tag cloud and add tags to the cloud**

> **Important** This procedure assumes that items are in the tag cloud. If you do not have any items, you should work through the section "Adding Tags for a List or Library" earlier in this chapter before continuing.

1. Access My Site.

2. On the top-level menu, click the **My Profile** link to display your profile page.

3. Click the **Tags and Notes** tab to display the tag cloud (tags and notes you have defined). The tag cloud is displayed to the left of the screen by default.

4. Note the message displayed directly beneath the tag cloud, titled **Add SharePoint Tags and Notes Tool**. The last paragraph in that message says "Right-click or drag this link into your browser's favorites or bookmarks toolbar to tag external sites." This link displays the **Tags and Notes** dialog box, as described in the "Adding Notes on the Note Board for a List or Library" section earlier in this chapter. Click that link to display the **Tags and Notes** dialog box.

5. In the **Tag** text box, type the terms you want to add and then click **Save**.

6. Click the Back button on your browser to return to your profile page and the **Tags and Notes** section.

➤ To review tags in the tag cloud

1. Access My Site.

2. On the top-level bar, click the **My Profile** link to display your **Profile** page.

3. Click the **Tags and Notes** tab to display the tag cloud (tags and notes you have defined). The tag cloud is displayed to the left of the screen by default.

4. Click one of the tags in the tag cloud. At the right of the screen, you see all the notes posted and all the tags associated with this content.

➤ To manage tags

1. To delete a tag (or note), click the **Delete** link that is displayed at the bottom of each note or tag.

2. To make a tag private, select the **Make Private** check box, which is displayed at the bottom of each tag.

3. To view any related activities on content that has been tagged or has a note associated with it, click **View Related Activities**. This displays the **Tag and Notes** dialog box, which lists all related tags or notes that are public.

Practice Tasks

Practice the skills you learned in this section by performing the following tasks on your site:

- Upload a document to a document library, and ensure that Rating Settings is applied to the document library. Set the rating of the uploaded document to two stars.
- Add a tag and note to the uploaded document.
- Visit your My Profile page, and add a tag to your tag cloud.
- Delete a note assigned to a document.

Objective Review

Before finishing this chapter, be sure you've mastered the following skills:

3.1 Configure My Site

3.2 Collaborate through My Site

3.3 Tag and note content

4 Configuring and Consuming Site Search Results

The skills tested in this section of the Microsoft Office Specialist exam for Microsoft SharePoint 2010 cover configuring and consuming site search results. Specifically, the following objectives are associated with this set of skills:

- **4.1** Administer search at the site level
- **4.2** Search SharePoint for content
- **4.3** View search results
- **4.4** Perform advanced searches
- **4.5** Search for people

Search is everywhere in SharePoint. Typically, a search box appears in the top right portion of a SharePoint site and is displayed above every page you browse to. (If you place a page in editing mode, you will not see the search option.) When you search, SharePoint returns information from pages, documents in your sites, and, depending on how your site has been configured, results from external sites and data sources such as shared folders and public folders.

A key feature of SharePoint 2010 search is the ability to refine results. For example, you can refine a set of search results by document type, site, author, or other criteria. Also, SharePoint can be connected to the Windows Explorer search capability so that you do not need to open a browser to search for content. Additionally, you can preview content in the search results, which lets you view the content in the browser instead of having to open a document in the relevant application. Here is an example of the search results you'll see in SharePoint.

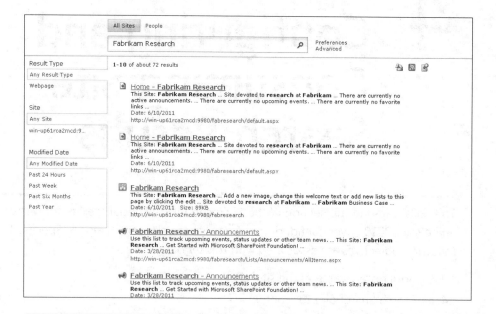

> **Important** To work through this chapter, you need to be a site collection administrator to enable a number of features that are available only to that role. To confirm that you have those permissions, access the site settings of your SharePoint site. If you see the section Site Collection Administration, you have that role enabled for your account and can proceed. If you do not have that level of permission, ask your site administrator to grant you that level of permission.
>
> Also, keep these points in mind when working through this chapter:
>
> - In references to document libraries and lists where a feature or option being discussed is present in both, we use the term *repository* to refer to both libraries and lists.
>
> - You will be directed to access a repository to carry out tasks listed in the procedural steps. For example, "Access a repository's settings" means that you need to open a document library or list and then access the library or list settings for that repository. To review how to access a document library or list, please refer to Chapter 1, "Creating and Formatting Content," for more information.
>
> - Search ability should be configured and operational on your site collection.

4.1 Administer Search at the Site Level

Part of successfully managing content stored on a SharePoint site is having the ability to locate that content and provide users with mechanisms that allow them to search the content. There is no point in creating areas for documents to be stored if there is no easy way for users to find that content.

Users are able to locate content directly on the site and then, at the Enterprise level, use a SharePoint Search Center site to carry out searches into other content sources.

> **See Also** We describe content sources, the Search Center, and how to perform content source searching in the section "Search SharePoint for Content" later in this chapter.

All content in SharePoint has metadata (information that describes information) associated with it. For example, a document stored in SharePoint has metadata stored in columns that describe its title, the date it was created, the date it was modified, who modified it, and other pieces of information associated with that content. When users search for content, most or all of those columns can be used to allow a user to locate the information easily.

Searching for data in SharePoint is a fundamental aspect of the platform. It is vitally important that you understand the options available at the site level for searching, how to administer search, and how to configure search.

This section teaches you how to define the columns to be searched by indexing them, how to search a list in a site, and how to view and understand search results.

> **Important** To work through this section, you need to configure the Search Settings site collection feature. Carry out the following steps to ensure that the search settings for the site collection have been set to display the scopes available in your site collection:
>
> 1. Navigate to the top-level site of your SharePoint site.
> 2. Click **Site Actions**, **Site Settings**.
> 3. In the **Site Collection Administration** section, click **Search Settings**.
> 4. In the **Site Collection Search Dropdown Mode** section, select **Show scopes dropdown** from the **Specify the dropdown mode for Search Boxes** drop-down list.
> 5. At the foot of the page, click **OK**.
>
> After you have completed these steps, return to the home page. Examine the search feature at the top of the page. Notice that SharePoint now provides a drop-down list that allows you to select which aspect of the site you want to search. This ability becomes important when you want to search for content in a particular repository.
>
>

Setting Up Columns to Be Searched

When a user performs a query, whether by using code or for a Web Part view, each item in the repository is examined individually for a match. As the amount of information in a SharePoint site grows, this operation can take longer to complete and can cause performance issues to surface. (For example, it might take longer for information to be displayed from the relevant list.)

For users to find information more quickly by using key columns, you can set columns so that they are indexed. This effectively means that SharePoint uses those columns instead of the default columns when searching in a repository. SharePoint lets you index the information within individual lists or libraries.

Before starting to configure the relevant columns, you need to be sure that the repository has search capability switched on. If this setting is enabled, the repository is included when users perform a search and items located in that repository are visible in search results. Then you need to access the metadata options for the repository to configure the columns you need to include in the search features.

Search	
Specify whether this document library should be visible in search results. Users who do not have permission to see these items will not see them in search results, no matter what this setting is.	Allow items from this document library to appear in search results? ◉ Yes ○ No

> **Important** In cases in which confidential information is stored in a repository, you might want to turn off the setting allowing items in that repository to be visible in search results. This prevents the possibility of content from the relevant repository being displayed to a user carrying out a search.

The following procedures teach you how to enable search results for a repository and how to define a number of columns as indexed.

➤ **To enable search results for a repository**

1. Navigate to the home page of your SharePoint site.
2. Access the repository from **Quick Launch** or from the **All Site Content** page.
3. Click the **Library** or **List** tab on the ribbon.
4. Click the **Library** or **List Settings** button in the **Settings** section.
5. Click the **Advanced Settings** link in the **General Settings** section.
6. On the **Advanced Settings** page, select **Yes** for the **Allow items from this document library to appear in search results?** option.

➤ To set up indexed columns

1. Navigate to the home page of your SharePoint site.

2. Access the repository from **Quick Launch** or from the **All Site Content** page.

3. Click the **Library** or **List** tab on the ribbon.

4. Click the **Library** or **List Settings** button in the **Settings** section.

5. Scroll to the **Columns** section.

6. At the foot of the **Columns** section, click the **Indexed Columns** link to display the **Indexed Columns** page.

7. When you visit this link for the first time, the page displays the message "You have created 0 of maximum 20 indices on this list," and shows the **Create a new index** link below the message.

8. Click **Create a new index** to display the **Indexed Columns Edit** page.

9. In the **Primary Column** section, select **Title** from the **Primary column for this index** drop-down list. When you do this, SharePoint disables the **Secondary column for this index** list.

10. Click the **Create** button.

Searching in a List

You can use the search tool at the top right of the SharePoint window to select what content source (for example, the site or repository) you want to search. (You can search a repository directly by displaying the repository and then using the search tool.)

Another method is to create a search scope targeted at the relevant repository so that users can search the repository from any part of the SharePoint site where the search tool is displayed.

This section describes how to search a list. The instructions also apply to a document library. The procedures that follow assume that you (or a site collection administrator) have configured search settings so that scopes are displayed. (If you have not already confirmed this, see the introductory section of this chapter for more information.)

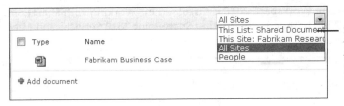

➤ **To perform a search in a list**

1. Access the repository you want to search.

2. In the **Search** drop-down list, select **This List: <Name of List>**, where *Name of List* is the title of the list you accessed in step 1.

3. Enter the information you want to search for in the search prompt to the right of the **Search** drop-down list.

4. Click the **Search** button (the one that looks like a magnifying glass) to carry out the search for the information entered in the previous step.

Configuring Site Search Visibility

By default, all content in SharePoint is indexed and visible through searches carried out by users who have access to the content. However, in some situations you might want to prevent items from appearing in search results. Content should be excluded from being indexed when it poses an information disclosure risk. For example, an administrator managing 100 SharePoint sites might be contacted by the Human Resources department and asked to ensure that all data on the Human Resources site is not displayed in any search results because the content on this subsite is confidential.

> **See Also** In addition, the administrator would have to protect access to the data by ensuring that only users who should have access to the data are set up to access it. For more information on how to do this, see "Manage Users and Groups" in Chapter 2, "Managing SharePoint Sites."

At the site level, you use the Search And Offline Availability page (accessed through the Site Settings page) to prevent the index server from crawling a particular site. Additionally, if the site's content is made visible in search results but some content is secured by using permissions that are more restrictive than the page itself, you can set an option to prevent the restricted Web Parts from being indexed. The Search And Offline Availability page also includes a section named Offline Client Availability, which contains an option you can set to allow content to be taken offline for offsite work using SharePoint Workspace 2010.

> **See Also** SharePoint Workspace 2010 is discussed in "Working with SharePoint Workspace 2010" in Chapter 5, "Integrating SharePoint 2010 Services and Microsoft Office 2010 Applications."

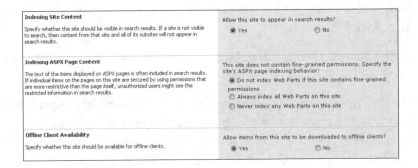

> **To set search visibility for the site**

1. Navigate to the top-level site of your SharePoint site.

2. Click **Site Settings** on the **Site Actions** menu.

3. Click **Search and Offline Client Availability** in the **Site Administration** section.

4. In the **Indexing Site Content** section, select **Yes** for the option **Allow this site to appear in search results?**.

5. Click **OK**.

> **To set search visibility for Web Parts**

1. Navigate to the top-level site of your SharePoint site.

2. Click **Site Settings** on the **Site Actions** menu.

3. Click **Search and Offline Client Availability** in the **Site Administration** section.

4. In the **Indexing ASPX Page Content** section, select **Always index all Web Parts on this site**.

5. Click **OK**.

> **To set offline client availability**

1. Navigate to the top-level site of your SharePoint site.

2. Click **Site Settings** on the **Site Actions** menu.

3. Click **Search and Offline Client Availability** in the **Site Administration** section.

4. In the **Offline Client Availability** section, select **Yes** for the option **Allow items from this site to be downloaded to offline clients?**.

5. Click **OK**.

Practice Tasks

Practice the skills you learned in this section by performing the following tasks on your site:

- Create a new Task list called ProjectJobs. Add a column of the single line text type to this list. Name the column **Job Type**. Index this column. Add two items to the list, and be sure that you enter information in the Job Type column.

- Search for information in the Job Type column using only the ProjectJobs list as the search scope.

- Prevent any indexing from occurring on the site.

- Prevent any items on the site from being downloaded to offline clients.

4.2   Search SharePoint for Content

The previous section covered searching for content within a particular repository and using SharePoint internal features to locate the content. This section covers using external features provided by the Microsoft Windows operating system and Microsoft Office products. The tasks in this section are based on using Windows 7 search features and Microsoft Word 2010.

Searching SharePoint Content with Windows

In Windows 7, you can quickly and easily search a SharePoint site from Windows Explorer. This capability offers a new and convenient way to search for content on a SharePoint site.

Note Windows 7 search is a fast and easy method for searching from the Windows desktop. It is most useful when users know what they are looking for. An example of using this type of search is when you search by using the title of a document. SharePoint search, on the other hand, offers powerful features, such as Advanced Search, Refinement Panel, and Query suggestions. SharePoint search is useful when you are doing research or when users do not know what they are looking for (for example, when a user is researching project analysis data).

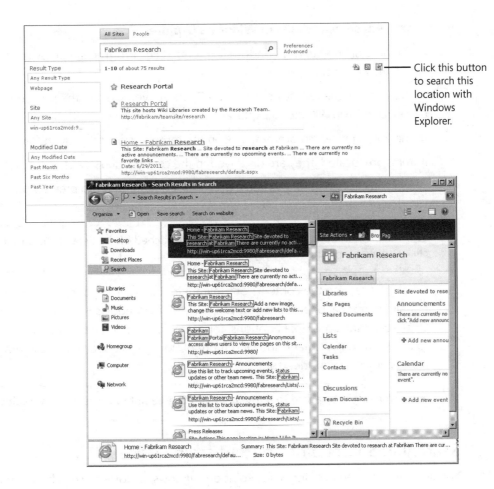

➤ **To set up searching with Windows Explorer**

1. Access your SharePoint site.

2. Carry out a search to display the search results page.

3. On the search results page, click the button that looks like a Windows Explorer icon to search the site location again in the future.

   A dialog box is displayed that adds the search center to your Windows Explorer Favorites list. You need to confirm that you want to add the Search Connector to Windows; click the **Add** button when this message is displayed.

   Windows Explorer is displayed. At this point, you can type the term you want to search for in the Windows Explorer search prompt.

After you have completed the preceding procedure, you can use Windows Explorer whenever required to search the relevant SharePoint site.

➤ **To work with search results in Windows Explorer**

1. From the **Start** menu, run Windows Explorer. (Click **Programs**, **Accessories**, **Windows Explorer**.)

2. In the pane on the left, select the SharePoint site you used in the procedure "To set up searching with Windows Explorer."

3. In the top-right search prompt, type in the term you want to search for.

   If items are located, they are displayed in the center results pane.

   When you click an item, you see a preview of that item in the preview pane in Windows Explorer.

   > **Tip** The preview pane in Windows Explorer is switched off by default. To turn it on, click Organize, and then click Layout, Preview Pane.

   When you can see the contents of the item in the preview pane, you can carry out all the normal operations you can perform in Windows Explorer (by using the Organize, Print, and E-Mail options, for example), and you can right-click the item to display a context menu showing more options. Additionally, you can drag the file to copy it to your desktop.

   > **Note** You might be asked to authenticate to SharePoint to access search results.

Searching SharePoint Content from Office 2010

You are not restricted to using SharePoint or Windows Explorer to search for content in SharePoint. The Microsoft Office research pane gives you the ability to search SharePoint directly from Office 2010 applications. Having this ability is very useful because you can search for material stored externally without having to leave the relevant application.

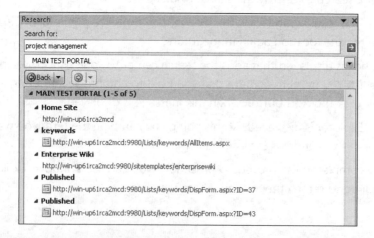

> **Important** To complete the following exercise, you must have access to the Internet, a fully functional copy of Microsoft Word 2010, and full access to the SharePoint site that you want to search.

➤ **To set up the Research pane in Microsoft Word 2010**

1. Open Microsoft Word 2010.

2. Click on the **Review** tab on the ribbon.

3. Click the **Research** button in the **Proofing** group to display the **Research** pane.

4. Click **Research options** at the bottom of the pane.

5. In the **Research Options** dialog box, click **Add Services**.

6. In the **Add Services** dialog box, in the **Address** box, type the URL to the SharePoint search service web service for the relevant SharePoint site collection. The URL should be similar to *http://[your_server]/_vti_bin/search.asmx*. For example, if the SharePoint Site collection is at *http://fabrikam*, the URL to the SharePoint search service web service is *http://fabrikam/_vti_vin/search.asmx*.

   After you complete step 6, Word adds the service to the Research services list under the section **Intranet Sites and Portals**.

7. Click **OK** to close the **Research Options** dialog box.

Practice Tasks

Practice the skills you learned in this section by performing the following tasks on your site:

- Set up Windows Explorer to consume searches from SharePoint 2010.

- Search for SharePoint content. From the results list, drag a file to your desktop.

- Set up research on your SharePoint site from Microsoft Excel and then use Microsoft Word to locate data on that SharePoint site.

4.3   View Search Results

When a SharePoint search operation has completed and listed the results, each result is displayed with an associated link. When you click this link, SharePoint displays the relevant item (if it's a list item) or loads the document into the associated application.

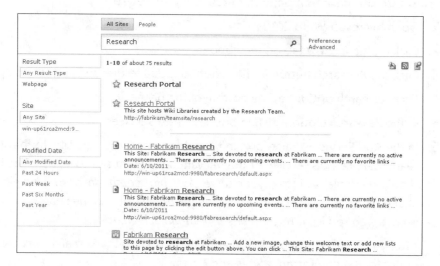

This section teaches you how to display search results and then work with those results to open an item or a document. You will also learn how to create quick search methods to find information by applying keywords and creating best bets.

Browsing Search Results

When you are unsure where to look for content about your organization, use the Search Center. This is the ideal way to carry out a broad search of SharePoint content in an organization. The Search Center provides a single prompt for entering the information that you want to search for and two tabs:

- **All Sites** Search for content across all SharePoint sites you have access to.

- **People** Search for people in the organization

When you type information in the search prompt, SharePoint displays a list of search suggestions or similar words that have yielded results for other users. You can turn search suggestions on or off by using the Preferences link displayed at the top right of the search prompt. Clicking this link displays the Preferences dialog box, where you can clear the check box for the option Show Search Suggestions In The Search Box.

To start a search after entering information, click the Search button (the one that looks like a magnifying glass). When results are displayed, they show the following:

- An icon, which tells you the type of document
- The title of the content, which is a link to the source
- A description called a *snippet*
- The name of the author, the date the item was last modified, any tags, and the item's size
- The URL where the item resides

When you have several pages of results, the Refinement Panel is displayed to the left of the page. (The Refinement Panel is discussed in more detail later in this section.) At the foot of the page are the page links you use to navigate between the result pages.

In SharePoint 2010, you can also use Boolean searches to construct logical and relational operators. Logical operators are AND, OR, and NOT (in uppercase). You need to use uppercase characters in the query syntax; otherwise, the operators are considered additional search words. You can, for instance, search for "project AND analysis" or "project NOT analysis". Table 4-1 describes the relational operators.

Table 4-1 Relational Operators

Operator	Description
=	Equal to
<	Less than
>	Greater than
<=	Less than or equal to
>=	Greater than or equal to
<>	Not equal to

You can also search using SharePoint properties:

- Filename
- File Type
- Date and time
- Server Name
- * wildcards

Note the use of NOT and AND in the search.

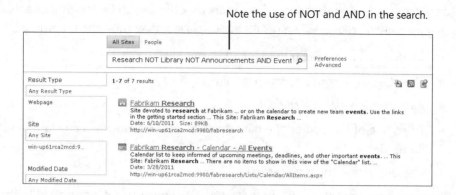

► To search using Boolean logical operators

1. In the **Search** prompt on your SharePoint site, enter, for example, **project management AND schedules NOT costing**.

   This example locates content that includes *project management* and *schedules*, excluding any content that includes the term *costing*.

2. Click the **Search** button.

Using Best Bet Results

To enhance search results, you can define keyword terms. These keywords can be used in queries from the Search box or the Search Center site or in Advanced Search. When a query includes a keyword or one of its synonyms, the definition for that term and links to its featured locations or documents, called *best bets*, are displayed prominently on the search results page.

The keyword.   A best bet.   A search result that includes the word "Research."

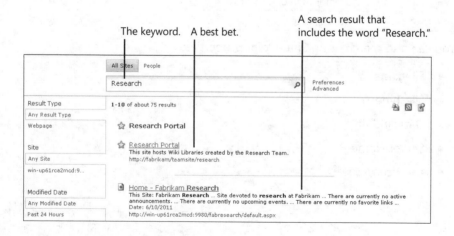

By defining terms that are often used in searches as keywords, a site collection administrator can provide a standard glossary of names, processes, and concepts that are part of the common knowledge shared by members of an organization. When keywords have synonyms and associated best bet links, they also become handy tools for guiding users toward recommended resources.

Best bets are created in the Search Center on the Add Keyword page. You must be a site collection administrator to create best bets. For example, assume that the SharePoint administrator for Fabrikam Inc. is contacted by the Human Resources department. The department wants employees to easily find travel expense documentation. From its research, the department discovers that people search using terms such as *expenses*, *travel*, *business expenses*, *travel expenses*, and *expense log*. The administrator can create a keyword with those search terms as synonyms and set the best bets to the location of the travel expense documentation, which might have a URL such as *http://fabrikam/hr/guidelines/travelexpense.docx*.

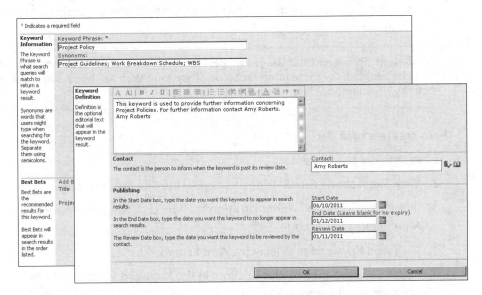

Keywords have start, end, and review dates, which are set in the Publishing section at the bottom of the page. The start date is when the keyword should start appearing in search results and defaults to the current date. The end date is when the keyword should no longer appear in search results. The review date is when the keyword should be reviewed by the contact. The Contact text box is where you enter the user account for the owner of the keyword. The owner is notified when the keyword is past its review date.

You do not need to set a contact or an end date or review date. These settings are optional and can be used when you want to provide further management features to the keywords.

> **Tip** When you add best bets, you can select an existing best bet to associate with the keyword. For example, if you have a best bet for Traveling Costs and a best bet for Traveling Expenses, you can create a keyword called Traveling Guidelines and assign as best bets the existing Traveling Costs and Traveling Expenses best bets.

When you need to modify a best bet, you use the Manage Keyword page, where you also can refine the keyword list and gather analytics about the usage of keywords and suggestions for best bets.

On the page, you'll see the following:

- Expired Keywords, which displays keywords whose end date has passed
- Keywords Requiring Review, which displays keywords whose review date has passed
- Best Bet Usage and Best Bet Suggestions, which provide reports showing how often the best bets are displayed on search results and suggestions for best bets you might add

> **Important** To use Best Bet Usage and Best Bet Suggestions, the Web Analytics feature must be enabled. For more information on SharePoint Web Analytics, see "Analyze Site Activity" in Chapter 2, "Managing SharePoint Sites."

➤ **To create a best bet**

1. Access the Search Center.
2. Click **Site Actions**, **Site Settings** to display the **Site Settings** page.
3. In the **Site Collection Administration** section, click **Search Keywords** to display the **Manage Keywords** page.
4. Click **Add Keyword** to display the **Add Keyword** page.
5. In the **Keyword Information** section, in the **Keyword Phrase** text box, type the keyword you want to define.
6. In the **Keyword Information** section, in the **Synonyms** text box, type the synonyms for the keyword.
7. In the **Best Bets** section, click **Add Best Bet** to display the **Add Best Bet** dialog box.
8. Select the **Add new best bet** option.

9. In the **URL** prompt, type the best bet location.

10. In the **Title** prompt, type a title.

11. In the **Description** prompt, type a description for the best bet.

12. Click **OK** in the **Add Best Bet** dialog box.

13. Click **OK** on the **Add Keyword** page.

➤ **To modify a best bet**

1. Access the Search Center.

2. Click **Site Actions**, **Site Settings** to display the **Site Settings** page.

3. In the **Site Collection Administration** section, click **Search Keywords** to display the **Manage Keywords** page.

4. In the **Find Keywords where** drop-down list, select **Keyword**.

5. In the **Contains** text box, type the keyword you want to work with.

6. Click the **Search** button to find the keyword.

7. Click the keyword to display the **Edit Keyword** page. The details of the keyword are displayed.

8. In the **Synonyms** text box, type the new synonym.

   In addition to modifying the synonyms for the keyword, you can modify its best bet, contact, and start and end dates.

9. At the foot of the page, click **OK**.

Using the Refinement Panel

The Refinement panel shows the categories (or metadata) for the first 50 items in the search results list. You can change the results displayed by clicking the links in the panel.

For example, click on the name of an author to display all items written by or containing the author's name. Or click the name of a site to display all the documents on that site that contain the keywords in the query. You can also use the Refinement panel to show documents of a specific type.

➤ **To refine a search result to show only Microsoft Word documents**

1. Access the Search Center.

2. Carry out a search to display search results.

3. In the **Result Type** section of the **Refinement** panel, click **Word** to show Microsoft Word documents.

Using Alerts and RSS Feeds

Search alerts provide users with the ability to receive e-mail and SMS text message notifications when specified search query results change or are updated. Search alerts are configured on the search query page when a query is completed and results are displayed. Search alerts can be configured and viewed only by the user who creates them.

Really Simple Syndication (RSS) is a widely used technology for transmitting information across the Internet and intranets. The search results page provides an RSS feature that provides users with a method of getting an automatic update related to a search result. For example, if the users of the Fabrikam SharePoint Project Management Office subsite want a page that shows the results of a search related to *project guidelines*, the team can create a page that includes the RSS Web Part and set the RSS Feed URL property from the RSS search feed URL.

> **See Also** For more information concerning RSS, see "Setting Up RSS Feeds" in Chapter 3, "Participating in User Communities."

> **Important** Search alert functionality is turned off by default and must be enabled by your SharePoint administrator.

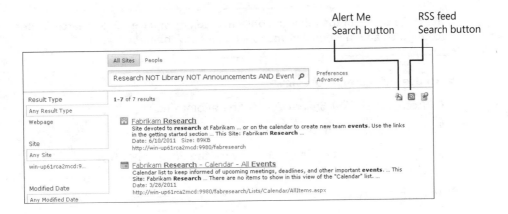

> **To set an alert for a search result**

1. Access the Search Center.
2. Carry out a search to display search results
3. Click the **Alert Me** button to display the **New Alert** page.
4. Enter the details of the alert: the title, who to send the alerts to, the delivery method, the change type, and when to send the alerts.
5. Click **OK**.

> **To set an RSS feed to a search result**

1. Access the Search Center.
2. Carry out a search to display search results
3. Click the RSS button to display the search results page for the content you searched for in step 2.
4. Click the **Subscribe to this feed** link. This adds the feed to the **Common Feed** link (available as Feeds from the Favorites option) in your web browser.

Viewing Document Previews

SharePoint FAST Search provides document preview capabilities when you search for information in SharePoint. Document previews allow users to view documents within their browser by using Office Web Apps. Users don't have to launch the associated

Office application or even have the application installed on their local computer. Using document previews is useful when users are browsing a SharePoint site in kiosks and Internet cafés on computers that might not be running Microsoft Office.

> **Note** To carry out the following objective, you must have a FAST Search Center configured and functional in your SharePoint environment.

➤ **To use a document preview**

1. Access your FAST Search Center SharePoint site.

2. Carry out a search for content.

3. Click on the content hyperlink to view the document preview.

Practice Tasks

Practice the skills you learned in this section by performing the following tasks on your site:

- Carry out a basic search. Locate content that includes the words *project management* (or a term that is suitable for the content on your site), and then refine that content so that only Excel documents are displayed.

- Create a search alert for a search result based on a search for the term you used in the first step.

- Create an RSS feed from a search result based on a search for the term you searched for.

- Carry out a search and then refine that search so that only Word documents created in the last 24 hours are displayed in the search results.

- Create a keyword called *SharePoint* with the synonym *Collaborate*. Create a best bet for that keyword with a URL to *http://sharepoint*, a title of *SharePoint*, and the description *Microsoft SharePoint Home*.

4.4 Perform Advanced Searches

To perform a highly targeted search across all sites in an organization, use the Advanced Search page in SharePoint. The Advanced Search Page is separated into four areas:

- The words you want to find or exclude
- The language you want to search by
- The type of results you are looking for
- The properties of the content you want to find

You can use one or all four areas for your query.

Setting Up and Running an Advanced Search

To understand the relevant areas of the Advanced Search page, imagine that you need to find content related to project management. The following list describes the search results for the words you want to find or exclude when you choose one of the following options:

- **All Of These Words** The search results will contain items for which the words *project* AND *management* exist.

- **The Exact Phrase** The search results will contain the phrase *project management*.

- **Any Of These Words** The search result will contain items for which the words *project* OR *management* exist.

- **None Of These Words** The search result will contain items for which neither word exists.

The Language section allows you to choose the language the document was created in. The default options are English, French, German, Japanese, Simplified Chinese, and Traditional Chinese.

In the Result Type area, you can select the type of document to include in your results. The default options selected are Documents, Word Documents, Excel Documents, and PowerPoint Presentations.

And finally, in the Property Restrictions section, you can carry out powerful queries by specifying a particular property—for example, author, description, name, size, URL, last modified date, created by, and last modified by. You can include and exclude individual properties by using query syntax. Default options include Contains, Does Not Contain, Equals, and Does Not Equal. You can add multiple properties when building a query.

By combining advanced search options, you can, for example, create a query to locate Word documents about project management in the English language, not authored by John Doe, and that do not include the word *schedule*.

> **Note** Keep in mind not to use too many exclusions (on words or properties) because doing so can exclude the documents you want and can cause the search to take longer to generate results.

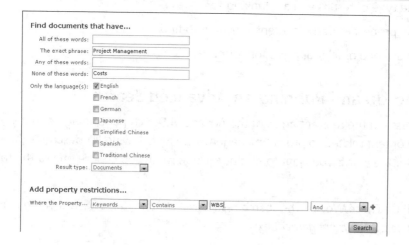

> ### To locate a document using advanced search

1. Access your Enterprise Search Center page.

2. Click the **Advanced** link located at the bottom right of the **Search** prompt.

3. In the **The exact phrase** text box, type the term you are searching for.

4. In the **None of these words** text box, type any words you want to exclude.

5. Select the **Only the language(s)** check box.

6. In the **Result type** drop-down list, select **Word Documents** or the result type option you want to use.

7. In the **Property Restrictions** section, select **Author** or another option from the **Pick Property** drop-down list.

8. In the **Property Restrictions** section, select **Does not contain** or another option from the **Query Syntax** drop-down list.

9. In the text box adjacent to the **Query Syntax** drop-down list, type the value you want to exclude.

10. At the bottom right of the page, click **Search**.

Practice Tasks

Practice the skills you learned in this section by performing the following tasks on your site:

- Find all Excel documents that were modified before the year 2011.
- Find all PowerPoint presentations authored by a particular author.
- Find all English Word documents that are related to the terms *projects* or *schedules* (or terms suitable for the content on your site).

4.5   Search for People

People are an organization's key asset. The more easily and quickly people can locate each other, the more they share ideas and expertise. SharePoint includes a people search feature that ensures that people-specific factors are balanced in search results. Profile information from My Sites is used to generate result summaries, and metadata-based refiners help quickly locate the right person.

> **See Also** My Sites is described in "Configure My Site" in Chapter 3.

To find people in an organization, you can use the Search Center's People search facility. This facility helps locate people on the basis of their name and any other properties in their user profile that have been indexed by SharePoint. For example, searches can be carried out on company name, department, and phone number.

The search system indexes names by using phonetic spelling and also includes common nicknames. This way, searches for *Geoff* return results for *Jeff*, while searches for *Bill* also show results for *William*.

When you carry out a people search and view the results, the following information is shown for each person:

- Name
- Job title
- Department
- Phone number
- Location
- E-mail address

Three links appear beneath each result:

- **Add as colleague** SharePoint knows who you work with only if you supply that information by using the Colleagues feature. This feature allows you to specify who you work with from the search results (by using the Add To Colleagues link) or from your personal site. SharePoint automatically recognizes some colleagues, such as your manager, people you manage, and other people who have the same manager.

> **See Also** For more information about setting up colleagues, see "Setting Up My Site" in Chapter 3.

- **Browse in Organizational Chart** Another item that is unique to people search results is the Browse In Organizational Chart link, which might appear for each result. Clicking this link directs you to a page that shows an organizational chart and the selected user's location in it.

- **By <Person's Name>** When you click this link, SharePoint displays a dialog box listing recent documents the person has stored in SharePoint that you have access to.

> **See Also** User profiles describe the kind of properties associated with people in SharePoint. See "Configuring Profiles" in Chapter 3 for more information.

> **Important** To carry out the tasks in this section, the SharePoint User Profiles Services application and People Search must be functional.

Searching for People

SharePoint Server has a user profile database that stores information about users. If this feature has been set up, you have the ability to search for people and view their details. Also, if someone has created a personal site, you can see the public view of that personal site.

You can perform a people search from most SharePoint Server sites by choosing People from the Scopes drop-down list (if this list appears next to the site's Search box). You can also navigate to the Search Center and choose the People tab.

Use this tab to search for people
in the Search Center.

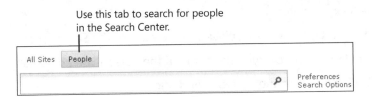

➤ To search for people from a SharePoint site

1. Access your Enterprise Search Center.

2. In the **Search** prompt, click the **People** tab.

3. Enter the name of the person you want to search for.

4. Click the **Search** button (which looks like a magnifying glass).

5. The search results page that appears shows you the people search results.

Using Advanced Search Features for People

When you search for people, the advanced search features behave slightly differently from how they apply to documents and list items. Unlike the results for documents and list items, results for people are ordered by social distance. This view shows you the people you work with first, the people they work with second, and then anyone else.

For example, to look for someone whose first name is Marina and whose job title is Procurement Manager, type **Marina** in the First Name text box and **Procurement Manager** in the Job Title text box. Click the Search button, and the search results page that appears shows you the people search results.

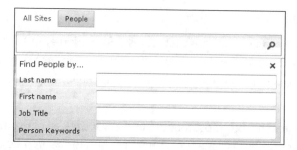

➤ **To use the advanced search feature to search for people**

1. Access the Search Center.

2. Click the **Search Options** link displayed to the right of the **Search** prompt.

3. In the **First Name** text box, type the name of the person you are looking for.

4. In the **Job Title** text box, type the person's title.

5. Click the **Search** button (which looks like a magnifying glass).

   The search results page that appears shows you the people search results.

Practice Tasks

Practice the skills you learned in this section by performing the following tasks on your site:

- Carry out a basic people search. From the search results page, add one of the resulting names as a colleague.

- Carry out a people search. From the search results page, find out what documents have been created by one of the people displayed there.

- Carry out a people search. From the search results page, display an organization chart for one of the people listed.

Objective Review

Before finishing this chapter, be sure you've mastered the following skills:

4.1   Administer search at the site level

4.2   Search SharePoint for content

4.3   View search results

4.4   Perform advanced searches

4.5   Search for people

5 Integrating SharePoint 2010 Services and Microsoft Office 2010 Applications

The skills tested in this section of the Microsoft Office Specialist exam for Microsoft SharePoint 2010 cover the integration of Microsoft SharePoint 2010 Services and Microsoft Office 2010 applications. Specifically, the following objectives are associated with this set of skills:

5.1 Configure SharePoint 2010 Services

5.2 Run Microsoft Office 2010 applications with SharePoint 2010 Services

5.3 Create dashboards

In this final chapter, we cover objectives related to configuring SharePoint Services, using Microsoft Office applications with those services, and creating and managing site dashboards.

To work through this chapter, you need to have site collection permissions and the ability to access the SharePoint Central Administration facility on the server. Some of the features you need to work with are available only in SharePoint 2010 Server, so you should be sure you have access to a fully functional version. This chapter assumes you are familiar with SharePoint site administration (using the Site Settings page) and that you know how to access the SharePoint Central Administration page on SharePoint 2010 Server or from your computer. You also need the following Microsoft Office 2010 applications:

- Microsoft Word 2010
- Microsoft Access 2010
- Microsoft Excel 2010
- Microsoft Outlook 2010
- Microsoft Visio 2010
- Microsoft InfoPath 2010
- Microsoft SharePoint Workspace 2010

5.1   Configure SharePoint 2010 Services

This section explains the fundamentals of SharePoint 2010 Services. You will learn how to configure and use the SharePoint Services features related to Microsoft Access 2010, Microsoft Excel 2010, and Microsoft Visio 2010. You will also learn the fundamentals of configuring and using Microsoft InfoPath 2010 Form Services.

Understanding SharePoint Services

SharePoint Services is the backbone of the SharePoint environment, providing the key functionality required for the platform. This section provides a brief introduction to three of these services: Visio Services, Access Services, and Excel Services.

> **See Also** To learn more about the array of SharePoint Services, see *www.sharepointgeoff.com/sharepoint/sps2010sertvapps.aspx.*

Visio Services

Visio Services enables you to view and refresh Visio diagrams in a web browser. These services provide collaborative content management, and they give you the ability to connect Visio diagrams to external data sources and then view information from those sources in formats compatible with SharePoint. When a web drawing is connected to an external data source, Visio can update the appearance of the drawing on the basis of changes to the underlying data.

Access Services

Access Services lets you host Access databases within SharePoint. For example, you might implement Access Services in cases where users have many Access databases located on file shares and their individual systems and you want to centralize the databases to manage them more efficiently.

The ability to view, edit, and interact with databases in a browser via Access Services enables users to build their own applications using programming languages such as Microsoft Visual Basic for Applications (VBA) without directly requiring programmers to build an Access application in SharePoint.

> **Important** Because Access Services lets users develop their own applications and centralize where databases are stored, you need to be aware of issues related to managing the data and related to the growth rate of the data. For example, you need to consider what level of governance you need to apply to control and locate the data.

Excel Services

Excel Services allows you to publish Excel client workbooks on a server running SharePoint Server. Users can then view and interact with the Excel files in a browser. Excel Services in SharePoint Server 2010 is designed to let users analyze business data and increase business intelligence. Any published workbook can be managed and secured according to your organizational needs and then shared throughout the enterprise.

With business intelligence, you can store data that represents your organization's key business processes, organize that data in a useful manner, and present that data as meaningful information. Knowledge workers can act on that information to increase their productivity and to provide feedback that improves underlying business processes.

Configuring SharePoint 2010 Services for Excel, Access, and Visio

This section teaches you how you might use the features provided by Excel Services, Access Services, and Visio Services in SharePoint 2010. To work through this section, your SharePoint environment must have the SharePoint Services applications configured by your SharePoint administrator.

You can use these services in many ways. In this section, we provide examples of how to publish content created in Excel, Access, or Visio so that the content can be stored and worked with in SharePoint. For information concerning other operations you can carry out with these services, see the following online sources:

- Excel *Office.microsoft.com/en-us/sharepoint-server-help/introduction-to-excel-services-and-excel-web-access-HA010105476.aspx*

- Access *Office.microsoft.com/en-us/sharepoint-server-help/build-an-access-database-to-share-on-the-web-HA010356866.aspx?CTT=3*

- Visio *Office.microsoft.com/en-us/sharepoint-server-help/add-data-driven-web-drawings-to-your-dashboard-with-visio-web-access-HA101791927.aspx?CTT=3*

Publishing a Workbook to Excel Services

Let's say you are a product manager at the company Fabrikam and are working on an Excel spreadsheet that shows product analysis details. You need to present the data on the Project Management SharePoint site so that other people in the company can use it for various needs. You want users to be able to look at and work with the data, but you don't want other users editing the original data in Excel because your workbook is the master version and should not be compromised. One solution is to publish the Excel spreadsheet to a SharePoint site.

➤ **To publish an Excel spreadsheet to a SharePoint site**

> **Important** You need to have access to Microsoft Excel 2010 and Contribute permissions to a SharePoint site to complete this section.

1. Access your SharePoint site and the document library where you want to save the Excel worksheet.

2. Confirm that you are able to publish documents to the document library. If you can see the **New Document** button on the **Documents** tab on the ribbon, you have the permissions required to continue.

3. Copy the URL for the document library from the address box in your browser. Copy only the portion of the URL that includes the target to the document library—the string */Forms/Allitems.aspx* is not required. For example, if the document library URL is *http://fabrikam/sites/pm/pmdocs/Forms/Allitems.aspx*, the target to the document library is *http://fabrikam/sites/pm/pmdocs*.

4. Open Microsoft Excel, and then open the workbook you want to publish.

5. In Excel, click **File**, **Save & Send**.

6. Click **Save to SharePoint** in the **Save & Send** area.

> **Important** The Save To SharePoint section includes a Publish Options button, which displays the Publish Options dialog box. In this dialog box, you can specify whether to publish the entire workbook, specific sheets, or particular items. Additionally, you can specify whether users can enter information into any of the cells by using the Parameters tab. Enabling this feature is useful if you have a worksheet that uses formulas for interactive calculations. The user can enter values that Excel then uses in the formulas. For example, for reimbursement of travel costs based on distance traveled, the user could enter the distance and have Excel calculate the expense.

7. In the Locations section, double-click the **Browse for a location** button to display the **Save As** dialog box.

8. Paste the URL you copied from the web browser address box in step 3.

9. Click the **Save** button.

10. This displays the SharePoint document library in the **Save As** dialog box.

11. Enter a name for your spreadsheet, or accept the default name.

12. Click **Publish Options**, and then define what you want to publish and what cells can be edited.

13. Click the **Save** button.

Adding an Access Database to a SharePoint Site

One type of database you might consider adding to a SharePoint site is a contacts database. You can add a contacts database, for example, to give users access to the SharePoint site to view contact data without requiring them to have Access 2010 installed on their computers.

When you publish a database to SharePoint, Access creates a subsite and then creates all the repositories, properties, and code. At the end of the process, the Publish Access Application dialog box appears confirming that the site has been created. The URL of the database is displayed as a link you can click to open the database in SharePoint.

> **Tip** The Report Center for a web database requires Microsoft SQL Server Reporting Services to be enabled. This must be enabled at the site-collection level.

The following procedure describes how to create a contacts database using Microsoft Access 2010 and publish the database to a SharePoint 2010 site by using Access Services.

➤ **To publish an Access database to SharePoint**

> **Important** You need Access 2010 and site-collection administration permissions for a SharePoint site to complete this procedure.

1. Open Microsoft Office Access 2010.

2. On the Access ribbon, click **File** to display Backstage view, and then click **New** if necessary to display the available templates

3. In the list of available templates, double-click **Sample templates**.

4. Click the **Contacts Web Database** template.

5. On the **Contacts Database Pane** on the right side of the page, click the **Create** button.

   Microsoft Access creates the Contacts Web Database.

6. Click the **File** tab.

7. In the **Information about Contacts Web Database** section, click **Publish to Access Services**.

8. In the **Access Services Overview** area, click **Run Compatibility Checker.**

   This operation checks the database for web compatibility and identifies items and settings not supported by the web. This step is useful if you are going to migrate an existing Access database or use a template that is not a web database type.

9. In the **Publish to Access Services** section, in the **Server URL** text box, type the URL of the SharePoint site collection where you want to publish the Contacts Web Database. As you do this, the **Full URL** area displays the complete URL of the contacts database.

10. In the **Site Name** text box, leave the site name as **Contacts**.

11. Click the **Publish to Access Services** button displayed to the left of the **Server URL** text box.

Publishing a Visio Diagram to SharePoint

You can use a SharePoint list for many purposes, among them to list statistics that show the current progress of a project team. Your list might include man-day resources for project tasks, for example. You can create graphical depictions of data such as this in Microsoft Visio 2010, connect the drawing to the SharePoint list, and display the Visio diagram in a web browser. Doing so lets users who don't have Visio 2010 on their computers view the information.

> **Important** You need to have access to Microsoft Visio 2010, owner access to a SharePoint document library, and a SharePoint custom list to complete the following procedures.

➤ **To set up the site and list**

1. Create a document library called **VisioDrawings**.

2. Create a custom list called **ProjectProgress**, and add the following two columns to the list:

Column	Type	Value(s)
ManResourceDays	Numeric	0
Job Title	Choice	Procurement Manager, Core Project Manager, Scheduling Analyst

3. Add the following sample data to the ProjectProgress list:

Title	ManResourceDays	JobAllocatedTo
Buy Resources	10	Procurement Manager
Hire Business Analysts	5	Core Project Manager
Build Schedule	10	Scheduling Analyst

> **Tip** Copy to Notepad the URL of the site where the ProjectProgress list has been created. You will need this when you work in Microsoft Visio.

➤ **To create the Visio diagram and set up the ProjectProgress list as the SharePoint list data source**

1. Open Microsoft Visio 2010.

2. On the **File** tab, click **New** and select the **Basic Diagram (Metric)** template.

3. In the **Shapes** pane, click in the **Search for Shapes** text box and type **People**.

4. Click the search button (which looks like a magnifying glass). A list of people-related shapes are displayed in the **Shapes** pane.

5. Click the **Data** tab.

6. Click the **Link Data to Shapes** button to display the **Data Selector** dialog box.

7. Click **Microsoft SharePoint Foundation list**.

8. Click the **Next** button.

9. In the **Site** text box, type the URL for the site where you created the list. (Paste the URL if you copied it earlier.)

10. Click **Next**.

11. Select the **ProjectProgress** list from the **Lists** list.

12. Click **Link to a list** in the **Link Options** section.

13. Click the **Next** button.

14. Click **Finish**.

   The contents of the linked list are now displayed under the drawing page. This is the data source.

➤ **To connect the data source to the shapes**

1. Click the Person—Torso shape in the **Stencil** pane.

2. Drag the Person—Torso shape to the drawing page.

3. Click the row next to the relevant ID for the data source.

4. Drag the row from the data source to the Person—Torso shape on the drawing page.

5. Repeat steps 1 through 4, until you have populated the page with the shapes and data that you want to include.

➤ **To show the Job Title next to the linked Person—Torso shapes on the drawing**

1. Click and then right-click one of the Person—Torso shapes on the drawing.

2. Click **Data, Edit Graphic Data** from the shortcut menu.

3. In the **Edit Data Graphic** dialog box, click the **New Item** button at the top of the dialog box.

4. In the **New Item** dialog box, select **Job Title** from the **Data Field** list.

5. Select **Text** from the **Displayed as** list.

6. Click **OK** in the **New Item** dialog box.

7. Click **OK** in the **Edit Graphic Data** dialog box.

   The job title is now displayed under the ManResourceDays field along with the associated data.

➤ **To publish the Visio diagram to a SharePoint 2010 document library as a web drawing.**

1. In Visio, click **File**, **Save & Send**.

2. Click **Save to SharePoint** in the **Save & Send** area.

3. Double-click the **Browse for a location** link in the **Save to SharePoint** section to display the **Save As** dialog box.

4. If you do not have the URL for the library where the document is to be published, visit the SharePoint site and copy the URL in the browser. Press the Enter key to force an update to the contents displayed in the **Save As** dialog box.

5. Double-click the **VisioDrawings** document library.

6. Enter **ProjectProgress** in the **File name** text box.

7. Select **Web Drawing (*.vdw)** from the **Save as type** list.

   If necessary, you can also select a different type of Visio drawing, including a drawing file (.vsd), a stencil (.vss), or a template (.vst), among others.

8. Select the **Automatically view files in a browser** check box.

9. Click the **Save** button at the bottom of the **Save As** dialog box.

   The Visio diagram is then displayed in a web browser. Buttons for opening the diagram in Visio and refreshing the display are shown at the top of the page. Whenever data is altered in the ProjectProgress list and the Visio diagram is refreshed, the data is updated in the Visio diagram.

Configuring Form Services

In this section, you learn how to configure and create forms using Microsoft InfoPath 2010. With InfoPath 2010, you can create user interfaces for Office business applications. InfoPath 2010 provides the design platform, and SharePoint 2010 InfoPath Forms Services can render these forms in the browser. This section teaches you how to enable Form Services, customize an existing list using InfoPath, publish a form based on that list, and then use that form.

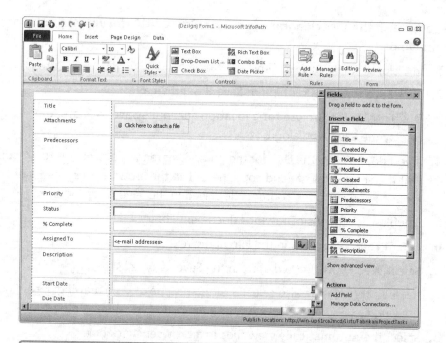

> **Tip** For the following procedure, we recommend that you create a list that you will customize to create an InfoPath form. You can customize any list, but creating a list specifically for this procedure will help if you need to repeat the exercise later.

➤ **To enable Form Services on the site collection**

> **Important** Form Services is part of the SharePoint Server Enterprise Site Collection features. These enterprise features must be enabled at site-collection level.

1. Access your SharePoint site collection.

2. Click **Site Actions**, **Site Settings**.

3. In the **Site Collection Administration** section, click the **Site collection features** link.

4. Locate **SharePoint Server Enterprise Site Collection features**, and then click the **Activate** button to this item's right.

   Form Services is now available to the site collection. The next step is to customize a list so that you can create and then publish an InfoPath form.

➤ To customize a list to create an InfoPath form

1. Access the SharePoint site where you want to customize the list. (Remember this must be in the site collection where the Enterprise Site Collection features are enabled.)

2. Access the SharePoint list in which you want to build an InfoPath form.

3. Click the **List** tab on the ribbon.

4. Click the **Customize Form** button in the **Customize List** section. If you do not see Customize Form, click the drop-down arrow beneath the **Customize List** button and then click the **Customize Form** button.

   This launches Microsoft InfoPath 2010 and places the default form into the display panel.

   Now the form can be customized using InfoPath 2010. For more information on customizing and building forms using InfoPath, see the following video, which describes how to build custom InfoPath forms for a SharePoint list, publish the InfoPath form, and then connect the InfoPath form to another list as an additional data source: *msdn.microsoft.com/en-us/ Office2010DeveloperTrainingCourse_ListFormsInfoPath*.

➤ To publish a customized form back to SharePoint

1. In Microsoft InfoPath 2010, click the **File** tab.

2. Click the **Info** link to display the **Form Information** section.

3. Click the **Quick Publish** button.

   The form is published back to the list where you originally clicked the **Customize Form** button.

➤ To access an InfoPath form

1. Access the SharePoint list where the InfoPath form has been published.

2. Click the **Add New Item** link.

   The InfoPath form is displayed.

Practice Tasks

Practice the skills you learned in this section by performing the following tasks on your site:

- Create a web database in Microsoft Access, and publish the database to your SharePoint site.

- Create a Visio diagram, link it to a SharePoint list, and publish the diagram to your SharePoint site.

- Deploy an Excel spreadsheet so that the document can be displayed in a web browser.

- Create an InfoPath form by customizing a custom list.

5.2   Run Microsoft Office 2010 Applications with SharePoint 2010 Services

In this section, you learn how to use Microsoft Outlook 2010 and Microsoft SharePoint Workspace 2010 with SharePoint 2010 Services. You learn how to configure key features of both of these products as they relate to their integration with SharePoint 2010, including how to synchronize libraries and lists in Outlook and SharePoint and how to use SharePoint Workspace 2010 to take SharePoint content offline and then have that content automatically synchronized when you next connect to your network. You also learn how to use Microsoft Office Web Apps. Office Web Apps give you the ability to work with Microsoft Office files in your web browser.

Using Microsoft Outlook with SharePoint

This section teaches you how to synchronize Outlook 2010 features and functionality with SharePoint.

Document Libraries

When you synchronize a document library between Outlook 2010 and SharePoint 2010, the library appears as a folder in the Outlook Navigation pane under SharePoint Lists.

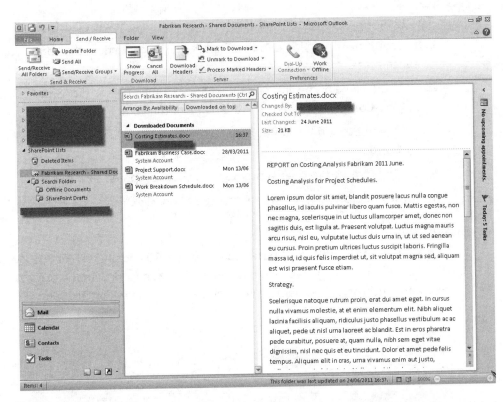

The Instant Search feature in Outlook includes synchronized SharePoint documents in the content it searches. You can preview documents returned in the search results in the Outlook Reading pane. You can also take libraries offline, work with Office files that a library contains, and then go back online and synchronize the changes.

> **Important** Changes you make to files in the SharePoint library can be downloaded to Outlook. You cannot make changes to non-Office files in Outlook and upload them back to the SharePoint library. When you work with Outlook offline, you can edit Office files and then upload your changes to the SharePoint library when you come back online. Outlook does not track changes made to these Office files in the SharePoint library.

If you want access to all the files in a library and that library has subfolders, be sure you view the library at its top level and then connect it to Outlook. By default, if you are viewing a subfolder of a library and connect the library to Outlook, only the contents of the subfolder are connected.

> **Tip** You can invite team members or colleagues to share a library you've connected to in Outlook. Right-click the library name in Outlook, and then click Share This Folder.

➤ To synchronize a SharePoint 2010 document library with Outlook

1. In your browser, navigate to the SharePoint site containing the library you want to synchronize.

2. Click the name of the library on the **Quick Launch** bar, or click **Site Actions, View All Site Content** and then click the name of the library.

3. On the ribbon, on the **Library** tab, in the **Connect & Export** group, click **Connect to Outlook**.

4. When prompted to open a program on your computer, click **Allow**.

5. If you are prompted to confirm the operation, click **Yes**.

Contact Lists

By synchronizing a contact list between Outlook 2010 and SharePoint 2010, you can store, share, and manage SharePoint contacts. You can work with the contact list offline and then synchronize it either from Outlook 2010 or SharePoint 2010.

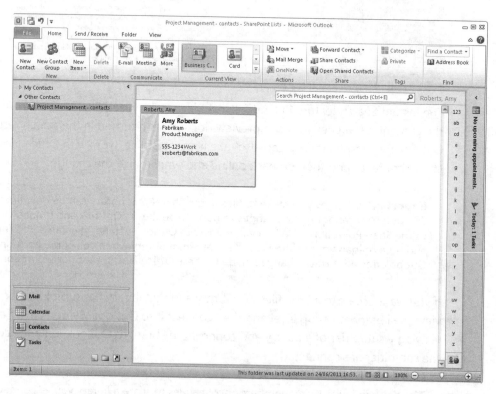

In Outlook 2010, the synchronized contact list appears as an Outlook contact folder. You can work with this folder as you would any other Outlook contact folder.

> **Important** Contact list synchronization is a two-way process. Changes you make in Outlook or SharePoint are automatically synchronized in the other application.

➤ To synchronize a SharePoint 2010 contact list with Outlook

1. Navigate to the SharePoint site containing the contact list you want to synchronize.

2. Click the name of the contact list on the **Quick Launch** bar, or click **Site Actions**, **View All Site Content** and then click the name of the contact list.

3. On the ribbon, on the **List** tab, in the **Connect & Export** group, click **Connect to Outlook**.

4. When prompted to connect the SharePoint contacts to Outlook, click the **OK** button.

Task Lists

In synchronizing a SharePoint task list between Outlook 2010 and SharePoint 2010, you can work with a standard task list or a project task list. As with a contacts list, you can work with a task list offline and then synchronize the list from Outlook.

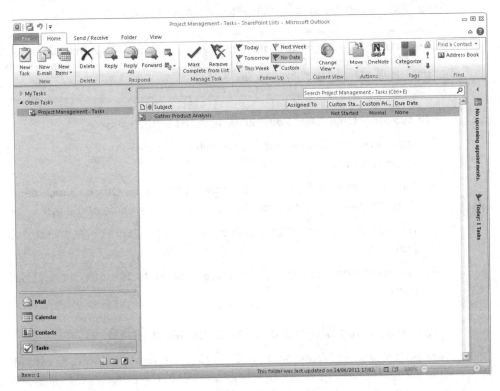

The items in a synchronized task list appear under Other Tasks in the Navigation pane in Outlook and are consolidated in the To-Do Bar. To track the status, progress, and history of projects, you and your colleagues can create, assign, update, respond to, and delete tasks when working in Outlook. After you connect a task list or project task list to Outlook, you can send a message to team members or colleagues and invite them to connect to the tasks. (Right-click the list name in Outlook, and then click Share *Tasks List Name*.)

You can apply flags and categories to synchronized tasks as you do with your Outlook tasks. The flags and categories do not appear on the SharePoint site but are available when you work with tasks in Outlook. SharePoint task notifications are fully integrated with tasks and calendars. You can specify settings to automatically generate notification e-mail messages and reminders.

Task list synchronization is a two-way process. When you open the task in Outlook, or open the SharePoint task list or project task list in SharePoint 2010, you see the latest changes. If changes are made to a task in Outlook while the SharePoint task list is opened, you must refresh the browser to see the latest changes in the list. If changes are made to the SharePoint task list while the task is opened in Outlook, you must use the Send/Receive command to see the latest changes in the Outlook task.

> **Important** To synchronize SharePoint 2010 libraries and lists with Outlook 2010, you must have Outlook 2010 installed on your computer and have Collaborate permission for the relevant SharePoint library or list.

➤ To synchronize a SharePoint 2010 task list with Outlook

1. Navigate to the SharePoint site containing the task list or project task list you want to synchronize.

2. Click the name of the task or project task list on the **Quick Launch** bar, or click **Site Actions**, **View All Site Content** and then click the name of the task or project list.

3. On the ribbon, on the **List** tab, in the **Connect & Export** group, click **Connect to Outlook**.

4. When prompted to connect the SharePoint contacts list to Outlook, click the **OK** button.

Working with SharePoint Workspace 2010

Microsoft SharePoint Workspace 2010 is a client application (included with Microsoft Office Professional Plus 2010) for SharePoint 2010. The program provides offline access to SharePoint documents and lists from the desktop and lets you synchronize content on a local computer with content in SharePoint. When you are connected to the SharePoint server, all content updates on the server and in the workspace are automatically synchronized. When you are not connected, changes you make in the workspace are cached locally. The next time you connect to the SharePoint server, the changes are automatically synchronized.

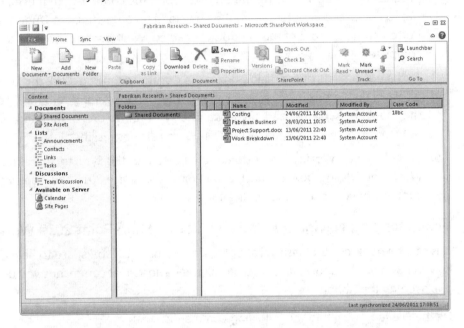

In the following sections, you learn how to do the following:

- Create a SharePoint 2010 workspace.
- Understand the navigation and layout of a SharePoint 2010 workspace.
- Disconnect, reconnect, and synchronize the SharePoint 2010 workspace with a SharePoint site.

To carry out the procedures in this section, you must have Contribute access to a SharePoint site and SharePoint Workspace 2010 installed on your local computer.

➤ To create a SharePoint 2010 workspace

1. Access your SharePoint site.
2. On the ribbon, click **Site Actions** to display the **Site Actions** menu.
3. Click **Sync to SharePoint Workspace** on the **Site Actions** menu. The **Sync to SharePoint Workspace** dialog box is displayed and prompts you to confirm that you want to create a SharePoint 2010 workspace.

4. Click the **OK** button displayed at the bottom of the **Sync to SharePoint Workspace** dialog box.

    The **Sync to SharePoint Workspace** dialog box is displayed, which shows a description of the function, a confirmation of the site to be synchronized, and the progress of the download operation that copies the content from the SharePoint site to the local computer. When the download is completed, the **Open Workspace** button at the bottom of this window is enabled. Wait for the download to complete.

    At the bottom left of the dialog box is the **Configure** button. Click this button to display a dialog box in which you can fine-tune what content from the SharePoint site should be synchronized. If you want to synchronize one or more documents but not the entire site, you use the Configure Settings facility.

5. Click the **Open Workspace** button at the bottom of the **Sync to SharePoint Workspace** dialog box to launch SharePoint Workspace 2010 and display the contents of your site in the application.

Understanding Navigation and Layout of a SharePoint 2010 Workspace

This section describes the basic layout of a SharePoint 2010 workspace to help you learn how to navigate the application. Virtually all the navigational commands you use are displayed on the ribbon.

On the File tab, you'll find the following commands:

-   **Connection Settings** Provides information such as the URL of the SharePoint site the workspace synchronizes with, when the last synchronization occurred, and technical information concerning the workspace installation. Additionally, this command can be used to tell SharePoint Workspace 2010 to go offline (meaning that SharePoint 2010 Workspace is disconnected from the SharePoint environment).

-   **Manage Alerts** Displays settings you can use to change how SharePoint Workspace alerts you to unread content in the workspace.

-   **Manage Account** Displays settings you can use to modify your account settings.

-   **Manage Messages and Contacts** Provides options you can use to view and manage your message history and contacts.

-   **Other commands include New, Print, Save & Send, Help, and Options.**

The Home tab displays commands relevant to the type of repository clicked in the Content pane (described later in this section). If a document library is selected, the Home tab looks like the following:

When a list is clicked, the Home tab appears as shown here:

> **Tip** When Available On Server is clicked in the Contents pane, all options on the Home tab are disabled.

The Sync tab is the tab you use to ensure that content altered in SharePoint 2010 Workspace and content altered in the connected SharePoint site are kept up to date. If, for example, a document has been altered or added to the workspace, the Sync command ensures those changes are echoed to the site. If another user is reviewing a document that you need to see offline and that document is on a SharePoint site, here again you need to use Sync to ensure that document is available in the workspace.

Sync has just three key buttons: Sync, Change Sync Settings, and Sync Status. You must click Sync to carry out synchronization with SharePoint 2010 Workspace and the SharePoint site. By clicking Change Sync Settings, you can disconnect and connect the repositories being synchronized. When you click Sync Status, a dialog box is displayed that shows all the repositories in the workspace that have been synchronized, whether the synchronization was successful, and the date and time when the last synchronization took place.

Use the View tab to change the layout of the SharePoint workspace depending on what section you are working in. For example, the following screen shot indicates that the section being worked on is the Documents section. If the Current View list showed Lists, Contacts, or Calendars, the section being worked in is in the Lists section.

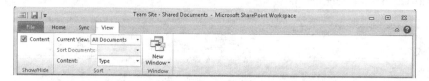

Below these tabs are three sections divided into panes: the Content pane, the Folders pane, and the Items pane.

The Content pane displays the structure of the SharePoint site being synchronized, which is organized under the headings Documents, Lists, Discussions, and Available On Server. Documents displays a list of the available document libraries, and Lists shows the titles of the available list repositories. Discussions lists discussion boards, and Available On Server lists areas of content that cannot be synchronized. You can still view the contents of these repositories by clicking on them. For example, if you click the Calendar link in the Available On Server section, the contents of the calendar are displayed in a web browser.

The Folders pane is displayed when you click one of the titles in the Documents section of the Content pane. This pane displays all the folders for the selected document library. The folders that are displayed have other options associated with them. When a folder is right-clicked, a menu is displayed with a range of options. The Copy To option lets you copy entire folders.

This area is displayed only if there are any
document libraries selected in the Content pane.

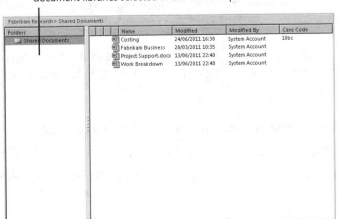

> **Tip** When a list is clicked in the Content pane, the Folders pane is not available.

To the right of the Folders pane and the Content pane, the Items pane displays the
content of the selected document library or list. In the Items pane, you see information similar to the contents displayed when you are viewing a document library or list
in SharePoint. There are rows showing each item and columns showing information
relevant to the item. Each item can be managed by using the commands available on the
tabs or via the menu that's displayed when you right-click an item.

This is the Items pane. Columns shown here reflect
the contents of the document library or list.

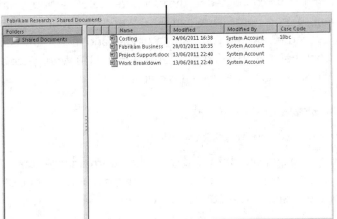

> **See Also** This section covers the basics of using SharePoint 2010 Workspace. You can find additional information at *office.microsoft.com/en-us/sharepoint-workspace-help/ sharepoint-workspace-2010-an-introduction-RZ101972732.aspx*.

As an example of navigating the SharePoint 2010 Workspace, the following procedure describes how to copy a document displayed in the Shared Documents repository to the local computer's desktop.

➤ To copy a document from a SharePoint site to a local computer

1. In SharePoint Workspace 2010, click the **Home** tab.
2. In the **Content** pane, click **Shared Documents** (located under the **Documents** heading).
3. In the section to the right of the **Folders** pane, right-click the document you want to copy to display the selected document's context menu.
4. In the context menu, click **Copy To** to display the **Browse for Folder** dialog box.
5. In the **Browse for Folder** dialog box, select **Desktop** from the list of available locations.
6. In the **Browse for Folder** dialog box, click **OK**.

   The document selected is copied to the desktop.

Go Offline, Go Online, and Synchronize the SharePoint 2010 Workspace with SharePoint

You can take SharePoint 2010 Workspace offline when you want to work on the site content without having to be connected to the computer network. You return to online status when you want to reconnect SharePoint 2010 Workspace to the computer network, and you use Synchronize when you want to upload and merge any changes with the content of the SharePoint 2010 workspace. SharePoint 2010 Workspace automatically synchronizes with the SharePoint site when it is online.

➤ To take SharePoint Workspace offline

1. In SharePoint 2010 Workspace, click the **File** tab.
2. On the menu on the left, click **Info** to display the **Information About <SharePoint Site Name>** page. *<SharePoint Site Name>* is the title of the site you are synchronizing SharePoint 2010 Workspace with.
3. Click the down-facing arrow to the bottom right of the **Connection Settings** button, which will display three links: **Pause Workspace**, **Work Offline**, and **Communication Settings**.

4. Click **Work Offline**. A tick symbol appears to the left of this link signifying the SharePoint 2010 Workspace is offline and disconnected from the site it is set to synchronize with.

➤ **To place your SharePoint Workspace online**

1. In SharePoint 2010 Workspace, click the **File** tab.

2. Click **Info** to display the **Information About** *<SharePoint Site Name>* page, where *<SharePoint Site Name>* is the title of the site that you are synchronizing SharePoint 2010 Workspace with.

3. Click the down-facing arrow to the bottom right of the **Connection Settings** button, which will display three links: **Pause Workspace**, **Work Offline**, and **Communication Settings**.

The **Work Offline** link will have a tick to the left of it, signifying that the workspace is not connected to the computer network.

4. Click the **Work Offline** link. The tick disappears from the left of this link to indicate that SharePoint 2010 Workspace is online and connected to the computer network where SharePoint resides.

➤ **To synchronize your SharePoint workspace**

1. In SharePoint 2010 Workspace, click the **Sync** tab.

2. In the **Sync** section, click the **Sync** button.

At the bottom of the SharePoint 2010 workspace, the status line shows that the site is being synchronized and also displays any errors. Additionally, use the **Sync Status** button to identify what has been synchronized on the site and the time when the last synchronization took place.

Using Office Web Apps

Office Web Apps are the online companions to Microsoft Word, Excel, PowerPoint, and OneNote. Office Web Apps enable users to access documents from anywhere by using a web browser. Users can view, share, and work on documents with other users online across personal computers and mobile devices. This section takes a brief look at Office Web App functionality. Here you learn about some of the key features and use the Editing and View options.

> **Important** The Office Web Apps feature must be activated on the relevant SharePoint site collection where you want Office Web Apps to be available.

Office Web Apps have limited functionality compared to the desktop versions of these applications. When users attempt, for example, to edit a document in the browser, they are notified if the relevant Office Web App is unable to open the file and also see an explanation of why. As with the desktop applications, Office Web Apps display a ribbon, which is located at the top of the browser window. In an Office Web App, the ribbon offers only the Home and Insert tabs, which provide commands for making simple edits to a document.

> **Important** When you make changes to an Excel spreadsheet or PowerPoint presentation by using Office Web Apps, changes are immediately saved; there is no Save button.

One method you can use to edit a document using an Office Web App is to click the View In Browser link, which is displayed when you right-click a document in a document library. When you click this link, you see how the document looks. Near the top of the browser window, you can click Edit In Browser to modify the document.

> **Tip** Word Web App hides pictures, themes, and other formatting, but it still allows you to edit the text. Note also that changes need to be saved with Word Web App by using the Save button or by clicking Save on the File tab displayed at the top of the browser.

➤ To edit a document using Office Web Apps

1. Access the SharePoint site and document library where Office Web Apps have been enabled.

2. Click the drop-down arrow that appears to the right of the document to display the context menu.

3. Click **Edit in Browser** to open the relevant document in the web browser.

Practice Tasks

Practice the skills you learned in this section by performing the following tasks on your site:

- Display a Word document using Office Web Apps.

- Create a contact list, document library, calendar, and task list in a SharePoint site, and then practice synchronizing Outlook with each of these repositories.

- Synchronize your SharePoint site using SharePoint 2010 Workspace.

- Create a contact list in a SharePoint site, and then synchronize Outlook with that contacts list.

5.3 Create Dashboards

To create a dashboard in SharePoint 2010, you can integrate part of the SharePoint Server 2010 Enterprise featured called PerformancePoint. PerformancePoint Services is a performance management service you can use to create a dashboard with which you can monitor and analyze your business. You can define key performance indicators (KPIs), scorecards, reports, filters, data sources, and dashboards. You also use the Dashboard Designer to deploy your finished dashboards to SharePoint.

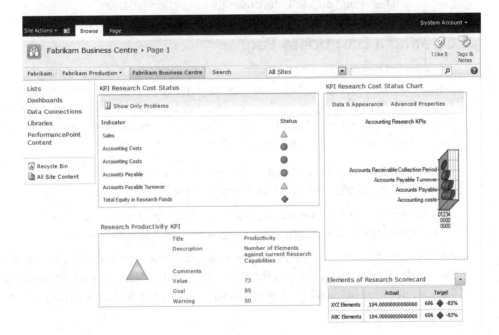

You can also build basic versions of dashboard elements from within the SharePoint site and then use the Dashboard Designer to enhance these basic elements at a later stage. We introduce how you can use the Dashboard Designer to create a dashboard in this section, although full coverage of the Dashboard Designer's features is outside the scope of this chapter.

> **Important** More information concerning PerformancePoint dashboards and the Dashboard Designer is available at *technet.microsoft.com/en-us/library/ee661741.aspx*. More information concerning the building of elements such as KPIs, reports, filters, and scorecards using the Dashboard Designer is located at *office.microsoft.com/en-us/dashboard-designer-help/CH010355796.aspx*.

To complete this section, you or an administrator must enable several features and complete the following procedure.

➤ **To enable site collection features**

1. On the ribbon, click **Site Actions**, **Site Settings**.

2. In the **Site Collection Administration** section, click **Site collection features**.

3. Active the following features:

   ○ PerformancePoint Services Site Collection Features

   ○ SharePoint Server Publishing Infrastructure

   ○ SharePoint Server Enterprise Site Collection Features

Creating a Dashboard Page

A dashboard is stored in a special document library (called the PerformancePoint Content document library) on a business intelligence site. (A business intelligence site is a special site template designed for creating dashboards and using PerformancePoint.) The basic design of a dashboard is carried out in Dashboard Designer. In the following procedures, you'll learn how to do the following:

- **Create a business intelligence site.** This is a special site that will house all of the elements created through the Dashboard Designer.

- **Launch Dashboard Designer.** Dashboard Designer is the tool required to build the dashboards that will appear on the business intelligence site.

When the dashboard is available on the SharePoint site, you can add other Web Parts to the dashboard. This is covered in the following section, "Adding and Configuring Web Parts for Your Dashboard." First, you'll learn to create the business intelligence site and the dashboard.

➤ **To create a business intelligence site**

1. Access the SharePoint site collection on which PerformancePoint Services has been enabled.

2. On the ribbon, click **Site Actions**, **New Site**.

3. On the **Create** page, select the **Business Intelligence Center** template from the **Sites** list.

4. Enter the name of the site in the **Site** text box.

5. Enter a URL into the **Web Site Address** text box.

6. Click **Create**.

   The Business Intelligence site displays three tabs on its home page. You use commands on these tabs to create, design, and format the site.

➤ To launch Dashboard Designer

1. Access the business intelligence site created in the previous procedure.

2. Click the **Create Dashboards** tab displayed on the site's home page.

3. Click the **Start using PerformancePoint Services** link to display the **Dashboard Designer** page.

4. Click the **Run Dashboard Designer** button. When you do this, a dialog box is displayed informing you the product is being downloaded. Note that you must be logged on to the same domain that the SharePoint Server is a member of to launch the Dashboard Designer.

5. When the Dashboard Designer has been downloaded and installed, PerformancePoint Dashboard Designer will run.

   As Dashboard Designer loads, the application displays a new workspace within which the business intelligence site is synchronized. The two key document libraries on the business intelligence site appear in the workspace: Data Connections and PerformancePoint Content. Data Connections is where all the data sources used to give information to your KPIs are stored. PerformancePoint Content is where the elements created in Dashboard Designer (that can be displayed on your dashboards) are stored.

Adding and Configuring Web Parts for Your Dashboard

The dashboard can be populated with Web Parts to show business data from various data sources, SharePoint lists, Excel Services, SQL Server databases, and fixed data. In this section, you learn how to perform the following tasks:

- Create a status list to hold a key performance indicator (KPI).
- Create a key performance indicator (KPI).
- Configure the Key Performance Indicator (KPI) Web Part.
- Configure the Chart Web Part.
- Configure the Current User Filter Web Part.
- Configure the Excel Web Access Web Part.

The first step is to create a status list to hold key performance indicators. The business intelligence site has a sample list available (called Sample Indicators), but for the purposes of this exercise we will create a new status list you can use if you decide to repeat this procedure.

> **Important** The following procedure assumes that you are comfortable adding Web Parts to a SharePoint page. If you need more information, see "Manage Web Parts on a Page" in Chapter 2, "Managing SharePoint Sites."

➤ **To create a status list**

1. Access the business intelligence site.

2. On the ribbon, click **Site Actions**, **More Options**.

3. On the **Create** page, click **List** in the **All Types** section.

4. Click **Status List** in the list of available templates.

5. In the **Name** text box, enter the name of the status list.

6. Click the **Create** button.

➤ **To create a key performance indicator from the status list**

1. Click the drop-down arrow to the right of the **New Button** link.

2. Select **SharePoint List Status Indicator** from the drop-down menu.

3. In the **Name** text box, type a title for the indicator.

4. In the **Description** text box, type a description that explains the purpose or goal of the indicator.

5. In the **Comments** text box, enter some comments to explain the current value or status of the indicator

6. In the **SharePoint List and View** list, choose the list you want to associate with the indicator.

7. In the **View** drop-down list, select the view that represents the data you want to use.

8. Under **Specify the indicator value**, choose whether you want to total the number of items in the list or show a percentage of items against a criteria. If you want to show a percentage of items against a criteria, you need to also specify the columns and the kind of filtering you want to apply against the column.

9. In the **Status Icon** section, choose the rules under which the colors of the icons are displayed. For example, you might want to specify whether a status is better if the values are higher or lower.

10. In the **Color of the icons** section, which shows Green and Yellow, indicate the value you want the green icon to show when a value has met or exceeded the goal. Enter a value for the yellow icon when a value has met or exceeded a warning.

11. In the **Details link** section, you can select a page that displays additional information about the indicator.

12. In the **Update Rules** section, choose whether the value should be recalculated for every viewer, or whether the value should be manually updated by clicking on a link.

13. Click **OK** to create the indicator.

➤ **To configure the Key Performance Indicator (KPI) Web Part**

> **Important** The following procedure describes how to display key performance indicators from a status list on a dashboard page using the Key Performance Indicator Web Part. To complete this objective, you must have already created a dashboard page and you should already know how to place Web Parts on a page.

1. Access the business intelligence site.

2. Click the **Dashboards** link on the **Quick Launch** bar.

The contents of the **Dashboards** document library are displayed.

3. Access the folder related to the dashboard, and click on the page displayed in that section to display the dashboard page.

4. On the ribbon, click the **Page** tab.

5. Click the **Edit** button to put the page in Edit mode.

6. Click **Add a Web Part** in a Web Part zone.

7. Click the **Business Data** folder in the **Categories** section.

Web Parts relevant to the business data are displayed in the Web Parts list.

8. Click **Status List**.

9. Click the **Add** button.

The Status List Web Part is added to the zone.

10. In the Web Part, click the **Open the tool pane** link.

To the right of the page, the tool pane for the Status List Web Part is displayed.

11. Click the icon to the right of the **Indicator** list box to display the **Select an Asset** dialog box.

12. On the left side list box, click the title of the status list that holds the KPIs.

The **Location (URL)** text box contains the relative URL for the status list you select.

13. In the **Select an Asset** dialog box, click **OK**.

14. In the **Change Icon** drop-down list, select the kind of symbols you want to use to represent the changes of values on the KPI. The options available are **Default**, **Checkmarks**, **Flat**, and **Traffic Lights**.

15. If you want to show only the change icon, select the **Show Only Status Icon** check box.

16. If you want to show only problems where KPI values have not met their targets, select the **Show Only Problems** check box.

17. If you want to hide the toolbar at the top of the KPI (which provides the user with the ability to create new indicators, update and change the icons, reset the order, and show only problems), select the **Hide the toolbar** check box.

18. To save the KPI, click **OK** at the bottom of the tool pane.

➤ **To configure the Chart Web Part**

1. Access the business intelligence site.

2. Click the **Dashboards** link on the **Quick Launch** bar.

3. In the **Dashboards** document library, access the folder related to the dashboard and click on the page displayed in that folder to display the dashboard page.

4. On the ribbon, click the **Page** tab.

5. Click the **Edit** button to put the page in Edit mode.

6. Click **Add a Web Part** in a Web Part zone.

7. Click the **Business Data** folder in the **Categories** section.

8. Click **Chart Web Part**.

9. Click the **Add** button.

10. In the Web Part, click the **Open the tool pane** link.

    A default Chart Web Part is displayed.

11. Click the **Data & Appearance** link at the top of the Chart Web Part.

    A **Chart Wizard** page appears. The **Connect Data to Chart** link on this page allows you to connect the chart to various data sources. The **Customize Your Chart** link allows you to customize the layout, type, and elements of the chart.

12. Click **Connect Data to Chart**, and then work through the wizard to connect to the data source.

13. Click **Data & Appearance** at the top of the Chart Web Part, and then click **Customize Your Chart** to choose customize the layout of the chart.

➤ **To configure the Current User Filter Web Part**

> **Important** This procedure describes how to configure the Current User Filter Web Part, which displays only the key performance indicators created by you. To complete this procedure, you must have displayed some KPIs on the dashboard page that you created and have access to the status list where those KPIs are stored.

1. Access the business intelligence site.
2. Click the **Dashboards** on the **Quick Launch** bar.
3. Access the folder related to the dashboard, and click on the page displayed in that folder to display the dashboard page.
4. On the ribbon, click the **Page** tab.
5. Click the **Edit** button to put the page in Edit mode.
6. Click **Add a Web Part** in a Web Part zone.
7. Click the **Filters** folder in the **Categories** section.
8. Click **Current User Filter** in the **Web Parts** list.
9. Click **Add**.

    The Web Part is added to the zone.

10. Click the drop-down arrow to the right of the **Current User Filter** title.
11. Click **Connections**, **Send Filter Values To**, *<the status list holding the KPIs>*.
12. In the **Configure Connection** dialog box, the **Filter** text box displays **Current User**. Below this, **Filtered Parameter** is displayed. Select **Created By** from the drop-down list.
13. Click **Finish**.

➤ **To configure the Excel Web Access Web Part**

1. Access the business intelligence site.
2. Click the **Dashboards** link on the **Quick Launch** bar.
3. Access the folder related to the dashboard, and then click on the page displayed in that folder to display the dashboard page.
4. On the ribbon, click the **Page** tab.
5. Click the **Edit** button to put the page in Edit mode.
6. Click **Add a Web Part** in a Web Part zone.
7. Click **Business Data** in the **Categories** section.
8. Click **Excel Web Access** in the **Web Parts** list.

9. Click **Add**.

The Excel Web Access Web Part is added to the zone.

10. Click the drop-down arrow to the right of the Excel Web Access Web Part.

11. Click **Edit Web Part**.

The tool pane for the Web Part appears to the far right of the page.

12. In the **Workbook** text box, enter the URL of the workbook. To help you locate the URL, click the symbol to the right of this text box, which will display the **Select An Asset** dialog box.

13. If you want to display only a named range defined in the workbook, enter its name in the **Named Item** text box.

14. Scroll to the bottom of the tool pane area, and click **OK**.

> **See Also** This Web Part has many options that allow you to further configure how it is displayed and its functionality. You can find more information at *office.microsoft.com/en-us/sharepoint-server-help/introduction-to-excel-web-access-web-part-HA010377880.aspx*.

Practice Tasks

Practice the skills you learned in this section by performing the following tasks on your site:

- Create a dashboard that connects to a SharePoint list data source.
- Add a KPI in a status list.
- Display an Excel 2010 Workbook using Excel Web Parts.
- Connect the Current User Filter to a KPI status list.

Objective Review

Before finishing this chapter, be sure you've mastered the following skills:

5.1 Configure SharePoint 2010 Services

5.2 Run Microsoft Office 2010 applications with SharePoint 2010 Services

5.3 Create dashboards

Index

Symbols

symbol, 366
? wildcard character, 366

A

absolute cell references, in macros, 276
absolute values, calculating, 51
.accde file name extension, 318–319
Accept menu, 81
Accept Or Reject Changes dialog box, 181–182
access
    restricting (Word), 15–17
    to workbooks, 161
Access deployment files (.accdc), 317
Access Options dialog box, 326–331
    Add-Ins page, 329
    Current Database category, 327–328
    Datasheet category, 328
    General tab, 326
    Language page, 328
    Object Designers category, 328
    Proofing page, 328
    Trust Center page, 329–330
Access Services, 635
    publishing databases to, 315, 321–322
Access 2010. *See also* databases; database records; database tables
    application parts, adding, 339–346
    Backstage view, 309–330
    built-in forms, 340
    calculated fields, generating, 461–465
    compatibility issues, 316
    data connections with Excel, 262–263
    data macros, creating, 357–359
    databases, creating and managing, 309–330
    databases, publishing to SharePoint sites, 637–638
    Datasheet view, 347. *See also* Datasheet view (Access)
    Design view, 347–359. *See also* Design view (Access)
    expressions, 353
    fields, creating and modifying, 360–369
    file format, 316
    form design options, applying, 408–421
    forms, arranging fields and objects on, 422–426
    forms, creating, 396–407
    forms, formatting, 426–434
    Home tab, 370–371
    importing data into, 384–393
    Live Preview, 489
    navigation pane, configuring, 331–339
    Open dialog box, 313–314
    options, setting, 326–330
    queries, constructing, 435–451
    query fields, manipulating, 454–457
    records, sorting and filtering, 370–377
    Report Arrange tab options, applying, 483
    Report Design tab options, applying, 475–482
    Report Format tab options, applying, 486–488
    Report Page Setup tab options, applying, 488–491
    reports, creating, 468–474
    Save & Publish command, 315–323
    Save Object As command, 313, 320–321
    source tables and relationships, managing, 451–454
    table relationships, setting, 378–383
    tables, creating in Design View, 347–359
Accessibility Checker, 177–179
action macros, creating, 287–289
ActiveX command button controls, 300
ActiveX controls, 300–303
    adding to forms, 144–145
    Caption property, 301
    command buttons, 138–141
    configuration settings for (Word), 7
    inserting, 300
    Name property, 301
    order form, creating with, 303–305
    properties, setting, 300–301
    security settings, 302–303
ActiveX image controls, 300
ActiveX text box controls, 300
ActiveX toggle button controls, 300
Add Existing Fields command (Access), 401, 417–422
Add Gallery To Quick Access Toolbar command (Access), 409
Add Help Text button, 157
add-ins
    configuration settings for (Word), 7
    in databases, managing, 329
    installing, 8
    managing (Word), 6
    managing, 329 (Access)
    unloading, 8
Address Block command (Word), 107
address blocks
    inserting, 109
    modifying, 107–108
address lists
    creating, 105–107
    fields, customizing, 107
addresses, mailing, validating, 119
Add Scenario dialog box (Excel), 231
Add To Quick Style List option, 43
Add Trendline dialog box (Excel), 213
Add Users dialog box (Word), 14
Advanced Filter/Sort window (Access), 372, 375

S

About the Authors

Geoff Evelyn is a Microsoft SharePoint MVP, Fellow of the Institute of Analysts and Programmers, Member of the Institute for the Management of Information Systems, and enjoys more than 25 years of work in information technology, with more than 10 years' experience with SharePoint. Geoff's main areas of work are SharePoint information systems design, architecture, implementation, planning, governance, and automation. He has published many articles and guides about SharePoint and makes other resources available on his website, SharePointGeoff.com (*www.sharepointgeoff.com*). Geoff is also the author of *Managing and Implementing SharePoint 2010 Projects* (*oreilly.com/catalog/9780735648708/*).

John Pierce worked as an editor and writer at Microsoft Corporation for 12 years and is the author or coauthor of *Microsoft Access 2003 Inside Track*, *Microsoft Office Groove 2007 Step by Step*, *Microsoft Small Business Kit*, and other books. He is now a freelance editor and writer who frequently works on books and articles related to Microsoft software and technologies.

How To Download Your eBook

![Microsoft]

Thank you for purchasing this Microsoft Press® title. Your companion PDF eBook is ready to download from O'Reilly Media, official distributor of Microsoft Press titles.

To download your eBook, go to
http://go.microsoft.com/FWLink/?Linkid=224345
and follow the instructions.

Please note: You will be asked to create a free online account and enter the access code below.

Your access code:

HQVRZXW

MOS 2010 Study Guide for Microsoft® Expert, Excel® Expert, Access®, and SharePoint®

Your PDF eBook allows you to:

- Search the full text
- Print
- Copy and paste

Best yet, you will be notified about free updates to your eBook.

If you ever lose your eBook file, you can download it again just by logging in to your account.

Need help? Please contact:
mspbooksupport@oreilly.com
or call 800-889-8969.

CERTIPORT®

What do you think of this book?

We want to hear from you!
To participate in a brief online survey, please visit:

microsoft.com/learning/booksurvey

Tell us how well this book meets your needs—what works effectively, and what we can do better. Your feedback will help us continually improve our books and learning resources for you.

Thank you in advance for your input!